LADY ANTONIA FRASER

The Weaker Vessel

Lady Antonia Fraser is the author of *Mary Queen of Scots*,
Cromwell, *King James VI and I*, *Royal Charles*,
The Weaker Vessel, *The Warrior Queens*,
and *The Wives of Henry VIII*.

The
Weaker
Vessel

ANTONIA FRASER

The Weaker Vessel

VINTAGE BOOKS

A DIVISION OF RANDOM HOUSE, INC.

NEW YORK

VINTAGE BOOKS EDITION, JANUARY 1994

Library of Congress Cataloging in Publication Data
Fraser, Antonia, 1932–
The weaker vessel.
Bibliography: p.
Includes index.
ISBN 0-394-73251-0 (pbk.)
1. Women—England—History—17th century.
I. Title.
HQI 599.E5F73   1985   350.4'0942   85-40131
CIP

Author photograph © Sophie Baker

Manufactured in the United States of America
5 7 9 8 6 4

FOR
LECTISSIMA HEROINA ELIZABETH LONGFORD

Contents

Illustrations

Author's Note

'*Were* there any women in seventeenth-century England?' This question was put to me by a distinguished person (male) when I told him the proposed subject of my new book; like another jesting interlocutor, he did not stay for an answer, but vanished up the steps of his club. This book is in part at least an attempt to answer that question.

Wherever possible I have quoted the voices of women themselves, in letters, in the few but poignant diaries, and in the reports of others. Obviously there are enormous difficulties with the written record where women of this period are concerned, in view of the fact that the vast majority below the gentry class were, through no fault of their own, illiterate. Nevertheless I have battled to breach the walls of this artificial silence. Indeed, if I have had a bias, it has been towards the unknown rather than the known; believing strongly in what we owe to 'the number who lived faithfully a hidden life, and rest in unvisited tombs', in the words of George Eliot's moving conclusion to *Middlemarch*.

The idea of writing such a book first came to me in 1970 when I was working on a biography of Oliver Cromwell; it occurred to me that a study of women in the English Civil War would produce some interesting results, in view of the spirited nature of the women in question, whether petitioning, defending castles or fighting alongside their husbands – a variety of activities, none of them particularly passive. Working on a life of Charles II, following these women through to the next generation, did nothing to diminish my ardour, but did show me how much more complicated the subject was than I had supposed.

After ten years of working on the seventeenth century I felt more enthusiasm than ever. But I did come to the conclusion that I must confine my study to England alone; although I had at an early stage wistfully contemplated including Scottish women, until the many differences in the laws as well as the society of the two nations convinced me that this was a separate subject. I also realized how important it was to take the hundred odd years from the death of Queen Elizabeth I to the accession of Queen

Anne as a whole, if only to explore to what extent woman's position in society did or did not improve with the passage of time.

This, then, is a study of woman's lot: it is not intended as a dictionary of female biography in the seventeenth century, nor for that matter as an encyclopedia of women's topics. I have selected those characters who interested me; omissions were not only inevitable, if the book was not to be of mammoth size, but also deliberate.

Obviously, no one writes in a vacuum, and to boast of being unswayed by the currents of opinion swirling about in one's own time would be, like most boasts, foolish. During the twelve years in which I have been taking notes towards this book, the growth of feminism both as a force and an influence has been a spectacular phenomenon. But this book is, I hope, a historical work, not a tract. After all, to write about women it is not necessary to be a woman, merely to have a sense of justice and sympathy; these qualities are not, or should not be, the prerogative of one sex.

I have taken the usual liberties in correcting spelling and punctuation where it seemed necessary to make sense to the reader today. For the same reason I have ignored the fact that the calendar year was held to start on 25 March during this period, and have used the modern style of dates starting on 1 January throughout. This is an age which presents considerable problems to the writer, where the nomenclature of women is concerned. On the one hand, many of them bore the same Christian name: in a host of Marys, Elizabeths and Annes, one learns to be grateful for the odd Jemima. On the other hand, equally confusingly, women at this period changed their surnames with frequency, due to marriage and remarriage. Sometimes, therefore, it has proved convenient to use a pet-name or diminutive consistently for a particular character; sometimes I have used the same surname or rank for a woman throughout the book (as for example Margaret 'Godolphin', antedating her marriage, and Margaret 'Duchess' of Newcastle, despite the changes in her husband's title). My aim in all this has been clarity for the reader.

I wish to thank the Marquess of Bath for permission to quote from the Longleat MSS, and Miss Jane Fowles, Librarian and Archivist to the Marquess of Bath; Miss Cathleen Beaudoin, Reference Librarian of the Public Library, Dover, New Hampshire, for letting me see the John Scale MS on Quaker women; and the Wardens, Melvin and Sandra Roberts, of the Religious Society of Friends, Nottingham Meeting, for permission to quote from the letter of Isabel (Fell) Yeamans. I am grateful to the staff of numerous libraries, principal among them the Bodleian Library, the British

Library, the Institute of Historical Research, the London Library and the New York Public Library.

I should also like to express my thanks to the following, who helped me in a variety of different ways over the years, from answering queries to conducting stimulating conversations: Dr Maurice Ashley; Professor John Barnard; Mr G.P. Bartholomew; Dr Chalmers Davidson; Mr Fram Dimshaw; Lt. Col. John Dymoke of Scrivelsby; Mr Peter Elstob; Miss Jane Ferguson, Librarian to the Royal College of Physicians, Edinburgh; Mr John Fowles; Ms Valerie Fildes; Reverend Mother M. Gregory IBVM; Pauline Gregg; Mrs Cicely Havely; Mr Cyril Humphris; Sir Oliver Millar; Mr G.C.E. Morris; Sir Iain Moncrieffe of that Ilk; Mr Richard Ollard; Professor Elaine Pagels; Mr Derek Parker; Professor J.H. Plumb; Mr Anthony Powell; Dr Mary Prior; the Duke of Rutland; Ms Sally Shreir; Lady Anne Somerset; Emma Tennant; Miss Dorothy Tutin; Brigadier Peter Young.

Over the years I have much appreciated professional support from my publishers on both sides of the Atlantic, John Curtis of Weidenfeld and Nicolson and Robert Gottlieb of Knopf. In addition, I am deeply indebted to my daughter Flora Powell-Jones for her assiduous researches; to Mrs Hatherley d'Abo who showed herself a heroine typing the manuscript; to Linden Lawson of Weidenfeld's for patient editorial overseeing; to Dr Malcolm Cooper for the Chronology and to Gila Falkus for the Index.

Lastly I would like to acknowledge with affection and gratitude three early readers of the book: my mother, to whom it is justly dedicated; my daughter Rebecca; and my husband, who was, as he is fond of pointing out, 'the first'.

ANTONIA FRASER
All Hallows Eve, 1983

Chronology of Important Events, 1603–1702

1648   Start of the Second Civil War; Battle of Preston (17 August); end of the Second Civil War; Pride's Purge

1649   Execution of Charles I; formation of the Commonwealth; Cromwell's expedition to Ireland

1650   Cromwell leads campaign against Scots; Battle of Dunbar (3 September)

1651   Battle of Worcester (3 September); escape of Charles II

1652   Start of the First Dutch War

1653   Dissolution of the Rump Parliament; the Barebones Parliament; Cromwell becomes Lord Protector

1654   End of the First Dutch War

1658   Death of Cromwell

1660   Declaration of Breda; Restoration of Charles II; Act of Indemnity and Oblivion; marriage of the Duke of York and Anne Hyde

1661-5 Enactment of the 'Clarendon Code'; Corporation Act (1661); Act of Uniformity (1662); first Conventicle Act (1664); Five Mile Act (1665)

1662   Marriage of Charles II and Catherine of Braganza; foundation of the Royal Society

1665   The Great Plague; start of the Second Dutch War

1666   The Fire of London

1667   End of the Second Dutch War; fall of Clarendon

1670   Enactment of the second Conventicle Act

1672   Charles II's Declaration of Indulgence; start of the Third Dutch War

1673   The First Test Act; marriage of the Duke of York and Mary of Modena

1674   End of the Third Dutch War

1677   Marriage of Princess Mary and William of Orange

1678   The Popish Plot

1682   The Rye House Plot

1685   Death of Charles II; accession of James II; the Monmouth Rebellion; the Bloody Assizes

1687   James II dismisses Parliament and issues his first Declaration of Indulgence

1688   James II's second Declaration of Indulgence; imprisonment of the
        Seven Bishops; birth of James's son; overthrow of James II and
        arrival of William and Mary

1689   Start of joint rule of William III and Mary II; Bill of Rights and
        Toleration Act passed; start of the War of the Grand Alliance

1694   Death of Mary II; Triennial Act passed

1697   End of the War of the Grand Alliance

1701   Act of Settlement passed

1702   Death of William III; accession of Anne

Prologue: How Weak?

It was a fact generally acknowledged by all but the most contumacious spirits at the beginning of the seventeenth century that woman was the weaker vessel; weaker than man, that is.

The phrase had originated with Tyndale's translation of the New Testament into English in 1526 and was given further prominence by the King James Bible. St Peter, having advised wives in some detail to 'be in subjection to your own husbands', urged these same husbands to give 'honour unto the wife, as unto the weaker vessel, and as being heirs together of the grace of life', founding his remarks on those of St Paul, in his Epistle to the Ephesians.

By 1600 the phrase was freely employed – by Shakespeare amongst others – to denote either a particular female or the female sex as a whole. Throughout the century following, the words of St Peter, founded on those of St Paul, might form part of the Protestant marriage service as an alternative to a sermon: so that there was a fair chance that most women would listen to them at least once – on the most important day of their life, their wedding-day.

Man then was the stronger, woman the weaker vessel. That was the way God had arranged Creation, sanctified in the words of the Apostle. About the precise nature of this female 'weakness' there was however a good deal less agreement.

Was woman *morally* weaker than man? And if she was accepted as such – for Eve's audacious behaviour in the Garden of Eden certainly seemed to hint at some innate tendency to depravity in the female sex – what followed? Many of those of both sexes who accepted woman's innate moral inferiority deduced from this that man had a particular duty to protect the weaker sex. Furthermore, it could be argued that for man, the stronger vessel, to sin was a good deal worse than for woman, the weaker – her own frail nature, while inevitably leading her towards temptation in that fatal way she had inherited from her 'Grandmother Eve', also to a certain extent excused her.†

It was a point made by the Rev. Robert Wilkinson in a wedding sermon of 1607, 'The Merchant-Royal or Woman a Ship', which provided a classic exposition of the duties of the married state: where sin was concerned 'he that imposeth so much upon the Weaker Vessel, importeth much more to the stronger'. Equally if a husband was exacerbated by a particular fault of his wife's: 'Yet you must remember she is the Weaker Vessel: God therein exerciseth your wisdom in reforming, and your Patience in bearing it. . . .'[2]

Few however would have gone as far as the sultry and intelligent Emilia Lanier, who at the beginning of the century dared to pursue the question of 'my Grandmother Eve's' feminine frailty to its logical conclusion:

> But surely Adam cannot be excused,
> Her fault though great, yet he was most to blame;
> What weakness offered, strength might have refused,
> Being Lord of all, the greater was his shame.[3]

The majority of those who accepted the notion of woman's moral inferiority simply concentrated on the eternal vigilance necessary to keep the devil from tempting the woman and causing her to fall – yet again. As William Perkins wrote in 1608, on the vexed subject of witchcraft: 'the woman being the weaker sex, is sooner entangled by the devilss illusions with this damnable art than the man'.[4] Witchcraft and sorcery represented perhaps the extreme forms of the devil's attentions to womankind: Elizabeth Josceline, laying down precepts for her unborn child in 1622, expressed the more conventional view that a girl would inevitably be in greater danger from the sin of pride than a boy; to her hypothetical daughter she wrote: 'thou art weaker and thy temptations to this vice greater'.[5]

If morally weaker, was woman necessarily spiritually *inferior*? From the notion of woman's susceptibility to temptation, certain propagandists did slide casually towards the notion of woman as inherently evil – tempted as it were in advance of her birth, born already beguiled. Joseph Swetnam provided a notorious example of this in *The Arraignment of Lewd, Idle, Froward and Unconstant Women*, first printed in 1615. 'Then who can but say, that Women spring from the Devil,' he inquired, 'whose heads, hands, hearts, minds, and souls are evil?'[6] This type of fulmination, however,

†Prayers for women's use, composed by either sex, often referred apologetically to 'my Grandmother Eve'. Men in the seventeenth century were not, it seemed, descended from Eve.[1]

tended to elicit a fierce barrage of objections, and although Swetnam's book had gone through six editions by 1702, his views were violently attacked.

These interesting discussions concerning woman's possible spiritual inferiority were rooted in uncertainty rather than bigotry. The question of the female soul was crucial. Once again, the notion that women were actually born without souls represented the extreme view, generally denounced whenever it was stated.[7] For example, in 1646 George Fox, the founder of the Society of Friends, met some people in Nottingham 'that held women have no souls, adding in a light manner, no more than a goose'. He reproved them by adducing the text of the Magnificat: how could the Virgin Mary's soul magnify the Lord if she did not possess one?[8]

The equality of the male and female soul was another matter. At the beginning of the seventeenth century it was by no means taken for granted that the respective souls which dwelt in the bodies of men and women were identical. It was for this reason that William Austin, in a book of 1637 praising the female sex, took so much trouble to stress the point: 'in that the soul there is neither hees nor shees'.[9] It was significant that throughout the seventeenth century educators and other friends of the female cause felt the need to state and restate the principle: God 'gave the feeblest woman as large and capacious a soul as that of the greatest Hero', declared Richard Allestree in 1673 in *The Ladies Calling*, a best-selling guide to conduct.[10] Despite St Peter's statement that the strong and weak vessels were 'heirs together of the grace of life', not everyone agreed with Allestree even then. In 1600 there would have been a good many who instinctively flinched from such a proposition.

Perhaps the idea of the woman as merely *physically* weaker was the simplest notion to entertain, as Rosalind, in man's apparel in the Forest of Arden, knew it was her duty to check her tears and 'comfort the weaker vessel [her cousin Celia] as doublet and hose should show itself courageous to petticoat'. It is true that women were regarded as more susceptible to ailments than men; the midwife Jane Sharp, in a popular book of 1671 based on forty years' experience in her profession, pleaded for greater medical care for women for that very reason.[11] Obviously the general sufferings of women in childbirth, although not strictly speaking produced by disease, and the high rate of maternal mortality encouraged this view.

Yet there was an unexpected corollary to the notion of woman's physical weakness, her 'fairness', her 'softness' – for as the century wore on, phrases

like 'the softer sex' – used by John Locke for example – and 'the fair sex'
hung delicately like perfume in the air. By the 1690s in the popular *Ladies
Dictionary*, females were referred to unhesitatingly as 'being made of the
softest mould'.[12] The identification during this period of outward beauty
with inward beauty, reaching its extreme form in the doctrines of the
'Platoniques', took the argument further. If women were indeed softer,
physically 'smoother' as William Austin had it, might they not also be
softer and smoother in spirit? Better than men?

In a very different context, to present woman as physically inferior to
the male was to ignore one potentially menacing aspect of her strength
well known at the beginning of the seventeenth century. This was
woman's carnality. 'Though they be weaker vessels, yet they will overcome 2, 3 or 4 men in the satisfying of their carnal appetites' – thus the
Elizabethan musician Thomas Wythorne.[13] Female sexual voracity was a
subject of frequent comment. It was axiomatic that a woman who had
once experienced sex would wish to renew the pleasure as soon as possible
and as often as possible – hence the popular concept of the 'lusty widow'.
The relative facts concerning the male and female orgasm being well
understood, women were regarded in an uneasy light for being undeniably
weaker – yet in certain circumstances insatiably stronger.

Where intelligence was concerned, there was a great deal more unanimity. At the time of the death of Queen Elizabeth I, almost everyone of
both sexes agreed that the female intelligence was less than that of the man:
women themselves were wont to refer as a matter of form to the strength
of their passions, apt to rule over their weaker reason. The intellectual –
and childless – Duchess of Newcastle was described in an elegy on her
death as being the exception to the rest of 'her frail sex ... who have
Fruitful Wombs but Barren Brains'. The Duchess herself subscribed to one
contemporary supposition that the female brain was somehow biologically
different: 'mix'd by Nature with the coldest and softest elements'.[14]

And yet ... there was something troubling here too, which could not
be altogether overcome by referring automatically to clever women as
having a masculine intelligence. The great Queen who died in 1603 had
played that game herself with consummate skill, describing herself in a
famous passage as having the body of a weak and feeble woman but the
heart and stomach of a king – that is, her masculine counterpart. As the
century progressed, obstinate voices would point out that women were
not actually intellectually inferior to men – merely worse educated. Other
voices would be raised to the effect that if woman's intelligence was really
inferior, she might logically need more, not less education than a man.

For those who pondered on such subjects, it must have been a relief to come to the absolute certainty of the English common law, or as a cynical assessment of women's position, *The Lawes Resolutions*, put it, 'The common law here shaketh hand with divinity.'[15] Under the common law of England at the accession of King James I, no female had any rights at all (if some were allowed by custom). As an unmarried woman her rights were swallowed up in her father's, and she was his to dispose of in marriage at will. Once she was married her property became absolutely that of her husband. What of those who did not marry? Common law met that problem blandly by not recognizing it. In the words of *The Lawes Resolutions*: 'All of them are understood either married or to be married.'[16] In 1603 England, in short, still lived in a world governed by feudal law, where a wife passed from the guardianship of her father to her husband; her husband also stood in relation to her as a feudal lord. This had serious consequences for those wives foolish enough to be detected plotting to kill their husbands: for the act thus counted as treason. Like servants who plotted the death of their master, the wife was subject to the death penalty in its severest form – being burnt alive.

Here was the weak vessel with a vengeance – weak at law. Yet even here there was a respite. The wealthy widow might or might not be racked with lust as the popular imagination believed (one of those 'young brisk widows who cannot be satisfied without that Due Benevolence which they were wont to receive from their Husbands').[17] Her position was none the less, as we shall see, in many ways enviable. City wives were particularly well treated: by the Custom of London a wife had the right to one third of her husband's property at death, and if there were no children, their one third share also. The potential strength in the position of the wealthy widow, if her settlement was unencumbered, her children free from restricting guardianship, may stand as one example of those possibilities which did exist for womankind in the real world, outside the dream or nightmare of her theoretical weakness....

For it is at this point that we notice history holding the door ajar; through this door we glimpse prophetesses, businesswomen, nuns, bluestockings, radicals, female labourers, prostitutes and courtesans, good women, holy women, the immoral and the amoral, criminals, wayward heiresses, unhappy wives, purposeful mothers, heroines – great ladies who defended besieged houses and castles in the Civil War and others, no less brave, who fought as soldiers themselves – nurses, midwives, adventuresses, educators, and that new breed, the actress.

The contemplation of these faces, in their variety and vitality, whether suffering or triumphant, summons questions to the lips. Now the sound of the female voice too is heard: the writers including poets and playwrights, the diarists – the first diary by a British woman was written at the turn of the sixteenth century by Lady Margaret Hoby[18] – the memorialists, the letter-writers from the sublime and literary to the humble, the latter all the more fiercely poignant for being so often without name or number; Dante's *la gente perduta*,[19] a phrase which can cover too easily 90 per cent of English womanhood in the first half of the seventeenth century.

Were these vessels all really so weak as society ostensibly supposed? What kind of lives did women really lead in England between the death of one Queen Regnant and the accession of another?

PART ONE

As It Was – This Blessed Knot

'Marriage, O Lord, is thine own holy and sacred ordinance: Thou sawest in thy wisdom, that it was not fit for mankind to be alone. Upon this, it was thy pleasure to appoint this blessed knot. . . .'

SAMUEL HIERON, *Prayer for those intending marriage*, 1613

1 *A Wife Sought for Wealth*

'House and possessions, wealth and riches, land and living is that, that most men regard, and look after: yea men are wont to seek wives for wealth. But saith Solomon, as a good name, so a good wife, a wise and a discreet woman is better than wealth; her price is far above pearls. . . .'

THOMAS GATAKER, 'A Good Wife Gods Gift', 1624

Let us begin with a wedding. That was after all how most women in the early seventeenth century were held to begin their lives. 'All the Time of your Life you have been gathering for this Day', Honoria Denny was told at her wedding to James Lord Hay at Twelfth Night in 1607, 'therefore learn to practise now that [which] you learned before; that is, to honour, to love and to obey. . . .'[1] Thus was Honoria, only daughter and heiress of Lord Denny, dispatched into the arms of her bridegroom with the aid of a masque devised by Thomas Campion and a prolonged banquet.

It was all held in the presence of the King. James I enjoyed these pretty wedding celebrations of a young couple, particularly when as on this occasion he had acted as matchmaker. In the course of the masque, characters such as Flora, Night, Hesperus and Zephyrus emitted suitably nuptial sentiments, to the dulcet sounds of violins, a harpsichord, the odd double sackbutt and several bandoras (an early form of guitar or banjo) twanged by 'two Sylvans'.[2] The King looked on with sentimental satisfaction. James Hay, a good-natured but extravagant young man, was the first of his favourites at the English court: King James sought to cure his financial problems with the aid of Honoria Denny's rich expectations. Although the bride's father had for some years opposed the match – for exactly the same reason as the King was promoting it – he had finally succumbed to royal blandishments which included a title and the grant of a patent. So the new Lord Denny handed over Honoria.

At the wedding ceremony, the Rev. Robert Wilkinson, chaplain to the Prince of Wales and rector of St Olave's Church, chose to denounce marriages based on mercenary considerations in the course of his sermon. It was 'the Manner of the World' he proclaimed angrily, to seek wives 'as Judas betrayed Christ, with a *Quantum Dabis*? (How much will you give?)' Later, for the benefit of the young couple – and the world in general – he had printed 'what so lately sounded in your ears'.[3] This sermon was reprinted in a collection entitled *Conjugal Love* as late as 1725. Despite the genesis of the Hay marriage, Wilkinson's words would not have echoed ironically in the ears of his fashionable audience in 1607, or plagued the consciences of his readers in the ensuing decades.

Throughout the seventeenth century marriages for money were regularly denounced from the pulpit and in guides to behaviour of all types. The Puritan handbooks in particular pointed to the perils inherent in such money-based matches. In another wedding sermon of 1624, 'A Good Wife Gods Gift', the Puritan divine Thomas Gataker was as firm as the royal chaplain had been: 'House and possessions, wealth and riches, land and living is that, that most men regard, and look after: yea men are wont to seek wives for wealth. But saith Solomon, as a good name, so a good wife, a wise and a discreet woman is better than wealth; her price is far above pearls: For house and possessions are the inheritance of the fathers; but a prudent wife is of the Lord.'[4]

At the same time in real life, the inquiry '*Quantum Dabis*?', far from being regarded as the cry of Judas, was a question seldom off the lips of any respectable and dutiful father. A girl brought with her a dowry or 'portion' as it was termed; in return she would be promised a 'jointure', something to support her should she survive her husband. An heiress not only brought with her a larger portion at the time of her marriage; her jointure would also be larger, since there was considered to be some mathematical relationship between the size of the dowry and the size of the jointure. That however lay ahead – it was always possible she would predecease her husband. At the time of the marriage it was more relevant that, in the words of *The Lawes Resolutions* (an exposition of the law concerning the female sex printed in 1632 but thought to have been written by two lawyers at the end of the sixteenth century), 'That which the husband hath is his own' and 'That which the wife hath is the husband's.'[5] Marrying an heiress, or at least a bride with a decent portion, was therefore a recognized – and respectable – path to material advancement at this date, one which a good parent did not hesitate to recommend to his offspring.

Henry, fifth Earl of Huntingdon, laying down some ground rules by

which his son Ferdinando might choose a wife in about 1613, advised him
not to bother too much about her exact rank, since he was 'already allied
to most of the nobility'; the boy would do better to 'match with one of
the gentry where thou mayest have a great portion'. The true interests of
a noble family were at stake: 'without means thy honour will look as
naked as trees that are cropped'. Oliver Cromwell, by birth a member of
the gentry, set to with a will to secure an heiress – Dorothy Mayor – for
his unsatisfactory elder surviving son Dick; he regarded getting the best
terms out of Dorothy's father as a kind of holy task, devoting a great deal
of correspondence and worry to it at two crucial periods in his political
career. At one point there was a question of £2,000 in cash being handed
over: 'I did insist upon that ... The money I shall need for my two little
wenches.'[6] In other words, as the pattern of the prudent Puritan father,
Cromwell wished to do his best by Dick, in order to promote the interest
of his own unmarried daughters Mary and Frances.

A coarser view was expressed by Richard Lane. Hearing that his friend
Christopher Lord Hatton had a mistress, he gave the following advice:
'Well Kitt, do anything but marry her, and that too if she have money
enough; but without it you shall never have my consent, since this is to
reduce you to a filthy dowlas [very coarse linen] and bread and cheese,
which, whilst the love lasts, is fancied partridge and pheasant, but when
that is gone (and we know it will go) then it turns to cheese again; and
what will you do then?'[7]

It is true that the seventeenth century also witnessed a cautious development of the law of equity in the Court of Chancery, where an heiress's
financial interests were concerned. A judgment of 1638, for example,
indicated that where a deceased person's estate was 'thrown into Chancery'
for administration, the interests of any married woman who might be
amongst his beneficiaries obtained indefeasible protection. (Previously,
although the dating of the change cannot be pinpointed precisely, the
Court of Chancery had followed the common law courts in upholding
the doctrine of conjugal unity where finance and property were concerned.)[8] But this modest and gradual amelioration of the female lot at
law applied of course only to those few women whose affairs somehow
reached the august precincts of Chancery. Where the majority of women
were concerned, their lives were lived within the depressing and total
restrictions of the common law.

So, in an age before the English had properly discovered the rumbustious
sport of fox-hunting, heiresses were hunted as though they were animals

of prey. But these vulnerable creatures, unlike foxes, were neither wily nor predatory. For the most part they were very young. The age of consent for a girl was twelve (fourteen for a boy),[9] but the exciting whiff of a glittering match, particularly if the girl was an orphan, was often scented long before that; then the chase was on. The mention of 'unripe years' might mean the postponement of such routine accompaniments to the marriage as consummation; but the contract itself was made, even though a bride was theoretically entitled to her own choice of husband at the age of consent, without a previous betrothal to inhibit her.

The peculiarly confused state of the laws of England concerning valid marriages and the marriage ceremony before the Hardwicke Act of 1753, helped to make the chase still more exciting when much was at stake. Throughout the seventeenth century a girl might well have been forced into a marriage against her will, by parental pressure, or even outright violence from a stranger, and have found herself thereby robbed of her freedom and her money.

Under these circumstances, the heiress's lot could hardly be described as invariably happy, despite the fact that her hand was so avidly coveted by her male contemporaries. Moreover, where the law was concerned, there was yet another sinister rider on the subject of adultery. *The Lawes Resolutions* had something pithy to say about that too: adulterous wives, if convicted, lost their 'dower'; men, on the other hand, could commit adultery with impunity where finance was concerned. 'They may lope over ditch and Dale', for the fortunate male there would still be no 'forfeiture'.[10] This provision relating to the adulterous wife was particularly ominous where an heiress was concerned. Married when still virtually a child for her 'house and possessions', a wife sought 'for wealth' in Gataker's phrase, it might be easy and even natural for her to look elsewhere for affection. But the consequences, as we shall see, could be disastrous.

*   *   *

On Michaelmas Day 1617, ten years after the wedding of Honoria Denny and James Hay, King James presided over another magnificent nuptial celebration. The bride was Frances Coke, daughter of the great jurist Sir Edward Coke. She was fourteen years old. The bridegroom, Sir John Villiers, was twenty-six. In this case it was not upon him but upon his younger brother George Villiers, recently created Earl of Buckingham, that the King's affections were passionately focused. (As for Honoria, she was by this time dead, during her brief life having fulfilled one normal female destiny by providing her husband with a male heir – and property; the spendthrift Lord Hay was on the verge of taking a seventeen-year-old girl, Lucy Percy, as his second wife; at their wedding the King would be once again 'exceeding merry'.)[11]

At Frances Coke's marriage, James I himself gave away the bride. Splendid court festivities ensued and the King rounded off his own enjoyment of the proceedings by sending a directive to the newly married pair to the effect that they should be in no hurry to end their wedding-night. He intended to visit them personally, lying in bed, sometime after noon the next day, to hear details of what had transpired. Such visits were a royal hobby: in 1612 James had paid a similar visit to 'two young turtles' (doves), his sixteen-year-old daughter Elizabeth and her husband the Elector Palatine.[12]

Yet what a world of trouble, pain and unhappiness lay behind the formal proceedings by which the fourteen-year-old Frances Coke was wedded and bedded with Sir John Villiers![13] It is true that Frances herself was quite beautiful enough – if not sufficiently docile – to be compared to a turtle-dove. As one of the late flowers of the Jacobean court, Ben Jonson would hail her:

> Never yet did Gypsy trace
> Smoother lines in Hands or Face;
> Venus here doth Saturn move
> That you should be Queen of Love....[14]

John Villiers, on the other hand, shortly to be ennobled as Viscount Purbeck, the name by which he is known to history, was nobody's idea of an appealing bridegroom. The man suffered from periodic fits of insanity of a manic nature which might lead him to smash glass and 'bloody' himself. The matching of this disparate pair had nevertheless become the dearest project of the bride's father, Sir Edward Coke.

Coke, in political disgrace, saw in the alliance of his child with the all-powerful Buckingham-Villiers clique a means back into the King's favour. The Villiers family was at this point headed by an ambitious matriarch, Lady Compton, mother of both Villiers and Buckingham, now the wife of the wealthy Sir Thomas Compton. Having persistently married for money herself, Lady Compton intended her sons to do likewise. For her part, she saw in Frances Coke's enticing portion and still more savoury expectations just the kind of fortune her son needed.

As it happened Frances Coke's expectations owed much to her mother as well as to her father. Elizabeth Lady Hatton had been the young rich widow of Sir William Hatton when she married the elderly Coke a few months after Hatton's death in 1597. (Lady Hatton was generally known by the title of her first husband even after she married Coke.) From Hatton Elizabeth had received endowments including Corfe Castle in Dorset and Hatton House in London, with its tranquil garden containing fishponds, fountains, arbours and a dovecot. Much of this might accrue to John Villiers if he married Frances; and then there was the question of the additional fortune of Queen Elizabeth's favourite, Christopher Hatton, which Sir William had inherited from his uncle.

Unfortunately for the smooth resolution of Coke's plan, neither Lady Hatton nor for that matter Frances Coke happened to represent that kind of modest submissive female, full of 'bashful shamefastness' which was the masculine ideal of the time.[15] Lady Hatton had no particular wish to fall in with Coke's plans, having come to dislike her second husband; in any case, quite reasonably, she did not regard John Villiers as a suitable bride-groom for the child described by a contemporary as 'the Mother's Dar-ling'. Furthermore Lady Hatton detested the ambitious Lady Compton, with whom she had recently quarrelled.[16]

Coke, however, paid no attention to his wife's objections, and as for Frances's feelings, they were judged to be quite irrelevant. Negotiations with the Villiers family went on apace. 'I would have been pleased to have taken her in her smock', declared Sir John Villiers gallantly of the lovely Frances; in fact the bride was to be dressed a great deal more richly, metaphorically speaking. Coke proposed a down payment of £10,000, and an allowance of £1,000, with the magnificent prospect of her Hatton expectations to come.[17]

Lady Hatton's next move was swift. Her pleas being unavailing, she suddenly removed Frances by coach to Oatlands, near Weybridge, which had been rented for the summer by one of her cousins. Here Lady Hatton tried to get Frances personally committed to another suitor, Henry Earl of Oxford (an official betrothal in those days – or 'spousals' in front of witnesses – having arguably the validity of a marriage).[18] To help matters along, Lady Hatton first forged some love letters from Lord Oxford and then obliged her daughter to sign a document pledging herself to him entirely: 'and even if I break the least of these [vows]' it ran, 'I pray God Damn me Body and Soul in Hell fire in the world to come'. It was signed by Frances on 10 July 1617 'in the presence of my dear mother Eliza Hatton'.[19] Presumably as the result of the forged letters, Frances herself now felt a clear preference for Lord Oxford over Sir John Villiers.

The great Sir Edward Coke was not, however, so easily outwitted. Arming himself with a search warrant of sorts – its validity was very doubtful – he arrived at Oatlands to reclaim his daughter. When he was refused admittance, Coke simply battered down the door and then searched the house from top to bottom until he found Frances and her mother cowering in a dark closet. A physical tug-of-war between the rival parents ensued. Coke won. Frances was dragged weeping away.

Now it was Lady Hatton's turn. In hysterics, she got a warrant from the Council, signed by the Lord Keeper Bacon (whom she had woken in the middle of the night), and set off to rescue her daughter with men and pistols. In return Coke summoned his wife for kidnapping and counterfeiting the Oxford engagement and planning to seize the girl again. Lady Hatton was more than equal to this one: 'Who intended this [i.e. force]? The Mother. And wherefore? Because she was unnaturally and barbarously secluded from her daughter – and her daughter forced against her will contrary to her vows and liking to the will of him she disliked.'[20]

The Council felt some cautious sympathy for the plight of Lady Hatton and Frances – the caution being due to the fact that King James was absent in Scotland and his reaction to the prospective match was as yet unknown. When the King returned, making it clear that in his eyes Buckingham could do no wrong, the Council attempted to strike some kind of compromise which would soothe the outraged Lady Hatton and yet not risk offence to the favourite. So Frances was officially restored to Hatton House, and there amidst its arbours and fountains, it was ordained – perhaps rather optimistically – that Sir John Villiers should be allowed to win her hand for himself. Even more optimistically, his mother should be allowed to support him.

But Frances was not to be wooed. Lady Hatton, maintaining her opposition to the match to the last, was finally put under house arrest at the lodging of an alderman of the City of London. Lord Oxford, nervously aware of Frances's preference for his suit, backed away at the prospect of Buckingham's powerful displeasure. Even so, the fourteen-year-old Frances would not give in.

In the end she was 'tied to the Bedposts and whipped' – possibly more than once – 'till she consented to the Match'. Only now did Frances surrender and write a pathetic dictated letter to her mother, saying that she was a mere child, 'not understanding the world nor what is good for myself'; besides, Sir John Villiers was a gentleman and she saw no reason to dislike him. She ended with an ironic postscript: 'Dear mother, believe there has no violent means been used to me by words nor deeds.'[21]

This then was the grotesque preamble to the ceremony on Michaelmas Day – 29 September – at which the King presided so magnificently, drinking many a health to the bride and inquiring so eagerly after the details of the wedding-night the next morning. Lady Hatton, the mother of the bride, still under house arrest, was at first refused permission to attend and then ordered to do so – at which she declined to come, saying she was sick.

A marriage begun with such a gorgeous sham of a ceremony was not necessarily doomed by the standards of the age. It was Buckingham – and Coke's – cold ruthlessness in condemning Frances to such a demonstrably unsuitable bridegroom, which led to the next fatal episode in the heiress's story. Lady Hatton still refused to bestow certain Dorset properties on her new son-in-law, as a result of which the King felt obliged to create Villiers Viscount Purbeck to atone (the title being derived from those properties he had not yet acquired). As Viscount and Viscountess Purbeck, the newly wedded pair might be hoped to sparkle, he as Master of the Robes to the Prince of Wales, she as one of the reigning beauties of the court.

Instead, Purbeck's madness grew steadily worse. (It is interesting to note that Richard Napier, the clergyman-physician who began to treat Purbeck in 1622, seriously blamed his mother for his condition.) He was already 'weak in mind and body'; when his worst fits were on him, he needed to be restrained from doing violence to himself.[22] Buckingham's reaction was brilliantly rapacious. Announcing that his brother was mad, he proposed to take Purbeck's estates into his own care to administer them – which of course had the effect of denying Frances altogether the use of what had once been hers.

At the same time, Frances's beauty brought its own natural temptations, all the harder to resist in view of the unsatisfactory nature of her husband. 'You will turn all Hearts to Tinder', wrote Ben Jonson of his 'Queen of Love'. One heart in particular Frances's charms burnt up – that of Sir Robert Howard. Handsome and unmarried, Howard was ten years Frances's senior. Their adulterous liaison was not a very well-kept secret.

It was said afterwards that Howard had been seen coming by water in the evenings to visit Lady Purbeck at York House, 'there being a private and secret passage to her chamber'; he would also be seen slipping away early the next morning.[23]

Adultery was at that date still officially a matter for the church courts (even though the common law was beginning to establish its jurisdiction in certain cases).[24] An ordinary couple so convicted could expect to perform some form of humiliating and arduous penance at least. However, cuckoldry was hardly unknown at the Jacobean court and under normal circumstances Lady Purbeck and Sir Robert Howard might have been left more or less free to pursue their liaison. The circumstances were made abnormal by two things: first, Buckingham's determination to secure Lady Purbeck's fortune on behalf of his mad brother; second, Lord Purbeck's presumed inability to beget a child – certainly he was unable to do so while living under restraint, apart from his wife.

Frances's petitions concerning her poverty after Buckingham seized Purbeck's estates make piteous reading: she could not even get 'relief in her necessities'; she declared herself 'most barbarously carried by force into the open street'. Buckingham in reply merely suggested that Frances's conduct had been the cause of Purbeck's madness. Frances really had no alternative but to declare herself willing to return to her unsatisfactory husband; 'though you may judge what pleasure there is in the conversation of a man in the distemper you see your brother in'. Otherwise she would be completely poverty-stricken, despite the injustice of the situation: 'for you know very well I came no beggar to you, though I am like so to be turned off'.[25]

Even the King seems to have felt that Buckingham had gone rather far on this occasion, for he intervened. Frances secured an annual income on condition that she left Purbeck for good – which of course also meant abandoning the estates to Purbeck, or rather Buckingham.

Frances now became pregnant by Sir Robert Howard. Given the lack of any effective form of birth control at the time, this development was perhaps inevitable, but it did undoubtedly complicate her cause. For one thing the law of the time, so cruel to wives, was very much softer towards children born, if not necessarily conceived - within wedlock. If the husband was testified to have been 'within the four seas' (i.e. not in foreign parts) at the time, the child was deemed to be his. The hysteria of the Villiers family at the prospect of Frances's pregnancy – which they maintained could not possibly be attributed to Lord Purbeck – was made still worse by the fact that Buckingham had at this point no male heir; a Purbeck son might actually inherit from his legal uncle Buckingham as well.†

Frances first of all denied that she was pregnant. When the story leaked out to Buckingham, via a necromancer called Dr Lambe, whom Howard and Frances had rather unwisely consulted, Frances bolted. Under the assumed name of Mistress Wright, she gave birth in lodgings to a baby which was secretly baptized as 'Robert Wright'.[26] Nevertheless she still swore when taxed that the baby was her husband's child. Afterwards Frances justified this guilty flight by saying that it had been caused by a brutal gynaecological 'search' of her person, at the hands of midwives employed by her mother-in-law. Given the latter's character, that was quite believable. Frances's explanation for the conception of her baby demanded more of an act of faith: she explained that Lord Purbeck had somehow eluded his captors for a short period, in the course of which a secret encounter with his wife had resulted in her pregnancy.

Here was an adultery with a fortune at stake. Frances and Robert Howard were called in front of the Court of High Commission; on and off the proceedings would continue for three years before both were found guilty and condemned to public penance. Frances throughout behaved with characteristic defiance. Some of her sayings have a biblical ring. In front of the court, 'with bitter revilings', she called on the prelates concerned 'that they should make their own Wives set the good example, by swearing that they were free from all Faults'.[27]

One of the last acts of James I, who died in the spring of 1625, was to sign a warrant by which Frances, her baby, its nurse and her other servants, were committed to the care of Alderman Barkham of the City of London, the same kind of house arrest to which Lady Hatton had been subjected. Unfortunately the new King, Charles I, was equally intoxicated by the personality of Buckingham; Howard received a coronation pardon but by 1627 there seemed no way in which Frances could avoid carrying out her destined penance. As well as paying a £500 fine, on a Sunday she was to walk barefoot and dressed in a white sheet from St Paul's Cross to the Savoy, and there stand at the door of the church for all to see.

But Frances still did not see fit to perform her penance. With the connivance of the Ambassador of Savoy she managed to escape, dressed as

† Divorce – keeping the bride's dowry, which was the aim of the Buckingham family – was virtually impossible at this date, as will be described in Chapter 15.

a page-boy. She was next heard of living with her lover Robert Howard on his Shropshire estates. It was not until the mid 1630s that the guilty pair felt it was safe to return to the capital – by which time an assassin had removed Buckingham from their path, and his mother was dead. Their return was, however, a misjudgement. Frances was imprisoned once more on the old warrant and placed in the Westminster prison known as the Gatehouse.

This time it was a venal turnkey who enabled the dauntless Lady Purbeck – still determined not to perform her penance – to escape. She headed for France. Sir Robert Howard had also been confined, but in June 1635 was released on his promise not to 'come at' Lady Purbeck. Promptly breaking his promise, Howard was happily reunited with his mistress in Paris. Both became Catholics. Now perhaps, with French society ready to receive them, the couple might be allowed to rest. It is good to know that Sir Kenelm Digby, meeting the notorious Lady Purbeck in Paris, discovered in her 'Prudence, sweetness, goodness, honour and bravery' beyond any other woman he knew: *'vexatio dat intellectum'*. He was full of indignation that this enchantress should be obliged to live in exile.[28]

Frances Purbeck's adventures were however not concluded. King Charles I, in an unwise gesture, attempted to have the writ served on her in Paris, which aroused French nationalist fury. Then Frances withdrew into a nunnery, but finding it not to her liking, resumed her life in Paris, where she lived in considerable penury. By 1640 she was back in England petitioning for the return of her marriage portion from Buckingham's sister Lady Denbigh; only to find whatever estates she had secured sequestrated by Parliament in 1644. Frances Lady Purbeck died in June 1645 at Oxford, where the King was then holding his court and Parliament; she was buried in St Mary's Church. Sir Robert Howard, who had stuck to his mistress through all these traumatic events with admirable constancy, remained a bachelor until after her death, marrying for the first time at the age of fifty-eight.

The story of Frances Coke had a curious postscript. Lord Purbeck married again but never succeeded in begetting legitimate issue. The love-child Robert Wright, or Robert Villiers as he was alternatively termed, did make some claim to the title; but his real political sympathies were elsewhere. Under the Commonwealth he abandoned the Royalist name of Villiers for Danvers, that of his wife, daughter of one of the judges who tried Charles I. After the Restoration he became involved in an anti-governmental conspiracy and fled the country. But his widow, children and grandson resumed the claim to the Purbeck title, and also that of Buckingham after the second Duke of Buckingham's death, in a long-running *cause célèbre*.[29] The claim only ended properly in 1774 with the death of the last male descendant of that doomed union between Frances Purbeck, the wife sought 'for wealth', and Robert Howard, who sought her for love.

*   *   *

Mary Blacknall, heiress to a large amount of property in Berkshire including the Abbey of Abingdon, was, unlike Frances Coke, an orphan.[30] The lack of a father to hector her was however not necessarily to her advantage. In the first half of the seventeenth century the Court of Wards still engulfed heirs to the Crown's tenants-in-chief who inherited at the age of fourteen (if a girl) or twenty-one (if a boy). It was the right of the Court of Wards to sell off these orphans in marriage, the Crown receiving a fat fee in return; the Master of Wards could be just as unsympathetic a matchmaker as Sir Edward Coke, indifferent to the feelings of his wards where pecuniary concerns were at stake.

The Court of Wards and its procedure was one of the abuses of the Crown's position most resented on the eve of the Civil War: swept away by Parliament in 1645, it was officially abolished at the Restoration. Before that date interested relatives sometimes bought the wardship of a child back from the Crown. It would be nice to relate that this argued concern for the orphan's free choice of a spouse, but in most cases the transaction was once again financial. The relatives hoped themselves to benefit from administration of the properties and, sooner or later, the arrangement of a match.

This was the fate of Mary Blacknall. Four of her maternal relations – Richard Libb, Charles Wiseman and two Anthony Blagroves, father and son – paid a £2,000 fine to the Crown for the lease of her lands. Ostensibly they were securing for Mary not only a good education, outside the impersonality of the Court of Wards, but also freedom of choice of bridegroom when she reached the age of fourteen and was free from their guardianship. But somewhere along the way, three out of her four guardians forgot these fine feelings and married Mary off when she was ten to her first cousin, the son of Uncle Libb.

The fourth guardian, Uncle Wiseman, then proceeded to appeal to the Court of Wards on the grounds that Mary was under the age of consent.

The appeal was successful. Orders were given that Mary should be delivered forthwith to the house of Sir John Denham, one of the barons of the Exchequer, at Boarstall; there she would be brought up with his own daughters. Despite her recent experiences, Mary was officially pronounced 'unmarried, unaffyed, and uncontracted'. At this point Uncle Wiseman evidently felt that he had frightened Uncle Libb sufficiently; the order was not enforced and Mary remained with the Libbs – the possibility of a £5,000 fine hanging over the guardians' heads if they indulged in any further conspiracies before Mary reached the age of fourteen.

If not her Libb cousin, who was Mary to marry? The guardians set to with a will once more to see if some more congenial prospect could be envisaged. Of various offers made for Mary, that of Sir Edmund Verney on behalf of his son Ralph was held to be the best. So Mary was ordered to be delivered once more, this time to the house of Sir Francis Clarke, as the future bride of Ralph Verney. Sir Edmund Verney engaged himself to protect the guardians against any penalty imposed by the court, and also paid that half of the guardians' discharge to the Crown which remained outstanding. Still Mr Wiseman was not satisfied that Mary would retain her right of free choice at the age of fourteen; so Mary lingered on at the house of Mr Libb. Whereupon Sir Edmund Verney himself appealed to the Court of Wards, anxious that this prize should not slip through his – or rather his son's – fingers. The Court of Wards ruled in his favour. This time Mary really was delivered. And on 31 May 1629 Mary Blacknall was married to Ralph Verney.

There was still some explaining to do. First, Sir Edmund had to draft a letter for Mary to write to Mrs Wiseman: 'Good Aunt – Besides the desire I have to hear of your health and my uncle's, I think it fit to acquaint you that now I am married.' Since Aunt Wiseman's main preoccupation was to outwit Aunt Libb in the matter of the marriage – and Aunt Libb's plans for her son – Aunt Wiseman was not too much put out. She did hope however that the Wisemans would not be blamed 'when she [Mary] shall come to understand what she hath done': that was because Sir Edmund should have made a settlement for Mary before the marriage and had not yet done so. Aunt Libb on the other hand vowed that Aunt Wiseman would repent this matter as much as anything she did.

The second aspect of the affair was more serious. Mary referred in her letter to her marriage having been 'privately done' at her own request, to explain why the Wisemans had not been invited. Her mother-in-law wrote in the same vein: 'She desired so much to have it privately done . . . .'

Weddings at this date were not necessarily the grandiose court affairs of Honoria Denny and Frances Coke – nor the similarly celebratory if less magnificent occasions which in villages and country districts constituted one of the main features of social life. There was a good deal of vagueness as to what constituted a valid union in the first place.[31] It was naturally even more difficult to ascertain the validity of a marriage which had been 'privately done'. In the case of Mary Blacknall the obscurity of her wedding was surely deliberate. For on 31 May 1629 Mary Blacknall was still only thirteen years old. Once she was fourteen it would be theoretically possible for her to repudiate what had earlier been done in her name.

There is some evidence that efforts were made by her maternal relatives to persuade her to do so after her fourteenth birthday on 14 February 1630. How were the Verneys to prevent Mary from being once more wrested away? The obvious and natural solution was to persuade young Ralph Verney, by now a student at Magdalen Hall, Oxford, to win with soft words the prize which had hitherto been his solely in terms of a contract. Ralph was therefore tipped off that now, if ever, was the time for a gallant courtship of the young lady, 'rather than let slip this occasion, which if not now performed is not likely ever to be ended'.

Ralph Verney set to with a will. Shortly afterwards his tutor was hastily pointing out the inadvisability of total concentration on 'Hymen's Delights'; he must not neglect his work at university entirely for Mary's sake: 'the sweetness of a kiss will relish better after the harshness of a syllogism'. Happily for Mary, if not the tutor, Ralph preferred kisses to syllogisms. Mary Blacknall remained – or rather became in the fullest sense – his bride. Nearly twenty years later Ralph would refer to her as 'my dear, discreet and most incomparable wife'.[32]

We shall meet her again, this gallant supporter of her husband through all the tumult of war, exile and sequestration. At the present time it is enough to quote Ralph Verney's own description of his married life: 'We who ever from our very childhoods lived in so much peace, and christian concord. . . .'[33] The practical common sense which dictated that, heiress as she might be, Mary must have her consent wooed not wrested from her, was responsible in no small measure for this happy union.

*   *   *

The worst of Mary Blacknall's fate was to be the object of gentlemanly bargaining among her adult relatives. The affair of the orphan Sara Cox represented an altogether darker aspect of the heiress's life. In August 1637

Sara Cox was fourteen years old. Being 'fatherless and motherless' and 'of a good portion' she had been made 'orphan of the City of London' (that is, placed under their guardianship).[34] She had then been sent to a well-known girls' boarding-school run by Mrs Winch at Hackney – a favourite area for such schools at the time, because although pleasantly rural, it was also convenient for the girls' parents, many of whom were merchants and other dwellers in the City of London.

One of Sara's schoolfriends was called Katherine Fulwood. It was Katherine's brother, Roger Fulwood, who, hearing of Sara's 'good portion', conceived from afar the notion of transforming his fortunes by marrying her. Using Katherine as an intermediary, Roger tried to persuade Sara to share in this brilliant scheme – without success. On 22 August therefore, as Sara and a few of her schoolfriends were taking the air on Newington Common, an array of horsemen with drawn swords suddenly emerged. From out of the midst of her friends, Sara was seized and bundled off into a waiting coach. Here lurked Roger Fulwood. In this coach, Sara Cox, a latter-day Europa with Roger Fulwood as her bull, was 'carried off Screaming'.[35]

Her destination proved to be Winchester House in Southwark on the south bank of the Thames, residence of the Bishop of Winchester. At first her reception here seemed reassuringly respectable: for she found Roger's mother Lady Fulwood presiding, and spent the night under her protection. The next morning however matters took a grimmer turn. On the pretence of being shown over the Bishop's dwelling, Sara was inveigled into the chapel. Here, to her dismay, she found a waiting minister of religion and she was forthwith – and forcibly – married to Roger Fulwood in the presence of Lady Fulwood.

Worse followed. Lack of consummation being a well-known ground for establishing the nullity of a marriage, it was important to the Fulwoods that this enforced union should be seen to be a full one. So Sara's clothes were pulled off her and Sara herself was placed in bed with Roger Fulwood. (From what follows, it seems that this was done more as a formality than with the serious intent of consummating the marriage, but the experience must have been none the less terrifying for the fourteen-year-old Sara.)

Fortunately at this critical juncture the help of the law was at hand. Sara's abduction from Newington Common had led her friends to institute a furious search: that night Roger Fulwood and his accomplice, named Bowen, were at last located by the Lord Keeper's Sergeant-at-Arms and apprehended. Fulwood and Bowen, accompanied by Sara, were brought before the Lord Mayor of London at one o'clock in the morning. Poor Sara flung herself on her knees before him: 'she beseeching him ... and for God's sake, to deliver her out of the hands of these people'.[36]

The horrified Lord Mayor complied. Sara was given back into the custody of her friends. And now the full extent of Fulwood and Bowen's duplicity – and that of the Bishop of Winchester's housekeeper, one Nicholas Young – was known. The marriage licence for the wedding of Sara and Roger Fulwood had been secured on Young's false affidavit that the intended bride was neither heir nor ward. It was further affirmed that Sara had given her own consent to the match, because her friends had been planning to marry her off to a Dutch doctor – another fabrication.

The erring Roger Fulwood was arraigned for his life on 3 September: by an Act of the reign of Henry VII taking of women against their wills for 'the lucre of their substance' and either marrying them or 'defiling' them had been made a felony.[37] The events of this sordid abduction were outlined to King Charles I in a petition from the Lord Mayor on 17 September. The King's indignation was promptly expressed.

In the end Roger Fulwood and his friend Bowen did not pay the harshest penalties. Lady Fulwood weighed in with her own petition to the King at the beginning of November: on the one hand she complained that the matter was 'not nearly so barbarous as had been bruited' (presumably a reference to the fact that Sara had not actually been 'defiled' by Roger, whatever appearances might suggest); on the other hand she begged for mercy. On 25 November Fulwood and Bowen were both pardoned for their lives and for their estates, which as felons they had forfeited.[38]

Still, the troubles of Roger Fulwood were not over. Obviously Sara's friends' chief concern was to secure a declaration of the nullity of this 'marriage' so that Sara's future prospects were not impaired. They were clearly reluctant to see Roger Fulwood leave prison until this matter had been settled in Sara's favour, for the following June Roger was still in prison, despite his pardon. He issued a desperate petition to the King: 'the said Sara and her friends desiring to question the said marriage', he had agreed in advance to give his consent to a suit of nullity, whenever it would be required by the court concerned. If he was not released now, he would have to lie in prison throughout the long vacation of the courts. Finally Roger offered a surety of £2,000 that he would consent to the annulling of the marriage when the time came, and was released.[39] Thus Sara Cox was officially restored to her maiden state.

This cautionary tale showed that young men who were 'wont to seek wives for wealth' needed to have the weight of the establishment, royal and legal, behind them. Roger Fulwood had transgressed not so much in his intention to marry an heiress – which was that of many respectable men of his time – as in the rash and violent manner in which he tried to carry it out. As a result, Sara Cox suffered a fearful ordeal at the hands of strangers; all because she epitomized that seventeenth-century object of desire, a young lady 'of a good portion'.

2 *Affection Is False*

'"Affection!" said the Queen, "Affection is false." Yet her Majesty rose and danced; so did my Lady Marquess of Winchester.'
ROWLAND WHYTE TO SIR ROBERT SIDNEY, JUNE 1600

'Poor greenheads', wrote the Puritan Daniel Rogers of those who married purely for love: when a year or two had passed and they had skimmed the cream of their marriage, they would soon envy the good fortune of those whose union was built on stronger foundations. In *Matrimoniall Honour* Rogers even went so far as to argue that over-passionate marriages might actually result in contaminated offspring: 'What a cursed posterity such are likely to hatch ... what woeful imps proceeded from such a mixture.'[1]

During this period, the emotion we should now term romantic love was treated with a mixture of suspicion, contempt and outright disgust by virtually all pundits. From the Puritans in their benevolent handbooks of domestic conduct to the aristocrats concerned to see that society's pattern was reproduced in an orderly fashion, that tender passion which has animated much of the great literature of the world (including those plays of Shakespeare and the Jacobean dramatists familiar to theatre audiences of the time) received a hearty condemnation. Nor was this a revolutionary state of affairs in seventeenth-century England, the arranged marriage as opposed to the romantic union having been preferred by most societies in the history of the world.

Only briefly at the court of Henrietta Maria did the cult of Platonic love (imported from the Queen's native France) hold sway. Then the elaborate paraphernalia of gallantry which attended this philosophy merely helped to underline the chasm which existed between the Queen's small coterie and the rest of the country. In his play of 1629, *The New Inn*, Ben Jonson cheerfully mocked the cult. Lady Frances Frampul was a 'Platonique' who desired nothing more than 'a multitude of servants', i.e. platonic admirers to worship at her shrine. Love itself was defined as

> ... a spiritual coupling of two souls
> So much more excellent, as it least relates
> Unto the body....[2]

Outside this make-believe little court – and the realms of satire which fed upon it – public advocacy of romantic love was unknown.

James Houblon was the son of a Huguenot refugee who rose to wealth and success in the City of London, identified with the new Royal Exchange. He married, in 1620, an eighteen-year-old girl also of Huguenot descent, Marie du Quesne – 'in a happy day' as he later described it. When Marie died nursing a child of plague in 1646, she left her husband with seven young sons to bring up, her daughters being already married. (One of these sons, Sir John Houblon, was the first Governor of the Bank of England.) In his old age James Houblon was quite clear how his daughters should 'undertake the matching' of their children. 'Beg first the Assistance of God, and see that you match them in families that fear the Lord and have gotten their Estates honestly.' There was nothing here about inclination or susceptibility.[3]

It was not a question of rank. At roughly the same date as Jonson's play appeared, Henry, ninth Earl of Northumberland, was appalled to discover that his son, Algernon Lord Percy, had secretly engaged himself to Lady Anne Cecil, daughter of the Earl of Salisbury – and all for love!

It was true that in 1628 the families of Northumberland and Salisbury stood in roughly the same friendly relationship to each other as Montagues and Capulets in the opening scene of *Romeo and Juliet*. The 'ancient grudge' which existed between them, or as Lord Northumberland put it, the family wounds 'fresh smarting in my sides to this day', originated at the time of the Gunpowder Plot. Then Salisbury's father had been instrumental in having Northumberland imprisoned in the Tower of London for several years, although nothing had been proved against him; Northumberland had also been forced to pay an enormous fine. Twenty years later it was particularly galling for Northumberland to find that his son had secretly chosen a bride in whose veins ran the hated Cecil blood; which in Northumberland's opinion 'would not mingle [with his] in a basin, so averse was he from it'.[4]

The fact that Lord Percy had actually fallen in love with Lady Anne, far from being an extenuating circumstance, only made things worse. Lord Northumberland expostulated to Lord Salisbury: 'My son hath abused your Lordship, himself and me too. If I had had a daughter and your son had engaged himself in this sort, I should not have trusted his words ... *nulla fides est in amore* [there is no faith in love].' While it is difficult not to detect a note of gloomy satisfaction in his prediction of Anne Cecil's future: 'Poor lady, [she] I fear, will have the least good in the bargain, how so ever pleasing for the present. Loves will weave out and extinguish when the knot that ties them will not do so.'[5]

Lord Percy's reckless behaviour had also of course made it difficult for Lord Northumberland to strike that kind of hard bargain over the marriage settlement on which a father might pride himself – one excellent reason for distrusting love in the first place. Beauty, because it might incite a susceptible Romeo to love, as Lady Anne's beauty had won Lord Percy, was not to be trusted either. Joseph Swetnam, in that violent attack on women first printed in 1615, paid particular attention to the turpitude of beautiful women who represented traps for men. 'The fairest woman', he declared, had 'some filthiness' in her; beautiful women in general he compared to glow-worms, 'bright in the hedge, black in the hand'. Even the far more temperate Thomas Gataker referred to beauty as having 'a bait to entice' while adding that it had 'no hook to hold'.[6] Certainly Lord Northumberland, who had already given his views on the likely impermanence of his son's 'hooked' affections, would also have agreed with Gataker that beauty was 'a bait to entice'. Throughout his negotiations with Lord Salisbury before the marriage finally took place, he constantly bewailed the expensive settlement he was obliged to make because 'the beauty of your daughter fettered my son'. (The marriage was however a happy one, cut short by Anne Cecil's death ten years later.)

Another celebrated infatuation of the time aroused echoes not so much of an ancient 'grudge' as of an ancient scandal. In 1634 the twenty-one-year-old William Lord Russell was described as being 'all in a flame of love' with the nineteen-year-old Lady Anne Carr.[7] Unfortunately this modest and charming young girl was the daughter of that notorious beauty of the Jacobean court, Frances Countess of Somerset, her father being Robert Carr, Earl of Somerset, yet another of the favourites of King James I. The fact that the ancient scandal – almost too light a word – concerned the bride's mother in this case made Anne Carr's descent even more unfortunate than that of Anne Cecil. Anne Cecil's grandfather might have had Lord Northumberland imprisoned, but Anne Carr's mother was a self-confessed murderess – and an adulteress too – who had spent some years in the Tower of London for conspiring to poison Sir Thomas Overbury.

'Cat will after kind' – so ran a popular saying of the day. There was a dire suspicion that a girl's moral character was inherited directly from her mother (it was the same kind of logic which held that all women were contaminated by their descent from Grandmother Eve). Anne Carr could be held to have been bred for depravity – for her maternal grandmother Katherine Countess of Suffolk had been another notorious woman.

Lord Russell's father, the Earl of Bedford, a leading Puritan, was of a notably harsh character. He had himself been present in the House of Lords on that fatal occasion in January 1616 when the lovely Countess of Somerset, all in black with 'cobweb lawn ruff and cuffs', had confessed her guilt 'in a low voice, but wonderful fearful'.[8] Only a few weeks earlier she had given birth to a child. That child was Anne Carr. Subsequently the Countess was imprisoned in the Tower of London. Who would welcome a girl of such flagrantly unfortunate antecedents as a daughter-in-law?

Yet this was the bride on whom William Lord Russell, 'a handsome genteel man' wrote the Rev. George Garrard, a contemporary observer, had set his heart. When William came back from the Grand Tour in 1634 he announced to his father that he would have Anne Carr or no one; this despite the fact that there was, in the words of the same observer, 'much looking on' the handsome and eligible young man – the names of the far more suitable Dorothy Sidney and Elizabeth Cecil (Anne Cecil's cousin) being mentioned in this connection.[9]

Lord Bedford utterly refused to entertain the idea of the marriage. With regard to Anne Carr he had given his son instructions 'to choose anywhere but there'. Equally William Russell refused to give way. Then Lord Bedford, faced with an only son who threatened not to marry at all, tried to scupper the match in another way by demanding a portion from the bride's father, which he believed Somerset – who was known to be financially embarrassed – would not be able to pay. Heroically, the Earl of Somerset decided that if 'one of the two must be undone', he would rather it was himself than his daughter, and he decided to pay the price asked.[10] Still the match lagged. Even King Charles I, on a visit to the Earl of Bedford at Woburn Abbey, failed to persuade the angry father to give way.

After four years of wrangling, the marriage finally took place in July 1637. It was a victory for love – not heredity – that Anne, Countess of Bedford and chatelaine of Woburn Abbey after her father-in-law's death, proved a pattern of gentle virtue; she was blessed with nine surviving children and enjoyed nearly fifty years of happy marriage. (Only her own life ended in a tragedy, as dramatic in its own way as her beginnings in the Tower of London – with the execution of her son William Lord Russell for treason – but to that we shall return.)

*   *   *

So for all the fulminations of fathers and the directives of handbooks, love, as it always has done, did find a way. What the prevailing climate of opinion on the subject did induce, however, was a distinct feeling of guilt on the subject, even when romantic love triumphed over such normal considerations as financial prudence and personal suitability.

Lettice Morrison was eighteen years old when she captured the heart of Sir Lucius Cary, later Viscount Falkland. The daughter of Sir Richard Morrison of Tooley Park, Leicestershire, she was an exceptional character, not only for her beauty, but also for a genuine love of study, which marked her out from most girls of her time: 'oft-times at a book in her Closet when she was thought to be in bed'. After Lettice Falkland's death, her chaplain wrote a eulogistic biography of her: here at last was one descendant of Eve who 'in her cradle' had 'strangled the serpent'.[11]

Scorning the contemporary fashion of wearing her hair 'in loose braids' in order to ensnare men, Lettice did none the less unwittingly ensnare Sir Lucius Cary; for she offered a far more unusual attraction than floating hair: a character which combined 'Piety, wisdom, quickness of wit, discretion, judgement, sobriety and gravity of behaviour'. Unfortunately, as her chaplain succinctly put it, Lettice brought with her no dowry beyond these 'riches'.[12] Such qualities might be portion enough for her lover, but her lover's father took a more worldly view and expressed strong disapproval. Father and son quarrelled. Even so Cary persisted in his suit – helped by the fact that he, not his father, had been made heir to his rich grandfather Lawrence Tanfield. Shortly after Easter 1630 Cary was married to this lovely but penniless girl. A short while after that Cary succeeded to the Falkland title; under which name his story, with that of the wife at his side, became woven into the political, religious and literary life of England on the eve of the Civil War; whether at his estate of Great Tew near Oxford, or in Parliament itself.

Despite Lettice's admirable character, Falkland's contemporaries were amazed that this 'incomparable young man' should marry in this rash way. Clarendon, who adored Falkland and thought that his death alone was enough to make the whole Civil War accursed, summed up the general feeling: Falkland had 'committed a fault against his father in marrying a young lady whom he passionately loved'.[13] Others, for whom mere love seemed an insufficient explanation, developed a theory that Falkland had married Lettice for her strong resemblance to her brother Henry, Falkland's friend, who had died young.

Interestingly, Falkland himself clearly felt a kind of honourable guilt about the whole matter. He was prepared to stand by his affections: at the same time he did not pretend he had behaved altogether correctly. According to Clarendon, he offered to resign the estate inherited from his grandfather and depend solely on maintenance from his father in order to atone 'for the prejudice he had brought upon his fortune, by bringing no fortune to him'. But his father's anger caused him to refuse this handsome offer.[14]

Had Falkland been influenced in his choice of Lettice Morrison by the example of his own mother? Elizabeth Tanfield, Viscountess Falkland, accorded the supreme compliment of having 'a most masculine understanding',[15] was one of those remarkable late Tudor women, educated in the great tradition of female learning of that time. Her accomplishments included a knowledge not only of French, Italian, Spanish, Latin and Greek but also of Hebrew and Transylvanian. Perhaps Falkland had early discovered in his mother the charms of the company of a well-educated woman.

Or was it on the contrary Lettice's natural seriousness – a sense of the sadness at the centre of things – which struck an answering chord in Falkland's heart? There had been a streak of melancholy in her make-up even as a girl, when some had criticized her 'lack of joy'. Aubrey tells us that during her married life she deliberately used her ready tears to obtain favours for her servants; but then Aubrey disapproved of a man of Falkland's reason and judgement being 'stormed' by a woman's tears for what he deemed an unworthy purpose.[16]

At the onset of the war, Falkland's own 'natural cheerfulness and vivacity' grew clouded. Having believed in the possibility of a simple Royalist victory, he watched instead the country being torn apart. Clarendon paints an unforgettable picture of the agonies of a man of conscience in a world of war: 'Often, after a deep silence and frequent sighs, he would, with a shrill and sad accent, ingeminate the word Peace, Peace.' Falkland was killed at the age of thirty-three at the first Battle of Newbury: he rode into the heart of the fighting – looking at last 'very cheerful', as he always did 'upon action'[17] – and was shot down.

Lettice Falkland never recovered from the blow. 'The same sword which killed *him*, pierced *her* heart also', wrote her chaplain. She lived another four years, spending her time in rigorous works of philanthropy, not all of which commended themselves to her friends. Her scheme for helping widows was one thing, but she was much criticized for encouraging layabouts by her charity.

'I know not their hearts', Lettice replied with spirit. 'I had rather relieve five unworthy Vagrants than that one member of Christ should go empty away.'[18] Her desire, as a Royalist, to help Roundhead prisoners in Royalist gaols aroused further suspicion.

Examples of her growing melancholia were more disquieting. Lettice became increasingly scrupulous in her piety, full of fears of the devil. Having already banned all rich clothing on her husband's death, and even looking-glasses, in order to extinguish personal vanity, she further abandoned that household pomp 'which her quality might have excused'. Lastly she turned on that very affection which had been the foundation stone of her own life. Urging the other wives not to be too fond of their husbands, she insisted that there was 'no real comfort from any espousals but from those to Christ'.[19]

Lettice Viscountess Falkland died in 1647 at the age of thirty-five 'without twitch or groan or gasp or sigh' of what was surely a form of broken heart. (Her two surviving sons succeeded in turn to the title of their father.) It was notable that even in the elegy on her death the strange circumstances of her marriage, including Lord Falkland's waiving of a dowry, were solemnly commemorated:

> Nor did He wed her to join Fortunes and
> Lay Bags to Bags, and couple Lands to Land
> Such Exchange Ware he scorn'd, whose Noble eye
> Saw in her Virtues, Rich Conveniency.[20]

*   *   *

It would be quite wrong, however, to describe the general distrust of love among the upper classes as a purely masculine conspiracy. Those few women before the Restoration with the opportunity for self-expression did not hesitate to join in the chorus. Both Margaret Duchess of Newcastle and Dorothy Osborne, whatever the reality of their private lives, shuddered away from the concept of love, and above all from its devastating consequences.

The Duchess of Newcastle was that extravagantly-dressed woman of letters who in later life would alternately fascinate and appal Restoration society. As a young woman, she prided herself on never having felt 'amorous love' for her husband. 'I never was infected therewith', she wrote. 'It is a disease, or passion, or both, I know only by relation.'[21] This was not a matter of mere cynicism towards the state of marriage - for the Duchess also prided herself with justice on her devotion to her husband; condemnation of 'amorous love' was a matter of principle.

William Cavendish, in turn Earl, Marquess and Duke of Newcastle, was over fifty and a grandee at the court of Charles I, when he began to woo Margaret Lucas, thirty years his junior, as his second wife. For all his seniority – he was well past middle age by the standards of the time – Newcastle displayed surprising vigour in his suit. It was his very enthusiasm which Margaret regarded with suspicion. First she was concerned that her own declarations should not be too explicit: 'I am a little ashamed of my last letter more than the others,' she wrote on one occasion, 'not that my affection can be too large but I fear I discover it too much in that letter, for women must love silently.' Then she was obsessed by the essentially ephemeral nature of any ardent protestation: 'If you are so passionate as you say,' she continued, 'and I dare not but believe [it], yet it may be feared it cannot last long, for no extreme is permanent.'[22]

Another lively and articulate young lady, Dorothy Osborne of Chicksands, never ceased to identify 'passion', that is, strong feeling, as the enemy of all mankind – and womankind in particular. Yet her beguiling and chatty love letters to William Temple, later an important diplomat in the reign of Charles II, seem to us to breathe a very romantic form of affection.[23] This was another star-crossed match, for Dorothy was the daughter of the Royalist Governor of Guernsey, while William Temple's father sympathized with Parliament. Even the lovers' first meeting was suitably exotic. On the Isle of Wight, on his way to France, Dorothy's brother rashly inscribed a piece of pro-Royalist graffiti on a window pane in hostile territory: Temple witnessed with admiration how the sister saved the brother from the consequences of his audacity by taking the responsibility for the inscription upon herself. Then family opposition to the marriage confined Temple and Dorothy to an apparently eternal courtship, while Temple travelled abroad, and pretty witty Dorothy was courted by a series of other men.

Through all this, the lovers remained true to each other. As this seventeenth-century Penelope rejected a number of eligible suitors, including the Protector's son, Henry Cromwell, she had to endure the vehement reproaches of her family, led by her youngest brother. Then Dorothy was struck down by that dreaded scourge of female beauty, smallpox, and much of her early physical charm vanished. Still William's fidelity held him to his vows. Finally in 1655 they were married.

The romantic elements in this story, including the constancy under trial of both parties, make an interesting contrast to Dorothy's oft-professed scorn for 'passion'. As much as Margaret Duchess of Newcastle, Dorothy prided herself that she had not been seared by that awkward emotion, amorous love. In her letters she was quick to denounce those who, by coming too close to its perilous flames, had been burnt or branded. When Lady Anne Blount, daughter of the Earl of Newport, ran off with one William Blunt (no relation), Dorothy bewailed her fate to Temple. She was also quite clear where the responsibility for Lady Anne's 'fall' lay.

'Ah! if you love yourself or me', she wrote to Temple, 'you must confess that I have reason to condemn this senseless passion; that whereso'ever it comes destroys all that entertain it; nothing of judgement or discretion can live with it, and [it] puts everything else out of order before it can find a place for itself. What has it not brought my poor Lady Anne Blount to?', Dorothy went on. 'She is the talk of all the footmen and boys in the street, and will be company for them shortly, who yet is so blinded by her passion as not at all to perceive the misery she has brought herself to ....' As for William Blunt, Lady Anne's partner in the affair, 'if he had loved her truly he would have died rather than have been the occasion of this misfortune to her'.[24] Once again we hear the Cassandra-like voice of Lord Northumberland, condemning his son's infatuation for Anne Cecil, because it would certainly lead to her undoing.

As it happened, Dorothy Osborne was probably right about the peripatetic Lady Anne Blount. By the next year William Blunt, her erstwhile partner, was petitioning against her, saying that she had only run off with him to obtain some money, so that she was presumably home again. The year after that Lady Anne had taken flight once more without her father's consent – this time with Thomas Porter, son of Endymion Porter, who had been Groom of the Bedchamber to Charles I. Yet Dorothy's own fear of 'this senseless passion' obviously runs deeper than mere condemnation of a flighty young lady's self-destructive behaviour.

There is a malaise here, seen again in her yearning for a peaceful life in another letter to Temple: 'Do you remember Herm [a Channel Island]', she wrote, 'and the little house there? Shall we go thither? That's next to being out of the world. There we might live like Baucis and Philemon, grow old together in our little cottage, and for our charity to some shipwrecked strangers obtaining the blessing of dying both at the same time.'[25] Some of this desire for an existence dominated by tranquillity – as opposed to some more excitable emotion – even with her lover, can of course be attributed to the troubled nature of the times. Nevertheless Dorothy and the rest of her generation, whatever the political strife about them, still drew back in apprehension from love itself, especially love in marriage.

'No passion could be long lived, and such as were most in love forgot that ever they had been so within a twelvemonth after they were married.'[26] The words are those of Dorothy's brother Henry, trying to convince her that the very nature of this type of affection was to be impermanent. Dorothy, by her own account, was puzzled at the want of examples to bring to the contrary. Throughout the whole of Dorothy's correspondence, one detects a wistful hankering that Temple himself should somehow represent the settled convenient match of her family's desires. He did not. He represented something more dangerous. And in the end she married him.

*   ★   ★

At the marriage of William Herbert and Anne Russell in 1600, in the time of Queen Elizabeth, the traditional masque followed: 'delicate it was to see eight ladies so prettily and richly attired'. Mary Fitton, a lady-in-waiting, led the masquers. After they had finished, and it was time for each lady to choose another to tread the measure with her, Mary Fitton went up to the Queen and 'wooed her to dance'. The Queen asked Mary Fitton what allegorical character she represented; Mary Fitton replied that she was Affection.

'Affection!' said the old Queen. 'Affection is false.' Yet all the same Queen Elizabeth rose up and danced.[27] Many of the dancers in the pageantry of marriage in the seventeenth century believed that affection was false; yet trod to its measure all the same.

For love, like cheerfulness, kept breaking in, and ever with love came guilt. In July 1641 the fifteen-year-old Mary Boyle, daughter of the great Earl of Cork, made a match which at the time was conspicuous for its unworldliness. She married, very privately, Charles Rich, a 'very cheerful, and handsome, well-bred and fashioned person'. Then merely a younger son without prospects, he promised to make up for 'the smallness of his fortune' by the 'kindness' he would ever have for Mary. Previously 'unruly Mary', in her father's disapproving phrase, had rejected the suitor chosen by him in Ireland, the wealthy Mr Hamilton 'who professed great passion for her', on the grounds that her 'aversion for him was extraordinary'.[28]

It was unexpected that (by the deaths of several relations) Charles Rich should eventually succeed to the title and property of the Earl of Warwick, establishing Mary Rich, Countess of Warwick, as the great lady her father had always intended her to be. Despite this fortunate occurrence, and despite an affection for her husband which persisted throughout their married life, Mary Countess of Warwick still felt it necessary to apologize for the circumstances of her marriage in her autobiography. 'My duty and my reason having frequent combats within me, with my passion', she wrote, she had acceded to the latter. In so doing she had gone against her father's wishes, and years later she still regarded this piece of defiance as 'an ill and horribly disobedient answer' for a daughter to give to a father.[29]

Not all stories where love and duty tugged in different directions ended as happily as that of Mary Countess of Warwick, especially when the financial arrangements could not be satisfactorily sorted out (finally the Earl of Cork did give his daughter her large dowry). From the Oxinden papers, the intimate records of a family living in East Kent, emerges the sad story of Dorothy Denne, who fell in love with a personable serving-man.[30] Dorothy Denne, an Oxinden cousin, was one of the five daughters of the Recorder of Canterbury; William Taylor worked for her brother Captain John Denne.

Propinquity led to a mutual attraction, but the question of privacy for the courtship was another matter. A rendezvous indoors was virtually impossible at a time when even the wealthy lived without any privacy in the modern sense. Under the circumstances ladies such as Mary Countess of Warwick and Dorothy Osborne turned to nature for spiritual retire-ment. Mary Warwick's 'wilderness', an artificial creation of trees and shrubs which she called her 'sweet place', was her favourite resort for meditation. Dorothy Osborne would dream of William Temple at night alone in the garden – 'a place to roam in without disturbance'; with the jasmine smelling 'beyond all perfume'.[31] Dorothy Denne and William Taylor too were compelled to turn to the outdoors, in a series of trysts.

Dorothy's letters, making the arrangements for them, can still be read: 'Friend', she begins, 'My sorrow and vexations [at not meeting] are as great as yours. I would fain speak with you therefore any fair day about four o'clock in the afternoon, if you send Jack Munday or Jane to me ... I will venture to speak with you in the orchard.' Somehow Dorothy and William were surprised at this rendezvous, possibly because William had told a 'lying ... prating wench' (Dorothy's description) who was his official sweetheart about it. Great was Dorothy's lamentation, principally on the subject of the scandal: 'I think there lives not a sadder heart than mine in the world, neither have I enjoyed scarce one hour of contentment since we happened to be discovered at our last meeting.... If you had borne any true and real affection to me and valued my reputation you would never have run that hazard, knowing that a woman which has lost her good name is dead while she lives....'[32]

The romance continued, with Dorothy persistently preaching the su-perior claims of duty (and financial security) to those of passion, yet by her conduct encouraging very different expectations in her admirer. She main-tained that it would be 'a sin of a high nature' if she ran off with her

William, and neither of them could expect the blessing of God on such an enterprise. She had heard that William might secure 'a gentlewoman worth a thousand pounds' as a wife: 'for the Lord's sake take her or any other, and make not yourself and me ever miserable'. As to William's romantic notions – 'You speak of having me without any clothes or one penny in my purse' – Dorothy made short work of them: 'people would think me either stark mad or a fool ... to bring myself to beggary and contempt of all that know me'. Yet at the end of this long letter recommending prudence on both sides is a note in another hand – presumably William's: 'We did meet the same time.'[33]

Dorothy was appalled when news of their clandestine relationship began to leak out, which might mean that her father would reduce her inheritance; only God could protect them from the 'poverty and misery' which their sinful relationship deserved. At the same time Dorothy suffered agonies because of the news – reported maliciously by her maids – that William was courting another lady in the same village: 'They say it is a great disgrace for me to love such an unworthy fellow as you are ...' Nevertheless at the end of the letter Dorothy signed herself William's 'true and faithful yoke fellow so long as my life shall last'.[34]

William's letters have vanished but they must have been comparatively ardent since at one point Dorothy exclaimed: 'Dear Love, you write in such strains of rhetorick I know not well how to answer them. Your compliments term me a goddess ... I am not divine but a poor mortal creature, subject to all kinds of miseries, and I account myself the more miserable in losing thy sweet company.'[35] The end of the affair was however on a less elevated plane, since Dorothy eventually married a rich London draper named Roger Lufkin, whereupon William Taylor's mother tried unsuccessfully to blackmail Dorothy by producing the compromising correspondence. At least Captain John Denne, Dorothy's brother, still remembered William Taylor kindly in his will, while it is to William's mother's malevolence that we owe the preservation of Dorothy's agonized letters among the Oxinden papers.

Dorothy Denne accepted her destiny and made in the end a prudent match, the charms of William Taylor forgotten. The moral tale of Henry Oxinden of Barham's refractory daughter Peg demonstrated – from the point of view of the period – exactly what could happen to a young woman who refused to conform.[36] Peg had already declined one suitor produced by her father in 1647, when she was just over twelve. Henry Oxinden took her rejection ill, raging on in his letters that 'the folly of a girl' was preventing 'her own happiness' as well as making her 'assuredly miserable' in the future; he also punished Peg by denying her new clothes. Then Peg did worse still by selecting her own suitor, in the shape of John Hobart, son of a Lady Zouch by her first marriage; he was attending school at Wye nearby, and lodging at Barham.

Although the marriage did take place finally in 1649, Lady Zouch was quite as disapproving as Henry Oxinden. In vain her son pleaded for her forgiveness: 'I must confess that I have married one whom I have loved ever since I saw her', he wrote. Lady Zouch got her revenge by acting the tyrannical mother-in-law to Peg when the young couple came to lodge with her in London. As for Henry Oxinden, he continued to denounce Peg's 'neglective demeanour' to him, and when the marriage started – perhaps inevitably – to go badly, he took Lady Zouch's side. Peg, he decided, was growing 'too headstrong' and needed 'such a one as the lady [Zouch] to break her if possible of her wilful courses'. So Peg was not allowed to leave the house without permission, a sad fate for one who had led a comparatively unrestricted life in Kent. Poor Peg's troubles only increased when she became pregnant: she was still part of the Zouch household, Henry Oxinden insisting that she should not leave of her own accord, for then 'she would not have been allowed any maintenance by law'; a message also came from him, saying that Peg could expect nothing from her father. John Hobart's early love had also clearly faded: Peg's husband, wrote an observer, minded her pregnancy 'as much as my cows calving'. No money was supplied for the lying-in or baby linen: 'she is as unprovided [for] as one that walks the highways'. Such was the unhappy end of Peg's defiance, based on impetuous affection.

*   *   *

Only at the bottom of society was some kind of proper independence enjoyed. Women of the serving or labouring classes were in theory subject to exactly the same pressures where love was concerned. 'This boiling affection is seldom worth anything' when making a choice of a husband, wrote Hannah Woolley in her commonsensical handbook for 'the Female Sex' which included 'A Guide for Cook-Maids, Dairy-maids, Chamber-maids, and all others that go to the service'.[37]

Nevertheless in practice these toiling females enjoyed a good deal more freedom of choice where their marriage partner was concerned than their well-endowed sisters, simply because they lived below the level where such considerations as portions and settlements could be relevant. With freedom of choice came obviously the freedom to marry for love, if so desired, simply because no one else's interests were at stake. Richard

Napier was a consultant clergyman-physician who kept notebooks of his cases between 1597 and 1634; they reveal, according to their editor, many instances of romantic love (and its problems) 'among youth of low and middling parentage'.[38]

The lack of acute concentration on the matches made in the lower ranks of society did not of course mean that love suddenly became the paramount blinding emotion which guided them: the eternal practical consideration of the wherewithal on which to marry remained. This could take many different forms, according to the type of society in which a couple lived, urban or agricultural. The brother of Adam Martindale, a Nonconformist minister of Lancashire, disappointed his father grievously when he set his heart on 'a wild airy girl ... a huge lover and frequenter of wakes, greens, and merry-nights, where music and dancing abounded', with a dowry of only £40 when he could have had a bride worth £140. Although the wild airy girl proved an excellent wife, the sense of disappointment remained.[39] (Perhaps only women of the vagrant classes enjoyed total freedom to follow their fancy – and they very often, so far as can be made out, did not bother to marry at all.) This lack of concentration did mean that women outside the propertied classes of the aristocracy and gentry married really quite late – according to recent research – at an average age between twenty-three and twenty-four.[40] Whatever the manifold disadvantages of the poor, that was another freedom they enjoyed, when one thinks of the ordeals of the wealthier young ladies, torn between 'duty and reason' and 'passion' in their early teens.

It was fashionable to gaze from outside at the innocence of the fresh country world, and marvel at it, as though with nostalgia for some lost paradise, as in the picture presented by the ballad of 'The Happy Husbandman':

> My young Mary do's mind the dairy
> While I go a howing and mowing each morn ...
> Cream and kisses both are my delight
> She gives me them, and the joys of night.

A good deal of this was sentimental: Sir Thomas Overbury's 'fair and happy milkmaid', dressed without benefit of the silk-worm, being 'decked in innocence, a far better wearing', would with reason have envied the material lot of a court lady.[41] But there was one respect in which the milkmaid possessed an advantage to which the court lady could not aspire.

Robert Herrick wrote of the carefree celebrations of the country life:

> For Sports, for Pageantry and Plays,
> They hast their Eves, and Holidays:
> On which the young men and maids meet,
> To exercise their dancing feet.[42]

It is true that Herrick's young men and maids enjoyed a kind of guiltless freedom in the sphere of the affections unknown to their social superiors (even if it would never be expressed in literature or letter), especially when one bears in mind that this was a sphere in which enormous attention was not paid to the subject of the bride's virginity. Furthermore that simple betrothal before witnesses which constituted a valid precontract of marriage justified in many people's opinion full sexual intercourse.

Dorothy Osborne described how she would walk out of a hot May night to a common near her house, 'where a great many wenches keep sheep and cows, and sit in the shade singing of ballads'. When she walked over to them, she found their voices and appearance vastly different to 'some shepherdesses that I have read of'. But when she fell into discussion with them, she found that despite these deficiencies, they wanted 'nothing to make them the happiest people in the world but the knowledge they are so'.[43]

If not the happiest people in the world, Dorothy's wenches were, in the single instance of their emotional independence, ahead of the majority of their female contemporaries.

3 Crown to her Husband

'I with great thankfulness acknowledge she was my crown and glory....'

DR ANTHONY WALKER, *The Holy Life of Mrs Elizabeth Walker*

'A virtuous woman is a crown to her husband'; so Elizabeth Walker, wife of the minister Dr Anthony Walker, would emphasize to her daughters, quoting from the Proverbs. Samuel Hieron, a London preacher whose printed sermons were so popular that they had run through eight editions by 1616, referred to marriage as 'this blessed knot' appointed by God; a 'holy and sacred ordinance' since He had seen in His wisdom 'that it was not fit for mankind to be alone'. Woman was intended to act as man's helpmate. Elizabeth Walker succeeded triumphantly in this pious ambition according to her husband, who wrote her *Holy Life* after her death: 'I with great thankfulness acknowledge she was my crown and glory....' Similarly, a poetic obituary upon Mrs Anne Mors, a merchant's wife of King's Lynn, referred to the support she had given her husband's business in her lifetime:

> If women's souls be Planets in the air
> And rule like potent Constellations there
> Surely the Merchants' wives will there reside
> Darting kind beams their husbands' ships to guide....[1]

There were many other wives in the seventeenth century – not only among the ranks of the Puritans and the merchants – who were adjudged to have reached the status of an ideal wife; women whose funeral elegies might run like that of Lady Katherine Paston who died in 1637. On her monument it was written that her 'sad Consort' had 'reared this structure here':

> That future Ages might from it collect
> Her matchless merit, and his true respect.

The (extremely long) memorial to Elizabeth Cavendish, Countess of

Bridgwater, who died in 1663 at the age of thirty-seven and was described amongst other things as 'a most affectionate and observing wife to her husband, a most tender and indulgent mother to her children, a most kind and bountiful mistress to her family' (i.e. her household), ended: 'In a word she was so superlatively good, that language is too narrow to express her deserved character.'[2] There was indeed a remarkable unanimity in the nature of such tributes. For all the religious differences which bedevilled the structure of society, the qualities which went to make up a right royal 'crown to her husband' were not much in dispute.

Modesty, that preferred female attribute of the time – for all women, not only wives – received its due mention. Gervase Markham in *The English Huswife* of 1615 expected his 'compleat woman' to be 'of great modesty and temperance'; Thomas Fuller's *The Good Wife* of 1642 was also to be remarkable for her 'modest carriage' (although she could at the same time 'bind her children with a look' which might imply a slight contradiction in terms).[3] But if modesty and deference were to be displayed in theory, in practice a woman needed a formidable combination of organizing ability and sheer physical dexterity if she was to act as a proper crown to her husband.

Thus Gervase Markham's 'compleat woman' possessed skill in 'bakery, cookery, physic, banqueting stuff and distillation'. As to organization, the fact that the phrase 'the family' was so often applied to the household of the time, be it large or small, expresses the wide responsibilities of its effective ruler – the housewife. In 1631 in *The English Gentlewoman*, Richard Brathwaite wrote of 'the office of a Mistress' that 'winning Modesty' at all times should prevent its occupant from becoming an 'imperious Governess'. Instead, the mistress of a household should know 'when to put on a smooth brow, and to cherish industry with moderate bounty. Her discreet providence makes her family look with cheerful countenance.... The open field she makes her Gallery; her Labourers her living pictures.'[4] Modesty and submission might be persistently demanded – Elizabeth Walker was fond of quoting to her daughters another biblical precept: 'ye wives, be in subjection to your own husbands, even as Sarah obeyed Abraham, calling him Lord'[5] – but it was strength and executive ability – even perhaps a touch of the 'imperious Governess' – which were actually required in the 'compleat woman' if she happened to be a wife, as the great majority of women of this period were at one time or another during their lives.

To outsiders, the City wives with their rich costumes – grotesquely rich according to playwrights like Dekker who mocked them – affluent furnishings and groaning boards, were figures of fun. Even the old magnate James Houblon, larding his daughters with good advice, begged them to have a care not 'to puff up' their children with 'pride of apparel'.[6] It was a commonplace to discuss the magnificence with which wealthy citizens adorned their homes, and at the same time to deride the social ambitions of their wives. Mocked as they might be, or lusted after (Pepys never failed to report a sighting of a pretty citizen's wife, including at church, if he had reason to suppose she might be available to his advances), the lives these women led ill accorded with the contemporary notion of the wife as modest silent helpmate. *Hic Mulier: Or, The Man-Woman*, in 1620, paid special attention to 'the demy-Palaces of Burgers' which harboured vivacious painted wantons – 'these Apes of the City'. The citizens' wives, like all good women, were urged to bear in mind the following salutary quatrain:

> Those Vertues that in women merit praise
> Are sober shows without, chaste thoughts within,
> True Faith and due obedience to their mate,
> And of their children honest care to take.[7]

The fact was that strong independent characters were often concealed beneath the finery worn by the citizens' wives. What was more, this was in keeping with the true demands of such women's position, which entailed not only running their affluent household, but sometimes acting in virtual partnership with their husbands in business. Dekker, in *The Shoemaker's Holiday*, depicted Mrs Eyre, wife of the future Lord Mayor Simon Eyre, at work, bustling away amidst her husband's apprentices. The Custom of London gave to citizens' wives one third of their husband's estate on death, and also allotted to them a further one third if there were no children of the marriage; the last third was bestowed at the testator's wishes and so might also go to the widow. This meant that a merchant's wife never expected to be a mere cipher on his death (and as we shall see, this had an important influence on the remarriage of City widows). Nor did she behave as one in his lifetime. A traveller from the Continent noted about City wives: 'In all banquets and feasts they are shown the greatest honour; they are placed at the upper end of the table, where they are first served.' In mercantile society in cities elsewhere – nearly a million people at this period lived in towns other than London – in Bristol, for example, in 'the high and spacious Halls' of the Bristol merchants, wives were leading active lives in which submission, practically speaking, was the least of the qualities required.[8]

This was also true in the urban households lower down the social scale, those of the tradesmen and artisans where young (male) apprentices were taken. Here a wife, living above the shop, became her husband's active assistant, and effective partner; tales of wives beating apprentices were sufficiently common to prove that the weaker vessel could wield a strong arm on occasion, when she fancied she had the authority to do so. Young Valentine Pettit wrote a sad tale of Mrs Newman, the wife of the man to whom he was apprenticed, to his cousin Richard Oxinden. She was, he complained, 'a strange kind of woman' whose hold over her husband was so great that since his marriage he had terrorized his apprentices and would now 'beat them for any small occasion'.[9] There was clearly nothing very submissive about Mrs Newman.

Other tradesmen's wives deployed their energies more salubriously: borough records reveal them as energetic participants in their husbands' affairs, and in some minds they were rated their superiors: 'Your citizens' wives are like partridges, the hens are better than the cocks', was a contemporary comment.[10]

In the country the picture of industry – necessary industry – continued. Where rural practices were concerned, indeed, James Howell did not see why the country squires selling 'Calves and Runts' and their wives selling 'Cheese and Apples' should be held to be more 'gentle', that is refined, than the great merchant-adventurers of the town selling silks and satins, diamonds and pearls, with silver and gold. George Herbert's poem in memory of his mother gives a description of the life of the country clergyman's wife. The day began with some 'active kindling prayers' and a discreet toilette:

> . . . as good women rightly use, she'd braid
> Her hair with simple art and sparing aid
> Of jewels . . . .

This was the prelude to a busy schedule:

> Then on her family forth she shone, and spent
> On kitchen, garden, house due management;
> To every thing its time and place disposed,
> And with her needlework the late day closed.
> Her life and household shared her constant plan,
> 'So many days for this' each task began.[11]

When a woman was married not to a clergyman but to a farmer her 'constant plan' would also include traditional and important responsibilities such as the garden and orchard and the poultry; many farmers' wives were also pig farmers. On the wife too fell the responsibility of training the servants, both male and female. (Dorothy Osborne's carefree shepherdesses might have to reckon with an irate farmer's wife, the reverse of modest in her carriage, if any of their charges strayed while they sang their ballads in the shade.)

John Banks, a Quaker farmer imprisoned for his religion at Carlisle in 1648, who described his separation from his wife as 'the greatest trial that ever I met with', specifically termed her 'a Meet-Help and a good Support to me' in his work; he worried how she would cope at harvest-time.[12] In fact it was not only the tasks close at home which fell to the woman: at harvest-time it was customary for all those capable to lend a hand, including the wives of husbandmen, who might generally tend the pigs and cows after their marriage, or work in the garden. Women could plough and sow; other specifically female tasks were 'weeding the corn' and shearing sheep. In his autobiography William Stout of Lancaster tells us that in the absence of his mother, his sister had to look after him as a child: 'our mother not only being fully employed in housewifery, but in dressing their corn for the market, and also in the fields, in hay and corn harvests, along with our father and the servants'.[13]

Dairy management was another traditional preserve of the farmer's wife, commemorated in Richard Brathwaite's picture of another busy woman like William Stout's mother:

> Oft have I seen her from the Dairy come
> Attended by her maids, and hasting home
> To entertain some guests of Quality.

The financial side of the farm's affairs was often undertaken by the wife; and it was frequently the wife on her own who performed the vital role of selling the farm's produce at the market. The fact that these activities were not without their attendant dangers is demonstrated by the awful story of Maud, the wife of another Quaker farmer, Thomas Collar of Woolavington. Returning from the market at Bridgwater alone, Maud was struck and called 'ugly toad' by one Adrian Towes. Then he demanded her purse (presumably containing the farm's takings); finally he bullied her into kneeling and swearing on the Lord's blood that she was not a Quaker.[14]

The housewife, if she was literate, was not totally dependent on the traditional lore of domesticity handed down by word of mouth. There were some printed manuals (as there had been since the Middle Ages) and with the slow – the very slow – rise in female literacy, these increased. The desire to cash in on a famous name for commercial purposes being no modern phenomenon, these were generally launched with some fairly high-sounding credentials: *The Queens Closet Opened*, for example, printed in 1655, attested to the universal lure of royalty even under Cromwell's Protectorate.[15] It offered 'Incomparable Secrets in Physick, Chirurgery, Preserving, Candying and Cookery as they were presented to the Queen [Henrietta Maria]. Never before Published. Transcribed from the true Copies of Her Majesties own Recipe books, by W.M., one of her late servants.' The author, while admitting that some might view 'with a kind of indignation' his action, as a servant who had been entrusted with 'so sacred a custody', in making these copies public, gave the classic defence that 'corrupt copies' of the same recipes were already circulating. He threw in for good measure the plea that any mistakes should be overlooked, since he lived in the country and due to his age and infirmity had not been able to oversee the printing.

For all its boasted royal provenance *The Queens Closet Opened* offers merely the conventional remedies of the time for the usual ills. Here is Dr Stephens' Water (a cordial frequently mentioned) and Dr Read's perfume against the plague – a fragrant mixture of red rose-water, treacle, cloves and angelica. Recipes for breaking the stone in the kidneys, for curing piles, for alleviating colic ('Take a turf of green grass and lay it to the Navel . . .') jostle with purges, cordials to suppress Melancholy (borage and bugloss with juice of pippins) and other cordials for the heart. Some recommendations, like drinking a camomile infusion to induce sleep, still sound sensible to the modern ear; others, like swallowing the juice of sage or pimpernel to cure dumbness, must have needed a good deal of faith to make them work. However, 'The Lord Spencers Cherry Water' – a bottle of sack fortified by four pounds of crushed cherry-stones – certainly has a jolly sound, and one can well believe it might have cured fainting.

Elizabeth Talbot, Countess of Kent, author of *A Choice Manuall of Rare and Select Secrets in Physick and Chirurgery*, first printed after her death in 1651, was a daughter and co-heiress of the seventh Earl of Shrewsbury. In herself the Countess provided an interesting link with history: she was a granddaughter of that redoubtable bastion of Tudor womanhood, Bess of Hardwicke; her sister had been a goddaughter to Mary Queen of Scots, then a Shrewsbury captive; and both in childhood and later she herself was close to her unhappy cousin Lady Arbella Stuart. As a married woman, the Countess of Kent acted as a generous patron to Samuel Butler, but her outstanding role was as hostess and patron to the great Stuart jurist, John Selden.

A Choice Manuall was popular and ran through several editions.[16] Frequent remedies against the plague remind us that its outbreaks were not so much a dread as a reality in most people's lives: epidemics of varying severity occurred throughout the century, by no means confined to that notorious one of 1665. 'A Medicine for the Plague' begins well with 'Take a pint of Malmsie', before departing for the realms of spice and nutmeg. 'To break a Plague sore' involved the soberer process of roasting an onion and combining it with a white lily root. Another widespread scourge was the contagious disease known as 'The Itch'; for this a judicious mixture of unsalted butter and the juice of red sage, with additives of walnut and ginger, was recommended.

There is continuous mention of 'Melancholy' ('two spoonfuls of Sirrup of Gilliflowers ... this will cheer the heart'), 'the Green Sickness' (from which the young were often considered to suffer), and 'fits of the Mother' (i.e. a form of hysterical convulsion to which all women were subject), not only in the Countess of Kent's manual but in other similar collections. These were the kind of sufferings, many of which would now be considered psychological in origin, which the mistress of a household would expect to combat with herbs, spices, wines and whatever else took her particular fancy.

In this connection 'The Countess of Kent's special Powder', otherwise known as 'Gascons powder', must have been a useful household requisite: a child of five troubled with much phlegm, a gentlewoman of forty troubled with 'crude and flatulous humours', a girl of about eighteen troubled with 'fits of the Mother', a young woman of twenty-four 'not without some suspicion of the Plague', were all cured by grains of this powder dissolved in assorted liquids. It was also said to be good against smallpox, measles, spotted or purple fever, 'good in swoonings and passions of the heart, arising from malignant vapours or old causes, as also in the Plague or Pestilent Fevers'. The Countess of Kent concluded with a sweeping recommendation worthy of her grandmother Bess: 'These and many other Experiments have I with good success tryed, and with Gods blessing recovered divers severall Patients.'[17]

*   *   *

Provision of her own necessities and medicines was only one part of the duty of the mistress of the household: the housewife in a financial position to do so must also act as 'An Over-seer for the poor'. 'She takes a Survey daily and duly of them,' wrote Richard Brathwaite, 'and, without any charge to the Hamlet, relieves them.' A good housewife, he concluded, would think 'that day wholy lost, wherein she doth not one good work at least'.[18]

That 'crown and glory' to her husband, Elizabeth Walker, was the daughter of a pharmacist in the City of London named Sadler, and was born in 1623 and married in 1650. Her husband in her biography did refer to the spiritual aspect of the marital partnership: let 'man and wife be meet helps to one another' in order to assist each other to reach Heaven. This was one refinement of the concept of the helpmate where Puritan thinking, with its stress on woman's spiritual capacity, was in advance of its time. However, Elizabeth Walker was aptly described by her husband as 'both Martha and Mary';[19] it was as Martha, with her conscientious housekeeping and her personally administered charities, that she exemplified the perfect wife of the time, whatever her religious persuasion.

True, it was as Mary that Mrs Walker began the day, at four o'clock in the morning, and sometimes as early as two or three, in order to obtain some hours of solitary meditation before the household was awake; in fact Mrs Walker was specially commended in the *Holy Life* for taking the trouble to light her own fire at that godly hour and not requiring some servant to do it for her! (The servants were first summoned at six for readings from the Bible, and prayers for the day-labourers came after breakfast.) After that Martha took over from Mary.

Indoors there was work with the needle, outdoors inspection of the dairy. Afternoons were spent visiting the sick, distributing salves and medicines. Mrs Walker would also visit women in childbirth, rising at any hour of the night, because of 'the commands of the Litany'. She was an excellent businesswoman, referred to jokingly by Dr Walker as 'my landlady' because he allowed her £19 worth of rents to handle a year. And he took particular pride in his wife's skill at cookery; she was 'clerk of her little kitchen, if I may so speak', making her own pastry and cream cheeses.[20]

On the last wedding anniversary which they celebrated – honoured by the presence of 'three coronetted heads' – this prodigious caterer managed to envelop thirty-nine pies in one dish which she had made herself. Afterwards the fragments were used to feast the many poor families who thronged to the house, pretending to seek Dr Walker's advice, actually desiring Mrs Walker's food. At Christmas everyone was offered hospitality, rich and poor; people were even encouraged to bring their children, for whom there was a special table: 'Trouble not yourselves', she would say, 'I love to see this little fry.'[21]

Mrs Walker also concocted 'English wines' and ciders to give away to her friends as presents. One is relieved to discover that this latter-day saint, who as a minister's wife always wore black without a redeeming knot or ribbon of colour, reacted most humanly when all the guests' praise for the cider was directed towards her husband.

'His cider!', she would exclaim, according to Dr Walker half way 'betwixt jest and earnest', ' 'Tis my cider: I have all the pains and care, and he hath all the praise who never meddles with it.' But then on many counts Elizabeth Walker showed herself a woman of independent view. Dr Walker also tells us – 'however much it might lessen her in people's esteem' – that his wife was in the habit of observing that 'Blacks and Tawnys as well as Whites were descendants of the first Adam'.[22]

The household routine of Mary Rich, although on a far grander scale, particularly after she became Countess of Warwick, conformed to the same ideal. Here, like Mrs Elizabeth Walker, is Brathwaite's paragon of domestic energy. It is true that her autobiography was ostensibly written as a record of the 'providences' in her life after she had undergone a 'conversion' and embraced the stricter Puritan faith of her husband's family (charting spiritual progress in written form, what Isaac Ambrose called 'a Register of God's dealings', was a popular task with Puritan ladies).[23] However, so many of these 'providences' occurred within the household, such being the intimate pattern of her existence, that we have here a picture that is as much domestic as spiritual.

Even her avowedly spiritual writings have a charmingly domestic flavour, an appreciation of the small mercies of life in terms of the small beauties of the daily round: 'Upon walking in autumn among dead leaves', 'Upon seeing a silk worm spin', 'Upon seeing a hog lie under an acorn tree, and eat the acorns, but never look up from the ground to the tree from which they fell'. 'Upon a Hen of my Lady Essex Rich' described a chick which was hatched in the stillroom by her niece and afterwards 'this poor grateful creature' persisted in returning to the house to lay its eggs there (a lesson to those less thankful for benefits received). Fish, mowers in the fields, her pet dog, canary birds and linnets that learnt to sing like canaries, these were the kind of domestic sights seen at Leighs Priory, the Rich family property in Essex, which provoked edifying reflections from Mary.[24]

A typical day, on which Mary would rise at about six for two hours of solitary meditation, would include not only a lengthy ordering of her household with all its ramifications between breakfast and dinner, but also a visit to the sick servants, and another visit to the village girls' school. These activities were not purely gracious. On the contrary, the cure of the sick (as Mrs Walker had distributed salves) and the administration of medicines generally, were an important duty on a level with the relief of the poor; most of the remedies, of a herbal nature, being prepared at home in the stillroom.

As for education, Mary Warwick was in the habit of catechizing her maids daily and reading to them books of devotion, in addition to her diurnal visits to the village girls' school. The educative abilities of a mistress of a household - including those on a much smaller scale than Leighs Priory - were of enormous potential importance in an age when girls' schooling as such hardly existed since the disappearance of the Catholic convents in the previous century (the Leighs Priory neighbourhood being fortunate in their patrons). Obviously the Puritans, with their emphasis on Bible reading, had a particular incentive to increase the spiritual capacity of their dependants by teaching them to read: Mrs Walker had her maids read holy texts to her. But in general, as we shall see when we return to the subject of educational opportunities for women, any conscientious housewife would expect to exert some kind of good influence in this respect - that is, when she could read herself.

*   *   *

'Dost thou love me?', Elizabeth Walker would ask of her husband, smiling.

To which he would reply: 'Most dearly.'

'I know it abundantly,' she would answer, 'to my comfort; but I love to hear thee tell me so.'

On another occasion Dr Walker was telling Elizabeth why he loved her and began: 'First for conscience -'. She stopped him:

'I would have thee love me, not because thou must, but because thou *wilt*, not as a duty but delight. For,' she added, 'we are prone to reluctate against what is imposed, but to take pleasure in what we choose.'

'Our mutual compellation', wrote Dr Walker, 'was always "My dear", not spoken automatically nor as an empty compliment, but the sincere interpretation of the language of our hearts.'[25] This affectionate, even slightly flirtatious relationship between the Walkers, which emerges so beguilingly from the pages of the *Holy Life*, serves as a salutary reminder that the ground rules of seventeenth-century marriage, while they threw up a number of hard cases, did not preclude the formation of many very happy unions.

The intimacy which flourished in the 'sturdy oaken' matrimonial bed-stead, destined to last 'one whole Century through' in Mary Evelyn's phrase in *Mundus Muliebris*, could be passionate and idyllic as well as fulfilling God's 'own holy and sacred ordinance'. (The importance of the marriage bed as a symbolic and enduring piece of furniture was attested by Henry Oxinden when he took the seventeen-year-old Kate Culling as his second wife, and had no bedstead of his own to share with her: he commissioned his cousin Eliza Dallison who lived in London to have a vast bed made, seven foot seven inches in breadth, six foot three inches long, with four posts at the corners one foot round. 'We would willingly have of the latest fashion,' he wrote, 'for this is all the beds we are like to make in our time.')[26] Marital sex, far from being frowned upon, was generally approved as leading to health and happiness in the husband; while the generally straightforward attitude of the time included the sensible notion that women too, once introduced to the pleasures of the marriage bed, could and would enjoy them.

'Dear Niece, Now that you know what's what, and the best and worst that man can do unto you, you will give me leave to wish you joy', wrote Lord Monmouth cheerfully to his niece Philadelphia Carey, now Lyttel-ton, shortly after her marriage. Philadelphia's sister was ill at Winchester; Lord Monmouth went on to suggest the same remedy for her: 'You may tell her that such an ingredient as you have had of late would do her more good than any physick she can take. But she is too good and too handsome to lack it long if she have a mind to it; and therefore she may thank herself if she continue to be ill. But you will be better to preach this doctrine to her than I, now that you have tried it yourself. Well, sweet niece, to leave raillery. . . .'[27]

Jane Sharp, the midwife, writing for popular consumption, agreed with Lord Monmouth that the 'Green Sickness' which occurred in unmarried girls would be cured by the physical delights of marriage. What was more, this was an age when the possibility of the female orgasm was not only appreciated and encouraged, but also, in the rather muddled state of thinking on the subject of the procreative process, believed by some people to help it along. Jane Sharp, for example, writing quite frankly about the private parts of a woman's body such as 'a little bank called a mountain of pleasure near the well-spring', thought that a woman's imagination, when aroused, helped her to produce the seed. The French believed that the womb then opened to enable conception.[28]

The Puritan handbooks were equally forthright, seeing in marital sex part of the divine plan which helped to save the soul as well as keep the marriage together. As William Gouge wrote in *Of Domesticall Duties*: 'To deny this duty being justly required, is to deny a true debt and to give Satan a great advantage.' Milton, declaring that there was nothing inher-ently sinful about sex itself 'whatever hypocrites austerely talk', envisaged in *Paradise Lost* an Adam and Eve before the Fall who did not want for 'youthful dalliance as beseems Fair couple, linkt in happy Nuptial league'.[29]

There were prohibitions: excessive 'dalliance' even in marriage was to be avoided. Evelyn, in his advice to his son John on his wedding-night, particularly advised against the kind of 'intemperance' that would exhaust him (and might also create 'unfortunate expectations' in his bride . . .). But then Evelyn also advised against making love on a full stomach, by day and in very hot or very cold weather: in short 'too frequent embraces dulls the sight, decays the memory, induces the gout . . . and shortens life'.[30] The recommendation against sex in hot weather was general – in advice given in the almanacs the dog days of July and August were thought to be particularly hazardous. However, recent research into baptismal registers, while it does show a correlative drop in baptisms in May and June, has not yet pin-pointed the cause, which may have been simply due to the exhaustion of the harvest work. Even here the point was well taken, that 'if husband wont, another must'.[31] Although we must depend on guesswork, there is no reason to suppose that in a frank and earthy age these recommendations to sexual moderation in marriage were heeded by any who were not physically predisposed to it in the first place.

Married love is a more difficult subject to chronicle with certainty than the lack of it – if easier than married sex. Yet there are revealing vignettes such as that of Lady Oglander, the wife of Sir John Oglander, Deputy Governor of the Isle of Wight, who would rush eagerly out to meet her husband under the oaks on Matthew's Green when he returned to London from the Isle of Wight; merely to 'live lovingly' with his wife was Sir John Oglander's declared public ambition.[32] And true conjugal felicity can certainly be glimpsed obliquely through the conventional public tributes.

Sometimes it is the death of the beloved which provokes the revealing outburst, as when the Parliamentary lawyer Bulstrode Whitelocke wrote in his journal on 15 May 1649 (a time of extreme political tension for the new Commonwealth): 'This was the saddest day of all the days of my life hitherto; my brother William Willoughby brought me the direful news that my wife was dead.'[33] Anthony Ashley Cooper, later Earl of Shaftesbury, whose cool sense of intrigue enabled him to survive membership of Cromwell's Council of State into the high Whig politics of the next reign, made an advantageous marriage in February 1639 to Margaret, daughter of the Lord Keeper Coventry. His passionate encomium on her sudden death ten years later makes an extraordinary contrast with the taciturn jottings in his diary which precede it.[34]

'My wife, just as she was sitting down to supper, fell into an apoplectical convulsion fit: She recovered that fit after some time, and spoke and kissed me, and complained only in her head but fell again in a quarter of an hour, and then never came to speak again; but continued in fits and slumbers until next day. At noon she died.' Shaftesbury continued: 'She was a lovely beautiful fair woman, a religious devout Christian, of admirable wit and wisdom, beyond any I ever knew, yet the most sweet, affectionate and observant wife in the world. Chaste, without a suspicion of the most envious, to the highest assurance of her husband, of a most noble and bountiful mind, yet very provident in the least things, exceeding all in anything she undertook, housewifery, preserving, works with the needle, cookery, so that her wit and judgement were expressed in all things, free from any pride or forwardness. She was in discourse and counsel far beyond any woman.'

Ashley Cooper, who was now a childless widower, did not long remain so; but his entry for that day in April 1650 on which he made a second marriage – for sound political reasons – is once more extremely taciturn: 'I was married to Lady Frances Cecil, and removed my lodging to Mr Blakes by Exeter House.' This time the match seems to have remained one of pure political convenience, for when a few years later the new wife also died, there was no outburst and no eulogy.

Lady Essex Rich was that niece and ward of Mary Countess of Warwick who as a girl had kept the 'grateful hen'. She was married off by Mary, after due investigation of his moral suitability, to Daniel Finch, later second Earl of Nottingham. Lady Essex died not long after, leaving her husband with a single daughter. Finch wrote to the minister who had married them a distraught letter: 'for I have lost surely a better friend, a wife without her equal, one that I loved as myself, for she was willing even to die to wean me from this world ... that we might meet in a better, and live together eternally.... Henceforward I will not think she has gone from me, but that I am going to her ... no man can be so proud of what he has, as I am that I can say I once had the best woman in the world.'[35] Like Lord Shaftesbury, Finch married again shortly – to the heiress Anne Hatton – who presented him with an enormous family. But he called his eldest daughter by his second wife Essex – after she who had been 'the best woman in the world'.

Oliver Heywood, a Puritan minister, was even more explicit after the death of his first wife Elizabeth Augier, 'the mirror of patience and subjection in her relation, as a child, as a wife, and of tenderness and care as a sister, and as a mother'. He wrote: 'I want her at every turn, everywhere, and in every work. Methinks I am but half myself without her.'[36]

Letters too reveal affections beyond the normal conjugal respect which spouses were supposed to feel for each other.

On this evidence Brilliana Lady Harley, 'that noble Lady and Phoenix of Women', to whose heroic story we shall return, had enjoyed a married life abundant in tenderness at its inception. 'I pray you remember that I reckon the days you are away ...', she wrote to Sir Robert Harley on 30 September 1625, when they had been married two years. Throughout his absences she expressed a constant wish to see him, culminating on 5 October 1627 with the cry: 'Believe me, I think I never missed you more than now I do, or else I have forgot what is past.'[37]

In 1642 Basil Lord Feilding, the Parliamentary commander, married as his third wife Elizabeth (Betty) Bourchier. The next year he succeeded to the title of his Royalist father, the Earl of Denbigh. It was no doubt an arranged match: despite his two previous marriages, the new Lord Denbigh was childless; Betty herself was a daughter and co-heiress of Henry Bourchier, fifth Earl of Bath. Nevertheless her letters breathe with her desire for him: 'My dear heart, my dear life, my sweet joy ...', she begins, ending with 'PS A hundred, thousand kisses I give thee, as I might be so happy as this paper. I long much to see you.' Sometimes Betty becomes petulant: surely he doesn't really love her, otherwise he would come back and see her? At other times she is more resigned. In 1644 she writes: 'Dear Joy ... I should have been glad to have been with you on the 8th July, because it is our wedding-day' but instead she will eat three cherry pies and drink her husband's health with his niece Su Hamilton. (For Lord Denbigh's own delectation, Betty dispatched presents of cakes and candied flowers, borage and marigolds.) It is all summed up by another ecstatic postscript: 'Dear! how thy Betty loves thee!'[38]

It is good to be able to record that the loving Betty, unlike so many wives in the seventeenth century, lived to enjoy nearly thirty years of married life (although, like all the Earl of Denbigh's other wives, she was childless).

★   ★   ★

Lastly, in the private memoir written by Ann, wife of Sir Richard Fanshawe, can be found in a humbler prose form the kind of lyrical sentiments about love and separation which Richard Lovelace, the admired Cavalier poet of his generation, poured into his volume of 1649, *Lucasta*:

> . . . Though seas and land betwixt us both,
>   Our faith and troth
>   Like separated souls
>   All time and space controls:
>   Above the highest sphere we meet
> Unseen, unknown, and greet as Angels greet.[39]

Ann, daughter of Sir John Harrison of Hertfordshire, described herself as being 'that which we graver people call a hoyting girl' (i.e. a hoyden) when she married Richard Fanshawe in 1644, he being a bachelor of thirty-five, and she a mere seventeen years old. She wrote the memoir after his death, in 1665, to be circulated in the family, and for the special attention of her only surviving son, so that he might understand the kind of man his father had been – and the kind of relationship of perfect trust which existed between them.[40] Fanshawe had been a man 'so reserved that he never showed the thought of his heart in the greatest sense, but to myself only', wrote his wife, but 'this I thank God with all my soul for, that he never discovered his trouble to me but went from me with perfect cheerfulness and content, nor revealed he his joys and hopes, but would say that they were doubled by putting them in my breast'.

Richard Fanshawe was a highly educated man, with a deep love of reading, especially history and poetry; he would even go for a walk with a book in his hand, generally poetry. He was a minor poet himself, a translator of Horace, and of Camoens's *The Lusiads* from the Portuguese. Indeed his career, as a courtier-politician and diplomat in the Stuart cause, through good times and bad, fully justified his wife's description of it after his death as 'nearly thirty years suffering by land and sea, and the hazard of our lives over and over. . . .' There were also 'seven years of imprisonment' as Lady Fanshawe phrased it: for Richard Fanshawe was captured after the fatal Battle of Worcester in 1651, which ended the cause of Charles II in England, and imprisoned at Whitehall. Although he was released on bail in November, it was not until 1658 that he was properly free once more and permitted to go abroad.

When the Fanshawes were married at Oxford in 1644, where the court then was, Richard had just been created Secretary for War to the Prince of Wales (the future Charles II, then a boy of fourteen); King Charles I hoped to use his son's position as a titular leader in order to pacify his squabbling rival commanders in the West. Clearly fierce love existed between the Fanshawes from the first, despite the seventeen-year gap in their ages and the allegedly austere nature of Richard. The first day they were parted after their marriage – Richard Fanshawe had to go to Bristol on the King's business – the 'reserved' husband was 'extremely afflicted even to tears, though passion was against his nature'. When he was able to send for Ann from Oxford, the letter of summons made her feel so faint with joy that she 'went immediately to walk, or at least to sit, in the air (being very weak) in the gardens of St John's College'.[41]

At Bristol, after Richard Fanshawe had joyfully hugged his young wife, he showed his trust in her practical sense by entrusting her with his store of gold. He told her: 'I know that thou that keeps my heart so well will keep my fortune, which from this time I will ever put into thy hands as God shall bless me with increase.' After this, Ann Fanshawe wrote, 'I thought myself a queen, and my husband so glorious a crown that I more valued myself to be called by his name than born a princess.'[42]

Equally clearly, it took a little time before the 'hoyting girl' realized the limits of the position of such a queenly wife, who could be trusted with her husband's fortune, but not his State secrets. Lady Fanshawe tells the story of how her kinswoman at the court – the Countess Rivers, an older woman – tacitly convinced her that in these troubled times it had become fashionable for women such as the beautiful Lady Isabella Thynne to display deep interest in matters of State and that to do so would make her even more beloved by her husband – 'if that had been possible' adds Lady Fanshawe quickly.[43] Impressed by this reasoning, the gullible girl proceeded to question her husband about his confidential business as Secretary for War, and in particular about the contents of a packet which had recently arrived from the Queen in France; all this was with a view to passing on the information to Countess Rivers.

So: 'When my husband returned from Council, after welcoming him home, as his custom ever was, he went with his handful of papers into his study for an hour or more. I followed him. He turning hastily said: "What wouldst thou have, my life?"' Ann Fanshawe then told him that she guessed he had the recent packet from the Queen in his hand and would like to know what was in it.

'He smiling replied, "My love, I will immediately come to thee. Pray thee go, for I am very busy." When he came out of his closet, I revived my suit. He kissed me and talked of other things.' At supper Ann declined to eat, although Richard carried on discoursing as usual, 'and drunk often to me, which was his custom'. Then it was time to withdraw. 'Going to bed, I asked again, and said I could not believe he loved me if he refused to tell me all he knew, but he answered nothing, but stopped my mouth with kisses, so we went to bed. I cried and he went to sleep ... next morning very early, as his custom was, he called to rise, but begun to discourse with me first, to which I made no reply. He rose, came on the other side of the bed and kissed me, and drew the curtain softly and went to court.'

When Richard returned that night for dinner, Ann took his hand and accused him of not caring about seeing her so upset. 'To which he, taking me in his arms, answered, "My dearest soul, nothing upon earth can afflict me like that; and when you asked me my business, it was wholly out of my power to satisfy thee ... the trust I am in may not be revealed."' He then assured her that in everything else 'my life and fortune shall be thine, and every thought of my heart'.

Richard Fanshawe kept his word, although some of the turns of fortune which he offered his wife might have broken the spirit of a lesser woman. In Galway they found themselves in a plague-ridden town, having narrowly escaped seizure in Cork at the time of Cromwell's campaign, as the Irish, 'stripped and wounded', were with 'lamentable shrieks' turned out of the town. On their subsequent sea journey to Spain at the request of Charles II, Ann Fanshawe, as a woman, was in danger of being taken as a slave by a Turkish man-of-war. While the master of their ship was parleying with the Turks, trying to convince them of his innocence, Ann was locked in her cabin. She stole out by bribing the cabin boy to let her have his clothes: 'I crept up softly and stood upon the deck by my husband's side as free from sickness and fear as, I confess, from discretion; but it was the effect of that passion I could never master.' When the danger had passed and Sir Richard realized who it was beside him, 'looking upon me he blessed himself and snatched me up in his arms, saying "Good God, that love can make this change!" And though he seemingly chid me, he would laugh at it as often as he remembered that voyage.'[44]

Leaving Spain for France, they were very nearly shipwrecked in the Bay of Biscay in a violent storm which lasted for two days and three nights, and ripped both sails and mast from the ship, so that crew and passengers thought all hope was lost. Afterwards, at Nantes, they had some white wine, butter, milk, walnuts and eggs, and 'some very bad cheese'. But, commented Ann: 'I am sure until that hour I never knew such pleasure in eating, between which we a thousand times repeated what we had spoke when every word seemed our last. We praised God; I wept, your father lifting then up his hands admired so great a salvation. Then we often kissed each other, as if yet we feared death....'[45]

Richard Fanshawe had been made a baronet in 1650; after the Restoration he was made a Privy Councillor and appointed Ambassador first to Portugal and then to Spain (where he died, although his body was finally reburied in Ware Church near his home in Hertfordshire). Diplomacy apart, he enjoyed the role of ambassador, having a great taste for hospitality, 'and would often say it was wholly essential for the constitution of England. He loved and kept order with the greatest decency possible.' Here once more Ann Fanshawe was the perfect helpmate and housekeeper, as we can appreciate, reading between the lines of her own modest disclaimer: 'though he would say I managed the domestics wholly, yet I ever governed them and myself by his commands, in the managing of which I thank God I found his approbation and content'.[46]

When she tried to sum up her married life for her son, Lady Fanshawe wrote: 'Now you will expect I should say something that may remain of us jointly, which I will do, though it makes my eyes gush out with tears, and cuts me to the soul, to remember and in part express the joys I was blessed with in him.

'*Glory to God* we never had but one mind throughout our lives, our souls were wrapped up in each other, our aims and designs one, our loves one, and our resentments one. We so studied one the other that we knew each other's mind by our looks; what ever was real happiness, God gave it me in him. . . .'[47]

Fourteen years after her husband's death, when 'what ever was real happiness' had ended, Ann Lady Fanshawe was laid beside him, at the age of fifty-five, in the family grave at Ware. So for them both at last those lines which Richard Fanshawe had written half a century ago came true:

> White peace (the beautifullest of things)
> Seems here her everlasting rest
> To fix, and spreads her downy wings
> Over the Nest.[48]

4　*The Pain and the Peril*

'My God and my Lord, my defender and protector, receive I most humbly beseech thee my acknowledgements of thy mercy, and my thanksgivings for my safe deliverance from the pain and the peril of Childbirth. . . .'

PRAYER OF ELIZABETH VISCOUNTESS MORDAUNT AFTER THE BIRTH OF HER SON JOHN, 1659

If we try to envisage the appearance of the women of the seventeenth century in relation to our own, we should allow of course for the evil effects of diseases now vanished such as smallpox, or dental decay in an age before competent dentistry. Both of these depredations, taken for granted at the time, might come as a shock to the curious time-traveller. But the fact that most of the leading female characters of the seventeenth century were in a state of virtually perpetual pregnancy would probably come as a far greater surprise.

Let us take the reigning goddesses of the courts of Charles I, Charles II and James II. Henrietta Maria, the exquisite sloe-eyed pearly Queen of Van Dyck's portraits and the court masques of Inigo Jones, was in fact pregnant almost without intermission from the autumn of 1628 until January 1639, when she bore her seventh child Katherine. After that, absence from the King's side in wartime accounted for a gap, but a last child Henrietta-Anne was born in 1644. Barbara Duchess of Cleveland, tempestuous mistress of Charles II, and Lely's voluptuous beauty, produced five children in as many years during the very height of her ascendancy over the King's affections (as well as a sixth somewhat later, about whose paternity there was undignified dispute). Mary of Modena, second wife of James II, gave birth as Duchess of York to four children in four years between 1675 and 1678 and another in 1682. None of these survived. James ascended the throne in 1685. It was the birth of a son in 1688, after what was considered to be (by James's supporters) an alarmingly long gap, which precipitated the Protestant Revolution.

As the great ladies fructified, so did their humbler sisters. There too we should retain a floating image of motherhood. Once the blessed knot had been tied, a married woman was expected to shoulder forthwith that special burden of motherhood bequeathed to her by Grandmother Eve. It did not need the incentive of a royal succession (or a king's favour); the desire for children in marriage, as many children as possible, to be born as quickly as possible, was universal. Puritan doctrines emphasized the importance of God's ordinance to increase and multiply and cover the earth (which had the beneficial effect of increasing the number of the Elect).[1] At the other extreme, the Catholic Church had reaffirmed the teaching of St Thomas Aquinas, that the whole end of sex was procreation, at the Council of Trent in the previous century.

Most married couples, however, scarcely needed a scriptural or doctrinal backing to carry out such natural activity. Thus 'big-bellied' or 'great-bellied' women were considered to be the norm, the happy norm; indeed the very use of such a straightforward term as 'great-bellied' (the common phraseology of the time, being neither vulgar nor jocular) indicates the way in which perpetual gravidity was taken for granted during the long child-bearing years of a married female. Pregnant, 'she seems to me, Diana in her crescent majesty', wrote Nicholas Hookes, in *Amanda* in 1653, describing the various aspects of his loved one's beauty.[2]

Most of the admirable wives referred to in the last chapter spent their adult life, in addition to their other duties, bearing, rearing and – all too often – burying children, in a great cycle of birth and life, birth and death, but at any rate birth and birth and birth, which meant that they were generally either crescent or descendent.

Of Mrs Elizabeth Walker for example, her husband wrote that 'her posterity cannot choose but prosper'; he might have added – those of them that survived. In the course of her energetic and charitable life Mrs Walker gave birth to eleven children, and there were abortive or 'untimely' births in addition. Of these eleven, explained Dr Walker, 'I say nothing of the eight lost but only the last three.' These were all daughters. Little Mary died when she was six, but even at that tender age was established as a passionate reader, spending an hour or two every night at her books by candlelight; young Elizabeth died at the age of sixteen (the sins to which she used to confess were the sympathetic adolescent ones of lying in bed too long on Sundays and 'slubbering' over her duties). Mrs Walker's last daughter died in childbirth, although the baby – Johnny – for whom she gave her life, survived. To this beloved grandson, Mrs Walker in old age was wont to proffer a good deal of sage advice. 'Dear Johnny', she would write, 'let not the length [of this letter] be tedious unto thee ...'

- twenty pages follow - but then we must remember that Johnny was the only 'posterity' left to her after eleven births, she who was used to declare that children were 'the nurseries of families, the church and the nation'.[3]

The background to the many dangerous adventures endured by Ann Lady Fanshawe was one of virtually unceasing pregnancy, child-nursing - and child-burying.[4] Her first son Harrison was born in February 1645 and died in March. The next year, when the Fanshawes had arrived in Jersey, in retreat from England with the Prince of Wales, was born Ann (the first of two daughters who bore their mother's name); she died when she was nine. A son (the first of two to be christened Henry) was born the year after, and died at the age of two. In 1648 - by which time Ann Fanshawe had been married four years - was born the first of three babies to be christened Richard; he died at the age of eleven. In 1650, while she was in Madrid on her husband's mission seeking aid, Lady Fanshawe gave birth to the first of her three daughters who would be called Elizabeth; the baby, whom Ann Fanshawe was carrying at the time of their perilous Irish experiences, died immediately. (It was also shortly after this that the Fanshawes were virtually shipwrecked on their way to Nantes.) The second Elizabeth was born the next year; she died at the age of five.

It was during the years of Richard Fanshawe's nominal captivity in England that Katherine, Margaret and Ann were born, all of whom survived; this was surely not unconnected with the fact that during these pregnancies Lady Fanshawe did not travel abroad. However, a fourth daughter Mary, who was born in 1656, died in 1660, and a son Henry, born in 1657, died in 1658. After the Restoration, when the Fanshawes' life was equally nomadic, if far more gloriously so, three more children were born. Elizabeth, born in 1662, survived, but the second Richard, born in 1663, died at birth; it was not until August 1665 that the third Richard Fanshawe, that surviving son for whom Ann wrote her memoir of her husband, was born in Madrid. The following June, when his son and heir was not yet a year old, Sir Richard Fanshawe himself died; among other problems faced by his widow in a foreign land was the task of conveying very young children homeward.

Not only Lady Fanshawe but very many of the married women whose deeds of heroism during the Civil War we shall consider, were struggling at the same time with the additional burden of repeated pregnancies. These include the wives of the Levellers - Mary Overton and Elizabeth Lilburne - whose sufferings were similar in kind to those of Mary Lady Verney or the Yorkshire heroine, Lady Cholmley, or her sister-in-law Dame Isabella

Twysden, or Lucy Hutchinson, wife of the Roundhead Governor of Nottingham Castle, but whose privations through poverty and imprisonment were even worse.

*　　*　　*

It was the 'barren Hannah or childless Elizabeth', in Samuel Hieron's phrase, who bewailed her fate. Some real connection was seen between child-bearing and grace: for what was woman's best chance to redeem herself from the sin of Eve and restore herself to honour but by fulfilling this natural female role? This philosophy had the backing of the New Testament: 'Adam was not deceived, but the woman being deceived was in the transgression. Notwithstanding she shall be saved in childbearing.'[5]

Conversely, infertility might come to be equated with sin. Thus Samuel Hieron's prayer for the barren woman began with an acknowledgement of the sinfulness which had brought the petitioner to such a state ('It is just, I confess, with thee, to punish my barrenness in grace, and my fruitlessness in holy things, with this want of outward increase'), before proceeding to the heartfelt plea: 'let me be as the fruitfull Vine on the walls of my husbands house, and let (at the least) one Olive plant spring out from me, to stand about his table. ...'[6]

In 1644 Anne Murray was jilted by her lover Thomas Howard for the sake of a much richer bride, whom the unfaithful lover married 'privately' without letting Anne know. When the news leaked out, Anne's indignant maid Miriam lifted up her hands and cursed the new wife: 'Give her, O Lord, dry breasts and a miscarrying womb.' In her memoirs, Anne tells us that she reproved Miriam. However, she adds: 'But it seems the Lord thought fit to grant her [Miriam's] request, for that lady miscarried several children before she brought one to the full term, and that one died presently after it was born; which may be a lesson to teach people to govern their wishes. ...'[7]

Under the circumstances every manual and every almanac offered remedies for infertility, many of them allegedly with a long history of success; for as William Sermon wrote in *The Ladies Companion, or The English Midwife* of 1671: 'the Ancients (not being ignorant of what this Sex principally desire) have left several ways for the accomplishment of the same'. Sermon's recommendations 'to make Women fruitfull' included doses of white ginger taken in a powdered form, and more imaginatively, sitting over a bath in which skeins of raw yarn had been boiled in the water and then mixed with ashes. Otherwise the infertile wife might bathe herself in water in which 'Ale-hoof, oaten and pease straw have been boiled together – then let her dry herself, and presently let her Husband do his best endeavour.'[8]

It is easy to be cynical and suggest that of all these remedies, only the advice to the husband was likely to be remotely helpful; the number and extent of such cures advocated on every side bear witness to the passionate wishes of every wife to fulfil this other part of her bounden duty. Sir John Brownlow of Belton believed in the drinking of mares' milk every morning in March and April. Rules suggested to Samuel Pepys (anxious that his wife should conceive) ranged from the drinking of sage juice – a popular remedy of the time – and the 'wearing of cool Holland-drawers' to the propping up of the marriage bed at a slant or even better 'to lie with our heads where our heels do'.[9] In spite of this, Mrs Pepys never did bear any children.

It was hardly surprising that Margaret Duchess of Newcastle, whose husband had children by his first marriage, consulted the celebrated physician Sir Theodore Mayerne when she failed to conceive after two years. His advice was sensible: 'Be in good health and then you may till your ground, otherwise it will be time lost if you enter that race frowningly.' But Margaret did not conceive. As a result she came to write with considerable acerbity about her fertile sisters – women like 'Lady S.M.' who had only been married for four weeks, but knowing herself to be with child was already proudly 'rasping wind out of her stomache ... making Sickly faces ... and bearing out her Body, drawing her Neck downward, and standing in a weak and faint Posture as great bellied Wives do. ...'[10]

Margaret Newcastle poured further contempt on the great fuss which was made about the business of childbirth itself: the making and buying of fine and costly childbed linen (although one should perhaps point out that the heiress Lady Anne Clifford used her husband's three-year-old shirts as 'clouts'). Then there was the fearful fuss over the baby, including an expensive christening – the money, she suggested, would be better spent on the child's education – swaddling clothes, baby mantles, cradles, baskets and so forth.[11] In Margaret Newcastle's general scorn for women who prided themselves on their 'great bellies', one can detect the jealous voice of one who would never be able to form the centrepiece of such a celebration herself.

The constant emphasis on the virtuous work of bearing children – in which the mothers, as well as the fathers, preachers and advisers all concurred – casts the whole subject of contraception within marriage (never wholly clear of the shadows in any age) into a particular obscurity. The pathetic case of Mistress Augier, mother of Elizabeth Heywood, provides an extreme example of how a large family was regarded as a mark of God's favour. In 1642 Mistress Augier had been suffering from cancer of the breast for two years, enduring pangs 'so painful that she often said she would be content to have her breast ripped open for a little ease'. Under the circumstances it might seem fortunate rather than the reverse that there had been a long gap in her child-bearing; however, her husband, a Puritan minister, did not view the situation in that light. When Mistress Augier conceived once more, her husband attributed it to divine intervention. She was delivered of her child a month early, with a very long hard labour, in the course of which the midwife pronounced – correctly – that there was no hope of saving the mother's life. Mistress Augier died in terrible agonies. 'God gave her conception after almost eight years' respite,' wrote her husband after her death, 'having often put it into my heart to pray for the enlarging of my family.' He went on: 'Yet after her conception her weakness and weariness increased.'[12]

Elizabeth (Betty) Viscountess Mordaunt, who kept 'a Private Diarie', probably at the request of her spiritual adviser, also referred constantly within it to 'the Great Blessing of many Children'.[13] It was a blessing she herself certainly enjoyed, giving birth to seven sons and four daughters in under twenty years. It was, however, a tumultuous period, not only in the history of England but in her own life story and that of her husband, in which her repeated pregnancies can only have been an additional burden.

Betty Mordaunt was the only daughter and heiress of Thomas Carey, a son of the Earl of Monmouth. Besides that she was a beauty of whom it was said as a young girl:

> Betty Carey's lips and eyes
> Make all hearts their sacrifice.

John Mordaunt was a staunch supporter of Charles I and Charles II in turn. Clarendon paid Betty this tribute: quite apart from her physical charms, she was 'of a very loyal spirit and notable vivacity of wit and humour', sharing her husband's 'honourable dedication' to the Stuart cause.[14] Betty needed all her wit and loyalty when John Mordaunt was among three men condemned to death by the High Court of Justice in the spring of 1658, for conspiring against Oliver Cromwell in favour of Charles II. Betty was pregnant with her second child at the time, but behaved with great courage and enterprise throughout the trial; not only was she present in court, but also tried – vainly as it turned out – to bribe the members of the Court of Justice. It was however Betty who managed to get a note to her husband that while it was useless to question the court's jurisdiction (the normal Royalist reaction) the damning evidence against him was in fact comparatively slight.

For all this, Mordaunt was condemned to death. Now Betty Mordaunt paid a personal visit to the ageing Protector to plead with him for her husband's life; she remarked afterwards that the Protector 'played the gallant so well' that she believed he would have been as good as his word, and 'waited upon her the next morning' had she encouraged him. Whether Betty's pretty face, unaffected by pregnancy, and legendary lips and eyes ensnared the ageing Protector (who, contrary to the report of history, was never averse to an encounter with a pretty woman),[15] at all events John Mordaunt was the only conspirator who was reprieved. He survived to continue his intrigues on behalf of the King, being created Viscount Mordaunt of Avalon in 1659.

On her husband's tombstone, which listed his deeds of daring on behalf of the two Stuart monarchs, a gracious allusion was made to his wife: *lectissima Heroina Elizabeth Carey.* The private diary of this most excellent heroine, amid various ecstatic outpourings of a religious nature, chronicles a series of births which alone might justify the title. Betty Mordaunt wrote a prayer of thanksgiving after the birth of her son John in 1659 (the baby she had been bearing at the time her husband was condemned to death), 'for my safe deliverance from the pain and the peril of Childbirth'. And for her daughter 'Cory', born on 29 July 1661, she recorded her gratitude for 'the blessing of a live and perfect child'. But when she miscarried twins in 1674, on her birthday, she attributed this grave loss to her own spiritual transgressions. Pregnant once more at the time of her husband's death, Betty prayed passionately: 'preserve the child within me, the time it has to stay, from every ill accident ... bless my child with perfect shapes'. Little George was born safely in January 1676: Betty called upon 'my dearest Lord' [God] to be his father, 'he that was born without father, brought into the world by an afflicted mother'.[16]

It is obviously highly unlikely that women of this calibre or families like the Walkers and the Fanshawes practised any form of limitation whatsoever, given the rapid pattern of births. But was no attempt ever made to avoid the consequences of unlimited married sex, if only for the sake of the mother, condemned to what Betty Mordaunt aptly described as 'the pain and the peril' of childbirth? Or for that matter for the sake of the father and breadwinner, whose economic burden, when his numerous progeny actually survived infancy, might be well nigh intolerable during the years of their upbringing?

The subject of contraception within marriage at this date is complicated by the fact that the most effective form known (until the invention of the Pill in the present day), the sheath or condom, was not introduced to England generally until the eighteenth century. Its original purpose was prophylactic: the good news arrived in English aristocratic circles as early as the 1680s via France (where Madame de Sévigné for example wrote in praise of this hygienic measure in 1671). But Pepys, whose promiscuous life with the unofficial whores of Westminster Hall would have benefited from such a form of protection, was ignorant of it: instead he spent some anxious time calculating whether he could have been responsible for one particular pregnancy.[17]

At the same time herbal medicines which might either prevent or cure – the line between a contraceptive and an abortifacient being not always an easy one to draw – were, as they had always been, part of the folkloric knowledge of the times. Swallowing a hot mixture of spices was advocated for both contraception or abortion, as was the juice of the herb savin; hence its nickname Cover Shame – it being a 'notorious Restorative of slender shapes and tender reputations', as a pamphlet described it at the end of the seventeenth century.[18] Marjoram, thyme, parsley, lavender and 'brake' (bracken) were all proposed with the general object in view of preventing birth. Nicholas Culpepper's edition of the *College of Physicians' Directory* suggested that honeysuckle was able to 'procure barrenness, and hinder conception'. John Swan's almanacs also suggested that the juice of honeysuckle, drunk continuously by a man for thirty-seven days, would make him so that he could 'never beget any more children'. In Defoe's *Conjugal Lewdness*, early in the next century, there was advice concerning powders 'in Warm Ale'; after taking these 'she shall be out of danger'.[19]

Some of the advice on the subject might be surreptitious. It did not take much wit to appreciate that those herbs described as best avoided to prevent miscarriage, would, if administered, have exactly the opposite effect. (Women were warned, for example, that proximity to sowbread would cause abortion.) Similarly, herbs to be carefully avoided by the barren – such as rue – could be enthusiastically swallowed by those who did not wish to conceive. Violent movements during intercourse were said to inhibit conception; these same movements, if indulged, might ward off the danger.

Many of the herbal remedies were based on the sensible if slightly drastic premise that the dampening of masculine desire prevented the problem from arising in the first place: rue once again was said by the female astrologer Sara Jinner to make a man no better than a eunuch. One emetic mixture proposed consisted of radish root, agarick, and saram, boiled in barley water, to be drunk when cool.[20] Castor oil was suggested for the same purpose, as was lettuce (the purgative effects of the one and the soporific effects of the other must certainly have given them a high rate of success in extinguishing ardour).

Other measures recommended, of varying degrees of unpleasantness to the modern ear, included pessaries for the female – rue featured here again, or ground-up bitter almonds – and a uterine clyster (what would now be called a douche) employing such herbs as camphor, castor oil and rue. The male organ might be anointed with salves of a vaguely anaesthetic nature or bathed in cold liquids, vinegar, or the juice of nightshade or henbane. For the desperate, there was always blood-letting. According to the medical theories of the time it was the special heat of the blood which was responsible for producing that superior male seed which was considered to be 'the generative faculty'. A woman was generally believed to have 'seed' too, the ovaries being the equivalent of the testicles, but just as 'her heat is lesser and weaker than his', so her 'seed' was thought to be cold and watery, in short far less important in the procreative process. (The biological role of the female in procreation was only properly understood after the invention of the microscope revealed the existence of the female 'egg' as opposed to 'seed'.)[21]

The existence of this ancient twilight world of folkloric preventives demonstrates that both contraception and abortion were underground preoccupations of the seventeenth century – at least where sexual intercourse outside marriage was concerned (not a very surprising conclusion in view of the social consequences to both parties if illicit love resulted in pregnancy). The question of whether the same preventives were taken within marriage is far more difficult to establish; clearly the same medicines were available to be swallowed, applied, or otherwise employed, by the married as by the single. The whole subject of contraception within marriage is ignored by contemporaries, even by those whose revelations are otherwise fairly intimate. The diaries of the Puritan Ralph Josselin, as their editor has remarked, leave us to guesswork on this subject.[22] For instance he records his wife's miscarriages and these do tend to coincide almost exactly with the first moment when she could have known she was pregnant (and thus used an abortifacient), but since this early stage of pregnancy would also be the likeliest time for a spontaneous miscarriage, the mystery remains unsolved.

In any case many of the above remedies have something of an air of desperation about them; even if employed they would not have affected overmuch the child-bearing capacity of a healthy and fertile woman having regular sexual intercourse. It seems far more likely that those married couples who did for any reason wish to limit their families practised coitus interruptus, a method of birth control which, as it has been observed, it is possible for each generation to rediscover for itself.[23] Once again, first-hand information about the subject is hard to come by.

It has recently been suggested, albeit with caution, that the use of this type of family limitation was gradually rising among the middle classes as the century progressed. There are certain significant statistics: the fertility among women over thirty generally, and the age at which women bore their last child in particular, fell in the second half of the seventeenth century. Other researches point to a significant gap between the birth of the penultimate and the ultimate child.[24]

Mary Rich, Countess of Warwick provides one of the few direct references to family limitation in her autobiography (although she does not state the method used). The giddy young girl who got married at fifteen to a younger son, against her father's wishes, did not immediately ripen into the benevolent Puritan matron at the head of her household; as has been mentioned, a spiritual conversion had to intervene. Immediately after her marriage Mary Rich gave birth to two children in rapid succession: Elizabeth, who died as a baby, victim of two careless nursemaids who 'tossed' her between them, and a son called Charles after his father. She was not yet seventeen.

Twenty years later, young Charles Rich died at the age of twenty-one. Not only was his father, now Earl of Warwick, left without a direct heir, but the cousin who would inherit the title by default was considered by Mary to be of a highly unsuitable character. We have Mary's own account of the stricken couple's passionate wish to start a new family. Although she was still only thirty-seven, these hopes were not fulfilled, leaving Mary prey to further remorse that she had deliberately refrained from having further children in her youth. She gives two reasons for this resolve: first, at the age of seventeen, one of the youthful beauties of the court of Charles I, she feared to ruin her figure 'if she childed so thick'; secondly, Charles Rich, as a younger son, had worried that if he had 'many to provide for, they must be poor'.[25] Certainty is impossible; but if abstinence in a young couple, who had married for that troublesome emotion, love, is ruled out, one may suppose that coitus interruptus was the method by which Mary preserved her lissom figure, and Charles Rich his modest fortune – with ultimately such disastrous results.

*   *   *

In 1622 a woman of twenty-six expecting her first baby, called Elizabeth Josceline, wrote how she dreaded the painfulness of 'that kind of death' during childbirth. Born Elizabeth Brooke of Norton in Cheshire, she had been brought up by her grandfather William Chaderton, Bishop of Lincoln, a friend of Coke and Lord Burghley. In 1622 she had already been married for six years. *The Mothers Legacy to her Unborn Child* was an attempt to overcome that justifiable dread which possessed so many women of the time – how would the child fare if the mother did not survive the ordeal? Elizabeth Josceline carefully garnered all the advice she would proffer her child in advance, to obviate that 'loss my little one should have, in wanting me'. It proved a popular subject: by 1625 *The Mothers Legacy* had gone through three editions, and it was reprinted unaltered in 1684.[26]

Naturally the child would have to be put out to nurse, but despite its tender age, this was to be in a house where there was no swearing or speaking 'scurrilous words' (Elizabeth Josceline wrote: 'I know I may be thought too scrupulous in this'). Later the servants were to address the child by its Christian name, without the prefix 'Master' or 'Miss', to teach it proper respect. Throughout the book, Elizabeth Josceline modestly reminded herself that she was only writing for 'a child's judgement', although at the same time she begged her 'truly loving and most dearly loved husband Taurell Josceline', to whom the book was dedicated, not to pardon its faults through fondness but to correct them.

Reading *The Mothers Legacy* today, in manuscript, still has the power to touch one, for nine days after the birth of her child Elizabeth Josceline did undergo just 'that kind of death' she had feared. And she was wrapped in that very winding-sheet which she had already secretly bought for herself.[27] At least in bequeathing to posterity a book, she had succeeded in her declared ambition to do something more for her child than 'only to bring it forth'.

None at this time doubted that childbirth itself, whatever the desirability of founding a family, was both a painful and a dangerous ordeal. 'These are doubtless the greatest of all pains the Women naturally undergo upon Earth', wrote the midwife Jane Sharp. Margaret Duchess of Newcastle, herself of course barren, wrote that a husband who had heirs by his first wife should not complain if his second did not conceive children since 'she hazards her life by Bringing them [children] into the world'.[28]† Nor was

† But the joint monument to the Duke and Duchess of Newcastle in Westminster Abbey still records this failure on her part, ahead of all her manifold virtues: 'Here Lyes the Loyall Duke of Newcastle And his Dutches his second wife, by whom he had noe issue . . .'

Elizabeth Josceline alone in her apprehensions. Anne Harcourt, in her diary, confessed to her 'exorbitant fear' of labour, 'notwithstanding the former experiences of God's goodness in helping me at like times'. The jilted Anne Murray, finding happiness at last in marriage with Sir James Halkett, gave birth for the first time at the age of thirty-four. She drew up a *Mother's Instructions* before the birth of that child, and of each subsequent arrival, although in fact she lived safely on, dying in 1699 at the age of seventy-seven.[29]

Margaret Blagge, the lovely yet earnest Maid of Honour to Catherine of Braganza, John Evelyn's adored young friend, was not so lucky.[30] As a girl she had been markedly reluctant to abandon her virgin state; one of her reasons was her fear of childbirth. Evelyn hastened to reassure her: 'Little women, I told her, had little pain.' Even after marrying the young courtier Sidney Godolphin, Margaret remained full of melancholy presentiments. First she did not conceive for two years, and then when she did, she too, like Elizabeth Josceline and Anne Halkett, laid all her plans in the eventuality of her death. Enduring a very difficult pregnancy and 'growing bigger', her public life was gradually reduced to visits to the chapel.

Margaret Godolphin went into labour during the night of Monday, 2 September 1678; about noon on the Tuesday 'a Man Child' was born, her husband, in attendance at court at Windsor, was informed. On the Thursday the child was baptized Francis. On the Sunday Evelyn, who was at his house at Deptford, received a letter while at church from Sidney Godolphin: 'My poor wife is fallen very ill of a fever, with lightness in her head.' Evelyn's prayers were implored. But Margaret's delirium increased. Matters were made worse when the doctors hung back and refused to act except in the presence of other physicians. Evelyn then arrived, with his wife, and by his own account took charge. (Even in her delirium, he noted, his chaste young friend said 'nothing offensive'.)

But poor Margaret was now, as Evelyn wrote, 'in a manner spent'; she had already endured 'the pigeons' – a medieval remedy by which live birds were applied to the patient's feet, generally to reduce fever – and bloodletting; the latter, from a vein in the arm, was commonly believed by doctors to stop haemorrhage.[31] The momentary respite which was granted by Betty Viscountess Mordaunt's famous strengthening cordial was soon over. Erysipelas, a kind of hot red rash described by Evelyn as 'a fiery Trial', began to spread over her back, neck and arms (it was in fact produced by the acute streptococcal infection causing her 'puerperal' fever). She lasted like this in 'all the circumstances of pain and weariness' until the morning of the next day. Then her paroxysms grew worse and she died at noon on Monday, 9 September, one week after the birth of her child, being in her twenty-fifth year.

Margaret Godolphin's last letter to her husband was full of that submissive melancholy which had animated so much of her short life: 'In the first place, my dear, believe me, that of all earthly things you were and are the most dear to me . . . and do not grieve too much for me, since I hope I shall be happy, being very much resigned to God's will.' In her letter to him concerning her legacies, however, she revealed that other apprehension which haunted the dying wives of the seventeenth century: if Sidney Godolphin married again, he was to 'be kind to that poor Child I leave behind, for my sake, who lov'd you so well'.[32] But Sidney Godolphin, rare among his contemporaries as we shall see in the next chapter, never married again.

*   *   *

Lord Falmouth, who was madly in love with his beautiful wife Mary Bagot ('His Dearest Deare'), wanted her labour to be over before he returned from the Dutch war at sea, since he could not bear to see his beloved suffer: 'I cannot endure to see you in pain or trouble.' Later he wrote: 'You are in my thoughts the first thing in the morning and last at night. 'Tis certain my Dearest Deare Child that, let your pain have been what it will, my torment in the belief of it has not been much inferior to it.' (Falmouth's daughter had in fact been born four or five days earlier, but Falmouth, killed at the Battle of Lowestoft a short while later, never saw her.)[33]

How were these harrowing ordeals and deathbeds familiar to every household, and (unlike the state of pregnancy) never glossed over in contemporary accounts, to be explained in the divine order of things? Samuel Hieron made the origin of such sufferings quite clear in his prayer to be uttered by a woman in labour: 'the smart of the punishment which thou [Lord] laidst upon me being in the loins of my grandmother Eve, for my disobedience towards thee: Thou hast greatly increased the sorrows of our sex and our bearing of children is full of pain'. The poet Edmund Waller put it another way when he threw a light-hearted curse over Lady Dorothy Sidney, who had rejected him for another: 'make her taste the first curse imposed on womankind – the pains of becoming a mother'.[34]

If woman redeemed herself from the sin of Eve by child-bearing, she was none the less condemned to suffer the pains of childbirth in order to fulfil that prophecy made in Genesis: 'Unto the woman he [God] said, I will greatly multiply thy sorrow and thy conception; in sorrow thou shalt bring forth children.' This doctrine, upon which Catholics and Puritans were alike agreed, gave at least some spiritual context to the agonies of women. (It was Catholic belief that after Eve's Fall, only the Virgin Mary, being born without original sin, did not suffer the pangs of childbirth, when she gave birth to the Infant Christ.) Faced with the perpetual prospect of their wives' sufferings, there was even some relief for loving husbands in accepting the link with the sin of Eve; it alleviated a burden which was otherwise unacceptable.

The penitential element in childbirth could even be carried further. The ceremony of 'churching' had, in its Judaic origins, been intended to 'cleanse' a woman after her delivery, but by the seventeenth century it was intended quite simply as a ceremony of thanksgiving. Certain women evidently believed that Archbishop Laud, in his plans for the Anglican Church, was attempting to bring back this penitential element to the ceremony, by insisting on a handkerchief or veil being worn; with indignation, protesters compared this head-covering to the white linen sheet which had to be worn by the 'unchaste'. There are entries in the Essex and Colchester Courts for women refusing to cover their heads in this manner. In 1639 Dorothy Hazzard, wife of a Bristol parson, received women to her house for their lying-in, because they could thus avoid the more disagreeable churching ceremonies elsewhere.[35]

If the cruel pangs of labour could be blamed upon Grandmother Eve, that other affliction endured by so many mothers of the seventeenth century, the death of the child itself in infancy, could hardly be laid directly at her door. Yet such a harrowing experience, as has been seen in the case of the Walkers and Fanshawes, was an inseparable part of parenthood in the seventeenth century. It might be the death of one child, of many children, of the entire flock; it was a rare and fortunate parent who escaped this tragedy altogether.

It has been suggested in recent years, notably by Lawrence Stone in *The Family, Sex and Marriage in England 1500-1800*, that the low expectation of infant life meant that people were as a whole less attached to their children, or at any rate during the child's first year of life, when its ability to survive the rigours of infant disease had not been established. He does however comment that the popular psychologist Richard Napier treated women disturbed by the deaths of infants; Napier's notebooks concerning his patients (who were drawn from every social class) certainly include 134 cases of disturbing grief – nearly half of which were attributed to a child's death. The vast majority of these sufferers were mothers, such as Ellen Craftes who 'took a fright and grief that a door fell upon her child and slew it. Presently head, heart and stomach ill; eyes dimmed with grief that she cannot see well.'[36]

In general one can only observe that this suggested indifference is not the attitude of those women literate or lucky enough to be able to express themselves. Since the maternal instinct of one sort or another is a universal one (if anything enhanced rather than diminished by the proximity imposed by poverty), it seems unlikely that a woman wailing without words for her baby felt the death less because she was inarticulate. As in any natural disaster, only the voice of the privileged (generally male) was heard, but everyone suffered alike.

Ralph Verney's wife Mary was delirious for two days and nights with sorrow when her baby died suddenly of convulsions; when the news of the death of her daughter Pegg reached her she felt totally unable to care for two little girls, relations of Ralph's, because to do so would simply exacerbate her own grief. Oliver Heywood, in his account of the life of his mother, described 'how great an affliction' was the death of her first-born. The poet Katherine Philips (known as the 'Matchless Orinda') wrote of the death of her baby son in 1655 in a poem entitled 'Orinda upon little Hector Philips':

> I did but see him, and he dis-appeared,
> I did but pluck the Rose-bud and it fell. . . .[37]

In the simple pain of the sentiment she spoke for all the countless women who had also glimpsed their babies only once, and mourned in silence.

As for the slightly older children, the desperation of many contemporary comments on these deaths speaks for itself. Sir Hugh Cholmley of Scarborough described how when one of their children, known as 'little Betty', died aged four and a half 'to the great grief of my wife and myself', he took the stricken household away on a holiday to try and recover from a sorrow unendurable amid the familiar surroundings[38] – a reaction to loss which does not alter down the ages.

A comment by Samuel Clarke, who wrote *The Lives of Sundry Eminent Persons in this Later Age*, printed the year after his death, in 1683, explains the difference in the approach to suffering of that period. There is a parallel to be drawn between the public guilt felt about the emotion of love (although love itself was undoubtedly experienced), and the guilt felt about grief over the death of a child. Clarke included among his pious ladies his own wife Katharine Overton, whom he married in 1625, when she was twenty-four. He tells us that she experienced the most terrible grief at the deaths of her children, but thought it her duty to try and overcome it.[39] Poor Lettice Falkland felt that the devil himself was tempting her because she was overcome with desolation at the death of her son Lorenzo; she began to imagine herself responsible for his death by her own transgressions – a guilt which can only have added to the natural despair of the stricken mother. Anne Digby, the cool Countess of Sunderland, provided a glimpse into the reality of contemporary suffering when she wrote to John Evelyn over the death of his beloved grandson at the age of a year: 'We are so comfortably sure that the poor innocent babies are taken out of a naughty world to be very happy, that I have often wondered at the excessive sorrow I have sometimes seen on these occasions.' She added piously: 'but ... we always prefer our own satisfaction, be it never so transitory, to the most solid good for others'.[40]

Sir William Brownlow was a brother of that Sir John Brownlow of Belton who recommended mares' milk for conception; no such expedient was necessary in the case of his wife, Elizabeth Duncombe. William Brownlow kept a meticulous record of her child-bearing from 27 June 1626 when their first child Richard was born, who died in the October of that year, down to the birth of their nineteenth child twenty-two years later; a daughter who lived – unmarried – till 1726. One third of this vast progeny survived – two sons and four daughters – which on a larger scale was something like the average survival rate for upper- and middle-class families of the time, in so far as it can be estimated.[41]

At one point, between 1638 and 1646, *seven* children, born at almost exactly yearly intervals, died in a row; Thomas, Francis, Benjamin, George, James, Maria and Anne. William Brownlow's exclamations of grief as each new tragedy struck show some attempt at reconciliation to the workings of providence – 'Though my children die, the Lord liveth and they exchange but a temporal life for an eternal one' – but absolutely no diminution in grief. Little George, for example, his fifteenth child, managed to live from October 1641 to 29 July of the following year; when he died, his father wrote: 'I was at ease but Thou O God hast broken me asunder and shaken me to pieces.' That was doubtless the truth. Parents, in their heart of hearts, could not reconcile themselves to a doctrine which left the little one happier in heaven – and their arms empty.

'My dear mother, why do you mourn and weep so much for my

brother Willy?' asked Alice Thornton's little daughter Naly. 'Do you not think he is gone to heaven?'

'Yes, dear heart', replied Alice Thornton, 'I believe he is gone to heaven, but your father is so afflicted for his loss, and being a son he takes it more heavily, because I have not a son to live.' At this Naly asked the logical child's question: 'Would you then have him out of heaven again?' Alice Thornton in her autobiography does not record her reply, only that she felt reproved out of 'the mouth of so young a child' for her 'immoderate sorrow'.[42]

Alice Wandesford was born at Kirklington in Yorkshire in 1627 a member of the minor gentry of the North Riding, and married William Thornton of East Newton in 1651. A woman of strong character emerges from the pages of her autobiography; she declared that her motive for writing it was to make some sense of her husband's failure in life (he ended up a bankrupt), and her own subsequent struggles to bring up her family in poverty. Memories of a golden girlhood in Ireland, when her father's cousin the Earl of Strafford was Deputy, provided a bitter contrast. Nevertheless Alice Thornton does not write bitterly, although her financial worries were compounded by her sufferings as a mother. Her sister Catherine, wife of Sir Thomas Danby, had given birth to sixteen children, of whom six were stillborn, and died as a result of a long and painful delivery at the age of thirty.

Alice hesitated for some time before accepting the suit of William Thornton through a personal wish to be single; possibly affected by the spectacle of her sister's sufferings. Conceiving shortly after marriage, she was very sick in the early stages of her first pregnancy, and the child died after half an hour. Her second child was nearly 'overlaid' by its nurse – a gruesome contemporary fate, whereby the wet-nurse fell asleep and stifled or crushed the baby. Hearing the baby 'groaning troublesomely' Alice rushed in and extricated the infant from its perilous position. As a result of this, Alice suckled the next child – 'my sweet Betty' – herself, being 'overjoyed' to do so. However, at the age of eighteen months sweet Betty died of a combination of rickets and a cough: 'When Mr Thornton and I came to pray for her, she held up those sweet eyes and hands to her dear Father in heaven, looked up and cried in her language, "Dad, dad, dad" with such vehemency as if inspired by her holy father in heaven to deliver her sweet soul into her heavenly father's hands.'[43]

Then there was the son who died because the midwife lacked skill. After this Alice, fearing that she might now be barren, went to Scarborough Spa. She did conceive a child. This was 'my dear Willy Thornton' whose death at the age of fourteen days was taken not only by his father but by Alice herself very hard.

In giving birth to her next child Robert, Alice suffered repeated haemorrhages, although she was able to feed him herself for two years. Expecting her eighth child, Alice nervously worried herself over their fate if she should die, and Mr Thornton married again: 'as I had been told that it would be necessary for him for his health'.[44] But it was William Thornton who died, not Alice. Despite the fact that the birth of her ninth child left her very weak, with gangrene of the breast, Alice Thornton recovered after four months spent in bed. She lived on until 1706.† Three out of her nine children survived. Little Naly was evidently a highly strung as well as a precocious child: she fell into convulsions when taken by the maids to see the show put on to celebrate the coronation of King Charles II at Richmond – soldiers, drunks, noise, and firing muskets provoked from her a series of paralysing screams. Despite this, at the age of fourteen she was 'spoken for' by the curate of Stonegrave, Thomas Comber, later a venerated Dean of Durham, and Naly lived, like her mother, to a great age.

*   *   *

The true figures for deaths in childbirth at this time cannot be established with certainty, owing to what one scholar has called the 'exasperating rarity' of evidence in the parish registers as to why the person buried there died. One estimate gives a figure varying from 125 to 158 per 1,000 in the first half of the seventeenth century and from 118 to 147 in the second half. Research among aristocratic women has produced the statistics that 45 per cent died before the age of fifty, one quarter from the complications of childbirth; these figures do not however allow for the debilitations caused by constant parturition.[45] Many women must have died of diseases and conditions related to 'the pain and the peril', worn through by ceaseless child-bearing, who did not actually die in labour.

It was ironic, if a subtle form of social justice, that the one natural form of contraception in existence at this time was the breast-feeding of the previous baby. While lactation did not give universal protection, it certainly afforded some.[46] What was more, the general prohibition against intercourse while the woman was still feeding her baby at the breast (even

† This remarkable woman was buried in the nearby Church of the Holy Trinity at Stonegrave, where the Chapel of St Peter is still dedicated to her memory, a chapel which she had wished to restore; but through her husband's failure she had not sufficient funds to do so. The arms of the Thorntons and Wandesfords can be seen there combined.

if not universally respected) exercised its own restraint. But the great ladies, and even those much further down the social scale, such as the Lancaster grocer's wife Mrs Coward, to whom William Stout was apprenticed, did not propose to feed their own children; it being customary to pay someone else, known as a 'wet-nurse', to do the job (the word was first introduced in 1620; before that the general term 'nurse' was used).[47] So the richer women enjoyed – endured might be a better word – a higher rate of fertility than their poorer sisters, who not only nursed these wealthy cuckoo babies for money, but also suckled their own children. Both processes gave the women of the poor some kind of short respite from the eternal process of giving birth, which brought so many women of the time into mortal danger, pain and peril year after year.

In general, breast-feeding was so unusual in that section of society where the mothers could afford to pay others to perform the duty for them as always to be worthy of remark. It was the subject of comment for example when Sarah, daughter of the Quaker Margaret Fell, nursed her son herself, born when she was forty-two. Lucy Hutchinson's mother was said to love her 'above the rest of her children' just because she had suckled her. Essex Cheke, third wife of the second Earl of Manchester, had her prowess in that respect commemorated on her tombstone when she died in September 1658. She had left Lord Manchester with six sons and two daughters, seven of them suckled 'with her own breasts'. The memorial added: 'Her children shall rise up and call her blessed.' On the other hand another Essex, that Lady Essex Rich who was the beloved first wife of Daniel Finch, Earl of Nottingham, was criticized for her rashness in feeding her own child; this eccentric behaviour was thought to have contributed to the baby's death.[48]

Why did the mothers of this time refuse to feed their own children, except in rare cases? This was after all a time when the alternative of animal milk was not used except for syphilitics. Baby bottles as such were also virtually unknown, although there were drinking horns (and nipple shields also existed, made of lead, tin or silver).[49]

It was not as if the character of the wet-nurses in themselves inspired much confidence. Every domestic handbook abounded in advice on how to choose a wet-nurse; the constant reiteration that she should be healthy and full of milk shows how often the contrary was discovered to be the case. (Complexion was rated exceptionally important: red hair and freckles for example were dangerous because they betokened sour milk; a healthy 'brown' was best.) Sexual relations between the wet-nurse and her husband (or anyone else) were also considered dangerous but it is highly doubtful that such prohibitions actually brought about celibacy. Babies in

general seemed to be in constant threat from 'overlaying', the fate of Alice
Thornton's baby. Under the circumstances Mary Lady Verney probably
made a prudent decision when she chose the wife of Ralph Rode to wet-
nurse little Ralph Verney on the grounds that her own family appeared
healthy: 'she [Mrs Rode] looks like a slattern but she sayeth if she takes the
child she will have a mighty care of it, and truly she hath two as fine
children of her own as ever I saw'.[50] Yet the circumstances in which a
feeling mother would surrender a beloved baby to a woman who looked
'like a slattern' are difficult for the modern imagination to encompass.

On the one hand the importance of the bond was understood: mental
and spiritual qualities also were believed to be imbibed with the wet-
nurse's milk, as Oliver Heywood wrote of his wife Elizabeth that 'she
being nursed and nourished at home partook of her natural parents'
excellent dispositions'. The wet-nurse to two monarchs, Mrs Katharine
Elliott, appealed for a grant to sell silk stockings as a reward for such
intimate services, while her own daughter petitioned Charles II at the
Restoration for some financial recognition of the fact that she had sucked
'at the same breast as so great a monarch'. Mrs Martha Farthing claimed a
pension of £300 when her former nursling Queen Anne ascended the
throne, on the grounds that she was 'the only wet-nurse to her present
Majesty'. Martha Farthing had fed the Princess for fifteen months, which
was slightly longer than the median age established by contemporary
reports, although some medical authors recommended weaning as late as
twenty-one months.[51]

On the other hand, desperate laws, like that of a foundling hospital,
which declared that any nurse who had imperilled the lives of two children
might not take on the nursing of a third, show how low the standards sank
for all the efforts to maintain them.[52]

To explain this phenomenon, it is too simple to say that a bunch of
unfeeling women, bereft of the normal maternal instinct, had mysteriously
emerged at a particular moment of history. The prejudice against lactation
on the part of the mother was in fact far more a matter of social usage than
maternal instinct.

Breast-feeding had its theoretical advocates, particularly among the
Puritans. Perkins, Gouge, Cleaver and Dod (who believed that the breast
was not an erogenous zone) all recommended it as part of a good mother's
duty in their Puritan publications. But for all this preaching, there is
evidence that the ideal was seldom realized: it has been pointed out, for
example, that William Gouge's wife only nursed seven out of her thirteen
children, Gouge himself admitting that the practice could be forsworn if

it proved dangerous to mother or child. It is noticeable that the midwife Jane Sharp, who had experience of the difficulties of nursing, was a good deal less positive in her advice than the male pundits.[53]

The recommendations against marital sex during the period of lactation may well have had something to do with the matter, where the feelings of the husband were concerned. The casual (masculine) point of view was exhibited by Sir William Knollys at the turn of the sixteenth century, in a letter of advice to his goddaughter Anne Fitton, Lady Newdigate. He told her that he would not like it 'that you play the nurse, if you were my wife'. He admitted that 'it argueth great love, but it breedeth much trouble to yourself'. However Anne Newdigate ignored her godfather's advice; she did breast-feed her first child and went on to suckle four more (as a result of which achievement she was considered as a possible wet-nurse to the children of Anne of Denmark and James I). In a petition as a widow, she boasted that her children were born of her own body and nursed of her own breasts ('they never suck other milk').[54]

Elizabeth Knyvet, wife of the third Earl of Lincoln, wrote a defiant plea that the mother should suckle her own child in a book called *The Countess of Lincoln's Nursery*, first printed in 1622.[55] Her motive for her crusade was the same as that of Alice Thornton, who nursed her own child after her fright with an incompetent nurse. The Countess had given birth to eighteen children herself, and at least one of her 'Babes' had died through the neglect of nurses, who had falsely pretended 'willingness, towardness, wakefulness'. In fact, in the upbringing of eighteen children, the Countess of Lincoln declared she had only encountered two careful attendants.

A foreword by Thomas Lodge contained the encouraging rhyme:

> Go then, great Book of Nursing, plead the Cause;
> Teach Highest, Lowest, all, it's God's and Nature's Laws.

The Countess swept away all the possible objections that nursing was 'troublesome ... noisome to one's clothes, makes one look old, endangers health' (making the prevailing attitudes among her contemporaries clear). Such weak women, she observed, should not have married in the first place. She also pointed out triumphantly that the period of peace while nursing provided a woman with an excellent opportunity for prayer.

As in every controversial issue in the seventeenth century, the Bible was searched for precedents. Did not Sarah – 'a great Princess' – suckle Isaac? What of Hannah? Above all, what of the Virgin Mary, suckling the Infant Christ? But in proving that breast-feeding by the mother was according to God's holy ordinance, the Countess of Lincoln played her trump card in citing the example of Eve, who must surely have suckled Cain and Abel and Seth, since no other woman existed in the world to act as a nurse on her behalf.

'We have followed Eve in Transgression', declared the Countess of Lincoln on behalf of the female sex. 'Let us follow her in obedience.' But most women of her time who had the choice, unaware of the protective value of such a practice, declined to imitate this rare piece of good behaviour on the part of Grandmother Eve.

5 *Are You Widows?*

> 'Again, are you widows? You deserve much honour, if you be so indeed.... Great difference then is there betwixt those widows who live alone, and retire themselves from public concourse, and those which frequent the company of men.... In popular concourse and Court-resorts there is no place for widows.'
>
> RICHARD BRATHWAITE, *The English Gentlewoman*, 1631

Once widowed – the third stage of her projected life – a woman was expected to add a further virtue in the shape of fidelity to the long list of feminine virtues she already possessed, including modesty, meekness, patience and humility. The fidelity was to the memory of her deceased spouse, for the ideal widow did not seek to alter her state by marrying again. Instead, in a favourite comparison of the time, she emulated the turtle-dove by mourning her late husband in solitude; as Mary Countess of Warwick was thankful when she had married off her late husband's nieces: her worldly duties being over she could spend the rest of her life a widow devoted to God's service.[1] That at least was the theory of widowhood. The reality as we shall see was often very different.

Lettice Viscountess Falkland, on top of all her other virtues, was formally commended for being:

> A Scripture Vestal, one whose chaste desire
> Call'd it adultery not to watch one fire...

Eschewing 'all second loves' she displayed herself until her death 'One made of ice toward Venus, and her doves'. Lady Alice Lucy, who died in 1648, was considered such an outstanding example of female virtue that Samuel Clarke chose her for one of his subjects in *The Lives of Sundry Eminent Persons in this Later Age*, published in 1683. Lady Alice began with a thoroughly submissive approach to her union with Sir Thomas Lucy of Charlecote: 'She knew that her taking of a second self, was a self-denying work; and therefore she resigned both her reason, and her will unto her Head, and Husband....' After Sir Thomas's death, she never even contemplated remarriage, for the good reason that God 'made himself her Husband, supporting her, comforting her, and enabling her prudently to manage her great Estate, and to order her numerous family'.[2]

Another 'ideal of the true mourning turtle' was Anne Lady Newdigate, she who as a widow boasted that all her children were 'nursed of my own breasts'. Petitioning in 1610 to be allowed to have the wardship of her son and his lands during his minority, Lady Newdigate hotly denied that she should ever be so 'accursed a woman [as] to marry again'. She kept her word, despite various offers for her hand, devoting her life to her children and their business interests. Her friend Lady Grey proposed a less severe attitude to remarriage – 'I must needs tell you that your too infinite care may take away that happiness which might give much content to you and yours.' Lady Newdigate's constancy was nevertheless considered heroic. Here was the reverse of the Pygmalion image: 'a fair woman' was 'turned into a marble stone'.[3]

Conversely, some very peculiar attitudes can be detected towards those widows who did take a second husband. There was an idea that marrying a widow might constitute 'bigamy', and if a widow had two spouses dead, it might even be termed 'trigamy'. John Aubrey ascribed an even more complicated view to William Harvey, the physician who discovered the circulation of the blood: 'He that marries a widow makes himself Cuckold' (that is, by the woman's dead husband). Harvey was supposed to have suggested that the children of the second marriage might even resemble the husband of the first, just as 'a good bitch', if first mated with a mongrel, would still bring forth 'curs' even after she had been mated with a dog of a better strain.[4]

The attitude of Edward Lord Herbert of Cherbury to his mother Magdalen's second marriage was positively eccentric: in his autobiography he paid a glowing tribute to her character, how 'she lived most virtuously and lovingly with her husband [his father] for many years ... brought up her children carefully and put them in good courses for making their fortune....' At no point did he mention that in 1608 the widowed Lady Herbert had married Sir John Danvers – she being forty and he twenty years old. Danvers himself is also mentioned by name, but the relationship between the two men is not. One might well wonder what this Hamlet was endeavouring to conceal on the subject of his mother's second union, except that John Donne (who preached the funeral sermon for Lady Danvers in 1627) tells us the marriage was in fact a very happy one. It seems therefore that nothing more than a theoretical distaste for abandoned widowhood was at stake.[5]

This revulsion against the notion of remarriage could also take the form of sentimental surprise when it actually took place. Dorothy Countess of Sunderland was widowed at the age of twenty-five. As a girl Dorothy Sidney had been the idol of her generation, one who succeeded in her professed aim to her father, the Earl of Leicester, to be 'the perfectest good child upon earth'. For her, his Sacharissa, Edmund Waller wrote that classic lover's apostrophe:

> Go lovely Rose
> Tell her that wastes her time and me,
> That now she knows,
> When I resemble her to thee,
> How sweet and fair she seems to be.

Having rejected not only the poet (who then wished on her that first curse of womankind, 'the pains of becoming a mother') but another aristocratic suitor for his addiction to debauched company, Dorothy Sidney made what seemed the ideal marriage to Henry Lord Spencer, later created Earl of Sunderland, a man who combined handsome looks with great taste – and great possessions. Four years later he was killed at the first Battle of Newbury (that same battle into which Lord Falkland rode looking 'very cheerful'), leaving Dorothy with a son and two daughters, but also heavily pregnant: she gave birth to a second son a fortnight later.[6]

After Lord Sunderland's death, Lord Leicester gave a classic piece of advice on the behaviour of a desolate widow to his 'dear Doll': she must cease damaging herself by her unhappiness since 'you offend him whom you loved, if you hurt that person he loved'. Her children remained – 'those pledges of your mutual friendship and affection which he hath left with you' – and if she did not recover enough to take care of them, she was betraying 'their father's trust' which had been reposed in her: 'For their sake, therefore, assuage your grief....'[7] For the next ten years or so the young Dowager Countess did devote herself in approved widow's fashion to the upbringing of her family, especially her son, and the management of the Spencer family estates at Althorp.

The consternation of the world when Dorothy married Robert Smythe in 1652 may seem by modern standards ludicrous. He was a Sidney family connection, a neighbour to the Leicester property at Penshurst (where Dorothy had spent her first widowhood), and although some years younger than the Countess had probably been in love with her for years. The contemporary consternation was none the less real. The Countess tactfully suggested to Dorothy Osborne that she had been swayed by pity for Smythe, although the fact that Smythe was 'a very fine gentleman' was surely at least as relevant. Even though Dorothy Osborne admitted that the Countess of Sunderland – still only in her thirties – might be growing 'weary of that constraint she put upon herself', her verdict was unforgiving: 'She has lost by it [the marriage] much of the repute she had gained by keeping herself a widow. It was then believed that wit and discretion were to be reconciled in her person that have so seldom been persuaded to meet in anybody else. But', concluded Dorothy Osborne sadly, 'we are all mortal.'[8]

*   *   *

This yearning for fidelity beyond the grave – the ideal of the devoted widow – makes strange reading put side by side with the nature of the society in which these men, women (and widows) lived. While there was general agreement, except by a few generous-minded or realistic spirits, that a second marriage for women was to be avoided, the facts about life in the first half of the seventeenth century give us a very different picture. Pepys, in one of the earliest entries in his diary, was much moved by a sermon he had heard on the subject of St Anne, mother of the Virgin Mary, only seven years married, who had lived to the age of eighty-four a widow. It neatly expressed the contrast between the ideal and the actual. The preacher 'did there speak largely in commendation of widowhood, and not as we do, to marry two or three wives or husbands one after another'.[9]

This was, after all, an age in which the life expectancy at birth was not much more than thirty-five years.[10] Each sex was subject to its own special threat. Women had to face the continuous peril of childbirth. Men on the other hand appear to have been more prone to disease, while the male population was also periodically decimated by war, whether at home or abroad.

Under these circumstances remarriage, far from being a distasteful aberration, was in fact a very common occurrence, it having been calculated that about a quarter of all marriages were a remarriage for either the bride or the groom. In the upper echelons of society – that is to say, those ranks where the interests of money and property were at stake in any given marriage – it has been further estimated that about 25 per cent of the population married again in the late sixteenth and seventeenth centuries, and about 5 per cent married three times. Four or even five marriages in a lifetime were as likely to be achieved then in a society with a high rate of mortality as they are today in a society with a high rate of divorce.[11]

The career of Eleanor Wortley, who married in turn Sir Henry Lee of Quarendon in Buckinghamshire, the sixth Earl of Sussex, the second Earl of Warwick, and the second Earl of Manchester, was notable more for the fact that she married a series of aged husbands than for the number of her bridegrooms. Sir Ralph Verney (he was knighted in 1640 but made a baronet at the Restoration) actually used to refer to her in code in his letters as 'Old Men's Wife'.[12]

Lady Sussex was a woman of tempestuous character whose tribulations – as well as marriages – enlivened the existence of her friends. She also had a rather beguiling vanity. She recommended Mary Lady Verney (Mary Blacknall, the heiress, now a contented married lady) to use myrrh water for her complexion, explaining: 'I have long used it and find it very safe. 'Tis good for the head and to make one look young long. I only wet a cloth and wipe my face over, at night with it.' However, it says less for Lady Sussex's artistic sense that when Van Dyck wanted to paint her she was torn between vanity and avarice: 'I am loth to deny him, [but] truly it is money ill bestowed.' (Van Dyck got £50 for the job.) Later Ralph Verney had to intervene, in a common problem, alas, with portraiture: he prevailed upon Van Dyck at Lady Sussex's request 'to make my picture leaner, for truly it was too fat'.[13] Later, after her third marriage, Lady Sussex tried to get hold of the picture for her new husband, but perhaps deservedly, failed.

The 'Old Men's Wife' was not, however, an unloving character. As the aged Lord Sussex lay on his deathbed at his estate at Gorhambury during the Civil War, she declared: 'I will not stir from my good old Lord what soever becomes of me.' She assured the Verneys: 'Now I must tell you that which maybe you will hardly believe, that I heartily suffer for my good old lord who truly grows so very weak that I fear he will not hold out very long.' She then spent a considerable sum of money – £400 – on his funeral as a mark of her respect. 'Good man', she wrote of Lord Sussex after his death, 'I am confident he is happy.'[14]

Lady Sussex's third husband, Robert Earl of Warwick, was approaching sixty – a vast age by the standards of the time, when thirty was held to mark middle age. She was frank about her reasons for choosing him. 'Wanting a discreet and helpful friend . . . made me think of marriage', she told the Verneys, 'being unable to undergo what I found continually upon me.' The Earl of Warwick was not only 'extreme kind' as she put it, but in the view of his daughter-in-law Mary Rich one of the 'cheerfullest persons'. He was also a grandee who did not allow his religious and political Puritanism to stand in the way of the great state he kept at

Warwick House in Holborn. Nine months after his death in 1658 Eleanor married another Parliamentary leader, the fifty-six-year-old Earl of Manchester, a double which won for her the sobriquet of 'the Peeress of the Protectorate'. She still, however, kept Warwick House, which had been willed to her by her third husband. It is a tribute to Eleanor's warm character that Mary Rich, by now Countess of Warwick in her turn, wept bitterly at her death in 1667. 'I was much affected for the loss of my poor mother-in-law', wrote Mary; she found it no consolation that her husband would now at last be free to use the family residence of Warwick House.[15]

By her two matches with the Earl of Warwick and the Earl of Manchester, Eleanor had entered into a remarkably complex network of relationships. At the time the situation was summed up by the saying that the Earl of Manchester, following his first wife's death, had married 'Warwick's niece, Warwick's daughter and Warwick's wife':[16] that is to say his third wife, Essex Cheke, 'Warwick's niece', that philoprogenitive lady who had fed seven children at the breast, was the daughter of Warwick's sister; she was thus a first cousin of Manchester's second wife, who had been 'Warwick's daughter', Lady Anne Rich; Manchester's fourth wife was of course Warwick's widow, Eleanor. (After Eleanor's death, the ever-game Lord Manchester went on to marry for a fifth time, the widowed Countess of Carlisle, who survived him.)

The marital career of the second Earl of Warwick, straightforward compared to that of the Earl of Manchester, was not without its own incidents. His first marriage, which had taken place as long ago as 1605, was to Frances Hatton, step-daughter of that spirited Lady Hatton who was the mother of Frances Coke. His second wife was Susan Halliday, the widow of a rich London alderman; of her Mary Rich wrote: 'Because she was a citizen, she was not so much respected in the family as in my opinion she deserved to be.' Warwick's other daughter-in-law, Lady Anne Cavendish, a haughty scion of the house of Devonshire, had been particularly unpleasant to her. Mary, however, found her 'as good as my own mother', sympathized with her ill-health, and 'when God called her away, [I did] much mourn for losing her'.[17]

Remarriage, then, was a fact of contemporary life and it was not only the great Parliamentary magnates, the leaders of their society, who indulged guiltlessly in this potentially acquisitive pastime.

That same Lord Herbert who refused to acknowledge in print the second marriage of his mother, relates in his autobiography a cold-blooded conversation with his own wife. When they had established a family of three, he called the children in front of their mother and asked her how she liked them. 'Well', she replied. In which case Herbert requested his wife to settle her estates on these children in her lifetime, because there was a strong possibility of one or other of them dying, and the survivor marrying again; he being young for a man and she 'not old for a woman' (she was thirty-one, four years older than he was). Future offspring of these hypothetical second marriages might damage the financial prospects of their existing family. Although Lady Herbert refused, on the grounds that she did not wish to find herself in the power of her own children – 'she would not draw the cradle upon her head' – her husband's premise concerning death and remarriage was not in itself surprising or shocking to her.[18]

In reality it was more often the question of the children's financial future – the children of the first marriage, that is – which bedevilled the prospect of a widow's remarriage, than the notion of her fidelity to her first husband. William Blundell quoted with approval in his diary the Latin tag of a certain widower:

> *Liberorum causa duxeram uxorem*
> *Liberorum causa rursus non duxi*

('I had married a wife for the sake of children; for the sake of my children I have not married again'). Widows too were adjured to bear in mind the consequences of a second marriage for those who had something to lose from it, such as their children. (Later the Quakers would make it a feature of their religion that proper provision should be made for the children of first marriages before a second marriage took place.) Brilliana Lady Harley summed up the two sides to the question with good sense in 1642 when she described herself as 'glad' that her cousin Catherine, widow of Oliver St John, was remarrying: 'I believe it is for her advantage; tho' in my opinion, when one has children, it is better to be a widow.'[19]

* * *

From the opposite point of view – those with something to gain from a woman's remarriage, notably her prospective second husband – no spectacle was more stirring than that of a wealthy widow. A Tally-Ho would go up when one of these creatures was sighted, followed by a pursuit which can only be compared to the contemporary chase after an heiress; except that the fox in this case was older and therefore wilier.

'If a widow happens to fall in the mean time she shall be kept in syrup for you', wrote a correspondent to Framlingham Gawdy in 1637, at the end of a list of available widows which included their incomes. Sir John

Eliot, the leading spirit in the forcing of the Petition of Right upon King
Charles I, a man who was imprisoned for his opposition to arbitrary
power, left the question of his second marriage entirely in the hands of his
friend Sir Henry Waller, who knew of a wealthy widow who had recently
'fallen', i.e. become available. Eliot made no inquiries concerning his
bride's moral character.[20]

In 1653, about the time of Dorothy Countess of Sunderland's second
marriage, Dorothy Osborne went to dinner with a rich widow, middle-
aged and 'never handsome', who had 'broke loose from an old miserable
husband' with the avowed intention of spending all his money before she
died. Whereas Sacharissa's fall from grace had shocked Dorothy, the
widow's palpable state of siege thoroughly amused her. For all the widow's
frank words concerning the use to which she intended to put her late
husband's money, and despite her lack of physical attraction, she was,
wrote Dorothy, 'courted a thousand times more than the greatest beauty
in the world that had not a fortune'. They could hardly get through dinner
for the disturbance caused by letters and presents pouring through the
door in order to persuade the widow to change her mind.[21]

Other widows made a different use of their opportunities. Francis
Kirkman described in his autobiography how his thrice-married step-
mother had had a dubious past, diddling another step-son out of his estate
by forging her first husband's seal on a will. But Francis Kirkman's father
was hardly interested in such details. 'My father married her upon small
acquaintance'; he only knew that she had a considerable estate, 'that being
the chief care of most thriving citizens to inquire into that'.[22]

City widows (like Susan Halliday, the second Countess of Warwick)
were a particular target, because the Custom of London concerning the
disposition of a man's estate was so favourable towards his relict. Marriage
to an important widow (in the commercial sense) was the basis of one of
the most successful businesses built up in the City in the seventeenth
century. William Wheeler was a goldsmith; a profession incidentally
where there was a tradition of bright-eyed and quick-witted wives, including that famous mistress of Edward IV, Jane Shore, who displayed her
'beauty in a shop of gold'. Wheeler transferred the Cheapside shop inherited from his father to the Marygold, formerly a tavern, in Fleet Street
near Temple Bar. When Wheeler died his widow Martha married one of
his two apprentices, named Robert Blanchard, who then succeeded to the
business. (Wheeler's daughter Elizabeth married another apprentice,
Francis Child; he later inherited the business in his turn, and as Sir Francis
Child, was reckoned 'the father' of the banking profession.) It was appro-

priate that Blanchard, who owed so much to the Widow Wheeler, should leave £200 in his will to the Goldsmiths' Company to pay £4 a year to two widows of good repute, over the age of fifty, who were less well endowed.[23]

When Sir William Craven died in 1618, his was the largest fortune known at the time from a will – at least £125,000. In turn Lady Craven at her death was reputed by John Chamberlain to be 'the richest widow (perhaps) that ever died, of London lady'; she was said to have left an income derived from land worth £13,000 a year between her two sons. The Vyners were another remarkable City dynasty. Pepys gazed in awe at Mary, wife of Sir Robert Vyner, but for once not for her looks; it was true she was still handsome but from having been 'a very handsome woman' he reckoned her at the age of thirty-four 'now old'. No, Pepys's awe arose from the fact that Lady Vyner, a wealthy widow at the time of her marriage, was reputed to have brought her husband 'near £100,000'.[24] The prize did not however have to be on quite such a lustrous scale for the competition to be keen, as is manifested by the case of the Widow Bennett.

Elizabeth Cradock – the Widow Bennett of the story – came of a decent Staffordshire family and her father had probably been some form of mercantile agent.[25] She was still a young and attractive woman when her husband, Richard Bennett, a well-off merchant and son of a former Lord Mayor of London, died in April 1628. The widow was left with a four-year-old son, Simon, doubtless named for her husband's brother Sir Simon Bennett, who had been created a baronet the previous year. With respectable if not brilliant connections, the Widow Bennett was certainly well placed to make a sound second marriage, especially as she was the sole executrix of her husband's will, under which she received two-thirds of his estate. That was not all. She also inherited her husband's coach with its four grey coach-horses (mares and geldings), to say nothing of jewels which included chains of pearl and gold, and diamond rings. In short, the Widow Bennett was in a position to cut just that type of 'ladyfied' figure alluded to by Massinger in his satirical play *The City Madam* who wore:

> Satin on solemn days, a chain of gold,
> A velvet hood, rich borders, and sometimes
> A dainty miniver cap, a silver pin . . .[26]

Only six months after her husband's death the Widow Bennett had acquired three established suitors. Like some latter-day Paris, the widow was expected to bestow the golden apple of her fortune on one of the trio. There however the mythical comparison ends and a more homely note is

struck, for, to the general amusement of society, these three suitors happened coincidentally to bear the names of Finch, Crow(e) and Raven.

Finch was undoubtedly the best of the flock. Sir Heneage Finch came of
an excellent Kentish family, he had been Speaker of the House of Commons in 1626 and was now Recorder of London, and his establishments
included a handsome house and garden in that countrified outpost of
London called Kensington (where Kensington Palace and Kensington
Gardens now lie). Crow, in the shape of Sir Sackville Crowe, was em-
barrassingly eager that this 'Twenty thousand pounds widow' should help
him to make up that gap in the public accounts which would shortly cause
him to retire from his office of Treasurer of the Navy. Raven was a doctor,
and a dashing fellow – but as it proved, rather too dashing a fellow for the
widow's taste.

One night Dr Raven bribed the widow's servants to let him secretly
into her house. He then entered her bedroom, where the widow was
sleeping, and proceeded to make passionate love to her. It was a
commonly-held assumption of the time that a 'lusty widow', as the
Duchess of Malfi was termed by her brother Ferdinand, must be ever on
the lookout for sexual fulfilment. Ferdinand expressed the reason thus:
'You know already what man is.' Joseph Swetnam, for example, in *The
Arraignment of Lewd, Idle, Froward and Unconstant Women* laid it down that
no widow, 'framed to the conditions of another man', could possibly
'forbear carnal act' if an opportunity came her way, since she was habitually
deprived of it.[27] One can only observe that the Widow Bennett's behaviour would have proved a sad disappointment to anyone proceeding
on this assumption.

Far from showing herself unable to forbear carnal act, the widow
immediately sprang out of bed, and began to shriek such unamorous
words as 'Thieves!' and 'Murder!' She managed to summon her venal
servants, and in the course of time the dashing doctor was arrested by the
parish constable. Haled before the Recorder of London the next day, the
Raven found himself facing none other than the Finch. The latter having
sent him into custody until the next sessions, it was some time before the
unfortunate Raven, having pleaded guilty to 'ill-demeanour', was finally
set free.

At this point a fourth bird joined the flock, in the shape of a recent
widower called Sir Edward Dering. Much of Dering's journal of his
campaign to secure the widow's hand survives; it supplies vivid details of
all the necessary preparations for such an assault. Here are the Widow
Bennett's servants bribed (again! it must have been a lucrative position)

and supplying Sir Edward with tit-bits of encouraging gossip to spur him on. One servant would whisper 'Good news! Good news!', and Sir Edward's heart would leap. There would be a hint that 'the widow liked well his carriage and . . . there was good hope', provided that Sir Edward's land was not already settled on his son by his first marriage.

Sir Edward's own efforts included the dispatch of rich presents for the widow herself, as well as her servants, and visits to the church where he might spy her – and presumably be spied. These could be quite demanding, for the good widow was a great church-goer: 'Nov 30: I was at the Old Jewry Church, and saw her, both forenoon and afternoon.' Then there were his advisers, who included the Widow Bennett's cousin Cradock, and even Sir Heneage Finch (who appeared at this point to have withdrawn from the campaign). The two men had dinner together. Others who interested themselves in Sir Edward's cause were his cousin, the Dean of Canterbury, and his late wife's mother and sister (who far from advocating any form of fidelity to his dead wife had clearly decided that Sir Edward's family would benefit generally from the supplement of the Widow Bennett's estate). When Sir Henry Wotton, the Provost of Eton, happened to meet Sir Edward in the Privy Chamber, he expressed the general interest in the pursuit by genially wishing Sir Edward 'full sail'.

Of course there was the continuing anxiety of the other suitors. Front-runners were the newly created Viscount Lumley and a Mr Butler. The latter was rejected by the widow for being 'a black blunt-nosed gentleman', but Lord Lumley also prosecuted his suit by going to the widow's church. In all of this, Sir Edward's interviews with the widow, as opposed to ecclesiastical sightings of her, were really rather disappointing, but somehow no one seems to have noticed this fact in all the excitement of rumour and counter-rumour. At one interview Sir Edward could get 'no answer of certainty, nor yet indeed any denial'. At another the widow protested that she would not marry at all, or at any rate she would make no answer to his proposal at the present time. At yet another meeting, in February, Sir Edward 'intreated of her' to grant him at least one suit: 'viz., to love herself . . . viz., to choose that man with whom she might live happiest'. The widow's reply was scarcely encouraging: 'Say that you left me, and take the glory of it.'

When the dreams of the Widow Bennett – and of Sir Edward – were introduced into the proceedings as relevant evidence by her cousin Mrs Norton, another of Sir Edward's informants, they were not exactly encouraging either. The Widow Bennett dreamt that as Mrs Norton was bringing her 'a mess of milk' in bed, Sir Edward came into the room behind her, at which the Widow Bennett sprang out of bed – with that same strange lack of carnality with which she had eluded Dr Raven – and ran out of her bedroom into the parlour 'in her smock', whereupon she caught cold. Sir Edward, more prosaically, dreamt that the widow had sent him a Twelfth Night cake.

But what were these lack-lustre portents compared to the glittering prospect of her fortune? Sir Edward gloated over it: 'George Newman [her servant] says she hath suits of silver plate, one in the country and the other here, and that she hath beds of £100 the bed.'

The trouble was that the widow herself was not totally without cares in her new state. It has been mentioned that she had a small son, Simon. The wardship of this boy had been sold by the Crown to a man named Steward, according to the custom – so much resented – of the time. Throughout Sir Edward's courtship, the widow was engaged in trying to buy back the wardship of her boy into her own hands for £1,500; but having paid the amount, she then discovered that Steward himself had already sold the wardship into another's hands. Was it this problem which was causing the widow to hang back so unconscionably from matrimony? Sir Edward, like many would-be second spouses, was well aware of the importance of little Simon in his mother's favours. He ambushed the child at his daily walk, when he was out with his nursemaid Susan and George Newman. 'Susan professed that she and all the house prayed for me, and told me the child already called me "Father"', Sir Edward reported joyfully in his journal.

Perhaps little Simon was the key to the situation. With the question of the wardship at last settled in the spring, the widow was to be found 'in a merry plight', according to her cousin Mrs Norton. The two women were drinking beer and chatting together: 'Well, Thomas,' she said to her servant, 'I must have one glass of beer more.' The widow agreed to drink a toast to Sir Edward 'as one that loved her'. And shortly afterwards in April 1629, a year after the death of her first husband, the Widow Bennett did duly marry again. She married however not patient aspirant Sir Edward, but the Finch.

It has been suggested that Sir Heneage had been advising the widow all along on the provoking matter of the wardship. The Finch may have allowed Dering's blatant courtship to conceal his own more discreet suit.[28] Be that as it may, with the marriage the dramatic story of the Widow Bennett and her suitors ends. It remains only to say that though the Finch marriage was short-lived (Sir Heneage died in December 1631 and this time the widow did not venture to remarry), it lasted long enough for the new Lady Finch to bear one daughter and conceive an even more remarkable child, born after her father's death. But the story of Anne Finch, Viscountess Conway, belongs to another chapter.

*   *   *

The Widow Bennett, seen through the pages of Sir Edward Dering's journal, was no pliable character on whom the masculine sex necessarily imposed: in the end she secured a distinguished second husband (of considerably higher social rank than her first) who supplied her need for 'a discreet and helpful friend', as Eleanor Lady Sussex had described her protective third husband the Earl of Warwick.

This is where the figure of the wealthy widow, that contemporary object of desire, begins to emerge as one vessel who was in practice by no means quite so weak as the rest of womankind. Widows by their very nature presented considerable problems to those pundits who postulated that obedience was the female's essential lot. If unmarried girls obeyed their fathers, and wives obeyed their husbands, whom should a widow obey? There was no clear answer to that question. Widows, indeed, could be held to be technically 'masterless', especially if their jointure or other form of inheritance was free from legal restraint.

It was a point made by a headstrong young widow, Mrs Margaret Poulteney, who was actually Ralph Verney's aunt, although only a year older than he. Enjoying a handsome jointure without encumbrances, Margaret Poulteney went and married herself secretly to a Catholic soldier named William Eure; this despite the prolonged negotiations for a conventional second marriage, made on her behalf by her family. Eure's proscribed religion, the secrecy of the event, the embarrassment felt towards Margaret Poulteney's other suitors who had been assured she was 'a free woman'; all these contributed to a feeling of collective indignation in the Verney family breast.[29]

Sir Edmund Verney hoped gloomily that 'some lucky bullet may free her of this misfortune'. Margaret Poulteney was felt to have behaved particularly badly because she had tricked Ralph's wife Mary into buying her a form of trousseau – a black taffeta waistcoat and petticoat trimmed with handsome lace – and delivering Margaret's favourite red damask petticoat and waistcoat from Claydon. Margaret used the excuse that she needed a new outfit for a christening. Instead she rushed off with her finery to meet William Eure on his way back from Scotland, where he had been serving in the King's Army.

To all these reproaches Margaret, now Mrs Eure, had an irrefutable as well as disdainful reply: 'The town makes havoc of my good name, but let them do their worst, I defy them all. None in the world can call me to account for my actions; for I am not in any one's tuition.'[30]

By the 1670s *The Ladies Calling* was trying to get round this awkward possibility by suggesting that God did not set the same value upon their being 'masterless' as some over-independent widows did: 'He [God] reckons them most miserable when they are most at liberty.'[31] This last shot was presumably mere conjecture on the part of the Anglican divine who wrote *The Ladies Calling*; the feelings of the widows themselves, which can be established with more certainty, were very different. Liberty, if accompanied by affluence, could be very sweet.

Lady Anne Twysden was a widow with two fine houses, one in London and the other at East Peckham, Kent. In her youth she had been a beauty, tall but very slender. Her own son, Sir Roger Twysden, paid this tribute to her: 'She was the handsomest woman (at least as handsome) as I ever saw', with 'skin exceeding fair' and 'light brown hair'. After forty, although she continued to look young for her age, 'fatness' was 'much trouble to her'.[32] Despite this hampering weight, ill-health generally and a lame foot where she had been dropped by her nurse as a child, Lady Anne ruled her domains with a rod of iron. Endowed with an excellent business brain, aided by a fluent epistolary style (and that female rarity, good handwriting), Lady Anne Twysden hardly accorded with the prevalent notion of woman as the helpless sex. At the time of the ship-money crisis in the 1630s, Lady Anne at one juncture had the courage to refuse to pay the tax – a development which deeply worried her son on her behalf, but which he could not affect.

Even though she was physically unable to move about the house, somehow Lady Anne, according to her son, managed to know 'every egg spent in it'. Her thriftiness was combined with a chastity, one might almost say, prudery, which prevented her from being alone with a man – even her own son when grown up – without a maid present. Thrifty and prudish as she might be, Lady Anne was also, wrote Sir Roger, 'full of motherly affection'.[33] She must have been warm-hearted, for she managed to make herself beloved to those around her, including the young gentlewomen of little fortune whom she employed as attendants (no doubt to report on the egg-spending).

One of these, the thirty-year-old Isabella Saunders, was finally selected by Lady Anne as a bride for Sir Roger, still a bachelor at the advanced age of thirty-seven. Isabella tended her mother-in-law with devotion and wept copiously at her deathbed in 1638, although after her marriage it was still Lady Anne, not the new Lady Twysden (generally termed Dame Isabella, perhaps to differentiate her), who ran Roydon Hall. Sir Roger Twysden's notebooks also leave us an exact record of the financial restraint which Lady Anne imposed upon him under the heading 'Reckonings between me and my mother'; as for example, 'The 6th July 1629 I owed her £46.12.10. pd her £20. 20 July and pd. her £40. 10 Sept and told her where she cd have another £100 in London.'[34]

The reason that Lady Anne Twysden was able to exercise such command over every aspect of life surrounding her, including the life of her son, was simple. It was not connected with her beauty, motherly affection, or even her thriftiness. It was because Anne Twysden had been born Lady Anne Finch, another member of that large Kentish family to which Sir Heneage Finch belonged. Her mother was the heiress Elizabeth Heneage, 'a Lady of great Fortune; and having a Mind suitable to it',[35] who married Sir Moyle Finch and after his death was created Viscountess Maidstone and Countess of Winchilsea in her own right as a mark of her status. Anne Finch's husband, Sir William Twysden, died in 1629. After that, as a widow with an unencumbered estate, Lady Anne Twysden was able to enjoy personally that very fortune which she had brought to her husband on marriage.

Lady Anne Clifford, like Anne Twysden, was an heiress, but on a vastly grander scale. She was born in 1590 but true happiness only came to her late in life in her role as a magnificent widow, mother and grandmother, one of whom V. Sackville-West, the editor of her autobiography, aptly wrote that she was 'born to matriarchy'. After Anne Clifford's first marriage to Richard Sackville, Earl of Dorset, in 1609, Emilia Lanier serenaded her as

> ... that sweet Lady sprung from Cliffords race,
> Of noble Bedford's blood, fair stream of Grace;
> To honourable Dorset now espous'd ....[36]

However, much of life with 'honourable Dorset' turned out to be torment for his young wife.

Her role as chatelaine of the historical Sackville palace at Knole was often invidious since Lord Dorset was openly unfaithful – even bringing his inamorata Lady Penistone – 'a dainty fine young lady' – to stay at Knole. Almost worse from Anne's point of view was the fact that Dorset refused to support her in her struggle to claim her own northern inheritance from her father's brother (since the estates had been entailed in her father's will on a child of either sex). Lord Dorset wanted to commute these rights for cash; his wife wanted to cling to the lands. Most people blamed her for her obstinacy and at one point during the row her son was removed from her care. Anne described herself in her autobiography as being 'like an owl in the desert'; while Lord Dorset went to 'Cocking, to Bowling Alleys, to Plays and Horse Races ... I stayed in the country having many times a sorrowful and heavy heart, and being condemned by most folks because I would not consent to the agreements.'[37]

Death removed Lord Dorset in 1624, but Lady Anne Clifford's second marriage, in 1630, to Philip Earl of Pembroke and Montgomery, owner of sumptuous Wilton House near Salisbury, was no happier. Notorious for his rough ways in youth, Lord Pembroke sided with Parliament in later life – possibly to secure his possessions – and was much pilloried by the Royalist pamphleteers in consequence. Fortunately – from Anne's point of view – his death in 1649 left her a widow for the second time. From now until her own demise nearly thirty years later at the age of eighty-six, she was able to enjoy not only the fruits of two rich jointures, but also those northern properties she had so much desired, released to her at last by the death of her uncle.

'The marble pillars of Knole in Kent and Wilton in Wiltshire were to me oftentimes but the gay arbours of anguish', wrote Anne of her two marriages. How different, how formidably different was the life of the Dowager Countess! Clad usually in black serge, 'her features more expressive of firmness than benignity', as a nineteenth-century local historian tactfully expressed it after studying her portraits, 'the Lady Anne', as she is still remembered in the north, gave full vent to all her tastes in a way she could never do throughout two unhappy marriages.[38] Her two surviving children being daughters, by her first marriage, they offered no impediments to her will.

These tastes included the restoration of ancient castles and chapels, part of her inheritance, on which it has been estimated that she must have spent at least £40,000. 'The Lady Anne' also took particular pleasure in raising monuments in stone: among others she was responsible for the classical monument to the poet Spenser in Westminster Abbey executed by Nicholas Stone, and a medieval type of altar tomb to her own mother which can still be seen in the Church of St Lawrence, Appleby, in Cumbria, alongside the monument which she erected to herself. John Donne had paid tribute to her conversation in youth: she was a woman who 'knew well how to discourse of all things, from predestination to flea-silk [a plant], a wonderful housekeeper who could still open her mouth with wisdom'. In later life the Lady Anne shared the conversational gifts which had so much impressed Donne with those poorer widows whom she had installed in a residence at Appleby in Westmorland; she made a point of dining with them once a week and talking as freely 'as with persons of the highest rank'.[39]

The Lady Anne was a great reader; as she grew old, she kept two 'well-educated females' constantly at her side to read aloud. The Psalms and the Old Testament were favourites, but she also enjoyed classical authors and had a particular love of Chaucer. When engrossed in his works, she wrote, 'a little part of his bounteous spirit infuses itself into me'. Bounteous she certainly was, and not only in spirit. She made the giving of presents her hobby, buying books of devotion, for example, in bulk – up to fifty at a time – to give away. And she was a prodigious tipper: £3 to a man who brought her a letter from her daughter, a sum which represented something like the man's annual wage. Even if her autobiography gained a good deal from the work of certain literary ghosts,[40] that in itself was a form of patronage which few women of the time other than a very rich widow could have exercised.

*   *   *

Even for the less privileged, widows' rights were one area where the law was by no means so unfavourable to women as it was elsewhere. For those outside the wealthier world of the marriage settlement made in advance of the ceremony, there existed the traditional widow's 'thirds', that is, a third share in the husband's estate which under common law was her due.[41] A widow's inheritance could take many different forms, some of which could enable her to make a convenient second marriage on her own terms if she so wished, while others allowed her a position of her own in commercial society.

In cases of trouble a widow's dower lands were protected if the late husband's creditors fell upon the rest of the estate. These lands could only be forfeited by the widow voluntarily. There were other perquisites: Alice Thornton, dealing with her husband's virtually bankrupted estate, was advised by her brother to cling on to her valuable 'widow-bed' instead of selling it to pay the debts. Unlike the beds left to her by her mother, which formed part of her estate – and thus part of her husband's – and so could be 'prized' away by creditors, the 'widow-bed' could not be touched.[42]

Manorial court rolls show that it was customary for a widow of a copyhold tenant to remain in occupation of his land until she remarried or died – this was called her 'widow's estate'.[43] As a new grant of a piece of copyhold land was customarily made for three lives, the widow of the first named – if she did not remarry – might survive the other two. (The fact that remarriage meant loss of the copyhold kept many widows from remarrying.) But women were also copyhold tenants in their own right in some of those manorial court rolls that have survived from the seventeenth century: thus one Henry Hellier put his wife and son's name into the copy in 1626 – a demonstration of equality. This meant that Anne Hellier could enjoy the copy after her second marriage.

Certain corporations of the period still recognized the wife's position as a business partner (even if that recognition was dwindling as the century progressed).[44] In contrast to unmarried girls who were rarely allowed to be apprenticed to the guilds, the wives of guild members could have their husbands' rights and privileges conferred upon them: as widows, they were thus often in a position to run the business, for the assistance of a journeyman still meant that the widow was in practical control. Carpenters' widows, for example, could receive apprentices. Weavers' widows were especially well treated, being able to continue to work in their own right. After the Restoration, when many similar privileges were vanishing, Charles II still upheld the rights of the weaver's widow by decree 'to use and occupy the said trade by herself'.

Widows' names appear in the contracts of the shipping trade: in 1636 Susanna Angell and her daughter Elizabeth petitioned to land fourteen barrels of powder, and another thirty-eight barrels expected to arrive in the ship *Fortune*, and either sell it or send it back to Holland, from whence it came. In *Tom of all Trades*, published in 1631, Thomas Powell recommended young men not to seek employment in the provision businesses which he termed 'the housewives' trades (as brewer, baker, cook and the like)' because the wife so often acted as her husband's business partner. Where the wife had demonstrably shared the work during the husband's lifetime, her position was often entrenched on his death. The names are known of brewers' widows, bakers' widows, and butchers' widows still plying the family trade (not all, one hopes, of the type of Elizabeth Chorlton, who was fined in the 1650s for selling 'stinking meat'). A widow could even be a vintner, if she inherited the business, an unlikely opportunity for a woman on her own account.[45]

Strongest of all was the position of the printers' widows. Membership of the Stationers' Company, which included booksellers, binders and printers, was strictly limited to twenty-two persons. Widows actually retained their freedom of the Stationers' Company not only after their husband's death, but following remarriage. In this way a printer's widow presented an eligible match for an aspirant printer, printers' businesses frequently travelling sideways in this manner, as when the widow of

Francis Simson married in turn Richard Read and George Elde, carrying the vital membership of the Stationers' Company with her.[46]

These energetic women were certainly not carrying out that ideal of the widow's conduct proposed by Richard Brathwaite in *The English Gentlewoman*: 'Again, are you widows? You deserve much honour, if you be so indeed.... Great difference then is there betwixt those widows who live alone, and retire themselves from public concourse, and those which frequent the company of men. For a widow to love society ... gives speedy wings to spreading infamy ... for in such meetings she exposeth her honour to danger, which above all others she ought incomparably to tender.' What if a widow needed to plead in a law court for her inheritance, family fortunes which might 'all lie a-bleeding'? Here widows were simply reminded of the promises of Christ: 'Your Lord maketh intercession for you, rendering right judgement to the Orphan and righteousness unto the widow.'[47]

The women described in this chapter would have preferred to take Christ's parable of the importunate widow as their text; which advocated a far less passive code of behaviour.

6 Poor and Atrabilious

'[I] could see nothing in the evidence which did persuade me to
think them other than poor, melancholy, envious, mischievous, ill-
disposed, ill-dieted, atrabilious constitutions.'

ARTHUR WILSON ON THE CHELMSFORD WITCHES, 1645

When the fifth Earl of Huntingdon succeeded to the title of his grandfather
in 1604 he specifically ordered that great respect should be paid to 'my
ould lady' – Dorothy Port, Dowager Countess of Huntingdon. Fifty years
later a cheerful young lady, proposing to marry a peer who was on his
deathbed, saw it as an undoubted advantage that she 'might be a widow in
a very short time, and not be troubled long with him'.[1] But the independence of a wealthy widow, and the honour generally paid to an elderly
aristocrat, found no parallels in the condition of the poor women who
made up the vast majority of the widow class. The contrast between the
fate of the haves and the have-nots in seventeenth-century society is
alarmingly illustrated by the relative prospects of the rich and poor women
in widowhood.

The very sight of a poor old woman lacking an obvious protector
aroused many different primitive fears in the breast of society (nor were
these fears exclusive to the male sex). To begin with, such a woman presented a social problem: where the 'masterlessness' of the wealthy widow
was her opportunity for independence, the unsupported state of her poorer
contemporary could all too easily mean suffering, if not actual destitution.

Recent research has dispelled the cosy notion of a society where old folk
lived side by side in the same dwelling with their descendants: very few
married children lived with their parents, let alone with a single surviving
parent; such a household was the exception rather than the rule. At the
same time the old style of welfare, based on the charity of the church or
the manorial organization, had either vanished or was breaking down. A
series of Tudor statutes, culminating in the Poor Law of 1601, made the
succour of the weak the business of the parish, by means of compulsory
rates levied on its members.[2]

There were also far more women than men at the bottom of society economically: most of the adult pensioners in the City of London were widows (however, their treatment here seems to have been benign).[3] The frequent mention of poor widows in the social projects and wills of the charitably inclined (the efforts of Lettice Viscountess Falkland and Lady Anne Clifford have been observed) makes the continuous nature of the problem clear. These and other private beneficiaries were the lucky ones. In general, the sight of a poor old woman might raise implications of possible financial responsibility in fellow members of her community – guilt never being an agreeable sensation.

Nor was the phenomenon of old age a particularly rare one, despite the short expectation of life at birth. Every village, wrote Francis Bacon in 1623, had at least one person in it over sixty; Gregory King, in his account of the English population written at the end of the century, estimated that one person in ten would be aged sixty or older.[4] The fact was that those members of society who did survive the perils of accident, disease and childbirth might live to a great age.

These figures do not refer of course peculiarly to women; nevertheless accounts of women attaining an exceptional age, even by today's standards, spatter such annals as we have. George Ballard, born in 1706, was a self-educated antiquary; his diligence at research makes his *Memoirs of Several Ladies of Great Britain who have been celebrated for their writings or skill in the learned languages, arts, and sciences*, first published in 1752, a valuable source-book for the previous century. He quotes among his heroines Elizabeth Legge, who was born in 1580 and died in 1695; her two sisters lived to 100 and 112, her brothers to 109 and what must have been under the circumstances a disappointing eighty-two, respectively. Some of the early Quaker women, for all their trials, lived to an astonishing age. It has been suggested that it would be not so much the lack of aged persons as the lack of a large middle-aged group which would surprise us about the seventeenth century, in contrast to our world today.[5]

An old woman, then, as well as being an unwelcome spectacle for social reasons, was also a comparatively common one. Still further to her detriment was her actual physical appearance. Beauty, while it might be condemned by the preachers as an unstable basis for marriage, continued naturally to exercise its eternal lure; dislike of the aged physique, on the other hand, also widely inculcated, was a genuine passion of the time. It could even be justified. This was after all an age in which there was a subtle conspiracy to agree that beauty of outward form expressed an inward virtue; a view promulgated for example by Milton in *Comus* praising the

appearance of The Lady – 'so dear to Heaven is saintly chastity' – or by
Ford in '*Tis Pity She's a Whore*:

> So, where the body's furniture is beauty,
> The mind's must needs be virtue....

Hic Mulier in 1620 suggested that 'good women, modest women' were
'ever young because ever virtuous'.[6] There was an obvious corollary to be
drawn: physical ugliness (that common woe of the old) signified a base
moral nature, if not something worse.

'The bodies of aged persons are impure', wrote William Fulbeck in his
account of witchcraft in 1618; in general the breath and sight of such
persons was regarded as 'being apt for contagion'.[7] The seven-year cycle
after the age of sixty-two was sometimes known without much compassion as the Crooked Age. In the important seventeenth-century concept of
the humours which went to make up the body, dryness and melancholy
were held to be characteristic of the constitution of the aged.

The prejudices aroused by the sight of such dilapidated creatures were
unquestionably worse in the case of old women than of old men. This was
where many dark forces of the subconscious came into play. The ancient
susceptibility of woman – the weaker vessel – to 'the devil's illusions' was
the form in which these turgid fears were generally expressed in public.
Woman's sexual voracity was another subject on which there was a
conspiracy to agree in the seventeenth century, a period when, as has been
mentioned, the potentially repetitious and thus demanding nature of the
female orgasm was fully understood. As Robert Burton wrote in 1621:
'Of women's unnatural, insatiable lust, what country, what village does
not complain?' We have noted that the lusty widow was a favourite
concept of the times; sometimes economic necessity might become mixed
up with lust. The village whore might be a widow, one such as Isott Wall
of Tolland in Somerset who, according to evidence presented against her
in court, boasted that 'she would open her door at any time of the night
either to a married man or a young man'. Another convenient arrangement
of a slightly different ilk might take place when a widow, needing a milker
for her cow, paid for the work in kind.[8]

These women, evidently still in their sexual prime, were, if lusty, also
ingenious in fulfilling their own needs. But what of the case of an old
widowed woman, of hideous physical appearance, prone by her very sex
already to the temptations of the devil? Secretly voracious, might she not
be slaking her lust at some diabolical source, deprived of any other? In the
writhings of the popular imagination concerning the old, all these webs –

woman's weakness, her voracity, ugliness and Satan – became darkly and menacingly entangled.

The bodies of old women, twisted and gnarled by time like tree trunks, marred perhaps by protuberances and growths of different sorts including harmless warts and lumps and dangerous tumours – might the dissolving eye of fantasy not see in these ugly excrescences and bumps strange teats which the devil could suck? Was a particular wart or discoloration a mark of old age – or the witch's mark, which when pricked did not hurt?[9]

The notorious loquacity of the female – also taken for granted throughout literature, correspondence and popular report – was another characteristic where the devil's influence might be detected. Sir Thomas Overbury wrote wistfully in 1614 of *A Good Woman*: 'Her language is not copious but opposite ... She sings, but not perpetually, for she knows, silence in a woman is the most persuading oratory.' However, a great many women at the time evidently did not choose to employ silence's persuading oratory, since cases concerning the common scold, worse still a scold and brawler, and worst of all, a scold, brawler and curser, abound. A wife like that of Adam Eyre of Yorkshire: 'This morn [in June 1647] my wife began, after her old manner to brawl and revile me for criticizing her clothing and stepping on her foot and she kept on till noon', was the sort of wife every man dreaded. The words of Solomon were quoted with approval: 'It is better to dwell in the corner of the housetop than with a brawling woman.'[10]

The scold was by definition female. A woman presented to the courts for the offence and condemned faced a series of punishments: she could be fined; more picturesque and more humiliating was the practice of confining a scold in a brank or padlocked bridle; more spectacular still and on occasion more dangerous was the employment of the cucking-stool (the word was a corruption of the French *coquine* for a hussy). The occupant of the cucking-stool, otherwise known as the ducking-stool, was frequently cooled off in the village pond – whatever the season. Apparatus for the immersion of a scold was part of the social organization of the time: at Gravesend in 1636 for example, porters were paid 2s for ducking Goodwife Campion and 8d for laying up the cucking-stool afterwards. The popular almanacs of the time, containing advice by physicians as well as astrologers, all seriously defended the use of the cucking-stool; less seriously, one hopes, the cutting-out of the tongues of persistent offenders was also advocated upon occasion.[11]

Such women were Alice, wife of Thomas Crathorne, a victualler of Seasalter, Kent, who was charged in 1616 with being 'a common swearer and a brawling scould, and withal will be drunk exceedingly'. Or Isabel Richardson and Alice Worthington, 'Common Scoulds and disturbers of their neighbours' whom the jury of the manor court in Manchester directed should be confined in the 'Cucking Stool' and ducked several times in the horse pond in mid-October. Or Jane Withers of Weldon in Northamptonshire, who was sent to gaol in 1630 till she could find sureties for her next appearance at the general sessions; on her return to Weldon, the constable was ordered to 'cause her to be brought with the cucking-stool to some convenient place within the town and ... there be doused and ducked in the manner of scoulds'.[12]

It was when scolding slid into the far more serious social crime of cursing (against which Parliament even legislated in 1624) that the devil's influence was once more detected. Scolding, like other manifestations of bad temper, was frequently an end in itself, whereas curses implied a wish to injure the person concerned. It was when the devil overheard the Witch of Edmonton cursing her enemy Banks that he exclaimed joyfully: 'Now thou art Mine Own', and he prophesied concerning the churlish Banks:

> The witch of Edmonton shall see his fall,
> If she at least put credit in my power,
> And in mine only, make orisons to me,
> And none but me.[13]

It was dangerous, if you were an old woman, a beggar perhaps, of disagreeable appearance, to curse your uncharitable or unkind neighbour, or even to allow your lips and what Hannah Woolley called 'that slippery glib member the tongue' to move in some possible version of a curse. For then if your neighbour suffered a loss, grief or other form of injury, you might be suspected of having caused it ... with the aid of the devil. It would be suggested either that he had brought about the injury himself or that he had endowed you, as his partner, with the powers to do so. Thus by cursing, even muttering gibberish in a way characteristic of many harmless senile persons,[14] a friendless old woman imperilled her own safety. Her danger was even more acute if her maledictions had some justification because she had suffered some real damage or slight at the hands of the person against whom she railed. A wealthy widow without encumbrances was a potential independent; a crone without protection was a potential witch.

*   *   *

Attention has been drawn to the fact that in many cases of witchcraft tried in the seventeenth century the alleged witch had a genuine grievance against the persons who declared themselves bewitched. This in turn draws attention to the fact that a poor old woman might well have no form of retaliation against the society which persecuted her, other than the hopeful practice of enchantment. One need not go as far as John Stearne, who in 1648 explained witchcraft as a female phenomenon on the grounds that women were more 'easily displeased and revengeful' than men, due to Satan 'prevailing with Eve'. More simply one can see that the social circumstances of many old women might well point them in that direction, out of desperation.[15]

Some form of blackmail, for example, might be exercised in order to secure an old woman a living, something otherwise difficult for her to do, as emerges from the evidence at the great Lancashire witch trials of 1612–13. It was said that none could escape the fury of Elizabeth Southernes (known locally as 'Old Demdike') if her family were 'given any occasion of offence' or denied 'anything they stood need of'. John Device was supposed to have been so afraid of Anne Chattox – 'a very old, withered, spent and decrepit creature, her sight almost gone' – that he covenanted to pay her a yearly dole of meal on condition she hurt neither him nor his goods; on his deathbed he considered that he had been bewitched by her because he had left one instalment unpaid.[16]

It was a point made by Reginald Scot in his classic exposure of 1584, *Discoverie of Witchcraft*: in the case of certain old women 'their wrongs' gave them leave 'to chide and threaten' (as being void of any other way of revenge).[17] The case of the Belvoir witches indicates that not all those arraigned on charges of causing injury were innocent of the *intent* to harm – if a more rational society remains doubtful of their ability to do so.

The story begins like a fairy tale with a castle and a happy, prosperous and noble couple. (It ends like one too, with the deaths of some wicked witches.) Belvoir Castle, in Leicestershire, set augustly on a natural prominence dominating the surrounding countryside, was the seat of the powerful and ancient family of Manners, headed by the Earls of Rutland. In 1612 Francis, sixth Earl of Rutland, succeeded to the title on the death of his childless brother. Not only did the new Earl and Countess lack for nothing either of wealth or prestige, enjoying close connections with the court of King James I, but the succession was now secure, since they had two young sons, Henry Lord Roos, the heir, and Francis Manners; in addition the Earl had a daughter, Catherine Manners, by his first wife. When he succeeded to the earldom, Lord Rutland was described as one who took such honourable measures in the course of his life that he neither displaced tenants, nor discharged servants, but made strangers welcome; his wife was similarly benevolent, 'so that Beaver-Castle was a continual place of Entertainment'.[18]

Among the early objects of the benevolence of the Earl and Countess was an old woman known as Mother (Joan) Flower, and one of her daughters, Margaret. Mother Flower's poverty was relieved and she was employed as 'Char-woman' (the word, then as now, was applied to a domestic help who came in by the day) at the castle. Margaret Flower was put in charge of the 'poultry abroad and the wash-house indoors'. It cannot be said that the Flowers, mother and daughter, sound very satisfactory employees. Margaret Flower purloined provisions, and while some servants' perks were obviously tolerated, these provisions were taken out of the castle in excessive quantities. Margaret Flower also crept out of the castle, 'returning at such unreasonable hours' that mischief was suspected. This mischief was no doubt connected with the fact that Mother Flower's house was supposed to be a local bawdy-house; at any rate it was always full of 'idle and debauched company'. Here Mother Flower's other daughter, Philippa, held sway, and among other activities was 'lewdly transported with the love of one Thomas Simpson'.

As for Mother Flower, she would be described a few years later as 'a monstrous malicious woman, full of oaths, curses, and imprecations, irreligious, and for anything they [her neighbours] saw by her, a plain atheist'. The general impression left by Mother Flower was certainly gruesome: 'her very countenance was estranged, her eyes were fierce and hollow, her speech fell and envious, her demeanour strange and exotic, and her conversation sequestered'. In short, both in her appearance and in her speech, Mother Flower corresponded closely to Reginald Scot's stereotype of the breed of witch: 'commonly old, lame, bleare-eyed, pale, foul and full of wrinkles ... lean and deformed, showing melancholy in their faces ... doting, scolds, mad, divelish'.[19]

Furthermore Mother Flower had a pet cat called Rutterkin, and in that respect too she conformed to the stereotype of the witch. 'I come, Graymalkin ... Paddock calls ...', cry the witches to their familiars in the opening scene of Macbeth before they vanish. It is her dog Tomalin – 'My Tommy, My sweet Tom-boy!' – actually the devil in disguise, who lures the Witch of Edmonton to her destruction. The 'brindled cat' which mewed thrice, the toad of Macbeth, the devilish dog of Edmonton, find a hundred parallels in the witch trials of the seventeenth century, which also featured a multitude of rats, and even the occasional wasp or butterfly. During the famous case of the North Moreton witches, for example, tried at Abingdon in 1605, Agnes Pepperwell was accused of having a 'whitish mouse with a man's face called Sweat' who was a Spirit, Elizabeth Gregory had a black rat with a swine's face and a boar's tusk called Catche, and Mary Pepperwell had 'a whitish toad' called Vizett.[20]

Who knew what devilish familiar might lurk inside the humble shape of a black dog seen by the roadside or a tame white mouse on an old woman's shoulder? No domestic animal, glimpsed prowling in the shades of evening, slinking through the night, was to be totally trusted, never mind the fact that such a pet might be the natural companion – solace even – of a lonely old woman, never mind the nocturnal habits of so many such creatures, notably cats, for this was an area where common sense had taken flight before the onslaughts of fear and prejudice. So Mother Flower's pet cat Rutterkin was destined to play his part in the accusations against her.

What with Margaret Flower's light-fingeredness and her 'indecencies', and the maledictions of her mother, it was hardly surprising that the Flower family in general made themselves extremely unpopular with the household at Belvoir Castle; very soon 'nobody but the Earl's family loved them'. And then that love too faded: the Earl of Rutland turned against Mother Flower 'and used not that Freedom nor familiar conferences with her as usual'. When a certain Peake wronged Mother Flower, the Earl of Rutland, hitherto her patron, paid no attention to the injustice, which was thus not remedied.

As for the Countess, she too became disillusioned with Margaret Flower for her neglect of her duties, so that to the pleased derision of the neighbours, Margaret Flower found herself ejected from her comfortable billet at the castle. The Countess of Rutland seems to have behaved with financial generosity over the dismissal, giving Margaret Flower 40s (as much if not more than a year's pay), a bolster, and a mattress of wool. Nevertheless the feelings of Mother Flower and her family towards the Earl and Countess of Rutland now turned to 'Hate and Malice'.[21]

For all this, when in 1613 the heir to Belvoir, Henry Lord Roos, sickened and died of a disease for which the doctors could find neither cure nor explanation, witchcraft was not suspected. It was only when the second boy Francis, now succeeded to his brother's courtesy title of Lord Roos, sickened, and the girl Catherine Manners also went into some form of decline, that doctors and desperate family alike, interested neighbours and dependants, looked round for some explanation outside the natural world as to why this tragedy should be threatening the house of Rutland.

By an unfortunate coincidence – from the point of view of the Flower family – there was at this juncture a witch trial in progress at the nearby

Leicestershire Assizes, at which three women who knew the Flowers, Anne
Baker, Joan Willimot and Ellen Green, were being accused. Familiars
played their part in this drama. Anne Baker revealed that Joan Willimot
had given her two spirits in the likeness of a kitten, which went with
deceptive innocence under the name of 'Puss', and a mole called 'Hiffe'.
Both animals had leapt on her shoulder and immediately sucked at her
ears (sucking was an acknowledged attribute of familiars). Anne Baker
bestowed the kitten upon a baker who had struck her and the mole on one
Anne Dawse who had termed her 'witch, whore, jade'. Within a fortnight
both the baker and Anne Dawse were dead.[22]

Intensive examination of the three women also produced a number of
weird accusations against Mother Flower concerning the vengeance she
had vowed to take on the Earl of Rutland. Later the Flower daughters
provided further details of the affair. Possibly in their case some form
of physical torture was used,[23] but generally speaking where suspected
witches were concerned, relentless questioning by the authorities, combined with the other harsh deprivations associated with imprisonment,
produced confessions readily enough. Mother Flower was by this time,
as we shall see, beyond human aid or punishment, but the story of her
vengeance, as pieced together from the various confessions, went as
follows.[24]

After Margaret Flower's dismissal the devil had seen an excellent opportunity to use the family as 'Instruments to enlarge his kingdom'. He
therefore offered them whatever they might want, accommodatingly
suggesting that he should attend them in the guise of a dog or cat or rat,
in order to allay suspicion. 'Abominable kisses' and 'an odious sacrifice of
blood' sealed this unpleasant compact. Although the Flowers did take the
opportunity thereafter to produce the occasional 'Tempest' for the ruin of
the crops, it was of course personal vengeance against the Earl of Rutland
which chiefly preoccupied them.

Joan Willimot, herself a widow, like Mother Flower, testified to the
latter's boast that though she could not have her will of the Earl of Rutland
'she had spied my lord's son and stricken him to the earth with a white
spirit'. Spitting on some earth and working it with her fingers, she
announced herself well satisfied that 'though she could not hurt the Lord
himself, yet she had sped his son'. Margaret Flower supplied further details
as to how her mother had carried all this out. Mother Flower had asked
her daughter to procure a glove belonging to the young Lord Roos, and
Margaret had duly picked one up which she found lying 'on the Rushes
in the Nursery'. Mother Flower then first used the glove to stroke her cat

Rutterkin, then dipped the glove in hot water, 'pricked it often' and within a week, lo and behold Henry Lord Roos was 'tormented'.

The glove of Francis Lord Roos was discovered by Margaret Flower on a dung-hill; she brought it to her mother where it received similar treatment of immersion in hot water and rubbing on the belly of Rutterkin. However in the case of Francis, because the boy, although sickly, was still alive in 1619, it was stated that Mother Flower had merely threatened him 'a Mischief' and had predicted (inaccurately as it turned out) that he would mend again.

A piece of handkerchief belonging to Lady Catherine Manners was similarly applied to the belly of Rutterkin, at which point the cat was ordered to 'fly and go'. According to Margaret Flower, Rutterkin merely replied with the word 'Mew' and did not either fly or go; however, this refusal was somehow interpreted as evidence that even her familiar did not have power over a witch like Joan Flower. The lewd Philippa Flower confirmed her sister's confession concerning the glove and its treatment; ultimately her mother had buried it 'wishing the owner might never thrive'. Philippa also contributed that her mother frequently cursed both the Earl and Countess of Rutland, boiling 'feathers and blood together, using devilish speeches and strange gestures'.

We do not have to accept the wilder statements of Margaret and Philippa Flower in order to suppose that Mother Flower had not only threatened to be revenged on the Earl of Rutland, but had actually indulged in some form of witchcraft to do so. Nor was her successful form of vengeance intended to be kept secret. Anne Baker had been told three years earlier by 'two wives of Belvoir' concerning the death of Lord Roos that a glove had been buried and as it 'rotted and wasted, so did the liver of the lord'. Writing towards the end of the eighteenth century, when descendants of the deponents were still living, John Nichols in his *History and Antiquities of the County of Leicester* wrote that there was 'no doubt of their intentional guilt . . . In short they believed themselves to be witches.'[25] For a malevolent old woman, ranged as she saw it against the powerful Rutland family interest, witchcraft represented not so much one possible form of revenge as the only possible form. The coincidental (as we must believe) sickenings and deaths of the Manners children represented therefore at once Mother Flower's triumph and her downfall.

After the Leicestershire accusations against the Flowers had been heard, the family were fetched by the Justices of the Peace, who bound them over to appear at the Assizes at Lincoln. Margaret and Philippa reached Lincoln, but Mother Flower died suddenly *en route* and was buried at Ancaster.

Even the manner of her death was appropriate to one whose 'whole course of life gave grave suspicion that she was a notorious witch'. It was remembered that Mother Flower had predicted that she would be 'neither hanged nor burnt'. This time her prediction was certainly successful although there is no evidence that she had additionally foreseen the precise manner of her death. This came about as Mother Flower was eating a piece of bread and butter. She called on the morsel to choke her if she was guilty of being a witch. She was and it did.[26]

The Flower sisters were less fortunate. A series of Tudor statutes against witchcraft had culminated in the toughest one of all at the beginning of the new reign. By the Act of 1604 it was no longer necessary to have actually caused the death of a person by the use of witchcraft, the mere practice of it if proved was sufficient to ensure guilt. This law, which was not repealed until 1736, also made any form of consultation with or feeding of an evil spirit a felony; so much for Rutterkin and his kind, the kitten called Puss, the mole called Hiffe and so forth and so on, an endless stream of evil spirits masquerading as domestic animals who were undeniably being harboured by their mistresses. By this standard, Philippa Flower too, like her mother, was probably guilty of practising witchcraft - in her case to cause Thomas Simpson to love her; Margaret by her own account had supplied the fatal gloves belonging to Lord Rutland's sons.

Margaret's confessions in general sounded that pathetic note of hysterical delusion which marks so much of the evidence at the witch trials.[27] She admitted that she had two familiar spirits 'sucking on her', one white, the other black and spotted. The white spirit sucked under her left breast, and its black-spotted fellow 'within inward parts of her secrets'; they had agreed to carry out all her wishes in return for the promise of her soul. While Margaret was in gaol at Lincoln, four other devils also appeared to her, one of whom had a black head like an ape; unfortunately Margaret could not recall anything about their encounter except that she had been angry that the devil had not been 'plainer' in the manner of his speaking. The other three took the forms of Rutterkin, 'little Robin' and another spirit.

Philippa Flower too bore witness to the existence of a white rat sucking at her own left breast - in fact a spirit - for three or four years, to which she had promised her soul if it would cause Thomas Simpson to love her. And Philippa confirmed that Rutterkin, now recognized for what he was, a devil in disguise, had persistently bitten and sucked at her sister's neck over the years.

In March 1619 the two daughters of Mother Flower were executed at

Lincoln 'to the terror of all beholders'. The Earl of Rutland, hearing them cry out against the devil 'for deluding them' and now breaking his promise of assistance 'when they stood most in need of his Help', no longer felt any difficulty in believing in their 'Wickedness and horrible Contracts'.[28] A year later when their sickly son Francis died in his turn, the Earl and Countess, now left without male heirs, must have felt themselves still further convinced that justice had been done.

We can follow the rest of the sad story in the Rutland family accounts. In 1619 £20 had been given to Mr Jephson for prosecuting the witches at Lincoln, and another £20 had been spent on 'my Lord's journey to the Assizes'. With the death of Francis in March 1620 £26 was the total sum incurred for breaking the ground for his burial, and payments to the chanter, the Dean, choristers, vergers, grave-makers, as well as eight dozen torches and sufficient frankincense. The coffin itself cost 10s. In July payments were noted relating to a journey by 'my lady' to take the waters at Tunbridge Wells. She went 'for Barrenness', the waters there being celebrated for relieving that unhappy condition.[29] The cure did not work. It turned out to be one of Mother Flower's less successful predictions that after a long while the Earl and Countess 'should have more children'. No more children were in fact born to the stricken Rutlands.

This absence of male heirs did, however, have the unlooked-for effect of improving the fortunes of the Earl's daughter by his first wife, Lady Catherine Manners. About the time the Flower sisters were being put to death at Lincoln, Lady Catherine, already an heiress from her own mother's property, had found herself courted by the most glittering figure of the age, George Villiers, Duke of Buckingham. It had been suggested that Buckingham sought Catherine as much for the satisfaction of her Manners connection – the Villiers had once been minor gentry in the area dominated by the Manners family – as for her money;[30] 'that puir fool Kate', as she was dubbed by King James I, was certainly not pretty.

At first the match hung fire; despite her love for Buckingham, Catherine, who was a Catholic, declined to change her religion, while 'the mother Countesses', that is the Countess of Rutland and Buckingham's baleful mother, the former Lady Compton, now created Countess of Buckingham in her own right, quarrelled. But the death of Francis transformed Catherine from a considerable into a magnificent heiress; Buckingham was now far more likely to receive the vast dowry he was said to be asking for 'the sister' – £20,000 ready money and land worth £4,000 a year, the latter figure to be doubled if Lord Roos died.[31] At last in May 1620 Buckingham succeeded in marrying the 'puir fool', who bestowed upon him not only her heart but a fortune hugely augmented by her brothers' deaths.

The transformation of the daughter of the Earl of Rutland into the Duchess of Buckingham, wife of the King's splendid favourite, cannot have been what Mother Flower intended to bring about with her spells and curses.

*   *   *

'[I] could see nothing in the evidence which did persuade me to think them other than poor, melancholy, envious, mischievous, ill-disposed, ill-dieted, atrabilious [that is, black-biled] constitutions' – so wrote the historian Arthur Wilson charitably, and doubtlessly accurately, of the Chelmsford witches at their trial in 1645.[32] For if Mother Flower had a genuine grudge against the Earl of Rutland and tried to practise some kind of vengeance, there were many old women throughout the seventeenth century who suffered simply because they corresponded to the stereotype of the witch.

In many ways it was a circular argument. Whatever the present disagreements about the precise nature of seventeenth-century witchcraft, it is at least common ground that the vast majority of witches actually tried were both female and old (with widows at a special risk).[33] Contemporaries were well aware of the fact. King James I put the proportion of females to males at 20 to 1 and Alexander Roberts put it at 100 to 1. In his pamphlet of 1648, John Stearne, a close associate of the witch-hunter Matthew Hopkins, wrote that it was 'evident' that of witches in general 'there be commonly more women than men ... especially of the hurting witches'. Reginald Scot had connected witchcraft with the menopause, a phenomenon peculiar to the female, when women suffered delusions because of 'the stopping of their monthly melancholic flux'. Witches were also believed for the most part to live 'in most base esteem and beggary', a supposition also borne out by the figures available.[34] Thus was the stereotype constructed in both literature and public opinion.

This meant that while some younger women and a few men were certainly tried for or suspected of practising witchcraft, they were considered as individuals; the species to which they belonged was not of itself under suspicion. (Pregnancy incidentally saved a woman from being hanged, at least for the time being; a woman who was not pregnant would sometimes plead so in order to save herself – a claim which would be investigated by the local midwives.) But because the agreed characteristics of a witch were those of an old woman, any old woman might be suspected of being a witch owing to characteristics over which she had no control.

A family group *c.* 1645, in part by William Dobson; the four skulls on the broken column at which the father gazes mournfully refer to his dead children, evidently not forgotten despite the high incidence of infant death.

A rich merchant, Sir Robert Vyner, and his family: Lady Vyner had been a wealthy widow when he married her. Pepys admired her both for her looks and her fortune. Painted by John Michael Wright.

Margaret Duchess of Newcastle, from the frontispiece to her book, *The Worlds Olio* (1655).

Mary Countess of Warwick.

Ann Lady Fanshawe.

Lettice Viscountess Falkland (who was esteemed for not making a second marriage after her husband's death, unlike many of her contemporaries) depicted in her widow's weeds.

Mrs Margaret Godolphin, John Evelyn's adored friend, who died young as a result of childbirth.

A milkmaid: one of the better-paid jobs for women which also led to some kind of independence.

Susanna Perwick, who died unmarried in 1661 at the age of twenty-four, from the frontispiece to her biography by John Batchiler, *The Virgin's Pattern* (1661).

A countrywoman, showing the kind of agricultural implements that women regularly used.

The housewife and the hunter, from the *Roxburghe Ballads*.

The title page of *The Needles Excellency* by John Taylor (1634).

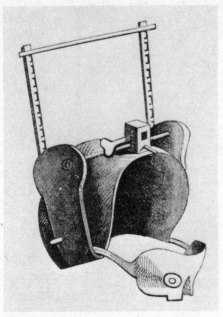

A scold's bridle.

A BOVLSTER LECTVRE.

Dum loquor icta, taces?

Surda canis

This wife a wondrous racket meanes to keepe,
While th' Husband seemes to sleepe but do'es not sleepe:
But she might full aswell her Lecture smother,
For ent'ring one Eare, it goes out at t'other.

Will: Marshall. sculpsit.

The title page of *Ar't asleepe Husband? A Boulster Lecture* by Richard Brathwaite (1640). The talkativeness of women was axiomatic at this time.

A witch and her imps, from a drawing of 1621.

Execution of witches, 1655.
A: hangman. B: bellman. C: two sergeants. D: witchfinder, taking his money.

Dorothy Sidney, Countess of Sunderland (Edmund Waller's 'Sacharissa'), painted by Van Dyck.

Below: One of the remarkable series of paintings made to illustrate the career of the Catholic nun and reformer Mary Ward. A legend in German accompanying the picture reads: 'When Mary was recovering from a very dangerous illness, that she had at St Omer, she was lying one day in bed enjoying unusual rest and quiet, when she became aware of a voice within her, revealing to her most plainly in what way she was to organize her Institute.'

Another witness to the witch-hunting forays which produced the Chelmsford trials wrote that suspicion fell on 'every old woman with a wrinkled face, a furred brow, a hairy lip, a squint eye, a squeaking voice, or a scolding tongue, a skull cap on her head, a spindle in her hand, a Dog or Cat by her side'.[35]

The Bideford witches – three crazed old women who were put to death in the West Country in 1682 – provide tragic examples of persons who were probably guilty of little except advancing age, destitution and wandering wits. Temperance Lloyd, a widow, Susanna Edwards, a widow, and Mary Trembles, a single woman, were tried at the Devon Summer Sessions in front of Sir Francis North, the Lord Chief Justice, and Sir Thomas Raymond. North described them later: they were, he wrote, 'the most old, decrepid [sic], despicable, miserable creatures that ever he saw. A painter would have chosen them out of the whole country for figures of that kind to have drawn by.' They were in fact damned by their own confessions, which as North pointed out, exceeded even the testimonies brought against them, which of themselves were 'very full and fanciful'.[36]

Certainly there was much which was 'fanciful' about the evidence produced against the three women.[37] Temperance Lloyd was subjected to a crude physical examination. This was a routine procedure for a suspected witch, in order to discover either the devil's mark – which could be pricked without pain – or some form of teat – which could suckle a familiar (described as 'a common token to know all witches by'). Mrs Anne Wakeley, wife of a Bideford husband, headed the body of women who found in Temperance Lloyd's 'secret parts' two teats 'hanging right together like unto a piece of flesh that a child had sucked. And that each of the teats was about an inch in length.' Temperance Lloyd herself confessed that a 'Black man', sometimes in the shape of a magpie, had sucked at them. The devil had also helped her to disguise herself as a 'grey or braget' (honey-coloured) cat, in order to deposit a child's puppet in the chamber of one Grace Thomas to whom she wished to do harm.

Anne Wakeley testified that while nursing Grace Thomas, 'something in the shape of a magpie' had come into her chamber. Grace Thomas contributed that Temperance Lloyd had fallen on her knees and wept in Bideford High Street allegedly for joy at seeing her, Grace, 'so strong again'; however, that night, clearly as a direct result of the encounter, Grace Thomas had been overcome by agonizing pricking pains from head to foot. Significantly, in her opinion, Grace Thomas recovered once Temperance Lloyd had been hauled off to prison.

The old woman further testified that she had disguised herself 'in the form of a red pig' to bewitch one Lydia Burman who had given evidence against her in another trial (Temperance was however acquitted on this particular charge). Some of Temperance's revelations cast a pathetic light on the nature of her daily round. The devil, she said on the eve of her death, had appeared to her while she was fetching some brooms, 'This poor woman has a great burthen', he exclaimed, offering to ease her of it. But Temperance refused the devil's offer: 'I said The Lord had enabled me to carry it so far, and I hope I shall be able to carry it further.' Sometimes she revealed an understandable sense of grievance: 'I sold apples, and the child took an apple from me, and the mother took the apple from the child; for the which I was very angry.' But, added Temperance piteously, the child itself died of smallpox, not witchcraft.

Another routine test of a witch was to compel her to recite the Lord's Prayer or the Creed; a test incidentally that a confused and illiterate old woman was all too likely to fail. Failures of memory, stumblings or mumblings indicated the devil at work. Old Temperance recited both the Lord's Prayer and the Creed most imperfectly.

As for Susanna Edwards, she recounted how she had met the devil about two years ago 'in the Parsonage Close' in the shape of a fine gentleman 'apparelled in black'. Hoping to get some money from him, Susanna curtseyed. The devil, discovering from her what he was apparently not sufficiently omniscient to know, that Susanna was very poor, promised her that she would not want for meat, drink or clothes in future if she placed herself in his power; after this encounter, the devil – 'something in the shape of a little boy' – sucked at her breast. Then it was Mary Trembles's turn: she confessed that she had been persuaded by Susanna Edwards to follow her into mischief. She had then had carnal knowledge with the devil in the shape of a lion: he had sucked her 'and caused her to cry out with pain'.

In the end Susanna Edwards was convicted of bewitching one Grace, wife of John Barnes, and Mary Trembles of bewitching a mariner's wife called Dorcas Coleman, whose violent internal pains her doctor had been quick to ascribe to witchcraft. Both these women incidentally were alive and healthy at the time of the trial, so the witchcraft had evidently done little permanent damage. The reason Susanna and Mary gave for 'tormenting' Grace Barnes was a significant one: it was to punish her for having refused them 'meat and tobacco' when they begged for it. Like Temperance's fury with the child and its mother who robbed her of payment of her apple, these admissions were evidence of the kind of low-level village grudge which must have existed in multitudes. It was when a child died, a woman rolled in agony and the slighted person corresponded to the black-biled – 'atrabilious' – stereotype of a witch, that the hue and cry of prejudice frequently followed.

A pamphlet printed shortly after the deaths of the three old women (which accused them amongst other things of sneezing a woman to death and causing a boy out at sea to fall to his doom from the main mast of his ship) gives the following account of the execution scene.[38]

Old Temperance Lloyd went on her last journey from the prison quite unconcerned, 'eating all the way'. She does not even seem to have comprehended the danger she was in. Mary Trembles, on the other hand, 'lay down' and had to be tied on to the back of a horse before she could be moved.

Just before the hangman did his work, the Rev. Mr Hann, a local clergyman, subjected the three women to one last cross-questioning on the subject of their diabolical past. Mary Trembles protested her innocence. While admitting that she had seen the devil once (although no longer quite sure of his shape – 'looking, I think, like a lion') she denied what had been sworn at the Grand Inquest, that she had 'a teat in her privy parts', and denied too that she had had carnal knowledge of the devil.

In so far as Temperance Lloyd had any understanding of what was happening to her, she seems to have made a last ditch attempt to blame Susanna Edwards:

MR HANN: 'You say you never hurt ships nor boats: did you never ride over an arm of the sea on a cow?'
TEMPERANCE LLOYD: 'No, no, Master, 'twas she' (meaning Susanna).

At this Susanna burst out in her turn that Temperance 'lied'. And so after a prayer by the Rev. Mr Hann, Susanna Edwards suggested to Mary Trembles that they should sing part of the Fortieth Psalm (which ends, appropriately enough, 'But I am poor and needy; yet the Lord thinketh upon me: thou art my help and my deliverer; make no tarrying, O my God'). As Susanna Edwards mounted the ladder, she said: 'The Lord Jesus speed me; though my sins be as red as scarlet, the Lord Jesus can make them as white as snow; The Lord help my soul.' In the words of the pamphlet, 'Then was executed.'

Mary Trembles went to her death with similar piety: 'Lord Jesus receive my soul; Lord Jesus speed me.' Then Mary too 'was executed'.

This left old Temperance Lloyd, whom the sheriff described to her face as 'the woman that has debauched the other two'.

SHERIFF: 'Did you ever lie with the devils?'
TEMPERANCE: 'No.'
And later:
SHERIFF: 'Did the devil never promise you anything?'
TEMPERANCE: 'No.'
SHERIFF: 'Then you have served a very bad Master, who gave you nothing.
Well, consider you are just departing this world; do you believe there is a God?'
TEMPERANCE: 'Yes.'
SHERIFF: 'Do you believe in Jesus Christ?'
TEMPERANCE: 'Yes; and I pray Jesus Christ to pardon all my sins.'
'And so was executed.'

It is quite possible, as was stated by a later pamphlet, that the judge
actually tried to get Susanna, Mary and Temperance off: 'these three poor
old women [as he supposed] were weary of their Lives and that he thought
it proper for them to be carried to the Parish from whence they came, and
that the Parish should be charged with their Maintenance; for he thought
their oppressing Poverty had constrained them to wish for Death'. But in
another version, the judge, while referring to the harmless effects of
'melancholy or delusion', regretted that mercy could not be shown to the
old women in the present state of the law: 'we cannot reprieve them
without appearing to deny the very being of witches'.[39]

*   *   *

Not all old women witches who practised some form of primitive magic
suffered as cruelly as the Bideford witches. The mysterious nature of 'black'
witchcraft, as it was regarded in the seventeenth century, is underlined by
the fact that 'white magic' co-existed with it, as indeed forms of 'white
magic' had always been practised since ancient times (and are, in various
forms from fortune-telling to herbal healing, still practised today). 'Cunning folk', who unlike witches were often male, existed in abundance: in
The Anatomy of Melancholy, Robert Burton wrote that there were 'Cunning men, Wizards and white-witches ... in every village'. Their protection was quite simply that they were believed to do good. Thus a 'cunning
woman', one with certain curative arts at her disposal from which black
magic was specifically excluded, might pursue an active and even lucrative
career, provided she kept herself carefully free from the taint of witchcraft.
Sir Ralph Verney's son and heir Edmund, generally known as 'Mun', had
a 'distracted' wife called Mary. It was decided to send for a cunning
woman called Old Judith.[40]

First of all Mun Verney asked Old Judith to assure him that she did not
'use any manner of Charms, Sorceries, or Magic whatsoever'. Old Judith

hastily gave 'devout assurances' to the contrary. She was then permitted to carry out her experiment. This was to take a hare's head – 'Jack Hare' – and wrap it in a cloth; she then bound the wrapped hare's head round the patient's own head for three days and three nights. When the hare's head was finally removed, it was inserted into the patient's pillow, amid the feathers, to lie there 'so long as they live'. The idea of the cure was that there was a 'sympathetical Virtue' in a 'melancholy Hare's Brain' which would 'draw away all Melancholy out of that hare-brained people' (i.e. the mad).

The cure did not work. As Mun Verney wrote: 'It would be very pretty if so slight a thing could cure.' Poor mad Mary Verney never fully recovered her wits. All the same, Old Judith suffered no ill consequences for her efforts, while Mun Verney in his slightly sceptical attitude to the whole affair represented a kind of tolerance which not only co-existed with harsh prejudice but also grew as the century progressed.

Among rational people, it had always seemed strange that the devil should choose the 'poor and atrabilious' and invest them with such colossal powers. As the newspaper *The Moderate Intelligencer* put it in 1645, it was 'a great wonder' that devils should be conversant with 'silly old women that know not their right hand from their left'. In 1641 Henry Oxinden of Barham, father of the headstrong Peg, wrote with marked good sense about the case of one Goodwife Gilnot, who was accused by a man called Brake of having lost his sheep. Oxinden pointed out that he too had frequently lost sheep – without going to the trouble of thinking himself bewitched.[41]

As for Goodwife Gilnot, who was accused of having a teat upon her upper body – actually a small wart – 'believe it', he wrote, 'there is none so familiar with her as to receive any sustenance from thence'. He went on: 'Such deep root hath the fables of witchcraft taken hold in the heart of this and other silly men ... they will not with patience endure the hand of and correction of God ...' It was being suggested 'that certain creatures here on earth, called witches, be the authors of men's miseries, as though themselves were innocents and had deserved no such punishments ...' Henry Oxinden concluded: 'Moreover I cannot see how any rational man can persuade himself that a simple woman should do such things as these.'

The progress in scepticism on the subject has been summed up by Christopher Hill in these terms: 'In 1600 most respectable people believed in witches ... by 1700 this was no longer true.'[42] The last execution of a witch occurred at Exeter in 1685, three years after the deaths of the three 'decrepid' Bideford women; Jane Wenham, the last person to be condemned (in 1712), was reprieved. Yet as late as 1704 *The Athenian Oracle*, a magazine for answering popular queries whose view on life was otherwise quite enlightened, when asked whether it was permissible to kill a witch to preserve oneself, answered: as to those 'wretched and malicious Creatures . . . we should make no scruple to strike or stab them'.[43]

But these old women, wretched and malicious as they often were, might have framed on their own behalf the bitter question posed by the Witch of Edmonton:

> Cause I am poor, deform'd, ignorant
> And like a bow buckled and bent together . . .
> Must I for that be made a common sink
> For all the filth and rubbish of Men's tongues
> To fall and run into?[44]

7 Unlearned Virgins

> ... But think you, Helen,
> If you should tender your supposed aid,
> He would receive it? ...
> A poor unlearned virgin....
>
> COUNTESS OF ROUSILLON TO HELENA, *All's Well That Ends Well*

'Thou mayest perhaps think I have lost my labour': thus Elizabeth Josceline to her husband in 1622 on the prospect of her giving birth to a daughter. The best way to palliate the blow would be to think of those biblical exemplars, Elizabeth, Esther, and chaste Susanna. Betty Viscountess Mordaunt was equally frank on her own account: 'If it be thy blessed will, let it be a boy' – this was her fervent prayer when she was once more pregnant in 1665, although she already had six sons. And when a seventh boy was indeed safely born, Betty Mordaunt apostrophized the Almighty in verse:

> To all the rest, thou hast this added more
> The blessing of a son, to increase my store.

Anne, wife of the Royalist commander Sir Simon Harcourt, shared the primitive feelings of her husband who wrote back to her from the campaign in Ireland: 'with God's blessing bring me another lusty boy'. After his death Anne Harcourt married the Parliamentary general Sir William Waller, a widower with sons. Her diary, kept like that of Betty Mordaunt for spiritual reasons, is a long record of public and private trials and her own 'transgressions'. Throughout, whenever pregnant, she pleads for the safe birth of a living child with all its parts and limbs – 'and a son'.[1]

The experience of Agnes Sim, a servant of East Brent in Somerset who had become pregnant by her master, was on a cruder level. She 'asked him [her master] who should father the child. He said he would, if it was a boy, but if it was a maid, she should lack a father for it.' (Servants did sometimes undertake the responsibility of providing their sonless masters with male heirs; the sex of the child being, it was believed, determined by the female.)[2] Nevertheless Agnes Sim discovered for herself what Betty Mordaunt and Anne Harcourt expressed so eloquently in their spiritual diaries, that primitive desire for a boy which in a sense disadvantaged the girls of this period even before their birth.

Cary Verney was one of the five sisters of Ralph Verney and as a child had been the 'she-darling' of her father Sir Edmund. Married at fifteen, but with the settlement never completed owing to the difficulty of wartime conditions, Cary found herself at the age of eighteen a pregnant widow, when her husband Captain Gardiner was killed in 1645. Then, 'My sister was brought to bed of a girl to all our griefs', wrote Ralph Verney. Having provided no male heir, with no proper marriage settlement, even her own jointure in peril, poor Cary was grudged her very food at the Gardiner home at Cuddesdon; finally she fled back to her own family. Cary Verney did enjoy an exceptionally happy second marriage to John Stewkeley of Hampshire; but it was no wonder, as one of the jolly, gambling, gossiping ladies of the Restoration court, that she regretted hearing the news that her nephew John Verney's wife (already the mother of a son) had given birth to a daughter: 'for I find our sex is not much valued in our age'.[3]

One of the primary reasons why the average female was 'not much valued', as Cary Verney lightly but aptly expressed it, was that she was not much educated – in comparison, that is, with the average male, her brother as it might be, that child who had fulfilled his parents' primitive expectations by being born of the favoured sex.

Even women despised other women for their silliness. Margaret Duchess of Newcastle was sharp enough to see the reason for this foolishness: in 1655 in *The Worlds Olio* she wrote that 'in Nature we have as clear an understanding as Men, if we were bred in Schools to mature our Brains'. Nevertheless in practice she found the tittle-tattle of women intolerable.[4] Conversely, even those women who did for a number of individual reasons receive a proper education might well be scorned for their attainments. In principle, society rewarded the learned woman with disapproval or at best suspicion.

Anne Lady Newdigate, that devoted mother, unconsciously summed up the contemporary attitude to the education of the sexes when she wrote in her will, dated 1610: 'that my boys may be brought up in good learning and both they and my daughters to be bred up in virtuous and godly life'. Elizabeth Josceline, laying down instructions in *The Mothers Legacy to her Unborn Child* for the education of that hypothetical daughter for whose arrival she had apologized in advance, hoped she would be taught 'The Bible, housewifery, writing and good work'. (She herself, incidentally, had been highly educated by her grandfather, learning both languages and history in the enlightened tradition of the late sixteenth century.) Elizabeth Josceline added: 'other learning a woman needs not, though I admire it in those whom God hath blest with discretion yet I desire it not much in my own, having seen that sometimes women have greater portions of learning than wisdom'. And if her husband himself wanted to have 'a learned daughter'? At least: 'my dear ... I pray God give her a wise and a religious heart'.[5]

Where a highly educated woman did escape censure, it was generally for some extraneous reason which might be exceptional piety, of the sort which Elizabeth Josceline hoped would redeem her own 'learned daughter'. Or it might, in a more worldly fashion, be due to her high position in society. In private Dorothy Osborne poked fun at Margaret Duchess of Newcastle, who admittedly did cut a fairly weird figure in society, at any rate where her costume was concerned. In 1653, Dorothy was 'satisfied that there are many soberer people in Bedlam', and she wrote that the Duchess's friends were 'much to blame to let her go abroad'.[6] In public however, Margaret Newcastle's rank (that of a very rich Duchess, wife of a Royalist grandee who had been Governor to Charles II as a boy) obtained for her some handsome tributes from academics at both universities.

The Duchess used to present favoured colleges with her own works. Expressions of gratitude were published after her death in a special volume: *Letters and Poems In Honour of the Incomparable Princess Margaret, Dutchess of Newcastle*. A letter from the Master and Fellows of St John's College, Cambridge, sets the tone: 'In your Poesy we praise that Life and native Verdure, every way Confident with its self, Castilian like, it stands not still, nor boils over, but with a gentle stream doth touch our Ears and slide into our Minds. In your Philosophy we praise that lightsome and piercing acuteness, nothing constrained, nothing obscure; you render all things clear and genuine ...' However, Trinity College, in wondering aloud 'how it came to pass that Eloquence, Poetry, Philosophy, things otherwise most different, should without the help of a Tutor, without the Midwifery of a University, at length, agree in a Woman' showed that the Duchess was very much the high-born exception to the general rule.[7]

It was not a rule which showed signs of lapsing as the century progressed. On the contrary, the prejudice against education for girls – and its dreaded end-product, the learned woman – had derived fresh impetus from the presence of a male sovereign after 1603. It had always been rather tactless to attack the learned woman with too much zest so long as that paragon of female erudition Queen Elizabeth occupied the throne. As the poet Anne Bradstreet wrote in memory of 'our dread Virago' forty years after her death:

> Let such as say our Sex is void of Reason,
> Know 'tis a Slander now, but once was Treason.

Not only were men freed from the inhibition of the 'dread Virago's' intellectual example by her death, but that male sovereign, James I, had himself a scant opinion of the female intelligence. Perhaps the frivolity of his Queen, Anne of Denmark, had something to answer for; at any rate when it was suggested that his daughter, another Elizabeth, should learn Latin, the King replied that 'To make women learned and foxes tame had the same effect: to make them more cunning.' And he forbade it.[8]

Such sentiments would have come as a marked surprise to his English royal relations of yore: those Tudor princesses of the Renaissance, not only Queen Elizabeth herself who could translate Latin into Greek, and the famously erudite Lady Jane Grey, but Queen Mary Tudor, celebrated at the time for her knowledge of science and mathematics. For that matter James's mother Mary Queen of Scots, whose intellectual attainments have been overshadowed by her dramatic life story was, as a princess, automatically instructed in the classics. We know from the English Ambassador to Scotland that she used to read Livy regularly for pleasure after dinner, with George Buchanan.[9]

In the sixteenth century Sir Thomas More had written: 'I do not see why learning ... may not equally agree with both sexes.' At the end of Queen Elizabeth's reign, a classical education was a mark of elegance in the circle round Mary Countess of Pembroke: William Wotton, in his *Reflections on Ancient and Modern Learning*, wrote of that period: 'It was so very modish, that the fair sex seemed to believe that Greek and Latin added to their Charms: and Plato and Aristotle untranslated, were frequent Ornaments of their Closets.' Such a tradition lingered on at a place like Little Gidding. Here the many daughters of the house, in the tranquil religious retreat founded by the Anglican theologian Nicholas Ferrar in the 1620s, were carefully educated in Latin, as well as arithmetic, writing and music (and such practical matters as book-binding). But it was in the seventeenth century that George Herbert was able to list among well-known proverbs: 'Beware of a young wench, a prophetess and a Latin woman.'[10] While women themselves were often contributing a note of ritual apology whenever they felt they had stepped outside the modest mental boundaries which circumscribed their sex.

Lady Elizabeth Hastings, carefully educated by her 'Vigilant Mother' Lucy Countess of Huntingdon to know French, Latin and Italian, was advised by her on marriage merely 'to make herself fit conversation for her husband'. As a result, Lady Elizabeth showed herself so modest – that favourite epithet again – throughout her short married life with Sir James Langham that he never had 'all those inconveniences which some have fancied, so necessarily accompany a Learned Wife'. She died still young in 1664. This model existence on the part of one who might otherwise have caused Sir James a great deal of trouble with her accomplishments, was summed up in a quatrain:

> That Skill in Scripture, and in Tongues she got,
> Made her a living Bible Polyglot.
> These did not puff her up, she did descend
> To the kind offices of Wife and Friend.[11]

It was not that women did not read the books where they had the ability or the opportunity to do so. In 1647 we find Adam Eyre of Yorkshire spending 1s 8d on a book at a fair at Wakefield for his scold of a wife – presumably to palliate her bad temper on his return. There was, as might be expected, a heavy bias towards what Lettice Falkland's biographer called 'good authors'. Mary Countess of Warwick's tastes ran to the works of Jeremy Taylor, Foxe's *Martyrs*, and Baxter's *Crucifying of the World by the Cross of Christ* (which she described as her favourite book) as well as the poetry of George Herbert – who often features in ladies' reading at this time. But Lady Anne Clifford read Turkish history as well as Chaucer, and had Ovid's *Metamorphoses* read aloud to her by her cousin Maria. Lady Cholmley, wife of Sir Hugh, the Governor of Scarborough Castle during the Civil War, was 'addicted to read and well versed in history'.[12]

Nevertheless an atmosphere of excuse was apt to prevail when a female achieved anything out of the ordinary of a literary nature. Mrs Dorothy Leigh, author of *The Mothers Blessing*, which had reached its seventh edition by 1621, dedicated it to her three sons (she was a widow). Writing, she admitted in this dedication, was 'a thing unusually among us' since women generally used words to exhort. The book itself contained a lot of advice on the sort of wives her boys should marry, and the need to exhibit patience towards them subsequently: 'Bear with the woman,' she pleaded, 'as with the weaker vessel.'[13]

*   *   *

It was not a coincidence that one of the few Englishwomen in the first half of the seventeenth century who believed, without apology, in the need to educate girls properly was a Catholic nun: Mary Ward.

The disappearance of the convents at the time of the Reformation had deprived English girls not only of convenient local places of learning, but also of a pool of women teachers in the shape of the nuns themselves. Indeed, when the convent of Godstow near Oxford was being disbanded, a petition for its preservation (unsuccessful) was mounted on the grounds that 'most of the gentlewomen of the county were sent there to be bred'.[14]

At home in England the position of the woman teacher had not recovered from the collapse of the nunneries. (Again, it was no coincidence that the Anglican Little Gidding, derided by opponents of its high church sympathies as a 'Protestant nunnery', also placed a value on female education.) Many of the daughters of the English Catholic families however continued to be sent abroad to convents in the Low Countries to receive their education. These girls – Knatchbulls, Gages, Vavasours, Blundells – embarked on journeys of much danger and difficulty, defying the authorities to reach their goal abroad.[15]

It was their parents' intention in sending them that they should be preserved in the ancient faith. A Petition of the House of Commons of 1621, which asked for all children of Catholics to be recalled from abroad and given Protestant teachers at home, also had in mind re-educating such children religiously. But these girls who wended their way to the Low Countries, often remaining there as nuns, also found a kind of independence unknown to their sisters still at home – paradoxically in view of the black reputation of such convents back home in Protestant England.

Mary Ward's obsession with women's education (which has been shared by most people through history who have wished to improve the female lot in a permanent fashion) had as its ultimate objective the reconversion of her native England to Catholicism. But as a woman of remarkable independence of judgement, Mary Ward was quick to see that women in religious orders could not carry out their proper part in this apostolate, if they were not correctly prepared for it. As she told Pope Paul V, when she pleaded with him to be allowed to found an order of 'English Virgins': 'the education of girls is congruous to our times'. Nor was this education intended to fit girls solely for the religious life. Mary Ward's memorandum to the Pope on the subject of the 'English Virgins' described their aim as being to instruct young girls in 'piety, Christian morals and the liberal arts' so that they could 'profitably embrace either the secular or the religious life'.[16]

Mary Ward was born in Yorkshire near Ripon in 1585: her baptismal name was Joan (she took Mary at her confirmation).[17] She came of a prominent recusant family, related to half the other Catholics in England: two of her Wright uncles were involved in the Gunpowder Plot and her father was one of the many Catholic gentlemen arrested on suspicion immediately afterwards. On Mary herself the influence of her grand-mother, with whom she lived for five years, was probably even more powerful since Mrs Wright was famous for being 'a great prayer'. As a young girl, Mary became engaged to a member of the Redshaw family, but on his premature death, despite her 'extreme beauty' which attracted new suitors, she abandoned all thoughts of marriage. Instead she joined the Poor Clares at St Omer.

It was at this point that Mary encountered a completely new world from that of the hunted recusant Catholics in which she had been brought up. Women as a whole, and particularly women of rank – whether in religious orders or not – led much freer lives in the Low Countries. This was something on which travellers commented, including the fact that women here participated equally in conversation and argument with men. At the same time the generally passive or secluded role of women within the Catholic Church itself had begun to be questioned in certain quarters after the Council of Trent. The spirit of the Counter-Reformation, incar-nated by the career of the great Spanish nun, St Teresa of Avila, suggest-ed that women could achieve much not merely by prayer and contem-plation but by direct participation in the worldly work of the Church. As Mary Ward was to put it later, women were proposing 'to follow a mixed kind of life, such as Christ and his Blessed Mother lived on earth'.[18]

At Gravelines Mary Ward attempted to found a Poor Clare convent for Englishwomen out of her own resources, and later she did found a boarding-school for English girls at St Omer, where she was aided by five English friends, including her sister Barbara. On one occasion at St Omer the nuns' confessor made an unwise observation, ascribing their diminish-ing religious fervour to the weakness of their sex. Mary Ward strongly rebutted him. Was their failure 'because we are women? No, but because we are imperfect women. There is no such difference between men and women', she went on, 'that women may not do great things!...' As for the Catholic religion, 'It is not *veritas hominis*, verity of men, nor verity of women, but *veritas Domini*' – the truth of God. Mary went on to quote the example of the (female) saints: 'And I hope in God it will be seen that women in time will do much.'[19]

Certainly Mary Ward herself fulfilled her own prophecy that women in time would 'do much'. Her life story was one marked by unusual reverses and dangers even by the standards of the seventeenth century; she was also dogged by ill-health. None of this stood in the way of her determination to prove that the education of girls was 'congruous' to the times in which she lived.

As time went on, an increasing number of English girls were sent abroad to be taught under the auspices of Mary Ward and her friends. This had the double effect of increasing Mary Ward's contacts with the English Catholic world she had left behind via these young ladies, and also necessitating journeys to England itself to seek out new pupils, or in certain instances annuities to pay for their board and tuition.

The account of these travels, made by Mary Ward between 1608 and 1618, makes exciting reading: a sort of *Westward Ho!* in reverse. London at that period was a honeycomb round which government informers buzzed, seeking to rout out secret Catholics. The 'English Virgins' came to be nicknamed the Apostolicae Viragines or the Galloping Girls by their pursuers. The technique of Mary Ward and her friends was to come in plain clothes, as it were, and blandly to hold open house, as though there was nothing to hide. Then they pursued their mission under the noses of the Government and its spies. But the 'plain clothes' were in fact deliberately splendid garments such as ladies of quality would have worn if they had *not* been nuns. We have a description of Mary's sister Barbara 'in a bright taffeta gown' with a starched yellow ruff 'à la mode' and richly embroidered petticoats.[20] When Mary Ward herself was hauled to the Guildhall to answer for her missionary work, she abandoned concealment and carried a rosary in her hand in defiance of the law – and her own safety. In the court she denounced the magistrate for blasphemy, and recited the litanies of the Blessed Virgin Mary in her coach on her way to prison.

It would be nice to be able to record that Mary Ward, allowed to vanish beyond the seas once more, was warmly received on the Continent. Unfortunately for all her energies and perseverance in the cause of female education there, she was destined to arouse quite as much – and in a sense more – damaging hostility abroad. Here her enemies lay within her own Church. 'Runaway nun!' 'Visionary!', and worst of all, 'False Prophetess!' had shouted the townspeople of Gravelines. The spirit of the Counter-Reformation, where women were concerned, had its ardent supporters and also its furious detractors. While the immediate reaction of Pope Paul V to Mary's idea of a new Institute of women following 'a mixed kind of life' in the world had been favourable, and his successor Gregory XV received her kindly in 1621, the atmosphere in Rome soon changed for the worse.

It was Mary's intention to place her Institute under a superior general directly dependent on the Pope (on the model of the Jesuits). That was an unpopular notion with the Catholic Church as a whole, and in particular the bishops. But her conviction that women could 'do much' was equally unpopular with that section of the Catholic Church which remained convinced that women *could* do much – at home or in a secluded convent. Exaggeration is always a skilful weapon of attack. Mary Ward was accused of wishing women to rival men in the ministry, that is to say, usurp their functions as preachers; Mary Ward had in fact deliberately made the point that women could not and should not preach or administer the sacraments, and wives should also be subject to their husbands.[21] Yet the unfair charge succeeded in its aim.

Mary Ward's convents and schools, founded as far apart as Liège and Cologne, Vienna and Prague, Rome and Naples, flourished. But opposition to the new Institute intensified until in 1631 a decree was issued by Pope Urban VIII dissolving it; its members were only allowed to continue their ordinary work of religious education if they took purely private vows.†

Mary Ward herself was imprisoned in Germany, in a tiny airless filthy cell at the orders of the Church (but not the Pope – who had her released when he heard the news). Subsequently she lived quietly in Rome, and in 1639 she returned to England.

Here, the patronage of the Catholic Queen Henrietta Maria seemed to promise her the opportunity of continuing her work of female education. There were 'common schools for girls in London' to be founded, and young women needed to be taught Latin; unlike King James I, Mary Ward was a fervent believer in the importance of Latin studies for girls. Or perhaps it would be accurate to say that Mary Ward approved of such studies for exactly the same reason as King James disapproved of them: she thought it important that women should become 'more cunning' – in the service of God. As Mary Ward wrote of a young nun in her care: 'Let Kate perfect her Latin with all possible care, without loss of health.' She added: 'no talent is so much to be regarded in them [young nuns] as the Latin tongue'.[22]

The outbreak of the Civil War and the flight of the English royal family from London put an end to Mary Ward's new London apostolate. She

---

† It was not until 1703 that Mary Ward's congregation received papal approval, and not until 1877 that the then Pope officially described Mary Ward as its foundress. Finally, in 1951, Pius XII described Mary Ward, with St Vincent de Paul, as the outstanding pioneer of the lay apostolate of women. Today Mary Ward's Institute of the Blessed Virgin Mary, a mainly teaching foundation, spreads across five continents.

went north to her native Yorkshire, and died in 1645, having lived through the siege of York. Most of her adult existence she had suffered torments from gall-stones, and the last twenty years of her life she was in such pain that she could not lie down, but had to sleep in a rocking-chair. Yet in her last hours, with characteristic spirit, she insisted on the sisters round her singing to stop their tears, and managed to sing with them. Her last recorded words were firmly practical: 'It matters not the who, but the what.'[23]

In general, with her independence and her gallantry, as well as her excellent sense of humour in the most trying circumstances, Mary herself stands for the best kind of English spinster. 'From my palace', she headed a letter written in her filthy German cell. The Elector of Bavaria, in her private code, was known as 'Billingsgate', a slang term of the time for bad language. 'When she travelleth she is extraordinarily jovial', complained one of her contemporaries, who was shocked by her apparent light-heartedness. But Mary Ward had her answer: 'Mirth at this time is next to godliness', she observed of one particular tight corner. When she did travel - crossing the Alps four times, frequently in winter and through snow - Mary Ward retained a kind of splendid English curiosity which sent her sightseeing in Prague and buying silks in Venice. She was notably fond of 'a fine view', yet shocked the fashionable Romans by proceeding on foot all the way to Perugia, wearing old clothes and leading a sick sister on her own donkey.

Above all education, and the need for education in women if they were to perform God's work, aroused her fervour. 'She was a great enemy of ignorance', wrote a contemporary.[24]

*   *   *

In general, if an English girl, regardless of rank, did receive a good education, it was very much a matter of individual luck. Alice Heywood, Oliver Heywood's saintly mother, made herself responsible for sending the children of her neighbourhood to school as a work of charity, buying the 'poor ignorant sottish creatures' books. A maidservant might become an accomplished reader if she happened to fall into the employment of a benevolent mistress, such as Elizabeth Walker or Mary Countess of Warwick, both of whom saw it as their evangelical duty to instruct their maids to read (so that they could at least read the Bible and Psalms). A forlorn creature came to Elizabeth Walker's door, who only knew her name was Mary Bun, 'almost eat up with scabs and vermin, with scarce rags to cover her, and as ignorant of God and Christ as if she had been born and bred in Lapland or Japan'. Elizabeth Walker decided to save her not only by stripping her, washing her and curing her of 'The Itch', but also by teaching her to read, so that finally a rich farmer took Mary Bun as his apprentice. The formidable Lady Anne Clifford also delighted in giving her maids 'such a book as they had not before'.[25]

As a result intelligent and forceful maids often feature prominently in the life stories of their mistresses: as 'Honest Dafeny' Lightfoote, Alice Thornton's maid inherited from her mother, who both could and did write and became as a result the mainstay of the beleaguered Thornton household after Mr Thornton's death as a bankrupt. 'God hath sent me a friend after my own heart', wrote Alice Thornton. Bess, maid to Sir Ralph and Lady Verney, who accompanied them into exile in France at the time of the Commonwealth, learnt French easily.[26]

A good Free School or benevolent patronage or both might account for sudden unexpectedly high figures of local literacy. A recent study by David Cressy quotes women as a whole (they are not analysed by class) as displaying the same high level of illiteracy as labourers and husbandmen; a figure of 90 per cent illiteracy amongst women is given for London – the most favourable area – in 1600, declining in 1640 quite sharply to around 80 per cent; in East Anglia at the same period female illiteracy is given as nearly 100 per cent.[27] The accounts of the Russell family headed by the Earls of Bedford at Woburn Abbey in Bedfordshire, over a considerable period during the seventeenth century show that the skills among the maids varied. One year, out of seven or eight maids there would be two or three who could write well, another year none (whereas amongst the male footmen there would always be two or three who could write well). One housekeeper, Ann Upton, wrote well; her predecessor could not write at all. Apart from contact with the Russell family themselves, some of these literate servants had probably been educated at the local Free School founded by the second Earl of Bedford.[28]

Where a girl of the upper classes was concerned, it was a happy accident if she came from a large family of brothers spread out over a number of years; she might then enjoy the services of their tutor, who would not automatically vanish when the eldest boy went away to school or university. In this way the disparity between the education offered to brother and sister might be somewhat lessened. The Ladies Diana and Margaret Russell were the daughters of William, fifth Earl of Bedford, he who married Anne Carr, worthy daughter of the unworthy Frances Somerset, for love. The education of these little girls, like the literacy of the maids, can also be traced in the accounts for Woburn Abbey.[29]

Anne Countess of Bedford, like Betty Mordaunt, was the proud mother of seven sons, as well as four daughters. As a result, for a number of years

Diana and Margaret were taught by their brothers' tutor, the Rev. John Thornton, a remarkable pedagogue and a man of formidable intellect who came straight to the services of the Russell family from Cambridge in 1646. The influence of this dissenting divine on the character of the girls' brother William Lord Russell (the celebrated Whig martyr of the reign of Charles II) is a matter for the history books; but for the Russell girls, especially Lady Diana, who was Mr Thornton's favourite, a rare opportunity occurred for instruction.

Mr Thornton believed in the new principles of education introduced by Comenius, which amongst other things supplemented teaching by pictures. One entry in the accounts reads:

Pictus Orbis Comenii for Mr Robert	2s	
The Assemblies Pieces in Latin for Mr Robert	2s	4d
Small Catechisms at several times for them and for Lady Diana	2s	6d
Paper and Quills for them all for these five years	3s	6d

It will be seen that even under Mr Thornton's care Lady Diana did not learn Latin (something which would have grieved Mary Ward). However, Lady Diana did receive the best Bible: an edition in 'fair minion print' costing 12s 6d where the other children's Bibles cost 3s 6d.

Ultimately the gorgeous brothers departed – for Westminster, for university, for the Grand Tour – and when the last of them was gone, it was time for the Ladies Russell to be given over to the dancing master, music teacher and French master who would give them that education deemed in principle suitable for young ladies of their station. Lady Diana grew from the beguiling little girl painted by Lely with another sister Anne (who died of eating poisonous berries at the age of five) into a woman of resolute character. She married twice: first at the age of fifteen, being left a childless widow a year later, and secondly to Lord Alington of Wymondley. Lady Diana maintained however a lifelong friendship and correspondence with Mr Thornton. In later life Lely's charming child came to believe sternly in total abstinence from food as a cure-all for sickness. 'If he would come down to me, I should quickly cure him by fasting', she wrote of one troubled member of the family.[30]

Outside the aristocracy both the educationalist Basua Makin and the scholar Elizabeth Elstob benefited from early association with gifted brothers. Basua Makin was born in 1612, the daughter of the rector of Southwick in Sussex, and the sister of the astonishing scholar John Pell – at the age of twenty he was reputed to know Hebrew, Greek, Latin,

Arabic, Italian, French and both High and Low Dutch. Influenced by his example, Basua herself by the age of nine was said in some measure to understand Latin, Greek, Hebrew, French and Italian; we shall consider the conclusions she drew for female education as a whole from this exceptional upbringing in a subsequent chapter. At the end of the century Elizabeth Elstob, the pioneer of Old English studies, was able to work in Oxford because she had accompanied thither her brother William, who was at the university. The antiquary George Ballard, who knew the Elstobs at Oxford and included Elizabeth among his celebrated ladies, was another with an erudite sister who at the age of fourteen had 'an extraordinary genius for Coins' and had made a collection of them.[31]

It was no wonder that the sisters, watching the world through their brothers' eyes, often developed passionate attachments to these young gods who could roam freely, while they were kept confined at home. Ann Oglander, daughter of another happy marriage, that of Sir John and Lady Oglander, described by her father as '*Très belle* Ann' – the most beautiful of all the family – was in despair when her brother George left for Caen on the Grand Tour. Her sorrow was premonitory, for he died abroad shortly afterwards.[32]

As a child Anne Viscountess Conway, daughter of the Widow Bennett by her carefully selected second husband Sir Heneage Finch, worshipped her step-brother John Finch, who was five years older – all the more so because her father had died before her birth. Little Anne hung around at home and in the gardens of Kensington House, plagued with sick head-aches. Her family put her frequent maladies down to too much reading, unsuitable to her sex.[33] Given the intellectual achievements which marked the adult life of Anne Conway despite this handicap, it is more likely that a proper education (her step-brothers went to Westminster and Christ Church or Eton and Balliol) would have helped rather than hindered her health.

The most celebrated example of a sister's devotion to a brother was that of Katherine Viscountess Ranelagh for Robert Boyle, the famous physicist and chemist who arrived at the eponymous Boyle's Law (which stated that the pressure and volume of a gas were inversely proportional). Bishop Burnet proclaimed after her death that 'Sister Ranelagh', otherwise known as 'the incomparable Lady Ranelagh', had cut 'the greatest figure in all these revolutions of these kingdoms, for above fifty years, of any woman of her age'.[34] It was significant that this one woman whose learning merited universal respect not censure was not only well-born and pious but chose to exercise her powerful influence privately rather than through the writing and publication of books, spending the last forty years of her life caring devotedly for her brilliant brother. In her decency, her active kindness – she was both hospitable and charitable – and above all in her acceptance of the self-abnegatory nature of female intelligence, Sister Ranelagh incarnated the masculine ideal of a good woman. Her learning therefore, far from being a disturbing quality, became an added grace. As a result she had the distinction, perhaps a slightly dubious one, of being the one woman of whom Milton actually approved.

Katherine Boyle was born in 1614, one of the vast brood of children of Richard Earl of Cork. Four sons and four daughters survived the original family of fifteen; others besides Robert Boyle were talented. Mary Rich (née Boyle), Countess of Warwick, was Katherine's younger sister; Roger Boyle, Lord Broghill, later Earl of Orrery, author of the play *Mustapha*, was a writer as well as a soldier. 'Precious sister Kate', married at fourteen to an Irish nobleman, the second Viscount Ranelagh, quickly displayed that mixture of liveliness and godliness which would later captivate Commonwealth London. 'The sweetest face I ever saw' and 'the best company in which to be merry' – these were some of the compliments she attracted as a young married woman in Dublin.[35]

Her own arranged marriage was unhappy: unlike wilful Mary she had not made a choice for love. The best thing that could be said about Lord Ranelagh, remarked a contemporary, was that he seldom came sober to bed. But 'that excellent sister of mine', as Mary Warwick called Katherine, showed no signs of envying Mary's superior happiness. On the contrary, it was Sister Ranelagh alone in the family who forgave Mary instantly for her imprudent love match; it was Sister Ranelagh alone who visited Mary when she was laid low with smallpox; it was Sister Ranelagh who enabled Mary to bear the long strain of her husband's protracted death-bed, the agonies of gout producing little serenity of temperament in the dying man. Mary's verdict on Sister Ranelagh was as 'the most useful and the best friend, for soul and body, that ever any person I think had'.[36]

Separated from her unsatisfactory Irish husband, Sister Ranelagh came to make her life in England instead; her house in Pall Mall, Westminster, now became a home-from-home for her brother Robert Boyle at Oxford. Katherine was already acquainted with John Milton: in the late 1640s she dispatched her nephews to be educated by him at the Barbican. It was when Milton moved to Petty France, becoming Sister Ranelagh's close neighbour, that the friendship properly ripened; Milton describing her as standing to him 'in the place of all kith and kin'. At this point Lady

Ranelagh's son Richard Jones was also sent to Milton, probably to read Greek and Latin with him.[37]

In London Sister Ranelagh, gifted with a memory, according to Mary Warwick, 'that will hear a sermon and go home and pen it after dinner verbatim' took lessons in Hebrew from 'a Scotch teacher'. He later dedicated his *Gate to the Holy Tongue* to her, congratulating Lady Ranelagh on her 'proficiency' in the language considering the short time she had learnt it and 'amidst so many abstractions as she was surrounded with'. However, at the end of Robert Boyle's life (when he was living with his sister) we are told that weak sight forced him to give up reading the Scriptures in Hebrew 'since he had none about him that could read it to him', so perhaps the 'abstractions' of Sister Ranelagh's busy life had proved more formidable than her teacher supposed. On firmer ground, Sister Ranelagh expressed herself as well satisfied with the new Experimental Philosophy which her brother and others were trying to institute, believing it would help mankind to understand 'this great frame of the invisible world', and thus the power of Almighty God. And it was her suitably bountiful task to distribute gratis all the 'noble Medicines' which Robert Boyle compounded in his laboratory in her house.[38]

A priggish note creeps into some of Sister Ranelagh's later letters; or perhaps too many years of acting as the fountainhead of good advice to a wide circle, with Roger Lord Broghill as well as Robert Boyle hanging on her judgements, had corrupted her. Sometime in about 1658 Robert repeated to his sister a compliment paid to her by the poet Edmund Waller, whom Boyle had visited at Hall Barn, near Beaconsfield. But Sister Ranelagh was no Sacharissa. She responded: 'I know his calling as a poet gives him licence to say as great things as he can, without intending they should signify any more than that he said them or to have any higher end than to make him admired by those whose admirations are so volatile as to be raised by a sound of words ...' That category did not include Sister Ranelagh. Why should Waller, so eloquent 'upon things that so little deserved them ... be so unwilling to apply that faculty to those subjects that were truly excellent?' she wrote. For this reason she returned 'his great professions' with a 'plain hearty wish' that he should employ them 'for the time to come' upon higher topics than herself.[39]

So much for Waller's compliments. Was this the same woman who had once been 'the best company in which to be merry'? One is not altogether surprised to learn that one of Sister Ranelagh's three daughters, perhaps finding the high moral tone unendurable, ran off with a footman. 'Niece Jones' as Mary Warwick and Robert Boyle described her, did not however

gain much happiness from this plunge into passion. Robert Boyle, referring to his six nieces in his will, left property to Niece Jones, now Mrs
Melster, and the daughter of the *mésalliance* Catherine Melster, the latter's
portion to be held till she was twenty-one 'because of her peculiar circumstances'.[40]

Lady Ranelagh's experiences as a mother were in general disheartening.
Her son Richard Jones, the third Viscount Ranelagh, was a spendthrift
who succeeded in being expelled from the House of Commons (although
his reputation rests more pleasantly with posterity, since he built Chelsea
House and laid out Ranelagh Gardens). Her favourite daughter – 'a good
person' according to Mary Warwick – died unmarried in 1672; another
married daughter died young.[41]

It was as the beloved hostess to Robert Boyle, the centre of a distinguished and learned circle hanging on her good sense and judgements, that
Lady Ranelagh enjoyed her true happiness. As late as 1687, when she was
well over seventy, Sister Ranelagh was advising John Locke's friend
Damaris Lady Masham on how to cure melancholy, acting as 'her physician' in this cause, as Lady Masham told Locke. When Sister Ranelagh
died at the age of eighty-seven in December 1691, Robert Boyle, her
companion of forty years, only survived her by a week; it was popularly
believed that he had died of grief. The brilliant brother and his 'dearest
sister and constantly obliging friend' as he had termed her in his will, were
buried together in the chancel of St Martin-in-the-Fields.[42]

*   *   *

If the fraternal association was a fortunate chance, the advantage of a
supportive parent at this period, where female education was concerned,
can hardly be overestimated. Elizabeth Walker, for example, took particular care to teach her daughters to read. The modest yet learned Lady
Elizabeth Hastings was described as being educated in 'a School or rather
Academy' – in short, by 'her Vigilant Mother' Lucy Countess of Huntingdon.[43] It is notable how many of that slender band of female writers on
whose autobiographical works we depend pay tribute to a mother who
actively encouraged them to learn.

The mother of Anne Murray, Lady Halkett, was governess to the
younger children of King Charles I, but did not neglect her own family:
she 'paid masters for teaching my sister and me to write, speak French,
play on the lute and virginals, and dance, and kept a gentlewoman to teach
us all kinds of needlework'. The mother herself oversaw her daughters'
Bible reading: five a.m. in the summer and six a.m. in the winter. Ann

Lady Fanshawe's mother saw to it she was offered 'all the advantages that time afforded, both for working all sorts of fine works with my needle, and learning French, singing, lute, the virginals, and dancing'. Alice Thornton's mother had her taught to read the Bible and the Psalms, also writing, singing and dancing, playing the harpsichord and the lute, and everything else thought fit for a lady.[44]

The ultimate advantage, however, for a daughter, was to be born of an erudite father, one who for whatever motive – possibly seeking a son-substitute – set out to provide her with a 'masculine' education. When Helena, the heroine of *All's Well That Ends Well*, offered to cure the King of France of his fistula, the Countess of Rousillon suggested with alarm that her aid was hardly likely to be accepted – that of 'a poor unlearned virgin' – where so many celebrated doctors had failed; Helena, however, armed with her father's 'prescriptions of rare and prov'd effects' went on to cure the King, and win the hand of her desired Bertram.[45] There were a few Helenas in the seventeenth century, although their contemporaries tended to react with the same alarm as the Countess of Rousillon at the idea of such accomplishments in 'a poor unlearned virgin'.

Like Katherine Ranelagh, Lucy Hutchinson had 'a great memory' as a girl and put it to the same pious use: 'I was carried to sermons', she tells us and, 'while I was very young could remember and repeat them so exactly, and being caress'd, the love of praise tickled me and made me attend more heedfully'. Lucy Hutchinson, born in 1620, the daughter of the Royalist Sir Allen Apsley, is one of the most attractive of the gallery of seventeenth-century women.[46] Although she sprang into print in order to write a justificatory memoir of the husband she adored, Colonel John Hutchinson, Governor of Nottingham Castle and judge at the trial of Charles I, it is the witty, independent, ever courageous character of Lucy which animates the text, rather than that of the Puritan John Hutchinson.

In Lucy's case she began life well with a mother who actually did want a daughter after bearing three sons. Lucy was also delicate, and received special care (including breast-feeding) from her mother, who feared she would not live. Furthermore, Lady Apsley began to dream of having an 'eminent' daughter when she found that Lucy could read perfectly by the age of four. Being given a Frenchwoman as a 'dry-nurse' as soon as she was weaned, Lucy was also bilingual in French and English at an early age.

At this point her mother lost confidence and began to worry that so much study would ruin Lucy's health. It was Lucy's father who had her taught Latin. Thus encouraged, Lucy began to outstrip in her progress her three brothers who were at school, despite the fact that her father's chaplain, who acted as her tutor, was in her own words 'a pitiful dull fellow'. Lucy became an avid reader: 'every moment I could steal from my play I would employ in any book I could find'; at the same time her mother took to having her daughter's own books locked up, to preserve her health. Her mother also worried at Lucy's lack of progress in dancing, and at the lute and harpsichord, and 'for my needle', wrote Lucy, 'I absolutely hated it'.

In an autobiographical fragment,[47] Lucy confesses that she was disliked by the other children for her solemnity, and her tendency to give little knowledgeable lectures. She was not however a prig, and passion always had a high priority. The maids fortunately were more appreciative of Lucy's lectures, as a result of which she was delighted to find herself their confidante in their love affairs. It was to Lucy's great satisfaction that her learning, far from depriving her of a husband as was generally prognosticated, actually won her the love of John Hutchinson. Idly, he spied some Latin books lying on the shelves at Lucy's parents' when she was away in the country; hearing they belonged to a mere girl, he became curious about this unusual character and asked a series of questions about her. The other girls, thinking to belittle her, told Hutchinson 'how reserv'd and studious she was, and other things which they esteem'd no advantage'.

They had mistaken their man: thus was ignited a lifelong love, John Hutchinson and Lucy being married in 1638, when she was eighteen. Many years later, after Hutchinson had died in the prison to which his allegedly treasonable activities had brought him (only Lucy's energies in tackling her Royalist relations saved him from death), she summed up her feeling for her husband as follows: 'So, as his shadow, she [Lucy] waited on him everywhere, till he was taken into that region of light which admits of none, and then she vanished into nothing.'[48] It was a romance stirred not by a pair of gloves, a favour or a fan, but by a shelf of books in the Latin language.

Although one should perhaps add that Lucy Hutchinson, like that other clever woman Margaret Newcastle, never evinced a very high opinion of the rest of her sex: doubtless the behaviour of her early companions rankled. The influence of Queen Henrietta Maria, for example, she thought to be disastrous: it was an 'unhappy kingdom' where the hands which were made only for 'distaffs' affected 'the management of sceptres'. And Lucy praised Queen Elizabeth for acceding to her male counsellors.[49]

*   *   *

We have dealt with the exceptions, the products of fortunate chance. What happened to those who were not singled out in this way?

No one was very interested in the formal education of the daughters of the poor for the obvious reason that reading and writing were not likely to be skills which would enable them to support themselves in later life. Where provisions had to be made by the authorities, as in the case of foundlings, emphasis was very much on the practical – knitting rather than reading or writing. A Free School was endowed at Great Marlow in Buckinghamshire in 1626 to teach twenty-four girls to knit, spin and make bean-lace – twenty-four boys, however, were to be taught to read. The well-known school for the 'Red Maids' of Bristol – daughters of 'decayed' (poverty-stricken) or dead freemen, so called after their uniform of red cloaks – had been intended by its founder to teach the girls either reading or plain needlework; the latter accomplishment, so much more economically useful, soon swallowed up the former.[50]

The quality of public education offered to girls also went downhill from the late sixteenth century onwards, as the practice by which a few girls had attended the grammar schools, if not to an advanced age, ceased. In 1594 for example Banbury Grammar School forbade the inclusion of girls above the age of nine, or when they could read English. Where girls did attend the grammar schools in the seventeenth century – their presence attested by girls' names in the margins of school books – this was where the curricula of the schools in question were not limited to a strict grammar course; girls were not permitted to take the ordinary public grammar course (with its heavy grounding in Latin).[51]

Richard Mulcaster was the first headmaster of Merchant Taylors' School, and subsequently High Master of St Paul's until his resignation in 1608 (he died in 1611). As an educationalist he was liberal compared to most of his contemporaries, believing in the value of such 'extras' as music, theatricals and physical training. He also viewed the education of girls with approval, generally advocating it in *Positions . . . for the training up of Children*, first published in 1581 and dedicated to Elizabeth – 'a Virgin and a Learned Queen'. Yet it is significant that to this champion (by the standards of the time) the education of girls was only as 'an accessory by the way' to the upbringing of youths.[52]

In no way therefore did Mulcaster approach the position of Mary Ward, who believed that there was nothing to stop women one day, like men, doing 'great things'. On the contrary, he qualified his general approval for female education in a number of important respects. First, he proposed that girls had a 'natural weakness'; using this to explain the awkward fact that they often 'ripened' intellectually earlier than boys. Since girls' brains were not so much 'charged' as those of boys, explained Mulcaster, 'therefore like empty casks they make the greater noise'.

Second, Mulcaster was careful only to 'allow them [girls] learning . . . with respect to their ends'. What were these ends? 'I meddle not with needles nor yet with housewifery,' wrote Mulcaster, 'though I think it and know it to be a principal commendation in a woman to govern and direct her household . . . because I deal only with such things as be incident to their learning.' Since these girls were to be in the future 'the principal pillars in the upholding of households' it was useful for them to learn to read; moreover reading was needful for the study of religion. But Mulcaster saw no point in the admission of girls to the public grammar schools or the universities.

There were a rising number of girls' boarding-schools, particularly in the environs of London (we have noted how the heiress Sara Cox was snatched from Mrs Winch's school at Hackney in 1637). To these the prosperous middle classes began to send their daughters; at the school of Mr and Mrs Robert Perwick, also in Hackney, which flourished from 1637 to 1660, there were as many as 100 girls at a time. Other such schools have been traced at Westerham in Kent, Manchester (where there were two), Oxford, Exeter (two) and in Leicester.[53]

The first public school actually recorded was the Ladies' Hall at Deptford in Kent; here in 1617 the 'young gentlewomen', fetchingly attired in loose green garments covered in silver and carnation lace, their shoulders bare, their arms half naked, their hair 'dishevelled' (but artistically so), wearing green pumps and gloves, were presented to Queen Anne, wife of James I. They bestowed on her examples of their needlework. The Queen was then hailed in delightfully zeugmatic terms;

> Then bright Goddess, with thy sweet smile grace all
> Our nymphs, occasion, and our Ladies Hall.[54]

This emphasis on needlework and graciousness was characteristic. In 1647 Unton Lady Dering summed up what was expected for Peg and Elizabeth Oxinden, aged twelve and eleven, at Mr Beven's finishing school at Ashford: 'And besides the qualities of music both for the virginals and singing (if they have voices) and writing (and to cast account which will be useful to them hereafter) he will be careful also that their behaviour be modest. . . .' In these boarding-schools, as in the homes of Anne Halkett, Ann Fanshawe and Alice Thornton, it was the education 'fit for her quality' in Alice Thornton's phrase, that is, 'lady's' quality, which was

being provided, rather than the sort of learning which Sir Thomas More
had had in mind in the previous century when he wrote that a wife should
be 'learned if possible, or at least capable of being so'.[55]

Some practical accomplishments were of course taught – a form of
shorthand for example (not so much for secretarial purposes as suitable for
taking notes on 'good' reading), enough arithmetic for household accounts
as Lady Dering suggested, legible handwriting, even tolerable orthography
was considered desirable – although any girl who actually succeeded in
these achievements would find herself way ahead of most of her female
contemporaries.† At the same time all this was a world away from the
kind of heavy grounding in Latin which was being automatically given to
the girls' brothers at the grammar schools: Latin being the key not only to
entrance to the universities, but to all forms of serious scholarship at the
time, as well as science and medicine (something Mary Ward had appreciated in her emphasis on the subject to her young nuns).

As the boys' grammar schools themselves improved with the progress
of the century, the rift between male and female education grew into a
chasm. Scholarship was not the only loss. By the Restoration, classical
knowledge was a prerequisite of the cultivated gentleman. It was left to
the playwright Aphra Behn to mourn on behalf of her sex:

> The God-like Virgil, and great Homer's verse
> Like divine mysteries are concealed from us.[57]

Dainty French was however thought to be a desirable female accomplishment at court and elsewhere. An early seventeenth-century French
grammar was written to enable women to 'parlee [sic] out their part with
men'. The arrival of a French Queen – Henrietta Maria – in 1625 continued
the trend. The influx of French Protestant (Huguenot) refugees into London resulted in the establishment of a few French schools, and provided
a number of French teachers. French maids and French nurses were
to be found in fashionable households. Later French romances began
to flood into England and were read avidly, sometimes in the original: Brilliana Lady Harley, ordering a book from her son at Oxford, in
1638, asked for it in French: 'for I would rather read that tongue than
English'.[58]

Humphrey Moseley, a leading bookseller, published a translation of
Mademoiselle de Scudéry's novel *Artamenes or The Grand Cyrus* 'now

---

† The editors of the Verney letters and Oxinden papers comment on the 'evident decline'
in female education and 'lack of advance' in female literacy respectively in the seventeenth
century as compared to the sixteenth.[56]

Englished by F.C., Gent' in 1653; he dedicated it to Lady Anne Lucas on the grounds that she was known to have a perfect command of French (thus presumably not needing the services of F.C., Gent). Moseley added: 'Were it a Discourse of the most profound Learning that Humane Nature is capable of, and written in Greek or Hebrew, I would make its Dedication to your Noble Lord....'[59]

That was the difference.

In 1650 the Eure girls, Ralph Verney's cousins, children of his aunt Margaret Poulteney's romantic second marriage to William Eure, were taught 'what is fit for them, as the reading of the French tongue and to sing and to dance and to write and to play of the guitar'. In contrast, when Sir Ralph heard that his goddaughter Nancy Denton, child of his friend and kinsman the learned Dr Denton, was going to be taught the classics, he read first the doctor, and then Nancy a lecture. 'Let not your girl learn Latin', he pronounced to the former, condemning shorthand too for good measure. 'The difficulty of the first may keep her from that vice, for so I must esteem it in a woman; but the easiness of the other [i.e. shorthand] may be a prejudice to her; for the pride of taking sermon notes, hath made multitudes of women most unfortunate.'[60]

Nancy, a girl of spirit, wrote back to her godfather that her cousins might out-reach her in their French, but she would outstrip them by learning 'ebri grek and laten' (let us hope that knowledge of Hebrew, Greek and Latin improved Nancy's spelling in English). Sir Ralph however refused to concede; in a further letter he condemned such unfeminine attainments once again: 'Good sweet heart be not so covetous; believe me a Bible (with the Common Prayer) and a good plain catechism in your Mother Tongue being well read and practised, is well worth all the rest and much more suitable to your sex; I know your Father thinks this false doctrine, but be confident your husband will be of my opinion.'[61]

Sir Ralph did put his seal of approval upon learning French. He offered to start a French library for Nancy on his next visit to Paris, since matters suitable for women's perusal were often written in that language; he included in that category not only romances, plays, poetry, but also all manner of subjects suitable to good housewifery such as recipes and gardening hints. In French could also be read profitably the stories of 'illustrious (*not learned*)' women from the past, wrote Sir Ralph firmly.[62] The distinction between the two was not one which would have been appreciated by that 'dread Virago', Queen Elizabeth I. Yet Sir Ralph was no fierce male brute: he was on the contrary a good husband, a loving and considerate brother to his five orphaned sisters, a caring father to his daughters. He was merely expressing the philosophy of his times; while Nancy Denton, the daughter of an enlightened father with a particular interest in female education, represented one of the fortunate exceptions.[63]

8 Living under Obedience

'Teach her to live under obedience, and whilst she is unmarried, if she would learn anything, let her ask you, and afterwards her husband, *At Home*.'

SIR RALPH VERNEY TO DR DENTON

Susanna Perwick, daughter of those Perwicks who kept a fashionable girls' school at Hackney, was one of the few Englishwomen of this time – the age following the death of Queen Elizabeth – to be glorified under the title of virgin. Susanna, an exceptionally talented musician if her biographer John Batchiler is to be believed, died in 1661 at the age of twenty-four. Batchiler called his work *The Virgin's Pattern: in the Exemplary Life and lamented Death of Mrs Susanna Perwick*[1] ('Mrs' was the title then applied to respectable unmarried females, 'Miss' except in the case of very young girls being reserved for the other sort). Her musical talents were early encouraged, since the Perwicks' school staff included such luminaries as Simon Ives, the collaborator of Henry Lawes, as singing-master, and Edward Coleman the song-writer. Batchiler mentions that first Thomas Flood, then William Gregory, taught Susanna; others would gladly have taken their place, such as Albertus Bryne, the composer and 'famously velvet-fingered Organist' of St Paul's Cathedral. Susanna's proficiency at the violin quickly attracted favourable attention and she was also skilled at composing extemporary variations on a given theme; in addition she played the lute and harpsichord, sang, and studied books on harmony.

It was no wonder that ambassadors and other foreign visitors attended the Hackney school as the fame of this paragon spread, lured further by her sweet face, and her conversation – which, unlike that of most women, was 'rather sententious than garrulous'. According to Batchiler, Susanna had other skills beyond music: calligraphy, accountancy and cookery.

Alas, at the age of twenty-four Susanna caught a violent fever from sleeping in damp linen on a visit to London from Hackney. When she realized she was dying, she bequeathed her belongings in the neat orderly fashion which had characterized her whole short life: her books went to the young gentlewomen of the school, with the dying wish that they would not read other 'vain books' or waste time dressing-up. Then in the course of her protracted deathbed, Susanna herself gave 'small silent groans', in between her 'smiling slumbers', while her family wept loudly around her. At her funeral, attended by the whole school, Susanna's velvet-clad hearse was carried by six white-clad maidservants; while the pupils who had known her best, dressed in black, with white scarves and gloves, held up the mourning sheet. She was buried in the Hackney church, in the same grave as Mrs Anne Carew, a schoolfriend, 'a fine costly garland of gumwork' being placed on the coffin. Susanna's epitaph made her ultimate destination clear:

> Here Beauties, Odours, Musicks Lie
> To shew that such rare things can die . . .
> From Heav'n she came with Melodies
> And back again to Heav'n she flies.[2]

And it was highly satisfying to an age which particularly enjoyed the significance of a good anagram that the letters of Susanna(h) Perwick's name could, with a little pious cheating, produce the words: AH! I SEE (C) HEAV'N'S PURE SUN.' †

Although the title of his work, *The Virgin's Pattern*, celebrated Susanna's unmarried state, Batchiler was careful to make it clear that she had by no means rejected altogether that 'blessed knot' of matrimony which was the lot of dutiful (Protestant) womankind. Admittedly after the early death of her fiancé, Susanna had dismissed various other proposed bridegrooms as wanting in spiritual riches; but Batchiler announced that Susanna had made another 'secret choice' before her death, and died in the arms of the man concerned.[4] It was a significant assurance in a work much closer to hagiography than biography; readers could feel confident that the conventional virgin's pattern of the seventeenth century – which was in fact to eschew virginity and marry – had finally been followed.

Yet Susanna Perwick's character, as it can be discerned beneath the veil of Batchiler's melancholy ecstasies, has something distinctly austere and as we should now say, nun-like about it; certainly her persistent rejection of her suitors, even if allayed by a deathbed change of heart, does not indicate any great enthusiasm for the matrimonial state. Like the Catholic Mary Ward, who suffered a similar loss, Susanna Perwick regarded the death of

---

† In the first half of the seventeenth century, about forty books concerning anagrams were printed in Latin alone; a preoccupation compared by one scholar to the modern love of palmistry.[3]

her betrothed as a significant affliction from God. For Susanna there followed a form of spiritual 'conversion'; Mary Ward decided to devote her life to God and took the veil. The option of the convent was of course not open to the Protestant girl; indeed Susanna remained very much opposed to the 'Romish' religion, which she considered to be positively 'anti-Christian'.[5] Susanna was compelled to construct her own life of retirement within the confines of her parents' busy boarding-school.

Susanna also resembled Mary Ward in that she had the gift of beauty: Batchiler refers to the contrast of her brilliant complexion – 'red and white, Mixed curiously gave great delight' – with her 'black, jetty, starry' eyes. And for once the frontispiece to The Virgin's Pattern does actually show a pretty face, although there is a hint of firmness as well as humour in the curved mouth, above the legend: 'Here's all that's left.' Nevertheless, after the death of her betrothed Susanna adopted a deliberately plain, neat garb, abhorring the black spots and patches which were just becoming the rage of fashionable London; not only for her own use, but also making her mother confiscate them from the giddy young ladies at the boarding-school. At least Susanna showed enough sympathy with adolescent frailty to wear the jewellery she would otherwise have eschewed in order to please the girls. Batchiler also eulogized her bosom – 'Her pair of round crown'd rising hills' – but these rising hills were, after Susanna's conversion, sternly covered with a whisk or handkerchief, contrary to the usual custom of the time.

It was easy for Susanna to refuse to attend public revels where there would be dancing; it was more difficult to find peace at home for prayer and meditation, with 100 girls, to say nothing of the servants, perpetually 'going up and down'. So Susanna, like so many of her serious-minded contemporaries such as Mary Warwick and Dorothy Osborne, turned to the garden and there would read her Bible for an hour or so, secure from interruption (she had read the whole of the New Testament twice in the year of her death). For Susanna too, like Elizabeth Walker, there was the period of early morning prayer which would leave her red-eyed; before supper she would regularly meditate on death. Even if complimented on her music in later years, Susanna was liable to reply – rather off-puttingly – that music was as nothing compared to the joys of heaven.[6]

Throughout the seventeenth century it was customary for stout English Protestants to condemn the Catholic convents with horror, as barbarous concomitants of the 'Romish' religion. Yet one cannot help noticing how much easier it was for a Catholic young woman, a Mary Ward for instance, to construct a life of serious purpose on her own terms, than it was for a Susanna Perwick.

'Convenient storage for their [the Catholics'] withered daughters' was how Milton dismissed the convents. Lettice Countess of Leicester was struck with horror when 'a Popish orphan' named Mary Gunter, whom she had taken into her household, persisted in wanting to go 'beyond the seas, to become a nun' on the grounds that this was 'the surest and most likely way to go to Heaven ... the nearest way'. There was however nothing withered about Mary Pontz, an associate of Mary Ward. She was an acknowledged beauty who was on the point of marriage when Mary Ward's mission captured her spirit; she sent her cavalier a bizarre form of dismissal in the shape of her own portrait in which one half of the face had been eaten by worms![7] For Protestant girls who experienced these or similar urges there was little outlet; and Milton's derisive comment omitted to state that for the withered daughters of Protestants – those who had probably been allowed to wither on the bough unmarried because they lacked dowries – there was no convenient refuge at all.

Some Protestant women, who thought for themselves, could see that it was by no means fair to condemn the Catholic nunneries wholesale. Margaret Duchess of Newcastle, for example, with her usual gift for stating the truth, however uncomfortable, thought it better for a girl to be 'walled up' in 'a monastery' than unhappily married. Margaret Godolphin, herself so earnest, so reserved, so worried by the implications of matrimony, went further. She was impressed by the convents she visited in France: 'Their Nunneries seem to be holy Institutions,' she reflected. 'If they are abused, 'tis not their [the nuns'] fault; what is not perverted? Marriage itself is become a snare.' Earlier she had wished that there might be some kind of similar Protestant refuge to which she might fly and eschew the claims of the world.[8]

It was a desire echoed by the youthful Anne Murray, at the end of her unhappy love affair with Mr Thomas Howard.[9] As a girl without a fortune (her portion was ensnared in a legal tangle), Anne was aware that her marriage to Howard would not be permitted by his parents, and she honourably refused the young man's passionate request for a secret ceremony. Despite this evidence of rectitude, even Anne's own mother poured fury on her daughter for her behaviour, on the grounds that it was financially necessary for Howard to marry a rich citizen's daughter. She made Anne promise not to see her lover again. Anne kept her promise to the extent of saying goodbye to Howard blindfold, when he was packed off by his own relations to France. Even so, the disgust of the mother was so great, that she refused to speak to Anne except in anger for fourteen months.

It was at this point that Anne inquired privately from her cousin Sir Patrick Drummond, who was Conservator (consul) in Holland, whether there was not some Protestant nunnery there, consistent with her religious principles, because if so she would retreat thither immediately. But Sir Patrick addressed his answer to the angry mother, leaving Anne to explain herself: 'for since I found nothing would please her that I could do, I resolved to go where I could most please myself, which was in a solitary retired life'. A further blow was in store for Anne when Howard returned from France and married another lady, having cut Anne publicly: 'Is this the man for whom I have suffered so much?' she cried, falling on her bed. Her unfeeling mother laughed. It was no wonder that Anne secretly approved when her maid Miriam, as it will be remembered, called down a curse of barrenness upon Howard's bride.

Gibbon pointed to the plight of the runaway slaves under the universal government of the Roman Empire: nowhere to flee for the victims of injustice, for whom the world thus became 'a safe and dreary prison'. English girls who could not or would not marry were similarly without refuge. In contrast the remarkable longevity of many of the so-called 'withered daughters' who made the adventurous journey to the Continent to become Catholic nuns is also worthy of note. Two abbesses of Rouen, for example, died at over ninety; one of whom, Mother Francisca Clifton, had completed seventy-five years in religion. This longevity argues a life of purpose very different from that which faced many of their sisters at home – and of course freed in addition from 'the pain and the peril' of child-bearing which brought so many of these other young women to an early death. Spiritual considerations quite apart, there was something to be said for the point of view of that 'Popish orphan' Mary Gunter (she was in fact not allowed to become a nun and died in England, still young, in 1633).[10] A life of chosen virginity, led in an ordered, secure and educated society, was certainly not the worst fate which could overtake a young woman in the seventeenth century.

*   *   *

In seventeenth-century England, neither legally nor psychologically was there a proper place for the unmarried female or 'maid' – the term generally in use in 1600 – except on her way to marriage. Psychologically, it was hard to look on a young woman as a heroine. The Blessed Virgin Mary was no longer the official pattern of English womanhood as she had been before the Reformation, no longer praised in nightly Ave Marias, daily or weekly masses as a chaste and sinless female. On the Catholic Continent, the position of respect she enjoyed was emphasized in the seventeenth century by the institution of a number of new Marian feasts in the church calendar.[11] Candles glimmered before the multitudinous wide-eyed depictions of the Virgin, painted by Murillo in honour of the growing cult of the Immaculate Conception. In England, the whole subject of the Virgin Mary was complicated by the fact that Marian devotion in any form – 'Mariolatry' – was regarded as High Church or Laudian, liable to lead directly to Rome.

There was justice in this contention. Anthony Stafford, for example, who wrote a book entitled *The Femall Glory* in 1635, in which he attempted to rescue the Virgin Mary as a figure to be admired and emulated – she was not to be considered 'a mere woman' – was a follower of Laud, as was his patroness, the learned Lady Theophila Coke, to whom he dedicated the book. Stafford described Mary's marriage to Joseph as being intended merely to 'serve as a bar to the importunity of other Suitors ... so she might the more freely enjoy the inconceivable pleasure she took in her vowed Virginity'. As for the conception of Jesus: 'most blessed Virgin ... let thy Modesty rest secure; for the Operation of God, and not of man is here required'.[12]

This kind of heady talk was anathema to the Puritans, to whom the Blessed Virgin Mary was no more than 'Mall [a nickname for Mary], God's Maid'.[13] So Protestant womanhood was left with Grandmother Eve alone – that fearful guilty ancestress – to represent them. There was no chaste heroine in their pantheon: Grandmother Eve being very much a wife and mother, in her own guilty way, as all women in the seventeenth century were supposed to be.

Legally, the position of the 'feme sole' was equally ignored: her legal rights were assumed to be swallowed up in those of her nearest male protector. This does not overlook the fact that young women of the labouring class (that is, the vast majority of the population) worked to support themselves by one method or another from an early age;[14] it was from the 'spinsters', for example, a considerable number of young women working at home, that the modern legal term for the unmarried female was derived during the seventeenth century. Certain professions such as that of dairymaid or milkmaid had a tradition of independence, based on the adventurous expeditions to market which such 'maids' carried out in the course of their work, a freedom of movement not enjoyed by their sisters at home in the village.

The bold girls admired by Pepys at Westminster in the May Day parade of 1667, garlands round their milk-pails, 'dancing with a fiddler before them' as they collected tips from customers, came of a long tradition of such independent lasses; they were probably from farms nearby (Westminster then being on the edge of a rural area) and on their way to the Maypole in the Strand. Dairymaids were also amongst the highest paid of women workers: in 1647 a dairymaid that brought a cow to Hatfield so that the Lord Cranborne of the day could drink its milk was given a 2s tip – at a time when women agricultural labourers were lucky to get 4d a day.[15] Nevertheless an unmarried milkmaid, even if she enjoyed some practical freedom, was still legally in the care of her father, like any other young woman, and on marriage passed into that of her husband.

The point has been well made that it was only at marriage that men entered fully into the society into which they had been born;[16] that was also true of women, who in taking up their destined place as wives, were filling that place most convenient for the rest of society – which was male. The concept of an unmarried female, beyond a certain age and not demonstrably in the care of a male, tended to bring about a kind of bewilderment at best.

'Are you a maid, or widow, or a wife?' asked a Suffolk magistrate of Sister Dorothea, an English Catholic nun and follower of Mary Ward, when she was brought before him in 1622.[17] At the time of her arrest, Sister Dorothea was posing as the kinswoman of Lady Timperley of Hintlesham Hall, near Ipswich; from this vantage point she had taught local children of 'the vulgar sort' their Pater, Ave, Creed and Commandments, but she had also done a great deal of good work among the sick and the poor, which had made her popular in the neighbourhood and somewhat inhibited the magistrate in his treatment of her.

'I am a maid,' was the answer of Sister Dorothea.

'So much the better,' the magistrate exclaimed with relief, feeling that the problem was now virtually solved, 'for then I hope a good husband will persuade you to change your religion.' In vain Sister Dorothea protested that she had no intention of changing her state: the magistrate, taking his stand on the fact that the nun had performed much service to the poor – 'to give you your due' – and armed with the comforting thought that her religious eccentricity could not be of long duration, dismissed her. It was a point of view robustly expressed by Sir Ralph Verney, echoing the words of St Paul (a favourite source where he was concerned) to the Corinthians. He remonstrated on the subject of Nancy Denton, that ambitious scholar, to her father: 'Dr Denton, teach her to live under obedience, and whilst she is unmarried, if she would learn anything, let her ask you, and afterwards her husband, *At Home*.'[18]

*   *   *

Obedience was thus the watchword.

One version of it was the obedience practised by the numerous serving-maids living in other people's houses as part of their 'family' – the significant term used for the household. The role of the serving-maid, as opposed to that of the free unmarried female, was a conventional one, fully understood by society. For one thing it was widely fulfilled: it has been suggested that between one quarter and a third of all households of the period contained servants, in view of the fact that the lowly as well as the mighty entertained them.[19]

Marriage – especially to another servant – did not necessarily bring this kind of obedience to an end in any case since, as has been pointed out, girls outside the moneyed or landed class married quite late.[20] Not only in the great social edifices such as Woburn Abbey but in the little country dwellings were maids to be found – often the daughters of friends, leaving their own family to practise obedience (and work for their keep) in the 'family' of another, not necessarily removed further up the social scale.

Domestic service in the seventeenth century was not only a common fate, it was also not a bad way of life and the horror stories of later times – the Victorian era, for example – should be dismissed from the imagination as anachronistic. The intimacy denoted by the use of the word family had considerable advantages: food was shared, and where plentiful, it was plentiful for maid as well as master (or mistress). Indeed, the free regular provision of food, and often clothing as well, placed the domestic in a privileged position not only compared to those many unfortunates at the very bottom of society, who seldom had either, but also to their social equals, day-labourers.

Moreover, such provision places the apparently low annual wage of about £2 a year given to maidservants in perspective. The board wages for food for the maids at Belton House, Grantham, seat of Sir John Brownlow, when the family went away to London were 6s a week; in a 1688 inventory of the fine new palace designed for the Brownlow family by Wren, all the rooms including the servants' rooms had feather-beds, besides three blankets and a quilt. The maids' rooms at Woburn Abbey had pictures on their walls.[21]

Servants featured prominently in wills, where quite large sums would be bequeathed; if these legatees were mainly older women, married or widowed, nevertheless such legacies betokened the care and affection lavished in general upon their maids by those whom they served. Mary Countess of Warwick left £80 to Martha Upsheer, a chambermaid, £70 to Ann Coleman, another old servant, and £40 to 'my ancient servant Mary Taverner', formerly her housemaid. Mary Warwick's executors were instructed to use the money to purchase annuities for these women. Dame Margaret Verney, wife of Sir Edmund and mother of Sir Ralph, mentioned all the women servants at Claydon when she made her will (and incidentally they were all still there in service when she died ten years later).[22]

As long as the concept of the domestic as part of the 'family', held by most people at the beginning of the seventeenth century, lingered, so the scale of the maids' existence remained in proportion to the people they served. In the 1680s Mary Woodforde, wife of a Prebendary at Winchester Cathedral, wrote of the marriage of her servant Ann: 'She lived with us thirteen years and a half.'[23] The idea of a maid as an inferior creature, entitled therefore to a far inferior standard of life, came later.

With so many domestic servants to consider, it was natural that the topic of their treatment should come under common discussion. Inordinate severity was generally frowned upon; the Puritan handbooks pointed to it as morally wrong. Winefrid, sister of William Blundell of Lancashire, busy engaging a servant at 15s a quarter for a lady of rank in London who wanted a Lancashire servant, had time to reflect that 'some sweet encouragement', not perpetual severity, was the way to treat servants. In 1688 Lord Halifax took pains to tell his daughter that as a newly-married mistress of a household of servants she must not abuse her position: 'The Inequality which is between you, must not make you forget that Nature maketh no such distinction.'[24]

What then were they like? What of Nell Duck, Mary Hearne and Mary Croast, maids and cook-maid to Dame Isabella Twysden? What of Betty Bushin, Lydia Long the laundry-maid, and 'Alice-about-the-house', all in service to the Earl of Bedford at Woburn Abbey?[25] In many cases the lives of these maids come to us merely in tantalizing glimpses, like the rustle of a petticoat or the turn of an ankle, in the incidental references of accounts of their employers.

In 1614 at Chartley Manor in Staffordshire, seat of the Earl of Essex, three maids fell into the moat as they were doing the laundry. Two were saved by long poles, but one continued to drown. The Earl of Essex stood on the bank as the girl struggled, crying in some excitement: 'Now she sinks! Now she's gone!' until another bystander, Arthur Wilson (who tells

the tale) plunged in and saved her. Thereafter the delighted Earl received Wilson 'in his private chamber' and made him his gentleman-in-waiting – which equally delighted Wilson. Of the bedraggled laundry-maid nothing more is heard.[26]

From the Woburn Abbey accounts, it is possible to know details such as the fact that they were often given clothes as presents, or part-presents ('To Abigail, towards a nightgown. £1 10s od'). The Woburn maids also took – or were given – a great deal of medicine, and they were constantly bled for hysteria.[27] About the emotions or even events which might have prompted the hysteria, it is far more difficult to know.

The fact, referred to by Lord Halifax, that nature made 'no such distinction' was sometimes wryly underlined by the sexual connections formed between master, or master's son, and maid; another side-effect of household intimacy. The opinion of the time held this to be a two-way hazard. Francis Kirkman, in his autobiography, confessed that he had a dread of being caught by a maid in marriage if he 'toyed' with one; for she might then try to prove he had already married her. It was considered to be a sign of madness in the son of Lord Grey of Wark, destined to marry the Earl of Northumberland's daughter, that he fell in love with his mother's chambermaid, or at any rate the experience was blamed for causing his 'weak brain' to 'turn over';[28] yet madness was not necessarily the explanation for such a socially unsuitable infatuation, propinquity being a more likely cause.

Another story told by Kirkman is probably more typical of the kind of blackmail which prevailed in which dismissal or worse was threatened if the maid proved obdurate. A certain married couple could never agree on a maid, for the master would not accept a plain nor the mistress a pretty one (a dispute no doubt as old as domestic service itself). In the end the master compromised by accepting a girl who was 'liquorish' hoping 'to have a lick at her honeypot'. When the 'liquorish' girl was duly discovered broaching her master's cask of Canary wine in the cellar, she had to submit to his advances under threat of imprisonment for theft in Bridewell.[29]

Fear of unemployment followed by destitution was surely enough to account for Alice Thornton's story of the goings-on in the *louche* household over which the Earl of Sussex and his 'most odious' Countess presided. Alice Thornton recounted with shocked surprise that when the Earl ordered six of the housemaids to dance naked, only one 'modest chaste maid' said she would not do it, and when 'pressed' by the Countess, immediately left her service. On the other hand Robert Hooke's maid Nell, who slept with him three times a month for no extra money in the

1670s, as he records in his diary, presumably found the bargain worth while (at £4 a year, and more for sewing, she was already well paid).[30] In her own way Nell was living under obedience.

But some fell through the net and some did not care to be confined by it. Jane Martindale was an independent-minded Lancashire girl who in 1625 revolted against the narrow life prescribed for a yeoman's daughter. (We happen to know her brief story because her brother Adam, the Nonconformist minister, wrote his autobiography.)[31] Jane, in her brother's words, had 'her father's spirit and her mother's beauty'. She objected for instance to the restrictions imposed on the dress of women of her class – freeholders' daughters customarily wore 'felts' (a covering garment) over petticoats and waistcoats with handkerchiefs round their necks, and white cloths covering a coif on their heads. ''Tis true the finest sort of them wore gold or silver lace upon their waistcoats, good silk laces (and store of them) about their petticoats,' wrote Martindale. 'But the proudest of them (below the gentry) durst not have offered to wear an hood, or a scarf ... not so much as a gown till her wedding-day.'

1625 was a year in which one of the major outbreaks of plague had taken place in London; as a result a number of refugees from its devastation had reached Lancashire. When the time came for them to return, Jane Martindale decided to go with them, leaving her home village of Prescot, and seek the more adventurous life of the big city; she hoped to get a place serving 'a lady' since she was 'ingenious with her needle'. Jane's parents pleaded with her, pointing out that she wanted for nothing at home, while the London atmosphere might well prove dangerous to one who was not very hardy, having been brought up in the pure air of Lancashire. If Jane wanted to get married, her father told her that he could afford that luxury for her too – being able to provide a dowry.

Jane persisted. She took a little money from her family to get established in London and off she went. Perhaps her plan to serve 'a lady' with her ingenious needle might have worked – a form, naturally, of domestic service, but the life of serving 'a lady' in London offered opportunities for advancement unknown to a yeoman's daughter in Lancashire. Unfortunately she herself caught the plague and the plan had to be abandoned. Even so, her spirit was not altogether extinguished; she sent for a goose-pie from her family, in order that she might make merry with her friends, and they duly sent one, encased in 'twig-work' all the way from Lancashire. Jane added that some money for drink would also be appreciated, that 'the goose might swim', without cost to herself. But the carrier took three weeks to deliver pie and money; in the meantime Jane was in such dire poverty that she contemplated selling her own hair; 'which was very lovely', wrote her brother, 'both for length and colour'.

Ironically it was 'this blessed knot' of matrimony which rescued Jane in the nick of time; not the independent life she had envisaged. One of the young men who had travelled back to London with her had fallen in love with the beautiful Jane. He now married her, and the newly-wedded pair set up to run an inn called the George and Half Moon, just outside Temple Bar, which divided the City of London and Westminster. Jane's parents assisted her to furnish the inn, and sent country produce down from Lancashire.

Jane's city life then ran smoothly until the spring of 1632 when her mother became seriously ill. Jane bought 'an excellent swift mare' and rode home to Lancashire; too late – her mother was dead on her arrival. At this point Jane and her husband decided to sell the London inn and set up again at Warrington, to be closer to her remaining family. During one of her journeys between London and Lancashire to arrange all this, Jane stopped off at an inn to have a drink, where some children were suffering from smallpox. She caught the disease and died, being buried at Prescot in August 1632, beside her mother.

Several of the little 'chapbooks' as they were later known, popular fiction sold by pedlars for 2d a story, centred upon strong-minded – and strong-bodied – heroines. *Long Meg of Westminster*, which first appeared in 1582, is a notable example,[32] Long Meg being an Amazonian Lancashire lass who comes to London on a carrier's cart at the age of eighteen, like Jane Martindale seeking a place in service. But although Long Meg takes to touring London at night, dressed in men's clothing and beating men in fair fight, she ends by marrying a soldier, just as Jane Martindale had in the end married. To please her readers, most of whom were, of course, male, Long Meg vows to be a submissive wife: 'It behoveth me to be Obedient to you, and, never shall it be said, though I Cudgel a Knave that Long Meg shall be her Husband's Master.'

Only the real-life heroine Mary Frith, subject of Middleton and Dekker's comedy *The Roaring Girl*, never succumbed to the economic necessity or social ideal of obedience. But then Moll Cutpurse, as she was known, did not succumb to the law either. 'She could not endure the sedentary life of sewing or stitching, a sampler was as grievous to her as a winding-sheet.' Dressed as a man, sword and all, she was first of all notorious as 'a bully, pickpurse, fortune teller, receiver and forger'. Later she became what it would be appropriate to term a successful highwayperson. Building up a gang of thieves, she used her house in Fleet Street as a centre for her operations, give or take a spell in Newgate. On Sundays this female Robin Hood would visit the gaols and feed the prisoners out of her haul. Moll Cutpurse, untroubled by obedience, lived to the ripe old age of seventy-five, and was buried in 1659 after an Anglican service at St Bride's.[33]

*   *   *

Moll Cutpurse was the exception, as is demonstrated by the popular wonder accorded to her – several books were written about her as well as Dekker's play, and her biography *The Life and Death of Mistress Mary Frith* appeared in 1662. Living under obedience, as most women did, married or unmarried, they might be as garrulous as they pleased – so the satirists averred – at home, but their voices were unlikely to be heard in the public forum. The undesirable talkativeness of the female sex in the domestic circle was axiomatic; the desirability of its silence outside was equally taken for granted. Yet even before the Civil War, certain individual women, whether wilful, eccentric or just plain deluded, had already discovered a way in which the female voice might be raised without immediate masculine control.

Women were of course forbidden to preach in the churches – on the direct authority of mighty St Paul himself. But when a woman started to 'prophesy' as did a pedlar called Jane Hawkins at St Ives near Huntingdon in 1629, the matter was somewhat more complicated. 'This rhyming preacheress', as she was later described, made a strong local impression.[34] For by claiming direct inspiration from God – and expressing this inspiration in trances, descriptions of visions and other 'prophecies' – a woman made it that much more difficult for her voice to be extinguished; there would always be those around her, credulous or sympathetic, who believed that this extinction was suppressing the direct message of God. If the politics of Church and State were introduced, the matter became more complicated still. At the same time the dreaded implication of witchcraft, ever present for a woman who refused to conform, was avoided if the language was sufficiently religious in its expression to suggest possession by the Almighty, rather than some more sinister power.

Jane Hawkins, 'having fallen into a rapture or ecstasy', foretold on the one hand such disagreeable eventualities for the Anglican Church as the downfall of the bishops; on the other hand she 'magnified' the ministry of the local vicar, the Rev. Mr Tokey. When her prophetic rhyming continued for three days and nights, it was perhaps hardly surprising that the 200 people who listened to her included Mr Tokey, his curate, and another 'scholar' who sat at the feet of Jane Hawkins's bed, rapidly copying out the verses – amounting to some thousands – which were emitted from the entranced woman. The plan was to make a fair copy of the verses later 'with intent to print them'. At which point however, the Bishop, less enthusiastic at having his downfall predicted than Mr Tokey at having his ministry magnified, had the verses seized.

When Mr Tokey refused to abandon the claims of his spiritual patroness to be a true visionary, he was suspended, while his curate was 'put quite away'; the Justices of the Peace were given a warrant by the Bishop to look after Jane Hawkins herself and ensure that the neighbours did not visit her. Reports said that the local people were deserting their 'rhyming preacheress'; soon they were said to 'cry out against her'. Finally the unfortunate vicar made a written acknowledgement that Jane was an impostor, and that he himself had been guilty of indiscretion.

It is noticeable that the Bishop's attitude to Jane Hawkins was from the first one of suspicion on the grounds of her sex. Here was 'a witty crafty baggage', who was deliberately stepping out of her low station in life to make trouble for the rest of the world; he was disgusted that she would not 'confess' to having written verses before, or to having written them of her own accord now. To the end he referred to 'this imposture' of the woman at St Ives; it was not within his cognizance that someone of Jane Hawkins's ilk could have genuinely believed in the strength of her own visions.

Yet there had been a brief moment of glory when Jane Hawkins, a 'poor woman (and she but a pedlar)' as she was contemptuously described, lay on a bed surrounded by 200 local people, led by the vicar, who hung on her words with bated breath, and even had them copied down for widespread publication. The point has been made by Keith Thomas that in an age when women were unable to attend grammar schools, let alone attend university, and of course unable to preach, the self-styled role of prophetess enabled a woman frustrated of any normal means of self-expression to make her voice at least heard.[35]

A far more notorious 'rhyming preacheress' – because of her high station in life – was the woman born Eleanor Audeley, daughter of the Earl of Castlehaven, and wife in succession to Sir John Davies, Attorney-General for Ireland, and Sir Archibald Douglas. By her first marriage Lady Eleanor Davies (the name by which she is generally known) bore a daughter Lucy, whose life was early affected by her mother's eccentricities. In 1623 at the age of ten Lucy was married off by her father (without a licence) to Ferdinando Lord Hastings, who succeeded his father as sixth Earl of

Huntingdon in 1643; the hasty ceremony was probably intended to save
Lucy from her mother's drastic influence. Sir John Davies's death meant
that the young couple went to live together much earlier than had been
anticipated.[36] Life in the wake of a scandalous parent had its predictable
effect on Lady Huntingdon: an intellectual, Lucy also had a strong regard
for the conventions. It was she who had prepared her own clever daughter
Elizabeth Hastings so well for marriage that her husband never suffered
'all those inconveniences' generally believed to accompany a learned wife
(see pp. 122–3).

'Inconveniences' certainly surrounded the career of Lady Eleanor
Davies.[37] In 1625, when she was in her mid-thirties, according to her own
account she received a revelation while lying in bed at home at Englefield
Manor: 'nineteen and a half years to the Judgement and you as the Meek
Virgin'. Sir John Davies died the next year, but since Lady Eleanor – who
shared the contemporary preoccupation with anagrams – made of her
husband's name DAVIS IUDAS, she can hardly have regretted his demise.
Sir John's particular betrayal was described by Lady Eleanor: it was her
first book which 'was sacrificed by my first husband's hand, thrown into
the fire'. Lady Eleanor responded with her own weapons, giving Sir John
details of his 'doom', telling him 'within three years to expect the mortal
blow'. To hammer the point in, she wore black – 'my mourning garment'
– from that time forward.

There had been other troubles in the marriage: Lady Eleanor's son by
Sir John, known as Jack, was an idiot. There is a great deal that is touching
about the mother's attitude to her son's deformity, including the conviction (in 1617) that if Jack 'were now put into the hands of some skilful
man ... [he] might be brought to speak'. Lady Eleanor went on: 'for he is
wonderfully mended in his understanding of late ... he understands anything that is spoken to him without making any signs, so as it is certain he
hath his hearing ... then the defect must be in his tongue'.[38] But in the
event poor Jack was drowned, leaving Lucy Davies, incidentally, as heiress
to an important fortune.

To the outside world, however, Lady Eleanor was clearly marked down
as a trouble-maker, even before she turned her attention, fatally, to matters
of Church and State. In 1622, for example, a certain man called Brooke
reproached her for abuse (not recorded) of his wife and innocent child.
Brooke declared that Lady Eleanor had by her behaviour abandoned all
'goodness and modesty', being not only mad and ugly, but also blinded
with pride in her own birth; in retaliation he threatened on the one hand
to 'scratch a mince-pie' out of her; on the other hand he wished Lady

Eleanor, as being the most horrible curse in his power, to remain exactly what she was.[39]

Lady Eleanor's second marriage to Sir Archibald Douglas was by her own account not much more successful than her first. It took place only three months after Sir John Davies's death 'contrary to a solemn Vow', and soon there was a recurrence of both the old trouble – 'he likewise burning my book' – and the old revenge. For Sir Archibald 'escaped not scotfree', being bereft of his senses while at Communion and 'instead of speech made a noise like a Brute Creature'.[40] In later life (he lived until 1644) Sir Archibald believed he saw angels, and became, like his wife, preoccupied with anagrams.

REVEALE O DANIEL! This, the transformation of her maiden name, if spelt ELEANOR AUDLIE, was the crucial anagram in Lady Eleanor's own opinion (how very different was this strident call from that meek cry – AH, I SEE HEAV'N'S PURE SUN – composed by her admirers out of the name of Susanna Perwick). Altogether this self-styled Daniel was responsible for twenty-eight tracts of a prophetic nature, which have been described in modern times as 'an almost unintelligible mixture of religion, politics and prophecy'.[41] Unfortunately for Lady Eleanor, in her own time they were not altogether unintelligible, and unfortunately too, she had the occasional Cassandra's knack of prophesying accurately some rather unlikely and extremely unpleasant event.

The first prediction which brought Lady Eleanor real notoriety was that of the impending assassination of the Duke of Buckingham, made in June 1628, with the rider that the Duke's 'time was not till August'. When Buckingham was duly struck down by John Felton on the twenty-third of that month, Lady Eleanor's stock as a prophetess was understandably high amongst the common people of London, who elevated her as 'a cunning woman'. (However, lest Lady Eleanor be credited too firmly with supernatural powers, it has been suggested that her prophecy was common knowledge that summer and Felton may actually have timed his blow to fit in with it.)[42]

Lady Eleanor's successful prophecies concerning the pregnancies of Queen Henrietta Maria, if less ostentatious, probably had more effect in gaining her a reputation as a seer in high places – and thus leading in the end to her downfall. It was the inevitable way of royal life that soon after Henrietta Maria arrived in England in June 1625 as a bride, her possible pregnancy should be the subject of speculation. When two years later there was still no sign of an heir to the throne, it was also inevitable that the Queen (and those around her) should be concerned about her possible infertility. According to the story, it was on All Saints' Day, 1 November 1627, that the Queen paused as she was leaving the evening service and asked Lady Eleanor when she would be with child. Lady Eleanor replied that the Queen's first child would be christened and buried all in one day. And in May 1629 the Queen's firstborn, a Prince named Charles James, did die more or less as Lady Eleanor had predicted. In response to a further emissary from the court, a Mr Kirk, Lady Eleanor struck lucky again by predicting that the Queen's next baby would be another boy, but an exceptionally strong child – as the future Charles II, born in May 1630, proved to be. The King was irritated by Lady Eleanor's influence over his wife but Mr Kirk among others spread the lady's fame.

Three years later the lady's 'prophesyings', which she had printed at Amsterdam (where she needed no licence) under the legend 'Reveale O Daniel', were of a more extravagant nature. Now it was a question of the 'doom' of Charles I; referring to the King as 'Belshazzar' and describing her vision of a Beast ascended out of the Bottomless Pit, having seven heads to signify the seven past years of the King's rule, Lady Eleanor foretold the final execution of the King. In addition Laud, newly appointed Archbishop of Canterbury, was picturesquely evoked as 'horned like the lamb, hearted like a Wolf'.[43]

The King's annoyance was pardonable. This kind of prophecy was in theory a grave offence (even to cast the monarch's horoscope without authorization was treason). Lady Eleanor was summoned to the Court of High Commission on 24 October 1633, and there committed for 'compiling and publishing certain fanatic and scandalous pamphlets'. At least two of the judges thought that Lady Eleanor should acknowledge her offence at St Paul's Cross, while the Bishop of Rochester suggested Bedlam – the madhouse. In the end Lady Eleanor was fined £3,000 and sentenced to imprisonment in the Gatehouse. Her books however did not get off so lightly, being burnt publicly: 'this is the third day their dead bodies throwed in loose sheets of paper lie in the streets of the great city', she wrote in anguish.[44]

Even more humiliating to her spirit was her actual experience in court. Efforts were made to convince Lady Eleanor of the meaninglessness of her prophecies, and in particular of her precious anagrams. To illustrate the point, someone had the happy thought of pointing out that DAME ELEANOR DAVIS could be transformed into NEVER SO MAD A LADIE, 'which happy fancy brought that grave Court in to such a laughter, and the poor woman into such a confusion' that Lady Eleanor herself never alluded to this particular incident subsequently.[45] It is an ironic scene in retrospect: the august body of judges, from whom the future was happily hidden, attempting in vain to convince the distracted woman that anyone who predicted the execution of Charles I must necessarily have their wits a-wandering.

The fine was probably not paid, but Lady Eleanor remained in the Gatehouse despite her daughter Lucy Countess of Huntingdon's petitioning for her release. Lucy was careful to admit that her mother had been confined 'by just censure', but she asked that she might have some free air, 'for womanhood' some female of her own to attend her, and perhaps a clergyman as well.[46]

In 1635 Lady Eleanor was released from her London prison and went to live in the cathedral town of Lichfield in Staffordshire. Here she found no peace. Flouting the conventions, she freely used those seats reserved for the wives of the bishop and the canons within the cathedral; worse still she sat herself down on the episcopal throne, and declaring that she was both 'Bishop and Metropolitan', sprinkled a mixture of tar and water on the cathedral hangings.

This time there was no escaping 'Bedlam's loathsome Prison' even for the mother of the Countess of Huntingdon. Here sightseers would come to gape at Lady Eleanor (and other inmates). Nor was Lady Eleanor's prophetic voice silent. Particular alarm was caused when she predicted a fire within Bedlam, and fires duly occurred – although the fire risks were so great, that was hardly a surprising occurrence. Finally, after a spell in the Tower, Lady Eleanor was released into the care of her daughter and son-in-law in 1640.

The prophesying – and the violent treatment – continued. In 1646 Lady Eleanor was sent to another London prison called the Compter and incarcerated in a black cell by the Keeper, an experience she described graphically: 'Not long after (she all unready, etc.) between two of them carried down thence, instantly shut and bolted was into the Dungeon-Hole, Hell's Epitomy, in the dark out of call or cry, searching first her Coats pockets: Frustrate that way, with the Key took away the Candle, there left in their Pest-house on the wet floor to take up her lodging.' Fortunately, so that Lady Eleanor could examine her cell all night long till dawn: 'the Heavens without intermission flashed out Lightnings, as Noonday'.[47]†

It seems unfair that for all her charitable treatment of her own 'dear mother' Lucy Countess of Huntingdon was the victim of a series of tragedies as a mother herself. Her first three sons all died; the fourth,

† In 1932 the editor of *Dougle Fooleries* compared Lady Eleanor Davies's 'obscurity of meaning and . . . freedom from syntax' to that of James Joyce or Gertrude Stein.[48]

Theophilus, who eventually became Earl of Huntingdon, was not born until 1650, when the Earl and Countess of Huntingdon had been married for over a quarter of a century. *Sion's Lamentation*, a powerful piece – and for once politically innocent – was written for the funeral of one of these boys, Henry Lord Hastings, in 1649, by the prophetic grandmother. Lady Eleanor described the eerie emptiness of the streets through which the funeral train passed. As when Joshua made the sun and moon stand still at his command at Gibeon, the Lord harkening to his request, so the cortège 'saw not the face of Coach, Cart or Car, which passed by, either that met us, or stood in our way'.[49]

But by this date the whole world, not only the world of the distracted Lady Eleanor, was turning upside down – never so mad a lady till the present, perhaps, but other prophetesses were coming forward to rival her. Lady Eleanor, like these other frustrated women living in theoretical obedience, who poured their bizarre imaginings into prophecies, looked to the new order in the shape of Oliver Cromwell. We shall meet Lady Eleanor again in 1648, presenting a copy of the notorious 1633 prophecies to the great man himself.

For war was coming, a time when many women, not only the strange and wilful, would lead lives of chaos and disruption; a time of war, when the great mass of women who simply expected to exist, as their fore-mothers had done, rejoicing in the cyclical happinesses, enduring the private sorrows of domestic life, living under obedience, would not be able to do so. War, the great challenger, was coming to them all.

PART TWO

With the War – Stronger Grown

> To most 'tis known
> The weaker vessels are the stronger grown.
> The vine which on the pole still lean'd his arms
> Must now bear up and save the pole from harms.

JAMES STRONG, *Joanereidos: or, Feminine Valour Eminently discovered in Westerne Women*, 1645

9 Courage above her Sex

'My dear wife endured much hardship ... and though by nature, according to her sex, timorous, yet in greatest danger would not be daunted, but shewed a courage even above her sex.'

SIR HUGH CHOLMLEY, GOVERNOR OF SCARBOROUGH CASTLE

At the beginning of the wars, which lasted on English soil from August 1642 until September 1651, when Cromwell finally routed the young Charles II at Worcester, it was taken for granted that woman, the weaker vessel, lacked not only the martial spirit but also courage itself.

After the wars the theory of woman's timidity continued to be preached: in 1653 Margaret Duchess of Newcastle's first published work contained *An Epistle to Souldiers*, preface to a long poem describing the battle between Courage and Prudence before the Fortress of Hope. The Duchess was careful to explain that 'these Armies I mention, were rais'd in my brain, fought in my fancy, and registered in my closet'. Anything else – from a woman – would be ludicrous. 'Great Heroicks!' she addressed the male sex, 'you may justly laugh at me, if I went about to censure, instruct or advise in the valiant Art, and Discipline of War ... according to the constitution of my Sex, I am as fearful as a Hare, for I shall start at the noise of a Potgun, and shut my eyes at the sight of a Bloody Sword, and run away at the least Alarm.'[1]

Reality in the previous decade had been very different. The Civil Wars threw up a considerable number of 'Great Heroicks' of the theoretically weaker sex: women of the calibre of the Countess of Portland who at Carisbrooke Castle 'behaved like a Roman matron' and rather than surrender 'declared she herself would fire the first cannon'. Or there was the lioness Lady Mary Winter, wife of the Royalist commander Sir John, who declined to give up Lidney House, near Gloucester, to the Parliamentary commander Colonel Massey with some well-turned words on the subject of her absent husband's 'unalterable allegiance to his king and sovereign'. Thus Massey's 'hopes were disappointed by the resolution of a female'.[2]

Of these the most celebrated were the valiant ladies on both sides who in the absence of their husbands found themselves withstanding the enemy's siege. Less celebrated, but in quite as much danger, were the ordinary women also involved in the siege, maidservants and so forth; these too threw themselves into the fray. So that far from being fearful as hares, women showed themselves capable, on many different levels, of gallantry at least equal to that of their menfolk; and if they were indeed inherently timorous, then it could be argued that their courage was correspondingly even greater.

This seemingly contradictory heroism of the weaker vessel was easily explained on the surface: an individual woman such as Brilliana Lady Harley was said to have exhibited 'a Masculine Bravery' or displayed that 'constancy and courage above her sex' which her memorial tablet ascribed to the valiant Lady Bankes of Corfe Castle.[3]

Elizabeth Twysden, Lady Cholmley, married Sir Hugh Cholmley of Yorkshire, later Royalist Governor of Scarborough Castle. Throughout the siege of the castle, following the Parliamentary victory of Marston Moor, she stayed resolutely at her husband's side; as he wrote later, she 'would not forsake me for any danger', although her daughters sailed for Holland and her sons were away in London. When the besieging commander Sir John Meldrum threatened total massacre, Lady Cholmley begged her husband not to consider her own safety; throughout the defence Lady Cholmley led the nursing of the wounded and numerous sick (scurvy soon broke out) with the aid of her maids. Sir Hugh Cholmley's tribute to his wife's gallantry stands for many: 'My dear wife endured much hardship, and yet with little show of trouble; and though by nature, according to her sex, timorous, yet in greatest danger would not be daunted, but showed a courage even above her sex.'[4]

Yet the conventional refusal to impute courage to the female sex as a whole (while granting it tenderly to individual members) did not survive the wars quite unaltered despite Margaret Newcastle's ostentatiously modest words. Indeed, one can detect a certain masculine desperation in the repeated claims that the heroines of the wars acted out their martial role with the greatest reluctance. As we shall see, not a few of the 'Great [female] Heroicks' accepted their unusual destiny with zest; nor did this enthusiasm escape notice at the time, especially when it reflected derogatorily on the lady's husband.

'Three women ruined the Kingdom: Eve, the Queen and the Countess of Derby': this comment from a Parliamentary source, by associating Charlotte de la Trémoille, Countess of Derby with Grandmother Eve and the hated Catholic Henrietta Maria, paid tribute to her pre-eminence as a Royalist heroine. But there were also sneers at her husband, James Stanley, seventh Earl of Derby: it was said that of the two she had proved herself the better soldier, or more crudely, that she had stolen 'the Earl's breeches'.[5]

Certainly the Countess was bred to be a heroine: in an age when royal women were among the few allowed to revel in public attention, she was by birth close to being a princess. A French Huguenot, daughter of the Duc de Thouars, she was a granddaughter of William the Silent (of Orange) by his Bourbon wife. Through her marriage to the Earl of Derby, himself connected to the English royal line, she had enjoyed the full richness of English court life before the war; and since the Earl of Derby was the greatest magnate of the north-west, there she found herself a queen by his side: mighty Lathom House being generally considered 'the only Court' in the north.[6] The habit of command then came naturally to her. (And it may also be noted that she was seven years her husband's senior.)

Early in 1643 the fall of the Royalist stronghold of Warrington in Lancashire brought neighbouring Lathom House to the attention of Parliament. At this point the Earl of Derby was in the Isle of Man (also part of his estates) at the request of the Queen, while the Countess, a woman in her early forties, remained at Lathom House with two of her seven children, the Ladies Mary and Katherine Stanley. The aim of Sir Thomas Fairfax, the Parliamentary General, was to secure the surrender of Lathom House without bloodshed; to this end on 28 February he sent an official summons to the Countess by the hand of a Captain Markland.

At this point the formal rules governing a seventeenth-century siege become relevant (and indeed remain so through all the sieges, major or minor, which will be discussed in the ensuing chapter). These rules, which could have barbarous consequences for civilians plunged involuntarily into a siege, were nevertheless framed for the preservation rather than the destruction of life.

In short: after the besieging commander had issued an official summons to the defenders of a stronghold to surrender, a choice had to be made. If the defenders promptly surrendered, then the civilians – mainly women and children – within the stronghold were generally allowed to depart peacefully, leaving the soldiers within the stronghold to negotiate the details of the surrender, including the surrender of their arms. Before he captured Bridgwater, in July 1645, Sir Thomas Fairfax was said to have shown particular 'pity and commiseration' for these non-combatants by sending them a free offer of quarter before his troops began to fire. 'Upon which there came out a whole regiment of women and children.'[7]

If, on the other hand, there was no surrender, then according to the rules of war, the besieged civilians were equally at risk with the military when and if the stronghold was taken by force; there need be no quarter given. (It was under these rules, incidentally, complying with contemporary procedure, if outraging the instincts of humanity, that Cromwell at Drogheda and Wexford in 1649 permitted the slaughter of civilians as well as soldiers, because neither fortified town, after repeated summonses, agreed to surrender.) At Sherborne, shortly after the successful siege of Bridgwater, Fairfax 'according to his wonted nobleness' sent a messenger to the commander, Sir Lewis Dyve that 'if he pleased to send out his lady, or any other women, he would give way to it'. Sir Lewis, while expressing himself grateful for the favour, gave no very positive answer, and Lady Dyve remained within the stronghold. It was not until the 'storm' of Sherborne had begun that a white flag was hung out; this was too late to stop the sack, in the course of which the soldiers acquired a great deal of booty and everyone (except Lady Dyve) was 'stripped'. Lady Dyve was lucky since by this point there was no theoretical guarantee of her safety. At Grafton House, near Stony Stratford, on Christmas Eve 1643, all the women of the house were 'stripped to their naked skins' by the troops of Major-General Skippon, after the fortress surrendered.[8]

It may be asked what justification there could be for this ritual; the answer lies in the nature of siege warfare at that time. Without such a proviso it was greatly to the advantage of the defenders, if they had sufficient food and water, to hold out as long as possible, or at least until these supplies had been used up; after all they were warmly sheltered, and the possibility of rescue from outside remained. Meanwhile the besiegers were leading a far less agreeable existence, enduring the rigours of exposure, which led quickly to disease; the prospect of attack from the rear, in the shape of rescuing forces, only increased as time passed. Under these circumstances, some grim inducement had to be offered to the defenders to obey the summons: hence the harsh rules of siege war. Given these conditions the 'Welsh howlings' of the women who wanted to urge surrender upon their husbands at the siege of Oswestry (a walled town about to be blown up) were perfectly comprehensible.[9]

Lathom House in the 1640s was a massive and ancient fortress. The walls were six feet thick; a moat, eight yards across and six feet deep, surrounded them; after that came a strong palisade. Nine towers dominated the walls, each containing six pieces of ordnance or mounted guns; mightiest of all was the Eagle Tower, over which flew the proud motto *Sans Changer*. There was an excellent water supply. Even the terrain favoured the defence, for the ground rose up round Lathom House like another natural fortification.

The Countess of Derby's answer to Captain Markland's summons was not outright defiance. Instead she played for time, while subtly reminding both the Captain and his superior of her own renowned social status. It was after all only six months since the outbreak of this 'war without an enemy', as the Parliamentarian Sir William Waller called it in a letter to a Royalist friend: the pre-war standards of courtesy and respect towards a great lady still prevailed. Not only did the Countess request further time to consider the summons, but she firmly declined to emerge from her fortress in order to 'treat' with the enemy; in the first of a series of magnificent communications she observed that 'notwithstanding her present condition, she remembered both her Lord's honour and her own birth, conceiving it more knightly that Sir Thomas Fairfax should wait upon her, than she upon him'.[10]

Various other summonses were equally rebuffed in the same high style. The Countess's final answer was as follows: 'That though a woman and a stranger divorced from her friends, and robbed of her state, she was ready to receive their utmost violence, trusting in God both for her protection and deliverance.'[11]

Apart from the protection of God, the Countess also had a considerable garrison of soldiers, under a Captain Farmer, and the men from the Derby estate, the keepers, fowlers and suchlike who, being by profession skilled marksmen, manned the towers. Nevertheless the bombardment which ensued, including 'flaming granadoes' (grenades) as well as the pounding of a great mortar, was severe and left its impact on the besieged: several women had their hands scorched. A contemporary diary of the siege pays tribute to the courage of Mary and Katherine Stanley, 'for piety and sweetness truly the children of so princely a mother'. Having inherited the Countess's spirit as well, 'the little ladies had stomack to digest canon', although 'the stoutest soldiers had no hearts for granadoes'.[12]

The Countess remained staunch. The pinnacles and turrets of Lathom House began to crumble to the pounding of the mortar, a culverin and a demi-culverin, but still she continued to refuse in ringing terms that safe-conduct for herself and her daughters which would have implied surrender. It was, she declared, 'more noble to preserve her liberty by arms than to buy peace with slavery'. As for negotiations: ''tis dangerous treating when the sword is in the enemy's hand'. Although the diary of the siege refers to the indignities the Countess and her daughters had to suffer, listening to the language and affronts of the besieging soldiery, the cowardice of her neighbours presented a more practical problem. One petition suggested that the Countess would do well to surrender – for the future of the surrounding countryside. The Countess of Derby made short work of it. There is no evidence that the more forceful comments of the Parliamentary preachers on her character, couched in biblical terms – the Scarlet Woman, the Whore of Babylon and so forth – made any impact on her spirit either.

The besiegers attempted to drain off the castle water supply, where the spring rose on the hill. But the real danger was presented by the great mortar loaded with stones thirteen inches across, eighty pounds in weight, daily, relentlessly pounding them to pieces. The successful sally of the defenders out of the gates to capture the mortar and drag it inside was therefore a triumph of the desperate – except that the Countess would not admit to being desperate. Instead she commanded a public thanksgiving.

It was not the least of her pleasures to discover that the commanding officer of the besiegers, Colonel Rigby, had summoned his neighbours to watch Lathom House either yield or be burnt. They were thus present to witness his humiliation. Lady Derby gave him instead 'a very scurvy satisfying answer, so that his friends came opportunely to comfort him' (instead of rejoicing with him). Her enemy was 'sick of Shame and dishonour, to be routed by a lady and a handful of men'.

Three months later it was the arrival of Prince Rupert at the head of a considerable force which relieved Lathom House. The Prince conveyed twenty-two of the enemy's colours to the great lady who had held fast. Although the actual military manoeuvres were conducted by Captain Farmer, it is evident that without a woman of the lofty courage – one might add the aristocratic arrogance – of the Countess of Derby, Lathom House would have fallen to the enemy almost immediately. As it was, when it did surrender in December 1645, the Countess was far away on the Isle of Man. After the Restoration, her daughter Katherine, who retained vivid childish memories of the siege, would take to task a historian who suggested that the Countess had been present at, and thus connected with, this final débâcle. Thomas Dugdale, in his widely read 1660 *Continuation* of Sir Richard Baker's 1637 *Chronicle*, perpetuated this error, based on two false Parliamentary reports. Katherine, now Marchioness of Dorchester, joined with Lucy Countess of Huntingdon and her son (anxious to refute the rather more substantiated charge that Lady Eleanor Davies had foretold the death of Buckingham). As a result, Dugdale, while retaining the error, inserted a slightly equivocal compliment to the Countess in the 1665 edition: 'in her defending of that place' (Lathom House) the Countess 'had manifested a more than Feminine Magnanimity' – that is, greatness of spirit. It was not until 1674 that the error concerning the 1645 surrender was eliminated and the Countess's role in the original victory enlarged.[13]

The 'Heroick Countess' herself lived until 1664, surviving not only the wars but the tragedy of her husband's execution at the orders of Parliament for his part in the Worcester campaign (she tried, despite the objections of the inhabitants, to surrender the Isle of Man in return for his life). As an old lady she would tell stories of the wars to her Lancashire neighbour William Blundell, which he found difficult to understand on account of her French accent: 'a defect' in 'my lady's English'. To the end she was something of a tartar: where the Quakers were concerned, for example, 'she shut out all pity and tenderness' when they were imprisoned for non-payment of tithes.[14]

The Countess, so confident in her birth, and the utter rightness of all her opinions, would have appreciated Dugdale's equivocal compliment to her 'more than Feminine Magnanimity'.

* * *

From the point of view of the enemy, a high-born heroine in charge of a siege represented a double hazard. Most obviously, her combination of gallantry and authority would fuel the chivalrous defenders to greater efforts; secondly, the hoped for effect of an official summons upon the defenders' nerves might be largely nullified by the presence of such a feminine figurehead. No one had any particular desire to kill, maim or wound her or her family: hence the constant pleading requests to the Countess of Derby to accept a safe-conduct. When the husband himself conducted the defence, his wife's presence at the siege was still embarrassing to the attackers, as in the case of the Marchioness of Winchester, another brave woman whose refusal to quit inhibited her opponents.

The siege of Basing House, magnificent dwelling of the great Catholic magnate John, fifth Marquess of Winchester, which lasted from August 1643 until October 1645, was one of the most famous and protracted of the war.[15] When finally captured, Basing House was found to number amongst its contents not only riches and pictures and art works and furnishing – but also the engraver Wenceslaus Hollar and Inigo Jones himself (who was carried out naked, wrapped in a blanket). A passionate supporter of the King's cause, Lord Winchester was said to have '*Aimez Loyauté*' engraved on every window of Basing House.

Honora Marchioness of Winchester was, as Clarendon wrote later, 'a

lady of great honour and alliance', being the daughter of the Earl of St
Albans and Clanricarde, and the granddaughter of Queen Elizabeth's
Machiavellian statesman, Sir Francis Walsingham.[16] From the point of
view of Parliament, however, it was more important that she was half-
sister to their own general, the Earl of Essex (to whom one of the besiegers,
Colonel Hammond, was also related). Here was the problem of a civil war
in a nutshell. The Parliamentary besiegers were understandably anxious to
have such a lady safely removed from Basing House.

So Sir William Waller duly invited the Marchioness to lead out her own
children (she was the mother of seven), and all the other women and
children in the house, during a parley. He used exceptionally courteous
terms, 'excusing the rudeness of his disorderly guns'. The Marchioness's
answer was, like that of the Countess of Derby to Sir Thomas Fairfax,
superbly scornful: 'she thanked God that she was not in that condition to
accept of fair quarter at Sir William Waller's hands, being resolved to run
the same fortune as her Lord, knowing that there was a just and all-seeing
Judge above, who she hoped would have an especial hand in this business'.
From this august judge, she added, Sir William Waller could 'pretend no
commission'.

Then the Marchioness and her ladies set to with a will, casting bullets
from lead hastily stripped from the roofs and turrets of the house. During
a lull in the siege she also visited Oxford (where the King was) and solicited
diligently for help for her husband.

By the autumn of 1645 time had run out for Basing House, and its
courageous defenders of both sexes. It was now the one remaining Royalist
garrison guarding the south-west, and as such received the attentions of
Oliver Cromwell himself, since the victory of Naseby that summer the
hero of the Parliamentary forces. During the final bombardment, one of
Cromwell's shells 'brake in' to the Marchioness's lodgings, killing a
waiting-woman and a chambermaid (demonstrating how perilous might
be the fate of such innocent anonymous females caught up in these great
events).

What happened to the Marchioness? Accounts vary. Either she escaped
from Basing House before the final stage of the siege on 8 October, or she
was captured and subsequently exchanged for another prominent (male)
prisoner. Either way her name was specifically mentioned in the Articles
of Surrender, as were those of other chatelaines. (At the surrender of
Bletchingdon House to Cromwell in April 1645, the eighth Article read:
'That the lady of the House [Mrs Windebank] shall enjoy her goods as
before....')[17] Thus was war in its own strange way bringing the names of

women to the fore. While the Marchioness of Winchester survived to bring comforts to her sick husband imprisoned in the Tower of London, Basing House was 'slighted', or razed to the ground, at the orders of Parliament and its gorgeous contents looted.

Where the Countess of Derby and the Marchioness of Winchester were already illustrious figures before the war, through the panoply of their high lineage, 'prudent and valiant' Lady Bankes, defender of Corfe Castle, made her own name by the sheer courageous obstinacy of her resistance; and like Lady Derby, she gave every impression of enjoying her role, for all its perils. Mary Bankes came of a good if not a brilliant family, being the daughter of Ralph Hawtrey of Ruislip; her husband Sir John Bankes, described as 'a grave and learned man in the profession of law',[18] had prosecuted John Hampden as Attorney-General, and later became Chief Justice of the Court of Common Pleas.

The law had proved lucrative. It will be recalled that in 1617, at the time of the disastrous marriage of Frances Coke to Buckingham's brother, Corfe Castle was part of the rich settlement Frances was expected to receive from her mother Lady Hatton; the failure of Lady Hatton to part with it resulted in the King creating the bridegroom Viscount Purbeck as a consolation (see p. 16). So Corfe Castle remained in the possession of Lady Hatton. About 1634, Sir John Bankes bought it from her.

Mercurius Rusticus, the Royalist newspaper, would call Corfe Castle 'one of the impregnable forts of the kingdom'. Its peculiar site close by the Dorset coast, on top of a steep hill which lay in 'the fracture' of another hill, guarding the only route inland, had ensured 'Corph' a place in history since Saxon times; it possessed its own kind of grim female tradition, for hereabouts had been the *domus* of Queen Elfrida and here her step-son King Edward the Martyr had been murdered, according to later allegations, at her instigation, that her own son Ethelred might succeed. The present massive structure, with its walls ten feet thick, was complete by the reign of Henry II. Later Henry VII had repaired Corfe Castle for his own mother, the Countess of Richmond.[19]

Lady Bankes retired to Corfe Castle on the eve of the Civil War, leaving her husband to follow the political fortunes of the King, first in London, later at Oxford. We have some picture of how she lived there.[20] There were suites of gilded green leather, and blue damask hangings, a silk quilted carpet for the withdrawing-room, a rich ebony cabinet with gilded fixtures, fine tapestries in the gallery and another tapestry in 'my lady's bedroom' with a white dimity bed and hangings. In the large windows were embroidered satin cushions, and other cushions of crimson velvet.

Everywhere there was crimson velvet – chairs and stools as well as cushions were covered in it – together with rich carpets from Turkey and Persia.

For all the splendour of Lady Bankes's circumstances, supported by her husband's earnings as a lawyer, it was perhaps a pity that the previous owner, Lady Hatton, being, as a contemporary account put it, 'one (you may imagine) rather of Venus than Mars his company', had sold the 'chiefest guns' out of the castle. When it became obvious that a Parliamentary siege was imminent, Lady Bankes found herself armed with maidservants a-plenty, but as a garrison had a mere five soldiers. She was however not only 'a virtuous' but 'a prudent lady'; in her portrait she shows an extremely determined face to the world, with her strong long chin, her well-chiselled nose, firm lips and fine brave eyes – and she clutches the keys of Corfe Castle in her hand. Lady Bankes had no intention of having these keys snatched from her, not by stealth and not by surprise.[21]

Lady Bankes's prudence was displayed in a number of ways: for example in acquiring a great store of provisions. Aware of the Parliamentary sympathies of the town, she also kept the castle gates securely locked: for example on May Day when the Mayor and 'barons' of Corfe had the right to course a stag on her domains. When some troops of horse from Dorchester thought of surprising her, Lady Bankes 'very wisely and like herself' called in a guard, although the commanders of the troops denied that any harm was intended. She bore the foul language used by the common soldiers outside the castle with stoicism – as the Countess of Derby endured the indignities and affronts of her own besiegers.

When the local Parliamentary Committee at Poole demanded the four small pieces of ordnance left inside the castle, Lady Bankes's prudence led her, like Lady Derby, to play for time, instead of indulging in the outright defiance for which she was not yet prepared. There was a great deal of questioning of the seamen's warrants, and finally when the guns were placed on their carriages, Lady Bankes had them taken off; the seamen were beaten off by the five men of the garrison assisted by the 'maidservants at their Lady's command' to 'the small thunder' of guns. Lady Bankes secured an additional and far more substantial garrison of over fifty men from the Royalist commander Prince Maurice, brother of Prince Rupert. This was headed by a Captain Lawrence.

Despite the installation of these soldiers, her neighbours (like those of Lady Derby) did not match Lady Bankes in their stomach for a fight: 'presently their wives came to the castle, there they weep and wring their hands and with clamorous oratory persuade their husbands to come home and not by saving others to expose their own houses to spoil and ruin'. In the end Lady Bankes did let the great guns go – and that was prudent too, because it gave her a respite in which she could revictual the castle; it also gave Parliament the false impression that the prizing of Corfe would present no problem.

In fact Lady Bankes absolutely refused to surrender the castle at her enemies' summons; and when she was informed that no quarter could now be expected for the women and children inside the castle, according to the rules of war, took that threat with equanimity too.

The first siege of Corfe began on 23 June 1643. The castle had to stand an assault of 500 or 600 men, armed with a demi-cannon, a culverin and two sakers (small forms of cannon). In order to approach the walls in safety, the besiegers constructed two engines, known as the Sow and the Boar: however the marksmen found their legs entangled in these structures and abandoned them. The besiegers, headed by Sir Walter Erle, were also able to fire at Corfe with great impunity from the neighbouring church. According to the Royalists, Sir Walter conducted the entire siege wearing a bearskin coat for fear of musket-shot, and since it was summer and since he additionally crept about on all fours to avoid stray bullets he must have presented a bizarre spectacle.

As with the siege of Lathom House, there were sallies; food, not a mortar, was the object here – in the course of one of them, the defenders captured eight cows and a bull. The final assault came on a misty morning and the besiegers divided themselves into two parts to attack the upper and lower wards of the castle. By this time their numbers had been swelled by a rabble of sailors, dispatched by the Parliamentary Admiral the Earl of Warwick (Mary Rich's father-in-law) who brought with them the dreaded fiery granadoes and also scaling ladders. These bellicose fellows were fortified with alcohol to make them 'pot-valiant' (£1 12s od features in the accounts for 'a firkin of hot waters')[22] and assured that Corfe Castle would provide rich booty. Among their number were former felons, released from the prisons (the brands on their limbs were visible), but the courage of these 'silly wretches' gradually diminished in view of the fierce nature of the defence. The watchword for the attack was to be 'Old Wat', an allusion to their commander Sir Walter Erle; but 'Old Wat' was also the hunter's traditional nickname for a timorous hare which would not leave the cover of the bushes, a coincidence which the defenders at least thought highly appropriate.

Lady Bankes herself – 'to her eternal honour be it spoken'[23] – defended the upper ward of the castle, with her daughters, her women and five soldiers. This motley but determined force heaved stones and hot embers over the battlements so successfully that the soldiers were prevented from scaling their ladders.

Finally the strength of the assault wavered and gave way: hearing a report that the King's forces were coming, the besiegers 'ran away crying'. Corfe had been saved, as *Mercurius Rusticus* reported, by a combination of 'the fears of Old Sir Wat' and 'the loyalty and resolution of this honourable Lady'.

For some time after that Lady Bankes lived unmolested. Sir John Bankes (still absent from her side) died in December 1644. It was not until 1645, in the collapse of the Royalist side following Naseby, when other isolated centres of resistance such as Basing House and Lathom House were also captured, that Lady Bankes found herself once again besieged. In December Sir Thomas Fairfax sent a regiment of horse and two of foot to take Corfe. Even so, Lady Bankes was still stoutly holding out in February of the following year. It also seems that the final surrender of the castle was in fact due to treachery, although the long blockade must have contributed to it.[24]

One of her officers, a Lieutenant-Colonel Pitman who had served in Ireland under the Earl of Inchiquin, was by now 'weary of the king's service'. Proposing to fetch reinforcements from Somerset, he left the castle and contacted the enemy's commander on the pretext of arranging an exchange for his brother, then a Parliamentary prisoner. 'Under this colour' between 50 and 100 men were introduced into the castle disguised as supporters, many of whom knew its lay-out extremely well. So Corfe Castle fell at last, the prey to Colonel Pitman's Trojan horse.

Lady Bankes and her children were allowed to depart in safety. The gallant lady lived on until 1661; her son Sir Ralph Bankes enjoyed a long political career as well as enriching Dorset by building the noble house of Kingston Lacey. It was typical of Lady Bankes's resolve that her son actually got married on the day of her death – because she had concealed her pangs so successfully. She was buried at her native Ruislip where a tablet in the church still records that she 'had the honour to have borne with a constancy and courage above her sex, a noble proportion of the late Calamities'.

Corfe Castle, and its luxurious contents, fared less well than Lady Bankes and her reputation. Like Basing House, it was 'slighted'.† As for the

---

† In 1774 John Hutchins wrote of Corfe Castle in his *History of Dorset*, 'The vast fragments of the King's Tower, the round towers, leaning as if ready to fall, the broken walls and vast pieces of them tumbled down into the vale below, form such a scene of havock and desolation as strike every curious spectator with horror and concern.'[25] The curious spectator today will find the scene scarcely changed.

trunkfuls of Bankes belongings carted away so joyfully by the besiegers during the sack of the castle, those would take Lady Bankes's descendants many years to recover after the Restoration. A broker named Stone in the Barbican in the City of London seems to have bought £1,000 worth of goods, including some tapestry hangings which he sold 'to a fine lord'. As for Sir Walter Erle – 'Old Wat', that timorous hare – in 1661 he was to be found writing to Ralph Bankes in the following terms concerning the missing building materials of Corfe, in which injured innocence and innocent surprise were oddly mixed: 'And when the spoil was made, and the materials were carried away, I never gave any direction by letter or otherwise for bringing any part of it to my house, nor knew any such thing done more than the child unborn, until a good while after, coming down into the country, I found some part thereof among other things remaining of the ruine of my own house, laid by for future use.'[26]

*   *   *

Compared to such an iron character as Lady Bankes, Brilliana Lady Harley, who conducted the defence of Brampton Bryan Castle near Hereford, presents an altogether gentler image. Indeed, with her touching modesty of character combined with her strong sense of duty towards her absent husband's interests and property (which inspired her to a defiant course she would not otherwise have contemplated), Brilliana Lady Harley is really the seventeenth-century masculine ideal of a wartime heroine. She played her martial role with genuine reluctance but play it she did, most honourably, and to the death. And then there was that other aspect of her militarism, which might be termed the chivalry factor. Brilliana Lady Harley, whose husband Sir Robert supported Parliament, had Royalist relations herself, and as we shall see, her very sex made King Charles I notably reluctant to press against her, where he would have moved mercilessly against a male commander. At the same time, Parliamentarian propaganda waxed indignant against the Royalist besiegers: 'those capon-faced cowards who have unmanned themselves in offering violence to so noble a lady'.[27]

Brilliana Conway was born in 1600; her unusual Christian name reflected the fact that her father was Lieutenant-Governor of the Netherlands town of Brill at the time of her birth. In 1623 she married, as his third wife, Sir Robert Harley; a marriage, as has been mentioned (see p. 54), which was characterized by tenderness from its inception. Thereafter her life appeared to be punctuated by childbirth, for she bore her husband seven children between 1624 and 1634 (her predecessor, Sir Robert's second wife, had borne *nine*). However, Brilliana's letters which have survived show her to have been a woman of education as well as piety: she knew not only French but also Latin.[28]

Brilliana's maternal affections were concentrated on her son Ned, to whom, when at Oxford University, she directed a stream of rather touching advice. She sent Ned liquorice for his cold, 'eye water' for sore eyes, recommended beer 'boiled with liquorice' first thing in the morning for the kidneys. She would also have sent him a cold pie, except for two things: first, his father had assured her that Ned did not want it and second, and more cogently, Mrs Pierson (wife of the rector at Brampton) told Brilliana that when *her* son was at Oxford, she too sent him such things, until 'he prayed her that she would not'. A little purse of money – 'if only so he will think of her' – was presumably a more welcome present.[29]

An occasional flash of spirit does however remind one that Brilliana, for all her douce maternal femininity, had another side to her nature. Ned's letters have not survived, but we can imagine the one which provoked this retort, in a postscript: 'Dear Ned, My age is no secret; tho my brother Bray is something mistaken in it.'[30]

All this while Sir Robert Harley, who was one of the MPs for Herefordshire, was busy with parliamentary affairs in London. In his absence his business became somewhat neglected; it is noteworthy that Brilliana made no attempt to gather the reins into her own hands at this juncture. She contented herself with sending him veal pies and pairs of shoes from the country. Sharing her husband's Puritan sympathies, in many respects Brilliana found the year 1642 highly exciting: 'It is the Lords great work that is now a-framing,' she wrote to Ned in May. Yet she agonized over her growing responsibilities: 'what is done in your father's estate pleases him not, so that I wish myself with all my heart, at London, and then your father might be a witness of what is spent'. The plumbers who were mending the house, for example, were charging 5s a day! (although Brilliana thought the cost worth it). In July Brilliana the good housewife sent off the Harley silver plate to London for safe keeping in a trunk marked as containing cake. On 19 July, barely a month before the outbreak of the war, Brilliana also wrote off desperately for instructions as to how to guard Brampton Bryan; she was particularly concerned about treachery within and without since so many of her neighbours in Royalist Herefordshire favoured the King's cause. One 'roguish boy' working at the castle was sent up to London with a letter to get rid of him, lest he join the other side and betray them.[31]

Still Brilliana did not want Ned to come down and protect her; that would endanger him. And still she refused to budge from the castle. 'If I go away,' she told her son, 'I shall leave all that your father has, to the prey of our enemies; which they would be glad of.' As for the danger of her present position, defending Brampton Bryan: 'I cannot make a better use of my life.'[32]

In December 1642 came the expected stern demand from the Royalist Governor of Hereford that Lady Harley should hand over Brampton Bryan to the King's cause. As the Royalist gentry all about her assembled their levies, confident that with Sir Robert Harley at Westminster the stronghold would soon be theirs, Lady Harley told Ned: 'They [her neighbours] are in a mighty violence against me.'[33]

Yet Lady Harley's public defiance, as her letters to Ned reveal, covered an inner turmoil. Was she really right to hold out? What was Sir Robert's desire? 'I will be willing to do what he would have me do,' confided poor Brilliana to Ned. 'I never was in such sorrows.' Her tenants now found an excellent excuse for not paying their rents: money and food were short. By January 1643 the fowlers were forbidden to bring her game, her young horses had been commandeered and her servants dared not go into the town. 'Now they say they will starve me out of my house,' she wrote in February, when her cattle were driven away. The alternative was to dismiss her garrison, but that would be to invite plunder by all the local rogues: 'If I leave Brampton, all will be ruined.'[34]

In March Lady Harley received a summons but declined to hand over the castle. In June, still not yet officially beset, she burst out in a letter: 'O! my dear Ned – that I could but see you ... you are both a Joseph and a Benjamin to me.' On 26 July 1643 the siege began in earnest, at about two o'clock in the afternoon, with the arrival of two or three troops of horse, who proceeded to stop all passage between the castle and the outside world. Then 200 or 300 foot arrived; a total of 700 faced the beleaguered garrison. In the evening a trumpeter, according to custom, officially summoned the 'honourable and valiant Lady Harley' to surrender the castle, in the name of the High Sheriff of the City of Hereford, and others. The summons was politely worded: the Royalist troops and their commander Sir William Vavasour wished to prevent 'further inconvenience' to her.[35]

Lady Harley's reply was more dramatic. 'I dare not, I cannot, I must not believe', she exclaimed at the sight of Sir William drawing up his forces before the house. What of the King's many solemn promises on the subject

of liberty? 'I have the law of nature, of reason, and of the land on my side.'
At this, Sir William, although still polite, showed himself more menacing.
He referred to his wish to keep from Lady Harley 'all insolencies that the
liberty of soldiers, provoked to it by your obstinacies, may throw you
upon'. However, he went on: 'if you remain still wilful, what you may
suffer is brought upon you by yourself, I having by this timely notice
discharged those respects due to your sex and honour'. It was left to
Brilliana to conclude this fruitless exchange with the protest that there was
no 'drop of disloyal blood' in her body.[36]

The next day, 27 July, some small shot was exchanged; the Royalists
plundered Lady Harley's sheep and cattle, and more dangerously invested
the town and church – from the latter they were well placed to bombard
Brampton Bryan. How much Lady Harley's bold words to Sir William
belied her own fears is demonstrated by her letter of 30 July: she believed
her state of misery was without parallel. That 'One of my condition, who
have my husband from me and so wanting comfort should be besieged,
and so my life, and the lives of my little children, sought after!' Yet, the
next day, when Sir William offered her a protective guard for the house,
and the guarantee of safety for herself and her family if they would
lay down their arms, Brilliana firmly declined on the grounds that this
would be betraying her trust to her dear husband who had confided his
home and children to her care. Lady Harley ended pointedly: 'I do
not know that it is his pleasure that I should entertain soldiers in his
house.'[37]

So the ordnance began to play upon the walls of the house; 'their loud
music' was heard daily, including on the Sabbath, which further shocked
Lady Harley. The fact that no one within this 'close house' became sick
during these 'dog-days' of August was regarded by her as the workings of
providence. However, a few days later Lady Coleburn lost an eye as a result
of the bombardment and another woman, Mrs Wright, wife of the doctor,
was injured. Fortunately news of a Parliamentary victory by Sir William
Brereton was smuggled into the castle; this made up for the fact that shots
fired from the church steeple had broken some precious Venetian glasses.
It is interesting to note that the language of the soldiery – abuse shouted up
at the castle inhabitants for being 'Essex bastards, Waller's bastards, Harley's bastards, besides rogues and thieves' – was, as at the Royalist strong-
holds Lathom House and Corfe Castle, regarded as being a major part of
the ordeal. Great earthworks had been thrown up by the besiegers in the
gardens and walks of the castle, which 'lay so near us that their [the
Royalist troops'] rotten language infected the air; they were so completely

inhuman, that out of their own mouths, and the mouths of their guns, came nothing else but poisoned words and poisoned bullets'.[38]

For all this, for all Sir William Vavasour's original announcement that nothing more was due to Lady Harley's 'sex and honour', the siege of Brampton Bryan had by the third week of August reached a stalemate; just because its defence was being conducted by one of the weaker vessels – and a respected one at that. The Royalists hesitated to press. The lady refused to surrender. On 24 August Sir John Scudamore was allowed into the castle by means of a rope ladder, a drum having announced a parley; he presented a letter from King Charles I to Brilliana Lady Harley.

The King declared himself 'very desirous' to believe that what had happened at Brampton had been due rather to Lady Harley's being seduced by evil counsel, than 'out of your ill-affection to us'. He was still willing to avoid 'effusion of blood' and he was 'unwilling that our forces – in respect of your sex and condition – should take such course for forcing or firing of the same as they must otherwise take'. Lady Harley read the letter, but refused to receive Sir John personally. Perhaps it was just as well, for Sir John observed later that he would have told her squarely not only of the King's victories (which made her defiance absurd) but also of other members of her sex in London, crying out in multitudes against the House of Commons: women 'who cry out for their slain and imprisoned husbands; divers women killed by the soldiers in this tumult, yet unappeased'.[39] The implication concerning Lady Harley's own unfeminine conduct was clear.

Brilliana replied to the King in comparatively humble terms: she reminded him that the castle was hers 'by the law of the land', but if he did require it of her, at least let him permit her, with her family, to pass somewhere where they would not perish. According to Lord Falkland (husband of Lettice) the King was much moved by this, 'so far [as] to reflect with pity upon the sex and condition of the petitioner'; he suggested that Brilliana should stay at Brampton Bryan, under the protection of a Royalist garrison, until she found new accommodation. However, the only answer Brilliana actually received was a letter from Sir William Vavasour, offering once again a free pass, and a convoy for the lady and her servants to march safely away. At this stage of a siege this offer was in theory a concession. Brilliana was not appeased; especially as Sir William's letter was followed in the evening by a sharp letter from Sir John Scudamore demanding the instant surrender of castle and arms.[40]

Buoyed up by secret intelligence that the Parliamentary forces were approaching, Brilliana prevaricated. She also protested when the Royalists moved their gun carriages during this period of cessation of arms, and shot at them to teach them a lesson; when the Cavaliers stole her bells: 'we sent some of his Majesty's good subjects to old Nick for their sacrilege'.

And relief was in sight. When Fairfax reached Gloucester, 'these bloody villains' were obliged to depart, leaving Brilliana to instigate a service of public thanksgiving for the deliverance of 'our poor family' from the 'malignants of seven counties'. There were public tributes also to the courage of her who 'commanded in chief, I may truly say, with such a masculine bravery, both for religion, resolution, wisdom and warlike policy, that her equal I never saw'.

So the fame of Brilliana Lady Harley spread throughout the kingdom; even her enemies greeted her story 'with admiration and applause'. And it was said that those who had proceeded against her – a mere woman, albeit a brave one – were jeered at in the opposing King's Army.[41]

What should she do now? Should she leave Brampton Bryan or remain? Brilliana confided her worries to Ned on 24 September, being already confident that Ned – by now in the Army himself – would thoroughly disapprove of 'all plundering unmercifulness'. By October the forces of the King were once again menacing the safety of Brampton Bryan. And there was another ominous development. Brilliana had never been strong; throughout the previous siege her health had been progressively weakening. In a letter of 9 October, Brilliana revealed that she had taken 'a great cold'. It was 'an ill time to be sick in' she told Ned ruefully, adding that her last wish was to see him: 'for you are the comfort of your B.H., yr. most affect. mother'.[42]

Her wish was not granted. Later the same month Brilliana had 'an apoplexy and defluxion of the lungs' and lay for three days in extremity. Still her temper remained resolute: she 'looked death in the face without dread'. On the fourth day she died, leaving behind 'the saddest garrison in the three kingdoms, having lost their head and governess'. Once her commands had 'carried us into the cannon's mouth', as a grief-stricken eye-witness, Captain Priamus Davies, wrote, now her death was saluted not with the thunder of guns but with 'volleys of sighs and tears'.[43]

Brampton Bryan did not long survive the loss of its 'head and governess': hideous tales of the fate of the defenders of Hopton Castle nearby scarcely encouraged the civilians left within Brampton Bryan, under Dr Wright, to proceed with their defiance now that the chivalrous protection due to

Brilliana's 'sex and honour' could no longer be expected from the King's Army. So Brampton Bryan, early in 1644, surrendered.

Prince Rupert – a legend to his opponents for his savagery – was said to have ordered its inhabitants to be put to the sword, but Sir William Vavasour, more of a gentleman, refused. In the event, as the Puritan defenders of Brampton Bryan were carried away to captivity at Ludlow they 'baited us like bears', wrote Captain Davies, 'and demanded where our God was'.[44] But worse did not befall. And Brilliana's bereft children, baby Tom, and Ned's 'sweet little sisters' Dorothy and Margaret, aged eleven and thirteen respectively, were well treated by the Governor of Ludlow Castle and also by the Royalist Sir John Scudamore – who was, incidentally, their kinsman.†

The castle itself was of course 'utterly ruined'. Sir Robert Harley estimated that he had lost nearly £13,000 worth of goods, for all his wife's frenzied wish to protect his property. At least the legend of Brilliana's heroism survived: 'That noble Lady and Phoenix of Women died in peace,' declared the minister at her husband's funeral, 'though surrounded with drums and noise of war, yet she took her leave in peace. The sword had no force against her.'[45]

*   *   *

From time to time, relating the exploits of the 'Great Heroick' ladies, contemporaries commended in passing the activities of their female acolytes: Lady Cholmley's maids who nursed the sick at Scarborough, Lady Bankes's chambermaids defending the upper ward of Corfe Castle, the Marchioness of Winchester's maidservants who turned lead into bullets at Basing House. . . . Where the women of the people were concerned, their Amazonian deeds in their own defence, if they attracted public notice, were certainly officially applauded.

After the siege of Gloucester in 1644, the town clerk John Dorney collected various pamphlet accounts of its defence. One referred to the 'cheerful readiness of young and old of both sexes . . . to labour in the further fortification of our city' as being admirable to observe. The young women who ventured forth to gather fuel were specifically commended: 'Nay, our maids and others wrought daily without the [earth] works in

---

† Ned's subsequent distinguished career – as Sir Edward Harley – eschewing the extremism of both Roundheads and Royalists, and sitting for Parliament throughout the reign of Charles II, would have heartened his adoring mother. It was his son and Brilliana's grandson, another Robert Harley, who was that celebrated Tory politician of the reign of Queen Anne.

the little mead, in fetching in turf, in the very face of our enemy.' The fortifications of the City of London were thrown up with the assistance of a number of women, not all as socially prominent as the Lady Mayoress armed with her own entrenching tool. This democratic spirit was celebrated by Samuel Butler in *Hudibras*, describing how women

> From Ladies down to oyster wenches
> Labour'd like pioneers in trenches.[46]

During the siege of Bristol by Prince Rupert, one Mary Smith valiantly took out provisions to the men on the out-works, and helped construct the fortifications. Joan Batten and Dorothy Hazzard helped to stop up the Frome Gate; and about 200 women were said to have gone to the Parliamentary commander Colonel Fiennes and offered to place themselves in the mouth of the cannon to ward off the shot. Women in Nottingham patrolled the streets, keeping a look-out for fires. During the siege of Nantwich in Cheshire, women were employed to put out the 'terrible fire' in the brush-wood ricks in a back-yard and saved Dorfold House.[47]

The most renowned of these group-heroines were the women of Lyme, on the Dorset coast, who in 1643 successfully helped to repel the attacks of the Royalists under Prince Maurice. Their fame was spread in a long poem by a local man named James Strong, the son of a tailor at Chardstock, who after being educated at Wadham College, Oxford, held livings at Bettiscombe and then Ilminster. *Joanereidos*, printed in 1645, declared its subject to be: 'Feminine Valour Eminently discovered in Westerne Women';

> To most 'tis known
> The weaker vessels are the stronger grown.
> The vine which on the pole still lean'd his arms
> Must now bear up and save the pole from harms.

Joanereidos was to be much satirized in later years:

> Which I should most admire, I know not yet
> The womens valour, or the Poets wit.
> He made the verses, and they threw the stones ...
> O happy stones which those fair fingers gripped![48]

Even at the time it was not altogether clear that the masculine pole relished the principle of the female vine's assistance – even if he enjoyed it in practice. (Never mind the fact that these intrepid women were already well equipped to defend themselves by the lives of physical endeavour they led at home or in the fields – war was different.) An uneasy impression that women were 'stronger grown' was one of the many disquieting feelings produced in the masculine breast by the course of the Civil Wars in England.

Camden in *Britannia* described Lyme as 'a little town situate upon a steep hill . . . which scarcely may challenge the name of a Port or Haven town, though it be frequented by fishermen' being 'sufficiently defended from the force of winds with rocks and high trees'. And then there was its Cobb, a long spit of stone cutting off the harbour from the open seas. In 1643 Prince Maurice paid his own kind of tribute to the town which managed to frustrate his advance by referring to it as 'the little vile fishing village of Lyme'.[49] The fact was that Lyme (the Regis came later, ironically enough for the town's loyalty in aiding the escape of Charles II after Worcester) held off Prince Maurice against all expectations; and contemporaries were agreed that this was owing to the exceptional enthusiasm of the defence.

On their arrival in the area in April, the Royalists had described the capture of Lyme as 'breakfast work . . . they would not dine till they had taken it'.[50] Thomas Bullen captured Stidecombe House, three miles from Lyme, and on 20 April Prince Maurice took some nearby dwellings. Weeks later 'little vile . . . Lyme' still held off the invader, although cut off from the interior by the Prince's forces.

The defenders consisted of some 1,100 men on day and night duty; but they were far from being well-equipped – they had not, for example, sufficient shoes and stockings to go round. Nevertheless their ferocity in their own defence was so great, and so many of the besiegers were slaughtered, that at one point their water supply was coloured rusty brown with blood. Some of the more affluent ladies inside Lyme when the blockade began were taken off – 'to the ease of the town' – in the Parliamentary ships of Lord Warwick, lying off the coast. It was left to the rest to suffer their casualties with the men. Following the bombardment, fire arrows were shot into the town, setting alight twenty houses. One maid lost her hand while carrying a pail to put out the conflagration, and another lost both her arms. A woman was killed while drying clothes on the strand near the Cobb-gate.[51]

This was suffering in the pursuit of ordinary domestic duty. The women of the town also filled the soldiers' bandoliers as they fought, which meant they shared the dangers equally with the men. They acted as look-outs, especially at night, work commemorated by Strong as follows:

> Alas! who now keeps Lime? poor female cattell
> Who wake all night, labour all day in Battle
> And by their seasonable noise discover
> Our Foes, when they the works are climbing over.

(The satirists later compared these faithful women to the geese who saved the Capitol:

> Geese, as a man may call them, who do hiss,
> Against the opposers of our Country's bliss.)[52]

In fact the women of Lyme threw stones with the best of the defenders; and with the best of the defenders it seems they too cursed the besiegers.

Finally, on 14 June the siege was raised and the Royalists departed. Then it was the women of the town, 400 of them, who fell upon Prince Maurice's earthworks and fortifications, and with spades, shovels and mattocks, levelled them. As a result of their efforts in 'throwing down ditches', the fortifications which had threatened them were removed in a week.[53]

Three years later, Parliament, by now in control, ordered £200 a week to be set aside for the relief of the wounded of Lyme, and of the widows and children. This the Puritan John Vicars, in his history *Gods Arke*, described as 'a good piece of State-Charity'. And Vicars gives us too the reaction of that unfortunate maid who lost her hand in the fire. When asked how she would now earn her livelihood, she is said to have replied: 'Truly, I am glad with all my heart that I had a hand to lose for Jesu Christ, for whose Cause I am as willing and ready to lose not only my other hand but my life also.'[54]

Vicars described this as 'A sweet and most Saint-like speech indeed', and perhaps it was. Or perhaps the tone, far from being one of sweet submission, was one of belligerence, new belligerence.

10 His Comrade

Her Husband was a Souldier, and to the wars did go,
And she would be his Comrade, the truth of all is so.

'The Gallant She-Souldier', 1655

'In my poor judgement these times can bring no good end to them', wrote
Sir Ralph Verney's aunt, Margaret (Poulteney) Eure on the eve of the war:
'all that women can do is to pray for better, for sure it is an ill time with
them of all creatures, for they are exposed to all villainies'. Three years
later, when the first phase of the hostilities was ending, a pamphlet entitled
The Scourge of Civil War and the Blessing of Peace seemed to indicate that
Margaret Eure's gloomy prophecy had been fulfilled: war was said to have
enforced the mother to behold the ravishment of her own daughter, and
made the sister mingle her tears with her brother's blood; on a more
mundane level, it was said to bring 'A Famine of Bread, Virtue scarce and
nothing public but disorder'.[1]

The helplessness of the female in wartime – falling on her knees in
prayer for want of anything better to do to protect herself – was another
article of conventional belief like her lack of courage; her passive suffering
was colourfully, even gleefully, described by both sides in the usual propagandist style.

In fact the women who lived through the period of the Civil Wars were
far from passive. Fund-raising was one activity: women brought their
jewellery to the Guildhall to aid the Parliamentary cause. In London,
Canterbury, Coventry and Norwich, women formed committees to
raise funds for troops of horse for Parliament. These were known in
consequence as Virgin or Maiden Troops: Cromwell took the Norwich
Maiden Troop into his own regiment in August 1643; 'I thank God for
stirring up the youth (your men and maids) to cast in their mite', he
wrote.[2]

Then as spies or 'intelligencers', or simple emissaries, women had a
mobility often denied to the other sex. Lady Byron, for example, was able

to escape from the siege of Chester in December 1645 and ask the King (then at Oxford) for assistance. An unknown 'poor woman' at Portsmouth acted as an agent between Charles I and Henrietta Maria at the beginning of the war. The handsome red-haired Jane Whorwood played a more sustained part in the efforts to free the King from his various places of detention and imprisonment. As such she earned the praise of Anthony à Wood for being 'the most loyal person to King Charles I in his miseries, as any woman in England'.[3] Indeed Jane Whorwood's various attempts to come to the King's assistance, by their very nature, could hardly have been undertaken by a member of the opposite sex.

At the beginning of the war Jane Whorwood was twenty-seven years old. Red hair was generally censured in the seventeenth century (traditionally it was a witch's colour; it was also to be avoided in a wet-nurse for fear of sour milk) but Jane Whorwood was generally held to be 'well-languaged', 'tall' and 'well-fashioned' – even if she did have pock marks on her face. She had strong, even intimate Royalist connections: her father had been Surveyor of the Stables to King James, and her step-father, James Maxwell, was one of the Grooms of the Bedchamber to Charles I. In 1634 Jane had married Brome Whorwood, eldest son of Sir Thomas Whorwood of Holton in Oxfordshire, and had given birth to a son (also red-headed, according to Anthony à Wood) the next year.[4]

In 1647, when King Charles I was held at Holdenby in Northamptonshire by orders of the English Parliament, Jane Whorwood, 'bold' as well as handsome, visited him in order to convey funds which had probably originated with her step-father. She was seized and searched, but released; later a letter in cipher was found behind the hangings where she had stood in the King's chamber.[5]

From Holdenby, the King was conveyed to Hampton Court, having been transferred into the power of the English Army from that of Parliament. Here again Jane Whorwood visited him, bringing money. She also took an enthusiastic interest in the possibility of the King's escape from the Army's 'protection', consulting the celebrated astrologer William Lilly as to his best destination. From Lilly came the suggestion of Essex, where he was 'certain he might continue undiscovered'. Unfortunately the King had already fled 'in the night-time westward'.[6] (In view of the disastrous consequences of the King's choice, Carisbrooke Castle on the Isle of Wight, one should not perhaps scoff at the workings of astrology.)

To Carisbrooke too came the faithful Jane Whorwood after more consultations with Lilly. Here the King found himself far more securely incarcerated under the control of the Puritan Colonel Hammond; at the same time the need for liberty in order to resume the royal juggling act between Army, Parliament and Scots was yet more urgent. Neither Jane Whorwood – nor anyone else – secured the King's escape; but Jane kept up a barrage of attempts, including an effort to get him secretly on to a ship 'to waft him to Holland'. On the advice of Lilly, she purchased aqua fortis, or nitric acid, to weaken the bars on the royal windows, so that they might be pulled from their sockets. Most of that was spilt on the way to the Isle of Wight; but at least Jane got as far as the King's stool-room with a file also procured by the astrologer. Throughout the autumn of 1648 Jane Whorwood conveyed messages to and from the King at Carisbrooke and according to Lilly, also advised him of the most favourable astrological hour to receive the Scottish Commissioners. 'I cannot be more confident of any', wrote Charles I. Since Colonel Hammond was warned of the intentions of this 'well-languaged' gentlewoman, it must have been her sex which protected her and allowed her the immunity of these frequent – if in the end unavailing – journeys.[7]

The disadvantage of Jane's sex lay in the fact that sooner or later she was accused of being the King's mistress. There is no evidence to support such a suggestion, which in any case would have been quite outside the King's character: Charles I was blamelessly uxorious. That however was the penalty Jane Whorwood paid for being an active helper to her sovereign – and at the same time a woman. Afterwards Anthony à Wood innocently increased the rumours by stating the King had bestowed a casket of 'precious jewels' upon Jane Whorwood – in fact they went to Lady Wheeler, the King's laundress. What was true was that Jane Whorwood ran forward to greet the King as he went to his execution[8] – but then that was in her 'bold' and loyal nature.

The romantic efforts of Jane Whorwood achieved in the end little. The partnership of Anne Murray, later Lady Halkett, and her lover Colonel Bampfylde, achieved in one respect much. For in 1648 this couple secured the rescue of James Duke of York from Parliamentary captivity in London. The what-might-have-beens of history are notoriously beguiling; all that can be said with certainty about the incident is that Charles I was extremely anxious his second son should not remain in Parliament's grip as a potential pawn. Beyond that one can only speculate what might have happened if James, next in line to the throne after the Prince of Wales, had lingered in London, a possible titular king in place of his father and brother.

When we last heard of Anne Murray, she had just been slighted by her reluctant lover Thomas Howard, and pined in consequence for some (Protestant) convent to which she could flee (see p. 146). This was in 1644.

Thereafter matters still did not mend for portionless Anne, since she fell victim to the charms of the dashing Colonel Bampfylde, a man who was certainly a Royalist agent, and later probably a double-agent as well.

The two-facedness of Colonel Bampfylde extended to his emotional life: a married man, he pretended that his wife was 'dead and buried' in order to overpower the scrupulous Anne. Wartime conditions made that kind of deception easier. Besides, the inventive Colonel gave as a reason for keeping this 'death' secret the fact that his wife's fortune would otherwise be sequestered by Parliament. It seems all too likely that the Colonel did overpower Anne's moral objections to his sexual advances by this stratagem. The truth was eventually discovered – the wife still lived – and Anne, telling the tale in her memoirs, without exactly admitting to her seduction, does react with the utter horror and mortification of one who has sacrificed her principles for a fantasy.[9]

In 1648 all this pain lay ahead. Anne had begun assisting Colonel Bampfylde in his operations since either early this year or late the preceding one. When Charles I indicated to Bampfylde his extreme anxiety that the fourteen-year-old James should be spirited away from St James's Palace, it was to Anne that Bampfylde turned for a vital part in the plan.[10]. The choice was approved in advance by Charles I, for Anne's mother had been governess to James's sister, the Princess Elizabeth, and her brother William Murray was in attendance on the King himself. It was also assumed that Anne as a young woman, like Jane Whorwood, would enjoy a kind of freedom of action certainly not granted to a known loyalist such as the Colonel.

So to Anne was entrusted the task of securing a suit of women's clothes in which the young Duke might make his escape. First she got the Colonel to take a ribbon with him to St James's Palace in order to mark 'the bigness of the Duke's waist' and 'his length'. Armed with this, Anne went to her tailor and inquired how much mohair would be needed to make a petticoat and waistcoat for 'a young gentlewoman' with these measurements.

There was a long silence. Then the tailor replied that he had made 'many gowns and suits but he had never made any to such a person in his life'. Privately Anne thought that the tailor was certainly right. However, his actual meaning was to do with the strange measurements which confronted him: 'he had never seen any woman of so low a stature have so big a waist'. Fortunately the tailor was more baffled than suspicious; he forthwith made a garment of mixed light and dark mohair, with a scarlet under-petticoat.

Now it was up to the young Duke. James, with some perspicacity, instituted a series of games of hide-and-seek in St James's Palace, so that his guardians should become accustomed to his absences. He also secured the keys to the gardens by a trick and had his pet dog locked up lest it should follow him. In this manner he managed to take advantage of his 'hiding' during a game to reach the Privy Garden and so the outside, where Colonel Bampfylde awaited him with the first stage of his disguise: a cloak and a periwig. They travelled first by coach and then by water from Westminster Bridge.

Anne's turn came next. With her faithful maid Miriam she was to await the arrival of the Colonel and his protégé at the house of a surgeon named Low near the next bridge down river from London Bridge. The Colonel's instructions were to remain till ten o'clock at night; after that, if he did not come that meant the plot had been discovered, and the women must save themselves as quickly as possible. As it was, ten o'clock came and went without the Colonel's arrival. But still Anne refused to flee.

Her confidence was rewarded. After a while 'a great noise' was heard; Anne imagined that the soldiers were coming to take her. In fact the first sight which met her eyes was the person of the young Duke himself, in those days, as the Grande Mademoiselle of France assures us, 'extremely good-looking and well made' (the saturnine looks of the future Charles II were considered much less appealing).[11]

'Quickly, quickly, dress me,' called the boy. So Anne did as the Duke commanded, finding him 'very pretty' in his woman's clothes. She also provided James with some food, including a Woodstreet cake, which she had procured because she knew he loved them. So the Duke, now outwardly a young lady if a somewhat oddly shaped one, departed for Gravesend in a barge 'with four oars'. And Anne and Miriam set off in a coach, helter-skelter, for the safety of her brother's home. At that moment all was confident action. The disillusionment concerning the Colonel's marital duplicity lay ahead.

*   *   *

If women were not passive, true it is that they suffered in the period of the wars (and so of course did the men). There was the most obvious suffering of all caused by the loss of the loved ones, bringing with it that grief which is the handmaiden of wars throughout history. Margaret Eure (for all her meek words a lady of some spirit, as her choice of the Catholic William Eure for her second husband had indicated – see p. 93) certainly found no 'good end' in the war. The 'lucky bullet', which her brother-in-law Sir Edmund Verney had once angrily hoped would free the headstrong young woman from the 'misfortune' of her second marriage to a Papist, found its mark. Colonel William Eure was killed in 1644. Margaret's romantic love for him had never faded: far from being relieved, she described herself as having suffered 'the greatest misfortune that could ever happen to me in this world . . . the Death of the gallantest man that ever I knew in my Life'.[12]

Grief struck equally at both sexes, but women were more likely to experience those pangs of divided loyalty peculiar to civil wars, brought about by marrying from one political allegiance into another. Thus Mary Rich, daughter-in-law of the Puritan Admiral of the Fleet, the Earl of Warwick, was also the sister-in-law of the Royalist Commander Lord Goring. She was alone at the Rich seat in Essex, Leighs Priory, when Goring arrived to help himself to the Warwick armaments stored in the house. Goring, blithely believing that Mary would favour her own family rather than that of her husband, sent a message to say that he would first take dinner with her, and then commandeer the arms. Mary did serve dinner – but thereafter did her level best to save the store from Royalist depredation.[13]

The agonies of a Royalist mother whose son joined the side of Parliament are affectingly recorded in the letters of Susan Countess of Denbigh.[14] 'Su' Denbigh was the sister of the magnificent Duke of Buckingham, favourite in turn of James and Charles I; she had thus been raised in intimate contact with the court, with kings and for that matter queens – she was now a lady-in-waiting to Henrietta Maria, and when the French Queen left for Holland to raise money and troops, Su Denbigh went with her. A friend and patron of the poet Crashaw, it was to Lady Denbigh that Crashaw recommended the Catholic Communion in the lines:

> What Heaven-entreated heart is this,
> Stands trembling at the gate of bliss?[15]

And she did subsequently convert to the Catholic Church.

William Earl of Denbigh, who had been Master of the Robes to James I, was equally a staunch Royalist. He was over sixty but he stood forth for the King at Edgehill; to the pain and humiliation of the mother her eldest son Basil Lord Feilding appeared on the opposite side of the battlefield for Parliament.

Clearly Basil Lord Feilding had the gift of inspiring affection (remember the adoration of his third wife, exclaiming 'Dear! how thy Betty loves thee!' – see p. 54). For Lady Denbigh loved while she agonized. 'I suffer [more] for the ways you take . . .' she wrote 'than ever I did to bring you into this world.' And again: 'Let my pen beg that which, if I were with you, I would do upon my knees with tears.' Or: 'I do long to hear my dear son Feilding speak once again to me in the duty he owes to his Master and dread sovereign [Charles I], the master of your poor afflicted mother, banished from the sight of you I do so dearly love.'

The Earl of Denbigh was severely wounded in the head by 'swords and poll-axes' at Birmingham, under Prince Rupert, in 1643; Lord Feilding visited him under a flag of truce – but by the time he arrived, his father was dead. Now let Lord Feilding give her 'the comfort of that son I do so dearly love', wrote Lady Denbigh from Holland from the depths of her grief. 'Leave those that murdered your father,' she pleaded, 'for what can it be called but so? ... there was no mercy to his grey hairs but wounds and shots, a horror to me to think of.' Before, her son had been merely in error; now his adherence to Parliament was 'hideous and monstrous'. Nevertheless Basil Lord Feilding remained true to Parliament; and Susan Countess of Denbigh remained true to the service of the Stuarts. She died in exile in Paris in 1652 without having seen her beloved son again.

* * *

Then there were the ordeals of the women who found themselves in the mindless path of the war. If divided loyalties were the painful prerogative of those somewhere near the political centre of things, it was aggravated distress which threatened those lower down the social scale. One Alice Stonier of Leek in Staffordshire was one member of this dejected flotsam, bobbing about between armies, countries and peoples – a lucky one as it turned out, since the righteous justices and churchwardens of Staffordshire eventually came to her rescue. Alice Stonier had been taken over to Ireland by her husband, an unsuccessful drover; there they had been robbed, their house burned, themselves driven out and stripped naked except for a ragged woollen cloak by the somewhat inhospitable native Irish population. The Stoniers slept in the fields at night till they reached Dublin; at which point Thomas was 'pressed' (conscripted) to be a soldier, and almost immediately killed. Because Alice and her five children represented Protestant victims of Irish Catholic aggression (a popular English concept at the time) the Stonier family were shipped back to Staffordshire, where Alice was granted 8d a week and her three eldest children were placed 'in good service'.[16]

Others were not so lucky. It has been pointed out that natural phenomena, common throughout the seventeenth century, such as harvest failure, disease and fire, had a far more disastrous effect on the lives of common

people than the wars themselves.[17] Plague pointed its finger and periodically decimated the population; a woman's lot, in an age when effective
birth control did not exist, comprised the ceaseless bearing of children, and
the perils thereof, wars or no wars. Nevertheless civil strife in one version
or another ploughed up the soil of England for nearly ten years. In
addition English soldiers, both Cavalier and Roundhead, fought and
continued to fight in Ireland; Cromwell installed an English Army of
occupation in Scotland after the victory of Dunbar which remained there
till the Restoration; under the Commonwealth English soldiers and sailors
were involved in military action against the Dutch, the French and the
Spanish, including an expedition to the distant West Indies. Women's lives
could hardly go unaffected by these hazardous peregrinations on the part
of their menfolk.

Alice Coles of Poole had the awkward problem of explaining how she
had conceived a child during her husband's absence serving in the Army
in Ireland; accused at the quarter sessions, she claimed, with some verve,
that he had paid her a miraculous visit! Another West Country wife was
propositioned by an enterprising gentleman after her husband likewise had
been away serving in Ireland for some time on the grounds that 'her
husband used the company and lay with women in Ireland and had the
carnal knowledge of their bodies and he would wish her to do the like
with men here in England'.[18]

These were mere hiccups compared to the financial sufferings often
experienced by the widows and families of soldiers, and the dependants of
the maimed, as the numerous petitions for their relief make clear. Towards
the end of the century Gregory King would cite the families of soldiers
and seamen among the three groups of the perpetually insolvent.[19]

Of course social disruption could affect every class, and it would be
insensitive to suppose otherwise. The death of the Royalist Sir Edmund
Verney in 1642, bearing the King's standard at Edgehill, left his five
unmarried daughters breathing in a climate of genteel despair, their portions sequestered along with the rest of the estates. Sue, Pen, Peg, Molly
and Betty Verney huddled together at Claydon; to be joined by a sixth
unhappy sister in the shape of the widowed Cary Gardiner and her pathetic
little daughter – for Cary had been so contemptuously treated by her dead
husband's family that she preferred to take refuge at Claydon (see p. 120).
So the girls spent their time with little prospect of a glorious match,
quarrelling peevishly amongst themselves in an attempt to keep up vanished standards. 'I did speak to Peg as her maid might serve both her and
Pen, but she will not it be so by any means', wrote a relative. 'I told her

now their father and mother was dead, they should be a helper one to the other . . . but all would not do [so].'[20] Without a man to protect them, the girls felt threatened by lawless soldiers on both sides while the King was at Oxford, since Claydon lay roughly on the borders of Royalist and Parliamentary territories.

Sir Ralph Verney's relations, the Denton family of Hillesden, suffered the capture of their house by the forces of Parliament. Sir Ralph wrote feelingly of 'the ruin of sweet Hillesden and the distresses that happened to my aunt and sisters'. Yet here it should be noted that the Dentons displayed a certain emotional resilience not granted to the Verneys. Susan Denton, walking in her distress over the fields to nearby Claydon, somehow captured the heart of one Jeremiah Abercromby, a member of the attacking force and himself a Covenanter. His love being returned, the unlikely pair got married. 'I think few of her friends like it,' wrote her brother gloomily, 'but if she hath not him, she will never have any, it is gone so far.' Alas, the next year the bridegroom was killed in a raiding party.[21]

More natural perhaps was the romance of Susan's sister Margaret Denton and Colonel Smith, the defender of Hillesden, who was taken to the Tower of London together with the Dentons, when Hillesden fell. There in the Tower a courtship took place which resulted also in a marriage. Margaret's aunt, Mrs Elisabeth Isham, wrote: 'I think it will be a happy match if these ill times doth not hinder it.' Although many thought it 'a bold venture' to wed a prisoner, Mrs Isham reflected: 'if these times hold, I think there will be none men left for women'. Finally the gallant Colonel escaped, abetted by the Denton women, who after a further confinement of eight days as a punishment, were themselves released.[22]

For all the disturbances endured by the Verneys and the Dentons, the fate of those lower down in society who found themselves robbed not only of their natural protector but also of an actual livelihood in the absence of their man, was undoubtedly worse; as in all periods of distress, those at the bottom of society's pile found themselves more woebegone than ever. The absence of the male – James Strong's 'pole' to whose authority the female 'vine' was supposed to cling – was a serious economic loss. Letters have survived from two wives of militia men. The latter were members of the so-called trained bands, not professional soldiers but supposed, since the time of Queen Elizabeth, to come to the aid of their county or city in a time of crisis. In 1642 these recruits were generally raw and frequently reluctant; it is noticeable that the two women share a pathetic sense of grievance against their husbands for subjecting them to an experience which they are convinced could somehow have been avoided.

In September 1643 Susan Owen, wife of John Owen serving under Lieutenant-Colonel West in the Blue Regiment, advanced a number of arguments as to why he should return to her side. First, she was pregnant and in danger of suffering a miscarriage. Second, the neighbours were mocking her for his departure: 'you did it on purpose to show your hatred of me'. Third – the most poignant plea – 'Why can everyone come [home] except you?'[23]

The letter of another Susan, wife of Robert Rodway, was addressed to her husband, a militia man in the Westminster Liberty Regiment; known as the Red Regiment (like the Blue) from the colour of its flag, it was one of those involved in the early unsuccessful assault on Basing House in 1643. Susan Rodway's letter was entrusted to 'Robert Lewington, the Hampshire carrier', but intercepted on its way by the Royalists and published as it stood in their newspaper *Mercurius Aulicus*:

Most dear and loving husband, my king love. I remember me unto you, hoping that you are in good health, as I am at the writing hereof. My little Willie have been sick this fortnight. I pray you to come home, if you can come safely. I do marvel that I cannot hear from you as well as other neighbours do. I do desire to hear from you as soon as you can. I pray you to send me word when you do think you shall return. You do not consider I am a lone woman; I thought you would never leave me thus long together, so I rest ever praying for your safest return
      Your loving wife
         Susan Rodway
Ever praying for you till death I depart. To my very loving husband, Robert Rodway, a trained soldier in the Red Regiment, under the command of Captain Warren. Deliver this with speed I pray you.[24]†

But Captain Warren had led the 'forlorn hope' of the Red Regiment in one of the fiercest assaults on Basing House. Robert Rodway was probably already dead by the time Susan wrote her poignant letter.[25]

The absence of the male 'pole' was the central hazard. This is not to say that episodes of violence, ravishings, assaults and the like, did not take place

† Susan Rodway's letter as printed is a good example of the spelling of a literate woman of the time: 'My little Willie have bene sick this forknight. I pray you to come whome, ife youe cane cum saffly. I doo marfull that I cannot heere from you ass well other naybores do. I do desiere to heere from you as soone as youe cane. I pray youe to send me word when youe doo theñke youe shalt returne. You doe not consider I ame a lone woemane; I thought you woald never leave me thuse long togeder, so I rest evere praying for your savese returne.'

on the part of the soldiery when discipline broke down; but then such episodes happened to unprotected women throughout the seventeenth century. However, few of the truly gloating propaganda stories, *pace The Scourge of Civil War and the Blessing of Peace*, bear up to close examination.

For instance the report by the Roundhead Colonel Edward Massey and Major John Bridges of the mayhem, including rapine and robbery, created by the Northern Horse of the Royalist Sir Marmaduke Langdale was certainly wildly exaggerated. The Northern Horse, about 1,500 strong, were to a great extent officers: 'This march of theirs was accompanied with many unheard-of cruelties. They robbed all the country people of their goods and took away their cattle. They ravished the women and bound men neck and heels together, and ravished their wives before their faces, and tied women in chairs and ravished their daughters in their sight. One woman they ravished who was within a week of her time ... etc. etc.' On the other hand it is substantiated that two Royalist soldiers, charged by their own side in Coventry with ravishing women, were stripped and given a public lashing.[26]

The xenophobic cruelty meted out to an old Irishwoman left behind by the Royalist forces after the unsuccessful siege of Lyme was the true type of atrocity which women had to fear in wartime. Unknown, unwanted, unprotected, the old woman stumbled into Lyme itself, not realizing that the troops to whom she had attached herself for some reason long ago forgotten, now never to be recorded, had departed. She was seized by the victorious defenders. Accounts as to the exact nature of her treatment vary; although all agree that it ended in a hideous death. First the old woman was robbed of her money – 20s or 40s. Then according to one version she was 'slashed' and her dead body thrown into the sea, from whence it was eventually cast up to lie 'till consumed' on the coast between Lyme and Charmouth. In another version the viragos of Lyme – heroines as they might be to their own side – pounced upon the stranger and incarcerated her in a hogshead full of nails, and then as in some frightful fairy tale, rolled her into the sea.[27]

*   *   *

How then was a woman to cope, she whose husband (or protector) had gone to the wars? It is clear that a great many women, out of a mixture of motives – commercial enterprise, loneliness, starvation or sheer love of adventure – went along too. The armies of the Civil Wars, and the various armies of occupation later, were attended by hordes of female campfollowers. Many of these adopted male clothing, more from convenience than caprice, which of course makes the numbers of this protean band hard to assess. All that can be said with certainty is that now in skirts, now in breeches, now as bawds, now as 'horse-boys', now as virtuous – and determined – wives, an amorphous mass of women went raggle-taggle along with those troops who comprised, for one reason or another, their means of livelihood.

Whores served the Army as – given the opportunity – they would have served the same men in civilian life; but here was a greater concentration of custom. One prostitute who had followed the King's camp from London was 'taken by the soldiers, and first led about the city [Coventry] then set in the pillory, after in the cage, then ducked in a river, and at last banished the city'. Others received a warmer welcome. 'There they had their whores with them', wrote Bulstrode Whitelocke of the sacking of his house, Fawley Court; and the troops subsequently quartered there by the Royalist Sir John Byron included some women who for convenience's sake 'counterfeited' their sex.[28]

On 13 July 1643 King Charles I issued a proclamation in which the general licentiousness, profanity, drunkenness and whoremongering of the Army was roundly castigated. Moreover the cunning adoption of male dress by females made it especially difficult to curtail the latter activity. These were the orders to be published at the head of every regiment: 'because the confounding of Habits appertaining to both Sexes and the promiscuous use of them is a thing which Nature and Religion forbid and our Soul abhors, and yet the prostitute Impudency of some women ... have (which we cannot think on but with Just Indignation) thus conversed in our Army; therefore Let no Woman presume to Counterfeit her Sex by wearing mans apparell under pain of the Severest punishment which Law and our displeasure shall inflict'.[29]

But there is no reason to suppose that King Charles I, for all his 'Just Indignation', any more than his predecessor King Canute, was successful in turning back this particular tide.

Wives as well as whores proceeded to 'counterfeit' their sex and adopt soldiers' attire. Sometimes they did so purely in order to follow their man. It was often better to be a man's comrade, however rough the going, than to be left as a charge on the parish at home, with all that entailed; a soldier's pay, a soldier's keep was at least a form of sustenance. Then there were the types of a seventeenth-century Fidelio. Sometimes, with despairing devotion, a wife or mistress or betrothed would set out to search for her beloved, vanished into the maw of the armed services; in this case male dress was not so much an economic convenience as a necessity – lest the unguarded female be thought to be displaying that 'prostitute Impudency' which had shocked King Charles I.

The 'Gallant She-Souldiers' saluted in contemporary song probably sprang from a mixture of these categories; once again their true numbers will never be known (the object of the exercise being after all anonymity rather than publicity). A newspaper of July 1642 told of a girl who disguised herself as a soldier to stay near her lover in the Earl of Lindsay's regiment, but was later detected. And when Shelford, near Nottingham, was taken by Major-General Poyntz of the New Model Army in November 1645, one of the Royalist prisoners there was said to be a woman corporal.[30] Jane Ingleby, who is said to have fought at Marston Moor in the cavalry, and being wounded, escaped on horseback to her home, was probably a Yorkshire yeoman's daughter.[31]

Eight years after the Restoration a play by the popular comic actor John Lacy called *The Old Troop* celebrated both types of camp-follower, the promiscuous whore and the faithful mistress. Lacy himself, who specialized in funny accents, played Monsieur Raggou the French cook; the character of Dol Troop was a prostitute, hailed by Raggou in the following terms: 'Begar, Madam Dol, you be de great whore de Babylon.' Dol's widespread generosity – if such it can be termed since she had saved about £400 out of her earnings – led her to remark when she discovered herself to be pregnant: 'I cannot say I am with child, but with children; for here has been all nations, and all languages to boot.' On the other hand Dol's tenderest feelings were reserved for the handsome young cornet's boy – who was of course a girl in disguise. Biddy had joined the Army for love and, unlike Dol, maintained her virtue throughout the play. It is legitimate to assume that Lacy, who began his career as a lieutenant of cavalry, had not only known Dols, but Biddys too.[32]

Dol Troop saw her pregnancy as a means of mulcting the entire regiment of payment. ('I mean to lay this great belly to every man that has but touched my apron strings.') But where the genuine she-soldiers were concerned, it was pregnancy which very often provided the means of detection. The popular ballad of 1655, 'The Gallant She-Souldier', described the real-life adventures of a woman who successfully masqueraded in the Army as 'Mr Clarke':[33]

> Her Husband was a Souldier, and to the wars did go,
> And she would be his Comrade, the truth of all is so.
> She put on Man's Apparel, and bore him company,
> As many in the Army for truth can testify.

No lewd camp-follower she: 'Mr Clarke' was not only 'upright and just'
but 'Modest still'. However, for all this vaunted modesty, 'Mr Clarke'
was just as good as any man at firing a musket or beating a drum,
until the untoward appearance of 'a pretty little son' upset her disguise.
She also took part in manly soldiers' recreations such as wrestling,
leaping, cudgels and cuffing, drinking and taking tobacco with the best
of them.

Indeed when 'Mr Clarke's' commander commented on his soldier's
surprising girth: 'Tom, why do you grow so fat?', the she-soldier answered
cunningly: ''Tis strong beer and tobacco which is the cause of that.' Finally,
when 'Mr Clarke' was in labour, concealment was no longer possible. The
she-soldier now became concerned to stress her own virtue: as for the
baby: ''Twas by her honest Husband, she could not be beguil'd.' At the
end of the ballad, those interested to see 'the young Souldier and his
mother' were asked to repair to the sign of the Blacksmith's Arms, in East
Smithfield near Tower Hill. 'Mr Clarke', one notes, was still the name to
ask for.

The moral drawn from the tale of 'Mr Clarke' was of a praiseworthy
fidelity, not always exhibited by the weaker vessel:

> I wish in heart and mind
> That Women to their Husbands were everyone so kind,
> As she was to her Sweet-heart, her love to him was so
> That she forsook all others, along with him to go.

Another conclusion can however be drawn from this and other ballads on
the subject, such as 'The Famous Woman Drummer', whose heroine's
devotion and courage, dressed in man's apparel at her husband's side, is
similarly stressed:

> They have been both in Ireland, in Spain and famous France, sir,
> And lustily she beat her Drum, her honour to advance, sir,
> Whilst Cannons roar'd, and bullets fly, as thick as hail from sky, sir;
> She never feared her foreign Foes, when her Comrade was nigh, sir.[34]

This conclusion, supported by cases of she-soldiers outside the realms of
ballad, concerns female physical strength and endurance.

Most women could obviously manage pistols, and a sword would not
have presented great problems (in any case soldiers' weapons tended to be
sorry blades, not particularly long or heavy). A halberd, a cross between
a spear and an axe, would also have been easy to manage. Muskets were
weightier, with barrels officially four feet in length, reduced to three in the

course of the Civil War, and had heavy – one and a half ounce – bullets. The arquebus, reduced from three to two and a half feet during the war, and the carbine which armed the light cavalryman would have been less of a burden. But what of the pike? Its proper length was eighteen feet, later reduced to sixteen; and although in practice often cut a good deal shorter by the soldiers on active service, one still might suppose it presented a challenge to the physique of the weaker vessel. But it is clear that women managed pikes too. The protagonist of 'The Female Warrior', for example, 'was at push of Pike some say, As good as ever struck'. The 'Famous Woman Drummer' was also said to have been adept with the pike, as well as the musket.[35]

It was traditional among the English to suppose that it was the women-folk of their Celtic neighbours who possessed a relentless ferocity. The Irishwomen in particular, attached to the Royalist armies, had a bad name (perhaps that contributed to the violence of the attack on the old Irishwoman found wandering about Lyme, although unconscious prejudice against her age and sex may also have had something to do with it). Irishwomen at the siege of Nantwich were said to have been armed with knives half an ell long – nearly two feet. After their capture it was recommended they should all be killed or thrown into the sea; it was Fairfax who had them exchanged for Roundhead prisoners instead.[36]

The Scots were thought to have included females among their forces when they marched towards Newcastle in 1644, to swell their numbers 'and their women (good Ladies) stood with blew-caps among the men' wrote the newspaper *Mercurius Aulicus*. When King Charles I moved against the Scots in 1639, the militancy of the Calvinist Lady Ann Cunningham – 'a notable Virago' – struck terror not only into the hearts of the English, but also into that of her own son, the Marquess of Hamilton, who did not share her religious convictions. At Berwick on 5 June, she rode with a case of pistols at her saddle, and her 'dags' (daggers) at her girdle, at the head of her troop of horse. All her attendant women had been obliged to become expert marksmen; the Marquess aroused her special ire. She threatened to shoot him personally if he came ashore with the King, and to that end, either with magic craft or with an aristocrat's due in mind, was said to have carried golden bullets with her.[37]

The truth was different: the Celts did not have the monopoly of Amazons. Any woman, desperate or convinced enough, English as well as Scottish or Irish, might find it in herself to play the 'Virago'. Commitment and necessity brought physical strength. (As indeed women have throughout history, in modern as well as ancient times, performed military service with success when circumstances demanded it.) Besides, whatever the mystique of feminine weakness, and even fragility, enjoyed by the ladies of the middle and upper classes, the women of the English labouring class were in their ordinary peacetime lives indulging automatically in feats of manual strength: a great scythe wielded all day at harvest-time was not such a bad preparation for 'push of Pike'.

It hardly needs stressing that at a time of sparse hygiene dress itself and concealment presented little problem: short hair (which was easily achieved) vanished in any case from the Roundhead philosophy shortly after the start of the war; the thick buff cassock coat and breeches of the average soldier was at once disguise and protection. Many must have acted as did Christian Davies, born in 1667, who, going in search of her soldier husband towards the end of the century, adopted the simple expedient of cutting her hair and donning his clothes 'having had the precaution to quilt the Waistcoat, to preserve my Breasts from hurt which were not large enough to betray my Sex'.

In her autobiography (sometimes ascribed to Defoe), *The Life and Adventures of Mrs Christian Davies, commonly call'd Mother Ross ... Taken from her own mouth when a Pensioner of Chelsea Hospital*, Christian Davies describes herself as one who as a girl had always enjoyed 'manly Employments, such as handling a rake, flail, pitchfork, and riding horses bareback'.[38] Such a one was perhaps the authenticated she-soldier Anne Dymoke, 'a young person' who turned up in the military garrison stronghold of Ayr, in 1657, during the occupation of Scotland by the Cromwellian Army. Anne described herself as the daughter to one John Dymoke of Keale, near Bullingbrooke Castle in Lincolnshire. The Dymokes, of which the main branch lived at Scrivelsby, were a distinguished family, headed by the King's Champion, who as Cavaliers had ruined themselves in the royal cause. But this was back in the bad old days of the Civil Wars; in any case there is no record of Anne in the main branch of the family, so perhaps either John or his daughter Anne was illegitimate. As it is, her adventures demonstrate that the ballads scarcely exaggerated in their dramatic descriptions of the she-soldier's life.[39]

Anne Dymoke's father and mother being both dead, she went to live with her aunt. Here she fell in love with one John Evison (or Ivison), like herself of Lincolnshire origin, but who had served in the Army in London. Her affection was returned. Unfortunately her friends would not hear of the match, and without their approval, Anne saw no way of 'accomplishing her end' – which was to throw in her lot with that of John Evison –

'but by putting herself into man's habit'. This she did in May 1655, and so attired went to London with her lover.

In London, however, John Evison proved to have no means of supporting her, so the couple decided to enter service together, describing themselves as two brothers, 'this maid still keeping in man's apparel'. As 'Stephan' Evison, Anne Dymoke lived at the house of a coachman in Chick Lane called Taylor for two years, while John Evison lived in Islington. John and 'Stephan' Evison then took a sea voyage. Tragically, in the course of this voyage, 'the said John was cast away', that is, washed overboard and presumed drowned. It was in this manner that the bereft Anne, 'keeping still her man's habit', arrived at Carlisle.

What was she to do, a young woman, friendless and alone in a strange city? The course Anne Dymoke adopted was to enlist as a soldier under a Major Tolhurst, using this time the name of her dead lover John Evison. And it was in this manner that she ended up at Ayr, where as Colonel Roger Sawrey was careful to make clear in reporting the incident: 'I can perceive nothing but modesty in her carriage since she has been with us.' Nor was Anne Dymoke any less keen to distinguish herself from Dol Troop and her ilk. In the garrison at Ayr she 'never was known to any, which she declares very solemnly to be all the way of her progress in her disguise'.

*   *   *

There was one particular woman's skill which in wartime made her man's valuable comrade, and that was nursing. The weaker vessel, just because her weakness also comprised softness, tenderness and compassion, was held to be a natural nurse (as man, the stronger vessel, was supposed to be a natural soldier). Sir Ralph Verney spoke as roundly on the subject of nursing to his son John as he had done on the subject of education to Dr Denton, only this time he found for women. ''Tis not a man's employment,' he declared of nursing, 'but woman's work, and they both understand it and can perform it much better than any Man can do.'[40]

There was a practical side to this as well. Before the war most nursing had been done at home, and as we have seen, housewives from great to humble regarded the provision of home-grown medical remedies as part of their essential duty. The wartime nursing of the wives among the body of camp-followers was in one sense merely an extension of this role; just as Lady Cholmley, the chatelaine of Scarborough Castle, nursed the sick during its siege, a task she would have performed, if on a lesser scale, in peacetime.

The field arrangements for nursing during the hostilities were on both sides also extremely sketchy. Commanders might rage – King Charles I might inveigh – against the peripheral nuisance of the camp-followers, but in this case at least, the value of their services was unarguable. General Venables's ill-fated expedition to the West Indies under the Protectorate was generally censured – rightly – for its lack of preparation. But when the General was also criticized for allowing some of the soldiers to be accompanied by their wives, he struck back with some justice, referring to 'the necessity of having that sex with an army to attend upon and help the sick and wounded, which men are unfit for'. Had even more women gone, he protested, 'I suppose that many had not perished as they did for want of care and attendance.'[41]

There were no movable hospitals during the campaigns, and a far from abundant supply of surgeons and physicians. There was also very little proper organization to get the wounded away from the field of battle afterwards to what hospitals did exist. Left too often where they had fallen, soldiers of both sides were fortunate to enjoy the natural nursing instincts and skills of some local woman. After Edgehill, for example, one Hester Whyte petitioned for reimbursement because she had taken charge of wounded Parliamentary soldiers 'in great misery by reason of their wounds' for three months and had laid out her own money to supply their wants.[42]

Royalist prisoners who were taken to Nottingham Castle and encountered Lucy Hutchinson were particularly fortunate. Lucy Hutchinson, 'having some excellent balsams and plasters in her closet', was busy attending to the wounds of her own side, and with the assistance of a gentleman that had some skill, she managed to dress all their wounds; 'whereof some were dangerous, being all shots, with such good success that they were all well cured in convenient time'. At this point the Governor's wife noticed three Royalist prisoners, 'sorely cut' and bleeding, being carried down to the castle's prison, known as the Lion's Den. Despite the protest of a Roundhead captain that these men were 'the enemies of God', the high-principled Lucy insisted on doing 'what she thought was her duty in humanity to them, as fellow creatures, not as enemies'.[43]

Another remarkable character in this respect was Elizabeth Alkin, otherwise known as 'Parliament Joan'. Elizabeth Alkin first came to prominence at Portsmouth when war broke out, and in the general chaos took it upon herself to take back the wounded to be cared for in London; for which humanitarian service she was paid £15 6s 8d. Later she went to Harwich, where she cleansed the bodies of the wounded, cut their hair and had their clothes mended. Like some earlier Florence Nightingale she demanded 'more hammacoes [hammocks], candles, wood etc.' for the needs of the sick; she also spent her own money: 'I cannot see them in want if I have it.' As a result of these further efforts, she was paid a further £15 by the Committee of Sequestrations in October 1647 (out of confiscated Royalist property) and granted a house for life. The later career of Parliament Joan, by now a 'fat woman ... about fifty', was as a spy or intelligencer for the Government, ferreting out illegal Royalist newspapers, and later still as a polemical journalist; but as a nurse it should be recorded that with Lucy Hutchinson, she saw it as her duty to tend the sick of all nations, treating Dutch prisoners equally with the English wounded.[44]

In the hospitals themselves, once again the pre-eminence of the softer sex in nursing was taken for granted. Amongst women, widows of soldiers were considered to be the best nurses of all; however, economic factors were probably at work here as well as the theory of compassion. For nursing wages were conspicuously low (including those of the Matron). For instance the joint salaries of thirteen nursing Sisters at the Savoy Hospital for sick and wounded soldiers, established in 1644, came to £52 a year. These wages being lower than those offered to the better-class domestic servant, it was not surprising that few women who had a choice expressed a preference for nursing.[45] The soldiers' widows, generally speaking in a depressed class, might be expected to have no choice.

As it was, women's traditional faults, as well as their virtues of mercy and tenderness, were not ignored in the rules made for nurses in hospitals. 'Scolding, brawling or chiding' were sternly forbidden. And those nurses who carried comradeship to the point of marrying soldiers within the hospital were thrown out.[46]

Colonel Bampfylde's erstwhile comrade, Anne Murray, put her practical abilities to good use nursing the injured and sick in Scotland. Her further adventures had led her here at the period when King Charles II, now allied with the Covenanters, was expected to land. In between there had been yet another humiliating interlude with a family at Nantwich Castle: the lady of the house suspected Anne of designs on her husband, designs which the husband in turn showed every sign of harbouring towards Anne; yet the poor girl had no money to leave. After the Royalist defeat at Dunbar in 1650, Anne was amongst those who tried to succour the wounded Scottish soldiers. She, like Lucy Hutchinson, had her own special balsam and plasters, which in this case she had brought with her from England. She treated at least sixty one day and twenty the next, some of them stinking with maggots and gangrene.

For the next two years Anne remained at Kinross, helping the sick. In later life as Lady Halkett her love of physics and surgery made 'things of her preparing' very popular; certainly she had scope enough in Scotland during the war and post-war years. It is good to record that her flight to Scotland resulted at last in that suitable marriage which Anne Murray had surely long deserved. She was by now a governess in the household of Sir James Halkett, her employer being a widower. As Anne observed demurely in her memoirs: 'It is so usual where single persons are often together to have people conclude a design for marriage, that it was no wonder if many made the same upon Sir James and me.'[47] Yet even now, because the matter of her portion was still unresolved, Anne hesitated. What was more, while matters were hanging fire, the duplicitous if fascinating Colonel Bampfylde made yet another appearance, with more tall tales about his wife, asking Anne soulfully whether she was yet married to Sir James Halkett.

'I am,' said Anne stoutly aloud, adding 'not' under her breath.[48]

Then at last, with a simple appearance in front of the Justice in Commonwealth style (who called for a glass of sack to drink their health) and a subsequent religious ceremony in front of the Minister, at the age of thirty-three Anne achieved the long-sought state of matrimony . . . .

11 *A Soliciting Temper*

> 'Certainly it would not do amiss if she [Lady Verney] can bring
> her spirit to a soliciting temper, and can tell how to use the juice
> of an onion sometimes to soften hard hearts.'
>
> SIR ROGER BURGOYNE'S ADVICE TO SIR RALPH VERNEY, 1646

'In these late Times', wrote Basua Makin after the Restoration, not only
did women defend their homes and 'play the soldier with Prudence and
Valour' but they also 'appeared before Committees, and pleaded their own
Causes, like men'. The necessity for women to make public appearances
in their own interests was one of the most surprising developments of the
wartime period. 'The customs of England' were changed as well as the
laws, as Margaret Duchess of Newcastle expressed it, with women 'running about' and acting as 'pleaders, attorneys, petitioners and the like'.[1]

What began as a necessity would later be regarded as an opportunity. A
decade or so later, Basua Makin was advancing this type of wartime
activity as evidence of the female's fitness for that education generally
denied to her. Yet ironically enough, women's influential role as 'solicitors'
actually developed out of their own supposed weakness.

The sequestration or confiscation of Royalist estates (and rents) had its
origin in the Parliamentary side's desperate need for money in the early
stages of the war, lacking resources to acquire supplies and pay troops. On
27 March 1643, Parliament passed an ordinance which sequestrated the
estates of all those giving assistance to the King; in practical terms, the
property of such a 'delinquent' was to be sequestered by a committee of
that county in which it was situated. In October of the same year, the lands
and houses of those Members of Parliament who had absented themselves,
or those who had neglected to pay Parliamentary taxation, were ordered
to be let, so that the rent might serve as a security for loans for Parliament.[2]

Women, however, were not delinquents, or if they were, it was a rare
state, more likely to be connected with their Catholicism than their
Royalism. Of the Kentish delinquents listed for example only 5 per cent
were female, and of those who did feature, about 93 per cent were Catholic

recusants; the tiny category of women sequestered in their own right, widows and spinsters, were accused of such offences as selling goods to Royalist garrisons.[3]

Women were not delinquents because of their own dependent legal status: there their dependency worked to their advantage. Technically, because all her rights at law were swallowed up in his, a woman's husband was also responsible for her crimes. Conversely his delinquency could not be laid at her door; there could be no guilt by association. This principle however had the awkward effect of leaving the weaker vessel not responsible for the crimes of the stronger, yet enduring all the same their practical consequences. So, the Parliamentary ordinance being framed to raise money rather than to impose suffering, delinquents' families had to be given some kind of protection from the complete destitution which would otherwise have been their lot following the sequestration.

For this reason, another ordinance was passed in August 1643 which set aside a special sum, not to exceed one fifth of the sequestered income of the delinquent, for the benefit of his wife and children. It was the right to this 'fifth', if she pleaded for it personally before the committee concerned at the Goldsmiths' Hall in the City of London, which gave to the wife – the woman – a new and special importance in that society where her public silence had previously been rated an eminent virtue. A Royalist ballad saluted the change:

> The gentry are sequestered all;
> Our wives you find at Goldsmith Hall
> For there they meet with the devil and all.[4]

At the same time the jointures of wives and the settlements of heiresses were not supposed to be sequestered along with their husband's own property, no matter how masterful a 'malignant' (as the Parliamentarians termed their adversaries) he had proved himself to be. It is a commentary on the postulated legal innocence of the weaker vessel that Lady Bankes complained bitterly – and with perfect justification – over the sequestration of her jointure along with the rest of her husband's assets after the fall of Corfe Castle. Yet, as we have seen, no one could have shown a finer sense of the need to assist the King than the woman who held the upper ward of the Castle and poured stones and hot embers on the heads of the invaders.

As Protector, Oliver Cromwell harkened to the plea of Lady Ormonde, heiress of the Irish Desmond estates, but also wife to the Marquess of Ormonde, the arch-Royalist leader, and as such condemned to poverty-stricken exile. A lady, he decided, should not 'want bread' for the bad luck of having 'a delinquent lord'; he ordered the Desmond inheritance to be restored to her. Indeed Cromwell, then the single dominant force in Britain, had 'a very general fame' for helping the weak, as Lady Ormonde pointed out hopefully in a letter from Caen; in most cases where he had made a personal intervention, the weak consisted of women, whom he regarded as innocent victims of their husbands' or fathers' wrongdoings.[5]

Of course the figure of the suppliant female being granted mercy by an all-powerful male was as old as history – or monarchy – itself. Cromwell as Protector was merely carrying on the tradition of the clement sovereign. As King James I passed graciously through his new dominion of England, to take up royal residence after the death of Queen Elizabeth, he presented an excellent opportunity for suppliance on the part of those whose relatives had offended under the previous regime. At Doncaster, a widow named Muriel Lyttelton flung herself at his feet and begged that the forfeited estates of her late husband might be returned, that she might somehow be able to raise and care for her children.

Muriel Lyttelton's husband, a Catholic, had been convicted of high treason under Elizabeth for his part in the Essex conspiracy and died in prison. As a result of Muriel Lyttelton's plea, the estates were returned and in the first year of James's reign, the act of attainder reversed. A careful businesswoman (she had some of the steely prudence of her father, the Lord Chancellor Sir Thomas Bromley), Mrs Lyttelton then tended her children's inheritance so well that she eliminated all debts. It was with some justice that an eighteenth-century history of Worcestershire wrote of this importunate widow that she 'may be called the second founder of the [Lyttelton] family'. Sir Edward Digby was another Catholic executed for conspiracy. His widow, Mary Lady Digby, twenty-four years old at his death, did so well with her suits and begging letters that in 1608 she was able to reclaim his forfeited properties for her sons; as a result of her perseverance, Sir Kenelm Digby inherited £3,000 a year.[6]

In the rising drama of the King's powers versus his subjects' rights in the 1630s, some of the most vivid incidents occurred when the Star Chamber sentenced men to physical punishments for the sake of the words they had spoken, written or printed. Wives played their convenient role here in appealing for mercy.

Henry Burton was a Puritan minister, denounced to the Star Chamber for preaching 'seditious sermons' at the same time as William Prynne was accused for his work *Histriomastix*; like Prynne, Burton was sentenced to have both his ears cut off while confined to the public pillory, and after that to be imprisoned for life. Sarah Burton was not allowed to visit him while he lay in prison in London, his wounds healing; but when he was deemed recovered and dispatched to a new prison in Lancaster, she followed him in a coach. On 7 November 1640, after he was transported to Guernsey, Sarah Burton petitioned to the House of Commons (now feeling its mettle against the practices of the Star Chamber) to allow him to return. Her language was carefully modest: 'as she knows not how to manage so weighty a business' she asked the House of Commons to take 'her distressed condition' into their serious consideration. On 10 November Burton was released. The language of John Bastwick's wife, asking at the same time to visit him in the Scilly Isles (he had been convicted of a scandalous libel under Archbishop Laud) because she could not provide for the children, was remarkably similar: 'your petitioner being a woman [is] no way able to follow nor manage so great and weighty a cause'.[7] Bastwick was released in December.

In January 1644, the Houses of Parliament at Westminster (as opposed to the King's Parliament at Oxford, a body whose validity they did not recognize) offered pardon to all Royalists who would submit before a certain date; the condition was that they should compound for their delinquency by payment of a sum, to be assessed, towards the public relief. After October 1645 when the capture of Bristol meant that the whole of England (with the exception, as we have seen, of a few fortresses) was at Parliament's mercy, this offer was renewed and extended.

The theoretical procedure was as follows: 'delinquents' who wanted to free themselves from sequestration by this method had to present themselves at the Committee for Compounding which sat at the Goldsmiths' Hall in the City of London, in Gresham Street near the Guildhall. The delinquent took an oath before the Committee binding himself not to bear arms against Parliament, and another (religious) oath, that of the Covenant. He then had to declare the full value of his estate, any mis-statement making him liable to a heavy fine. Rates of payment varied: MPs might lose half their estates, lesser delinquents only a sixth.[8]

In practice these negotiations were very often bedevilled by local jealousies - not forgetting that the original sequestration was carried out by the Committee of that county where the estates lay - as well as the separate but hideous complications attendant upon all bureaucracies, but particularly newly instituted ones. Some Royalist husbands were in prison - how were they to arrive at accurate figures concerning an estate and its rents? Others were in exile, not wishing to return until the principle of the compounding had been securely established. This was where the 'innocent' wives, already having the right to their 'fifth', might well be in a better position than the husbands to arrange for the compounding or obtain the vital certificate of sequestration from the local county Committee.

Above all, women had a mobility denied to the male; even if the word mobility has an ironic ring applied to persons who were often sick, often pregnant, often some combination of the two, yet finding themselves undertaking journeys which involved considerable physical hardship even for the healthy.

All this was as nothing compared to women's peculiar fitness to play the suppliant role. As the imprisoned Thomas Knyvett wrote to his wife in 1644: 'I think it will be fit for thee to come up and Appear in the business, for Women solicitors are observed to have better Audience than masculine malignants.'[9] It was in keeping with the contemporary estimate of the so-called weaker sex that any member of it could entreat most plangently without being accused of more than fulfilling her own feminine nature. This implicit social approval of 'Women solicitors' was the reverse side of that attitude which found excessive martial courage in wartime disquieting because it was considered masculine.

*   *   *

Lady Cholmley, she who had shown 'a courage above her sex' in her husband's estimation during the siege of Scarborough Castle, remained firmly in Yorkshire after its surrender.[10] Sir Hugh Cholmley was allowed to sail away to the Continent by the besieging commander Sir Mathew Boynton; Lady Cholmley however declined a pass to go abroad. It was important to establish that the Cholmley house at Whitby was hers, in order to avoid its sequestration with the rest of her husband's property.

Lady Cholmley's instinctive fear that in this case possession was nine if not ten points of this law was certainly right: the Roundhead Captain at Whitby refused to leave the house, despite Lady Cholmley's authority. Homeless, Lady Cholmley was obliged to take lodgings in Malton, with her young daughters, and wait on events. Fortunately for her – if not the Captain – plague broke out in Whitby, and one of the Captain's servants died; the Captain promptly fled. Seeing her opportunity, and unlike the Captain, careless of her own safety (although she left her daughters at Malton), Lady Cholmley then undertook a remarkable journey from Malton to Whitby, in the depths of winter. She was now in her late forties, but she went on foot 'over the bleak and snowy moorland' of North Yorkshire, a distance of some twenty miles as the crow flies, and rising to nearly a thousand feet. Attended by only one manservant and one maid, she took possession of her house again.

The plague vanished, the Captain tried to return. Lady Cholmley declined to be ousted. Finally, with the help of her brother-in-law, she secured officially that 'fifth' of Sir Hugh Cholmley's estate which was her legal right; the following February her son William Cholmley (upon whom the manor of Whitby had in fact been settled by his father) arrived to look after it. So at last Lady Cholmley was able to go to her husband abroad; at Rouen in March 1647 joyfully she re-encountered her son, another Hugh, whom she had not seen for five years.

A period of Cholmley family peace – albeit in exile – followed. However, in February 1649, shortly after the execution of Charles I had put an end to one set of Royalist hopes, it was Lady Cholmley who returned to England and arranged, with the help of some Yorkshire friends, composition of favourable terms for her husband's estate. Once the first instalment had been paid, Sir Hugh himself was able to come back in June 1649. After a period of helping William at Whitby, Lady Cholmley returned to her native south (she had been born Elizabeth Twysden, daughter of the grand Lady Anne Twysden, of East Peckham in Kent) and spent the rest of her days with Sir Hugh, mainly at her brother's home of Roydon Hall. She died in 1655. As a tribute to her fidelity Sir Hugh Chomley, who died two years later, elected to be buried with his wife in the south, rather than with his own forebears in Yorkshire.

Lady Cholmley's sister-in-law Isabella was another indomitable helpmate. We last heard of Isabella, the model daughter-in-law to Lady Anne Twysden, nursing the older woman with devotion through her last illness, having been picked by Lady Anne from amongst her gentlewomen, at the somewhat advanced age of thirty, as a bride for her son Sir Roger Twysden, the antiquary and MP (see p. 94). Sir Roger was a politician of independent mind: he had been sure that the demand for ship money had been wrong because the King had not acted in Parliament. But in the spring of 1642 he was one of the so-called Kentish Petitioners who protested to Parliament, amongst other things, on behalf of episcopal government and against religious 'heresy' in any form, a gesture which was extremely ill-received by the Puritan element in the House of Commons. According to Sir Roger, it was however owing to the private malice of his Kentish rivals Sir John Sedley and Sir Anthony Weldon that he was then imprisoned.[11]

Dame Isabella Twysden was now a woman of thirty-seven, her physique already wearied by child-bearing.[12] Nevertheless on hearing the ill news concerning Sir Roger she sent her babies to an aunt at West Mall and set off for London. It was not until Sir Roger was freed on bail that she returned to Roydon Hall with him. In the April of the following year, Roydon Hall was ransacked by soldiers. Sir Roger, having no wish to stand by while the extremists fought each other, tried to set out for a self-imposed exile in France with his son William; he was stopped. On 17 May 1643 the order was given for the sequestration of his estate, and Sir Roger himself was immured in the Compter Prison in Southwark.

It was now the melancholy duty of Dame Isabella to appeal to the county Committee – that of Kent – for that fifth which was her due for maintenance. But at this point the Kent Committee demanded that Sir Roger had first to acknowledge his own delinquency and thus by implication the justice of the sequestration, otherwise she would get nothing at all. This message, which was in effect an attempt to get Sir Roger to throw in his lot with Parliament, was duly passed on by Dame Isabella. Sir Roger refused to make the acknowledgement.

At this the Kent Committee set to and not only had Sir Roger's coppice woods felled – which if the sequestration order was accepted, was their right – but also certain trees which Sir Roger considered to be his standing timber. Sir Roger was convinced – no doubt with justice – that his old enemy Sir Anthony Weldon as Chairman of the Kent Committee was responsible; so that he in his turn decided to petition the central Committee of the Lords and Commons for Sequestrations, which sat at Westminster. For his emissary Dame Isabella, who was ill at the time, this involved daily journeys between Westminster and the Compter prison.

In late February 1644 Sir Roger was allowed to leave the Compter for a less formal confinement in Lambeth Palace, in the rooms of the former chaplain to the Archbishop of Canterbury. Moreover Dame Isabella was permitted to share with him the three rooms and a study, the latter 'a fair chamber with a chimney' in which Sir Roger was able to write and copy, following his antiquarian bent. The Westminster Committee also decided at last that the Kent Committee was not justified in their behaviour. However when Dame Isabella returned to Kent with this news, the local Committee merely greeted her with a yet more violent denunciation of her husband.

Sir Roger's petition was heard by the Westminster Committee in August: bitterly hostile witnesses from Kent testified against him, and Dame Isabella, with her counsel, was not allowed to remain in the room while judgment was reached. It was hardly surprising that the decision went against Sir Roger. Dame Isabella was privately informed of the reason: that 'for one man's sake', it would not do to disoblige the entire county of Kent. At least the Westminster Committee made an order to the Kent Committee at the beginning of September that they 'do allow the said lady a fifth part of her husband's estate'; a recommendation was added that Dame Isabella should be allowed the mansion house and the lands adjoining.

Dame Isabella's health was worse; she was also, in her fortieth year, in the early stages of pregnancy (altogether she bore six children between her early thirties and late forties). Nevertheless she battled down to Kent, and presented the order. All that happened was that the Kent Committee, under the hated Sir Anthony Weldon, refused outright to give her the lease, and furthermore put off granting her her fifth, on the pretext of requiring certain rentals from her – as Dame Isabella pointed out, they were in a better position than she was to supply these rentals, since they had confiscated the land concerned. So that it was back to Westminster, to the Committee of the Lords and Commons, and to Sir Roger; but the members of the Westminster Committee, saying frankly they had done all they could, ended by recommending her to return to Kent.

On 2 November the Committee of Kent treated Dame Isabella courteously. However, she was told now that she could not receive her fifth until she had supplied those vital details of the estate, which, it will be remembered, it was the duty of the owner of a sequestered property to provide. This was all very well in theory, but in practice was a prodigious labour since the estate had already been sequestered for eighteen months, with its master in prison, unable to keep a record of rents. Dame Isabella was undeterred. She set about visiting all the tenants herself and constructing a proper return. In this manner she was able to go back to the Committee of Kent on 2 December although it was not until 18 December that the certificate was finally made out. Ten days later the Committee of Kent allowed Dame Isabella one fifth of the rents and profits of the estate, and an allowance from the receipts of the rents since Michaelmas (which in fact constituted another piece of meanness, since most people were allowed a fifth of the total rents received since sequestration). But Dame Isabella was not to be permitted to occupy Roydon Hall; and the felling of the timber went on.

It was the latter injustice which caused Sir Roger, fretting impotently in his London confinement, particular pain. Once again it was the task of Dame Isabella to petition the Westminster Committee: '... the woods adjoining to the said house, being as she conceived in her fifth part, were then in felling....' Westminster did give out an order for this to stop; although privately once again they confessed that they could do little more to help her against the Committee of Kent.

At this point Dame Isabella started to keep a diary, which lasted for the next six years;[13] this document, besides charting the political rigours of the life of a 'Woman solicitor', gives small intimate glimpses of that domestic existence from which 'soliciting' distracted her. Thus are chronicled the coming and going of nurses, or matters such as the 'breeching' of young Roger Twysden at the age of six: this was a miniature nursery ceremony of the time, when the boy child officially deserted the 'skirts' of his sisters for masculine attire; on this occasion Roger's mother noted regretfully that although he was six years old, he was 'very little of growth'.

The return to Kent with the new order, on 8 February 1645, was recorded as follows (her own spelling): 'I came to Peckham great with child, and ride all the way a hors back, and I thank God no hurt.' Dame Isabella must have been in fact eight months pregnant, for her son Charles was born at the beginning of March; she rode pillion behind the loyal tenant George Stone, with whom the children had been boarded. At the beginning of the sequestration, her husband had kept a man for her but now he could no longer afford to do so. Her endurance was however fruitless, for the Committee of Kent simply nullified the Westminster order. Thereafter Dame Isabella's health took a long time to recover from the twin ordeal of childbirth and the journey. It was not until the end of May that she was well enough to return to London.

The fortunes of Sir Roger Twysden too mended slowly. In February 1646 he was allowed to leave his confinement for his London lodgings; in August 1647 he was further permitted to return to East Peckham, except that troops billeted there arrived the following week. In May 1649 Sir Roger was finally allowed to compound, at a rate of a tenth of his estate: and by this time 'a thousand oaks' had been felled. Dame Isabella reflected painfully in her diary how great her husband's sufferings had been; and all for that one 'Kentish' petition to Parliament before the outbreak of war. Even then their lives were not immune from brutal interruption: in April 1651 troopers burst into Roydon Hall at four o'clock in the morning. They took Sir Roger away, with his brother-in-law Sir Hugh Cholmley, to nearby Leeds Castle, in order to search 'as they said, for arms, and letters'. Dame Isabella commented: 'For no cause, I thank Christ.' Sir Roger Twysden was released, but Sir Hugh Cholmley, a more suspect figure, as the former Governor of Scarborough Castle and a returned exile, was kept shut up until June.

Dame Isabella gave birth to her last child, Charles, in 1655. The scene at her deathbed, two years later, is passionately described in his manuscript notebooks by Sir Roger. When the end was clearly near, she rallied briefly at three o'clock in the morning; although speechless she could still respond: 'When I kissed her which was the last I ever did whilst she lived, she gave me many kisses together so as I told her "here is the old Kisses still". She smiled as though she knew what she did use to do.' After her death Sir Roger kissed Dame Isabella again – one last time.[14]

In his notebooks Sir Roger praised his wife without stint – for her wisdom in her solicitations to the Committees: 'with what magnanimity she went through these miserable times', and for her courage later in facing death. A witness at Dame Isabella's deathbed was so impressed by this fortitude that she told her – a significant comment – 'she feared she was not a woman!' But Sir Roger was well aware of the cost to Dame Isabella of combining the two roles of wife and solicitor. For him she had submitted to the 'loathsomeness' of prisons; for him she had undertaken, heavily pregnant, 'great journeys in Kent', saying all the while she would endure more, 'much more for my sake'. 'She was the saver of my estate,' wrote Sir Roger, 'never man had a better wife, never children a better mother.'[15]

*   *   *

The pilgrimage of Mary Lady Verney to get the sequestration lifted from the estates of her husband, Sir Ralph, was arguably even more arduous than those of Dame Isabella since the Verney household had actually settled in France. Separation from her beloved spouse added a further distressing element to Mary Verney's story.

The marriage between the undergraduate Ralph Verney and the child heiress Mary Blacknall, described in the first chapter of this book (see p. 21 ff.), had proved one of remarkable happiness. As we have seen, Ralph had completed with 'the sweetness of a kiss' what had been begun under more mercenary auspices. Mary was Ralph's 'Budd', his 'Mischiefe' and he was 'her dearest Rogue'. Of course Mary – and Ralph's – life had contained its share of that endemic seventeenth-century sorrow, the death of a child. Mary's first child, a daughter, was born and died in 1632 when she was only sixteen; another daughter died at birth the following year; the year after was born Anna Maria, who died just before she was four. However their next three children all survived: Edmund, born in 1636, Pegg, born in 1638, and Jack, born in November 1640.

Ralph, who was knighted in 1640, sat in both Short and Long Parliaments as MP for Aylesbury. Unlike his father Sir Edmund, killed at Edgehill bearing the King's standard, he was not a passionate Royalist, but he was a devout Anglican. This was an unhappy combination of views for any

Member of the House of Commons to hold (we have seen the trouble it brought to Sir Roger Twysden) and in 1643 Sir Ralph Verney adopted that solution which Sir Roger Twysden had also sought – voluntary exile. By doing so, he certainly avoided taking the oath of the Covenant; but as an absent MP he also placed himself in that category of non-combatants whose estates were none the less liable to sequestration.

At Claydon remained Sir Ralph's pathetic unmarried sisters, together with the baby Jack, the 'saucy child', who was not yet three, so that Mary against her will was persuaded it would be safer to leave him; the real truth was that his aunts could not bear to let him go. To France went Mary, Ralph, seven-year-old Edmund and five-year-old Pegg. The ordinance for the sequestration of Claydon was duly dated 1644; Sir Ralph being named as a delinquent, and his tenants warned that rents in future should be handed over to the county Committee at Aylesbury. (Although it seems it was not totally carried through until September 1646.)[16]

It is the lot of the exile to be plagued by aggravating domestic detail, quite apart from the central fact of displacement, and the Verneys were no exception to this rule. They did have with them that bright maid from Claydon, Bess, who managed to learn French with ease, and a superior attendant, Mary's gentlewoman, Luce Sheppard; but in general French servants were violent and cheated them while 'no English maid will be content with our diet and way of living'. It was a question of good red meat. The Verneys had no money to keep up great state: 'Of late, I roast but one night in a week for suppers, which were strange in an English maid's opinion.' As a matter of fact, Luce and Bess, although loyalty kept them at Mary's side, did not care for her economical substitutes – un-English 'potages' and 'legumes' – either.[17]

Sir Ralph showed himself more accommodating by approving of French wine (although it is significant that when he had an opportunity to send for some 'dear old English sack' from Claydon, he did so). At least Mary could continue to make that good bread for which she was famous, and she had brought with her a portable oven for roasting apples. Meanwhile their friends at home took advantage of the Verneys' residence at the centre of things in one sense of the word, by sending for details of the latest Paris fashions. An English correspondent was to be found inquiring for some costly new-fangled aids to beauty: 'little brushes for making clean of the teeth, most covered with silver and some few with gold and silver twist', together with some little boxes to keep them in.[18]

The decision that Mary should return to England to get the sequestration lifted was, however painful for her husband, a natural one under the circumstances. Dr Denton, father and educator of Nancy, confirmed the increasing value of female solicitation in August 1646 in a blunt message to Sir Ralph: 'women were never so useful as now, and though you should be my agent and solicitor of all the men I know ... yet I am confident if you were here, you would do as our sages do, instruct your wife, and leave her to act it with committees'. He went on: 'Their sex entitles them to many privileges, and we find the comfort of them now more than ever.' Earlier in the same year another friend, Sir Roger Burgoyne, had given precise advice as to how Mary should behave if she did venture across the Channel. This was no place for emulating the staunch ways of the male sex. On the contrary: 'it would not do amiss if she [Mary] can bring her spirit to a soliciting temper and can tell how to use the juice of an onion sometimes to soften hard hearts'.[19]

To this Sir Ralph had replied at the time, 'I know it is not hard for a wife to dissemble, but there is like to be no need of that; for where necessities are so great the juice of an onion will be useless.' Certainly by the time Mary arrived in London, in late 1646, she scarcely needed an onion to provoke her tears. Everyone in the capital seemed cheerful, she told Ralph, 'yet I never had so sad a time in all my life'.[20] Bess stayed in France to look after Edmund and Pegg; Luce Sheppard accompanied Mary. The sea journey was delayed because of bad weather and high seas. When they arrived, Mary had to look for lodgings; for two rooms up two flights of stairs she was charged the exorbitant sum of 12s a week, fire, candles, washing and 'diet' were all extras. Mary was also pregnant (since her baby was born the following June, she must have known of her condition when she left France). Both maid and Mary fell ill.

Sir Ralph and Mary had arranged a code between them. This was the point at which their friend Eleanor Lady Sussex, newly married to that powerful Puritan grandee the Earl of Warwick and thus expected to play a crucially helpful role in the negotiations, was nicknamed 'Old Men's Wife' (see p. 85). The other code names were equally appropriate: sequestration was 'Chaine', the sequestrators 'Chainors', the Covenant was 'Phisick', money was 'Lead', and Newcastle was 'Coals'. Armed with this, Mary hoped to deal with the mountain of debts left behind by her father-in-law Sir Edmund Verney, and secure, like Dame Isabella Twysden, that vital certificate of sequestration from the Committee of the county in which Claydon lay – in this case Buckinghamshire. She then intended to petition the Committee of both Houses at Westminster 'after we have made all the friends that we possibly can', to get the sequestration lifted.[21]

If that failed, then there was nothing for it but the dreaded Goldsmiths' Hall. For all their praiseworthy endeavours, the experience of the Goldsmiths was much dreaded by the women petitioners (which made their courage that much the greater). The jaunty Royalist ballad quoted earlier referred to wives encountering there 'the devil and all'. We have Margaret Duchess of Newcastle's description of her own experience when she appeared on the arm of her brother (her husband being abroad) to plead for her due allowance; on receiving 'an absolute refusal' before she had even begun to speak, she whispered to her brother to take her out of such an 'ungentlemanly place' and left in silence.[22]

Thereafter Margaret was inclined to deride women who had done better, and expressed herself as indignant at reports that she had in fact pleaded before this and that committee. Women were chatterboxes – this was one of her favourite themes – and life at the Goldsmiths' Hall encouraged them in this regrettable tendency: 'if our sex would but well consider and rationally ponder, they will perceive and find that it is neither words nor place that can advance them but worth and merit'. But this was writing with hindsight ten years later, and perhaps with a little mortified pride. In fact a woman like Mary Verney by words – her own solicitation – and place – a London 'exile' far from her husband's side – stood to achieve a great deal more than by 'worth and merit' in France. Nevertheless she was human enough to dread the prospect of the Goldsmiths' Hall: 'where we must expect nothing but cruelty, and the paying of more Lead [money] than I fear we can possibly make'.[23]

Under the circumstances it was peculiarly distressing to find that 'Old Men's Wife', Eleanor Lady Warwick, was not prepared to exert that favourable influence with the new regime on which the Verneys had counted. 'I told her many times that it was friends which did all', Mary reported back to Ralph with indignation; and she proposed to sell the valuable watch which she had brought with her with the idea of rewarding Lady Warwick for her intervention. How differently the Verneys themselves had behaved to Eleanor, then Lady Sussex! They had even lent her the famous black Verney mourning bed with all its doleful trappings to mark one of her earlier widowhoods. This bed, used amongst others by Ralph's aunt Margaret Eure at the death of her husband William in battle, was accustomed to travel about England like an enormous raven, croaking its melancholy message. Now the new Lady Warwick, no longer having any such gloomy need, dispatched the raven back to its owners; but she made the Verneys pay for the carriage, which as Mary observed was 'not so handsomely done'. It is true that Lady Warwick subsequently explained to Mary that her life with her new husband was not quite the bed of roses that she had expected at her marriage: she lived in Lord Warwick's house 'like a stranger' and had to pay two thirds of her estate for her keep, receiving in return from her husband merely a diamond ring, no proper jointure. At the time, about the best thing which Lady Warwick did was to send round a pheasant and two bottles of wine when Mary and her maid were ill.[24]

The course of events for Mary Verney before the Committee of the two Houses in London followed the same dreary pattern of delay and frustration as it had for Isabella Twysden, and like Dame Isabella, Mary was tormented by a Committee in Buckinghamshire whom she described as 'very malicious and extremely insolent'.[25] 'The villains in the county might have given me a certificate if they had pleased', she told her husband, 'without putting me to this trouble.' When Mary visited Lady Warwick, her husband, the powerful Earl, sat 'like a clown' and said nothing. He did promise to turn up on Mary's behalf at the vital Committee but then failed to do so. It was not until April that Mary secured the all-important certificate giving the cause of the sequestration: 'it is for nothing but absence' she told Ralph – because Ralph Verney, as an MP, had vanished abroad.

By now Mary's pregnancy was far advanced; the prospect of childbirth alone in London further appalled her: 'to lie [in] without thee, is a greater affliction than I fear I shall be able to bear', she told Ralph. Already the Verneys had argued by post over the baby's name, Mary wanting Ralph if it was a boy, but Sir Ralph choosing Richard. They both agreed on Mary for a girl (the three little daughters who had died young or at birth when Mary was still in her teens had all been called some variant of Mary). Mary also had orders from Ralph to get a minister to the house to christen the baby as soon as possible in the old way; for this type of christening, together with godparents, had vanished under the new dispensation: the father was merely supposed to bring the child to the church 'and answer for it'. Mary complained: 'Truly one lives like a heathen here.' She found it impossible to find a decent service to attend in a London church.

On 3 June the child was born; it was a boy and Mary did call it Ralph. In France nine-year-old Pegg expressed herself dissatisfied because she had wanted a sister. But Ralph was thrilled to see Mary's own handwriting as a postscript to Dr Denton's letter breaking the news: 'I have borne you a lusty boy.' He fussed over her health: knowing that Mary being delivered would now try and get down to Claydon to sort out matters there, he begged her to go by coach, regardless of the cost; or if she insisted on going on horseback to save money, at least to lodge somewhere on the way. (Later when Mary visited 'Aunt Eure' in Leicestershire she reported the ordeal of 'a cruel trotting horse' because the coach was too expensive.) It was true that Mary was far from well: the 'lusty boy' was in fact quite weak, and Mary suffered from pains in the head.

Furthermore her journey to Claydon brought her small comfort, apart from the wonderful reunion with little Jack, whom she had not seen for four years. He trotted round after her as she made the inventories, enchanting her with his funny sayings and little songs: 'he is a very ready witted child and is very good company', she told Ralph, 'he is always with me from the first hour that I came'. Alas, Jack was also suffering from crooked legs due to rickets: a fate of many seventeenth-century children, however grand the nursery, including King Charles I. Jack also stammered and had been totally spoilt by his aunts. 'He would very fain go into France with his father', Mary told Ralph, and this time Mary was determined to take him with her.

Claydon itself was however in a disastrous state: the linen worn out, the feather-beds eaten by rats and the fire-irons corroded by rust. The soldiers quartered there had committed a series of crimes liable to grieve the heart of a careful housewife, such as ruining the cloth on the musk-coloured stools. Far worse than any of this was the death of baby Ralph from convulsions. Mary was delirious with sorrow for two days and two nights. It was fortunate that she did not then know that her daughter Pegg had died too about the same time in France; it was when the news finally reached her that Mary turned away in agony from those two other little girls, Peg and Mall, the children of 'Aunt Eure' and for the time being could not bring herself to care for them.

It was not until January 1648 that the Committee of both Houses at Westminster lifted the sequestration – and it seems that the Warwicks did in the end play some kind of helpful role. 'My dearest Rogue, it joys my heart to think how soon I shall be with thee', Mary wrote to Ralph in March, and she hoped to bring Jack safely to him. They were finally reunited in April.

The tenderness – and the teasing – of their married life was resumed. When Sir Pickering Newton, taking his wife abroad, asked Mary's advice as 'an old housekeeper in France' Sir Ralph reported that his wife was cross. 'Had you called her an old woman, she would never have forgiven you such an injury. You know a woman can never be old (at least not willingly, nor in her own opinion); did you dread her displeasure but half so much as I do, believe me you would run post hither to make your peace.'[26]

But Mary never did live to be old, neither in her own opinion nor in anyone else's.

She died at the age of thirty-four. The cause was consumption; but her condition must have been aggravated by her sufferings during that eighteen-month period of privation and worry in London. Sir Ralph's own calendar of his letters to Dr Denton in London (a list, combined with extracts, giving both Continental and English dating) relates the progress of his anguish:

15/5 May 1650. I write Dr [Denton] word I received his letter, but could write of no business, Wife being so ill.

22/12 May 1650. Oh my . . . my deare dear.

29/19 May 1650. Friday the 20/10 May (at three in the morning) Was the Fatal day and hour. The disease a consumption . . . I shall not need to relate with what a Religious and cheerful joy and courage this now happy and most glorious saint, left this unhappy and most wicked world. . . . I entreat you presently to pay one Mr Preswell (a silk man in Paternoster Row) about forty shillings, which he said she owed for something taken up there, though she could never call it to her remembrance.[27]

Mary's body was taken in its coffin for burial in England. Sir Ralph wrote: 'every puff of wind that tosses it at sea shakes me at land'. 'Ah Doctor, Doctor,' he wrote, 'her company made every place a paradise unto me.'

Later Sir Ralph wondered what sins he could have committed to deserve such punishments: the loss of two out of his three eldest children, his brother, his father and mother, and now his wife 'who was not only willing to suffer for and with me here, but by her most exemplary goodness and patience both helped and taught me to support my otherwise almost insupportable Burden. But, alas,' he concluded, 'what shall I now do!'[28]

What Sir Ralph Verney did not do was marry again. Luce Sheppard and Bess cared for the children. Unusually for his time – and responsibilities – Sir Ralph remained for the rest of his long life a widower. He died in 1696, nearly half a century after Mary, still faithful to the memory of his 'dear, discreet and most incomparable wife'. As with others who have tasted the matchless joy of a happy union, Sir Ralph worried over Christ's words of the New Testament concerning a marriageless Heaven. In the end he worked out his own form of faith: 'And although . . . in the Resurrection none marry nor are given in Marriage, yet I hope (without being censured for curiosity) I may piously believe, that we who ever from our very childhoods lived in so much peace, and christian concord here on Earth, shall also in our Elder years for the full completing of our Joys, at least be known to one another in Heaven.'[29]

It was this thought which comforted him during those terrible moments when he was 'almost swallowed up' by sorrow.

12 Sharing in the Commonwealth

> 'Since we are assured of our creation in the image of God, and of
> an interest in Christ equal unto men, as also of a proportionate
> share in the freedom of this Commonwealth. . . .'
>
> PREAMBLE, *The Petition of Women*, APRIL 1649

During the Civil Wars and after, it was axiomatic that women were
enjoying a new kind of freedom and strength, just as it was conventional
in many quarters to deplore the fact. On the one hand biblical women
who had assumed some kind of active role, such as Esther, Deborah and
Jael, became popular images of liberty, without such images being attached
to any precise notion of rights. On the other hand the idea of a Parliament
composed of ladies was generally mocked: in January 1642 some 400
women presented a petition to the House of Lords on the subject of the
decay of trade and their general distress:

'Away with these women,' cried the Duke of Lennox, adding sarcastically, 'We were best to have a Parliament of women.'[1]

This notion also provided a convenient metaphor for satirists to use to
attack other targets. The republican politician and pamphleteer Henry
Neville wrote two pamphlets in 1647, *The Ladies Parliament* and *The Ladies,
a Second Time, Assembled*, and another in 1650, *The Commonwealth of
Ladies*, aimed at the *louche* morals of the Cavalier aristocrats in a series of
double entendres in which the inherently absurd notion of such an assembly
was taken for granted – as well as woman's natural venality.[2]

The 'Rattel-head Ladies' were stated to have assembled at 'Kattes' in
Covent Garden – the notorious Oxford Kate's, a hostelry already half-way
to being a bawdy-house. The beautiful and dissolute Lady Isabella Thynne
resolved 'That no Roundhead dare to come into any of their Quarters.'
Ladies Montagu and Craven were thanked for favours to Cavaliers beyond
the seas. A complaint was officially registered against Sir Henry Blunt,
who was said to prefer the favours of common women to those of 'Ladies
of Honour'; other members of the Parliament discussed 'the common

enemy', their husbands. And in attendance, to help with the ladies' 'pressing affairs', were Doctors Hinton and Chamberlen – who were in fact fashionable obstetricians.

The Commonwealth of Ladies began: 'There was a time in England, when men wore the breeches ... which brought many grievances and oppressions upon the weaker vessels; for they were constrained to converse only with their homes and closets, and now and then with the Gentleman-usher, or the Footman (when they could catch him) for variety. ...' Now they have 'voted themselves the Supreme Authority both at home and abroad'. Lubricious details of their use of this new freedom followed.

Nor was this kind of gibing limited to Cavalier targets. The wives of the Army leaders were regularly and gleefully subjected to the scurrilous charge that they had 'usurped the general's baton' – as it was said of Sir William Waller's first wife, who was accused of being 'ambitious of the popular favour' and 'predominant' over her husband. Later Mrs Venables, wife of the commander of the disastrous West Indian expedition, would be arraigned in very similar language as one who had caused her husband to 'lower his topsail to a petticoat'.[3] Not much could be made along these lines of Oliver Cromwell's wife, a homebody if ever there was one (sneers at the economical housekeeping of 'Protectress Joan', as she was nicknamed, came closer to their target). But Fairfax's spirited wife Anne, daughter of Lord Vere of Tilbury, was regularly known to pamphleteers as 'Queen Fairfax' (as Elizabeth Lilburne was known as 'Queen Besse'). It was suggested that his wife's unfeminine ambition was causing Sir Thomas Fairfax to aim at the throne. 'Tell me not of gowns or lace nor such toys!', Queen Fairfax was supposed to have exclaimed to 'Madam Cromwell' in 1647, 'Tell me of crowns, sceptres, kingdoms, royal robes; and if my Tom but recovers and thrives in his enterprise I shall not say pish to be Queen of England.' When Fairfax later withdrew from the trial of the King, and in effect from the Parliamentary cause, it was once again conjectured – with more plausibility – that his wife had influenced him.[4]

Some of this freedom was genuine enough, even if it had only developed through the breakdown of traditional social organization either during or after the war. A member of the older generation like Clarendon deplored the fact that 'the young women' at this date 'conversed without circumspection or modesty'; that, perhaps, was only to be expected. Yet lack of chaperonage and in many cases lack of parents or at least fathers had led to the breeding of a rootless and thus independent generation. The Eure girls Peg and Mall, daughters of Ralph Verney's 'Aunt Eure' (whose father had been killed in 1644) dealt very saucily with efforts to marry them off in the

1650s. Peg broke off one alliance and announced that she would marry no one with living parents who might order her about! Her forthright words on the subject would surely have made Sir Edmund Verney turn in his grave: 'Sir, I am to lead my life with them [her possible in-laws] ... and know so well my own temper that I fear I shall never be happy with them.' She added that if dragged to the church, she would say no to her bridegroom at the altar. As for Mall, she turned down her cousin, Sir Ralph's son and heir Edmund, on the extraordinary grounds that she found him personally repulsive; although 'Mun' professed himself madly in love with her.[5]

This was the kind of behaviour to which Margaret Duchess of Newcastle drew attention in 1650 when she discussed women 'affecting a Masculinacy ... practising the behaviour (but not the spirits) of men'. Margaret Newcastle did not hesitate to ascribe this new confidence and boldness, or even impudence, as women began 'to Swagger, to Swear, to Game, to Drink, to Revell, to make Factions' to the evil effects of the recent conflict. Civil wars were, she wrote, 'the greatest storms that shipwrack honest Education', and especially for women, that are 'Self-admirers'.[6]

Unfortunately this new liberty enjoyed by women in the Civil War and Commonwealth period was frequently associated with two phenomena dreaded by sober citizens of whatever politics. The first of these was sexual licence. Certain extreme religious sects were accused of preaching sexual licence although such scandals were often the product more of rumour and prurient imagination than of knowledge. One hundred members of the Family of Love (a sect founded in Münster in the sixteenth century) were said to be living in Bagshot, in a broadsheet of 1641; the feast of Priapus being celebrated among their calendar of saints. The Familists *did* have their marriages arranged for them by elders, hence rumours spread that they practised sexual communism. And because the Anabaptists practised 'dipping' as a form of baptism, and sometimes 'dipped' at night, they were accused of public nudity and thus immorality.[7]

Not all the accusations were the product of misunderstanding or ill will. Some of the women among those sectaries known as the Ranters were unbalanced and hysterical. James Naylor was not a Ranter – he condemned them – but an extreme form of early Quaker who was at one point tried for blasphemy. Some of the women surrounding him were very wild in their behaviour, such as a couple known merely as Mildred and Judy, or Martha Simmonds, in whom 'an exceedingly filthy spirit ... got up; more filthy than any yet departed ...'. None of this was reassuring to those who feared excess in women in the first place.[8]

Ironically enough the few instances where free love was publicly advocated benefited in practice the male rather than the female. A Wiltshire rector named Thomas Webbe believed that he had rights to all women: 'there is no heaven but women, nor no hell save marriage' was the motto. Abiezar Coppe, a scholar of Oxford University, claimed that property was theft and pride worse than adultery: 'I can kiss and hug ladies and love my neighbour's wife as myself without sin.' One Laurence Clarkson preached that to the pure all things were pure, moving from place to place lying with 'maids' until he founded a little group in London called 'My One Flesh', a co-operative of willing maids; Clarkson justified himself by the example of Solomon. After returning to his wife in the country, Clarkson proceeded to travel England with another woman, a Mrs Star, until arrested by the Privy Council in 1650 for preaching the doctrine of free love.[9] Yet by seventeenth-century standards such incidents were as much to the discredit of the female sex as to that of the male, if not more so.

The second dreaded phenomenon was that of the 'Amazonian' all-female mob. This fear was not totally without reasonable basis: hopeful praise of female modesty and gentleness notwithstanding, such a force had a long history. To go back no further than the beginning of the century, women had led a successful revolt in 1603 at Market Deeping in Lincolnshire, against the draining of Deeping Fen, which threatened their own livelihoods. About 200 women had emerged from Langton and Baston 'and did cast down a great deal of the captain's ditch on the north side of the fen, threatening further to burn his houses, drown his servants, and if they had himself, to cut off his head and set it upon a stake'. It was only the intervention of 'a gentlewoman' who happened to be passing which dissuaded the women from their violent course, otherwise they would have done the captain, Thomas Lovell, 'some great mischief'. Thirty-four years later the women of the Fens had lost none of their vigour in defence of the lands on which their cattle grazed, when threatened with enclosure, and were among those who resisted the work of the 'overseers' at Holme Fen with scythes and pitchforks. Again in 1641, the crowd which broke into an enclosed fen at Buckden consisted mainly of women aided by boys.[10]

In Wiltshire in the 1630s the enclosure of Braydon Forest was resisted with what the Privy Council described as 'riotous insolencies ... committed in the night season by persons unknown, armed with Muskets'; when the principal actors were arrested, women's names featured as well as men's. At York in May 1642, women destroyed an enclosure and went to prison for their pains; like the she-soldiers, these particular viragos enjoyed tobacco and ale 'to make themselves merry when they had done their feats of activity'. Nor did the capital lack its own viragos: after the flight of the five members of Parliament in January 1642, King Charles I unwisely came to the City of London, hoping to secure their arrest at the instigation of the Lord Mayor. He failed (the members were not there) but after his departure certain citizens' wives fell on the Lord Mayor, pulled his chain from his neck, and at one point looked like pulling him and the Recorder of the City of London to pieces.[11]

A tract, *The Women's Sharpe Revenge*, which appeared in 1640, under the pseudonymous authorship of 'Mary Tattle-well and Joane Hit-him-home, Spinsters', was probably the work of middle-class women – trades-women for example. Here grievances were aired, many about education, which have a familiar sound to modern ears: if women were taught singing and dancing it was 'the better to please and content their [men's] licentious appetites'. Daughters in general were 'set only to Needle, to prick our fingers: or else to the Wheel to spin a fair thread for our undoings'. It was the policy of all parents in any case to subdue their daughters 'and to make us men's mere vassals, even unto all posterity'. Marriage was the be-all and end-all of the female existence: 'What poor woman is ever taught that she should have a higher Design than to get her a Husband?' At the same time it was claimed that the female character was infinitely preferable to that of the male, being for example far more chaste – the Virgin Mary, not Grandmother Eve, was cited here.[12]

When war broke out, however, these outwardly genteel preoccupations were swallowed up in the general disturbance. Those primitive cries of female protest which did make themselves heard tended to be on the basic subjects of food, money – and peace. All this had a raucous sound to frightened ears of both sexes (it was not only the men who shrank back in disgust or terror or both from the image of the Amazon). Certain groups of strong women who had long enjoyed the protection and even the encouragement of society now appeared to assume a more menacing aspect in these troubled times.

Of these the fishwives of Billingsgate market provided a striking – and strident example. Women had been connected with the sale of fish in London as far back as medieval times, if not further, since an act of Edward III allowed the 'continuance' of itinerant fish-women called 'billesteres' (the poor who sold their fish in the street, first crying up their wares).[13] These women were not however permitted to keep stalls 'nor make a stay in the streets'; they were also enjoined to buy their fish from free fishmongers. A similar liberty was granted to a category described as including both 'Persons and women' who came from 'the uplands' with fish, 'caught by them or their servants, in the waters of the Thames or other running streams'.

In the later years of the seventeenth century, the fishwives' trade became depressed in the face of the activities of salesmen who cut out these middlewomen and sold Thames fish directly on commission. To try and remedy this, in 1699 the Government ordered that Billingsgate be kept as an open market daily, and 'not permitting the fisherwomen and others to buy the said fish of the said fishermen, so that the fishermen were obliged to sell their fish to the fishmongers at exorbitant rates' was explicitly condemned.

However, in the early part of the century the fishwives flourished. In 1632 Donald Lupton gave a jovial picture of them in his *Characters of London*:[14] 'these crying, wandering and travelling creatures carry their shops on their heads', he wrote, their storehouse being Billingsgate or the foot of London Bridge and their habitation Turnagain Lane. As well as sorts of fish, their tiny shops – 'some two yards compass' – would hold 'herbs or roots, strawberries, apples or plums, cucumbers and such like' and sometimes even nuts, oranges and lemons.

Going on their rounds, they would first of all set up 'a good cry', hoping to sell the contents of their basket for 5s; 'they are merriest when all their ware is gone', he reported. Then they would 'meet in mirth, singing, dancing, and the middle as a Parenthesis, they use scolding'. If a particular fishwife was missing of an evening in a drinking house, it was suspected that she had had a bad return, or paid off some old debts, or gone bankrupt. If anyone 'drank out' their whole stock, the remedy was simple: 'it's but pawning a petticoat in Long Lane or themselves in Turnbull Street to set up again'. In short the fishwives were 'creatures soon up and soon down'.

Lupton's reference to the fishwives' 'scolding' in the midst of all their merry singing and dancing was significant. The fishwives' language was notorious. By the Restoration, the term 'fishwife' had become synonymous with one who swore (as 'Billingsgate' was already used to denote foul language); in the early eighteenth century 'a Billingsgate' was defined as 'a scolding, impudent slut', Addison making a whimsical reference to 'debates which frequently arise among ladies of British fishery'. During the Civil War period, James Strong, author of *Joanereidos*, stressed this aspect of their charms, saluting:

> ... ye warlike bands
> That march towards Billingsgate with eager hands,
> And tongues more loud than bellowing Drums, to scale
> Oyster or Herring ships, when they strike sail....

Those not sharing Strong's admiration for women who had 'stronger grown' were on the contrary much alarmed by the appearance of the stalwart and loud-mouthed fishwives among the women who petitioned the House of Commons. As Samuel Butler wrote in *Hudibras*:

> The oyster women had locked their fish up,
> And trudged away to cry 'No bishop'.[15]

The fact that the women's tongues probably were louder than 'bellowing Drums' did not add to the cogency of their case; on the contrary it confirmed that disgust for and fear of a scolding woman mentioned in connection with witches, and associated at a primitive level in society's consciousness with female activists.

The great women's peace petition of August 1643 – Parliament having recently rejected proposals which many had hoped would lead to the end of the war – was variously described.[16] The women arrived wearing white silk ribbons in their hats 'to cry for Peace, which was to the women a pleasing thing'. Numbers as large as 6,000 were mentioned although one contemporary report spoke more plausibly of 200 or 300 'oyster wives', who with other 'dirty and tattered sluts' arrived at the House of Commons and threatened to use violence to those there 'as were Enemies to Peace'. Another report referred to 'Whores, Bawds, Oyster-women, Kitchen-stuffe women, Beggar women and the very scum of the scum of the Suburbs, besides abundance of Irish women' (here were a number of prejudices neatly combined). Other reports spoke more simply of citizens' wives with their babies at the breast. Ironically enough, this was the peace-seeking mob – 'divers women killed by the soldiers in this tumult, yet unappeased' – which the Royalist Sir John Scudamore mentioned approvingly to Brilliana Lady Harley as an implied reproach to her unfeminine conduct in prolonging the siege of Brampton Bryan Castle (see p. 178). In London their violence had appalled both Houses of Parliament.

First of all the women forced their way into the yard at Westminster, beating the sentinels about and yelling at each dignitary who passed on his way to the House of Lords: 'We will have Peace presently, and our King'. Other women bewailed the loss of their husbands slain in the war. Sir Simonds D'Ewes, he who had, as we shall see, put an effective end to the voting of the women freeholders in Suffolk, displayed some cunning by declaring himself all for peace. In this manner he was able to pass through the mob easily, even receiving some 'benedictions'. Others were less wily and thus less fortunate. Violence continued to be shown; ministers and soldiers, especially those with short hair (still at this date considered a mark of a Roundhead), had it pulled. The women's especial venom was reserved for those MPs such as Pym who had received them favourably over earlier petitions in 1642, and promised them that their distress would be alleviated.

By the afternoon, despite the efforts of a trained band, the women had blockaded the House for two hours. When the militia men shot powder at them the women howled scornfully that it was 'nothing but powder' and hurled brickbats in reply. Another howl went up to produce 'the Traitors that are against peace, that we may tear them in pieces. Give up Pym in the first place', cried the women. A troop of soldiers was ordered up but the women simply tore their colours out of their hats and assaulted them in turn. Provoked, the soldiers began to use the flat of their swords: one woman was said to have been killed and another lost her nose. At last someone – it was not clear who – sent for a troop of horse, Waller's Horse, known derisively as 'Waller's Dogs', who cudgelled the petitioners with their canes. The women fled but before they could escape the pursuing horse further casualties were suffered, estimates of which varied from one or two to 100; and there were injured women as well.

Many of the women were sent to Bridewell, including 'a most deformed Medusa or Hecuba, with an old rusty blade by her side', whose hands had to be tied behind her back with 'Match' (the long fuse used for lighting the soldiers' muskets).

There were persistent rumours that this outburst, and other similar outbursts by women, were not in fact genuine if over-violent expressions of the misery caused by the war, but something far more menacing: highly organized demonstrations on behalf of the other side – in this case the Royalists. It was suggested that the Royalist Earl of Holland had egged on the campaign and even provided the white silk for the favours. As a rider to this, it was often suggested that any particularly virulent body of protesting women had contained men within its ranks, dressed up as women; Jenny Geddes, for example, the Scotswoman who hurled her stool at the preacher in St Giles' Cathedral in 1637, was alleged to have been an apprentice in disguise.[17]

It was of course impossible to disprove these propagandist allegations afterwards – which is why they were so effective. The mere possibility that a female mob might constitute an instrument to be wielded by the enemy, and even include the enemy itself concealed within, made yet more sinister a spectacle already disquieting enough to the male eye. It was not considered relevant that most of those women decked in white silk favours were probably sincere when they raised their voices and cried for peace – sweet peace 'which is to women a pleasing thing'. For if peace was pleasing to women (and to many men also) the sound of women's voices raised in tumult calling for it was not.

Woodcuts of the time show plenty of women present in the crowd of spectators which watched the execution of King Charles I on 30 January 1649, anticipating the *tricoteuses* of the French Revolution by 150 years. This was the type of 'Virago' from whom her contemporaries shrank back.

*   *   *

Hindsight – but only hindsight – has shown the importance of female suffrage in the elevation of women's condition; this importance was certainly not appreciated in the seventeenth century.

On 'an extreme windy day' in October 1640 the Parliamentary elections for the borough of Eye in Suffolk were being held according to the contemporary custom, in public – in 'Mr Hambies's field'. Some women, widows, arrived, to be 'sworn', as it happened on behalf of the two Presbyterian candidates, Sir Philip Parker and his uncle Sir Nathaniel Barnardiston. When the two knights were duly elected there were accusations of cheating from their opponents, amongst which was registered the fact that women had been allowed to be 'sworn'. At which point everyone, not least the knights concerned, made haste to point out that the women had not got very far in their endeavour, owing to the prompt conduct of the High Sheriff of Suffolk, Sir Simonds D'Ewes.

At first, it is true, the women did have their votes taken owing to the ignorance of the clerks concerned, but when D'Ewes heard what was going on, 'Mr Sheriff would have us take no women's oaths'. Both the knights requested the women's votes to be removed from the total, and when the High Sheriff 'cast up the Books, he cast out the women of the general sum'. Sir Simonds D'Ewes was quite clear in his own mind as to the reason for his behaviour: 'conceiving it a matter very unworthy of any gentleman, and most dishonourable in such an election, to make use of their [women's] voices, although they might in law have been allowed'.[18]

It was significant that the women in Hambies's field in 1640 were widows; once again, the widow, by her very status outside conventional male authority, occupied a position of potential strength. This was in any case a time of franchisal doubt concerning who could or could not vote (in those elections which were disputed and where public voting actually took place; undisputed nominations to Parliament were arranged behind the scenes).[19] It is important to realize therefore that these widows were not acting as agitators but freeholders.

It was the association of the vote with material wealth – the 'permanent fixed interest' in the country – which had enabled some women freeholders in the past to use their 'voice' in Parliamentary elections. It was in this sense that Sir Simonds D'Ewes at Eye admitted with some disgust that the Suffolk women's 'voices' might 'in law' have been allowed. In the remote medieval past, those Catholic abbesses who were early patterns of powerful womanhood had named representatives. Under Elizabeth there had been two cases of borough-owners, who happened to be women, returning Members of Parliament. More recently, in the reign of James I, a judge pronounced in the case of Coates v. Lyle that a 'feme sole', if a freeholder, could vote; in the cases of Catherine v. Surrey and Holt v. Lyle, the same judgment was given, although it was added that on marriage the right passed to the lady's husband. In 1628 Sir Henry Slingsby endeavoured – but in vain – to use the votes of widowed burgage holders in Knaresborough in Yorkshire.[20]

For all this, the little episode at Eye was not the harbinger of numerous occasions at which female freeholders attempted to be sworn; despite the fact that the Members elected were Presbyterians and that the Parliament concerned was that famous innovatory body which would be known as the Long Parliament. The incident in Mr Hambies's field on a windy day in 1640 was not a prologue but an epilogue to the subject of female suffrage. In 1644 the *Institutes* of Sir Edward Coke were published without challenge, in which it was laid down that 'Multitudes are bound by Acts of Parliament which are not parties to [the] election'. In this silent subject herd were to be included males under twenty-one, 'all they that have no freehold . . . and all women having freehold or no freehold'.[21]

It was true that at another Yorkshire election, that of Richmond in 1678, widows were explicitly disallowed in advance – 'it being against common right' – although they could assign their votes to others; but this was less an indication of potential female rights than of the vague nature of the English electoral roll at the time.[22] It was more significant that throughout a period of unparalleled radicalism – and radical debate – in English history, when so many revolutionary political ideas were discussed that to contemporaries it must have seemed that Pandora's Box had been opened, the serious question of giving a vote to Pandora herself was never even mooted.

At the Army's Putney debates in the autumn of 1647, the Levellers

among their number put forward startling demands for the extension of
the suffrage in their document *The Agreement of the People*, based on the
premise that the consent of the governed was needed for government: a
man could rule over other individuals 'no further than by free consent, or
agreement, by giving up their power to each other, for their better being'.
The Army's high command, including Oliver Cromwell and Henry Ireton, found this whole concept of a franchise based on rights rather than
property both dangerous and appalling. But this was *manhood* suffrage
which was being discussed, and those Levellers who did raise the question ·
of universal suffrage at Putney, envisaged it in terms of adult males.
Disconcerting as it may be to the modern inquirer, even male 'servants'
were to be excluded from the new franchise of the Levellers if they were
not householders, since roughly speaking household franchise was what
was required. It was not even thought worth mentioning that women,
whose legal rights were so obviously swallowed up in those of their
husbands, were excluded.[23]

Henry Ireton's answer came down firmly on the side of that freehold
qualification for voting which had been the founding notion of Parliament
since its earliest days in the time of Edward I (and was incidentally to
remain so for the next two centuries). No one had a right to choose those
'that shall determine what laws we shall be ruled by here', he declared,
who did not have 'a permanent fixed interest in this Kingdom', by which
Ireton meant the possession of freehold property, or some other form of
freehold such as an office or benefice (a fellowship at an Oxford or
Cambridge college entitled the holder to vote at county elections).

In the late 1640s even the extreme opinions of the Levellers did not lead
them to challenge the concept of a woman's legal subordination to her
husband. One scholar has written that no plea for female franchise was put
forward in the Civil War period so far as he can discover.[24] Towards the
end of the century, Locke omitted women from natural equality, and
James Tyrrell, one of Locke's associates, observed: 'There never was any
government where all the promiscuous rabble of women and children had
votes, as not being capable of it, yet it does not for all that prove that all
legal civil government does not owe its origin to the consent of the people.'
It was a contrast on which Mary Astell, the educationalist, would reflect
bitterly at the beginning of the next century: 'how much soever Arbitrary
Power may be dislik'd on a Throne, not Milton ... nor any of the
Advocates of Resistance, would cry up Liberty to poor Female Slaves or
plead for the lawfulness of Resisting a Private Tyranny'.[25]

The very few possible exceptions to this rule only serve to emphasize the monolithic nature of male supremacy at the time, at least in the political sphere, for none of them bore fruit. The short-lived Diggers' movement, whose members, extreme radicals, believed that land should be held in common, did result in some revolutionary suggestions on the subject of marriage from its leader Gerrard Winstanley. Article 56 of Winstanley's 'Laws for a Free Commonwealth' proposed that: 'Every man and woman shall have the free liberty to marry whom they love, if they can obtain the love and liking of that party whom they would marry, and neither birth nor portion' should hinder the match. The reason given was: 'for we are all of one blood, mankind, and for portion, the Common Storehouses are every man and maid's portion, as free to one as to another'.[26] Here was indeed a revolutionary suggestion; as we have seen, the disposal of the young in marriage for reasons other than affection was a cornerstone of society, without which the building could be expected in the minds of contemporaries to collapse. Marriage itself, in the same free style, was to take the form of a simple verbal declaration in front of witnesses.

Further Digger clauses on the subject of rape and the begetting of illegitimate children by men were even more startling. If a man lay with a woman forcibly and she cried out (as testified by two witnesses) he was to be put to death while the woman went free: 'it is robbery of a woman's bodily freedom'. If a man lay with a maid and she conceived, he was to marry her.

With the extinction of the Diggers' movement vanished Winstanley's revolutionary notions on marriage. Their effect on society as a whole had in any case been insubstantial; except to link radicalism still further with the upsetting of the natural order as regards the family. It was significant that the governmental – Puritan – legislation concerning sexual relationships between man and woman was of a very different order. The harsh new Act of 1650 made adultery a capital crime; however, the man could escape execution by pleading that he did not know the woman was married (a convenient loophole). The woman on the other hand could in theory only avoid execution if her husband had been absent more than three years. It seems that only one woman, Ursula Powell, brought before the Middlesex Quarter Sessions, was actually put to death under the law (and there is even some doubt about her fate); this was because juries refused to convict, or dealt out lesser penalties of imprisonment or whipping.[27] Nevertheless the principle of the greater guilt of the female was explicitly stated, in marked contrast to Winstanley's vision of justice.

In 1646, the year before the Putney debates, in *The Freemans Freedome Vindicated*, John Lilburne, the Leveller leader and theoretician, did at least

include women in his doctrine of consent. He wrote that of 'every particular individual man and woman ... by nature all equal and alike in
power, dignity, authority, and majesty' none had by nature any authority
over any except by 'donation, that is to say, by mutual agreement or
consent'. It has been proposed by one of his biographers that inclusion of
women in the franchise was at least 'consonant with Lilburne's actions';[28]
nevertheless he did not in fact postulate such an inclusion.

The early history of the Levellers was however marked by the courage
of their 'lusty lasses', as *Mercurius Pragmaticus* described them. Not all of
these lasses were as young as such a cheerful description implied. Katherine
Hadley was an old spinster who tended John Lilburne in the Fleet prison
in 1639, where he had been incarcerated the previous year for printing and
circulating unlicensed books, having been first fined, whipped and pilloried. She was subsequently accused of distributing Lilburne's pamphlet *A
Cry for Justice* at the Whitsun holiday to some apprentices, and another
Lilburnian appeal to both apprentices and clothworkers. Arrested without
a warrant, she was consigned by the Lord Mayor of London to the Poultry
Compter prison in the City, where she withstood seven months of harsh
conditions. When she petitioned for liberty, Katherine Hadley was transferred to Bridewell on 1 October – still without trial or even examination.
Here, to her chagrin and suffering, she was placed, as she put it, among 'the
common sluts, whose society is a hell upon earth to me, that fears the
Lord'. She was not set free until December 1640, in that newly liberal
climate which also led to the release of Burton and Bastwick. Thanks to
Lilburne, Katherine Hadley received £10 in compensation for what she
had endured.[29]

Mary Overton, the wife of the pamphleteer Richard Overton, who
under the name of Martin Marpriest attacked the Westminster Assembly
of Divines mercilessly, was another woman who suffered for a principle
with fortitude. At the time of the Long Parliament, Overton published
attacks on the position of the bishops anonymously; later he moved on to
theological matters and it was when he described, still anonymously, the
doctrine of immortality – 'the present going of the soul into heaven or
hell' – as 'a fiction' that his work incurred the displeasure of the House of
Commons, who ordered the licensing committee to inquire into its author,
printer and publisher. In August 1646 Overton was arrested for printing
some of John Lilburne's pamphlets and taken to Newgate.

Mary Overton's petition for her husband's release would later refer with
indignation to the fact that he had 'constantly adhered to the Parliament'.
She described his incarceration in Newgate as 'the high violation of the

fundamental Laws of this Land, the utter subversion of the Common Liberties of the people and of your Petitioner's husband's native Right and Inheritance in particular', quoting a list of protests starting with that of Magna Carta and going right forward to the Petition of Right in 1628.

She also described the traumatic moment of the arrest (she was sick in bed, having recently given birth), when the officers of the law broke open and ransacked their house, followed by another visit at which the officers were sent again 'to enter, search, ransack and rifle your Petitioner's house, her trunks, chests, etc. to rob, steal, plunder and bear away her goods, which were her then present livelihood for her imprisoned husband, her self, and three small children, her brother and sister'.[30]

In January 1647 Mary Overton herself was arrested, together with her brother Thomas Johnson, when they were discovered stitching the sheets of a seditious pamphlet written by her husband with the assistance of Lilburne, *Regal Tyranny Discovered*.[31] She was taken before the Bar of the House of Lords, but here she stalwartly refused to answer any questions or to take any oath against herself or her husband. At which point she was herself committed to prison. What was more she was literally dragged there 'on two cudgels ... headlong upon the stones through all the dirt and mire of the streets' with her six-month-old baby in her arms, and incidentally once more pregnant. As if this was not enough, the officers of the law abused her all the way, 'with the scandalous, infamous names of wicked Whore, Strumpet etc'. Finally she was thrown into the 'most reproachful gaol' of Bridewell, that 'hell upon earth' to decent women as Katherine Hadley had described it, where of course Mary Overton joined the company of all the genuine whores and strumpets (and lost the child she was carrying).

In Mary Overton's petition to the House of Commons of late March, she begged for a speedy sentence. If wrong had been done, then she was prepared to face execution; if not she should be granted her freedom; but arbitrary imprisonment at the orders of the House of Lords was utterly intolerable. Despite these cogent arguments, she was not released until July. And Richard Overton, issuing a number of broadsheets against his arbitrary imprisonment, continued to be associated both in and out of gaol with the Levellers.

*   *   *

Of all the Levellers' wives, Elizabeth Lilburne, born Elizabeth Dewell, excites at once the most sympathy for her sufferings and the most admiration for her endurance; these feelings being not unmixed with pity for the fate of anyone married to John Lilburne. (In general the story of Elizabeth Lilburne recalls that definition of a saint as one that is married to a martyr.) The kind of freedom which Elizabeth Lilburne shared with her husband was short-lived if it existed at all; the best tribute to her character being those words of Lilburne's in 1646 from *The Freemans Freedome Vindicated*, quoted earlier, in which man and woman were declared equal alike in dignity and authority; these sentiments – so much in advance of Lilburne's time – it must be plausible to ascribe to her husband's intimate knowledge of one splendid woman. His later treatment of her is not so edifying.

John Lilburne was about twenty-four when in 1638 he was sentenced by the Star Chamber. It has been suggested that Elizabeth Dewell, like Katherine Hadley, may have been among the women who visited him after his whipping. She certainly comforted him in the Fleet prison. Lilburne was released at the beginning of the Long Parliament and took to brewing. After his marriage, Lilburne described Elizabeth as 'an object dear in my affections several years before from me she knew anything of it'. At least these early days must have been a sweet period, for John could write later: 'I confess I partly know it by experience that divers months after marriage are most commonly a time of dotage.'[32]

At the beginning of the Civil War, Lilburne joined the Parliamentary Army and fought at Edgehill; Elizabeth was probably present too, quartered with the other women at Kineton, along with those baggage trains which the dreaded 'Prince Robber' Rupert plundered. John Lilburne was subsequently captured at Brentford, and having been tried for high treason for bearing arms against the King, was shut up in Oxford Castle in danger of execution. From there he smuggled out a letter to his wife; whereupon she, although pregnant, set out for the Royalist headquarters, which she reached after 'so many sad and difficult accidents to a woman in her condition, as would force tears from the hardest heart'. Lilburne's liberty was secured by exchange: he wrote later that by her 'wisdom, patience, diligence' Elizabeth had saved his life.[33]

On his release Lilburne's thirst for agitation proved to be in no way quenched by his ordeal. Elizabeth had secured him a government position at £1,000 a year; to her 'extraordinary grief' he rejected utterly the possibility of an easier life: he 'must rather fight for 8d a day'. It was true that Lilburne had an astonishingly quarrelsome nature, as well as passionate political convictions. He left the Army in the spring of 1645, refusing to take the oath of the Covenant. His contentiousness as much as his conscience soon led to further periods of imprisonment, this time at the orders of Parliament. Elizabeth, pregnant again, lived with him in Newgate prison in the autumn of 1645 until he was released in October; it was peculiarly painful to discover that when the Stationers' Company's agents had ransacked their house in Half-Moon Alley for seditious writings, they had also stolen the childbed linen which was carefully stored there (much as the Overtons had been robbed).

During a further period of more severe imprisonment in the summer of 1646, Elizabeth occupied herself in active campaigning on her husband's behalf. It was Elizabeth who undertook the presentation of John's defence in a letter to the Keeper of Newgate prison which was later printed with a characteristic challenge: 'as a free Commoner of England, I do here at your open Barre protest ...'.[34] On 10 July, Lilburne was committed to the Tower of London and not even allowed to receive food at his wife's hands. With about twenty other women, Elizabeth visited the House of Commons in September to present Lilburne's petition for justice, headed 'For J. Lilburne from his wife and many women', and she continued to protest at being barred from his side. Day after day this devoted body appeared at Westminster until a Committee of the House was appointed to hear Lilburne's case and Elizabeth was permitted to join him.

In February 1647 Elizabeth herself was arrested while at her husband's side for dispersing his writings. Unlike Mary Overton she did not remain silent: in court she gave vent to a furious outburst on the subject of 'a company of unjust and unrighteous Judges'. In this instance it was the quick-tempered John who demanded that what she had said should be overlooked: the court should 'pass by what in the bitterness of her heart being a woman she had said'. It was a perfect example of the weak but protected role of the female at law: Lilburne secured Elizabeth's discharge on the grounds that he, as her husband, must be held responsible for what had happened.[35]

Elizabeth Lilburne remained free to haunt the Army headquarters at St Albans and Kingston, petitioning for her husband's release and carrying messages to Leveller meeting places. But when Lilburne was offered bail in the autumn, his address to his family expressed the classic position of the man of conscience: 'Shall I for love of them, sin against my soul ...?'[36]

Elizabeth even had an opportunity to protect her husband physically. In January 1648 Lilburne was brought before the Bar of the House of Commons to answer further charges; in the lobby the soldiers turned on 'Freeborn John' with their musket butts until Elizabeth flung herself in the way. Lilburne was subsequently taken to the Tower, from which he was released in August. The great Leveller petition of 11 September is thought to have been largely his work. It was signed by 'Thousands of well-affected, dwelling in and about London'; in it the demands of *The Agreement of the People* were repeated, together with a demand for the abolition of the 'negative voices' of the King and the House of Lords.[37]

By the end of 1648, however, Lilburne had become disillusioned with the Army and its leaders, including Cromwell, seeing in its control of Parliament after Pride's Purge merely another face of tyranny. In the New Year, although he approved of the execution of the King in principle, he thought that an ordinary jury of the people should try him, following the establishment of a republic, rather than a High Court of Justice.

At the beginning of 1649 therefore, thanks to John Lilburne's temporary withdrawal from public affairs, a short period of domestic peace was enjoyed by Elizabeth and her family, now including three children, two of whom had been born while John was in prison (Tower was the unusual if appropriate name chosen for the youngest). But by the spring Lilburne, as the voice of the Levellers, had abandoned domesticity for strife once more. Once again Lilburne was demanding liberty of conscience, attacking the new Government. Once again he was clapped into prison. Once again it was necessary to petition for his release.

The presentation of *The Humble Petition of divers well-affected Women inhabiting the City of London, Westminster, the Borough of Southwark, Hamblets and places adjacent* to the House of Commons in April 1649, and the events surrounding it, represented the high point of political female activity at this period; just as the ardent demonstration at the funeral of the executed Leveller soldier Robert Lockyer was the most overt instance of public Leveller sympathies. The coffin was decorated with sprigs of rosemary dipped in blood. The long column of mourners adorned with black and sea-green ribbons – sea-green was the adopted colour of the Leveller cause – was brought up by a body of women at the rear, sea-green and black ribbons mingled at their breast.

The women petitioners for the release of Lilburne, Overton and the others, first tackled the House of Commons on 23 April, when they were simply told that the House was too busy to receive them. The next day the Sergeant at Arms dismissed them with the words that the matter was one 'of a higher concernment' than they understood. Besides the House had already given an answer to 'their husbands'; therefore 'you are desired to go home, and look after your own business, and meddle with your housekeeping'. Some angry repartee followed this condescending dismissal, in which the women gave as good as they got. One unwise Member attempted to say that 'it was not for women to Petition, they might stay at home and wash the dishes' only to be told smartly: 'Sir, we have scarce any dishes left us to wash, and those we have are not sure to keep.' Another MP ventured the milder observation that it was strange for women to petition; 'It was strange that you cut off the King's head', was the answer, 'yet I suppose you will justify it.'[38]

On 25 April twenty women were at last admitted to the lobby of the House of Commons bearing a petition, although the attendant soldiers threw squibs at them, and cocked their pistols. The women, with equal determination if not equal violence, grabbed Cromwell's cloak and began to lecture him on their grievances.

'What will you have?' cried Cromwell in answer to their tirade. 'Those rights and freedoms of the Nation, that you promised us ...' was the ominous reply. Whatever the public indignation of these furies, *The Petition of Women* was a considered document; it is likely that Lilburne had a strong hand in its production.[39] It called on all women who approved it to 'subscribe' (that is, sign or mark) and then deliver their signatures to women who would be 'appointed in every Ward and Division to receive the same'. Apart from the release of the Leveller leaders, grievances for which redress was sought included high taxes, lack of work, and arbitrary government in general.

The most interesting passage came in *The Petition of Women*'s preamble when the issue of women taking such an apparently unnatural step as to petition was squarely faced. There was a token reference to the 'weak hands' of women; but this was followed by the counter claim that 'God had wrought many deliverances for several stations from age to age by the weak hand of women' as they knew for their own 'encouragement and example'. Deborah and Jael were quoted in this context, as were the 'British' women who delivered the land from the Danes, and more recently the Scotswomen who fought against 'episcopal tyranny'. As for the charge that it was not the custom for women to address themselves publicly to the House of Commons, the Preamble began with the bold words: 'Since we are assured of our creation in the image of God, and of an interest in Christ equal unto men, as also of a proportionate share in the freedom of this Commonwealth ...'.

Was there perhaps, as has been suggested, an implicit demand here for a share in the franchise as well as the freedom? If implicit, it was once again not explicit. Two more petitions on behalf of Lilburne were presented at the beginning of May by 'bonny Besses in sea-green dresses' as *Mercurius Pragmaticus* picturesquely termed them. There were satirical mentions of 'my brave Viragoes, the Ladyes-errants of the Sea-green order ... so lately fluttering like flocks of wild Geese about the Parliament ears, for the liberty of their champion Jack and his confederates'.[40] Then the brutal quelling of the Burford mutiny in the middle of the month led to the collapse of the Leveller cause as a political force.

Petitioning on the part of Leveller women did not, however, fade away altogether. In October 1651 women were included in a Leveller petition that debtors should be released from prison to work off their debts (a favourite Leveller proposal and one of the many in which they were excitingly in advance of their times). In June 1653, a body of women, including the 'clamorous' Katherine Chidley, presented still further petitions for the release of John Lilburne, enduring yet another spell of imprisonment.

In July Katherine Chidley got into the pulpit at Somerset House and along with another sectary – a young man – 'preached to the people very much in Lilburne's behalf'. In the same month about a dozen women, headed by Katherine, presented a petition to Parliament on behalf of Lilburne, said to have been 'subscribed by above six thousand of that sex'.[41] This was that Little Parliament (sometimes known as the Barebones Parliament after one of its members, Praisegod Barebones, an Anabaptist leather-merchant) which was created following Cromwell's purge of the Rump Parliament of April 1653; it was disbanded when he became Protector in the following December.

The Leveller women 'boldly knocked at the door, and the House taking notice that they were there, sent out Praisegod Barebones to dissuade them from their enterprise, but he could not prevail; and they persisting in their disturbance, another Member came out and told them, the House could not take cognizance of their petition, they being women, and many of them Wives, so that the law took no notice of them'. The women issued a reasonable challenge to the notion of total female dependency based on wifehood by replying that 'they were not all wives, and therefore pressed for the receiving their petition'. The rest of the conversation was not quite on this high level. If their petition was refused, the women went on, the Members of Parliament 'should know that they [the women] had husbands and friends', who 'wore Swords to defend the liberty of the people etc.'. The members should 'look to themselves, and not to persecute that man of God [Lilburne] lest they were also destroyed, as the late King, Bishops, Parliament and all others that ever opposed him, who were all fallen before him'.[42]

But Lilburne was not released.

*   *   *

Brilliana Lady Harley, said to have exhibited 'a Masculine Bravery' during the siege of Brampton Bryan.

Brampton Bryan Castle, in north-west Herefordshire. From an early eighteenth-century engraving.

An illustration to the ballad 'The Female Warrior', 'Relating how a Woman in Mans attire, got an Ensigns place: and so continued till the necessity of making use of a Midwife discover'd her'.

A 'She-Souldier' from the ballad of 'The Valiant Virgin'.

Corfe Castle, near Wareham in Dorset, in 1643.

Mary Lady Bankes.

Below: The monument to Lady Bankes in St Martin's Church, Ruislip, calling attention to the 'constancy and Courage above her sex' which she displayed when defending Corfe Castle.

To the Memory of
The Lady Mary Bankes ẙ onely
Daughter of   Hawtrey of Rislip
in the County of Middx Esquir.
The Wife and Widow of the Honᵇˡᵉ Sʳ
Iohn Bankes Knight Late Lord Cheife
Iustice of his Late Maiestyes Court of
Comon Pleas, and of the Privy Councell
to his Late Maiesty King Charles the First
of Blessed Memory.
Who hauing had the Honnor to haue borne with
a constancy and Courage aboue her sex, a
Noble proporcõn of the Late Calamities, and
the happines to haue outliued them so farr
as to haue seene the restitution of the
Gouernement, with great peace of mind,
laid downe her most desired life the 11 day
of April 1661.
Sʳ Ralph Bankes her Sonne and heire hath
dedicated this

She left 4 Sonnes 1 Sʳ Ralph, 2 Ierom,
3 Charles, 4 William, (since dead
without iffue) & 6 Daughters.

Lucy Hutchinson, wife of Colonel John Hutchinson, with her son, painted by Robert Walker.

Charlotte Countess of Derby, who manifested 'more than Feminine Magnanimity' when she conducted the defence of Lathom House in Lancashire.

Eleanor Countess of Sussex in mourning, a frequent condition since she was widowed three times. She became in turn Countess of Manchester and Countess of Warwick, and was nicknamed 'Old Men's Wife' by the Verneys in their private correspondence.

Mary Lady Verney, wife of Sir Ralph Verney; a portrait attributed to Van Dyck.

A fishwife selling crabs, from a
drawing by Marcel Laroon.

'Grandmother Eve', as she was often
familiarly termed in the seventeenth
century, shown on an English
Delftware charger.

A satirical print, probably by Laroon, of a Quakers' Meeting in the seventeenth century showing a woman as the principal speaker.

Oliver Cromwell at the age of fifty, by Samuel Cooper.

Below: Cromwell's granddaughter, Mrs Bridget Bendish, in middle age; the resemblance to her grandfather, give or take 'female dress ... and a very little softening of the features', was the subject of much contemporary comment.

The story of Elizabeth Lilburne continued on more poignant if less dramatic lines as the petitioning woman of the 1640s gave way to the despairing – but still soliciting – wife of the 1650s; having much in common with Dame Isabella Twysden and Mary Lady Verney, despite the difference in their husbands' politics. To retrace our steps in John Lilburne's story: at the end of the Burford mutiny, he was still held in prison in the Tower of London. Elizabeth Lilburne therefore was still holding together the little household in London as well as she might in her husband's absence. At this point the family received 'a melancholy visitation' in the shape of smallpox; hardly an uncommon seventeenth-century occurrence, but the consequences in this particular case were heart-rending. Both of Elizabeth's sons died – 'the greater part of his earthly delight in this world', as John Lilburne would later describe them.[43] Elizabeth herself and her daughter hovered on the brink of death. Under these circumstances Lilburne was at least allowed to visit them from prison. Finally in November 1649 he was released.

It is understandable that the stricken Elizabeth now hoped that her husband would make his peace with the new Commonwealth and settle with what remained of his little household. (Another son, John, was born in October 1650.) She hoped in vain. As a result of a vendetta against Sir Arthur Haselrig, Lilburne was banished for life by an Act of Parliament in January 1652, and a huge fine was imposed. While he was in exile, Elizabeth found herself in great hardship, having to sell or pawn most of her household goods; she also suffered a miscarriage, and her other children were ill. Under the circumstances, she refused to send him papers which she believed would merely lead to more fruitless troubles. Lilburne referred to her letters as 'new paper skirmishes ... filled with womanish passion and anger'.[44] Outsiders may find it easier to comprehend the element of despair which was now creeping into her dealings with her intractable husband.

All the same, by May 1653 Elizabeth had scraped together enough money to visit John at Bruges; Lilburne had expected her to bring a pass for England from the newly installed Protector Cromwell. He was furious it was refused. Relations between husband and wife were evidently cool: in a letter to the Protector Lilburne blamed Cromwell for the fact: 'Your late barbarous tyrannical dealing with me hath exposed her to so much folly and lowness of spirit in my eyes, in some of her late childish actions, as hath in some measure, produced an alienation of affection in me to her ...' He referred ominously to 'that tenderness of affection that I owe to her whom I formerly entirely loved as my own life'.[45] Lilburne sent

Elizabeth to England once more for the pass and awaited her return at Calais. On hearing the news of a second refusal, he returned to England anyway, whereupon he was arrested, imprisoned once more in June 1653 and finally tried in July.

This was the celebrated trial which had the people roaring in chorus:

> And what, shall then honest John Lilburne die!
> Three score thousand will know the reason why!

John Lilburne did not die; in effect he was acquitted; but the Government declined to release him (provoking those petitions on the part of the Leveller women to which reference has already been made). By July 1655 he was in prison on the island of Guernsey. Elizabeth, her soliciting temper unabated by her privations – and John's recriminations – petitioned Cromwell that he should be released: 'Our grievous afflictions have obtained no remission!' she wrote. 'I beg you to take away all provocation from his impatient spirit, weared out with long and sore afflictions. I durst engage my life that he will not disturb the state.' John's own poor health lent plausibility to Elizabeth's last statement: it was probably she who got Fleetwood, Cromwell's brother-in-law and colleague, to persuade the Protector of Lilburne's newly pacifist frame of mind.[46]

When Lilburne reached Dover Castle, Elizabeth was living at the house of a friend who kept an inn at Guildhall; after years without a proper home life, or even a proper income, she had fallen into a state of depression, indicated by the fact that her newest baby, Benomy, had been a year old when she had had him baptized.[47] In London she received another startling piece of news concerning her husband's spiritual odyssey. He had now become a Quaker.

It was one thing for John to require Elizabeth to send him Quaker books down from London. But the language in which he hoped for Elizabeth's own conversion was scarcely such as to bring comfort to the weary homeless woman. He spoke of self-denial: 'even to a final denial of father, kindred, friends, my sweet and beloved (by me) babes'. Above all her conversion would enable her 'to go cheerfully and willingly along hand in hand' with her husband. Such a step, he wrote, 'abundantly would render thee more amiable, lovely and pleasant in mine eyes although thou wert then clothed in rags. . . .' Elizabeth had just escaped death by drowning in the Thames – John's sympathy with her plight was cursory. The fact that Elizabeth and the children *were* to all intents and purposes clothed in rags, John Lilburne treated with equal shortness. He wrote: 'I am also sorry that thou art so straitly put to it for money, but to live upon God by faith in the depth of straights, is the lively condition of a Christian: O that thy spirit could attain to it!'[48]

When the couple did meet again in November 1655, they had a bitter quarrel; yet even now, for the higher purpose of marital union, it was Elizabeth who agreed to a reconciliation on John's terms. By August 1657 John Lilburne, although nominally still a prisoner, was allowed to rent a house at Eltham in Kent; moreover Elizabeth was pregnant again (she underwent a total of ten pregnancies, five of her babies, including the boy named Tower, dying young). The house was for the *accouchement*, 'that I might be near my friends at my lying-in'. She duly gave birth. Then Cromwell, hearing of Lilburne's freedom, and being prepared to grant him an allowance but not to have him at large, called for his return. It was too late. John Lilburne was now 'sick and weak'.[49] On 29 August 1657, at the age of forty-three, he was dead.

Elizabeth was now in a state verging on destitution, with three children to care for, including a new-born baby. Her grief was not allayed by the Quaker funeral which followed. All that was left for her to do was to petition the all-powerful Cromwell, who, whatever his treatment of the dissident John, had as we have seen a merited reputation for helping distressed women. Cromwell responded with an order for the payment of the arrears due to Elizabeth, and a continuation of the 40s a week allowance granted to Lilburne. Unfortunately this was not to be the end of Elizabeth's 'piercing sorrows'. By the time Richard Cromwell succeeded his father as Protector, she was still petitioning to have Parliament repeal that Act of 1652 which had sentenced John to a colossal fine: 'Your late father professed very great tenderness to me', she wrote desperately to Richard.[50] The 1652 Act was finally repealed in February 1659.

This, little enough, was the material reward secured by Elizabeth Lilburne: in return for a small allowance (still being paid in March 1660) she surrendered John Lilburne's papers. If Lilburne himself would not have approved,[51] who can blame the exhausted widow, who had, as she told Richard Cromwell, endured 'seventeen years' sorrows' and longed for 'a little rest and comfort among my fatherless children'. A more equitable award lay in the earlier judgement of Lilburne himself. Dispatching a petition to Cromwell by her hand, he wrote: 'This I have sent by the gravest, wisest, fittest messenger I could think of.' He added, in this at least a conventional product of the seventeenth century, 'and, though a Feminine, yet of a gallant and truly masculine spirit'.[52]

13　When Women Preach

When women preach and cobblers pray
The fiends in hell make holiday.

'Lucifer's Lackey or The Devil's New Creation', 1641

'Let your women keep silence in the churches: for it is not permitted unto them to speak'; it was this verse from St Paul's First Epistle to the Corinthians which was at the root of the accepted condemnation of female preaching (and participation in church government) at the beginning of the seventeenth century. To conventional Christian ears, the mighty voice of the Apostle still thundered down the centuries with undiminished vigour and there seemed little distinction to be drawn between St Paul's admonition to the inhabitants of Achaea in the first century AD, and the will of God 1,600 years later.

For women, as a whole, there had to be a more private – and one might add less voluble – way of influencing their contemporaries; or as the epitaph of the pious and charitable Lettice Viscountess Falkland phrased it:

> And now, though Paul forbids her Sex to preach,
> Yet may her Life instruct, and her Death teach.

Richard Brathwaite, in *The English Gentlewoman* of 1631, that mine of advice on the conduct of the modest female, took the argument one stage further. Just as 'discourse of State-matters' would not become her, it was equally unsuitable 'to dispute of high points of Divinity': since women were forbidden to be speakers in church it was not right that they should discuss theological matters in private either.[1]

By October 1650 when Sir Ralph Verney was having his brush with Dr Denton (and Nancy) on the subject of a girl's rightful education, all this had changed. 'Had St Paul lived in our Times', wrote Sir Ralph gloomily, 'I am confident he would have fixed a Shame upon women for writing (as well as for their speaking) in the Church.'[2] Preaching among the women sectaries was a phenomenon of the English scene from the

1640s onwards; the shame that St Paul would or would not have felt being a subject of hot debate not only amongst outsiders hostile to the sects, but also within their ranks.

Women probably first began to preach in Holland in the 1630s in the Baptist churches, whose congregations had always included a large number of their sex. (There were said to be more women than men in the large body of English separatists who went to Holland in 1558; thereafter on the Continent women had held numerous church offices and taken some part in lay preaching.) In the New World – Massachusetts – women were known to have preached by 1636. In England in the 1640s women preached weekly at the General Baptist Church in Bell Alley, off Coleman Street, in the City of London. Anne Hempstall was described as preaching to 'bibbing Gossips' in her house in Holborn, and Mary Bilbrowe, wife of a bricklayer of St Giles-in-the-Fields, preached in her parlour, although the pulpit, which was made of brick, was so high that only her tippet could be seen. As early as 1641 a tract, *The Discovery of Women Preachers*, referred to their existence in Kent, Cambridge and Salisbury.[3]

Women were notable among the Brownists, those enthusiasts who led a tumultuous existence on the wing of the so-called Independent Church. (The name derived from one of their spokesmen, Robert Browne.) It was fear of these Independent sectaries which had led in March 1642 to the drawing-up of the Kentish petition, with Sir Roger Twysden as one of its leaders – that move to save the nation from 'heresy, schism, prophaneness, libertinism, anabaptism, atheism' which had led to all the subsequent troubles of the Twysden family (see p. 210). Later the division between Independents and Presbyterians would give way to a new type of alignment: because Brownists could not accept any form of central authority in religious matters, they now found themselves opposed to many of their previous Independent colleagues, as well as the Presbyterians.

The style of such pioneers could hardly be expected to be self-effacing. In London Mrs Attoway, 'Mistress of all the She preachers in Coleman Street', who was capable of preaching for well over an hour, seems to have run off with another woman's husband and in addition secured contributions to finance a journey to Jerusalem, a project which unlike her elopement remained largely in her imagination. Some of these women displayed undeniably an 'eerie spirit'; others were less 'eerie' than 'brazen-faced'.[4] The trouble was that the kind of woman who possessed the audacity to challenge the ruling of St Paul was not likely to combine it with that feminine modesty which would win society's respect for the cause of the woman preacher.

On the contrary, all the old gibes concerning woman's talkativeness – 'the natural volubility of their tongues' – proved useful yet again in the conflict over the 'preacheresses'. Prejudice could cause a woman preaching to be condemned first as 'a prater' or 'prattler', so by implication as a scold, and lastly even as some kind of witch – remembering the connection in the popular mind between scolding and cursing. Additionally, her 'Bible-thumping' could be held to demonstrate the perils of any form of education, however rudimentary, for women since they were clearly not capable of making good use of it.[5]

By 1645 the moderate Puritans were criticizing the Brownists for allowing women to take part in church government and to preach. Prynne attacked this implication of Independency, and in 1646 John Vicars, in *The Schismatick Sifted: Or, A Picture of Independents Freshly and Fairly Washt over Again*, deplored the fact that not only 'saucy boys, bold botching taylors' but also 'bold impudent huswives' were taking it upon themselves 'to prate an hour or more'. The principal attack was that mounted by Thomas Edwards in the same year in *Gangraena*, deploring the fact that these 'whirligigg spirits' of the Brownists included smiths, tailors, shoemakers, pedlars, and worst of all women who were giving 'constant lectures'. He thought this to be against not only the light of Scripture but that of nature.[6]

On 14 January 1646 aldermen and common councillors of the City of London delivered a petition to the House of Commons concerning the multitude of religious schisms in the City which they wanted eliminated. They claimed that in one parish there were 'eleven private congregations and conventicles who deserted the parish churches and have tradesmen and women preachers'. As a result, later that month several women preachers were committed to custody and others were brought before the Committee of Examinations of the House of Commons. Then in December 1646 the House resolved that no person should expound the Scriptures unless he be ordained in 'this or some other Reformed Church'.[7]

With due respect to St Paul, why did the question of women preaching arouse such extreme apprehension? A popular rhyme of 1641 entitled 'Lucifer's Lackey or The Devil's New Creation' ran:

> When women preach and cobblers pray
> The fiends in hell make holiday.

At the bottom, it was woman's demand for freedom of conscience rather than for freedom to 'prate' which caused concern. The crude mockery of 'Lucifer's Lackey' masked a real dread that a woman who placed conscience above husband and family might consider herself outside the former's control. The question as to whether a woman sectary had the right to leave a husband who was 'unsanctified' was never officially settled, though much discussed in the early 1650s. But the fact that some women sectaries such as Mrs Attoway did cast out or abandon 'unsanctified' husbands in the 1640s did nothing to relieve such fears.[8]

For this reason those women who were not 'eerie spirits' – and thus were in control of what they said – generally took care to emphasize their own weakness in advance of their message. This self-depreciation might be expected to win the sympathy of a masculine audience, or at very least avoid arousing its hostility. Elizabeth Warren, a pamphleteer, declared herself fully conscious of her own 'mental and sex-deficiency' in her preface to *The Old and Good Way Vindicated* of 1645, which bewailed the troubles of the times and defended a certain persecuted clergyman. In *Spiritual Thrift* she even went so far as to acknowledge that 'we of the weaker sex, have hereditary evil from our grandmother Eve'. Claiming for herself in general a 'silent Modesty', she defended her action in having her sentiments printed, aware that she might be accused of having deserted both this silence and this modesty.[9] As we shall see, even the redoubtable Katherine Chidley was not above pleading the weakness of her sex on occasions when it seemed politic.

*   *   *

Katherine Chidley lived in Soper Lane, off Coleman Street, a centre of Brownist activity, where St Pancras was one of the most famous of the Independent churches. Her son Samuel Chidley was also a leading sectary and later one of the treasurers of the Leveller party, hence Katherine Chidley's prominence among the women who had tried to secure John Lilburne's release. In the eighteenth century Ballard described Katherine Chidley as fighting as violently as Penthesilea, the Amazonian Queen, for the cause of Independency. The language in which she was described in her own time was less romantic if equally evocative. Thomas Edwards, a fanatical Presbyterian supporter, called her 'a brazen-faced audacious old woman', both 'talkative and clamorous', qualities as undesirable in a woman as they were in a witch.[10]

There is no reason to doubt the essential features of Edwards's picture (although it may be pointed out that the language of Edwards's attacks on the Independents certainly far exceeded in virulence anything the most 'clamorous' old woman could achieve). With Samuel, Katherine Chidley journeyed through England in 1641, and founded 'a small gathered church' at Bury St Edmunds where eight adults signed the Brownists' covenant. That took persistence and presumably a certain stridency too. In 1641 also Katherine Chidley wrote *The Justification of the Independent Churches of Christ*, to combat Thomas Edwards's attack upon Independency.[11] It was a sharply worded document. When Edwards argued that Independency would breed divisions within families, setting husband and wife against each other, Katherine Chidley countered that there had been a division in the first family, but that had been caused by Satan, not by toleration.

She wrote: 'Next you will say: "Oh! How will this take away that power and authority which God hath given to Husbands, Fathers and Mothers, over wives, children and servants."' To this Katherine Chidley answered that St Paul in the First Epistle to the Corinthians had plainly declared that the wife could be a believer in her sense ('sanctified'), and the husband an unbeliever ('unsanctified'). Why would he have advised husband or wife not to leave an unbelieving spouse if the Apostle had not at least envisaged the possibility? Furthermore St Paul also envisaged some unbelievers wishing to depart and added: 'A brother or a sister is not under bondage in such cases.'

Still, Katherine Chidley was careful to make it clear that an 'unsanctified' husband was not robbed of his ordinary rights, only of control of his wife's beliefs: 'It is true he hath authority over her in bodily and civil respects, but not to be a Lord over her conscience.' On the primacy of conscience, Katherine Chidley was unalterably strong, denying utterly the claims of the 'magistrate' to rule over it: 'I know of no true Divinity that teacheth men to be Lords over the Conscience.' (Although she herself would not tolerate the Catholics – but that, she declared, was because they had attempted by plots and treachery to 'ruinate the land'.)

At the end of the *Justification* Katherine Chidley challenged Edwards to a parley on the subject of Independency, each speaker to choose six people who in the presence of a moderator would thrash out the matter in 'fair discourse'. The sting was in the tail. Katherine Chidley was confident that she would defeat Thomas Edwards, but if by any chance she did not, that would represent no triumph for him: 'for I am a poor woman and unable to deal with you'. It was perhaps that thought which led Edwards to reject the encounter.

Katherine Chidley's second pamphlet, *A New Yeares Gift, Or A Briefe Exhortation to Mr Thomas Edwards*, contended that Independency alone followed the primitive pattern of Christ, and she argued that it should thus be instituted as the State religion, controlled by Parliament (not the Westminster Assembly of Divines) to form 'one entire government established upon sound principles, unalterable'. *Good Counsell to the Petitioners for Presbyterian Government that they may declare their faith before they build their Church*, of November 1645, which suggested that 'there is but one true Religion', attacked Presbyterianism for not being according to God's Word. The Chidleys, mother and son, were also said to have written the famous Independent tract *Launseters Launse* together; and Katherine Chidley may have had a hand in the composition of *The Petition of Women* in 1649.[12]

Unlike the retiring Elizabeth Warren, who said of herself that she disliked controversy (and about whom as a result nothing is known beyond her pamphlets), Katherine Chidley led a robust existence outside the confines of the printed page. In August 1645, for example, she rose up in church in Stepney, preached the tenets of Brownism and attacked various ministers 'with a great deal of Violence and bitterness'. Her particular grievance was the meeting of people in churches and other places where 'idolatrous services' had previously taken place. The incumbent minister, a Mr Greenhill, tried to rebuke her. Was no worship to take place in a church just because it had once been dedicated in the name of saints or angels? Did that imply that this church had been for ever 'set apart' for 'idolatry?' This encompassed the whole of England, which had been 'set apart' or dedicated to St George. At this Katherine Chidley's outburst of indignation was so overriding that Mr Greenhill was obliged to retire.[13]

In 1646 when Thomas Edwards issued his celebrated attack on Independency, *Gangraena*, he spared time to denounce the whole idea of women preaching, as well as the audacious Katherine Chidley in particular. As for claims of spiritual equality, this would mean that 'all women at once were exempt from being under government'.[14] In fact, as we have seen, Katherine Chidley had specifically excepted such a claim from her demands, nevertheless the fear remained and Edwards, in voicing it, exercised a more potent influence on public opinion than Katherine Chidley in denying it.

*   *   *

In contrast to the 'preacheress', the prophetess had always been treated with a certain nervous respect by society – remember Jane Hawkins, 'a poor woman (and she but a pedlar)', who in 1629 had for a period prophesied before 200 people (see p. 154). Claiming direct inspiration from God, the prophetess might challenge accepted notions concerning religion and society but she did not necessarily in her own person challenge the

accepted order. What differentiated the Civil War period was the substantial increase in the number of prophetesses and allied female seers. In this
time of hopes and dreams and visions, the attitude of authority itself – the
new authority: Army, Council, new Parliament, new rulers such as Cromwell – was equally more responsive.

In 1654 an Independent church congregation would debate at length
whether the average man had that dominion over prophetesses such as he
had over 'all Widows and Maids that are not Prophetesses'. The eventual
conclusion relied upon St Paul's remark in his First Epistle to the Corinthians that 'every woman that prayeth or prophesieth with her head
uncovered dishonoureth her head'; from this admonition it was deduced
that St Paul, since he did not explicitly forbid them, conceived of and
tolerated the existence of prophetesses, so long as their heads were covered.
So it was decided that 'a Woman (Maid, Wife or Widow) being a
Prophetess may Speak, Prophesy, Pray with a Veil. Others may not.'[15]

It was the good fortune of Lady Eleanor Davies, she whose desperate
rambling prophecies concerning the fate of King Charles I had brought
her first to the Gatehouse prison and then to Bedlam (see p. 158 ff.), to
survive into this more imaginative age. In 1648 she sought out Oliver
Cromwell. With her predilection for anagrams, Lady Eleanor was from
the first well disposed towards a man whose very name – O. CROMWEL –
suggested the words HOWL ROME. The 'O' of Oliver she envisaged hopefully as the splendid round sun, in contrast to the sickly crescent moon
which was the 'C' of Charles I. When the Army was at its headquarters at
St Albans in 1648, Lady Eleanor presented to him a book of her prophecies
first printed (with dire results) in 1633. She superscribed the book *The
Armies Commission*, adding the verse: 'Behold he cometh with ten thousand
of his Saints to execute judgement on all.' The splendid sun showed not
only more tolerance but more humour than the sickly moon – but then of
course Cromwell was not compared to Belshazzar as Charles I had been.
Smiling at the superscription, and putting on his 'specticles' (sic), Cromwell gently observed: 'But we are not all Saints.'[16]

As a result of this newly permissive atmosphere towards prophetesses,
Lady Eleanor was able to spend her last years in a state of happiness and
honour she can scarcely have expected in the bad old days of the King's
reign. She also had the sweetness of revenge: her old enemy Archbishop
Laud, 'horned like the lamb', was executed in 1645. When Charles I was
in prison in January 1649, shortly before his own execution, Lady Eleanor
took it upon herself to write to him: 'For King Charles, Prisoner, These'.
She reminded him of her sufferings at his behest 'because [I] took upon

me to be a Prophetess' and suggested that he make public acknowledgement of his 'high offence'. He should also implore her forgiveness, 'if so be you expect to find Mercy in this world or the other'.

In August that year, when the King, for better or for worse, had long exchanged worlds, Lady Eleanor's pamphlet was reprinted. In 1651 appeared *The Restitution of Prophecy*, restoring all her original revelations, and at her death in 1652 the Anglican divine Peter Du Moulin suggested she had indeed been 'favoured with some beam of divine knowledge of future things', while being in general '*erudita supra Sexum, mitis infra Sortem*': learned above her sex, humble below her fortune. The official epitaph put up by Lady Eleanor's family congratulated her on having 'in a woman's body, a man's spirit'.[17]

What was more, despite these Cromwellian connections, a dutiful daughter saw to it that Lady Eleanor's reputation was not blackened for ever after the Restoration. Lucy Countess of Huntingdon and her friend Katherine Stanley, Marchioness of Dorchester joined together to protest to Thomas Dugdale over the historical inaccuracies in his 1660 *Continuation* of Sir Richard Baker's *Chronicle*.[18] As has been noticed (see p. 168), Lady Dorchester succeeded in removing the slur against the courage of her own mother, Charlotte Countess of Derby, based on false Parliamentary reports. Lady Huntingdon's task was more delicate. Lady Eleanor Davies could hardly be whitewashed entirely but it was a matter of just how she was presented. Dugdale's statement that she was 'generally reputed little better than a mad woman' caused much distress; in particular Lady Huntingdon was anxious to rescue her mother from the charge that in predicting the death of the Duke of Buckingham she had been associated with the notorious popular astrologer of the time, Dr Lambe.

In the end Lady Huntingdon, supported by her young son Theophilus, seventh Earl of Huntingdon, was successful. Lady Eleanor's name was expunged from the account of the Duke of Buckingham's death. Even Peter Du Moulin's eulogy – learned above her sex, humble below her fortune – was removed from the new edition as being presumably distasteful to the Countess. One wonders what Lady Eleanor herself would have thought of that omission. More pleasing to her perhaps would have been her grandson Theophilus's measured yet tender judgement of her career.

Lord Huntingdon wrote that his grandmother – 'one not a little enthusasticall' – had 'obliged' his mother to give him his unusual Christian name (this occurred very shortly before Lady Eleanor's death, for Theophilus, the longed-for male heir to replace three dead sons, was not born until 1650).[19] He showed no signs of holding this against her. On the contrary, he accepted her own account that 'she heard voices supernatural, [so] that she was endowed with the gift of prophecy', but for censuring the ecclesiastical government and the Queen's Catholic practices, 'and her obstinate refusing any submission', wrote Lord Huntingdon, she was sentenced in the Court of High Commission 'as one that was out of her wits'.

Lord Huntingdon's chief indignation was reserved for the historian Sir William Sanderson, who in his account of the reign of Charles I had passed 'his own censure on this Lady as if she was either mad or possessed with delusions from the Devil'. This was indeed a 'Barbarous' judgement for a historian to deliver to posterity, complained Lord Huntingdon, 'considering her [Lady Eleanor's] extraction from a family of Ancient English Nobility...'.

*   *   *

Lady Eleanor Davies was an eccentric and an exception. The social standing of the other prophetesses of the period made it at least conceivable – by Lord Huntingdon's standards, that is – for them to be considered mad or deluded. Yet on the whole respect obtained. At Bodmin in February 1647, for example, a young girl was said to be busy foretelling things to come, most of which were said already to have 'fallen out true'. (Although one of her prophecies, that Charles I would shortly enjoy his crown again, being revenged on his enemies, was less successful.) She lived off a diet of sweetmeats, which were bought to her by 'small people clad in green, and sometimes by birds'. This girl was said to cure most diseases, as well as specializing in broken bones, which she mended with a touch of her hand. Examined by three divines, she gave a good account of herself, having the Scriptures by heart 'very perfectly'. Now under guard, she was seen to be fasting entirely, except on Christmas Day, when she had a feast of 'bread and water'.[20]

The prophetesses who interrupted the councils of Cromwell, the Army and later his colleagues in the new Government of England were an even more remarkable phenomenon. The point has been made that at least half a dozen times between 1647 and 1654 important deliberations were put aside, while some obscure prophetess (or prophet) delivered a message generally relayed by the Almighty via an apocalyptic vision.[21] Nothing underlines more clearly the weird atmosphere of these times. In the 1630s King Charles I showed first irritation, then outright anger, faced with the revelations of Lady Eleanor Davies. At the end of December 1648 – the most crucial period for the Army Council as the King's future swayed in the balance – an unknown woman named Elizabeth Poole appeared in front of them to communicate her visions concerning 'the presence of God with the Army'. She declared that the Army had appeared to her in the shape of a man and the country as a whole as a woman 'full of imperfection, crooked, weak, sickly'. The man it seemed was destined to heal the woman. This revelation was taken extremely seriously by the Army Council and much discussed. Elizabeth Poole's visions were described by Colonel Rich as 'that testimony which God hath manifested here by an unexpected Providence'.[22]

On 5 January God instructed Elizabeth Poole to return to the Council. There she handed in a paper arguing against the execution of the King, which was formally debated by the Council's members in her absence. She was then called back for further discussions. Elizabeth Poole repeated her conviction that the King should not be executed: 'you may bind his hands and hold him fast under' she announced, but he should not be put to death. She referred to the Scriptures to enforce her case, quoting the text: 'Vengeance is mine, saith the Lord.' She also described the King as the husband or head of the people; as such, citing the precedent of Nabal among the Israelites, he might be restrained but not cut down by his 'wife'.

Henry Ireton – the most intellectual of the Army leaders – questioned Elizabeth Poole at length about her revelations. If this King was not to die, was no King ever to die? Had she seen an angel or a vision? (The answer was: a vision.) A later Royalist pamphlet accused Cromwell of stage-managing the whole incident, coaching the woman in her answers to the Council; but this is manifestly absurd, especially in view of the King's fate at the hands of his 'wife' less than a month afterwards. The true significance of Elizabeth Poole lay in the exalted audience this humble woman was able to secure without difficulty, by invoking the awesome role of the prophetess.

*   *   *

The most extreme language was used by those prophetesses connected with the Fifth Monarchy movement. This was a millenarian sect so called because it looked forward to the establishment of the 'Fifth Monarchy' – that of Christ after his second coming. Among the Fifth Monarchists themselves particular reverence was accorded to any woman who 'appeared to be endowed with divine grace' – although no other category of woman other than a prophetess was in the end granted special rights within their church; nor, contrary to popular accusation, did the Fifth Monarchists attempt to elevate the status of the woman within the family, asking only for freedom of conscience from the husband's control.[23]

The determination of the Fifth Monarchists that the second coming of Christ would establish His political power brought them into natural conflict with the current rulers of England. The movement got under way after 1651 when it became clear that neither Parliament (nor Cromwell) was likely to set up the 'Rule of the Saints', as had once been hoped. In 1653 Cromwell's elevation as Protector was construed as a further insult to the true dominion of Jesus Christ, since to Him alone belonged the prerogative of single rule. Cromwell, hailed by Lady Eleanor Davies as a splendid sun in the early stages of his leadership, now found himself identified with something far less pleasant called the 'Little Horn', an odious excrescence on the head of the Beast. Despite this, and despite the violence of the prophetesses' invective, for some time the civil powers showed quite remarkable restraint towards them, genuinely hampered by their claims to be reporting the true intentions of God. The treatment of Mary Overton, dragged through the streets of London on 'cudgels' with her baby at her breast, and thrown into Bridewell among the vagrants and harlots for helping to sew up her husband's political pamphlets, contrasts remarkably, as we shall see, with that of the fervent Fifth Monarchist Anna Trapnel, including the comparative comfort allowed to the prophetess when she finally did reach Bridewell.

Anna Trapnel was the daughter of a shipwright in Poplar, and lived in Hackney.[24] By her own account, *A Legacy for Saints, being several Experiences of the dealings of God with Anna Trapnel*, her piety came to her early, 'when a child, then the Lord awed my spirit', and was encouraged by her 'godly mother'.[25] By the time she was fourteen, she was eager to hear the words of the Lord and to pray for herself, and it was while listening to the famous Independent preacher Hugh Peter on a text of Isaiah that her eyes were opened to 'the marriage covenant ... between God and his spouse'. Thereafter Anna went from minister to minister, and from sermon to sermon daily, but still did not find further elucidation. She could not sleep or even rest. In her depression she was even tempted to suicide, to which the devil tempted her by showing her a sharp knife. Her spiritual aridity only increased as she wrestled with the doctrine that Christ came not only to the righteous, but to all sinners. Finally she found herself able to accept it.

After this time of protracted perplexity, Anna enjoyed her true moment of revelation on New Year's Day 1642. It was a Sunday and she was listening to the Baptist minister of St Botolph's Church in Aldgate, John Simpson (later a prominent Fifth Monarchist), preaching on the text: 'Now if any man have not the spirit of Christ, he is none of his.' Suddenly Anna found herself saying: 'Lord, I have the spirit.' Then what joy she felt! 'Oh what triumphing and songs of Hallelujah were in my spirit.' Anna felt 'a clothing of glory' over her and saw angels, a clear flame without smoke and other 'christal appearances'. Sometimes 'the golden trumpet sounded higher, and sometimes lower, yet still it was sounding, and caused an echo to follow it'.

Thereafter there were still moments when Anna felt buffeted by Satan, as when she learnt of her mother's death. Yet many 'raptures' followed: sometimes she would fall down on the ground in public, at other times, alone in her room, she felt grace pouring over her 'like a fountain'. John Simpson, visiting Anna at home when she was sick, and her 'earthly tabernacle' – her body – was shaking with a fever, issued a caution: she might be deluded regarding the presence of God within her, as others in the past had been. But Anna had no such doubts. She knew that the Lord had chosen her so that 'out of the mouths of babes and sucklings he would perfect his praise'. She had a series of visions which ranged from the sun itself to Jesus taking up Peter and John into the Mount, the Transfiguration, and 'Revelations concerning the Government of the Nation, the Parliament, Army and Ministry'.

It was important to Anna Trapnel, as it was to an earlier prophetess and pamphleteer, Mary Pope, to point out the divine source of such outpourings. Mary Pope, author of *A Treatise of Magistracy*, referred to 'God having made me a Mother in Israel' and God 'as it were forcing me on ... for helping to settle these unsettled times'. Anna made a similar point. She felt a strong personal identification with 'that approved Hannah', the prophetess in the book of Samuel, which sometimes led to her being described as Hannah, not Anna, Trapnel (in fact she herself always signed her name Anna).[26]

The importance of the connection with the biblical Hannah, whom she declared herself desirous of imitating, was that Hannah too had been judged to be 'mad, under the administration of evil angels, and a witch'. Even the priest Eli had at first assumed Hannah to be drunk when he saw her lips moving – in prophecy – and no sound coming forth. Hannah had issued a dignified reproach to Eli telling him not to confuse 'thy handmaid' with 'a daughter of Belial'. In an age rich in citation of biblical precedent, all of this was very much to the advantage of any latter-day Hannah, who might expect to encounter several Elis, and even more

unsympathetic individuals, in the course of her divinely-ordained career as
a prophetess.

Anna Trapnel prided herself on two other aspects of her character, in
both of which one can detect a certain feminine defensiveness, as though
to meet predictable charges in advance. First, she was concerned to make
it clear that she was in no way a whore, being on the contrary, as her
friends put it, of 'beautiful and unblameable conversation'. Second, she
prided herself on the fact that she had not received any ordinary education,
since 'Christ's scholars', amongst which she included herself, were endowed with a far better type of learning 'from above'. Consciously or not,
this was a smart attitude to adopt for one who could well claim to be one
of 'Christ's scholars' but not the duller sort who had merely attended an
earthly university. So Anna, in her long rambling verses of prophecy,
pre-empted one accusation commonly made against the women who
preached – that they were silly uneducated females:

> Thou shalt not read what's spoke of Dragon and Beast
> With University-art;
> But thou shalt read with Kings seven eyes,
> And an enlightened heart.

> Thou shalt not run to Antichrists Libraries
> To fetch from thence any skill
> To read the Revelation of Christ,
> But be with knowledge fill'd.[27]

As for the other common charge – that the rise of women preaching
demonstrated the sheer foolishness of giving them an education – Anna
Trapnel, being untutored, was not liable to that. She after all had received
her education from the great university in the sky.

Anna Trapnel first came into public prominence as part of the violent
Fifth Monarchist reaction to the installation of Oliver Cromwell as Protector on 16 December 1653. On the eve of the event, she had had a vision
of Cromwell in the shape of a bull amidst a large herd of cattle: 'and of a
sudden there was a great shout of those that followed him, he being singled
out alone, and the foremost, and he looking back, they bowed themselves
unto him, and leaped up from the earth, and shewed much joy that he
had become their Supreme'. However, all did not end happily for the
joyful herd, for after mistakenly 'running at the Saints', they found
themselves scattered, with their horns broken, and finally they fell into
their graves.[28]

Three days later a Welsh preacher named Vavasour Powell announced in a sermon that Cromwell's Government could only be temporary (in view of the expected coming of Christ) and 'a small matter should fetch him down with little noise'. It was not the kind of remark calculated to reassure a nervous new regime, and in January Powell was summoned to Whitehall to explain himself before the Council. Along with him went 'a maid called Hannah'.

Anna Trapnel sat just outside the Council chamber in a little room with a fire, awaiting Powell's return from his examination. Just as Powell emerged, intending to go home, Anna was 'as it were seized by the Lord' and 'carried forth in a spirit of Prayer and Singing, from noon till night'. When she finally fell into her bed at Mr Roberts's lodging house near the Palace of Whitehall, at eleven o'clock at night, she lay there for twelve days. For the first five of these Anna remained without eating or drinking; thereafter she took a little toast soaked in small beer every twenty-four hours, sometimes merely to moisten her mouth. During all this period her eyes were shut, while out of her mouth issued a stream of prophecies, for two, three or even four hours at a time, by day or by night, and sometimes both.[29]

The sensational effect of such a daily performance in the heart of Whitehall, so close to the seat of the Protectoral power, may be imagined. 'Many hundreds' were said to be flocking to see her. Although very little of what she was saying could be understood when Anna was singing, her prayers were reported to be 'in exceeding odd method and order', and phrased in 'good language'. The effect of her 'excellent words and well placed' was that 'all that come, do much admire what they hear from her'. In view of some of Anna's topics for prayer – that the Lord Protector should be 'delivered from Carnal Councils' and should not be 'vain, nor regard earthly pomp and pleasure' – perhaps the obscurity of her singing was to be preferred, at least from the point of view of the Government. After twelve days of this, Anna rose up from her bed at Mr Roberts's lodging house and went home 'speedily and lustily'.[30]

Of course the sensation did not stop there. Since 1650 Anna Trapnel had belonged to the congregation of John Simpson, the minister of St Botolph's, now a leading Fifth Monarchist, who was one of the 'lecturers' at Allhallows Church. At the end of January Simpson was arrested and sent to prison at Windsor, along with other ministers, for making public a vision which predicted the fall of Cromwell within six months. At Allhallows, however, the new Protectoral regime continued to be denounced. Marchamont Nedham, the Commonwealth journalist, reported on this to Cromwell personally in February, making the point that 'This meeting much diminishes your reputation among foreigners, who expect changes, because they are proclaimed from the pulpit, and great things are made of it, though it is but a confluence of silly wretches.' Moreover, there was a plan to print Anna Trapnel's discourses 'which are desperate against your person, family, children, friends and the government', as well as sending her all over England to proclaim them. She is much visited, wrote Nedham, doing 'a world of mischief' since 'the vulgar dote on vain prophecies' such as she proclaimed daily in a trance.[31]

Still no action was taken against Anna Trapnel personally despite these subversive sentiments. Not everyone accepted the source of her visions without reservation: 'some say that what she doth is by a mighty inspiration, others say they suppose her to be a troubled mind'. Yet the general impression given was of some sort of communion with God, as one correspondent wrote who confessed himself baffled by the precise nature of her revelation and 'under what sort to rank it'.[32]

As for the attention Anna Trapnel received, Dorothy Osborne referred, humorously perhaps, but with a wry note beneath it all, to the prophetess's success in the world compared to her own. In March 1654 she wrote to her lover, William Temple: 'I am coming into my preaching term again. What think you, were it not a good way of preferment as the times are? If you advise me to do it, I'll venture.' After all, the woman (Anna Trapnel) 'was cried up mightily'. Dorothy Osborne's father had recently died, which affected the question of her long-delayed marriage (see p. 33); now Dorothy had to await her brother's arrival to know 'how I shall dispose myself'. Once more, Dorothy advocated patience to William Temple.[33] At the same time, rather more excitingly, Anna Trapnel awaited the arrival of the spirit of God and needed apparently very little other guidance as to how she should dispose herself.

The guidance which arrived from the Lord was that Anna should accept an invitation to tour the West Country.[34] When she first received the invitation, Anna exclaimed: 'There's a far journey indeed!' But the Lord over-persuaded Anna. As a preliminary she visited Simpson in his Windsor prison, having a vision of 'high rocky hills' at Hillingdon near Uxbridge on the way, and knowing that was how Cornwall would be. Still Satan tempted her not to set out; however, in the nick of time the birds singing outside the window of her chamber in the early morning reminded Anna of God's care for sparrows and restored her to her purpose.

The journey to the West Country certainly justified Anna's original reaction. She got a place in a coach at an inn but it took six days for the coach to reach Exeter; fortunately its 'rattlings' could not disturb her inner tranquillity. In the West Anna stayed at Tregasow near Truro with Captain Langdon, a Fifth Monarchist who had been a member of the recently defunct Barebones Parliament.

A later report would sum up the purpose of her visit as 'to asperse the government'. That was certainly too crude a summary from Anna's point of view, and she wrote back to the congregation at Allhallows denying that she had ever tried to stir up the people. However, her language on the subject of the Protector could hardly be interpreted otherwise. From the Government's point of view it was equally relevant that Anna, together with other Fifth Monarchists, took the line that the 'Saints' were not bound by legal precepts but by the commands of the Gospel 'and in this sense they are dead to the law, by the life of Christ in them'. People who considered themselves 'dead to the law' were not likely long to survive at liberty once they started to break it in any way that outraged the community. Thus when the local Presbyterian clergy showed themselves notably hostile to Anna and her prophecies, they were easily able to secure a warrant against her for subversion.[35]

On 11 April 1654 an order was given to take Anna Trapnel 'quickly' and send her up to the Council in London.[36]

Anna spent the eve of her apprehension in an all-night session of prayer and singing. She was still in a trance, and still singing the next afternoon when the constable with the justices came for her. Captain Langdon pleaded for her to be allowed to remain one more night, but the response was merely to pull the entranced woman from her pillow, first lifting up her eyelids to see if she was shamming. From the doorway a Presbyterian minister commented grimly: 'A whip will fetch her out.' Then at last Anna awoke and saying that she had had 'a sweet day', inquired if anyone had visited her.[37]

According to Anna, the people round about were on her side, telling the justices who came to take her that they would have to fetch their silk gowns and perform the deed themselves 'for the poor would not do it'. However, on her way to the sessions, a less enlightened mob of men and women, boys and girls, pulled at her as she passed and shouted: 'How do you now? How is it with you now?' And in the session house she was, as she put it, 'a gazing stock'.

One of those who gazed at her steadfastly in the face was the 'witch-trying woman'. But Anna survived this ordeal and although she heard whispers all round her that she would reveal herself to be a witch by being

unable to answer her judges, afterwards it was agreed by this same crowd
of whisperers that she could not possibly be a witch, since she had spoken
so many 'good words'. All the same the accusation of witchcraft – at least
by the ignorant – was never totally abandoned. Later, at Plymouth, words
like 'witchcraft' and 'a white Devil' were thrown at her.

In the main Anna Trapnel was courteously treated by her judges, despite
the fact that she refused to read aloud one of her own passages concerning
the Little Horn. A soldier who smiled when Anna related one of her
visions was sent out of court. Two women were produced who swore that
Anna had been well aware of the people's presence during her trance. One
of her judges termed Anna, not uncharitably, 'a dreamer'. ('So Joseph was
called', retorted Anna.)

Anna's true sufferings began in the course of her journey back to
London. There was no proper vessel to convey her to Portsmouth so that
Anna spent more than fifteen weeks in a 'man's prison' before being
shipped along with some prisoners-of-war (although she did have a maid
with her). When a storm blew up, Anna was accused by her shipmates of
causing the winds through witchcraft 'and they curst me there'. The same
storm caused an injury to her leg. Her company in the coach from
Portsmouth was rather more agreeable: a clutch of partridge eggs on its
way to the Protector as a present. The sight of the eggs inspired Anna. To
her companions in the coach 'I often told of a present from heaven',
she wrote afterwards, 'which was much better than the present of
partridge eggs, yea, it was costlier than the gold of Ophir, or Rubies and
Pearls from a far country'. Another comparison she was inspired to make
was between 'the Great Protector' in heaven and the inferior man who
had assumed the same title in England in the December of the previous
year.

On 2 June Anna Trapnel was committed to Bridewell.[38] She reached
the prison at eleven o'clock at night. The Matron told her sharply that she
had dealt with other 'ranting sluts', before admitting she had never received
one quite like Anna, since she had performed no 'base actions'. Anna now
insisted on sending for her friends, who would collect the maid that she
had brought from Cornwall to attend her. Despite the Matron's protests,
the friends arrived at midnight, and inspected Anna's lodging. They found
it large, but with only 'a hard flock-bed' and one little window in the
corner; the common 'shore' (sewer) ran beneath 'which sink smelt
grievously'. The rats 'that abode much in that room', running about like
cats and dogs, also contributed to the smell. Everyone, including Anna
herself, was horrified. The Matron however was inexorable, denied Anna's

right to a maid, and refused to leave her a candle, saying that she did not trust a prisoner to put it out.

To poor Anna, alone in the stinking darkness, Satan now returned. He suggested that everyone would point at her when she went out, saying 'There goes a Bridewell bird'; decent people would not associate with her 'because of Bridewell reproach'. The hard cold bed and the damp sheets gave her a fever. It was not until Anna's friends had clubbed together to buy a copy of the order against her for 16d that the Matron was convinced nothing had been laid to her charge. Thereafter, because Anna was not a criminal, the Matron allowed flowers and herbs to be strewn, to sweeten the room; her friends were now allowed to stay.

On the day Anna was supposed to appear in court, she was too weak to rise. The Matron showed a flash of her old form by threatening to send the man to fetch her who conveyed the harlots and thieves to beat hemp. Under the circumstances Anna's friends persuaded her to appear. Once again, she was treated courteously in court and allowed to sit down. After that relations between Anna and the Matron never progressed much further than an uneasy truce, the Matron accusing Anna of telling tales 'to wrong her', and Anna much resenting the Matron's suggestion that Anna wanted 'men to come at her'. Explaining herself, Anna said that her delight was not and never had been in men's company 'but in all people as they are godly'.

Yet compared to most criminals – that of course being the very comparison which she detested – Anna Trapnel was well treated. There was no question, as there had been with Mary Overton and Katherine Hadley, of suggesting that she belonged to their number. She was allowed to rent her own chamber at 5s a week – expensive but convenient – and when she was supposed to beat hemp, the other women did it for her. Seven out of the eight weeks she spent in gaol, Anna was accompanied by her sister Ursula Adman. For all that, she could hardly sleep because of 'such scolding' among the prisoners, especially when they were brought in at night. It was no 'pleasant prison' to those 'brought up tenderly', reflected Anna.

Anna Trapnel was released on 26 July after nearly eight weeks in Bridewell.[39] She had declared of herself: 'while I have tongue and breath it shall go forth for the Fifth Monarchy Laws, teaching and practice'. Nor would she give any undertaking about her public pronouncements on her release: on the contrary, she announced she would continue to speak out whenever the spirit moved her. Anna visited the West Country again the following year and with 'three young fellows' went to see the Fifth Monarchist John Carew in St Mawes prison. One of these fellows had a sword, and a soldier taxed him with it, saying that he was on the look-out for Cavaliers, and unless it was accounted for, he would remove it. Anna Trapnel and the young fellows together denied his authority: 'The Lord Protector we own not, thou art of the Army of the Beast.' But when the Governors of Pendennis Castle and the justices sent for her, Anna went into a convenient trance.

A quantity of her verses, which were probably given extemporaneously, were taken down by a reporter in 1657 or 1658.[40] Some of the imagery with Anna as the 'wife' of Christ recalls that of the Catholic mystics (whom Anna would have sternly condemned):

> For they did tear and rent the veil
> Of Christs beloved wife,
> She doth complain unto her King,
> What injuries and smites
> O spouse my Love, saith he, still sing....[41]

Some of it, which has been compared to the early hymns of the Methodists, touches with its simplicity:

> I shall be enclosed and kept
> I shall be very secure
> Unto eternity itself
> And through many strokes, endure.
> Though many strokes of death doth pain
> And make the body smart
> Yet thy presence, dear Jesus, doth
> Refresh and raise my heart.

Anna Trapnel did not however display much spirit of Christian forgiveness to her enemies:

> ... Bedone by as they did
> O they have laid them on the rack
> They have tormented by degrees
> And as they have done, so shall it be
> Saith Christ, done unto these....[42]

In *Voice for the King of Saints* of 1658 she developed the theme further:

> O come with vengeance, come Dear Lord,
> That their blood may drop out,
> That do now rob and steal from thee.

Nor did she regard the godly and the ungodly as in any way equal in an ideal society: under the 'Rule of the Saints', the godly alone would have been constituted 'earls and potentates'.[43]

Anna Trapnel was attacked in print as late as 1660, at which point, with the turn-about of the Restoration, she vanishes from history.[†]

*   *   *

After 1660 the voices of the prophetesses died away except for a few lonely exclamations; the female clamour of the Commonwealth, both sonorous and serious, gave way to the merry prattle of the ladies of King Charles II's England. The bells rang out for the restored King on 29 May, the cannons roared, and over 20,000 people jostled to greet him in London, so that the noise of it all was so great that it made Charles 'prodigiously dazed'.[45] Women were amongst these 20,000, as there had been women watching the execution of his father eleven years earlier. But the age when the female voice might be listened to with general respect – at least if it claimed to come from God – was over.

Did nothing remain – except memories, painful or otherwise – of this time when women had been 'stronger grown'?

It has been mentioned that among those women who caused public disturbances some of the wildest had been those 'eerie spirits' surrounding the strange Quaker enthusiast and preacher James Naylor. In some ways Quaker women, who were prominent in the sect from the start (giving rise to rumours that the sect was entirely composed of them), coincided in their behaviour with the worst prejudices concerning the uncontrolled female. Disruption of services, for example, by persistent crying out and 'quaking' during a minister's sermon – hence the popular nickname for what was in fact the Society of Friends – whenever moved by the spirit to do so, was not calculated to win the respect of the male authorities.

'Good Mistress Fell, go into your own pew, or else go your way', exclaimed a local justice to Margaret Fell concerning her repeated interventions at the local 'steeplehouse', in the course of which she called him 'a caterpillar' to be swept aside (and she was the sect's most respectable member).[46]

'Little Elizabeth' Fletcher, as she was generally known for her tiny physique, arrived in Oxford in June 1654 at the age of fourteen, on a self-imposed mission to speak to the undergraduates. After some ugly horse-play from her 'flock', which led to Little Elizabeth's being pushed under the pump 'with other shameful abuses', this 'virtuous maid of considerable

[†] Although she is just possibly to be identified with Anna Trapnel who married in Woodbridge in Suffolk in 1661.[44]

family', 'contrary to her own Will or Inclination, in Obedience to the Lord' ran naked through the streets of Oxford 'as a sign of the Hypocritical Profession they made there'. In the end, since she still persisted in speaking, the Vice-Chancellor of Oxford had Little Elizabeth whipped for blasphemy.[47]

There was however another aspect to the Quaker religion at its inception which was of more profound importance to the weaker vessel than these manifestations of unrest. George Fox, the founder of the Society of Friends, was a weaver's son from Leicestershire, whom William Penn described as 'an original, being no man's copy'. One of the marks of his originality was to face up to the uncomfortable implications of Christianity, that sex was not necessarily relevant where religion was concerned. Whereas an individual prophetess such as Anna Trapnel had merely claimed a special position for herself, in 1656 George Fox published the first defence in English of the spiritual equality of women since the Reformation. As for testifying, wrote Fox in 1652, 'I said that if the power of God and the Seed spoke in man or woman it was Christ.'[48]

Since Quaker testifying was dependent upon the arrival of the spirit of Christ in the breast, this doctrine of Fox's cast an entirely new light on the whole subject of women speaking in public. We shall meet the heroic if turbulent Quaker women again, their voices at least unstilled, their steps vigorous and defiant in adversity, as they not only travelled their own land but ventured to the New World of Puritan Massachusetts and the old world of the Sultan's Turkey. These women at least were confident that 'in the restoration by Christ' they were equal partners once again: 'Man and Woman, as they were before the Fall'.[49] Thus the most enduring claim made for woman during the period when the world was turned upside down proved to concern her soul, but that of course was invisible, as woman herself was sometimes supposed to be.

PART THREE

Afterwards – A Continual Labour

'Believe me, child, life is a continual labour, checkered with care and pleasure, therefore rejoice in your position, take the world as you find it, and you will I trust find heaviness may endure for a night, but joy comes in the morning.'

ADVICE OF RACHEL LADY RUSSELL TO HER DAUGHTER, 1695

14 *Worldly Goods*

'He is not a pleasant man – very few are; neither is [he] the very next sort for entertainment. One thing pleased: when he said "With all my worldly goods I thee endow", he put a purse upon the book with two hundred guineas.'

DOROTHY DOWAGER COUNTESS OF SUNDERLAND ON HER NIECE'S BRIDEGROOM, 1680

On the eve of the Restoration, Pen, Sir Ralph Verney's second sister, wrote: 'I pray God send we may live to see peace in our times and that friends may live to enjoy each other.' Pen had been one of that melancholy galaxy of unmarried Verney girls who remained at Claydon while Ralph went into exile, their portions caught up in the legal tangles caused by their father's death in the King's cause. For such dowerless young ladies, there were no brilliant matches available: it was more a case of 'thank heaven, fasting, for a good man's love'[1] – or any man's hand in marriage.

Sue Verney, for example, made do with a debt-ridden and drunken widower, spending her early married life at his side in the Fleet prison. Despite this, Sue loved her designated spouse most sincerely during their few years together, before she died in childbirth. Peg Verney was married off to Thomas Elmes – described as 'a very humoursome cross boy' who was soon to make her cry 'night and day'. Peg's own temper was not of the sweetest, and ultimately this cross-grained couple separated. Pen Verney, she who had quarrelled with Peg when asked to share a personal maid as an economy, drew her cousin John Denton; the best that could be said of him was that he *had* stopped drinking. . . . But Pen was in no position to be critical. 'Sir, she was sensible her portion lay in a desperate condition,' wrote her brother Henry to Sir Ralph, 'besides, she grew in years and was not to all men's likings'.[2]

That left Moll and Betty. Moll was said to be 'the plainest of them all', but blessed – or cursed – with 'a great deal of wit'; in addition she was 'wild as a buck' and thus 'too indiscreet to get a discreet man'. Moll, refusing the offer of an elderly bridegroom, ultimately made a disastrous match with one Robert Lloyd. (She was probably pregnant beforehand, for there was talk of shipping her to Ireland or even Barbados to avoid disgrace.) As for Betty, she was variously described as 'of a cross proud lazy disposition' and 'so strangely in love with her own will' that she loathed all efforts made on her behalf.[3] She was undeniably too cross and wilful for anyone who knew her to be willing to take her.

In 1662 cross-patch Betty bestowed herself privately upon a poverty-stricken curate named Charles Adams out of sheer despair. She had met him when he was preaching at church; none of her relations were asked to the marriage. Betty angrily rebutted charges that she had thrown herself away: 'I am not so much lost, as some think I am, because I have married one as has the reputation of an honest man, and one as in time I may live comfortably with.' All the same it was Betty's family which was faced with the problem of the Adamses' livelihood; meanwhile Betty managed to blame them not only for her present poverty but for almost everything that had happened to her since childhood. Her sister Peg Elmes wrote: 'Sometimes I am weary of hearing it, how she was cast off and forsaken and left to herself ... sent to a person's house to a school, like a baby.' Dr Denton referred to Charles Adams and Betty as 'Adam and Eve' in search of a living; it was not intended as a compliment. Only Betty's most charitable sister Cary Gardiner reflected that there were other examples of ladies marrying clergymen ... Lady Mary Bertie for example.[4]

The mingled sulks and despair of Betty Verney on the subject of marriage highlighted one problem of post-Restoration society: it was even more difficult for an ill-endowed girl to find a husband than it had been before the Civil War. And in cases where the possibility of a good dowry did exist, more not less money was required from the father in return for an adequate widow's jointure. It has been pointed out that the average ratio of dowry (given by the father) to jointure (settled on the girl by the bridegroom's family) rose from 4 or 5 to 1 in the middle of the sixteenth century to between 8 and 10 to 1 by the end of the seventeenth.[5]

The troubles of a gently-raised female at this period might be twofold. On the one hand her own portion was liable to have suffered from the effects of sequestration, confiscation and so forth like that of the Verney girls. Many different kinds of ruin had been brought upon families during the recent conflicts which made it difficult to provide a dowry for an unmarried daughter. At the same time these same families, or their equivalents, might well hope to remedy their fortunes by the time-honoured manoeuvre of capturing an heiress. But in this respect the daughters of the aristocracy and gentry were now meeting with what might be described as unfair competition from those richly-cargoed vessels, daughters of the City merchants.

Such brides could bring their husbands large and welcome amounts of cash. Few gentlemen's daughters could compete with this. 'Ours are commodities lying on our hands,' wrote Sir William Morrice of his daughters shortly after the Restoration, while 'merchants' daughters that weigh so many thousands' were sought out in marriage in their place. Sir William Temple blamed the first noble families 'that married into the City for downright money' for introducing 'this public grievance' by which the level of portions was raised all round, and landowners with many daughters were ruined. By the end of the century the agreeable whiff of good City money was to be detected in the grandest homes: the Widow Wheeler, she of the goldsmith's shop at the sign of the Marygold who married her husband's apprentice Robert Blanchard, would number the Earls of Jersey and Westmorland among her descendants; in 1682 the prudent marriage of the Marquess of Worcester with a Miss Rebecca Child, aged sixteen, daughter of the East India merchant Sir Josiah Child, secured at least £25,000 for the future ducal house of Beaufort.[6]

But if the young gentlemen were prepared to sacrifice birth for the sake of wealth – and the evidence shows that such marriages across classes were on the increase – their impoverished sisters were by tradition inhibited from making the same social leap. Although Lady Sandwich, wife of Pepys's patron, declared herself happy to settle for 'a good Merchant' for her daughter Jemima in October 1660, Lord Sandwich retorted that he would rather see her 'with a pedlar's pack at her back' so long as she married a gentleman rather than 'a citizen'. So the numbers of such girls' potential bridegrooms diminished, and the number of unmarried females of this class rose with the century.[7]

There was a further dismal element in the growing excess of women over men in the population as a whole. At the end of the seventeenth century Gregory King stated that women outnumbered men by a ratio of 28 to 27 (on his figures there were 100,000 more females than males in England and Wales as a whole). In 1662 John Graunt, in 'Natural and Political Observations ... made upon the bills of mortality', had noted that more males were born than females every year, and as a result 'every woman may have an Husband, without the allowance of Polygamy', notwithstanding the fact that men lived more dangerously than women, travelled more and adopted professions which demanded celibacy (such as Fellows of university colleges).[8]

Graunt was too optimistic. As Gregory King expressed it, the excess of males born annually – 7,000 – was 'not much more than equal to the males carried off extraordinary by wars, the sea and the Plantations in which articles the females are very little concerned'; while females in general enjoyed a greater life expectancy. A pamphlet of 1690, *Marriage Promoted in a Discourse of its Ancient and Modern Practice*, thought the neglect of marriage threatened the destruction of 'these Nations'. Nearly half the people of England were dying single and a third of the others marrying far too late: men should be *obliged* to marry at twenty-one.[9]

All this put a further premium on an heiress. Marriages were no more constructed on a basis of pure affection after the Restoration than they had been before the Civil War. During that wild period of the Commonwealth the Digger Gerrard Winstanley had actually declared that every man and woman should be free to marry whom they loved, with 'the Common Storehouses' as their portion:[10] such sentiments expressed exactly that kind of frightening radicalism which the post-Restoration world was anxious to eliminate from its memory. Nobody now believed – if anybody ever had – in 'the Common Storehouses', or in free liberty to marry for love.

In 1664 King Charles II wrote one of his racy, chatty letters about the scene at the English court to his sister in France: 'I find the passion Love is very much out of fashion in this country, and that a handsome face without money has but few gallants, upon the score of marriage.' At about the same date the Comte de Gramont, according to Anthony Hamilton, author of his *Memoirs*, was given a lecture on his arrival in England. 'Young women here expect serious intentions and a husband with landed property,' the exiled French writer Saint-Evremond told him sternly. 'You have neither.' He also warned Gramont that it would be 'a miracle' if any gallant proposition he made (other than that of matrimony itself) was considered.[11]

In the 1630s a cruel rhyme had celebrated the marriage of the rich but plain daughter of a Lord Chief Justice to John Lisle:

> Neither well-proportioned, fair nor wise
> All these defects four thousand pounds supplies.

Half a century later, Anne Killigrew, that sensitive observer of a materialist court, bewailed exactly the same situation in her *Invective against Gold*:

> Again, I see the Heavenly Fair despis'd,
> A Hag like Hell, with Gold, more highly priz'd. ....[12]

The difference was the rise of a weariness, a cynicism on the subject; that too perhaps a legacy of the Civil War and Commonwealth period when some kind of liberty had been enjoyed simply through lack of parental supervision. As a result, the state of marriage was mocked as though by universal agreement, especially in literature. (The English young ladies, married off according to worldly principles, also proved very much more susceptible to illicit offers of 'gallantry' than Saint-Evremond had predicted to the Comte de Gramont, the Comte himself experiencing quite a few of these delightful 'miracles'.)

'I rather fear you wou'd debauch me into that dull slave call'd a Wife,' observed Cornelia to Galliard in Aphra Behn's *The Feign'd Curtezans*. Another of Aphra Behn's spirited heroines, Hellena in *The Rover*, was equally forthright on the tedium of matrimony: 'What shall I get? A Cradle full of Noise and Mischief, with a Pack of Repentance at my Back.' Nor was a more romantic attitude to be expected from the other party to the contract. Willmore, Hellena's lover, responded for his own sex that marriage was as certain 'a Bane to Love' as lending money was to friend-ship. Keepwell, in Sir Charles Sedley's *Bellamira*, about to be married to the eponymous heroine, resolved to avoid 'the odious names of Man and Wife, In chains of Love alone we will be tied.'[13]

Yet few women looked to another fate. When Mrs Hobart, the oldest of the Maids of Honour to the Duchess of York, told a younger colleague, Anne Temple, that 'compared to the inconveniences of marriage, its pleasures are so trifling that I don't know how anybody can make up their minds to it', she was aware that her views were not commonly held. It might be 'the stupidest condition for a sensible woman which you can possibly conceive of', but Mrs Hobart was the first to admit that all the Maids of Honour were in fact desperately keen to get married. Besides Mrs Hobart was in the words of Anthony Hamilton 'susceptible only to the charms of her own sex'. It was all very well for such a plain and sharp-tongued woman to die unmarried in 1696 at the age of sixty-three (the title of 'Mrs' being honorific): Anne Temple on the other hand fulfilled a more normal feminine ambition, for all Mrs Hobart's warnings, by marrying the middle-aged widower Sir Charles Lyttelton in 1666 and giving birth to thirteen children thereafter.[14]

It was, however, no coincidence that the two Verney girls who ended their lives most happily did so as wealthy widows – as we have seen, an enviable position throughout the century. Cary lived at court cheerful and well provided-for, following her happy second marriage to John Stewke-ley of Hampshire. Thus were memories of her early humiliation at the hands of her first husband's family expunged by a life of good-natured and worldly ease in middle age. What troubles she had were caused by her passion for gambling, something which possessed many court ladies at the time.[15]

As for Pen, married life with John Denton scarcely seemed to justify the argument that any husband was better than none when one was growing older and 'not to all men's likings'. He too, like Sue's husband, was debt-ridden and imprisoned for it. He also had a vicious streak: Dr Denton referred to him as Pen's 'brute of a husband' who was apt to 'lay her at his feet' with his blows. After John Denton's death, however, Pen made a far more satisfactory match to the elderly Sir John Osborn, finding to her surprise that by her settlement she was now worth £6,000. 'I fear her good fortune will make all old women marry!' exclaimed Cary. When Sir John died in his turn, Pen was able to enjoy twenty good years at Whitehall, housekeeping for her brother and gossiping and playing cards with a series of aristocratic female cronies. She also used her position to boss about her Stewkeley nieces, Cary's daughters, in a way which added to her general enjoyment, if not to theirs.

In old age Pen boasted that she had lived her 'Laborious life' entirely to 'make a fine show to the world', never wasting one shilling to give herself pleasure. She died in 1695 at the age of seventy-three. Her will certainly made a fine show, for she left a series of bequests to those grand ladies whose company she had so much appreciated, so that it reads like some roll-call of the peerage: 'The Countess of Lindsay to have a silver scallop cup and grater, the Countess of Plymouth a serpentine cup with a silver cover, the Countess of Carnarvon a Silver Toaster to toast bread on' and so forth, and so on.[16]

*   *   *

In one sense the climate of the times had changed after the Restoration: parents in general no longer believed in exercising absolute authority over their children in the making of a match, however unwelcome. The ideal union was now one arranged by the parents to which the young couple concerned were consenting. Such an attitude was however very far from representing a new endorsement of that tender passion of love, generally condemned before the Civil War. It was quite simply practical: most sensible people had come to the conclusion that marriages forged on the anvil of agreement caused far less trouble to society in the long run; as Margaret Duchess of Newcastle put it, no one should marry 'against their own liking' because it led directly to adultery.[17]

The pre-war Puritan handbooks of domestic conduct had first pointed out this fact (so obvious to us now, so revolutionary then). As the years passed, the aristocratic fathers too softened: in 1650 Algernon, tenth Earl of Northumberland wrote of the projected marriage of his daughter to the son of Lord Grey of Wark that he would never use 'the authority of a father' to press his children 'to anything of this kind'; however 'if she likes the man', the parents on both sides were in agreement.[18] (Lord Northumberland's enlightened attitude proved a boon to his daughter, for this was the melancholy youth whose mind was distracted, as witness the fact that he had fallen in love with his mother's chambermaid.) Twenty years earlier his father, the ninth Earl, had flashed fiery words when Algernon, then Lord Percy, had defied him to marry Lady Anne Cecil (see p. 27).

In 1673 the most influential book on domestic conduct published after the Restoration – *The Ladies Calling*, the work of a divine named Richard Allestree – summed up the prevailing view as follows: 'As a Daughter is neither to anticipate, nor to contradict the will of her Parent, so (to hang the balance even) I must say she is not obliged to force her own, by marrying where she cannot love; for a negative voice in the case is sure as much the Child's right, as the Parents'.' Allestree even went so far as to say that it would be sacrilege for a maiden to make a vow of marriage where she hated. This was the principle to which Mary Countess of Warwick adhered, when arranging a match for her husband's orphaned niece Lady Essex Rich: having rejected certain suitors in advance for not being sufficiently 'viceless', Lady Warwick then allowed Lady Essex 'her free choice or not, to do as she liked or disliked' out of those she had already vetted. (The consequent match with Daniel Finch was, as we have seen on p. 53, extremely happy, but was cut short by Lady Essex's premature death.)[19]

In the 1670s it was the dearest wish of the childless Sir John Brownlow of Belton that his nephew and heir should marry his wife's niece Alice Sherard, a girl who was trained by her in household matters and whom she had virtually adopted.[20] Nevertheless in the codicil to his will Sir John was careful to make it clear that this pet plan should only be carried out if the young couple 'shall affect one the other' – there was to be no duress. In the event, eight months after this will was written, the couple *did* marry. Although Alice was only sixteen and her bridegroom was dispatched, probably on the same day, to his studies at Cambridge, the foundations had been laid for a stable dynastic union, to the satisfaction of all parties, old and young.

What would have happened to Alice Sherard if she had declined the honour of being chatelaine of Belton, for which she had been carefully groomed by her aunt? Nothing drastic certainly; but Sir John Brownlow's codicil also stated: 'if the said Alice Sherard shall dislike the said Match and by any refusal on her part the said Match shall not take place then this legacy to be void' – the legacy in question being 1,000 pieces of gold in a special box marked with the initials A.S.

That was the point. In the language of Hannah Woolley in *The Gentlewomans Companion*, published the same year as Sir John Brownlow's will was made, nothing, not 'affluence of estate, potency of friends, nor highness of descent' could make up for 'the insufferable grief of a loathéd bed'.[21] That might be so; but money, connections and birth were still the values which prevailed in the marriage market. While many parents had come to agree with Hannah Woolley both in principle and in practice about the need for consent, nobody seriously thought of substituting different values where the initial selection of partners was concerned.

Over children too, the theoretical authority of the parent remained intact in the second half of the century even if custom asked that it should be exercised more kindly. There was a pretty to-do in May 1667 when the eligible young Viscount Maidstone, heir to the third Earl of Winchilsea, was secretly married off at the age of fourteen to one Elizabeth Windham, without his father's knowledge, let alone his permission.[22] The whole affair sounded extremely dubious – at least to the ears of the outraged Earl of Winchilsea, then absent on a diplomatic mission in Belgrade. The boy had lived in the same house as his bride for some time while at Cambridge, and was encouraged by her relations to make advances to her. Still, the young Lord kept his head sufficiently not to consummate the marriage after the ceremony (or else was too frightened of his father to confess it). Writing back to King Charles II in a state of righteous indignation on the subject, Lord Winchilsea passed on his boy's account of the fateful afternoon: how he had been made drunk 'by their putting of wine into his beer' at the time of the marriage, but that as soon as the bride's mother left the chamber 'he ran out of the room'. Lord Winchilsea concluded triumphantly 'Nor doth he know whether she [the bride] be a man or a woman.'

To the Earl of Clarendon, Lord Winchilsea summed the matter up: this 'foulest piece of fraud and abuse' would shock all parents who claimed a title in 'the happy disposal of their children'. Still, a year later Lord Winchilsea had not succeeded in getting the marriage annulled. At some point the marriage was evidently consummated: Lord Maidstone died young, but left a posthumous son Charles behind him, the child of his Cambridge bride, who in time inherited his grandfather's title to become the fourth Earl of Winchilsea. When the time came for this boy to be married in the 1690s his widowed mother, Elizabeth Viscountess Maidstone, wrote a careful letter to his guardian Lord Nottingham about the possible choices: 'He has seen both these ladies and thinks them very beautiful, but if we were permitted to make choice, your Lordship knows our first desire. . . .' Lord Nottingham's eventual choice of Sarah Nourse, an heiress worth £30,000 in money and land, as the bride was acceptable to Lady Maidstone not only for financial reasons but also because 'My son has seen the lady and likes her very well.' Unlike the earlier Maidstone match, therefore, which had flouted the conventions, this projected union had everything to be said for it by the standards of the time.

In 1701 *The Athenian Oracle*, one of the early magazines for answering young ladies' queries, came down firmly on the side of parental authority. The questioner had vowed to leave her father and mother as soon as possible because they treated her so unkindly, and an opportunity presenting itself, wondered which obligation came first, her vow or her duty to her parents. The answer came back: 'Your Vow does not oblige you, for your Body is the Goods of your Father, and you can't lawfully dispose of your self without his knowledge and consent, so that you ought to beg God Almighty's Pardon for your Rashness' (in making the vow in the first place).[23]

Similarly the wife's legal position remained humble, as it had been at the beginning of the century. In the categorical words of John Evelyn to Margaret Godolphin on the subject: 'marriage entitles [the husband] to your person, and to all you bring with it of worldly goods, and he can do with it what he pleases without your consent'.[24] (The exception to this, already noted, was the development of the concept of the trust in Chancery, which if held for an heiress could not be swallowed up in the husband's property – see p. 11; but this of course only applied to a tiny percentage of women.)

*   *   *

The wedding of Lucy Pelham and Gervase Pierrepont at East Hoathly in Sussex in March 1680 celebrated a match made very much in this world; as a result it was not a very cheerful affair. The choice of Halland, the ancient seat of the Pelhams, was dictated by a mixture of economy and family pride. The bride's mother would have preferred the fun of a jaunt to London, but Sir John Pelham 'thought it would be more expense, and not handsome because of his great relations'.[25]

Gervase Pierrepont himself represented no maiden's dream. The bride's aunt was the former Dorothy Sidney, now styled Dowager Countess of

Sunderland (her second marriage to Sir Robert Smythe was conveniently swallowed up in the senior title). Lady Sunderland wrote tartly: 'He is not a pleasant man – very few are; neither is [he] the very next sort for entertainment.' The high point of the ceremony was that moment when the groom, by tradition, placed a purse upon the prayer book to accompany his vow: 'With all my worldly goods I thee endow.' A few years earlier at court the young William of Orange had deposited his own little heap of symbolic gold when wedding his cousin Princess Mary of York. King Charles II, the bride's uncle, had been in a merry mood and had commanded the fifteen-year-old Mary: 'Take it up, take it up. It's all clear gain to you.' In this case the congregation at East Hoathly was enchanted to see that Mr Pierrepont put down a purse containing 200 guineas! As Lady Sunderland commented: 'Everybody puts somewhat, but this is the most I have heard.'[26]

Whether this large sum was all clear gain to the new Mrs Pierrepont depends on one's attitude to that other sort of price she had to pay for it. At the time, commented Dorothy, she seemed pleased enough by events: 'but she loves more compliments and mirth than she will ever find. I prepared her, as well as I could, not to expect it. . . .'[27]

Lucy Pelham, one of the two daughters of Lady Lucy Sidney by her marriage to Sir John Pelham, a Member of many successive Parliaments, was born beneath that glittering net of aristocratic family relationships which spangled English society after the Restoration and onwards. When the time came for Lucy herself to be woven into this net by means of marriage the negotiations were entrusted to her mother's sister Dorothy – since both Pelhams were kept in the country, the one by inclination and gout, the other by illness alone.

Dorothy Sunderland's life had changed. Gone was the delicious magic of her youth which had led the poet Waller to make her his Sacharissa. Robert Earl of Sunderland, the ambitious rising politician, and his clever wife Anne, reigned at Althorp. Dorothy Sunderland was now in her sixties, living as she put it 'in twilight' in a little house in Whitehall. Gone too were the days when her own daughter Dorothy Spencer had reigned at Rufford in Lancashire as wife of Lord Halifax. Dorothy Spencer had died in 1670 and two years later Lord Halifax took Gertrude Pierrepont as his second wife. (Betty, for whom he wrote the famous *Advice to a Daughter*, was the fruit of this second union.) There is a story that Dorothy in these latter days asked Waller when he would write some more poetry for her. The poet is said to have replied: 'When you are as young again, Madam, and as handsome as you were then.' If true, the sourness was all on Waller's side – his poetry had gone sadly out of fashion. Dorothy, who described herself lightly as 'the poor old dolt in the corner' can hardly have been much put out by the rebuff; her correspondence shows that her humour and common sense remained pristine, with her Halifax grandchildren, Nan Savile in particular, close to her, and her friendship with their father uninterrupted despite his second marriage.[28] Indeed, far from living 'in twilight' Dorothy the Dowager Countess acted as the secret matriarch of this golden world, reconciling in herself the political differences which existed between its various members.

Romantic figure as she may have been in the past, Dorothy in old age displayed a brisk attitude to the whole subject of marriage. The selected bridegroom was a grandson of the Earl of Kingston and a first cousin of Halifax's second wife. Even more to the point was the fact that Gervase Pierrepont was rich. Apart from that, frankly there does not seem to have been much to say for him; and it is significant that Dorothy did not try to say it.

She wrote approvingly of Pierrepont's 'good fortune' – £200 a year and £5,000 more in 'money' – besides which there was an aunt of seventy in the offing, from whom more was expected, one who was conveniently suffering from a quartan ague. As to the rest: 'One finds that he does not talk ... another finds fault with his person who have little reason, God knows, to meddle with that.' In Dorothy's own opinion 'the worst of him is his complexion, and the small-pox is not out of his face yet; he had them but eight months ago'. His person was certainly not 'taking'. On another occasion she wrote even more straightforwardly that it was 'ugly'. Nor was this wealthy pock-marked Beast endowed with the kind of sparkling wit which would make up to Beauty for his appearance. He was 'well enough dressed and behaved', said Dorothy, but 'of few words', otherwise 'very bashful', certainly too bashful to speak to strangers. Nevertheless Dorothy was optimistic about the success of the match. After all Mr Pierrepont was no more ill-favoured than Edward Montagu, Lucy Pelham's sister's bridegroom; 'and his wife kisses him all day, and calls him her pretty dear'.[29]

What was Lucy Pelham's reaction to all this? Dorothy, who had a special fondness for her Pelham nieces, made it clear that she had no wish to ruin Lucy's life for the sake of a good fortune: 'I desired her to tell me if she had any distaste to him, and I would order it so it should not go on, and her father should not be angry with her. But,' Dorothy added, 'she is wiser than to refuse it.'

Nor did Lucy refuse the match negotiated by her clever aunt – which included a splendid jointure for the widow after her husband's death: 'I demanded a thousand a year and his London house and I have got it', wrote Dorothy triumphantly. The girl's father would never have thought of asking for the house as well: 'but a very pretty house so furnished as that will be very considerable to a woman'. Then there were six coach-horses to be bought, with Lady Halifax, Mr Pierrepont's cousin, to choose the coach. Lucy was to have her own page as well. In return the bride's father engaged to give a dowry in a ratio of 7 to 1 to the jointure: £7,000 pounds, £1,000 of which was payable on his death. Even Lucy's brother Tom, who disapproved of some of the financial clauses, admitted that his sister needed 'no persuasion' to marry Mr Pierrepont; although it should perhaps be mentioned, as an example of Dorothy Sunderland's famous wisdom, that she did not allow the pock-marked Mr Pierrepont to call on his future bride until her father had come to town to complete the arrangements.[30]

The only hitch which occurred concerned high politics, not the humble affections. It was unfortunate that the marriage negotiations, in early 1680, were taking place at a time of mounting tension over the possible 'Exclusion' of the Catholic Duke of York from the royal succession. In a complicated situation, Robert Earl of Sunderland and Lord Halifax represented, roughly speaking, rival political views. Sunderland naturally raised his eyebrows at the thought of his kinswoman marrying into the Halifax set. From the other point of view, Lucy's brother Tom Pelham, who had ranged himself far more violently against the King than the moderate Halifax, found the marriage equally unwelcome.

However, Dorothy Sunderland's granddaughter Nan Savile was said to be 'very comical' about the whole business, dangling invitations to Rufford before Mr Pierrepont's eyes.[31] Somehow all this was smoothed over, perhaps because Dorothy Sunderland's own political sympathies lay with her erstwhile son-in-law Halifax. Finally the wedding was allowed to take place.

At first Lucy seems to have been most contented with her new life. She was a giddy young woman, wrote her aunt, and 'delighted with liberty and money'. Of Mr Pierrepont she said that he was as kind as she could desire, allowing her to have everything 'to the uttermost of his fortune', and begging her to buy whatever plate or furniture she wanted, and he would pay for it. Dorothy was not quite as happy about all this extravagance as her earlier matchmaking might have indicated. She intended to advise her niece not to abuse her husband's generosity, for his grand relations would not think well of her if she proved herself too 'expensive'. She was also surprised – 'Pierrepont blood' not being famous for its open-handedness. Altogether it was a worrying situation, with Lucy 'a little too free and too merry in appearance', and Mr Pierrepont in contrast very grave and lacking altogether in self-confidence; he had 'an ill opinion of his own opinion', wrote Dorothy.[32]

Alas, poor Lucy. Mr Pierrepont, for all his wealth, was but a gilded sepulchre. By June, only a few months after the marriage, Dorothy feared that he would not prove a good husband. He was fond enough of his wife, but 'so unquiet in the house': that is to say he meddled with everything in the kitchen, and interfered with the servants, abusing them to such an extent that they had wearied of their positions and were all leaving. For his part, Mr Pierrepont was threatening to sack Lucy's personal maid, who had been overheard saying: 'God bless her mistress, she would be glad never to see her master again.' Above all, his Pierrepont blood had asserted itself and he was now very mean in everything that was not for show – so much for the visible splendours of the plate and furniture which Lucy had been encouraged to buy.

Lucy herself, according to Dorothy, was very depressed by this turn of events; still, she showed no signs of revolting against her fate. No great natural housekeeper, somewhat bewildered by that side of life, she was generally felt to have 'a hard task' coping with the demands of Mr Pierrepont. Yet she neither complained to nor confided in her aunt on the subject – rather to the latter's annoyance. On the contrary: 'she does observe him [Mr Pierrepont] as much as possible'. Dorothy added: 'Severity not well understood has no bounds.'[33]

Dorothy had originally been waspishly worried that this new 'fond' couple might take to kissing each other in public, and calling each other 'pretty dear', in the manner of Lucy's sister Elizabeth and her unprepossessing husband Edward Montagu. If so, she had intended to exercise her authority over her niece to put an end to such tasteless public exhibitions. In fact, the Pierreponts' married life was more reminiscent of the sad disgruntled marriages of late Restoration drama, that of Squire Sullen and Mrs Sullen in *The Beaux' Stratagem* perhaps ('O matrimony!' cries Mrs Sullen, 'Oh the pleasure of counting the melancholy clock by a snoring husband');[34] except that the Pierreponts' union was less colourful – no scandal smirched Lucy's name. Her earlier giddiness and love of liberty was presumably extinguished by the strain of housekeeping for Mr Pierrepont. Her husband was created an Irish peer – Lord Pierrepont of Ardglass – in 1703, and Lord Pierrepont of Hanslope in Buckinghamshire, in 1714. But Lucy Pierrepont never had any children, so the titles died out on his death.

*   *   *

The story of Elizabeth Percy, the child known as 'my lady Ogle', if its dénouement was less tragic than that of Frances Coke, Lady Purbeck (see p. 12 ff.), showed that the notion of the heiress had lost none of its power to lure in the intervening half-century. This was after all a venturesome - and mercenary - age in which the rumour of a girl's fortune was enough to incite some coarse spirits to extraordinary acts of boldness.

There was that Cornet Wroth who, dining with Sir Robert Vyner at his country house, took the opportunity to carry off an heiress named Miss Hyde in a coach after dinner. When a wheel broke, the egregious Cornet was still not checked: he put the girl across his horse and got as far as the Putney ferry, where another coach-and-six awaited, before his pursuers finally caught up with him. The girl, speechless after her ordeal, was recovered; but Cornet Wroth escaped. In February 1680 the mere rumour that one of Lady Tirrell's daughters possessed a considerable fortune was enough to encourage certain 'robbers' to break into her house in Buckinghamshire. The motive, it was explained afterwards, was not robbery at all, but the desire to lay hands on Miss Tirrell. One of the housebreakers, fearing not to be able to accomplish his design by ordinary means, 'did endeavour to have carried her away under some crafty pretence and to have married her'.[35] Matters had not really progressed very far since the presumptuous Roger Fulwood abducted the schoolgirl Sara Cox from Newington Common in the reign of Charles I (see p. 23).

The matrimonial affairs of 'my lady Ogle' were on an even more sensational level, owing to the particular combination of enormous wealth and high position in society. John Evelyn quoted a contemporary opinion: she was 'one that both by birth and fortune might have pretended to the greatest prince in Christendom'. This child's father was Joceline Percy, eleventh and last Earl of Northumberland of the ancient Percy creation. Her mother, Elizabeth Wriothesley, Countess of Northumberland - 'a beautiful lady indeed', wrote Pepys goggling at her at court in 1667 - was seldom mentioned without some allusion to her celebrated looks.[36] Certainly Lely's portrait of her among the Hampton Court beauties shows an angelic blonde docility; an impression borne out by the blameless quality of her personal life. A daughter of the Earl of Southampton by his second marriage, Lady Northumberland was one of the co-heiresses of the Southampton fortune with her step-sisters Rachel Lady Russell and Lady Noel. But through her mother, a Leigh, who had been the sole heiress of her father, the Earl of Chichester, Lady Northumberland was also extremely rich in her own right. Elizabeth Percy was her only surviving child.

At the death of the Earl of Northumberland in 1670, it was possible to see in Elizabeth Percy merely a little red-headed girl of three years old. More romantically, one could see in her 'the last of the Percies' (she inherited all those ancient resonant Percy baronies which could pass through the female line). It was also possible to envisage this small child as a prize to be captured. On the whole society took the latter view.

Still in her early twenties and quite apart from her beauty said to be worth £6,000 a year, Lady Northumberland was also now herself a natural target for a stream of suitors. In September 1671 bold Harry Savile found himself staying at Althorp at the same time as the lovely widow. Finding her door open, he entered in his nightgown, went right up to her bedside, and started to call 'Madam! Madam!' until Lady Northumberland awoke. He then acquainted her with the passion he had long nourished for her but had somehow been unable to confess in the hours of daylight. Lady Northumberland, in a fright, called her women, and Harry Savile was advised to leave Althorp as soon as possible. He did so, and subsequently went abroad rather than fight the duel which would have been proposed to avenge Lady Northumberland's honour.[37]

Thereafter the young Lady Northumberland resided chiefly in Paris, her valuable affections having been secured by Ralph Montagu, Charles II's Ambassador to the French court, who married her three years after her first husband's death. In 1696 Francis Viscount Shannon would dedicate the second edition of his *Discourses and Essays*, in which he strongly advocated against marrying for 'mere love', to Lady Northumberland, then keeping herself 'in a kind of religious retirement'; but there seems to have been something of love implicit in the widow's selection, for the unprincipled but fascinating Ralph Montagu had the knack of attracting the opposite sex. Ralph Montagu's motives were more cynical and the marriage was not a very happy one, any more than Lady Northumberland enjoyed her sojourn in France. Here the tart wit of Madame de Sévigné found an ideal target in the appearance of this famous English beauty - her features were not good, she looked surprisingly old and careworn and in case her dress might be supposed to atone for these defects: '*elle est avec cela mal habillée, point de grâce*'.[38] One of Lady Northumberland's problems abroad was not understanding the French language; one hopes that as a result she was at least spared knowledge of Madame de Sévigné's chauvinist criticism.

Meanwhile at home the child Elizabeth Percy fell into the care of her strong-minded paternal grandmother, widow of Algernon, tenth Earl of Northumberland. (She was his second wife; Lady Anne Cecil, that bride he had insisted on marrying for love, had died in 1637). Indeed, old Lady

Northumberland seized the opportunity of her daughter-in-law's second marriage to insist that the marrying off of Elizabeth Percy was to be her grandmother's sole concern.[39] The younger woman, being of a far gentler character, made no exaggerated counter-claim but protested that it was very hard that her own child 'should be disposed of without her consent' – especially since Elizabeth Percy 'if she had no other children must be her heir'. In the end some kind of accommodation was reached between the two Countesses of Northumberland on this important subject, by which the ladies both agreed not to marry off the girl without each other's consent – and without her consent as well. (It was also incidentally agreed that Elizabeth Percy should not be married below the age of legal consent.)

Nevertheless it was the old Countess, a redoubtable and scheming character, who in effect won out, since she retained control of the girl in England. The first match she arranged, in 1679, when Elizabeth Percy was only twelve, had at least the merit of dynastic suitability: this was with the thirteen-year-old Lord Ogle, heir to the Duke of Newcastle. Immediately on marriage, he assumed the surname of Percy. Dorothy Countess of Sunderland, however, thought him 'as ugly as anything young can be'.[40] Either for this or some more worldly reason connected with old Lady Northumberland's intrigues and Elizabeth Percy's tender age, her mother did not approve of the match. This led to a quarrel between young Lady Northumberland and the new Lady Ogle.

Rachel Lady Russell, Lady Northumberland's wise step-sister, tried to effect a reconciliation between the two in a letter to her niece on the subject of her marriage: 'You have my prayers and wishes, dear Lady Ogle, that it may prove as fortunate to you as ever it did to any and that you may know happiness to a good old age; but, Madam, I cannot think you can be completely so, with a misunderstanding between so near a relation as a mother. . . .' Lady Russell begged Lady Ogle to seek her mother's pardon. After all Lady Northumberland's advice had had but 'one aim and end . . . your being happy'.[41]

But Lady Ogle did not enjoy happiness to a good old age, at least not just yet, and not with this bridegroom.

A few months later Lord Ogle died. What was to happen to 'my lady Ogle' now? Rumours abounded, correspondence of the period avidly reporting the latest supposed developments in her situation as though the fate of 'my lady Ogle' was some major matter of State. Everyone was talking 'about Lord Ogle's death and Lady Ogle's position'.[42]

The person soon selected for Lady Ogle by old Lady Northumberland was Thomas Thynne Esquire of Longleat Hall in Wiltshire, and some kind of contract between the two was signed. This produced consternation in more than one quarter. The match was not considered worthy of Lady Ogle by the world at large, she whose name had been coupled with a bridegroom as august as the Prince of Hanover. Nor was Mr Thynne himself a specially savoury character, having seduced another girl under promise of marriage, before abandoning her for the lure of Lady Ogle. Lord Essex, Lady Ogle's uncle by marriage, believed that her grandmother had 'betrayed' her 'for money'; the Earl of Kingston or Lord Cranborne (Lord Salisbury's heir) would have been far more suitable.[43] Another unsavoury participant in the whole affair was the financier Richard Brett, who was rewarded by Thynne with valuable property for helping to bring about the 'sale' of Lady Ogle; Brett's wife being a connection of the heiress.[44]

As for Lady Ogle herself, it was said that 'the contract she lately signed rises in her stomach'. It may be that Lady Ogle had encountered a powerful counter-attraction in the shape of the handsome Count Königsmarck, who had been paying her court. At this point the drama increased when Lady Ogle herself vanished from her grandmother's house. On 10 November 1681, as Sir Charles Hatton wrote excitedly, no one yet knew with whom or to where she had fled. But it was generally believed that 'she went away to avoid Mr Thynne, whom she sometimes [that is, previously] married'. This marriage, which took place in the summer, had not been consummated before Lady Ogle's flight. There was now a rumour that it would be made void and that Lady Ogle would be wedded to George Fitzroy, one of Barbara Duchess of Cleveland's sons by Charles II, who had recently been granted that Northumberland title which had become extinct at Lady Ogle's father's death.[45]

The next stage of the drama took place when Mr Thomas Thynne, the unsuccessful husband – or suitor – of Lady Ogle was shot by a posse of Count Königsmarck's men; with five bullets in his belly he died next morning. Now the furore reached new heights. Had there been a duel? Duelling was against the law, and the King did all he could to enforce the prohibition, but it was at the same time a recognized social procedure where honour was concerned. Murder hardly came into the same category. Count Königsmarck's men tried to maintain that one of them – a Pole – had challenged Mr Thynne to a duel, but unfortunately this man was known to have asked the Swedish Ambassador the night before 'whether, if Mr Thynne was removed, his master might not marry the Lady Ogle according to the law of England'. The girl Thynne had betrayed was said to have played some part in the conspiracy, hence the satirical epitaph:

> Here lies Tom Thynne of Longleat Hall
> Who never would have miscarried,
> Had he married the woman he lay withal;
> Or laid with the woman he married.[46]

The responsibility of the Count himself – who had fled – was another much debated point.

In fact the Count only got as far as Gravesend where he was found in a boat 'disguised in a poor habit'. He was taken to Newgate and subsequently put on trial. However, his men loyally stuck to the story that there had been a challenge to a duel. It had actually been refused but one of their number, 'the Polander', had failed to appreciate this fact and thus fired the fatal shot.[47] So the Count was acquitted. (His men were hanged.)

None of this of course had improved the Count's chances of marrying Lady Ogle although, imperviously, he did renew his suit. In any case on 30 May 1682, the exciting chase was ended. Steps had been taken earlier in the year to render the Thynne marriage contract void at the Court of the King's Bench. In May Lady Ogle was married to the nineteen-year-old Charles Seymour, sixth Duke of Somerset. No one could deny that that was a splendid match: this latest bridegroom was dark and handsome, generous and cultivated. His only defect – an overweening arrogance on the subject of his ancestry, which led to his being termed 'the Proud Duke of Somerset' – was perhaps not such a defect after all for one who was herself 'the last of the Percies'. It showed tact on the part of the new Duchess that she did not finally hold the 'Proud Duke' to that promise which was part of the marriage contract, to change his surname from Seymour to Percy.

So the former Elizabeth Percy, Lady Ogle, lived in splendour for forty years as Duchess of Somerset, bearing her husband thirteen children, and ornamenting the court of William and Mary. Later her political influence was feared by the Tories under Queen Anne, when she became First Lady of the Bedchamber following the fall of Sarah Duchess of Marlborough. This incurred for her the enmity of Swift and thus was her red hair (and her dramatic past) angrily mocked:

> Beware of carrots from Northumberland;
> Carrots sown Thynne a deep root may get,
> If so be they are in Somer set.[48]

*   *   *

For all the *Sturm und Drang* which had surrounded the early years of 'my lady Ogle', it is appropriate to note that her aunt Rachel Lady Russell, the tragic much admired heroine of the same period, was herself an heiress and as such made a supremely happy marriage. It was possible in the second half of the seventeenth century, as it had been in the first, for love to flourish under rich bedcovers. The sorrows which came to Lady Russell, came from her husband's political convictions and his defeat at the hands of the established order. Her pleasures were on the contrary produced by her acceptance of the rules of society, within which framework she brought her own remarkable character and intelligence to play.

Rachel Wriothesley was born in 1636, the daughter of the Earl of Southampton by his first wife, a French Protestant noblewoman named Rachel de Ruvigny. Where her education was concerned, like her future sisters-in-law the Ladies Diana and Margaret Russell, she benefited from a domestic chaplain, Dr Fitzwilliam; at the age of seventeen she was married to Lord Vaughan, heir to the Earl of Carbery, a match later referred to as 'acceptance without choosing on either side'. In later years Lady Russell would describe herself as having been at this period fond of 'a great dinner and worldly talk', following a sermon which was not too long.[49] The only child of this marriage was born and died in 1665, in which year died also Lord Vaughan.

In a financial sense, however, the important event in the life of Rachel Lady Vaughan was the death of Lord Southampton two years later without a male heir. The three daughters who were his co-heiresses – 'my sister Noel, my sister Northumberland and myself' as Rachel described them – now cast lots for the valuable properties which formed part of his fortune. It was in this historic manner that Rachel acquired Southampton House and that area known then as 'the manors of Bloomsbury and St Giles' which was to provide the foundations of the great London property holdings of the Russell family. Rachel Lady Vaughan was now in the vastly desirable situation of being a wealthy and childless widow in her early thirties who had complete control over her fortune – and thus over her future. Although her fortune could not perhaps be compared with that of her step-niece 'my lady Ogle', certainly her immediate fate was likely to be preferable. And so it proved.

William Russell was in fact the second son of the Earl of Bedford, one of his immense brood of children by Anne Carr, the good Countess sprung from the bad mother, but his eldest brother was sickly and it was tacitly assumed that William was the heir; this brother died in 1678 and William then succeeded to the courtesy title of Lord Russell. Otherwise he was intelligent and charming if also, as time would show, of that steely stuff of which political martyrs are made. He was, however, a few years younger than Rachel Lady Vaughan. Still, a fortune glossed over such matters wonderfully. Although the wooing took some two years to complete, in view of the vested interests on both sides, it was finally successful. Rachel Lady Vaughan and William Russell were married on 31 July 1669. From his family accounts we know that William Russell spent lavishly on his own clothes for the occasion: £250 on cherry-coloured silk, scarlet and silver brocade and gold and silver lace.[50] (We do not know what the bride wore.)

William Russell now happily acquired control of Rachel's Bloomsbury properties, according to the laws of the time, just as her father's residence of Southampton House became their family home in London. In personal terms an equally blissful union was inaugurated. Two daughters – Rachel and Katherine – were born in 1674 and 1676; the Russells' joy was completed when a son, named Wriothesley in compliment to his mother's family, was born in 1680. Since Rachel Lady Russell was by now forty-four, there must have been some anxiety about the prospect of a male heir. Certainly the old Earl of Bedford at Woburn Abbey gave the messenger who brought him the news a present of sixteen guineas, nearly twice as much as had greeted the news of the arrival of the girls.[51]

The Russells were seldom apart, except when William went to visit the family estates at Woburn, and even then, as Rachel quaintly expressed it in 1675, she did not like to let 'this first post-night pass without giving my dear man a little talk', in the shape of a letter. Both were particularly fond of their own house (part of Rachel's inheritance) at Stratton in Hampshire. Rachel painted a placid domestic picture to William away at Woburn: the little boy asleep as she wrote, the girls singing in bed, with little Rachel telling herself a long story, 'She says, Papa has sent for her to Wobee, and then she gallops and says she has been there, and a great deal more.' Lady Russell ended her letter on a cheerful gourmet note: 'but', she wrote, 'boiled oysters call'. In June 1680 she told her husband more spiritually: 'My dearest heart, flesh and blood cannot have a truer and greater sense of their own happiness than your poor but honest wife has. I am glad you find Stratton so sweet; may you live to do so one fifty years more.' On another occasion she was writing with 'thy pillow at my back; where thy dear head shall lie, I hope, tomorrow night'.[52]

'I know, as certainly as I live, that I have been, for twelve years, as passionate a lover as ever woman was, and hope to be so one twelve years more.' Thus Rachel Lady Russell in September 1682. Less than one year after this declaration of an ideally happy wife, William Lord Russell was on trial for conspiring to kill the King and the Duke of York in what was known as the Rye House Plot. His specific guilt remains doubtful although with the other extreme Whig, Algernon Sidney, William Russell admitted he had declared it was lawful to resist the King on occasion. Significantly, when reasons were given to Charles II for leniency towards Lord Russell, the monarch tersely replied: 'All that is true, but it is as true that if I do not take his life he will soon have mine.'[53] In a test of strength between the King and the Whigs therefore, William Lord Russell was cast in the role of the Whig martyr, a role he was not unwilling to fulfil.

During the period between Lord Russell's arrest on 26 June 1683 and his trial which began on 3 July it was Rachel who beavered away, seeking support. And at the trial itself she caused a thrill of anguish by her appearance at her husband's side in the courtroom. Officially, the defendant in a treason trial at this date was not allowed a legal adviser; the Attorney-General, to anticipate Lord Russell's protests, declared that he could have a servant to take notes for him. A sensation of a different sort was caused when Lord Russell announced: 'My wife is here to do it', or in another version: 'I require no other assistance than that which the lady can give me who sits by my side.'[54]

'If my lady will give herself that trouble', was the embarrassed reply of the Chief Justice. The Attorney-General then offered two persons to write for Lord Russell if he so wished; the astonishment caused by Lord Russell's announcement being a striking commentary on the low level of female literacy at the time.

The predictable verdict was guilty and the sentence execution. Rachel's frantic efforts to bring about a reprieve, her own desperate pleas for mercy, the pleas of her relations and those of Lord Russell were all unavailing. The date was set for Friday 21 July. On the Thursday, Lord Russell told Gilbert (later Bishop) Burnet he wished for his own sake that his wife would cease 'beating every bush', and 'running about so' in the useless task of trying to save him; and yet when he considered that 'it would be some mitigation [to her afterwards] that she had tried everything he had to let her continue'. And there was a tear in his eye as he turned away. But he received his beloved children for the last time, according to Bishop Burnet, 'with his ordinary serenity' and Rachel herself managed to leave without a single sob.[55]†

Late that night the husband and wife said good-bye for the last time. Lord Russell expressed 'great joy' at that 'magnanimity of spirit' which he

† This touching family scene, together with 'The Parting of Lord and Lady Russell' and Lady Russell pleading for mercy from King Charles II, was to become a favourite subject among Victorian painters, figuring in exhibitions at the Royal Academy throughout the nineteenth century.[56]

found in Rachel to the last; parting from her was of all things the hardest one he had to do. As for her, he feared that after he was gone and she no longer had the task of his reprieve to buoy her up 'the quickness of her spirits would work all within her'. They kissed four or five times and still both managed a stoical restraint.

After Rachel's departure, William mused aloud on his great blessing in having had such a wife, one who had never begged him to turn informer and thus save his own life. How terribly this last week would have passed, he told Bishop Burnet, if she had been 'still crying at me'! God had showed him a 'signal providence' in granting him a wife of 'birth, fortune, great understanding, great religion, and a great kindness to him' – note the order even at the last in which these benefits were listed – 'but her carriage in this extremity went beyond all'.

After Lord Russell's death, Rachel Lady Russell's conduct in her be-reavement justified her husband's fears for her. Through the intercession of Lord Halifax, she was allowed to place a public escutcheon of mourn-ing over the door of Southampton House; this permission indicated that the King did not intend to profit from the forfeiture of Lord Russell's personal estate (a penalty which was generally exacted after the death of a traitor). In other ways Lady Russell withdrew into a more private world of lamentation. No visitors were ever allowed to call at South-ampton House on Fridays – the fatal day – and in addition 26 June, 3 July and 21 July were kept sacred to commemorate his arrest, trial and execution.

A few months after Lord Russell's death, Rachel's old mentor Dr Fitzwilliam advocated a recourse to the Scriptures for comfort. In reply, Lady Russell burst out that nothing could comfort her because of her lack of *him*. 'I want him to talk with, to walk with, to eat, and sleep with. All these things are irksome to me. The day unwelcome, and the night so too. . . .'[57] Even her children made her heart 'shrink' because she remem-bered the pleasure their father had taken in them. Two years later she was still torturing herself with thoughts that she could have done more to save him.

At the death of Anne Countess of Bedford (an event probably brought forward by the shock of her son's execution) Rachel took the opportunity to visit the family vault at Chenies in Buckinghamshire where her hus-band's body was entombed. She defended her decision to Dr Fitzwilliam. 'I had considered. I went not to seek the living among the dead. I knew I should not see him anymore, wherever I went, and had made a covenant with myself, not to break out in unreasonable fruitless passion.' She went deliberately to 'quicken my contemplation' as to 'whither the nobler part was fled, to a country far off, where no earthly power bears any sway, nor can put an end to a happy society'.[58]

When Lady Russell went to London for the sake of her little boy's future, she determined to be brave about visiting Southampton House: 'I think (by God's assistance) the shadows will not sink me.' Yet every anniversary destroyed her resolution by 'breaking off that bandage, time would lay over my wound'. In 1695, suffering in fact from cataract of the left eye, she was said to have wept herself blind. In extreme old age, listing her sins in shaky handwriting, Rachel included the fact that she had been inconsolable for the death of him who had been 'my dear Mr Russell, seeking help from man, but finding none'.[59]

It was natural that this tragic widow should resolve never to marry again; instead she resolved to see 'none but lawyers and accountants' in the interests of her children. Both decisions were much applauded by a society which admired Lady Russell's heroism in adopting such a stern and secluded way of life. So by degrees Lady Russell fulfilled the highest expectations of her time for a great lady.†

Her future efforts were entirely for her family. She succeeded in getting the attainder on her husband's title reversed so that her own Wriothesley could bear it. She carefully arranged, as we shall see in the next chapter, important worldly matches for her daughters. As for Wriothesley, he was not yet thirteen when old Sir Josiah Child, the magnate of the East India Company, described by John Evelyn as 'sordidly avaricious', but doubtless with compensating qualities, proposed the boy a bride in the shape of his granddaughter; this was Lady Henrietta Somerset, offspring of Lord Worcester and Miss Rebecca Child. Although Sir Josiah used a clergyman as his envoy, he found Lady Russell's reply disappointingly cold. As for the tactful response that the young lord was still being educated, that made Sir Josiah indignant: he wrote back that that had never been 'a bar to parents discoursing of the matching of their children, which are born to extraordinary fortunes'. City money was evidently not the problem, nor necessarily youth: for only two years later the young lord was duly married off to another Child granddaughter, Elizabeth Howland. This granddaughter was even richer, which may have been the point. The total of the young couple's ages came to twenty-eight years, wrote a

†This admiration for Lady Russell's thoroughly feminine withdrawal did not fade. In 1815 Mary Berry, Walpole's friend, editing her letters, referred to Lady Russell with approval as having spent the rest of her existence, unlike most heroines, 'within the pale of private life and female duties'; an example which should be more widely followed.[60]

contemporary; the bride alone, however, was worth a total of £100,000, a new Howland title being created for the Russell family as a compliment to her possessions.[61]

Rachel was clearly determined to show herself a sympathetic mother-in-law to the girl, only just in her teens; a year after the marriage she approved the news that Mr Huck the dressmaker had taken her in hand. While Lady Russell herself believed fashion to be 'but dross', she prayed constantly that her daughter-in-law might be 'a perfect creature both in mind and body; that is, in the manner we can reach perfection in this world'. In this perfection, Lady Russell was wise enough to see that Mr Huck the dressmaker had his place.[62]

As for Wriothesley, Marquess of Tavistock after the elevation of his grandfather to the dukedom of Bedford, when he turned out to be weak and an inveterate gambler – with a dead hero for a father and a doting mother did he ever have a chance? – Rachel Lady Russell was there to act as an intermediary in confessing his gambling debts to his dreaded grandfather.

At the death of the old Duke in 1700, Rachel only waited a few days before writing to King William and asking for the Garter 'his grandfather so long enjoyed' on behalf of her twenty-year-old son. 'Sir, I presume on your goodness to forgive a woman's troubling you,' she wrote: not only the new Duke 'but I know the whole family would always look upon it as a mark of your grace and favour to them'.[63] Even in her sixties with problems of eyesight Rachel could be relentless where the advancement of her family was at stake.

'Grandmamma Russell', as Rachel was ultimately known, lived to be nearly ninety, still keeping all Fridays as a day of recollection. She died in 1722. The *Weekly Journal* commemorated one who had been the heroine of her age, as well as being married to a hero, as follows:

> Russell, the chaste, has left this earthly stage,
> A bright example to a brittle age ...
> No arts her soul to second vows inclin'd
> No storm could frighten his unshaken mind. ...

She was in short, like her husband, 'Proof against all, inseparably good.'[64]

Divorce from Bed and Board

'A Divorce is from Bed and Board; and is not void in respect of the Marriage so as that the Injured [Party] may marry again.'
The Athenian Oracle, 1701

There was no such thing as divorce in the seventeenth century, at least not in the sense the term is understood today. This does not necessarily imply a starry-eyed view of human nature, still less a higher level of marital happiness: the pragmatic need for the separation of miserable or discordant couples was well appreciated, as it had always been, and such separations took place on a number of different levels of society.

In 1670 the Earl of Lauderdale, later created a Duke, Charles II's viceroy in Scotland and a member of the acronymic Cabal, was conducting a flagrant liaison with Bess Countess of Dysart. His wife separated from him and went to live in Paris; but Lauderdale paid for her and she was allowed to take with her not only her own jewels but also – to Bess's disgust – the Lauderdale family heirlooms.[1] After her death, Lauderdale and the flame-haired Bess were able to marry; as Duke and Duchess of Lauderdale they held proud court in Scotland.

A less grandiose form of separation occurred when one spouse absented herself or himself without formality from the other spouse's side. In the 1650s Tom Oxinden had married a fourteen-year-old heiress whom he brought home under proper supervision. As he wrote to his step-mother: 'I hope she carries herself civilly and dutifully towards you and lovingly towards my sisters, as I have often desired her to do.' A few years later the bond was not sufficient to prevent Tom falling in love with Mrs Zutphenia Ower, wife of Robert Ower of Sydal. The pair went off and lived together. In 1662 Elizabeth Oxinden, the deserted wife, heard to her satisfaction that 'the Lady' and her husband were not happy together, Tom looking lean and pale. It must have given her less satisfaction when the ne'er-do-well Tom took to being a highwayman, was apprehended and died in prison in 1668. At this point Elizabeth Oxinden was free to marry again, did so, and bore four children by her second husband.[2]

The Oxindens belonged, roughly speaking, to the middle class, and there was no question of Elizabeth Oxinden remarrying before Tom's death since details of his unfortunate existence filtered through to her. It was however quite possible in a ramified country like England for an errant husband (or wife) of a lower class to disappear altogether. Under such circumstances a second – bigamous – marriage might take place in the lifetime of the previous partner. Before the Hardwicke Act of 1753 which not only necessitated parental consent for minors but also made void those marriages performed without publication of the banns or a licence, such ceremonies were not too difficult to accomplish. In this manner it could be said that the propertyless classes enjoyed a kind of *de facto* liberty denied to their wealthier contemporaries. (Evidence of this popular 'divorce' in defiance of the rules is provided by the casebooks of Richard Napier.)[3]

The sort of marriage which had been preceded by a financial settlement, with negotiations for a dowry then and a jointure to come, presented more of a problem when its component parts began to fall apart. Money was a powerful shackle, particularly for the woman. A wife was unlikely to secure any kind of maintenance if she separated from her husband, and legally had of course no money of her own, all of this having been handed over to her spouse on marriage. When Lady Hatton, mother of Frances Coke, separated from her second husband Sir Edward Coke, part of their violent quarrel over money concerned her wish to preserve that property she had inherited from her first husband, Sir William Hatton.[4]

Influential relations were a help. Lady Isabella Rich, the daughter of the Earl of Holland and the heiress Isabel Cope of Kensington, married Sir James Thynne of Longleat. When Charles 1 was at Oxford, she acted the part of Egeria to the court (it was her knowledge of statecraft which had prompted Ann Lady Fanshawe's unfortunate intrusion into her husband's political affairs – see pp. 56-7). Lodged at Balliol College, Lady Isabella and Ann Fanshawe could cause 'a flutter' appearing in Trinity College Chapel 'half-dressed like Angels'. Dorothy Osborne described Lady Isabella as 'the loveliest thing that could be looked on'. And her talent for music, combined with her air of nonchalance, inspired Waller to a poem, 'Of my Lady Isabella playing on the Lute', beginning:

> Such moving sounds from such a careless touch!
> So unconcerned herself, and we so much!

Aubrey however put his finger on her disadvantage as a wife: 'most beautiful, most humble, most charitable etc.' as she was, Lady Isabella 'could not subdue one thing'.[5]

She became the mistress of the Royalist leader, the Marquess of Ormonde, finding him 'too agreeable', and bore him an illegitimate son (her marriage to Sir James Thynne was childless). Later she became involved in Royalist plotting, her father the Earl of Holland having been executed for his part in the second Civil War. Lady Isabella left England in 1650, finding refuge with Ormonde's charitable and sensible wife Elizabeth Desmond.[6]

It was hardly surprising under the circumstances that a formal separation was arranged between Sir James Thynne and his wife, the deed being dated 1 November 1653.[7] The real point of this extremely long and detailed document was not however that husband and wife should 'freely and voluntarily for ever hereafter permit and suffer each other to live separate and apart the one from the other'; nor even that Lady Isabella should be accounted, so far as her husband was concerned, as a 'feme sole', that is he should exercise no control over her; since both these states of affairs obtained already. Both sides were actually concerned to establish proper financial arrangements: Lady Isabella abandoned her claim on 'all her Jointures and title of Dower' settled on her at her marriage in 1640, in return for proper provision and maintenance.

Yet it was seldom that a woman, even supported by influential relations, secured more than the partial return of what had once been theoretically her own; Lady Isabella's allowance being a small part of what she had brought with her on marriage.

Not all the matches arranged by Mary Countess of Warwick for her Rich nieces were as happy as that of Lady Essex and Daniel Finch. Lady Essex's sister, Lady Anne Barrington, was made of flimsier stuff. Like many late seventeenth-century ladies Lady Anne heartily disliked living in the country. In 1658 wilful Betty Verney had written yearningly from the bedside of her sick sister of her London memories: 'Hyde Park and the cherries there is very pleasant to me.' It was also taken for granted that more estimable characters would share these sentiments: that admirable woman Lucy Countess of Huntingdon 'naturally loved London very well', wrote one of her children in 1664. But as time wore on, the connection between London and adultery (at least for wives) and the country and boredom (at least for wives) did not only exist in the plots of Restoration plays. Husbands punished their wives or alternatively secured the sanctity of their marriage beds in advance by dispatching their wives away from temptation. 'To send a man's wife to the Peak' was a phrase coined when the second Earl of Chesterfield sent his Countess back to his Derbyshire estates in a fit of jealousy.[8]

In 1679 Lady Anne's husband, Tom Barrington, made a stand after a lengthy period of unhappiness. 'But for your living in London', he told her, 'I shall not, nor ever will consent thereto. ...' For fifteen years he had conformed to her humour, and now she must conform to his and live 'a soberer life in the country'. Furthermore she must settle all her estates on their children. The negotiations were left to Lady Anne's brother-in-law Daniel Finch. He proceeded carefully: while not defending Lady Anne's rash conduct in London, he pointed out that she must receive some allowance in return for her estates; otherwise it was 'as if my Lady had committed so great a fault as that she must pay a thousand pounds a year per annum to repair it'. Lady Anne might have been a bad wife, but she had been a good mother, rising in the middle of the night to care for her child and visiting it while at nurse daily. Fortunately for Lady Anne the situation was resolved when Tom Barrington died; three years later she was able to marry again without hindrance.[9]

Unofficial separations brought their own problems, also financial. Peg Verney never really got on with her husband Sir Thomas Elmes – neither of them was sufficiently even-natured to make a go of it – and after a few years what amounted to a separation was tried. Sir Thomas believed that 'to part in Love', that is, amicably, might increase the affection they felt for each other; but he was concerned that it should be 'done in a way that nobody may know, certainly *guess* they will, but *know* they need not'. There was an attempt at a *rapprochement* which did not really work; for the rest of her life Peg was involved in arguments with Sir Thomas over the kind of money due to her, if any. At her death Sir Thomas angrily took the line that Peg had had no right to make a will leaving away money from him (because she was legally still his wife).[10]

When it came to an official arrangement it was possible to secure a form of divorce – *divortium a mensa et thoro*, divorce from bed and board as it was known – in the ecclesiastical courts. This was the kind of process threatened by the father of Mary Joyce in January 1661, as reported by Pepys, because she and her husband Will led 'a strange life together, nothing but fighting, etc.'.[11]

The word 'divorce' was generally applied to such cases, but we should in fact find the term judicial separation more accurate, since it was an important aspect of the process in the ecclesiastical courts that the parties concerned, including the injured party, were not free to marry again. This was in accordance with Canon Law. Although at the start of the century some preachers had been suggesting that remarriage might be possible for the innocent, this prohibition was strongly restated at the ecclesiastical conference of 1604.

Occasionally people did remarry, thus forfeiting the money which they had deposited as a security against doing so. In November 1605 the beautiful Penelope Rich, inspiration of Sir Philip Sidney and long-time mistress of Sir Charles Blount (by whom she had borne several children), obtained this type of divorce *a mensa et thoro* from Lord Rich in the ecclesiastical courts. It was specifically laid down that neither should remarry in the lifetime of the other. Despite this, six weeks later Penelope Rich was married to Sir Charles Blount. However, since this was a clear violation of Canon Law, her children by Blount were not made legitimate; and ironically enough Penelope Lady Blount, who had been happily received at court throughout her long adulterous liaison, was now debarred from it.[12]

William Whateley was a country vicar in the early seventeenth century, known as the Roaring Boy of Banbury for the power and vitriol of his sermons. In 1619, in a tract called *A Bride-Bush*, he stated that adultery and desertion annulled the marriage contract and thus permitted remarriage. He was promptly called before the Court of High Commission and obliged to recant; he withdrew the assertion in print in a second tract of 1624, *A Care-Cloth*. Only the Commonwealth Marriage Act of 1653 brought in a brief period of greater latitude; the notion of marriage as a purely civil ceremony denied the iron grip of Canon Law. The Act stated that the innocent party should be allowed to marry again according to the recommendations of the Westminster Assembly of Divines. (Milton's famous proposals on the subject of divorce were obviously framed with the idea of remarriage in mind.)[13] But although reformers continued to press for this possibility, with the Restoration this sophisticated Puritan interlude came to an end.

If the parties were anxious to remarry, the simplest method was for them to secure a decree of nullity which established that the marriage had been void *ab initio*, from the beginning. *The Ladies Dictionary* of 1694, a comprehensive work, referred to divorce 'in our Courts' as *only* being through nullity; grounds including Consanguinity and Affinity (of blood) as well as Precontract and Impotency. To be cynical, a decree of nullity was expensive but not impossssible to secure. Of the various grounds, non-consummation, if applicable, was the obvious one to choose; it was a subject however which might produce some strange assertions. When Frances, later Countess of Somerset, had been determined to get rid of her first husband, the Earl of Essex, she did so on the remarkable grounds that, although not impotent towards women in general, Essex was impotent towards her in particular. With the support of King James, Frances secured her decree of nullity and was able to wed Robert Carr, Earl of Somerset, the royal favourite. On the other hand when Lady Desmond sued Lord Desmond in 1635 it was on the more straightforward grounds that her husband had 'insufficiency to please a reasonable woman'.[14]

A marriage was also held to be void from the beginning if a previous contract existed. Since a pledge to marry in front of witnesses – spousals *de praesenti* as it was known – could be held to be a valid contract, this technicality might be brought into use. Aphra Behn for example used it to round off her play of 1676, *The Town-Fop, or Sir Timothy Tawdrey*, with a happy ending. Lady Diana's uncle Lord Plotwell promised 'to untie the Knot', and successfully did so on grounds of a precontract (it was helpful that Lady Diana's own marriage had not yet been consummated). In real life, it was not so easy. The familiar economic question remained: How was the woman to be supported in the future? At the end of another of Aphra Behn's plays, *Sir Patient Fancy*, a young woman who had chosen an old man out of financial necessity ('"Twas to that end I married you, good Alderman') succeeded in getting a separation from him, without having to return the money.[15] But this ideal – from the female point of view – was seldom realized in real life.

*   *   *

What if no possible grounds for nullity could exist? What, for example, if children had been born of the marriage so that consummation had demonstrably taken place? There was one further expedient which developed in the late seventeenth century, and that was *divortium a vinculo matrimonii*, literally a divorce from the bond of matrimony. This could only be obtained by a private Act of Parliament. A petition and Bill had to be presented to the House of Lords, which would be debated during its various readings, according to customary Parliamentary procedure. It was nearly always preceded by a separation *a mensa et thoro* in the ecclesiastical court; or an action at common law against the co-respondent for 'criminal conversation' with the plaintiff's spouse, or for assault and battery.[16]

The expense and difficulty of such proceedings were prodigious. The prolonged tribulations experienced by Henry, seventh Duke of Norfolk in ridding himself of his adulterous wife Lady Mary Mordaunt demonstrate that even the 'first Duke in England, installed Knight of the Garter, lord high Marshal of England, and one of the lords of his Majesty's Privy Council' was not immune from this general rule.[17] Only a little over 200 cases were heard before the Matrimonial Causes Act of 1857 made it possible to obtain a divorce in England other than by Act of Parliament; and only six of these were at the suit of the wife. In any case the wife was handicapped because adultery alone was not sufficient grounds for her to get her Bill through (whereas it was for the husband).† For the vast majority of the population other than the wealthy and privileged few, only the ecclesiastical form of 'divorce' was open to them, with no prospect of a happier second union. As *The Athenian Oracle* wrote in answer to a query in 1701, laying down the established practice of the time: 'A Divorce is from Bed and Board; and is not void in respect of the Marriage so as that the Injured [Party] may marry again.'[18]

The property laws made it difficult for women caught in an unhappy marriage to struggle free because there was no guarantee they would not end up poverty-stricken. But where divorce was concerned, men had their burden too. Because a valid marriage was indissoluble except by such an expensive protracted process as an Act of Parliament – which might be condemned by society for a variety of reasons unconnected with the marriage itself – it was not so easy for a man to dispose of a wanton wife. Ironically, the wanton wife had a peculiar advantage at this period which the legalization of divorce in 1857 took from her.

In particular, the offspring of her liaison with another man, if technically born within wedlock, were not so easily denied the inheritance of their legal father. As in the case of Frances Lady Purbeck and her child, unless the husband had been indisputably absent 'beyond the seas' for an agreed length of time, the burden of proof remained upon him to establish that the child could not possibly be his. In 1635 the Earl of Essex, prejudiced against womankind in general from the conduct of his first wife Frances, later Countess of Somerset, became convinced by spiteful gossip (in the manner of Othello) that the child his second wife was bearing was not his. He announced that he would not own it unless the baby was born by 5 November. When the baby was in fact born on that very date, neither suspicious husband nor innocent – and insulted – wife were any happier and the marriage collapsed. A deed of separation was arranged; even then Lord Essex tried to insert a clause in the deed saying that his wife would forfeit her jointure if she gave birth to any further children because

---

†It was not until 1857 that divorce was made generally available in England – to men on grounds of their wives' adultery alone, and to wives on grounds of their husbands' adultery, accompanied by cruelty or desertion.

'whosoever got them, yet my Lord must father them by the law', until the Countess of Essex indignantly refused to countenance it.[19]

In about 1632 Edward Scott of Scot's Hall married Catherine, the daughter of the first Baron Goring, but the couple only lived together for about two years. While her husband was serving at the front, Catherine Scott gave birth to children at Oxford and elsewhere. Her husband disowned them and brought an action in the ecclesiastical courts for separation, while she brought an action for alimony in Chancery. Then the husband brought a petition to Parliament in 1656. But a divorce was never obtained. Thomas Scott was thus perforce acknowledged by his 'father' as his heir, and succeeded to Scot's Hall at Edward Scott's death in 1663.[20]

The most notorious matrimonial case of the seventeenth century was however that of Lord and Lady Roos.

It could not be said that the title of Lord Roos was a lucky one. John Manners, who bore the courtesy title of Lord Roos, was the third and surviving son of John, eighth Earl of Rutland, who had succeeded to the title on the death of his cousin without male heirs in 1641. The two sons of Francis, sixth Earl of Rutland, who had earlier borne the courtesy title of Lord Roos, died in youth: as we have seen (on p. 105 ff.) these deaths were ascribed to the malevolent influence of the Flower family, the so-called Belvoir witches, who died themselves as a result.

Even the Roos title had a miasma of doubt attached to it. The ancient barony of Roos or de Ros, the premier barony of England, was, unlike the earldom of Rutland, able to pass through the female line. The sixth Earl's remaining child, his daughter Catherine, had married James I's favourite, the first Duke of Buckingham; her only surviving child, George, second Duke of Buckingham, was a prominent if maverick figure at the court of Charles II. The Duke of Buckingham claimed – as a matter of fact perfectly correctly – the ancient Roos barony through his mother. When pressed, the male line of the Rutland family based their use of the Roos title on another creation, that of Roos of Hamlake in 1616. But this new creation had been made specially for Francis the sixth Earl until such time as he should inherit the ancient barony on the death of a female cousin (which occurred in 1618). This new barony of Roos of Hamlake, which could pass to sons of the sixth Earl, had in fact become extinct at his death in 1632.[21]

This complicated and confusing squabble did not stop John Manners, heir to the eighth Earl of Rutland, bearing the courtesy title of Lord Roos at the time of his marriage to Lady Anne Pierrepont on 21 July 1658; but it was to have some bearing on his matrimonial affairs later.

In advance, the match had the air of being an ideal one. The bride was the daughter and heiress of Henry Pierrepont, Earl of Kingston and later Marquess of Dorchester, a highly eccentric figure as it happened, but that was considered less important in 1658 than the fact that the marriage united two families 'very noble in themselves, and of great fortunes, and allied to all the great families of the kingdom'. Anne Pierrepont was seventeen and brought with her a dowry of £10,000, £6,500 of it paid by Lord Dorchester on 21 July.[22] John Lord Roos was twenty and, as the last male heir of the ancient Rutland family, someone on whose future progeny many family hopes were pinned.

Around the time of the wedding lavish and traditional disbursements were made: £93 was spent on two pearl necklaces for the new Lady Roos, and £50 on crimson velvet for a coach. The famous miniaturist John Hoskins, described in the family accounts as the 'picture-drawer', was commissioned. A dozen pairs of 'gesiment' (jasmine, i.e. yellow) coloured gloves were ordered for distribution among the guests according to custom, and two dozen gloves for Lady Roos. Five shillings were 'given the poor at the gates the wedding-day' and six shillings went to the trumpeters.[23]

In spite of all this, the marriage was a disaster, virtually from the start. A daughter, born early in 1659, must have been conceived very close to the wedding (she did not live). Beyond that, there were few signs that Lord Roos and Lady Anne enjoyed any kind of marital happiness together. The Earl of Clarendon summed up the sexual problem between them with his usual magisterial concision: Lady Anne 'not finding the satisfaction she expected where she ought to have received it, looked for it abroad where she ought not to find it'. As for Lord Roos, he was indulgent enough, as men 'conscious of any notable defect' were wont to be, wrote Clarendon, 'not strictly inquiring how she behaved herself'. The picture was completed by the fact that Lady Anne was, at any rate in the opinion of Clarendon, 'of a humour not very agreeable' and made little effort to dissemble or conceal the contempt she felt for her husband.[24]

Not all Lady Anne's contempt was necessarily based on Lord Roos's sexual inadequacy. For Lord Roos had another interest – drink; he also gambled and led a life generally felt to be unsatisfactory by his contemporaries. When he related how Lady Anne accused her husband of 'debauchery' and 'being always in drink' Clarendon added: 'which was true'. At some point there was a tacit separation and at some point after that, after various 'acts of passion' (that is, anger) which gave both 'mirth and scandal' to the world at large, what purported to be a reconciliation but was in effect very much on Lady Anne's terms: 'the lady having the ascendant over the lord who was very desirous to live quietly upon any conditions, that he might enjoy himself though he could not enjoy her'.[25]

Once again Lady Anne slipped away from Belvoir to London. But on this latest occasion she overstayed her leave by several months; what was more she returned clearly pregnant, or as Clarendon phrased it, 'in so gross a manner that it appeared that she had kept company too much'. This at last stung the passive Lord Roos into making some kind of protest. He taxed Lady Anne 'that she was with child' and asked her: 'Who [be]got it?'

To this Lady Anne replied, with more spirit than tact, that 'whoever got it, if it proved a boy as she believed it would, he should be Earl of Rutland'.[26]

Lord Roos's reaction was to confide all to his mother, Frances Countess of Rutland, the daughter of the first Lord Montagu of Boughton and 'a lady of very great spirit and most exalted passion' (unlike the Earl of Rutland, a mild-mannered man from whom Lord Roos seemed to have inherited his desire for a quiet life). Already the Countess had noted how little 'kindness' Lady Anne showed to her husband at Belvoir and reproved her for it; either for 'want of wit' or out of some archetypal resentment at her mother-in-law's interference, Lady Anne had ignored the warning. Now the Countess took her revenge; grimly she confined the 'great-bellied lady' to her chamber, removing Lady Anne's own attendants and surrounding her with Manners vigilantes, in case Lady Anne tried to fudge the date of the baby's birth in some way, so as to falsify the date of its probable conception.[27]

Lady Anne although confined was not silenced. She managed to get a message of protest to her father the Marquess of Dorchester, describing how she was held prisoner, and feared for her life since the Countess was at the very least threatening to make her miscarry, if not to kill her. Nevertheless in the course of time Lady Anne did give birth safely to a living child. It was a boy just as she had predicted. That of course increased the complication of the situation, since this boy was now the eventual male heir to the earldom of Rutland. (A girl would have had no such inconvenient rights.) So the baby was rapidly baptized Ignoto, a name which left the whole subject of his paternity in abeyance. He was taken from his mother's side by the Countess of Rutland and placed with a poor woman locally to be nursed. Lady Anne herself, after she had recovered from the ordeal of childbirth, was allowed to travel to her father.[28]

In the Marquess of Dorchester, however, Frances Countess of Rutland had found a worthy adversary; she might be celebrated for her 'most exalted passion' but Lord Dorchester was notorious for his fits of irrational bad temper, sometimes accompanied by actual physical violence. In 1638 he had committed an assault within Westminster Abbey itself, and during a service; in 1641 he had been charged for the extremity of his language in the course of a debate in the House of Lords. A servant to Charles I – he had acted as one of his commissioners at the Treaty of Uxbridge – he had eventually come to terms with the Commonwealth regime; but he was back in the Privy Council of Charles II by August 1660.

Lord Dorchester's other claim to the attention of his contemporaries was that he was an amateur chemist. This brought him more ridicule than respect. When someone observed in 1676 that a man of his age was either a fool or a physician, Lord Dorchester – being one for litigation when physical violence would not serve – promptly brought an action of *scandalum magnatum* against him.

When Lord Dorchester received notification of his daughter's treatment at the hands of her husband and her family, he rushed into action. First he challenged Lord Roos to a duel, and when this was refused, an exchange of letters took place, subsequently published. Their tone was not temperate. Lord Dorchester referred to Lord Roos's 'Sottish and Clownish paper', written no doubt in one of his drunken fits, and charged him with cowardice as well: 'If I may see miracle, you with a Sword in your hand ... but if it was a bottle, none would be more forward.'[29]

Lord Roos for his part excoriated gleefully on the subject of Lord Dorchester's chemical experiments: 'Sir, sure you were among your gally-pots and glisterpipes, when you gave your choler so violent a purge, to the fouling of so much innocent paper, and your own reputation (if you had any, which the wise very much doubt)!' As for his own drunkenness, Lord Roos grandly dismissed it: how harmless were these 'Tertian fits of mine, which are easily cured with a little sleep' compared to Lord Dorchester's evident dottiness. (To this Lord Dorchester replied that they were not Tertian but Quotidian, daily.) In general Lord Roos sneered at his father-in-law for his challenge: 'If by your threatening to ram your sword down my throat you do not mean your pills, the worst is past and I am safe enough.'[30]

Lord Dorchester's next action was to appeal to the King. He wanted to see justice done not only to little Ignoto, still kept from the care of the only parent who was undoubtedly his, but also to his daughter in whose innocence the indignant Lord Dorchester continued to believe. He still believed in it following the hearing in front of Charles II at which some very dubious evidence of Lady Anne's conduct was produced. As well as Lady Anne, the Countess of Rutland and a host of other ladies appeared at the hearing, but there were 'so many indecent and uncleanly particulars' given, that many of the latter had to leave.[31]

A good deal of the evidence came from servants who sometimes contradicted indiscreet statements they were supposed to have made previously. Had Lord Roos ever said that 'although he lay not with his wife [at night], he did in the day?' Had Lord Roos ever observed that if only Lady Anne had arrived three weeks sooner or stayed three weeks longer 'then he would have owned the child'? Both these remarks were now denied by the men who were supposed to have passed them on.[32]

Despite all this washing of dirty linen, at the end of the hearings Charles II 'left it as he found it'. He refused to pronounce on the guilt of Lady Roos or the parentage of Ignoto. That is to say, although Lady Roos had clearly made some very rash statements to her husband, the King could not be sure that they had not been made out of a desire to provoke his jealousy (and thus perhaps secure that appropriate affectionate response which Lord Roos had hitherto been so laggard in making). 'He doth not find ground whereon to make judgement to condemn the lady.' On the other hand Charles II, a worldly man, could see that there was absolutely no question of a further reconciliation. He therefore suggested a separation, and a proper settlement by which the Rooses could live peacefully asunder. As for the child, that 'might be placed in the hands of some third person to be agreed on both sides, to prevent the apprehensions of either parties'. The King's last word on the subject was that if this tactful solution was not accepted, then there would have to be recourse to the law.[33]

Lord Dorchester interpreted this decision as a triumph. He carried Lady Anne home with him, convincing himself that her virtuous life in the future would vindicate her in the eyes of the world, and so that the point should not be missed gave instructions to his steward that the King's document should be read aloud, preferably in churches. As to the child, that should be restored to its mother; or if not to her, at least to someone on whom she could rely. Lady Anne should also be granted an allowance by her husband, and have her portion repaid (although she would relinquish the prospect of a jointure).[34]

Even if Lady Anne had been prepared to conduct herself discreetly as her father hoped, it is difficult to see how the situation could in fact have been resolved as Lord Dorchester and the King desired. There was the question of the boy Ignoto: either he was the legitimate issue of Lord

Roos, in which case he stood in line for the earldom of Rutland, or he was not, in which case Lord Roos lacked a male heir, and needed to provide himself with one. Before he could do that, he needed to get rid of his present wife. At first Lord Roos hung on to custody of the boy, saying that 'although the child be not of my begetting, so long as the law reputes it mine, I must and shall keep it'. But this, it is clear, was merely a manoeuvre in order to induce from Lady Anne a confession of the truth. The Earl of Rutland told Lord Dorchester that his son 'knows best that the child is none of his'; once Lady Anne had admitted to the King what she had already confessed to her husband, then she could have the child and do what she liked with it. Money was another matter: the Rutland family certainly did not take the line of Lord Dorchester that Lady Anne's portion should be restored to her father despite her behaviour. As for an allowance, 'I will give none but what the law determines', declared Lord Roos. And then he required the vital confession first.[35]

The first of a long series of legal proceedings to get rid of Lady Anne Roos was instituted in the House of Lords by the Rutland family. Lord Dorchester was said to be quite exasperated by their attitude, which combined the mercenary and the moral: why should he relinquish any part of his estate, i.e. the money that had constituted her dowry, to make up for 'the miscarriages of his daughter'?[36] Implicitly the Rutland family was fining Lord Dorchester for having sold them a bad bargain in the shape of Lady Anne in the first place.

Unfortunately Lord Dorchester's faith in his daughter's virtue was not justified. Lady Anne, growing bored with a discreet but dull existence under her father's roof, fled from his protection. Reverting to her former defiant ways, she led a life which became a public scandal. (Given her situation, one has to admire her courage if not her morals; or perhaps it was sheer miscalculation, based on her original contempt for her husband, which induced her to take such risks.) At some point she secured custody of Ignoto and she also gave birth to another child, also a son. These two boys went through life known as John and Charles Manners respectively, the family name of the man who was still in the early 1660s their legal father.[37]

Lady Anne's behaviour disgusted and infuriated Lord Dorchester. In one of those sudden volte-faces to which this passionate and peppery man was prone, he abandoned her cause altogether. He flung himself urgently on to the side of the Rutland family and was henceforth prominent among his daughter's attackers. It was certainly bad luck for Lady Anne that as well as having an inadequate husband, she was also saddled with a half-crazy father. Supposing as we must that she had inherited her own share of instability from Lord Dorchester., it was also bad luck that it manifested itself in her reckless sexuality; so much less socially permissible in a woman than violent arguments and ridiculous chemical experiments in a man.

At this point a divorce from bed and board was secured in the ecclesiastical courts, on the grounds of Lady Anne's adultery, without too much difficulty. The next step was to illegitimate Lady Anne's sons and any other children she might bear. This needed an Act of Parliament and a Bill was duly prepared relating details of Lady Anne's 'foul carriage' in full. This Bill was given its first reading in October 1666.

By this time Lady Anne herself had retreated to Ireland. When the Bill to illegitimate the children came to have its second reading in the House of Lords in November 1666, Lady Anne was summoned 'at the last place of her abode that can be discovered', but failed to appear.[38] The Bill seemed all set to go through when suddenly the ancient quarrel concerning the Roos title blew up again.

The Duke of Buckingham complained that the language of the Bill was prejudicial to his own claim to the Roos title. Lord Dorchester, now a fierce Roos partisan, first insulted Buckingham and then had a physical fight with him in the Painted Chamber (although he was nearly twenty years his senior). In the course of this Lord Dorchester had his periwig pulled off and the Duke had a handful of his hair pulled out. Both the fuming peers were clapped into the Tower to cool off, and only released on petitions of apology. The question of the Roos title was not so easily settled. The committee could not find a way of satisfying both parties, and the Bill as a result got further delayed.[39]

It was not until 8 February 1667 that the Act making the children of Lord Roos illegitimate finally received the royal assent.[40] In the meantime, in late January, the active Rutland family had seen to it that no trouble was experienced with the Bill in the House of Commons: no fewer than forty-six Members were entertained at their expense to a dinner at the Dog Tavern, and although Lord Roos himself had a fit of colic and had to rush away (festivities do not seem to have been his strong point), the Members stayed on. Then, 'as soon as they had dined, we carried them to the House of Commons', where the Bill was passed without amendments.[41]

As for the debated Roos title, that matter was not finally settled for a further 200 years. The Duke of Buckingham died in 1687 leaving no children of either sex; as a result the ancient barony of Roos or de Ros (which could pass through the female line) fell into abeyance between the descendants of his aunts; to one of these the barony was allowed in 1806. On the other hand the Earls and later Dukes of Rutland were permitted to bear the Roos title by both Parliament and sovereign until the late nineteenth century when it was quietly dropped.[42]†

*   *   *

Lord Roos was now once more in the happy position, as it seemed to him, of being without a legal heir. He was also separated from Lady Anne in the ecclesiastical courts. But the enormous hurdle of the divorce *a vinculo matrimonii* remained to be cleared. Even assuming that this type of divorce was secured by Act of Parliament, it was still by no means clear at this date that Lord Roos would be able to remarry in such a way that the offspring of such a second marriage would be unquestionably legitimate. And that after all was the whole object of the exercise. What point was there in dragging the family name through Parliament to obtain an expensive and controversial divorce if at the end of the day Lord Roos was simply free from Lady Anne? In most senses he was free from her already and he was certainly free from the presumptuous claims of her cuckoo sons. From the point of view of the Rutland family then, the Roos case in Parliament was entirely about remarriage, not divorce.

It was also in the nature of a test case, in quite a different respect. By the late 1660s hopes that Catherine of Braganza, the Portuguese wife of Charles II, would bear a living child were fading (she had suffered two miscarriages). The King however already had a large brood of illegitimate children, and was clearly capable of begetting a great many more (in fact several of his bastards were born in the 1670s). One way to solve the problem of the royal succession – his brother James Duke of York, already suspected of Catholic sympathies, was heir presumptive to the throne – would be for the King to divorce Queen Catherine and marry again. There is evidence that Charles II did at least passingly consider this solution; he certainly paid keen attention to the debates over the Roos case in the House of Lords, attending them sedulously, and observing in one of his characteristic asides that the whole thing was as good as a play. Once again, it was the question of the legitimacy of the children of a second marriage which obsessed the monarch: heirs to the throne of dubious legitimacy

†Today both titles are still represented in the ranks of the peerage: there is a Baroness de Ros (for the ancient barony is currently held by a woman) and Baron Roos of Belvoir is among the titles held by the Duke of Rutland; this new barony being created in 1896.

threatening a national disaster where for the Earls of Rutland it was merely a personal misfortune.

There were other interests at stake. Lords Anglesey and Ashley (the latter soon to be created Earl of Shaftesbury), whose sons had married Lord Roos's two sisters, 'drove in on the bill'; it was not in their sons' best interests that Lord Roos should be allowed to remarry, since if he could not both their wives were potential beneficiaries. Lord Castleton took the opportunity to demand a fourth part of the lands settled on his mother, sister to the Earl of Rutland, but later withdrew the claim.[43]

Remarriage then was the issue for most of the interested parties - most but not all. For Lady Anne Roos the issue was quite different: it was the uncomfortable issue of money, her money, her very livelihood. In February 1668 Lady Anne brought her own petition to the House of Lords stating that she had not received a penny from Lord Roos for four years and was thus destitute, yet she had brought a great fortune to Lord Roos on her marriage. None of this was now allowed to her, and she could not dispose of her own estate during Lord Roos's lifetime. Thus she was daily in danger of being arrested for debts, some of which had been contracted while she still lived with her husband. It was this dire state of poverty, she explained, which had caused her to flee to Ireland 'that her friends and relations might not be eye-witnesses of her misery'. While in Ireland she had been unable to travel to England to vindicate her honour. (Rumour said that Lady Anne had in fact travelled to Ireland with her lover; probably both stories were true.) Lady Anne implored Lord Roos to pay her reasonable debts, to give her yearly maintenance in proportion to the dowry she had brought with her, and enable her to dispose of her own estate so that she could support her children and keep them and her out of gaol.[44]

In the spring of 1670 a Roos Bill - for divorce - was once more before Parliament, and in society provided the main topic of conversation. Much turned on the precise interpretation to be given to various texts in the New Testament. The most favourable were those of St Matthew, in particular that verse where Jesus declared that 'whosoever shall put away his wife, except it be for fornication, and shall marry another, committeth adultery' - for this could be held to justify remarriage when fornication *had* been the cause of separation. (The versions given by St Mark and St Luke were less susceptible of such a favourable interpretation: 'Whosoever shall put away his wife, and marry another, committeth adultery against her'.) Then the various precedents were discussed, the most often quoted being that of the Marquess of Northampton in the reign of Edward VI. After his first wife had been put away for adultery, he had married 'the good and virtuous' Lady Elizabeth, daughter of Lord Cobham; the children of this marriage had been legitimated.[45]

On the second reading of the Bill, Lady Anne was once more called to the House of Lords. This time she did appear and had her petition for maintenance read. At the same time she was asked what she said to 'the scandals' laid upon her by Frances Countess of Rutland. Lady Anne's answer concerned money not morals: her petition she said was no scandal, as she hoped to prove if she had liberty of appeal. She asked to have counsel to speak for her. Lady Anne then left and the House considered the matter. However when Lady Anne was recalled the answer came back that 'she was gone'.[46] There is no evidence that she ever did get her portion returned – particularly in view of the hostility of her father – while her peripatetic way of life indicates that her debts continued to plague her. So Lady Anne ended by being penalized financially for her immoral behaviour; a development which was not exactly planned, but not disagreeable to society either.

As for the Marquess of Dorchester, he stood up in the House of Lords and publicly gave his assent to the Bill because of the 'foul blemish' done by his daughter to her husband. While the Earl of Rutland spoke eloquently of Lord Roos being the 'sole heir male' to the ancient Manners family, with whom the honour must expire if he was not allowed to marry – and procreate – again. Lord Rutland's appeal fell on receptive ears in the Lords. There was general compassion for his family's plight and general indignation that 'an impudent woman' should have brought it about. Although some peers still queried the important precedent which was being set, and the Duke of Buckingham continued to fuss about the use of his own title in the Bill, finally it passed through Lords and Commons.

On 1 March Lord Roos felt confident enough to spend 1s 10d on 'Fagotts' for a bonfire 'at the good accord of the King and the House of Parliament'. On 11 April 1670 the Bill for a *divortium a vinculo matrimonii* received the royal assent (although the Duke of Buckingham succeeded in getting the actual title of Roos left out of it).[47]

The decision created a sensation and was much discussed, often with a sense of unease. Although public sympathy lay with the injured and innocent Lord Roos, the words of the New Testament, especially those of St Mark and St Luke, had to be explained away. A pamphlet printed afterwards of a discussion between 'a clergyman' and 'a private gentleman' stressed St Matthew's text; of the Early Fathers, St Jerome had supported the view that a man could put away his wife for fornication; certain early

councils of the church had allowed remarriage. All of this was less convincing than the robust practical statement at the end of the pamphlet that
if a man were not allowed to remarry he were 'to be put into a kind of
Matrimonial Purgatory, and be rendered thereby incapable to enjoy, either
the advantages of a married one, or the freedom of a single man.'[48]

It was to free Lord Roos from the 'Matrimonial Purgatory' into which
the wanton behaviour of Lady Anne had cast him that the whole cumber-
some long-drawn-out process of the law, lasting one way and another for
nearly ten years, had had to be invoked.

*   *   *

As might have been predicted, it was not long before Lord Roos, freed
from his purgatory, essayed again those delights of heaven – would that
they might not prove once more the torments of hell – promised by
marriage. He had in fact been a target for matchmakers for some years,
who laid contingency plans just in case this rich prize became available. In
1671 he married Lady Diana Bruce. The choice, out of all the girls in
England, was an unlucky one; the next year she died in childbirth, and the
child, a boy, died too. (The payment for embalming the body of the
second Lady Roos appears in the family papers shortly after that joyous
expenditure of 1s 10d on faggots for a bonfire to celebrate freedom from
the first.)[49]

Eighteen months later Lord Roos married again: the new bride was
Catherine Noel, daughter of Viscount Campden. A son John was born in
1676, who bore in his turn the controversial title of Lord Roos when his
father succeeded to the earldom of Rutland three years later. So the
Manners succession was secure; too late however for Lord Roos's mother
– Frances Countess of Rutland had lived to see her son's divorce pass
through Parliament but died a year later.

John, ninth Earl of Rutland, a prominent supporter of William III,
was in his later years also famous for his dislike of the town of London; no
doubt his early traumatic experiences with Lady Anne had inculcated this
loathing. Mainly at Belvoir, he lived till 1711. As for Lady Anne, she was
dead before January 1697. She too married again – a Mr Vaughan, about
whom little is known except the fact that he was wounded in a duel by the
boorish seventh Earl of Pembroke in 1677. John and Charles Manners
were still living in 1699, but beyond that vanish from the pages of history.[50] The end of their lives is Ignoto – unknown – as once John Manners's
name had been.

Yet the trail of the Roos scandal was not totally obliterated, even in the next generation. If we return to Rachel Lady Russell, that 'bright example to a brittle age', we find that one of her primary aims in her dutiful widowed years was the splendid mating of her two daughters, another Rachel, and Katherine, as well as the care of her son Wriothesley. Rachel – little Rachel, she who had sung in bed and talked of Papa at 'Wobee' – was just fourteen when she married Lord Cavendish, heir to the Earl of Devonshire. Where Katherine Russell was concerned, the most eligible bridegroom in England in the early 1690s (other than her younger brother Wriothesley) was none other than John Lord Roos, offspring of his father's third and fortunate marriage to Catherine Noel.

Once again, as with the union of that other Lord Roos and Lady Anne Pierrepont nearly forty years earlier, everything seemed set fair for the match. John Earl of Rutland, as a Whig, was likely to look upon the daughter of the martyred Lord Russell with sympathy, and the Russells were likely to regard him with similar benevolence. There was a family connection: Catherine Countess of Rutland, born a Noel, was related by marriage to Rachel Lady Russell's 'sister Noel'. As for Katherine Russell herself, she was said to be 'of a sweet temper', had had a suitable education for her position, would be a good manageress, and 'wanted no wit':[51] in short, the ideal daughter-in-law. Nothing was known to the discredit of the young Lord Roos (he was the same age as his intended bride) and a great deal to his credit, including those vast Midland possessions he must one day inherit.

All the same Rachel Lady Russell hesitated. Twenty years later the memory of that frightful decade of scandal and divorce centred on the name of Roos had not utterly faded; besides there were those awkward Manners sons to be remembered, barred from the honours and the estates, but still in themselves constituting a reminder of those ugly days.

In the end, wise woman that she was, Lady Russell decided that it was wrong to avoid 'the best match in England for an imaginary religious scruple'. In characteristic fashion, she managed to sound a note which was both high-minded and worldly. 'If a divorce is lawful', she wrote, 'as agreeing with the word of God, I take a marriage after it certainly to be so. And as for the estate, as we enjoy that by man's law, and that man can alter, and so may alter again, which is a risk I am willing to run, if there should be enough left.'[52]

So John Lord Roos and Katherine Russell, both still just under seventeen, were married in August 1693. The wedding took place at Woburn Abbey. Afterwards the bridal pair made a triumphal progress to Belvoir Castle, something more like the journey of young sovereigns through their own country, than that of a bride and groom going to his father's house. The High Sheriff paid his respects at Harborough. As they approached Belvoir, thousands of people began huzza-ing. At the gates of the castle were to be found twenty-four fiddlers and twenty-four trumpeters. A magnificent banquet was followed by a visit of the bridal pair to the Great Hall where a vast cistern full of wine had been established. Healths were drunk – first in spoonfuls, then in cupfuls; after an hour the level of the cistern had hardly dropped an inch. After that the healths were drunk in great tankards.[53] The celebrations were in short even more magnificent than those which had heralded the arrival of Lady Anne Pierrepont into the Manners fold in 1658.

Rachel Lady Russell herself had to imagine the spectacle of her daughter's apotheosis since her eyesight was by now very bad; she followed to Belvoir more slowly and in some discomfort. Ultimately however, it was a great source of satisfaction to her that all three titles with which she was associated, Bedford, Devonshire and Rutland, were transformed into dukedoms. Bedford – her father-in-law – and Devonshire – her son-in-law – were created dukes in 1695. Transforming the earldom of Rutland into a dukedom took a little more time in view of John, ninth Earl of Rutland's obstinate dislike of London; despite Rachel's pleas he refused to attend the coronation of Queen Anne, the perfect opportunity for securing such titular advancement. Finally in 1703 John Manners, formerly the unhappy cuckolded Lord Roos, was made the first Duke of Rutland. His story had ended happily after all.

The story ended happily in another way. It had been written into Katherine Russell's marriage contract – oh shades of the past! – that she would forfeit her jointure 'if ever she lived in town without his [her husband's] consent'.[54] So amiable, so diligent and so virtuous did this Lady Roos prove herself that eventually her father-in-law relaxed the prohibition. When in 1711 Katherine died giving birth to her sixth child at the age of thirty-five not only Rachel Lady Russell but all her adopted family were cast into despair. It was appropriate that where woman's reputation was concerned, the ghost of the wanton and 'impudent' Lady Anne Roos should be finally laid by the daughter of the noble Rachel Lady Russell; for the one was the classic villainess, the other the classic heroine of the age in which they lived.

16 *Benefiting by Accomplishments*

> 'It is no ambitious design of gaining a Name in print . . . that put
> me on this bold undertaking; but the mere pity I have entertained
> for such Ladies, Gentlewomen and others, as have not received
> the benefits of the tithe of the ensuing accomplishments.'
>
> HANNAH WOOLLEY, *The Gentlewomans Companion*, 1675

What other course than marriage was open to the gently bred but dowerless female of post-Restoration society? Hannah Woolley, in a book of
domestic conduct, addressed herself to those 'many Gentlewomen forced
to serve, whose Parents and Friends have been impoverished by the late
Calamities, viz., the late Wars, Plague and Fire' (she was writing in the
1670s). Let them forget their glorious past! 'If your Father hath had large
Revenues, and could talk loudly of his Birth, and so [you] may think this
servile life beneath you, yet thank God you can do something for an honest
livelihood, and be never-the-less submissive.'[1]

What Hannah Woolley meant was that virtually the only respectable
profession open to such a relict was that of 'gentlewoman' or waiting-
woman to another more prosperous female. A natural chameleon, such an
attendant took on the worldly colouring of her employer: thus her status
varied considerably, and was not necessarily debased. At the highest level
a gentlewoman, acting as a companion, confidante or what would now be
termed personal secretary to a great lady, enjoyed a powerful and protected
position which had little of the menial about it; as Mrs Wall, confidential
servant to the King's French mistress Louise de la Kéroualle, Duchess of
Portsmouth, exercised her own form of petticoat patronage.[2]

In all cases however, intimacy was the rule not the exception. Sighing
over Dorothy Sidney, before the war, Edmund Waller took the trouble to
apostrophize her waiting-woman Mrs Brangton:

> You the soft season know when best her mind
> May be to pity, or to love, inclined.

Margaret Duchess of Newcastle dedicated her *CCXI Sociable Letters* to 'her friend and former maid' Mrs Elizabeth Topp. Dorothy Osborne had her 'sweet jewel' Jane Wright, daughter of Sir Peter Osborne's bailiff on the island of Guernsey (her sister Maria seems to have married the local rector at Chicksands, an example of delicate upward mobility).[3]

The female correspondence of the time bears witness to the existence of many such 'sweet jewels'. One who proved not quite so delightfully precious was the gentlewoman named merely as 'B—' by Evelyn, describing the testamentary letter of Margaret Godolphin. 'B—' (presumably Beck, her chief maid) was, it is true, to receive the princely sum of £100 from Sidney Godolphin; but this was merely a charitable endowment to enable her to live without employment at her father's house, since no one else would endure her lack of 'good service' with as much patience as had Margaret Godolphin.[4]

Very often the chosen companion would be some form of family connection, a poor relation perhaps, as in the case of 'Cousin Henderson' the intelligent and resourceful kinswoman of Bess Countess of Dysart, subsequently Duchess of Lauderdale. First Cousin Henderson instructed the young Bess Murray (she was the only child of Charles I's faithful servant William Murray, created Earl of Dysart, from whom Bess eventually inherited the title in her own right). Then Cousin Henderson settled down with Bess on her first marriage to Sir Lionel Tollemache, helping her with her business affairs – Cousin Henderson remaining a great deal more literate than her pupil. Finally when Bess's numerous Tollemache progeny began to create those problems in adolescence and later which multiplicity does nothing to alleviate, Cousin Henderson found herself with fresh responsibilities: when young William Tollemache, for example, got into trouble for killing a man in a duel in Paris, it was Cousin Henderson who went over to France to rescue William from the consequence of his rashness.[5]

The ultimate triumph of the poor relation in the guise of gentlewoman was however that of Abigail Hill, better known to history as Mrs Masham. Abigail Hill was the famous favourite who succeeded in supplanting Sarah Duchess of Marlborough in the affections of Queen Anne with disastrous political consequences for the Whigs. In fact the two women – Sarah Jennings, later Duchess of Marlborough, and Abigail Hill – were first cousins, and the ousted Sarah's furious claim that she had raised Abigail from 'a broom' had a great deal of substance to it.[6] Abigail's first appointment occurred before the Queen's accession, her father having been a merchant who ruined himself with unfortunate speculations. Sarah, hearing that she had a relative living in penury, secured for Abigail the post of

Bedchamberwoman to the then Princess Anne; Abigail's sister Alice was subsequently made laundress to the Princess's son, the little Duke of Gloucester.

Even then, Abigail's appointment was not made without some awkwardness, since it was known that Abigail had been working as a domestic servant in the household of Lady Rivers (an awkward example of downward mobility), and this would normally have ruled her out from the position of Bedchamberwoman to a Princess, where the work was, as we shall see, menial enough but the public prestige considerable. In principle a Bedchamberwoman had to display respectable antecedents, even if she was spared the haughty standards of a Lady of the Bedchamber: no one below the rank of an earl's daughter was considered.

Abigail was saved by the fact that none of the other members of the Princess's household were 'gentlewomen' – who might be supposed to be contaminated by the arrival of this former domestic servant – except one Mrs Danvers; but she had sacrificed the advantages of her birth by marrying a tradesman.[7] Once appointed, Abigail's duties as Bedchamberwoman included sleeping on the floor of the royal bedroom at night, and emptying the royal slops in the morning. From this – literally – lowly position, Abigail Hill was able to proceed upwards until she had as Queen's favourite achieved the glorious rank of Baroness Masham – Samuel Masham, her husband, being a Groom of the Bedchamber to Prince George of Denmark. The sympathetic approach by which Abigail as Bedchamberwoman was able to win the Queen's confidence stood in contrast to Sarah's natural loftiness of temperament; the attention paid by Abigail to the personal tribulations of the Queen's daily round, and her attempts to alleviate it, was particularly effective where a sick woman was concerned: Queen Anne was plagued with ill health – the consequence of her numerous pregnancies and other cruel afflictions – throughout her reign. This aspect of Abigail's rise, leaving aside her relationship to the Tory Robert Harley, was underlined when Queen Anne hesitated to create Samuel Masham a peer because it was not seemly for a peeress to lie on her floor 'and do several other offices' as Abigail was wont to do; yet Queen Anne was loath to relinquish Abigail's services. In the end a compromise was reached by which Abigail became Lady Masham but she also continued as Woman of the Bedchamber to the Queen.[8]

Thus the career of Abigail Masham stood not only for the triumph of the poor relation, but also for the possibilities of female advancement in the role of personal companion – one area outside marriage where such advancement was to be secured.

*　　　*　　　*

Where Abigail Masham emerges triumphant, Paulina Pepys – 'Pall' – the diarist's plain and rather pathetic younger sister, appears as a victim: both of the husband shortage, and of the use of domestic service to cope with the problem of a poor relation. When Samuel Pepys offered to have Pall come and live with him and his wife in London in November 1660, she received his offer with tears of joy; despite the fact that Pepys told Pall quite plainly that he would receive her 'not as a sister in any respect but as a servant'. This was because she had been living with her father in the country, virtually dowerless and with small prospect of finding a husband. Pall arrived the following January, but Pepys, unlike those great ladies such as Lady Sandwich who were graciously inviting their housekeepers to sit down at table with them, was quick to define her position downwards: 'I do not let her sit down at table with me', he noted in his diary with some complacency. 'Which I do at first, that she may not expect it thereafter from me.'[9]

Despite this cutting treatment, Pall was reported as having grown 'proud and idle' by July, and her brother resolved not to keep her.[10] The trouble was that at the same time as Samuel Pepys was trying to define his sister's position downwards (and thus solve the problem of her keep at the smallest expense to himself), his wife Elizabeth was in the process of defining her own position upwards – and since one of the marks of a lady was that she kept a waiting-woman, a waiting-woman was what Mrs Pepys would have. Poor Pall was not really able to fulfil the expectations of either Pepys. One of those unfortunate people, it is clear, who was rendered increasingly disagreeable by adversity, she scarcely added that note of social grace to the establishment desired by Mrs Pepys. Nor was she able to fit easily into the menial position conceived for her by her somewhat callous brother.

Home to the country went Pall. The next time Pepys saw her in October 1662 – still with no husband in view – he found her 'so ill-natured' that he could not love her, and 'so cruel an Hypocrite' that she could cry when she pleased.[11] (While we may accept the fact that Pall was by now thoroughly ill-natured, her tears at her situation were probably quite sincere.)

In the meantime, Elizabeth Pepys's search for the ideal refined attendant or 'woman' as she sometimes simply described her, went on apace; as with her other search for the perfect cook and perfect maid or some combination of the two, it provides one of the most fascinating and long-running of the great domestic dramas of the diary. Admittedly Pepys's particular sexual nature is one of the component parts of the drama: he could not be long close to any pretty young female, without wishing at very least to touch '*ses mamelles*' but such advances were, as we have seen, a recurring problem where female domestics were concerned; gentlewomen were not excepted.

The rise of the idea of the lady, too genteel or too languid or just too ladylike to do her own housework (as opposed to the robust working housewife, whatever her class, of the pre-war period), is amply demonstrated by the gathering domestic ambitions of Mrs Pepys. From a woman who did her own cooking, with the aid of perhaps one servant, she developed into the mistress of the household; one moreover who needed a gentlewoman at her side to sing with her and accompany her to plays. Pepys accurately drew attention to the fact that 'the increase of a man's fortune, by being forced to keep more servants ... brings trouble'. At the same time he criticized his wife for not looking neater now she had two servants; and noted that 'want of work' was one of his wife's problems.[12]

The first 'woman' hired was called Gosnell; Pepys hoped that she would make Elizabeth less lonely, and was himself impressed to find that Gosnell had a good singing-voice and was 'pretty handsome' (although he did have a dark suspicion that she might have been bred 'with too much liberty' for his household). Convincing himself, however, that Gosnell would cost nothing but her board and her small wages, as well as saving him a great deal of money by occupying his wife at home, Pepys purchased a book of country dances for her arrival.

Gosnell herself had put a different interpretation upon her post. Her singing did please, and she 'dressed' Mrs Pepys, that is, helped her with her toilette and did her hair. (This was beginning to be considered such an arduous job that Betty Verney at about the same date, angrily maidless, said that her arms ached with doing her own hair, and it would be scarcely less exhausting to go out to the plough.) But Gosnell was very put out to find that the Pepyses did not go to the court every week, nor often enough to plays, and she also claimed for herself the 'liberty of going abroad as often as she pleased'.[13] So Gosnell departed – to join certain other moneyless young ladies in another racier world than that of the respectable gentlewoman. With other actresses, we shall meet Gosnell again in the future.

The next suggestion was that Pall should be got back as Mrs Pepys's 'woman'; the economics of it pleasing Pepys, who did not like, as he put it, to spend money on a stranger when he could spend it on his sister. However, the girl who actually filled the position was called Mary Ashwell, a teacher from one of the fashionable Chelsea girls' schools who had the merit of singing well, dancing charmingly after dinner, and being in all respects 'a merry jade'. Too merry perhaps – she got into trouble with

Mrs Pepys over a ribbon which had or had not been stolen, and eventually went back to teaching, finding the duties of a 'woman' insufficiently stimulating and wanting a place 'where she might teach children, because of keeping herself in use of what things she had learned, which she doth not here or will there, but only dressing...'.[14]

Meanwhile the exiled Pall still wept. In the summer of 1664 she pleaded to be allowed to return to London to improve her chance of acquiring a husband; even Pepys had to concede that there was a danger in leaving her in the country to grow steadily older 'till nobody will have her' – then she would be 'flung upon' his hands for good. But now Mrs Pepys had set her heart on another symbol of gentility – a French maid; for along with French fashions, French songs, French dances, French wines and French cooking, French attendants had become the rage, as the returning cavaliers imported the civilized delights of their country of exile. (As a result, the absurd use of French by ladies of fashion was to be much mocked in Restoration plays. 'Affected? *Moi?*', exclaims Lady Fancyfull in Vanbrugh's *The Provok'd Wife*.) When this plan foundered, Mary Mercer was procured: a 'decayed' or ruined merchant's daughter, one of the newly poor, like Abigail Masham. For all Mercer's skill at the viol, however, there was soon trouble when Pepys was seen to pay too much attention to Mercer at table.[15] Mercer departed.

At least Mrs Pepys was beginning to see reason on the subject of Pall's dowry (the alternative of housing Pall was grimmer): in October 1665 she agreed that Pall should have £400, despite the fact that times were hard. As for Pepys, a mere three days after a certain Philip Harman's wife died in childbirth, Pepys was considering him as a bridegroom for Pall. With this in view, Pall was allowed up to London to be 'fashioned'. At the age of twenty-five, Pepys assessed her appearance as follows: even though she was 'full of freckles and not handsome in face, she was at least pretty good-bodied ... and not over thick...'. With the possibility of a portion to back up these charms, Pall also acquired another two suitors, even if one of them was 'drunken, ill-favoured and ill-bred'.[16]

Neither of these problems – Mrs Pepys's desire for a gentlewoman and Pall's desire for a husband – were however destined for immediate solution. It was not until 1668 that Pall, now aged twenty-seven, was finally married off to one John Jackson of Ellington in Huntingdonshire, a man with little to say for himself and of plain appearance, but a husband for all that. Pepys's relief was profound; there had been some desperate moments when he feared he would never find her a husband before she had grown 'old and ugly'. To his diary he confided that he could not love Pall, because she was so 'cunning and ill-natured'. However, her appearance improved on marriage, although she remained 'mighty pert'.[17]

As for Mrs Pepys, she heard of a very fine lady who would replace Mercer for £20 a year, able to sing, dance and play on four or five instruments; but this paragon proved on inspection to be 'tawdry' and was in fact perfectly prepared to come for £8. (The genteel importance of the role of gentlewoman is underlined by the fact that even a 'tawdry' one might command more than twice a maid's annual wage.) Under the circumstances Mrs Pepys preferred a girl called Barker; £7 or £8 was laid out on clothes for her by Pepys himself. Barker was 'very plain' but had good connections and a fine singing voice, two at least of the qualifications of a suitable gentlewoman. Barker duly accompanied Mrs Pepys on visits and learned part songs but proved to be a trouble-maker in the household. Her departure in May 1667 occurred when she was discovered to have been 'abroad' without permission and lied about it, so that Mrs Pepys found herself obliged to strike her.

Barker had one persistent complaint: she 'did always declare to her mistress and others that she had rather be put to drudgery and to wash the house than to live as she did, like a gentlewoman'. Pepys found this strange. Yet Barker's outburst explains what a strain might be imposed upon an employee when her mere presence was expected to bestow social prestige upon a household – 'qualities of honour or pleasure' as Pepys put it, while complaining that Barker had failed to provide them.[18] Like any equivocal role, that of gentlewoman could result in a failure of expectations on both sides.

So the way was cleared for the arrival of Pepys's great love, Deb Willet; a witness to the equivocal nature of the role (as had been in their different ways Pall, Gosnell, Ashwell, Mercer and Barker) but in yet another sense. At the beginning Deb only represented yet another attempt to find a suitable companion for Mrs Pepys; this time a mere child was chosen, the Pepyses hoping, no doubt, to avoid the independence of Gosnell and Barker. Deb had been at 'the school at Bow' for seven or eight years, and was said to be a model of good deportment. Mrs Pepys returned from a visit of inspection, reporting that Deb was 'very handsome'. Pepys regarded this as good news about the prospective companion: 'at least, that if we must have one, she should be handsome'. Alas, the handsomeness of Deb was his – and ultimately her – undoing. In vain she performed such duties as accompanying Mrs Pepys to the theatre, dancing and playing cards with admirable gravity and modesty. Her good looks aroused the passionate jealousy of Mrs Pepys, a jealousy which was certainly not

without foundation, since Pepys, finding himself quite unable to resist the
perpetual physical proximity of Deb, had embarked on a series of daring
amorous explorations.

One night after supper in October 1668 occurred an incident which in
Pepys's words' 'occasioned the greatest sorrow to me that ever I knew in
the world'. Deb was combing her master's hair – not in itself a proof of
intimacy, since this hygienic duty was usually performed by maids. Unfortunately Mrs Pepys, arriving suddenly upon the scene, 'did find me
embracing the girl con my hand sub su coats; and endeed, I was with my
main in her cunny', It was impossible even for Pepys to gloss over such a
flagrant discovery (although he tried). There was a violent scene; the
episode led in the end to Deb's dismissal. Pepys, full of 'love and Pity' for
her, accepted her departure with anguish; he also warned Deb solemnly
against allowing anyone else to take those same liberties to which he had
so freely helped himself.[19]

*   *   *

Hannah Woolley, author of several books on domestic practice and conduct under the name of her first husband, wrote out of her own experience.
She was born in 1623 (her maiden name is unknown), learning 'Physick
and Chirurgery' from her mother and elder sisters, but was early on left an
orphan. However, before she was fifteen, she was entrusted to keep a little
school of her own, by dint of her exceptional 'accomplishments'.[20] Hannah Woolley lists these (note the relatively low position of writing and
arithmetic):

> Needlework of very different sorts
> Bugle-work
> Framing pictures
> Setting out of Banquets
> Making salves and ornaments
> All manner of Cookery
> Writing and Arithmetic
> Sweet powders for hair, or linen

At the age of seventeen she was enabled by these same accomplishments
plus the additional asset of speaking Italian and playing several musical
instruments to attract a 'Noble Lady Patron' who took her into her
household to act as governess to her daughter. This lady taught her further
'Preserving and Cooking', introduced her to court and kept her for seven
years until the children had all grown up.

The original role of governess developed into something more conse-
quential. As Hannah put it: 'Time and my Lady's good opinion of me
constituted me afterwards her Woman, her Stewardess, and her Scribe or
Secretary. By which means I appear'd as a person of no mean authority in
the Family.' Hannah was proud of the fact that she read aloud daily to her
employer poems, plays and romances (for which she had to learn French,
one accomplishment hitherto lacking); she also took great trouble with the
letters which she wrote for her.

At the age of twenty-four, Hannah married the master of a Free School
at Newport Pond, Essex, by whom she bore four sons, as well as taking in
boarders to her school. The Woolleys then moved to Hackney, the centre
of genteel education at the time, where they kept over sixty boarders. Mr
Woolley died about the time of the Restoration, but in 1666 Hannah
married for the second time, one Francis Challinor, a widower of about
forty-five. In 1674 she was to be found living in the house of her son
Richard in London near the Old Bailey – as a Master of Arts and Reader
at St Martin's, Ludgate, he constituted an advertisement for an intelligent
mother – and she was probably still alive ten years later.[21]

Hannah Woolley began writing at the time of her first widowhood,
presumably in order to support herself. Unfortunately she found herself
enduring some of the less attractive aspects of an author's career: one rogue
publisher had her proofs revised by a different hand and another did not
pay her. The book in question was *The Gentlewomans Companion*, and
Hannah later issued a supplement to her second book, *The Queen-like
Closet*, to correct the record. Her first books were however centred on the
purely domestic arts; such as *The Ladies Directory in choice experiments
and curiosities of Preserving and Candying both Fruits and Flowers*, printed in
1661. She moved on to issues of social behaviour, and later related details
of her own life story, in order to enable other women to survive as she
herself had done. Apologizing for the personal details, she explained that
she had been prompted to write by 'the mere pity I have entertained
for such Ladies, Gentlewomen and others, as have not received the benefits
of the tithe of the ensuing accomplishments'.[22] It was to her knowledge
of these vital arts and artifices as listed above, as well as to her ability
to write and add up, that Hannah Woolley firmly ascribed her own
survival.

So that while Hannah Woolley wrote with the traditional and understandable bitterness of the female educationalist about the preference
shown to boys – parents cared for the 'barren Noddles of their Sons',
sending them to university, while the fertile ground of their daughters'

brains was allowed to go fallow – she did not herself ask for university education for women, or indeed anything like it.

Hannah Woolley complained indeed about the decline of standards of education among her own sex: 'Most in this depraved later Age think a Woman Learned and Wife enough if she can distinguish her Husband's bed from another's' was one of her gibes. She criticized the men who looked upon women merely as instruments to propagate their families, and were not interested in their minds. She was also, as we have seen, a strong believer in the 'treasury' to be laid up by education, 'by which they [unmarried women] may live without an Estate'. Education would enable such women to gain 'some honest and creditable Employment', she wrote; as a result 'their position will be so established that nothing almost but sickness and death can make an alteration therein'.[23]

But how far, how very far removed were the requirements of Hannah Woolley – based of course on those of society – from that 'modish' Latin and Greek which had once entranced the great ladies at court at the end of the reign of Elizabeth I, or indeed that 'ebri grek and laten' to which Nancy Denton had aspired in the Commonwealth period, to the disgust of Sir Ralph Verney! (See p. 140.)

Hannah Woolley put particular emphasis on the art of carving; she had acquired it herself early in life from her 'Noble Lady Patron', and it did of course enable a gentlewoman to exercise public authority over the rest of the household; Hannah gave elaborate hierarchical instructions on how to distribute the best bits in meat and fish (remember that the cod's head was considered a great delicacy). She reminded her gentlewomen that it would appear 'very comely and decent' to use a fork.[24] Her special plea that a gentlewoman should *not* lick her fingers at a meal not only suggests that many people of the period did, but also that a genteel manner at table was more likely to aid an unprotected woman to get on in the world in the reign of Charles II and his successor than all the knowledge which had once filled the august head of Queen Elizabeth I.

*   *   *

The fact that the developing special nature of female education was in itself a restriction was perceived by very few people of either sex at this time. During that period of Puritan revolution when exciting new ideas concerning universal education were promulgated – if not put into practice – by men such as Hartlib, Dury, Petty and Robinson, girls' education received scant attention. Only John Dury's 'Noble School' was adapted to the requirements of both sexes; although girls were intended to become 'good and careful housewives', those capable of learning 'Tongues and Sciences' were to be given encouragement. (Dury may have been influenced by the stern attitude of his wife Dorothy, who wrote a letter to the pious Lady Ranelagh headed 'Of the Education of Girls', attacking the general frivolity.) Hartlib, Winstanley and others were more interested in equipping girls from the lower classes in crafts such as weaving.[25]

One of the few who did appreciate the danger of the divide was Basua Makin. Like Hannah Woolley appalled by the decline in education, Basua Makin, unlike Hannah, was concerned to restore or at least promote the study of Hebrew and the classics. She determined to run a girls' school guided by this principle.

Basua Makin had excellent credentials to found the most fashionable establishment, apart from the fact that she may have been associated with a set of girls' 'schools or colleges' at Putney in 1649, visited by John Evelyn. The sister, as we have seen, of John Pell the learned mathematician (another brother, Thomas Pell, had been Gentleman of the Bedchamber to Charles I), she had a particular claim on the loyalty of the newly Royalist society in that she had been governess to Princess Elizabeth, that sad little sister of Charles II who had died in captivity at Carisbrooke Castle. As a result, this Princess at least had enjoyed an elaborate education including Hebrew as well as Latin and Greek (unlike her aunt and namesake Elizabeth of Bohemia, denied the classics by *her* father, James I, because Latin had the unfortunate effect of making women more 'cunning').

The education afforded to the next generation of Princesses, Mary and Anne, daughters of James II, then Duke of York and heir presumptive to the throne, stood in astonishing contrast. How ironic that Basua Makin's passionate plea of 1673, *An Essay to Revive the Antient Education of Gentlewomen, In Religion, Manners, Arts and Tongues. With an Answer to the Objections against this Way of Education*, should be dedicated to Mary, Princess of York, principal among all 'Ingenious and Vertuous Ladies'! For in the upbringing of Mary and her sister Anne, born in 1663 and 1665 respectively, domestic accomplishments were in fact stressed to the exclusion of virtually everything else. Yet these girls, as the children of the heir presumptive, stood in direct line to the throne from the moment of their birth, and in this age of high infant mortality there must always have been a distinct possibility that at least one of them would inherit it.

As a concession to their place in the Stuart family tree, it was thought important that these young Protestant hopes should be able to recite Anglican - as opposed to Catholic - prayers, but otherwise Mary and Anne could be safely abandoned to their favourite pastimes of whist and basset (another card game). Where education was concerned, the Princesses did learn French: Pierre de Laine's French grammar, published in 1667 when she was five, was written for Princess Mary, and a second edition for Princess Anne. Otherwise they were taught to sing and draw and dance (Mary was an especially graceful dancer), but that was the limit of their preparation for life. When Basua Makin wrote in anguish that all young gentlewomen were taught nowadays was 'to frisk and dance, to paint their faces, to curl their hair and put on a whisk'[26] she might have been describing the Princesses' own fate.

Tragically late, it seems to have been borne in upon Queen Anne that she was lacking in some of the essential equipment of a monarch; it was said to be 'an unhappiness' to her that she was not much acquainted with English history and the reigns and actions of her predecessors: 'she beginning to apply herself to it but a little while before King William died'. For all these last-minute efforts, Queen Anne as a monarch, with no magisterial co-ruler, no William III at her side, did display a lamentable ignorance of history and geography; while her grammar and spelling were both deplorable. (Only her good grounding in French, that traditional female accomplishment, but also of course the language of diplomacy, was to be admired.)[27]

As for Queen Mary, in effect a consort not a ruler, it was hardly surprising that in adult life she displayed few intellectual ambitions. Instead she concentrated on those gentle pursuits such as 'knotting', bugle-work to make bead bags, crewel-work and others forms of embroidery beloved of well-bred English ladies of her time. These were the refined accomplishments, the study of which Hannah Woolley advocated in order that a gentlewoman would appeal to her mistress; skill in such matters was certainly essential to the ladies surrounding Queen Mary. Celia Fiennes gives a picture of the Queen and her Maids of Honour embroidering away for dear life at Hampton Court.[28] The poet Anne Countess of Winchilsea was aware that she was a scornful exception when she described herself as one who would not participate in such trivially pointless crafts:

> ... In fading silks compose
> Faintly, the inimitable Rose,
> Fill up an ill-drawn Bird, or paint on Glass,
> The Sovereign's blurred and undistinguished face.[29]

To many women, to Mrs Pepys for example, who adopted the new fashionable passion for decorating objects with shell-work, such accomplishments betokened the leisure to have mastered them, and such leisure, like the employment of a gentlewoman, was the outward symbol of their rising social status. In this way amateur music publications rose as amateur singing extended, and the pursuit of painting – ever considered a suitable hobby for a lady – increased too. It was true that in certain rare cases painting might lead to professional employment. But the real motive which inspired a young lady to learn to paint or 'limn' as *The Ladies Dictionary* phrased it in 1694 (where 'limning' headed the list of a lady's permitted recreations, followed by dancing and music and finally reading) was hardly to support herself; it was to bequeath 'rare moments of her ingenuity to posterity'.[30] The moments of her actual ingenuity may have been rare; but the hours of leisure which stretched about them were not. So the lady limner also bequeathed to posterity, along with her creative efforts, the message that she had been gracefully unsullied by any other occupation.

It will be seen that the Princess Mary was indeed an inappropriate dedicatee for Basua Makin's *Essay* of 1673, a work in which she was much concerned to break the tacit embargo by which women were not allowed to study the classical languages. 'Tongues are learnt in order to [learn] things', she cried. As for the old witticism: 'Many say that one tongue is enough for a woman', Basua described that angrily as 'but a quibble upon the word'. Furthermore Basua pleaded for education so that women could 'understand Christ'. She did not suggest that women of 'Low parts' (the poor) should be educated; what she was anxious to do was to break down that dreadful idle way of life common to women in society, by which they learnt when young 'merely to polish their Hands and Feet, to curl their Locks, to dress and trim their Bodies ...' and so were incapable of any finer way of life, including the enrichment of their own souls, when older.[31]

Moreover in her *Essay*, Basua Makin was already toning down considerably her original demands concerning the scope of female education. In 1663 she had called for a curriculum based on that of the celebrated Dutchwoman Anna van Schurman, with whom Basua Makin had kept up a correspondence (in Greek). This included the study of grammar, rhetoric, logic, physics, mathematics, geography, history, and all languages, with Greek and Latin stressed, as well as painting and poetry. Anna van Schurman, the friend of Descartes and Richelieu, as well as the exiled Elizabeth of Bohemia, was another Helena who had been well instructed by her father; the vigour of her intellect equalled its emancipation: 'By what right indeed are certain things alone apportioned to us? Is it God's law or man's?' she wrote. Her influential work appeared in England in translation in 1659 as *The Learned Maid*, in which Anna van Schurman even suggested that women should be able to study the theory of military discipline if they so desired.[32]

In one respect however the great Anna van Schurman was mistaken. Citing the celebrated women of the previous century, such as Queen Elizabeth I and Lady Jane Grey, she supposed Englishwomen to enjoy exceptional freedom. In fact this kind of high-born female concentration on learning and learned discussion, and thus by implication on the preparatory education necessary, was by this period to be found far more widely on the Continent than in England.

Madame de Maintenon, the austere mistress of Louis XIV whom he married privately after his Queen's death, was as keen an advocate of the education of poor girls of good family as Hannah Woolley or Basua Makin, but with a great deal more influence to bring to bear on the subject. She had set up several little schools before the famous school for 250 girls at Saint-Cyr was founded under royal patronage in 1686, Louis XIV taking a keen interest in the details. After the King's death in 1714, Madame de Maintenon chose Saint-Cyr as her own place of retirement.[33]

A passionate interest in female education was not a marked characteristic of any of the mistresses of King Charles II, nor would it be appropriate to regard the King himself as obsessed by this particular aspect of the female development (although he did patronize the education of poor boys, particularly in mathematics, leading to his own pet topic of navigation).[34]

In the end Basua Makin herself was forced to compromise. When she founded her new school at Tottenham High Cross, described as 'four miles out of London on the Ware road', for which the fees were to be £20 a year, she found that it simply was not viable without the inclusion of numerous pretty arts on the syllabus. Basua Makin's new proposition was that half the time was to be spent studying 'Dancing, Music, Singing, Writing and Keeping Accounts', with the other half dedicated to Latin, French, Greek, Hebrew, Italian and Spanish – but those who insisted might 'forbear the languages' and learn only Experimental Philosophy.[35]

Unfortunately most people did wish that their daughters should 'forbear the languages'. The accomplishments which would enable a single woman to survive in the world remained, however regrettably from the point of view of female learning, those of Hannah Woolley. Where marriage was concerned the same standards prevailed. In vain Basua Makin protested against the contemporary belief that no one would marry an educated woman. Rather desperately she advanced the counter-proposition that learning in a wife was no disadvantage to a husband. Few gentlemen – and thus few parents – of the time would have agreed with her. In vain too Basua Makin denied that she was asking for 'Female Pre-eminence' and pleaded on the contrary that education would help women to understand even better that God had made Man 'the Head'. It was significant that she also denied that education would make women so proud that 'there will be no living with them'. Only in her proposition that since evil had begun with Eve and been propagated by her 'daughters', special care should be taken with their education, did Basua touch some kind of contemporary nerve.[36]

Even so, not many felt that Eve's daughters would be improved by a study of the classics or other serious topics. John Evelyn had his daughter Susanna taught Greek and Latin. Yet to his beloved Margaret Godolphin he gave the advice that she should read the Lives of Plutarch, Cyrus, Seneca, Epictetus, Virgil and Juvenal in English and French – 'More than this unless it be a great deal more, is apt to turn to impertinence and vanity.'[37]

John Locke benefited richly from the friendship of an educated woman: Damaris Cudworth, Lady Masham was the daughter of Ralph Cudworth, Master of Christ's College, Cambridge and Regius Professor of Hebrew (and incidentally the step-mother of Samuel Masham). She was Philoclea to Locke's Damon in a long personal and philosophical correspondence. She also provided him with a comfortable country retreat, despite a professed indifference to what she called 'the Impertinent Concerns of a Mistress of Family', which she assured Locke would never have 'Any place in my Heart; and I can at most do no more than submit to them'. As if in proof of this indifference, Lady Masham wrote two books herself as well as some very long letters indeed; 'you know I cannot write short letters'. It was Locke also who engaged Elizabeth Birch, who could speak Latin and Greek fluently, as governess to Lord Shaftesbury's grandson – another example of paternal encouragement to learning, for Elizabeth Birch's father had been a schoolmaster. Yet Locke did not believe in the female need to study grammar. Lady Masham, deploring women's lack of real educational attainments in one of her books, put her finger correctly on the reason: 'so few Men ... relishing these Accomplishments in a Lady'.[38]

Basua Makin, citing the usual historical stage army of eminent ladies to demonstrate the female's essential worth – Deborah and Hannah, down to Queen Elizabeth 'the Crown of All' – ended on some more recent examples including Rachel Lady Russell and Anne Bradstreet in America. Her reference to Margaret Duchess of Newcastle who 'by her own Genius, rather than any timely Instruction, over-tops many grave Grown-Men'

was perhaps in danger of destroying her own argument. Her tribute to her
own pupil, Lucy Countess of Huntingdon, was more to the point, suggesting she was unique:

> A president for Ladies of this age,
> So noble, humble, modest and so sage;
> For French, Italian, Hebrew, Latin, Greek
> The ornament of our Sex; where may we seek
> Another like her self?[39]

It was generally felt that the rest of Eve's daughters, given Lady Huntingdon's accomplishments, would sacrifice in modesty what they gained
in learning. Better far to take no risks and educate the softer sex more
softly.

*   *   *

Although the quality of education declined, the number of girls' schools
increased after the Restoration as the middle classes increasingly made use
of them. School under these circumstances was a worldly rather than an
instructive experience. Of course there were exceptions – the Quaker
schools were an exception, as the Quakers were the exception in so many
things. There were the Quaker 'women's schools' (after all, if women
were to be allowed to speak at Meetings they needed to be educated to do
it), and there was also a Quaker co-educational boarding-school at Wal-
tham Abbey, later moved to Edmonton, which George Fox visited in
both localities. A Quaker school at Shacklewell in Hertfordshire under
Jane Bullock was founded in 1667 on the advice of George Fox, for
instructing 'young lasses, and maidens in whatsoever things were useful
and civil in creation'; Rachel Fell attended it. There was another Quaker
school at Chiswick under Ann Travers. Quakers apart, the overall figures
for female literacy itself based on all classes also improved.[40] Nevertheless
the ludicrously sketchy nature of lessons learnt in most schools provided
the butt for satire in many Restoration plays.

A solemn young female cousin of Oliver Cromwell, born in 1654, who
kept a private diary for 'the help of my Memory, concerning the work of
God on my Soul, which I desire thankfully to commemorate', was placed
by her father at school in London; she recorded that the sparks of religious
life were almost extinguished within her as a result of this experience.[41]
Little Molly Verney, on the other hand, daughter of Edmund Verney by
his poor 'distracted' wife, who was sent to Mrs Priest's school at Chelsea
at the age of eight, found there exactly the training she wanted.

She desired to learn to 'Japann', a special course which cost a guinea entrance and about 40s for materials. Edmund was quick to extend the paternal blesssing: 'I approve of it; and so I shall of any thing that is Good and Virtuous, therefore learn in God's name all Good Things, and I will willingly be at the Charge so far as I am able – tho' they come from Japan and from never so far and look of an Indian hue and colour, for I admire all accomplishments that will render you considerable and Lovely in the sight of God and man. . . .' But then Molly's fate, as planned by her father, was to be placed in the household of a lady of quality, with her own maid and her board paid, as a kind of finishing process; then she would be married off to a country squire.[42]

Part of the problem was the lack of adequate women teachers to instruct girls in anything remotely taxing, because they themselves had not been so instructed. 'From an Ignoramus that writes, and a Woman that teaches, *Libera nos Domine*' – so ran 'The New Letanie', a satirical jingle of 1647. This was the vicious circle to which Margaret Duchess of Newcastle drew attention: 'women breeding up women; one fool breeding up another; and as long as that custom lasts, there is no hope of amendment', she wrote, castigating the kind of 'ancient decayed gentlewomen' at whose mercy girls found themselves.[43]

At a lower level in society there was a strange lack of interest in the subject, compared to the attention paid to the boys' teachers; women teachers occasionally coming to prominence for some misdemeanour, as one Isabel Reun was presented to the ecclesiastical court at Ely in 1682 for teaching scholars and at the same time keeping company with a man not her husband. The ecclesiastical licensing system which was supposed in theory to concern itself with petty teachers as well as grammar masters does not seem in practice to have concerned itself with women. The tendency towards teaching girls what was immediately economically useful remained: as in the case of the dame of a village school in Sussex in 1699 who put her children to making clothes in school (much as the 'Red Maids' of Bristol were put to embroidery); she contracted out reading and writing lessons, taking a distinctly lower place, to visiting schoolmasters. There is no evidence that Basua Makin herself was licensed as a teacher.[44]

So the girls tripped in dainty slippers down the ornamental paths of their education; so very different from the demanding courses of classics and grammar set for their brothers. Whatever the latter's application (Basua Makin answered the point that girls did not desire education with the perfectly accurate riposte: 'Neither do many boys'),[45] the intellectual difference between the two sexes was becoming ever more sharply defined;

as the quality of education offered to boys also improved, the gap only
increased. This had the makings of another vicious circle. A lady who had
received a lightweight education – in the words of Lady Chudleigh,

> As if we were for nothing else designed
> But made, like puppets, to divert mankind

– such a one was generally only capable of filling her mind with lightweight
matters. Charges of frivolity against the sex were thus all too easy to
substantiate, summed up by Rochester's sneer:

> Love a Woman! you're an Ass
>   'Tis a most insipid passion
> To choose out for your Happiness
>   The silliest part of God's Creation.[46]

At the same time, such outward frivolity, indolence even, became the
mark of a lady, to be aped by those (not only Mrs Pepys) who aspired to
rise higher in society.

The growth of 'frivolity' in this apparently secure and certainly leisured
society following the traumatic period of the wars was the subject of
widespread comment. Halifax gave to his daughter Betty his own zeugmatic picture of an idle lady of quality, 'wrapped up in Flattery and clean
Linen'. Mary Evelyn, John Evelyn's daughter, gives an amusing picture of
the world of the fashionable – and frivolous – in her *Mundus Muliebris: Or,
The Ladies Dressing-Room Unlock'd*, published after her death in 1690. Her
bedroom would include, in addition to its tea table, cabinets, screens,
trunks and silver plate:

> An hanging Shelf, to which belongs
> Romances, Plays, and Amorous Songs;
> Repeating Clocks, the hour to show
> When to the Play 'tis time to go,
> In Pompous Coach, or else Sedan'd
> With Equipage along the Strand....

Her 'Implements' would include, besides a mirror, 'one Glue Pot, One
for Pomatum, and what-not Of Washes, Unguents, and Cosmetics', while
of perfumes she would employ orange-water, millefleur and myrtle
'Whole Quarts the Chamber to Bequirtle'. As for the gallant courting this
cosseted beauty, he must pursue her to 'the Play, the Park and the Music',
even to Tunbridge Wells at the season of drinking the waters: 'You must
improve all occasions of celebrating her Shape, and how well the Mode
becomes her.'[47]

It was perhaps this kind of life that Rachel Lady Russell had led as a

young married woman, haunting the theatre, choosing a church with a
short sermon, impatient to reach the fashionable world of the park, and
occupying herself with telling her mother-in-law malicious stories; many
years afterwards she wrote of her frivolous conduct with regret.[48] But
Rachel Lady Russell had to endure exceptional sufferings; most women,
not subject to her tragic destiny, were also not subject to her regrets.

It is certainly a picture echoed over and over again in the plays of the
period. Victoria and Olivia, daughters of Sir John Everyoung in Sedley's
The Mulberry Garden, to give only two examples out of many, were said
to dance and play at cards 'till morning'; they were described as 'more in
their Coach than at home, and if they chance to keep the house an
afternoon, to have the Yard full of Sedans, the Hall full of footmen and
Pages, and their Chambers covered all with Feathers and Ribands'. In 1712
Addison, parodying the life of a society lady, began his account: 'Wednesday: from eight to ten drank two dishes of chocolate in bed and fell asleep
after them exhausted by the effort.'[49]

There were plenty of prototypes in real life; when one reads an account
of Ursula Stewkeley, daughter of Cary Verney by her second marriage, it
is difficult to suppose these pictures were much exaggerated. This energetic
young women loathed country life and was furious if she could not dance
twelve hours out of the twenty-four, and have music whenever she
wanted. After eight months of pleasure in London, she returned to her
country home in 1674 in the middle of the night, bringing a group of her
friends with her, including a certain disreputable Mr Turner, who had
been associated with a murder case; this uninvited party then proceeded to
sit up till three in the morning loudly roistering. The next day Ursula
borrowed a coach and took off for Salisbury races, returning that night
with the same merry crew to sit up once more till the early hours of the
morning.

'All this has sufficiently vexed me', wrote her mother, with feelings of
parental indignation with which it is easy to identify even at a distance of
300 years. But in addition the unwelcome Mr Turner's linen had had to be
mended and washed by her household and sent after him to London![50]

*   *   *

The first serious attempt to interest women in higher education as such
was that of Mary Astell at the end of the seventeenth century (as opposed
to Basua Makin's desperate avowal that she was only preparing women
properly for marriage, or such isolated ventures as a sympathetic paper on
the subject by the Anglican minister and writer Clement Barksdale in

1675). Mary Astell was born in 1666, to a prominent commercial family in Newcastle-upon-Tyne. Nothing is known about her own education, except that she came late to French; it seems it was her mother's death which brought her down from the north to London.[51] She lived in Chelsea, probably in Swan Walk, and included many of the clever socially prominent women of her time among her friends: Lady Betty Hastings, granddaughter of Lucy Countess of Huntingdon by her only son Theophilus and a tribute to the tradition of intelligent women in that family, was one. But the friendship which provoked Mary Astell into her first proposal for a form of women's college was a bird of a more gorgeous but less respectable feather. This was Hortense Mancini, Duchesse de Mazarin, ex-mistress of Charles II, a flamboyant woman with the looks of 'a Roman eagle'. She had acceded with pleasure to the advances of Charles II, but had not subsequently managed to stabilize her career, being the subject of numerous scandals, each one leaving her rather worse off than before.[52]

It was Mary Astell's conviction that the 'unhappy Shipwreck' of her friend had been due to 'the dangers of an ill Education and unequal Marriage', the former contributing to the latter. Had Hortense been properly educated, wrote Mary Astell, there would have been a 'right Improvement of her Wit and Sense, we should not have found her seeking Relief by such imprudent, not to say Scandalous Methods as the running away in Disguise with a Spruce Cavalier'. Perhaps in her generous assessment Mary Astell had not totally understood the character of her fallen friend; it is possible to argue that as long as there are spruce cavaliers, there will be at least some scandalous elopements. Nevertheless the conclusion which Mary Astell drew was in itself significant. She saw in her 'college' a refuge – an all-female refuge of course – where heiresses could elude the fate of an unwanted marriage, 'decayed' gentlewomen could teach, and daughters without dowries could be educated.[53]

Was there not something about Mary Astell's proposal which came very close to suggesting a kind of teaching convent? Of the sort only available since the Reformation to those Catholic girls like Mary Ward and her colleagues who were sent abroad. Ironically enough, this point was fully appreciated by Mary Astell's contemporaries, but only to denounce her suggested college for this very reason, as being 'Romanist'. Bishop Burnet in particular criticized her design on the grounds that it smacked of popery. It was only towards the end of his life, depressed by the 'ill methods' of the schools and colleges he saw around him, giving 'chief rise to the irregularities of the gentry as the breeding young women to vanity . . .' and being 'the source of corruption of that sex' that he came to see that Mary Astell had been right all along. 'Something like mon-asteries without vows would be a glorious design,' wrote the Bishop, 'and might be set on foot as to be the honour of a Queen upon the throne. . . .'[54]

Mary Astell herself was already drawing a distinction between the two different kinds of women. Upon those who loved their 'chains' she poured scorn: 'Let them Housewife or Play, Dress and be entertaining in Company . . .', these '*Very* women' as she termed them, whose accomplishments were 'most acceptable to all sorts of Men'. Then there were the other sort, who helped the poor and read pious books, who were accorded the honourable title of '*Good Devout Women*'. Mary Astell did not attack marriage as such, calling it 'the Institution of Heaven, the only Honourable Way of continuing Mankind'; it was however the plight of 'we poor Fatherless Maids and widows' which explicitly concerned her.[55] Yet by her distinction between the '*Very* women', acceptable to men, and those who were not, she helped to promote the notion of the learned lady as one who dwelt on the other side of some great divide; a more than slightly ridiculous figure, when viewed at a distance.

Elizabeth Elstob was that pioneer of Anglo-Saxon studies who had arrived at Oxford unofficially, by courtesy of her brother William's presence there. Described as 'the justly celebrated Saxon nymph', Elizabeth Elstob was responsible for the first Anglo-Saxon grammar, the first critical edition of one of Aelfric's sermons and the first attempt at a complete edition of Aelfric's homilies. With her brother, she formed part of a brilliant group at the university.[56]

Her work of 1709, *An English-Saxon Homily on the Birth-Day of St Gregory*, was dedicated to Queen Anne, hopefully relating her to such figures of history as Bertha the first English Queen, and the British born Empress Helena. 'I know it will be said, What has a Woman to do with Learning?', she wrote. 'Why therefore should those few among us, who are Lovers of Learning, although no better account cou'd be given of it than its being a Diversion, be denied the Benefit and Pleasure of it, which is both so innocent and so improving? But perhaps most of these Persons mean no more than that it makes them neglect the Theatre, and long sittings at Play, or tedious Dressings, and visiting Days, and other Diversions, which steal away more time than are spent at study.'[57]

William Elstob died prematurely. Whereupon Elizabeth had at once to leave the university town. For many years subsequently she struggled in poverty. When she was trying to found a dame's school at Evesham the distinguished scholar was obliged to issue a nervous apology concerning her lack of certain skills: 'There are some things to be taught in such a school which I cannot pretend to; I mean the two accomplishments of spinning and knitting. Not that I would be thought to be above doing any commendable work proper to my sex', she added hastily. 'And as an instance of the truth of this, the gown I had on when you gave the favour of a visit was part of it my own spinning, and I wear no other stockings but what I knit myself.'[58]

At one point Elizabeth Elstob was to be found 'in her sleeping room, surrounded by books and dirtiness'; one who had 'pursued too much the drug called learning'. This brilliant woman would in the opinion of her contemporaries have enjoyed a happier life if she had pursued instead the two accomplishments of spinning and knitting. As it was she became dependent on the patronage of the (female) great: Queen Caroline, wife of George II, was persuaded to make her a small allowance. After the Queen's death, it was arranged that Elizabeth Elstob should enter the household of the Duchess of Portland – as governess to her children. And here in 1756, after eighteen years as a governess, the 'Saxon nymph' ended her days.[59]

17 Petticoat-Authors

'I hate these Petticoat-Authors; 'tis false Grammar, there's no Feminine for the Latin word, 'tis entirely of the Masculine Gender, and the Language won't bear such a thing as a She-author.'

CHAGRIN THE CRITICK, IN *A Comparison Between the Two Stages*, 1702

If a woman did by any chance seek to educate herself, wrote Damaris Lady Masham, she was liable to be treated as 'a Scarecrow' by the Wits in London; Lady Masham (John Locke's 'Philoclea') added that in the country she would probably fare even worse. Scorn for the learned lady, generally expressed in cheerful ridicule rather than outright hostility but no less inhibiting for that, was one aspect of post-Restoration society with which every woman who pretended to achievements beyond the purely house-wifely – 'the dull manage of a servile house' in Anne Winchilsea's phrase[1] – had to cope.

Numerous English playwrights found in the idea of the pretentiously learned female an enjoyable inspiration for the stage. They included, it should be said, her whom Evelyn termed 'our Sappho ... the Famous Heroina Boadicia', Aphra Behn. In 1678 the character of Lady Knowall in Aphra Behn's *Sir Patient Fancy* was founded on that of Mary Astell. 'Oh, the delight of Books!' exclaims Lady Knowall. She goes on to describe her serious reading as Tacitus, Seneca and Plutarch or 'if in a Humour gay' Virgil, Homer or Tasso, all studied 'in the Excellence of their Original Language'. When the young Leander Fancy suggests that these authors can as well be read 'in our Mother Tongue, Madam', Lady Knowall turns on him: 'Faugh, Mr Fancy, what have you said, Mother Tongue! Can anything that's great or moving be express'd in Filthy English ...?'[2] So much for Mary Astell and her plans, so much for Basua Makin and her desperate plea that 'tongues are learnt in order to [learn] things'.

The success of Molière's plays, crossing the Channel in English versions (Aphra Behn for example in *Sir Patient Fancy* drew upon *Le Malade*

Imaginaire), added to the fun. Shadwell's *The Virtuoso* of 1676, an adaptation of Molière's *Les Femmes Savantes*, was itself pillaged by Thomas Wright
in 1693 for *The Female Vertuosos*: Philaminte, Armande and Bélise emerg
ing as Lady Meanwell, Mrs Lovewit and Catchat, three women of appropriately nonsensical achievements. Lady Meanwell has invented an engine
to keep the streets of London dry and clean (' 'Tis only Setting up Timber
Posts round about the City and then fixing a pair of Bellows on every one
of 'em to blow the Clouds away!'). Catchat is teaching a flea to sing opera.
Mrs Lovewit has made an exact collection of all the plays that ever came
out, and has devised an alembic by means of which the quintessence of wit
in them is to be extracted and sold to poets by drops. Congreve's *The
Double Dealer* of 1694 included the character of Lady Froth: 'a great Coquet
Pretender to Poetry, Wit and Learning', prone to apostrophize her servant
in banal verse:

> For as the Sun shines every day
> So, of our Coach-man I may say
> He shows his drunken fiery Face
> Just as the Sun does more or less.[3]

At least Catchat in *The Female Vertuosos* was allowed to retort on the
subject of female learning: ' 'Tis the partial, and foolish Opinion of Men,
Brother, and not our Fault hath made it ridiculous nowadays. . . .' The
trouble was that this 'foolish Opinion' grew rather than diminished in
strength towards the end of the century. By 1702 the prevailing attitude of
contempt for feminine achievement was summed up by the playwright
and essayist Charles Gildon in *A Comparison Between the Two Stages*,
through the mouthpiece of Chagrin the Critick: 'I hate these Petticoat-
Authors; 'tis false Grammar, there's no Feminine for the Latin word, 'tis
entirely of the Masculine Gender, and the Language won't bear such a
thing as a She-author.' Although another character, Sullen, is more reasonable (a woman has recently won a prize for poetry in France, and even in
England 'some of that Sex . . . have done admirably'), to Chagrin it is all
rubbish: 'Let 'em scribble on, till they can serve all the Pastry-cooks in
Town, the Tobacconists and Grocers with Waste-paper.'[4]

There is indeed a newly sour note about the mockery poured upon the
generation of female playwrights following Aphra Behn (who died in
1689 in her fiftieth year). *The Female Wits*, a play of 1696, said to be by
'W.M.', took as its target a trio of women, Catherine Trotter, Mary
Manley and Mary Pix, all of whom made their debut as petticoat-
dramatic-authors about this time, and castigated them; although the author

has not been identified, the piece was sufficiently appealing to the public taste to be published in 1704.[5]

In the following reign, all three of these women – Catherine Trotter at eighteen was the youngest, the others being in their early thirties – would have to learn to survive scathing male satire in the pursuit of their profession; a fate predicted by Mary Manley in her Prologue to her first play:

> The Curtain's drawn now by a Lady's hand,
> The very Name you'll cry bodes Impotence,
> To Fringe and Tea they should confine their sense.

One traditional way of dealing with petticoat-prejudice was for a female author to issue her works anonymously. Conversely, if a play under a woman's name was successful, it would be suggested, in the words of Mary Manley's Prologue once more, that 'Some private Lover helped her on her way.' Aphra Behn, a woman of extraordinary enterprise who after her father's death supported herself by journalism and even more daring forays into the world of espionage, before turning to plays and poetry, had to suffer the indignity of this suspicion: 'the plays she vends she never made'.[6]

What Aphra Behn eloquently asked for was 'the privilege for my masculine part, the poet in me' to be heard; for assuming that females were so endowed, she saw 'no reason why women should not write as well as men'. In a sense Aphra was right, for in so far as her plays triumphed over the contemporary denigration it was because they were witty, full of good characters and thus loved by audiences. However not even Aphra's spirit and talents were totally proof against the handicap of an inadequate female education: that ignorance of Latin which she herself mourned meant that her poems lost their appeal as classically-based poetry became popular.[7]

Most women who felt in themselves the creative lust were not as bold as Aphra.† Theodosia Alleine, wife of Joseph Alleine, a minister living in Taunton who died in 1668, was more typical in her bashfulness. After her husband's death, Mrs Alleine wrote an account of his life and sent it to one of his colleagues, 'she not imagining it should be put forth in her own words', as the printer subsequently explained. 'But that worthy Person, and divers others, upon perusal, saw no reason to alter it [the manuscript], but caused it to be printed as it is.'[8] In general, petticoat-authors, far from stepping forward in challenge, were inclined to retreat still further within

---

†Wonderful Aphra fully deserves both her place in history as the first professional woman author, and her place in Westminster Abbey where she is buried; she lies in the Cloister, however, near the actress Anne Bracegirdle, not in Poets' Corner.

the veilings of conventional female modesty, as though hoping to atone for the sheer flagrancy of their endeavours.

Dorothy Lady Pakington, who died in 1679, had once presided over a kind of Anglican salon at her house Westwood in Worcestershire. She was sometimes thought to be the author of *The Whole Duty of Man* (in fact the work of the Anglican divine Richard Allestree), because the book arose out of discussions held at her house: although she may have assisted him with parts of *The Ladies Calling*. Here was one who basked posthumously in the approval of society, since it was said by Anne Winchilsea that Lady Pakington

> Of each Sex the two best Gifts enjoy'd
> The skill to write, the Modesty to hide.

Sufficient modesty – and a sufficiently early death – could even gain undeserved reward: as Grace Lady Gethin, who died in 1696 at the age of twenty, was gravely admired for the essays *Reliquiae Gethinae* she left behind – in fact merely a number of Bacon's essays copied out.[9]

The most favourable kind of judgement was that accorded to Damaris Lady Masham, who herself gracefully eluded the hovering accusation of 'Scarecrow'; the existence of her books being somehow expiated by the parallel creation of a comfortable country house and the dispensation of hospitality not only to Locke but also to a wide circle of powerful connections. Aphra Behn's marble slab in Westminster Abbey was inscribed with the two lines:

> Here lies a proof that wit can never be
> Defence enough against mortality.

Damaris Lady Masham on the other hand was, on her tomb in the Abbey Church at Bath, described as one 'Who to the Softness and Elegance of her own Sex added several of the Noblest Accomplishments and Qualities of the Other.' Most petticoat-authors found it safer to be commemorated along the lines of Lady Masham rather than those of Aphra Behn.

Katherine Philips, an early example of the species, was known to her circle, according to the fashion of the time for slightly arch *sobriquets*, as the Matchless Orinda.[10] She was the author of one small volume of poems, one volume of letters and two translations from Corneille: *Pompey* and *Horace*. (Her version of *Horace* was the first woman's play to be professionally produced on the English stage, although it appeared after her death.) When *Pompey* was performed in Dublin – where Katherine Philips was then living – in 1663, the fact was celebrated in a cautious couplet:

> Yes, that bold work a Woman dares Translate,
> Not to provoke, nor yet to fear Mens hate.[11]

Throughout her life – she died in 1668 at the age of thirty-six – Katherine Philips showed indeed much care 'not to provoke' – as a result of which she was able successfully to avoid 'Mens hate'.

Katherine Fowler was born into the prosperous middle class, and educated at Mrs Salmon's school in Hackney, where she learnt both French and Italian. Her father had left her a respectable portion of £1,000 and in 1648 Katherine Fowler married James Philips of Cardigan. She was sixteen and he was fifty-four. Despite the disparity in their ages, it appears to have been a stable, happy marriage.

Katherine, being intelligent, was able to help her husband in business; thus the learning which enabled the wife to read Tasso, Michelangelo Buonarroti and Castiglione in the original (Florio's textbooks in the British Library have her name in them) caused no offence to the husband, himself benefiting from his wife's unusual qualities. Katherine Philips's French was even better than her Italian, John Davies dedicating his translation of *Cléopâtre* to her, 'a person so much above your Sex, in the command of those languages'. Nor did Katherine Philips's appearance present any kind of moral threat – 'very good natured ... pretty fat; not tall; red pumpled [sic] face', wrote John Aubrey.[12]

Conventional in her happiness, Katherine Philips was also conventional in her griefs, the reiterated tragedies of the time: the death of her only child, that little boy Hector of whom she wrote in 1655 'I did but pluck the Rose-bud and it fell'; followed by the death of her step-son Francis who died in 1660 at the age of twelve: 'Ah, beauteous Blossom, too untimely dead!'[13]

The personality of 'Orinda' was born during the Commonwealth, when Katherine Philips formed a circle in London, at the centre of which was a coterie of devoted female friends, men being permitted to enter, but on slightly less hectically intimate terms. (James Philips featured as 'Antenor'.) In these friendships, as in her poetry itself, Orinda was carrying on that Platonic tradition which had flowered at the court of Queen Henrietta Maria before the wars: the poets she admired and followed being Cartwright, Suckling and Waller, luminaries of that earlier age. It is in this context of strictly non-carnal love that Orinda's eloquent addresses to her female friends, 'Lucasia' (Anne Owen), 'Rosania' (Mary Aubrey) and later in Dublin 'adored Valerie' (Lady Anne Boyle), should be seen.[14]

Orinda was capable of showing possessive disgust towards her friends' attachments. When Lucasia married the widower Lord Dungannon, Orinda saluted the occasion in verse:

> You are so happy in each other's love
> And in assur'd perfection from above
> That we no wish can add unto your bliss
> But that it should continue as it is.

Unfortunately this perfect bliss seemed to preclude a relationship with Orinda on the old terms: 'I find there are few Friendships in the World Marriage-Proof', she wrote crossly, 'especially when the Person our Friend married has not a Soul particularly capable of the Tenderness of that Endearment ... we may generally conclude the Marriage of a Friend to be the Funeral of a Friendship.' So 'lovely Celimena' (the Countess of Thanet) replaced the renegade Lucasia.

It would however be wrong to read anything covertly sensual into these relationships, however overtly passionate. That would have been quite outside the Platonic tradition. As Orinda herself wrote on the nature of friendship, such 'flames' were free from 'grossness or mortality'.[15]

Orinda's personality was sufficiently distinguished for Jeremy Taylor to ruminate on the whole nature of friendship in a work entitled: *In a Letter to the most Ingenious and Excellent Mrs Katherine Phillips*. Dr Taylor explained in advance how much he differed from 'the morosity of those Cynics – who would not admit your sex into the communities of friendship'. Nevertheless in the body of the work, he himself differentiated carefully between the two sexes: 'a man is the best friend in trouble, but a woman may be equal to him in the days of joy: a woman can as well increase our comforts, but cannot so well lessen our sorrows: and therefore we do not carry women with us when we go to fight, but in peaceful Cities and times vertuous women are the beauties of society and the prettiness of friendship'.[16]

Where the merits of Orinda's poetry are concerned, it is unfortunately impossible to dissent from the view of her biographer: 'little enthusiasm is possible, even to one who has come to know her well'.[17] Although Keats was taken by her lines to Rosania:

> To part with thee I needs must die
> Could parting sep'rate thee and I –

the superbly banal wedding address to Lucasia and Lord Dungannon is quite as characteristic of Orinda's style: the touching simplicity of her grief for her dead son became her poetry best.

Her character is another matter. Katherine Philips, by dint of a personality which impressed but did not challenge, supported by a happily respectable private life, managed both to be known and to be respected as a she-author. She did so, unlike previous she-authors, without the benefit of aristocratic birth. This, in an age when it was the notion of the lady, with her carefully-nurtured, economically-protected languor, which captured the popular imagination, rather than that of her learned sister, was in itself a considerable achievement.

*   *   *

A gentle virtuous disposition in life, a life led none the less close to the highest in the land, an early much-lamented death leaving behind a deposit of poems to be printed thereafter in an atmosphere of mourning, these elements made of Anne Killigrew one she-author of whom it was not only safe but sentimentally delightful to approve. The fact that this Maid of Honour at court died in 1685 at the age of twenty-five unmarried contributed further to the sentimental picture: here was one who 'despised the Myrtle' (symbol of marriage) for the 'nobler Bay' (garland of the poet) in the words of Dryden. In an admonition to the reader the publisher of Anne Killigrew's work (to which Dryden wrote an introduction) drew attention to the same phenomenon, in slightly less graceful language:

> Know, that a Virgin bright this Poem writ,
> A Grace for Beauty, and a Muse for Wit!

But on the evidence of her secret poems, Anne Killigrew was a more complicated character than this salutation of 'a Virgin Bright' or Dryden's verdict – 'Wit more than Man, her Innocence a Child' – would indicate.[18] An obsessional fragment called 'Cloris' Charms' described a journey to be taken by the love-lorn:

> First take thy Hapless Way
> Along the Rocky Northern Shore
> Infamous for the Matchless store
> Of Wracks within that Bay
> None o'er the Cursed Beach e'er crossed
> Unless the Robb'd, the Wrack'd or Lost
> Where on the strand lie spread,
> The sculls of many Dead
> Their mingl'd Bones
> Among the Stones,
> Thy Wretched Feet must tread …

> For there's no Light
> But all is Night,
> And Darkness that you meet....[19]

Throughout her poetry a thread of melancholy, even bitterness runs, particularly on the subject of female unrequited love, a hint that 'Love the Softer Sex does sorriest wound.' In one of her pastoral dialogues, Anne Killigrew portrays a maiden who has been betrayed. She exclaims:

> Remember when you love, from that same hour
> Your peace you put into your Lovers Power:
> From that same hour from him you Laws receive
> And as he shall ordain, you Joy, or Grieve.

Anne Killigrew's 'Paragon' was the beautiful and chaste Duchess of Grafton, wife of one of Charles II's bastards and daughter of his minister Arlington. Here was a woman who for all her beauty kindled 'in none a fond desire'; this virtuous wife, admired but not courted, bonded by reason not the chains of passion, was the type of heroine she envied.[20]

In general there is a fastidious rejection of the worldly values of the court against the background of which Anne Killigrew led the whole of her short life. A very long and very pessimistic poem 'The Miseries of Man' pleads that reason, not passion, shall hold the reins of the chariot, so that anger, fear, pride, hope and desire may be harnessed. The poem, singularly modern in its approach to nature, points out:

> The bloody Wolf, the Wolf does not pursue;
> The Boar, though fierce, his Tusk will not embrue
> In his own kind, Bears, not on Bears do prey:
> Thou art then, Man, more savage far than they.[21]

'A Farewell to Worldly Joys' rejects among other things 'Ye Unsubstantial Joys, Ye Gilded Nothings, Gaudy Toys'. 'The Discontent' casts aside grandeur and fame, the pillars of the court, in favour of that repose which gold alone cannot purchase.[22] All of this suggests that the resignation saluted in another elegy on her death, probably by the poet and theologian Edmund Elys, was not achieved without emotional cost:

> O Happy Maid, who didst so soon Espy
> In this Dark Life, that All is Vanity.[23]

Anne's father was Dr Henry Killigrew, Almoner to the Duke of York, Chaplain to the King, and Master of the Savoy, one of three brothers all of whom combined an interest in the arts, specially the dramatic arts, with the royal service: Thomas Killigrew was manager of the Theatre Royal and head of the troupe of actors known as the King's Servants as well as Groom of the Bedchamber to the King; Sir William Killigrew, Vice-Chamberlain at court, also wrote plays. It was these connections which led Dryden to describe Anne as 'A Soul so charming from a Stock so good.'[24] However, the good stock also included Thomas's son, dissolute Harry Killigrew, Groom of the Bedchamber to the Duke of York, whose bawdy exploits served to *épater* the court, as well as Sir William's more conventional daughter Mary, who by marrying an illegitimate son of the House of Orange, established still closer Killigrew royal connections. Anne herself entered the household of the Duke of York, as Maid of Honour to his second wife, Mary of Modena.

It was significant of the relative public attitudes to female painting (approved) and female authorship (suspected) that the recognition Anne Killigrew did seek during her lifetime was for her artistic talent, not her poetry. Applauded in royal circles as a portraitist, she was reckoned to be particularly successful in capturing the likeness of the Duke of York: 'Her Hand drew forth the Image of his Heart,' wrote Dryden. From Dryden too we learn that Anne painted Greek and Roman scenes, and subjects such as Venus and Adonis, the Graces dressing Venus, and Judith and Holofernes.

Anne Killigrew looks out of her own self-portrait, displaying what Dryden described with not too much flattery as a 'well-proportion'd Shape, and beauteous Face'. In some ways this is the conventional late-seventeenth-century visage, so often painted by Lely, with its fine long nose, round cheeks, full mouth and lofty pure forehead, framed in thick curls; but there is something tighter and more disciplined here, compared to his flowering beauties (as well as a more restrained display of bosom). Anne Killigrew died of smallpox in the summer of 1685 and her father produced a memorial edition of her poems the following autumn. The modest yet firm self-portrait represents the public use of her talent. In private Anne Killigrew wrote poems like this *On Death*:

> Tell me thou safest End of all our Woe
> Why wretched Mortals do avoid thee so
> Thou gentle drier o' th' Afflicted Tears,
> Thou noble ender of the Cowards fears;
> Thou sweet Repose to Lovers sad despair....[25]

But then painting and drawing were the agreed feminine accomplishments, were they not? Psychologically, it was always possible to regard the female artist as merely extending the talents of a refined education into a wider sphere, even when as in the case of Mary Beale, who was influenced by Robert Walker and Lely, she was actually earning a good professional income from her efforts. Joan Carlile seems to have been the first of such female artists, said to have been presented with artist's materials (ultramarine) by King Charles I, and by 1658 known as 'a virtuous example' of painting portraits in oils, as well as copying Italian masters in miniature.[26] Mary Beale, born before the Civil War, the daughter of a clergyman called Craddock, lived to the end of the century; she produced water-colours and crayon drawings, portraits amongst others of Milton, Lord Halifax, the Duke of Norfolk and Bishop Wilkins. With a house in Pall Mall, her earnings rose from £200 in 1672 to a peak of £429 pounds – from eighty-three commissions – in 1677; although as Lely's pupil, her popularity declined with his death.[27]

Mary Beale, like Anne Killigrew, wrote poetry; not for her however the kind of hostility which might be shown to the more ostensibly learned 'Scarecrow'. Her brother-in-law Samuel Woodforde, a Prebendary of Winchester and himself a poet, described her with affection as 'that absolutely compleat Gentlewoman ... the truly virtuous Mary Beale', and Woodforde included two of her works in his *Paraphrase to the Psalms*, saying that she had made 'Painting and Poetrie ... to be really the same'.[28] Where painting was concerned, the distinction between the professional and the amateur was not really perceived; no modest apologies were felt necessary for the presumptuous female pen so long as it was wielded in the cause of art not literature.

Elizabeth Capel, Countess of Carnarvon, who died in 1678 at the age of forty-five, was one of the large family of that Royalist hero Arthur Lord Capel, executed in 1648. All the Capels loved flowers (as the great family portrait of 1637 bears vivid witness): another sister, Mary Duchess of Beaufort, a keen botanist and a friend of Sir Hans Sloane, developed the gardens at Badminton and commissioned an important florilegium by Everhardus Kickius. Flower-painting, inspired by her parents' garden at Little Hadam, was Lady Carnarvon's speciality. There is a small gouache in the Royal Collection dated 1662 (which may however be a copy of an existing flower-piece), and Lely's double portrait with the Duchess of Beaufort shows Lady Carnarvon holding one of her own works. In both cases the signature reads 'E. Carnarvon *fec* ...' under a coronet.[29] Here was a pursuit which no one resented: 'E. Carnarvon' would have many ladylike and floral-minded followers in the future, coroneted and otherwise, whom no one would think to criticize for being petticoat-painters.

*   *   *

There was another talented 'maid' at court who was an almost exact contemporary of Anne Killigrew.[30] That was Anne Kingsmill, later Anne Finch by marriage to Heneage Finch, a son of the third Earl of Winchilsea, and later still Anne Countess of Winchilsea when her husband succeeded to the title. (Heneage Finch was a great-nephew of that Sir Heneage Finch, Speaker of the House of Commons, who won the hand of the Widow Bennett in 1629.) Anne Kingsmill came of a good Hampshire family although both her parents died when she was very young; she began adult life as one of the six Maids of Honour to Mary of Modena, a body which included not only Anne Killigrew but also the witty and notorious Catherine Sedley, to whose very different use of her intelligence attention will be drawn in a subsequent chapter.

Anne's marriage was also made within the purlieus of the royal (York) household: Heneage Finch was Captain of the Halberdiers and Gentleman of the Bedchamber to James II, then Duke of York. The closeness of the connection meant that King James's flight from the throne threatened the Finch welfare: Heneage thought it prudent to take his wife to the family home of Eastwell in Kent, where his nephew Charles, fourth Earl of Winchilsea, gave his relations a retreat.

The secluded circumstances in which Anne now found herself, however galling in political terms, might be described as ideal for a serious (female) author. For one thing Anne lacked the joyous but distracting surroundings of a young family: she was childless and remained so, despite therapeutic visits to the spa at Tunbridge Wells. This was a negative asset. Then she had the positive advantage of a husband who was not only affectionate – 'They err, who say that husbands can't be lovers', she wrote – but also encouraging, making such gestures as asking her to write a poem for him ready for his return when he went to London. Heneage Finch was her 'Dafnis' and she was his 'Ardelia'.[31] Furthermore Heneage's nephew Charles, their young patron, also extended encouragement to Anne, before his death in 1712 left Heneage Finch to succeed to the title as fifth Earl of Winchilsea.

Anne certainly did not miss the busy life of the city. She said of herself that fashion meant nothing to her, wanting merely a new gown once a year in the spring and nothing more; her scorn for the feminine 'accomplishments' with which the idle and uneducated beauties of society filled their hours has already been quoted (see p. 322). What Anne enjoyed instead was the creative privacy of a country life, so much more conducive to the development of her poetry than the court where, as she pointed out, 'everyone would have made their remarks upon a Versifying Maid of

Honour'. She wrote some melancholy lines on this theme:

> Did I my lines intend for publick view
> How many censures, wou'd their faults pursue ...
> Alas! a woman that attempts the pen
> Such an intruder on the rights of men
> Such a presumptuous Creature, is esteem'd
> The fault, can by no virtue be redeem'd.[32]

Anne Winchilsea was right in her instinct that privacy was a further important asset to a she-author. For unlike Anne Killigrew, she lived out at least her natural lifespan, dying in 1720 in her sixtieth year. Chronologically if not stylistically (she was much influenced by Dryden) her poetry belongs to the eighteenth century; she first appeared in print in 1701, a small volume being published in 1713. Her reputation as a poet rests in consequence on more secure foundations: in the nineteenth century, Wordsworth fell in love with one of her poems, entitled 'Nocturnal Reverie', with its touching lines on the freedom of animals under cover of darkness:

> Their short-liv'd Jubilee the Creatures keep
> Which but endures, whilst Tyrant Man does sleep.

Commending its attitude to nature, he described 'Nocturnal Reverie' as 'often admirable, chaste, tender and vigorous'.[33]† But this also meant that unlike Orinda, a generation her senior, Anne Winchilsea survived to be printed in the keen-bladed age of Pope. And once her poetry was made public, it was open season for the hunt, as it was for the 'Female Wits'.

The trio of Pope, Arbuthnot and Gay together wrote a play, *Three Hours after Marriage*, in which Anne Winchilsea appeared as ludicrous Phoebe Clinket, ink-stained and with pens in her hair. Phoebe Clinket, unkempt as she might be, was also very much the lady of the house: she kept writing materials in every room in case inspiration seized her, and a compliant maid followed her about with a desk strapped to her back, so that Phoebe could even write on the move.[35]

Had Orinda been of a less charmingly tactful disposition, had Anne Killigrew cast modesty aside and made her secret feelings public, had both of them survived into the eighteenth century, one suspects that these ladies

---

†In recent years she has also been quoted with approval in a feminist context, as one who early protested against the idea of the 'natural' patriarchal order.[34]

might have found themselves in the literary pillory along with ink-stained 'Phoebe Clinket'.

*   *   *

Anne Finch, later Viscountess Conway, the little girl who had run about the gardens of Kensington House and worshipped her step-brother John, never did throw off those sick headaches which in her youth were ascribed to too much reading, unsuitable to her sex (see p. 131). Yet despite a lifetime of crippling illness necessitating virtual social retirement towards the end, Anne Viscountess Conway survived to write a philosophical work admired after her death (when it was printed) by Leibniz; the editor of her correspondence describing her as 'the most remarkable woman of that remarkable age' and comparing her to that mystic of the twelfth century, the Abbess Hildegard of Bingen.[36]

It is too easy to say that Anne Viscountess Conway was able to develop her original intellect just because her illness cut her off from the world and enabled her to avoid the hostility generally shown to the learned lady. Just as it is far too simple to ascribe her torturing headaches merely to an unconscious desire to withdraw from the jovial society favoured by her husband; the pain which would cause her at one point to seek trepanning as the lesser of two evils was evidently real enough. Besides, diagnosis, whether medical or psychological, is notoriously dangerous in the absence of the patient, especially when all symptoms are described in the very different medical language of 300 years ago. Nevertheless the story of Anne Conway demonstrates that a perpetual acknowledgement of her own weakness was one way, albeit a very painful one, in which a clever woman could avoid disapproval; the physical doing very well in the judgement of the world as a metaphor for the intellectual.

Anne Finch, born in 1631, was the posthumous daughter of Sir Heneage Finch by the Widow Bennett. (She was thus linked to Anne Countess of Winchilsea by marriage not blood.) She had numerous intelligent and successful relations on her father's side, including a formidable grandmother in Elizabeth Heneage, first Countess of Winchilsea. But if we seek a matrilineal descent for her intelligence, we may also turn to her mother, that pretty well-heeled Penelope who held off all suitors till she secured the one she wanted, and who proved to be a far more astute character than was generally suspected (see pp. 89–93). Or perhaps it was the cross between the two: the blood of the bright middle-class mother galvanizing into activity the more ancient strain of her father.

It was through her step-brother John that Anne first met the philosopher

Henry More, and was introduced to his Cambridge Platonist circle, More being John Finch's tutor at Christ's College. Anne's first letter to More, which precedes her marriage, enclosed her own translation of a piece of Descartes:[37] for it was More who was responsible for introducing to England the Cartesian Rationalism which postulated that the general nature of the world could be established by demonstrative reasoning from indubitable premises (in contrast to the Empiricists like Hobbes, who held that knowledge of the world came through experience, and not through reason alone). Anne became for More 'my Heroine Pupil'. Under his influence she read Plato and Plotinus, and studied such mystical works as the *Desiderata Kabbala*.

In 1651 marriage to Edward Conway made Anne into the chatelaine of Ragley Castle, Herefordshire; a position which enabled her, like Damaris Lady Masham, to dispense hospitality to her philosophical friends, principal among them More. For all Conway's taste for London society, it would be wrong to regard Anne Finch and her husband as intellectually mis-matched: here was no yoking of unhappy opposites. Edward, later third Viscount Conway, a man eight years older than his bride, was respected by More and himself a reader of Descartes. At Ragley he was happy to join in the discussions initiated by More on topics including spiritism and cabbalism as well as Rationalism. He was an early member of the Royal Society.

But Conway was also a man of action. The son of one of the principal Secretaries of State to James I and Charles I, he had distinguished himself in the north of Ireland in the recent wars. He could not see his own horizon, like that of his ailing wife, bounded by life at Ragley, whatever the stimulus of More's company. As a man pursuing a public career, his devotion to the social life at Whitehall was certainly defensible; one can also understand only too easily how a man with a taste for late-night suppers with the King and Nell Gwynn would not necessarily wish to spend every evening discussing Platonism in the country with a wife either crippled with or about to be crippled with a headache, a visiting philosopher and perhaps his wife's intellectually-minded gentlewoman – 'your library keeper Mrs Sarah'.[38]

Yet on the subject of Anne Conway's health, it should be remembered honourably in favour of Lord Conway, that he showed admirable stoicism when their only child, little Heneage Conway, died at the age of two and a half of smallpox. (Anne caught it too, enduring still further impairment of her fragile health.) He was advised that his wife would suffer agonies if she 'bred' again, and therefore trained himself not to wish for children: a piece of self-denial most uncharacteristic of his age. When the news was brought that Anne was possibly pregnant again, Lord Conway commented: 'My thoughts were long since sealed against any impetuous desires after children, and my mind disposed to that which was more diffusive than gathering together an estate for an heir, and this [news] will not alter me.'[39] His stoicism stood him in good stead, for Anne Viscountess Conway never did bear children.

It was fortunate for Anne Conway that she also had the benefit of those other affectionate relationships – in both of which she was encouraged in her learned studies – with her brother John and with More. Her intimacy with More lasted thirty years and was both platonic and 'Platonick'. Early on, More dedicated *An Antidote against Atheism* to Anne, as one who in 'penetrant Wit' and 'speculative Genius' had so far outstripped all her sex. To More, Anne Conway was not only his 'Heroine Pupil' but also 'Virtue become visible to his outward sight'. Sir John Finch, a physician at Cambridge who ended his life there with his lifelong friend and 'chevalier' Sir Thomas Baines (they were buried in the same grave) led in between a successful life as a diplomat. Anne Conway's girlhood attachment to her brother never waned. Here More consoles her for her grief at his departure: 'What you speak concerning friendship in reference to your brother, and in the behalf of a more passionate kind of affection as an inseparable concomitant of it [that is, grief], is true', he wrote. All the same the philosopher felt bound to point out: 'reason moderates these emotions'.[40]

Today Anne Conway's recurring headaches would certainly be regarded as migrainous in nature, particularly as they were often accompanied by sickness (but migraine today, even if understood, is still something for which no absolute cause, let alone an absolute cure, can be given). In those days, as the Conway correspondence amply demonstrates, Anne Conway's existence was bounded by remedies tried and failed, doctors approached and abandoned, healers of infinite variety solicited, whose increasingly bizarre nature indicates all too eloquently the desperation of the uncured – but surely not incurable? – patient with the passing of the years.

There was 'a red powder' and 'a blue powder'. Mercury was resorted to three times (something which worried More), once in the form of an ointment prescribed by the celebrated physician Sir Theodore Mayerne, twice in the form of a powder taken orally, made up by Charles Huis, a well-known chemist. Robert Boyle made up another powder, to be taken in a solution of sack and canary, which he prepared himself. Opium –

probably laudanum, at that time a novelty in England – was tried at the suggestion of Thomas Sydenham. Other doctors consulted included William Harvey and Sir Francis Prujean.

At one point Henry More proposed tobacco, which had a therapeutic reputation at that time and was not infrequently prescribed for headaches; he also suggested coffee.† Anne Conway's coach had to be stuffed with the softest down since even feathers threatened her acute sensibilities. She tried a special diet of 'husbandman's fare': woodcocks, pheasants and baked turkeys, and at the other extreme 'the experiment of water falling on your head'.[42]

The gruesome suggestion of trepanning actually originated with Harvey in 1656 (although he did refer Lady Conway to a board of specialists). Nevertheless the patient, in what state of torment one can only guess, took a sudden decision to go to France and have the operation, involving the sawing open of a hole in the skull to relieve pressure, performed forthwith. In the event the French physicians did no more than open Lady Conway's jugular arteries, although it is not clear whether the doctors drew back or in the end the patient shrank from the ultimate ordeal. In any case, there was a further ordeal to be endured of quite a different nature: Lord Conway, coming to join his wife, was captured at sea by the Dutch and thrown naked into a filthy prison until such time as he was ransomed.[43]

The episode of the Irish faith healer Valentine Greatrakes was less traumatic (although equally unsuccessful in its results). Greatrakes, known as 'the Irish stroker', came of a good family in Youghal; he never took any money for his cures in Ireland. His visit did have therapeutic effects for a good many of the tenants at Ragley, who found their ills alleviated. To Lady Conway he arrived on a morning when the sun was shining: 'for the sun, Madam, is a great healer and composer'. Greatrakes laid his fingers on her head while all around waited for the headache to vanish. It did not. Day after day he repeated the process. Still the headache maintained its vicious grip. After a fortnight the 'Irish stroker' like the previous doctors, admitted failure and departed.[44]

Lady Conway's condition aroused sympathy beyond her own country. From the Grand Duke of Tuscany, at whose court John Finch held the post of Minister, arrived 'a very ingenious contrivance to sit at all heights in the bed, and have the use of a table. It goes upon screws, and everything is to be unscrewed. The glass within the bed-pan is to be taken out by unscrewing the handle and taking the handle quite off, for then it opens.'[45]

---

†Coffee has not lost its reputation: Oliver Sacks, in *Migraine*, 1981, suggests that migraine sufferers take caffeine tablets, for the 'management' of migraine attacks.[41]

The particular stresses of Anne Conway's life, such as the death of little Heneage, naturally exacerbated her condition. 'Our passions are given us for certain uses and services which when they cease, our passions are to cease also,' wrote More.[46] That was easier advised than done. Yet it is notable and heroic – fully justifying More's praise of his pupil – that she pursued her studies throughout all these agonizing years; we find her for example attempting to learn Greek in 1665, when she was in the extremities of pain. In the winter of 1667 she was not only bed-ridden but reduced to an amanuensis in her correspondence with More at Cambridge; by the autumn of the following year, however, she was rising gallantly once more.

All this while More the philosopher had to contemplate the physical purgatory of his friend, and could do nothing to help her to pass from it. 'The pious and virtuous' came out of their travails as 'gold purified out of the fire', he declared. In 1671 More wrote to Anne Conway: 'And I hope your body will not prove a Tomb to you, but rather an holy Temple, an hallowed edifice for your soul to work in, those bodies that are most vigorously in health are the most devouring sepulchres to swallow down the soul into and to bury all the nobler faculties.'[47] Reflections such as these can have been as little true consolation to Anne Conway's agonized friend as they were to the suffering woman herself.

Perhaps there was more comfort to be found when More turned to philosophy. Lady Conway's headache, he wrote, might be good for the whole on the grounds that what is good for the whole may not be good for the part, and Lady Conway's headaches were certainly not good for one part – 'her particular friends'. The sentence: 'if her body were as well as her mind, it would be better for us all' only applied after all to these friends. Or perhaps after all poetry provided the true consolation. More sent Anne Conway a scribbled translation, done in bed, of his own *Aphoria, or The Perplexity of the Soul*, and then *Euphoria, or The Extrication of the Soul*, in a friend's translation which Anne had learnt by heart and of which she desired a copy. These lines in *Aphoria* apostrophizing Father Jove may have found some dark echo in Anne's heart:

> 'Tis rare, we mortals live i' the clouds like thee,
> Lies, Toys, or some hid fate, us fix or move.
> All else being dark, what's life I only see....[48]

In the autumn of 1670 Lord Conway and Henry More between them persuaded the Netherlander physician F. M. Van Helmont to visit Ragley. Van Helmont remained there for nine years, devoting himself to finding a cure for Lady Conway. Fresh medicines were sought from Germany; the headaches persisted but at least Lady Conway's general health, so much damaged by that fatal bout of smallpox which killed little Heneage, improved. At first Van Helmont's presence at Ragley had the agreeable side-effect that More could still visit the castle from Cambridge when Anne was too ill to receive him, since Van Helmont could act as host. But later Van Helmont's own interest in Quakerism reinforced Anne Conway's tendencies in that direction, and after some years of spiritual doubt she finally joined the sect in 1677. In the last years of her life she lived at Ragley surrounded by Quakers, and More's visits dwindled.

On several different levels, it is easy to see what attracted Anne Conway to the Friends; although the fact that Van Helmont regularly attended Quaker Meetings from 1675 onwards was clearly relevant in view of Anne's physical isolation brought about by her sickness, More's estimate of his friend's character must also be borne in mind: 'she was one that would not give up her Judgment entirely unto any'.[49] Her first interest was in that sect known as the Familists and the cobbler-poet of Bohemia, Jacob Boehme. Then she came to study the Quaker arguments through their tracts: like several of her friends, including More, she was prepared to believe that religion had been choked with irrelevant detail and speculate how it might be resuscitated.

Lady Conway was of course cut off by illness not only from the Quaker Meetings, but also from the more violent public manifestations of their religion, exactly those aspects which revolted her contemporaries. Thus Lady Conway did not perceive in the Quakers uncontrollable spirits who might interrupt a preacher in the midst of his sermon, but rather 'lovers of quiet and retirement'. On this ground, she sent away to London for Quaker maids: 'for if they prove what they seem to be ... they will fit the circumstances I am in (that cannot endure any noise) better than ordinary domestics'.[50] And she seems to have been lucky in her finds: for Quaker maids could be unreliable, suddenly inspired by the Lord to leave their position and go preaching; Lady Conway's maids on the contrary stayed with her to the end.

Lady Conway was also convinced that the Quakers understood the loneliness of pain and could comfort her when 'Reason' and 'Philosophy' could not, just because of their own frequent ordeals in the Lord's service: 'they have been and are a suffering people'. She wrote: 'The weight of my affliction lies so very heavy upon me, that it is incredible how very seldom I can endure anyone in my chamber, but I find them so still and very serious'; the Quakers' company would be acceptable to her so long as she could bear any company at all.[51] So in her dark room, surrounded by luxuries which could not cure, she harkened to their consolations and listened to their sufferings.

More, who had warned Anne against 'melancholy' (which has been described as the contemporary atheism), had failed to predict that she would turn to 'enthusiasm' (the contemporary fanaticism).[52] Before her death Anne did somewhat reconcile More to the Quaker cause; at least to understand her own attraction to it. Conversions, especially those to 'enthusiastic' or fanatical religions, are however notoriously difficult for the previous intimates of the convert. Lord Conway was by now occupying an important administrative position in Ireland; Anne dispatched a parcel of Quaker books to him 'to chalk out the way, by which all serious seekers after God may attain their desired satisfaction and true rest'. She signed her covering letter for the first time in Quaker style: 'Thine'. Although Lord Conway tried to plough his way through the books, despite eye-strain, and although he attempted honourably to assist the Quakers in Ireland (just as his wife in England tried to get George Fox out of gaol), he still pronounced them from the point of view of a government official a 'senseless, wilful, ridiculous generation of people'.[53]

At his last visit to Ragley in Anne's lifetime, Lord Conway was dismayed to find how the situation had changed: 'all the women about my wife and most of the rest are Quakers, and Mons. Van Helmont is governor of that flock, an unpleasing sort of people, silent, sullen and of a removed conversation'. George Fox on the other hand, the Friends' leader, found Lady Conway 'tender and loving', and in 1678 willing to detain him longer than he was ready to stay, in view of the call of his mission in other parts of the country.[54]

In February 1679, after days of terrible pain, Anne Conway was released into death; in her last agonies, she stoically refused to have Lord Conway sent for from Ireland, but her tiny wasted body was encased in an inner coffin of wood and glass so that he could see her face on arrival before she was wrapped in her outer covering of lead. A codicil to her will, clearly written with much physical difficulty, asked that the customary ostentation at the funeral of a lady of her quality should be forsworn, in accordance with Quaker practice. In addition, 'My Lady would have no Cerecloth to avoid the coming of any men about her, but desired that only Her Women with the two maids should lay her in the coffin'. In her will Lady Conway left £500 to Sir John Finch, £400 to Henry More, and £300 to Van Helmont, representing three stages of affection in her life.[55]

More spoke this epitaph upon her: 'I perceive and bless God for it, that

my Lady Conway was my Lady Conway to her last Breath; the greatest
Example of Patience and presence of Mind, in highest Extremities of Pain
and Affliction, that we shall easily meet with: Scarce anything to be found
like her, since the Primitive times of the church.' But the most telling
judgement on Anne Viscountess Conway, at least by the standards of the
century in which she lived, was pronounced by her brother Sir John Finch:
'I must never hope to see again in this World, knowledge enough to have
made a Man of Parts proud, in a more talkative Sex to be possessed without
noise.'[56]

*   *   *

The Principles of the Most Ancient and Modern Philosophy by Anne Viscountess Conway is thought to have been written by her when Van Helmont
first lived with her and her general health temporarily improved: it was
noted down with 'a Black-lead Pen' in 'a Paper-Book'.[57]

Like many others in the seventeenth century, Lady Conway was interested to try and reconcile the findings of the new science with the truths of
the Christian religion. She put forward a great many notes on Hebrew
and cabbalistic beliefs. Her work also included a disquisition on the nature
of God, who had created the world out of goodness, not out of necessity.
'In God there can exist no Passion.... For every Passion is something
Temporal.' She proposed that the time passed since the beginning of
Creation must be infinite (not 6,000 years as was popularly believed), as
could be demonstrated from the infinite goodness of God: 'Now how can
it be, that this Fountain shall not always plentifully flow, and send from
itself Living Waters?' As it was 'an Essential Attribute' of God, to be a
Creator, 'so by Consequence God ever was a Creator, and ever will be a
Creator'; otherwise his nature would be changed. Creatures themselves
ever were and ever would be: 'yet this Infiniteness of Times is not equal to
the Infiniteness of God's Eternity, because the Eternity of God himself,
hath no Times in it'. Christ she described as 'the Middle Being, not subject
to decay'.[58]

Lady Conway was of course a resolute opponent of Hobbes, who with
his associates 'grievously' erred in teaching that 'Sense and Knowledge'
were no more than 'a reaction of Corporeal Particles' one upon another.
Sense and knowledge, she wrote, were 'a Thing far more Noble and
Divine; in any Local or Mechanical Motion of any Particles Whatsoever'.
Rejecting Hobbes utterly, she described every creature as comprising both
a body and a spirit, or *Principium magis Activum, et magis Passivum* (a more
active and a more passive principle). Lady Conway thought these two

principles 'may fitly be termed Male and Female, by reason of that Analogy a Husband hath with his Wife. For as the ordinary Generation of Man requires a Conjunction and Co-operation of Male and Female; so also all Generations and Productions whatsoever they may be, require an Union.'[59]

More was probably responsible for the Latin translation of Lady Conway's *Principles*, in which form it first appeared in print in Amsterdam in 1690; two years later the book, re-translated into English, was printed in England. The English edition referred to a certain English Countess (Lord Conway was raised to an earldom in the year of his wife's death), 'a Woman learned beyond her Sex', whose work, found after her death inscribed 'in a very dull and small character' could only be read with the greatest difficulty. Leibniz probably heard of her work through Van Helmont: he declared himself greatly influenced by her and expressed his approval of her principles over those of Locke – *'Les miens en philosophie approchent un peu d'advantage de ceux de feu Mme la Comtesse de Conway.'*[60]

A postscript may be added concerning the fate of Lord Conway. He was now in his mid-fifties, a man with an important position in the world; in 1681, two years after his wife's death, he was created one of the Secretaries of State. Yet his house had no mistress and he himself had no heir. However valiantly Lord Conway may have reconciled himself to this disappointment twenty years earlier, he was now generally judged to be in need of a wife who would provide a son. Nor did the Finch family shrink from the prospect. Anne Conway's sister, Lady Clifton, was pleading with her brother-in-law to marry again only two months after Anne's death. Sir John Finch was also prominent in his persuasions, invoking the very name of his dead sister: let him remarry 'for her sake (whose dust could it speak, would join with me I am sure)'. Sir Thomas Baines, as the lifelong 'chevalier' of Sir John Finch, also interested himself in the affair: he gave it as his opinion that the ideal 'widower's wife' was small, thin and pale, albeit very healthy and coming of fruitful parents; she should also be 'of a feminine lax temper'.[61] A stream of young – or youngish ladies, generally in their early twenties, was paraded, most of whom possessed large or largish portions.

What did Lord Conway now do? Ignoring the parade (and the advice) he fell violently in love with a most unsuitable chit of seventeen – unsuitable because she was flighty – Margaret Poulett, daughter of the second Lord Poulett and niece of the Speaker of the House of Commons. What pent-up emotions, suppressed during his wife's long illness, what middle-aged desires, long believed quiescent, surged through the bosom of the admirable Lord Conway during this unexpected Roman spring?

Lord Conway's friends, trained to believe that a fifty-six-year-old widower was indeed a proper spouse for a young girl if his rank was sufficiently august, suggested various modes of attack, in all of which ultimate victory was assumed.[62] Perhaps he should emulate the methods of Julius Caesar who came and saw and conquered: cry *Veni, Vidi, Vici*, and then all the young gallants who surrounded Mistress Margaret would be blown away. Another friend advised him first to prepare his 'Wooing Countenance' and then reflect on St Matthew, Chapter One (this, which begins with a long recital of the begetting of the generations before Jesus, was presumably to be regarded as some kind of fertility chant). For this elderly Romeo a further confidant recommended 'a Handsome Dress'.

So Lord Conway had 'a riding-suit' ordered in order to call on his beloved at Bath. It was to be lined with black satin, and embroidered with black and silver; apart from the other black touches it was to be laced with black and white love lace, 'both mourning enough and fine enough for this expedition', a delicate way of emphasizing Lord Conway's status, at once a widower and a lover. Fifty pounds was disbursed on this outfit, not counting the sword and hat which were extra. But the whole effect was wasted, at least in Bath, when Margaret Poulett's brother would not let Lord Conway call upon her; he was himself perversely backing the suit of his own friend (and contemporary), the young Lord Arran. Lord Conway had to wait till London to call upon his beloved.

Gradually, very gradually, it was borne in upon Lord Conway that Margaret was merely playing with his attentions. He withdrew from the field. He did not however deny the force of that sweet fever which had ravaged him. He could have had many richer, nobler, handsomer and more discreet wives, he wrote, but 'I have still more inclination for her [Margaret] than for any woman that ever I heard of . . . I believe there is a fate in such things which I can give no account of'.

Lord Conway did marry again, a considerably older woman, someone presumably much closer to Sir Thomas Baines's recipe for the widower's ideal. But this second wife died in childbirth, as did the son she bore. Less than six weeks later Lord Conway married for the third time, a woman who brought him a portion of £30,000. By now Lord Conway's own race was almost run. He died in August 1683, only four years after the death of Anne. He died without an heir; but then he had long ago braced himself to accept that defeat rather than increase the physical burdens placed upon his precious jewel of a first wife; she who in the words of her brother possessed 'knowledge enough' to make the most intelligent man proud – and all 'without noise'.

18 Helping in God's Vineyard

'Here will be work and business enough for us all that none need to be Idle in God's vineyard, but as we have everyone received a measure of God's spirit and grace some may be fellow helpers and workers together with our brethren. . . .'

LETTER OF ISABEL (FELL) YEAMANS, 1676

Anne Viscountess Conway desired to have Quaker servants about her because this 'suffering people', so 'still and very serious' in their behaviour would make ideal sympathetic attendants for an invalid. Lord Conway on the other hand, in Ireland where he had to cope with the Quakers' sudden demonstrations according to the dictates of 'the Inner Light', found them 'senseless, wilful, ridiculous'.[1]

Certainly the stories of the early Friends, and their persistent testifying under the most hostile circumstances, more than justify Lady Conway's description of them as 'a suffering people': although her belief in their stillness might have been shaken by some of the events in the 'steeplehouses' and elsewhere when 'the Inner Light' inspired a Friend to interrupt proceedings. In the 1670s for example the charge brought against a Quaker woman called Ann Blaykling was that she had called the minister 'Priest, hireling and deceiver, greedy dumb dog, with many words of the same nature':[2] a by no means uncharacteristic selection of insults for an early Friend. In their opposition to the payment of tithes, because they believed in the separation of Church and State (hence Anglican ministers were 'hirelings'), their refusal to swear an oath (including an Oath of Allegiance in court), and in their insistence on their own form of marriage, the Friends, as Lord Conway discovered, also posed other problems to the State, beyond an awkward tendency to extemporary prayer.

At the same time the Society of Friends increased: it has been estimated that when its founder George Fox died in 1691, there were 50,000 Quakers in England, one in every 100 of the population.[3] In all of this, the sufferings, the agitations and the responsibilities, women continued to play that prominent role which had been theirs from the first inception of the sect. In 1656 George Fox had defended the spiritual equality of women with men (see p. 264): there was not only natural justice in this, there was also a practical recognition of the support women – including that despised, feared, disliked class, elderly women – gave him from the first.

Quakers were of course not alone among the sects which were nourished by the enthusiasm and energies of women. The force of women preachers, the original Baptists and Anabaptists of the 1640s, bore witness to that aspect of so-called heretical sects which enabled women to find liberation, both spiritual and social, in their midst. There were other examples, and early evangelism (unconnected with Quakerism) would continue to find women prominent. The history of the Quakers does however provide a microcosm of that liberation, with all the problems, as well as fulfilment, it brought. For one thing, their adoption of the Quaker religion hardly freed such women from the pressures to which their condition made them already subject. An 'ancient' widow inspired to step outside the traditional woman's role and speak publicly was for example more, rather than less, likely to be suspected of truck with the devil. As Margaret Fell, one of the most prominent of the early Quaker women, pointed out, there was always the danger of the Inner Light being mistaken for witchcraft; just as the prophetess Anna Trapnel, another female of independent voice, had been subject to the scrutiny of the 'witch-trying woman' (see p. 259). Barbara Blaugdone of Bristol, for example, who spoke out both in the West Country and Ireland, was forty-six when she was 'convinced'; in Cork some of her former friends termed her a witch and had their servants turn her out of doors. (But convincement brought strength: for all her sufferings, the dour sharp-tongued Barbara Blaugdone lived to the age of ninety-five, dying in 1704.)[4]

Nor did the presence of vociferous women in the Quaker midst allay hostility to a religion which relied on the worrying instrument of extemporary prayer – uncontrollable from the outside. In 1677 in *The Countermine*, the Royalist pamphleteer and historian John Nalson used this suspicious combination to deduce that such impromptu manifestations were in fact inspired by the devil. He gave an instance of a woman who had become generally admired for being 'so eminent especially in this Gift of Prayer'; subsequently she went to New England where she was discovered to be 'a most Abominable Witch'. At her trial she confessed that she had given up her soul to the devil in return for the gift of extemporary prayer. Concluded Nalson with satisfaction: 'Either now we must believe that this Extempore Way is not an infallible sign of the Spirit of God: or

that the Devil has the Power of disposing of the Gifts of the Spirit.' Had
not St Paul himself issued 'an express Command' against 'these Female
Doctresses'?[5]

As against this, George Fox, with that power which great conviction
allied to great personal strength always bestows, never ceased to push
forward the view that there was work for Quaker women to do as well as
men. He admonished the Women's Meetings: 'Encourage all the women
that are convinced, and minds virtue, and loves the truth, and walks in it,
that they may come up into God's service, that they may too be serviceable
in their generation, and in the Creation. ...'[6]

On the one hand therefore the Quaker women were able to exercise
responsibilities within their own religious organization denied to any other
Englishwomen of their time (and for a long time thereafter, if granted at
all). These women as a result were able to practise a certain kind of
admirable Nonconformist philanthropy from which so much reforming
richness has flowed in English social life. On the other hand where the
Inner Light drew Quaker women into a more challenging and adventurous
way of life, not only did they themselves suffer hideously, but they also
pulled down upon their whole sex still viler imprecations concerning the
nature of womankind.

*   *   *

Into the latter category of adventuresses falls the heroic Elizabeth Hooton
– it is surely impossible to deny her the epithet, on grounds of her age
alone.[7] She was nearly fifty when she first met George Fox, and over
seventy when she came to her death in a foreign land, still serving the cause
which she had made her life. Her age was indeed much remarked at the
time: most allusions refer to her as old or 'ancient'.

To George Fox Elizabeth Hooton was however 'a very tender woman'.[8]
The wife of a prosperous Nottinghamshire farmer, she was in fact George
Fox's first convert and his first preacher; that in itself was an indication
of the prominent role women would play in his mission. George Fox
met Margaret Fell a few years later. Elizabeth Hooton was then a Baptist,
and had probably been a preacher among the Baptists before her 'convincement'. Although Fox, like the Baptists (and other sectaries), shared
in the denunciation of tithes, he criticized them in his journal for being
'Jangling Baptists'; Elizabeth Hooton now testified against their 'deceit'.
By the end of 1648 Elizabeth Hooton had left her husband and family
to become a Quaker preacher. Carrying out in church, when moved
by the spirit, those kinds of interruptions which brought the Quakers

their early notoriety, Elizabeth Hooton suffered as a result a series of imprisonments.

As with all problems of civil order, when the disrupter absolutely declines to promise amendment, one can certainly feel sympathy for the authorities in the administrative problem which the Quakers presented.†
How were these interruptions – often of a frenzied and highly insulting nature – to be handled? On the other hand the rigorous treatment of the Quakers in prison can command no such understanding. George Fox was first imprisoned in Derby in 1650. This term initiated a period of close on forty years in which the Quakers were regularly confined for disturbing the public peace until the exemption of Dissenters (including the Quakers) from the penal laws in 1689 gave them relief: a Declaration of Loyalty was allowed to replace the Oath of Allegiance in court which the Quakers' religion would not permit them to swear.

There were periods of remission: at the Restoration a number of Quakers imprisoned under the Commonwealth were released from gaol. At the Declaration of Breda King Charles II had after all promised a liberty to 'tender consciences'. What happened however if liberty of conscience led to a breach of the peace – and some even more menacing manifestation such as rebellion? It was ill luck that the Quakers should become identified in the mind of authority with those rebellious millenarian relics, the Fifth Monarchists; a foolish rising of 1661, headed by a wine-bottler named Thomas Venner, led to wide-scale Quaker imprisonment. The tough Quakers' Act of 1662 followed, which imposed severe penalties on their Meetings, with transportation for a third offence. Then the first Conventicle Act of 1664 curtailed the activities of all Nonconformists by making it illegal for more than five persons outside a family to gather together for religious purposes. The Conventicle Act lapsed in 1668 but was re-enacted in 1670, bringing a fresh wave of imprisonments. As a result, thousands of Quakers passed through the prisons of England.

It was however from this experience, this wholesale incarceration of people who were not themselves members of the criminal classes, that the honourable Quaker commitment to prison reform sprang. It has been pointed out that in her letters from prison Elizabeth Hooton herself anticipated by 150 years the demands of the nineteenth-century Quaker

---

†Although one would hardly today go as far as Mabel R. Brailsford who, writing in 1915 in *Quaker Women 1650–1690*, was influenced – but unfavourably – by the actions of the suffragette movement; she compared the plight of the 'priest' faced by a Quaker woman to that of a Cabinet Minister faced by a suffragette, her sympathies being with the politician.[9]

reformer Elizabeth Fry.[10] Elizabeth Hooton's earliest extant letter to the Mayor of Derby contrasted the state of the prisoners with his own comfort and honour, warning him of the fate of Dives 'if he will not regard the poor and in prison'. Elizabeth Hooton was first shut up in the Fen Country; then in York prison (where she found a number of other Friends) on and off for two years; then in Beckenham prison for once again 'exhorting the people to repentance' for five months; finally she was imprisoned in Lincoln Castle, and here she found herself entirely among felons.

At Lincoln Castle too Elizabeth Hooton encountered a further hazard in the shape of a particularly malevolent female gaoler. The law permitted the magistrates to send the Quakers to prison, but they were not obliged to make provision for the Quakers' maintenance (nor for that of other prisoners of course). The Quakers then had to find their own board and pay fees for their lodging, something which brought them squarely within the power of their gaolers if malevolently inclined. It was easy for 'a malignant woman' like the gaoler of Lincoln Castle to persecute her Quaker prisoner, and also to whip up the other prisoners against her. *Elizabeth Hooton, Prisoner in Lincoln Castle, pleads to him in Authority to reform the Abuses of the Gaol* drew attention not only to the system of 'fees' but also to Brueghel-like conditions within the prison itself. Elizabeth Hooton described 'in drinking and profaneness and wantonness, men and women together many times part of the night ...' She asked that strong drink at least should be removed from the gaols.[11]

One of Elizabeth Hooton's fellow prisoners in York prison had been a Quaker servant-girl, originally from Pontefract, called Mary Fisher. She had probably been converted by George Fox in 1651 when she was about twenty-seven.[12] It was this Mary Fisher who was inspired by the Inner Light to carry the Quaker message to New England. Accompanied by Anne Austin, she reached Boston in July 1656. Her reward was to be 'searched' for being a witch. The hundred or so books on Quakerism which filled her baggage were confiscated. She was then flogged at the orders of the Governor of Massachusetts and expelled. In 1657 and 1658 the General Court of Massachusetts passed laws against Quakers landing. Elizabeth Hooton, once more at liberty, was moved in her turn to set forth for New England. She intended to carry on the work of Mary Fisher and the other Friends, regardless of the Governor's prohibition.

The death of Oliver Hooton in 1661 placed 'old Elizabeth' in that traditionally strong position of a widow with considerable property at her own disposal. At the age of sixty she determined, despite the opposition of her children, to set forth for Boston; Joan Brocksoppe of Derbyshire, reputedly about the same age, 'freely resolved to be her companion'. The two women, having taken this bold resolve, were however forced to kick their heels for a considerable time before a passage to New England could be secured; this because a new law had been passed in Boston fining the captain of any ship bringing a Quaker within its jurisdiction £100.

When Elizabeth Hooton and Joan Brocksoppe did reach Boston, by a sea and land route, they entered a town where one Quaker woman, Mary Dyer, had already been hanged on Boston Common in 1659, to say nothing of those who had been whipped at the cart-tail from town to town. None of this prevented the two 'ancient' Quakers from interrupting the preachers when moved to do so. Soon enough, therefore, old Elizabeth and old Joan found themselves shut up in that 'Lion's Den', Boston prison.

From here they were taken to confront the dreaded Governor Endicott. He roundly called both the old women witches, and asked them why they had come to Boston.

'To do the will of Him that sent me,' was the reply.

'What do you understand by that will?' demanded the Governor.

'To warn thee of shedding any more innocent blood,' answered Elizabeth Hooton. When the Governor countered that he would hang many more yet, Elizabeth Hooton pointed out that the Lord might spoil his plans by choosing to take him away.[13] Awaiting this happy event, she was put back into the Lion's Den, expecting to meet the same fate as Mary Dyer. In prison at the same time lay a Quaker man, Wenlock Christiansen, who was himself due to be hanged on 13 June. Unexpectedly all the Quakers – including Christiansen – were released the day before. It transpired that the execution of Mary Dyer was regarded with displeasure in England; for while no one could work out a plan for muzzling the Quakers, hanging was certainly considered an inappropriately harsh solution.

Perhaps there were moments when Elizabeth Hooton wondered if the fate which was substituted for it was not even worse than the gallows. Or on second thoughts, since there is no record of despair, we must assume her remarkable faith sustained her through the ordeal which followed. In Elizabeth Hooton's own words, another jury was called 'which condemned us all to be driven out of their jurisdiction by men and horses, armed with swords and staffs and weapons of war, who went along with us near two days' journey in the wilderness, and there they left us towards the night amongst the great rivers and many wild beasts that useth to devour and at night we lay in the woods without any victuals but a few biscuits that we brought with us and which we soaked in the water'.

By degrees the two old women reached Rhode Island, the centre of religious toleration since its foundation by the liberal-spirited Roger Williams. From Rhode Island they proceeded to Barbados, where Mary Fisher had also brought the message of Quakerism, and there were in consequence a number of Friends to receive them. Even at this point the two women were convinced that it was their duty to return to Boston; but having sailed back to New England, they were once more arrested in Boston and deported to Virginia. From here at last they took ship again for home.

In England however old Elizabeth's problems hardly diminished. She found herself returned to a land where Quakers were beset by the problems posed by the recent Acts comprised in the 'Clarendon Code' (which included the harsh Conventicle Act). A magistrate summoned Elizabeth's son at harvest-time, and when he would not take the oath in court, according to Quaker practice, fined him £5. When the son refused to pay, Elizabeth Hooton's property – to the value of £20 – was confiscated; to meet such demands the old woman was further forced into selling her farm at a severe financial loss. Then Elizabeth Hooton herself was imprisoned for twelve weeks, for not taking the oath.

At this point Elizabeth embarked on a relationship with King Charles II based – in her opinion – on her crying need for temporal mercy and his equally pressing need for spiritual conversion. Even if somewhat one-sided, this relationship does at least give some kind of lighter touch to her otherwise painful story. This lightness was not entirely due to the piquant combination of the earnest old Quaker woman with the playful womanizing monarch: 'KING CHARLES,' she would exclaim some years later, 'How oft have I come to thee in my old age, both for thy reformation and safety, and for the good of thy soul, and for justice and equity. Oh that thou would not give up thy kingdom to the papists nor thy strength to the women. . . .' Lightness was often King Charles's way with solemn events, as though good-natured mockery might palliate those ills which could not be eliminated. Pepys witnessed a scene when a pretty young Quaker presented an extremely long petition to the King. (She was probably the Kentish Quaker's wife who was debauched by an adventurer called John Scott; he got hold of her entire fortune to purchase an imaginary estate in Long Island, and then fled to America himself, taking with him her jewels and her eldest son.) Charles II listened to the petition and then observed that 'if all she desired was of that length, she might lose her desires'. The pretty Quaker declined to join in a conversation of such immodesty; it was not until it had returned to a more serious level that she began again, 'O King!'[14]

Yet the compassion of the King towards his 'tender consciences' was genuine enough, a feeling of mercy strengthened by his own sufferings in exile – so long as he did not consider that their deeds were threatening the security of the newly established stable state. The King frowned upon any possible connection between the Quakers and the Fifth Monarchists. But he chided his brother the Duke of York for an explosion against the Quakers and suggested that they might do better instead to amend the quality of their own lives. When the brave Baptist girl from the West Country, Hannah Hewling, presented a petition to James II in 1685 on behalf of her brothers William and Benjamin, implicated in the Monmouth rising, Lord Churchill warned her of the hardness of King James's heart: 'marble is as capable of feeling compassion'. (Nor did Hannah's pleas save the boys: both were hanged, although Hannah's money did at least spare their corpses the indignity of 'quartering'.)[15] There was nothing of this chill quality about the heart of Charles II.

Elizabeth Hooton first thought of coming to court in response to a revelation she had had at sea 'and in great danger of my life, that I should go before the King, to witness for God, whether he would hear or no. ...' But now she also asked for justice concerning the confiscation of her goods towards her son's fine. With the cry 'I wait for Justice of thee, O King', she now proceeded to follow Charles II wherever he went, including two visits to his tennis court, when she spoke to him as he went up into his coach, 'after he had been at his sport', and an encounter in another favourite place of royal relaxation, St James's Park, when she presented the King with two letters.

Familiarity bred in the soldiers round the King a rough sympathy for the persistent old lady, and the King's coachman actually read aloud one of her letters. In the park, the ordinary people murmured because old Elizabeth did not kneel before her sovereign. But one of the kindly soldiers did eventually get Elizabeth a kind of informal audience. She used it of course for a lengthy bout of preaching; and was in the end put once more outside the palace gates. The next morning Elizabeth Hooton returned, having devised a costume of sackcloth and ashes for herself in the meanwhile; once more she was pulled away from her preaching, but as she was being ejected, she continued to preach all the way through Westminster Hall and the palace yard, denouncing in particular the lawyers (who made professional use of that area).

Elizabeth Hooton's master-plan, apart from the need for justice, was to be able to buy a house and land within Boston itself, so that the Quakers of New England would have at once a meeting-house, a resting-place and a burial ground, all three being denied to them by the current laws. The fact that Charles II eventually granted the old woman a certificate to settle in any British colony will not surprise anyone who is familiar with the parable of the importunate widow (even she did not think to accost a man exhausted after his favourite sport). So Elizabeth Hooton sold her farm, and armed with the King's certificate succeeded in sailing to Boston, the certificate preventing the captain of the ship from being fined for transporting a Quaker. But the royal backing did not prevent her from having to put up to 20s a night for her lodging – to cover the fine which might be levied.

Elizabeth Hooton's subsequent experiences in New England, where she wandered about North Massachusetts preaching, were indeed even more harrowing than her previous ones, certificate or no certificate. In Cambridge, Massachusetts, the college boys, never as a class very sympathetic to Quakers, as 'Little Elizabeth' Fletcher found at Oxford (see pp. 263-4), mocked and pelted her.[16] She was then put into a stinking dungeon and left for two days and nights without food, before being sentenced by the court to be whipped through three towns and finally expelled from the colony. So she was tied to a Cambridge whipping-post and lashed ten times with a three-stringed whip, three knots in each string. At Watertown willow-rods were used; at Dedham, on a cold frosty morning, she received ten lashes at the cart-tail. Once more, but this time 'beaten and torn', she was carried into the wilderness: 'towards night they left her there, where there were many wolves, bears and other wild beasts, and many deep waters to pass through'. Once again, as on her first visit, Elizabeth Hooton made her way to friendly Rhode Island; she ascribed her preservation to the guidance of 'an invisible hand' and thanked God fervently that for His sake she had been able to endure 'beyond what her age and sex, morally speaking, could otherwise have borne'.

Still Elizabeth Hooton did not abandon her mission, continuing to assail Boston with her fervour, before being assailed in turn by the authorities and returning to Rhode Island to recuperate. A rare treat was provided by the funeral of Governor Endicott, taken away by the Lord just as Elizabeth had predicted five years earlier, in 1665. Elizabeth Hooton attended the ceremony; but since the Lord guided her to preach at it, she was removed from there to prison once more.

Elizabeth Hooton never succeeded in buying a house and land; after five years therefore she returned to England. Her experiences were summed up by her son Samuel, who later tried to continue her mission and told the justices: 'I had an old mother who was here amongst you and bore many of your stripes and much cruelty at your hands!' Back in England, Elizabeth Hooton was in time to witness the fresh wave of Quaker imprisonments consequent upon the second Conventicle Act of 1670, the penalties of which were still more severe than those of the previous one; Margaret Fell was one of these victims and Elizabeth Hooton lobbied her old friend the King on her behalf. In 1671 a London Meeting of the Friends made her one of the Overseers of the Fleet prison, to help care for the Quakers therein.

For all this useful work, the call of the New World still rang in the old woman's ears. When she learnt that George Fox intended to visit the West Indies in order to straighten out the somewhat chaotic affairs of the Quakers there, she decided to accompany him, one of twelve Friends to do so. She sailed with the rest on 12 August 1671, and arrived after a troublesome journey at Barbados on 3 October. In January the following year George Fox set off again for Jamaica where Quakerism, introduced in 1658, had recently been languishing. He was accompanied by Elizabeth Hooton and three male followers. This was to be old Elizabeth's last journey. A week after they landed, she died.

She went very suddenly, well one day and dead the next, according to George Fox's journal: 'in peace like a lamb'. A fellow Quaker, James Lancaster, was beside her when she died, and heard her give her last testimony 'concerning Truth'. But Elizabeth Hooton had spoken her own best epitaph when she explained, a few years before the end of her life: 'Yes, the Love that I bear to the Souls of all Men, makes me willing to undergo whatsoever can be inflicted on me.'[17]

*　　*　　*

Mary Fisher, the Yorkshire girl who introduced Quakerism to New England before being banished from it, was another of those early Friends whose travels 'for the Service of Truth Abroad' compel one's awe.[18] Her early spell in York prison had had one beneficial effect: she learnt to write while she was there. On her release Mary Fisher left Yorkshire for East Anglia. It was within the university town of Cambridge that Mary Fisher and her companion Elizabeth Williams met with an experience parallel to that of Elizabeth Hooton at Cambridge, Massachusetts, although some small provocation can be argued in this case. Observing the 'Froth and Levity' of the undergraduates' behaviour at Sidney Sussex, the two women told them that they were 'Antichrists' and that their college was 'a Cage of

Unclean Birds, and the Synagogue of Satan'. As a result the women were abused and pelted with stones.

Examined by the Mayor, Mary Fisher and Elizabeth Williams presented that familiar conundrum where problem women were concerned: under whose legal protection were they? 'He asked their names: They replied, their Names were written in the Book of Life. He demanded their Husbands' names.' (It was in essence the same question as that posed by the magistrate to the Catholic nun Sister Dorothea in 1617 – see p. 148.) The two women told the Mayor 'they had no Husband but Jesus Christ and he sent them'. At this the Mayor grew furious, denounced them both as whores, and ordered them to be whipped by the constable until the blood ran down their bodies. They were probably the first Quakers to suffer under the brutal application of the Elizabethan Act against rogues and vagabonds to the members of their religion. Throughout this ordeal Mary Fisher and Elizabeth Williams managed to sing: 'The Lord be blessed, the Lord be praised.'

In New England, as we have seen, Mary Fisher was flogged before being expelled. Curiously enough it was in her encounter with the 'Grand Seignior', as the Sultan of Turkey was known, that Mary Fisher suffered no ordeal beyond that imposed by her own adventurous progress. There was a certain irony in the fact that the low position of women in the Moslem world enabled the Turks at least to appreciate exactly how remarkable an individual Mary Fisher must be; they accorded her that amazed respect denied to her in the Christian world. On the other hand it is only fair to say that the converse is also true: Mary Fisher displayed a tact in handling the claims of Mahomet to divinity which she certainly did not choose to exercise when denouncing the frothy and light-hearted undergraduates of Sidney Sussex College.

Be that as it may, it is undeniable that this strange episode, like some kind of 'Turkish Nights', is one from which Sultan and Vizier of Turkey alike emerge with a credit quite alien to Governor Endicott of Massachusetts. The fate of Mary Fisher in Turkey was also a great deal preferable to that of two fellow Quakers, Katherine Evans and Sarah Chevers, who embarked for Alexandria but only got as far as Malta, where they were imprisoned by the Catholic Inquisition. There they remained for three and a half years until the efforts of the English Catholic Seigneur d'Aubigny, almoner to Queen Catherine, who had Maltese interests, effected their release in 1664. The two women then offered to serve d'Aubigny should it be in their power. He courteously replied that it was enough that he should be remembered in their (Quaker) prayers.

Mary Fisher originally set out for the Mediterranean in 1657 as part of a Quaker mission of six people: three men including the Irish Quaker John Perrot, another ex-Baptist, and two other women, Mary Prince and Beatrice Beckley. Hoping to reach Jerusalem, they got as far as Smyrna where the idea of converting the Turkish 'Grand Seignior' along the way seems to have first occurred. The English Consul, if amiable, was also discouraging, and sent the party back towards Venice by sea. However, Mary Fisher took the opportunity of a call along the coast of Morea to land and head none the less for the Sultan's court. Beatrice Beckley seems to have accompanied her at the landing, but Mary Fisher made her final prodigious journey alone. The first account published (by a Dutch Quaker in the early eighteenth century) said that she made it entirely on foot, which would have meant walking 500 to 600 miles through Greece and Macedonia and over the mountains of Thrace: this during a period when the prolonged war between Venice and the Ottoman Empire (and internal feuds within Turkey itself) caused either terror or xenophobia at the mere sight of strangers. It is more probable that the Friends took a Greek boat across the Aegean, before Mary Fisher set off alone on foot on her divinely appointed mission to the 'Great Turk'.[19]

The Sultan – the 'Great Turk' – was at this point lying together with 20,000 men at Adrianople, along the banks of the river Maritsa, whither he had repaired from Constantinople. The Sultan's tents were hung with rich gold embroideries: 'the magnitude of these Pavilions is such', wrote Henry Marsh in a survey of the Turkish Empire a few years later, 'that afar off they seem no less than Cities'. The Sultan himself, Mahomet IV, aged sixteen, was also gorgeously attired in gold and sable as he sat surrounded by his eunuchs. His appearance was however more terrifying than dazzling. The son of a half-witted father, he had been permanently marked by his father's savage attack upon him as a child. For all his majestic trappings here was 'a monster of a man' in the words of another English observer, 'a deformed sight both in body and mind, as if one strove with the other how to offend; stupid, loggerheaded, cruel, fierce as to his aspect'.[20]

Mary Fisher, on the other hand, was a thirty-five-year-old 'maid'; one whose 'intellectual faculties' were in the opinion of a contemporary 'greatly adorned by the gravity of her deportment'. Even to be granted an interview was in itself an achievement; Mary Fisher succeeded in persuading the Grand Vizier, to whom the Sultan left all business matters so that he himself could 'follow the chase of fearful and flying Beasts', to introduce her, despite the fact that the Grand Vizier, generally speaking, recommended the Sultan never to listen to women's 'Counsels and Advices'.

Surrounded by dragomans, who waited to interpret for her, Mary Fisher was introduced into the Sultan's presence. She then stood in silence. She was after all waiting for the guidance of the Inner Light. When the Sultan, mistaking her silence for modesty, offered to dismiss some of his suite, she declined his offer. Finally she spoke 'what was upon her mind'. The Turks listened to her 'with much attention and gravity' until she had done. The Sultan asked Mary if she had anything more to say, and she in return asked whether he had understood her message. According to the Quaker account which may have come from Mary herself, he answered, Yes, he had understood every word, 'and further said, that what she had spoken was truth'.[21]

The Sultan then pressed Mary Fisher to stay with them, saying that they could not but respect one who had taken so much pains to come to them so far from England, with a message from the Lord God. In view of the danger of travelling alone, he also offered her a guard to get back to Constantinople, if she persisted in that plan. Mary Fisher declined both offers. It was at this point that the Turks asked Mary Fisher what she thought of their prophet Mahomet, and she replied warily 'that she knew him not' although she knew Christ the true prophet. Concerning Mahomet she suggested that they should judge him to be true or false according to the words or prophecies he spoke: 'If the word that a prophet speaketh comes to pass, then shall ye know that the Lord hath sent the prophet; but if it come not to pass, then shall ye know that the Lord never sent him.' The Turks acknowledged the truth of what she said.

It is impossible to know exactly what interpretation the Sultan and his entourage put upon this amazing visitation; just as it is impossible to know exactly how Mary Fisher's words – and those of the Sultan – were transformed in translation. The Sultan never did mend his ways towards other Christians, or show any practical appreciation of Mary's message. Nevertheless Mary Fisher herself did return to Constantinople 'without the least hurt or scoff'.

Her gracious treatment at the Sultan's hands inclined her to believe of the Turks that 'there is a royal seed amongst them which in time God will raise'. 'The English are more bad, most of them', wrote Mary grimly. For in Constantinople the Quakers, including Mary, were treated much as they were in England and America, as a pernicious nuisance. The English Ambassador, Sir Thomas Bendish, drew weary attention to the Quakers' 'insufferable' disturbances of 'our divine exercises'. His successor was the third Earl of Winchilsea (father-in-law of Anne Countess of Winchilsea, and Anne Viscountess Conway's first cousin). He too complained that 'the carriage of that sort of people is ridiculous and is capable to bring dishonour to our Nation ...' when ordering the removal of the English Quakers.[22]

This particular Earl of Winchilsea, a man of great magnificence, was certainly not predisposed by his way of life to appreciate the Quaker message, unlike his cousin Anne. He was married four times and had twenty-seven legitimate children, of whom sixteen lived to maturity. His second wife, who accompanied him to Turkey, bore eleven of them. But Lord Winchilsea also kept a number of other women in Turkey, building little convenient houses for them, by whom he produced still further progeny. 'My Lord, you have not only built a town, but peopled it too', observed Charles II on Lord Winchilsea's return to England in 1669. 'Oh Sir, I was your Majesty's representative', retorted the prolific Earl.[23]

As for the grave and fearless Mary Fisher, she eventually reached England safely, where she later married a fellow Quaker, the master-mariner William Bayly, a romance begun when he was in Newgate. It was a very happy marriage, blessed by three children, and Mary Fisher preached no more. But in 1697, as an old lady, she was still pointed out as 'one whose name you have heard of, Mary Fisher, she that spoke to the Grand Turk'.

*   *   *

'God is thy witness', wrote Elizabeth Hooton to Margaret Fell in 1671, 'thou hast suffered more than many have expected. ...'[24] It was true that Margaret Fell, born Margaret Askew in 1614, might legitimately have expected a comparatively easy life by the (female) standards of the time. As a girl she had a portion of £3,000; she was married at sixteen to a much older man, Judge Fell, and left a wealthy widow on his death in 1658. Margaret Fell also enjoyed the blessing of an extremely large and affectionate family: she had no less than seven remarkable and intelligent daughters. Against these one ungrateful son weighed lightly in the emotional balance; although the practical consequences of his ingratitude, in the light of his sex, were heavy. She was blessed in addition with a constitution which would enable her to survive into her late eighties.

Nevertheless Margaret Fell from the first moment she heard George Fox preach 'saw it was the truth and I could not deny it'. Judge Fell on his return home was told that Margaret and her daughter Sarah had been bewitched. As Margaret Fell wrote: 'any may think what a condition I was like to be in, that either I must displease my husband, or offend God'. She chose to displease her husband (although Judge Fell was in fact to show

himself remarkably tolerant of his wife's earnest convictions). Now many
of the Fell female household, including 'little Mabby', Bet Drinkall, Peg
and her sister 'Old Jane', became Quakers. Margaret Fell herself was to be,
in George Fox's own words 'the nursing mother' of Quakerism.[25]

Her role as a nursing mother (she is addressed on occasion by her fellow
Quakers in quite lyrical language: 'O thou daughter of God, thou
art comely in thy beauty, clothed with the sun and moon under thy feet')[26]
was however essentially different from that of the itinerant Elizabeth
Hooton and Mary Fisher. Margaret Fell did not preach. She did not travel
the country. She did not venture abroad. The presence of this established
socially unassailable woman in the Quaker midst emphasized that other
side of female Quakerism: its organizational philanthropy towards its own
members. The hospitality which Margaret Fell dispensed, with her daughters, at Swarthmoor Hall in Lancashire, stood for more than mere material
need gratified, though that was important too; it also indicated that not all
female Quakers could be classed as wild spirits or even witches in the grip
of the devil's 'Extempore Way'.

It is suggested by Margaret Fell's biographer, Isabel Ross, that the
emotionalism of her first response to George Fox, and that of her daughters, enabled her to understand and cope with this phenomenon in Quakerism later. Postscripts in letters to Fox give some indication of the flavour
of this. Susan aged two [sic]: 'O my dear father, when wilt thou come';
Mary aged five: 'Thou art the fountain of life'; and Margaret Fell herself:
'We thy babes ... O thou bread of life ... O our life ... O our dear nursing
father ... O our life, our desire is to see thee again that we may be refreshed
and established'.[27]

But more practically it was Margaret Fell who led the first Women's
Petition of 1659, a supplement to the general Quaker protest against tithes.
She protested against the imprisonment of George Fox at Lancaster, and
was instrumental in securing from Charles II that release of Quakers which
attended the Restoration. Margaret Fell's social position enabled her to
write to such high-born ladies as Mary Princess of Orange and Elizabeth
of Bohemia (rumoured to have Quaker sympathies); she even tackled the
arch-Catholic Dowager Queen Henrietta Maria, presenting her with
Quaker books.

Even these connections could not free Margaret Fell from the problems
posed by her own conscience. She could not - would not - take an oath.
At the March Assizes of 1664 Margaret Fell was summoned for allowing
illegal meetings in her house. She refused to take the necessary oath in
court. Although Margaret Fell was courteously granted a stool and a

cushion by the judge (something not offered to Elizabeth Hooton and Mary Fisher), she was none the less threatened with the forfeiture of her estate, as well as life imprisonment, if she would not swear. At the death of Judge Fell, Margaret Fell had inherited Swarthmoor Hall for herself and her daughters; her son George received her own dowry of Marsh Grange, where he was probably already living. At this threat of forfeiture therefore Margaret Fell spoke up boldly: 'I am a widow, and my estate is a dowry, and I have five children unpreferred [unplaced]; and if the King's pleasure be to take my estate from me, upon the account of my conscience, and not for any evil or wrong done, let him do as he pleaseth.'[28]

Refusing to take the oath, or remove her glove, or promise to hold no further Quaker meetings, Margaret Fell was duly imprisoned in Lancaster Castle (where George Fox was already installed). There, in lodgings which let in the rain and the snow, she remained until the summer of 1668; she lay under sentence for *Praemunire*, that is, for rejecting the authority of the English courts in favour of some other (spiritual) authority. It was finally on the orders of the King and Council that she was set free.

Gossips had long connected the names of George Fox and the widowed Margaret Fell: 'I am so well used to them I know how to bear them', she told one of her daughters.[29] Contemporary satire was always rich – or poor – in jokes about the sexual morals of the Quakers. Some of this was owing to the unrestrained behaviour of the group surrounding James Naylor under the Commonwealth. Quaker inspiration was also mocked. Chapbooks (cheap popular fiction) of the 1680s included one story entitled *Love's Masterpiece*, which ended with a Quaker suggesting to his mistress that they should retire into the coal-hole: 'there only the light within will shine'. Quaker marriage was another fertile source of allusions, since the Quakers persisted in having their own form of ceremony at a Quaker Meeting, when the couple simply testified in the presence of the Friends. This led to accusations that the Friends 'went together like brute beasts', as was asserted at the Nottingham Assizes.[30]

Quaker marriage also led to troubles about inheritance: if the Quaker ceremony was not valid, then were the children of the marriage illegitimate? At Nottingham, where the inheritance of Mary Ashwell, daughter of the Quakers William Ashwell and Ann Ridge, was in doubt, the judge found for the Quakers. He compared the Quaker marriage to the union in paradise when Adam took Eve and Eve took Adam: 'it was the consent of the woman that made the marriage'. The general vagueness of the time about the state of marriage and the status of the ceremony which intro-

duced it acted in this case to the benefit of the Quakers. Even so it remained
a source of popular anxiety. At the end of the century *The Athenian Oracle*
was asked whether a Quaker marriage was valid. The reassuring answer
was that it *was* valid, if not strictly legal, and 'accordingly their children
are for inheritance'.[31]†

When George Fox did marry Margaret Fell – in October 1669 – he was
forty-five and she was fifty-five. It was a spiritual match. According to the
Quaker custom for the preliminary examination of the parties concerned
(which meant that Quaker marriages, far from being more loosely performed, were actually more carefully contracted), Fox was questioned on
the subject of his bride's age. Surely marriage was only for the procreation of
children? Fox answered his interlocutor: 'I told him I never thought of any
such thing [marriage] but only in obedience to the power of the Lord. ...'
He added: 'I had no command to do such a thing till a half year before,
though some people had long talked of it.' He also took the trouble to
make it clear that he was not interested in marrying a rich widow; carefully
asking his future step-children whether their rights under their father's will
had been respected. Fox also engaged himself never to meddle with the
estate.[32]

The intention of George Fox and Margaret Fell to marry was published
at three separate Meetings: a Man's Meeting where Margaret, her daughters and twelve women Quakers were also present: a Meeting of men and
women Friends; and a public Meeting. They were eventually married at
a very large public Meeting.

At the first of these Meetings, one of Margaret's daughters, Rachel,
testified: 'And I do believe, that the thing [the marriage] is of the Lord.'
Unfortunately George Fell, Margaret's only son, and his wife Hannah,
who were not Quakers, held the very opposite belief. George Fell felt
humiliated by the union of his mother with this weird and wild itinerant
preacher, *habitué* of prisons, and there were financial considerations as well,
for all Fox's precautions. Margaret Fell was after all in possession of
Swarthmoor. There is reason to believe that George and Hannah Fell were
instrumental in securing Margaret Fell's return to prison in 1670 when the
Conventicle Act was renewed.[33] And when George Fell died in 1670, he
specifically bequeathed the Swarthmoor Estate to his infant son, although
his father in his will had left it to Margaret to provide for the girls. Hannah
Fell, established at Marsh Grange, continued the vendetta. Whatever the
rights and wrongs of the legal position (by no means clear in view of a

†Between 1753 and 1837 the marriages of the Quakers and the Jews were the only ones
performed outside the Church of England which were legal.

wife's weak position at law), where Hannah Fell is concerned, it is difficult to disagree with the incensed judgement of old Elizabeth Hooton: 'What a rebellious daughter-in-law art thou! Was there ever such a wicked thing done in England or in any age before, that thou should ruinate thy husband's mother? The same hand that cut off thy husband will do the same by thee and leave thee neither root nor branch if thou do not speeedily repent.'[34]

In April 1671 Margaret Fell was released on the orders of the King, and her part of Swarthmoor Estate was granted to her daughters. The odious Hannah lived on at Marsh Grange. Nor was this family dispute thoroughly settled until 1691 when Daniel Abraham, husband of Rachel Fell, 'bought' the Swarthmoor Estate.

It would be wrong, however, to see life at Swarthmoor as dour, or Margaret Fell herself as priggish. She besought the Friends to think, where dress was concerned, that uniform dress and colour did not necessarily bespeak a pure life within. When disapproval of coloured and striped apparel was minuted at a Yearly Meeting (the beginnings of the so-called Quaker look of plain dressing) Margaret Fell exclaimed: 'This is a silly poor Gospel. It is more fit for us to be covered with God's eternal Spirit, and clothed with his Eternal Light.' She was probably less rigid in this respect than Anne Countess of Winchilsea, groaning at the demands of the fashionable life. Her clever eldest daughter Sarah wore red stockings and others of sky-coloured worsted. White wine, claret and brandy featured in the household accounts at Swarthmoor. Luxuries like oranges were sent for from London as were gloves and even frivolities like vizard masks,[35] so frequently employed by the courtesans of the capital to conceal their countenances, that the term 'vizard mask' became synonymous with their profession.

*   *   *

It was in 1666, during Margaret Fell's first spell in prison, that she wrote her defence of female preaching, *Womens Speaking*. Even among the Quakers themselves, the revolutionary proposition that a woman's voice might be heard in public on religious matters met with opposition.[36] Margaret Fell met the challenge boldly with quotations from the Acts of the Apostles and also from Joel: 'And it shall come to pass, in the last days, saith the Lord, I will pour out of my spirit upon all Flesh; your sons and daughters shall Prophesy.' Her basic message was that 'God hath put no such difference between the Male and Female as man would make.' She firmly blamed the devil – 'the Serpent' – whose ancient enmity towards

Eve had led to the general silencing of women since the Fall: 'and if the seed of the Woman speak not, the Seed of the Serpent speaks; for God hath put enmity between the two seeds, and it is manifest that those that speak against the Woman and her Seeds speaking, speak out of the enmity of the old Serpent's seed'. In short: 'all this opposing and gainsaying of Women's Speaking; hath risen out of the bottomless Pit . . .'.[37]

As for the message of St Paul, why should women be specifically ordered by the Apostle to have their heads covered when they prayed or prophesied, if the latter activity was not to be permitted? Margaret Fell was also free in quoting the many texts in which Jesus – or his predecessors the prophets – compared the Church to a woman: from that of Isaiah ('I have called thee as a Woman forsaken'), via David ('The King's Daughter is all glorious within') to the vision of St John concerning heaven ('a Woman clothed with the Sun, and the Moon under her feet . . .). She also pointed out that the most important revelations concerning Himself were spoken by Jesus to women, including that to Martha at Bethany: 'I am the Resurrection and the Life'. And was it not to a woman that Jesus first appeared on earth *after* the Resurrection?[38]

Like George Fox, who had early on pointed to the Magnificat as the supreme example of a woman 'speaking', Margaret Fell pointed triumphantly to the use of the words of Elizabeth, the mother of John the Baptist, and the Virgin Mary in the *Book of Common Prayer*: 'Are you not here beholden to the woman for her sermon, to use her words to put into your Common Prayer? And yet you forbid women's speaking.' But perhaps Margaret Fell's most telling point, at least from the modern point of view, was that men were trying to limit the power of Almighty God, by contending that it existed only in the male sex.[39]

The first organization of the Quaker movement was developed by George Fox out of sheer necessity to combat the effects of persecution (although there were those who continued to criticize him for abandoning his original conception of an unorganized religion). In some places women featured in this at an early stage; in about 1656 two Women's Meetings developed in London, the Box Meeting (for succouring the poor, so called because money was gathered in a box) and the Two Weeks' Meeting, on the model of the Men's Two Weeks' Meeting. Elsewhere in the country the participation of women was dependent on local prejudice – and no doubt on the availability of energetic women. It seems that it was not until 1671 that George Fox set in train the formation of the Women's Monthly and Quarterly Meetings to come together at the same time as the Men's. Fox, constantly using the word 'helpmeet' where the women were concerned, believed that they were intended for special work such as the care of Quaker servants and the examination of future spouses as well as the tending of the poor.[40]

It was a point of view well expressed by one of Margaret Fell's married daughters, Isabel Yeamans, writing from Swarthmoor in 1676 on the subject of Women's Meetings.[41] She thought these should be 'constant and frequent ... to wait upon the lord to feel his power to administer counsel, wisdom and Instruction that thereby your minds may be seasoned and fitted for the lords business'. This business was 'to inquire into the necessities of the poor and to relieve the widows and the fatherless and to visit the sick and the afflicted which is the pure practice of the pure religion'. The fallen should be reproved – but mildly. A private warning about 'undue conduct' should precede the reproof of the Women's Meeting. In general it was the duty of the 'elder and honourable women', in the footsteps of the holy women gone before, to be 'teachers of good things that they may teach the young women according to the holy apostles' exhortation and so to be good examples and patterns of prudence ...'.

Isabel Yeamans continued: 'Here will be work and business enough for us all that none need to be Idle in God's vineyard, but as we have everyone received a measure of God's spirit and grace some may be fellow helpers and workers together with our brethren in the work of the lord in these gospel days. ...' It was the distinguishing Quaker argument, first laid down by George Fox, that women too should be allowed to be 'serviceable' in their own 'places and stations'. Isabel Yeamans wrote: 'So every member of the body whereof Christ our lord is head may be serviceable and although we may be many members and some much more honourable than others yet no member though it be small is to be despised.'

George Fox himself defended his original contention concerning women's right to speak, both in England and on his travels abroad. In Flushing, New England, for example a minister's son disputed the subject with Fox at the end of a meeting in 1672. 'And as for women's speaking, such as the apostles did own, I owned, and such as they did deny, I did deny', was Fox's reply. In 1673 one Nathaniel Coleman spoke up against the whole principle of the Women's Meetings at Slaughterford in Wiltshire. Eventually Coleman flung out of the house 'in a rage and passion' vowing that 'he would rule over his wife' and so on and so forth.

To combat this, Fox explained that woman's lack of authority was part of the bad order of things, and had not existed in a state of innocence. Eve, by her transgression, her evil 'teaching' of her husband, had brought that about, but in the restoration, brought about by Jesus Christ, 'all the family of God, women as well as men, might know, possess, perform and discharge their offices and services in the house of God'. He also made the point, which arose in different forms throughout the seventeenth century, that if husbands such as Nathaniel Coleman could rule over their wives, which he did not seek to deny, 'neither he [Coleman] nor they must rule over widows and young women, and other men's wives'.[42]

In general, however, Fox attempted conciliation rather than provocation. So the arguments about the Women's Meetings and their precise purpose, and women's right to speak, continued within the Quaker movement itself: the very existence of such a controversy at that period being of course a tribute to the movement's early ideals concerning the spiritual equality of women.

Margaret Fell did not only enrich the Quaker movement with her own stalwart example of a woman whose conscience was unshackled by wealth, uncowed by adversity; she also bequeathed to it those further crusaders, her brilliant daughters. The possible influence of the mother for good at a period when few women were subject to influence outside the home is demonstrated at its fullest by the lives of the Fell girls. Sarah Fell, later married to William Meade, was said in her preaching to ravish 'all her beholders and hearers with admiration and wonder'. Margaret Fell herself had long shown an interest in Hebrew literature and teaching, leading towards the possible reconversion of the Jews. Sarah taught herself Hebrew to confound her critics, who claimed that she could not understand the biblical texts.[43] Isabel Yeamans accompanied her step-father on his travels to Europe.

George Fox died in January 1691 but Margaret lived on another eleven years, to benefit from the expanding atmosphere of toleration following the accession of William III. She was not bereft of the traditional joy of old age. Her eight children gave her twenty-four grandchildren, fourteen of whom survived childhood. As little John Abraham, son of Rachel, wrote in 1687: 'Dear Grandmot thou art oftener in my mind than I can menshon.'[44]

As for Margaret Fell's spiritual convictions, as late as 1695 she was reminding the Women's Yearly Meeting in London that the 'seed is one in male and female'.[45]

19   *The Delight of Business*

'Business is her sole delight in this world.... It is a charity to keep her in full employment.'

MRS CONSTANCE PLEY TO SAMUEL PEPYS, *Calendar of State Papers, Domestic,* 1666

'It is the Lord that creates true industry in his people ...'; thus Joan Dant, a pedlar, or rather a pedlar-extraordinary, and one of the few women *entrepreneurs* of the seventeenth century about whom some personal details are known. A woman pedlar in the seventeenth century was of course not necessarily indigent or despised, as the name might seem to indicate today. At one end of the market there did exist those women, close to beggars, who if sufficiently unsuccessful, old and quarrelsome, might be in danger of being accused of witchcraft. But at the other end were those enterprising women who travelled the country supplying haberdashery or provisions to the good wives unable or unwilling to make the journey to market. There was the Widow Elizabeth Doddington of Hillbishops, licensed by the Somerset justices in 1630 to use up to three horses in her work as a 'badger' of butter and cheese in Somerset, Wilts, Hants and Devon; or Hester Pinney, the unmarried daughter of a Puritan minister in Dorset who was ejected from his living at the Restoration: she sold lace in London, first as part of the family business (keeping in touch with her relations by letter) and then on her own account.[1]

When Joan Dant, who died in 1715 at the age of eighty-four, came to make her will she was worth rather more than £9,000. 'I got it by the rich and I mean to leave it to the poor,' she observed. In a letter to her executors she described herself as having 'through the blessing of God, with honesty and industrious care, improved my little in the world to a pretty good degree'. She therefore wished to help 'the fatherless and the widows in the Church of Christ'.

Joan Dant was a Quaker. Her husband had been a weaver who worked in Spitalfields. It was after his death that she took up work as a pedlar; carrying haberdashery, hosiery and the like from house to house in London and thereabouts. As a Quaker, and incidentally a woman of resolutely upright life, she was able to make good business use of her connections among the Friends. Soon the frugality of her own lifestyle (which she never altered) combined with the expanding nature of her business enabled her to save enough to start trading abroad. At her death, her executors found debts incurred, due to business pending, as far away as Paris and Brussels; while the amount of her fortune surprised even those who knew her well.

Joan Dant's industry – that 'true industry' whose creation she ascribed to the Lord – is an example of the fact that religions which encouraged women as well as men to work 'in God's vineyard' often encouraged them by implication to toil in other more commercial fields. The medieval abbesses of the great convents, confident in their religious office, had also been great businesswomen; in the same way Quaker women were sustained rather than depressed in the world of business by their beliefs: the knowledge that God intended them, in the words of George Fox, to be 'serviceable in their generation'.[2]

Katherine Philips, the Matchless Orinda, had been able to help her husband in his business as well as writing plays and poetry, in which capacity, wrote Ballard in the eighteenth century, 'few wives are supposed capable of serving their husbands'. But a Quaker dynasty, such as that of the Gurneys of East Anglia, would produce without comment women like Elizabeth Gurney, who in the 1680s kept the books of her husband's and brother's mercantile affairs, and acted as chief clerk. This energy can hardly be ascribed to lack of employment on her part: Elizabeth Gurney also bore eight sons, four of whom lived to adulthood.[3]

In part this ability was due to the Quaker emphasis on schools and education for both sexes, which meant that arithmetic was not a closed book to the female Friends. But since this emphasis on education was in itself due to the Quaker conviction that the Lord might move in any spirit, regardless of sex, one is back with the confidence granted at source, that is with the esteem given to women within the Quaker religion. Sarah Fell, Margaret's brilliant eldest daughter, had a good head for business, as well as being a 'ravishing' preacher, as the account books for Swarthmoor Hall show, during the years when she ran it.[4]

Where the women of the other dissenting sects were concerned, the connection, traced by the Puritans, between worldly success and divine approval, meant that there was nothing inherently abhorrent about the amassing of profits, particularly when they were used to forward God's purposes. (We detect a note of this in Joan Dant's letter to her executors, even if she was herself a Quaker.) But it is also noticeable in general that those women – often but not always widows – whose circumstances led them to indulge in business, could, whatever their rank or religion, expect approval if their efforts were successful. There was no trace here of that execration which attended the public endeavours of the 'petticoat-authors'. After all business practice in a woman could be seen as an extension of her role as the mainstay of her household, whereas learning and authorship were dangerously unfeminine pursuits. Just as the arithmetic necessary to do accounts (household accounts) was an esteemed part of female education, whereas the study of the classics drew forth angry male expostulations.

In the conduct of their affairs therefore, women paid far less lip-service to the gospel of female modesty than they did, perforce, in the pursuit of a literary career. The melancholy withdrawal of Anne Countess of Winchilsea, fearing contempt for poems from a woman's pen, may be contrasted with the zest displayed by Anne Russell, Countess of Bristol in the exploitation of her wine licence. Sister of William, fifth Earl and first Duke of Bedford, wife of George Digby, Earl of Bristol, the Countess was one of those rewarded with a licence to import goods at the Restoration, her husband having formed part of the Royalist administration-in-exile. She set to and sold her wine with a will, the Earl of Bedford being among her early customers. In 1691, when she was nearly eighty, the Countess of Bristol still managed to sell her brother six dozen bottles of red port for the sum of £5 8s.[5]

It was true, as the editors of Alice Clark's seminal study *Working Life of Women in the Seventeenth Century* (recently reissued with a new introduction) point out, that women's 'productivity and talents' depended on 'the domestic conditions which fostered them or precluded them'.[6] Pepys's diary provides an excellent insight into a world in which a variety of women were to be found working as shop-keepers, booksellers, ale-house keepers and the like. Nearly always family circumstances played some part in their situation.

The connection of women with the Stationers' Company and printing referred to earlier (see p. 98) found its natural extension in the existence of women booksellers, either independently or in working partnership with their husbands. One of Pepys's earliest entries concerns 'my bookseller' Mrs Ann Mitchell, who with her husband Miles sold not only books but pamphlets and newspapers in Westminster Hall. After Miles Mitchell died of the plague in 1665, Mrs Mitchell carried on the business. Also in Westminster Hall, plying their trade as linendrapers (not linendrapers' assistants) were the sisters Betty and Doll Lane, to whose activities as Pepys's unofficial mistresses we shall return.[7]

There had always been women among the brewers and ale-wives, with special rights to brewers' widows; ale-houses themselves being then enjoyed as meeting-places by women as much as men, at a time when ale was the drink of the poor and tea and coffee the luxuries of the rich.[8] Just as women might enjoy a pipe, there were numerous women among the tobacco-sellers (frequently unlicensed) keeping murky establishments where it was said of the inhabitants: 'their communication is smoke'. The mistress of the ale-house was a stock character in the popular chapbooks. Then of course at a less commanding level there was the 'lily at the bar' as the playwright and Wit Sir George Etherege described the barmaid at the Rose Tavern in Russell Street. Sometimes the lily was the ale-wife herself: Richard Gough, in his *The History of Myddle*, a portrait of a Shropshire parish begun in 1670, describes the lovely girl – 'very fair' – who helped her husband Samuel Downton keep an ale-house.[9] She was known as White Legs because she wore no stockings, and drew the customers irresistibly from miles around to the great benefit of her husband's business.

White Legs was actually the second Mrs Downton, Samuel Downton's first wife having left him a fair amount of money. She had been a maid. Unfortunately White Legs's character was not as fair as her complexion. First she decamped with her husband to Staffordshire, leaving behind three children to be maintained by the parish. Then the Downtons descended to becoming beggars: he 'an old decrepit person' and she with a box of pins and laces to sell. How unlike the worthy Joan Dant did White Legs show herself in her attitude to her trade! There was little of the 'true industry' given by the Lord to be seen here. Soon White Legs left her elderly husband for 'a new Sparke' who travelled the country. Old Samuel went back to Shropshire to be maintained by the kindly son of his first marriage.

Women, as we have seen, had always had strong connection with the provision business, where their work naturally complemented that of their male relations. In June 1690, a certain Widow Long was discovered who was prepared to give evidence to explain the adulteration of the soldiers' and sailors' provisions the year before. 'Bloody arts' had been practised, as a result of which many had become sick. The widow would give her evidence so long as she was protected from the consequences, since 'one of her nearest kindred was a practitioner of these arts; till his conscience troubled him'.[10]

Pepys, as Clerk of the Acts to the Navy Board, involved with the provisioning and equipping of the Fleet, came into contact with more than one 'she-merchant' in the course of his official duties, with pleasanter consequences. Mrs Elizabeth Russell had been the wife of a respected ship's chandler named Robert Russell. After his death in 1663, the widow took on the business – including the practice of sweetening those able to put business in her way. She sent Mrs Pepys a fine St George in alabaster, which the latter placed in her bedroom; Pepys himself received a case of knives with agate hafts, which he described as 'very pretty'.[11]

Far from showing any prejudice against the female in such a role, Pepys seems to have been both impressed and pleased by the phenomenon. Sarah Bland was the wife of a provision merchant named John Bland to whom Pepys went in December 1662 in order to discuss supplies for Tangier, a newly-acquired possession, part of the dowry of Queen Catherine. After the official business was over, Pepys stayed on to eat a dish of anchovies, and drink wine and cider: 'very merry', he commented, 'but above all, pleased to hear Mrs Bland talk like a merchant in her husband's business very well; and it seems she doth understand it and perform a great deal'. Two years later he was once again 'fain to admire the knowledge and experience of Mrs Bland, who I think as good a merchant as her husband'.[12]

*   *   *

Mrs Constance Pley was admired for her business sense and dealings not only by Samuel Pepys but by Colonel Bullen Reymes, a Dorset landowner and Member of Parliament, and a man with a reputation for financial acumen. He became Mrs Pley's business partner and – as a result of these transactions – intimate friend.[13]

Bullen Reymes, a Royalist, had been brought up in the service of the Duchess of Buckingham – Catherine Manners, widow of the first Duke and only surviving child of the sixth Earl of Rutland. Reymes married the co-heiress to extensive properties in Dorset and Somerset. After the Restoration, he was made Charles II's envoy to inspect Tangier after the Moorish invasion of 1664, and Surveyor of the Great Wardrobe (a financial post). At the time of the Dutch War he acted as the Portsmouth Commissioner for Sick and Wounded Seamen. A friend of John Evelyn, it was on the latter's nomination that in 1667 Reymes was made a Fellow of the Royal Society. A man of the world in every sense, charming, educated, well-travelled, Reymes paid no small compliment to Constance Pley at the end of his life: the first instruction which he left to his son, was to 'keep fair with Mrs Pley . . . he is sure she will not wrong him'. Yet by upbringing

Mrs Pley seemed destined merely for the obscurity of her own household
in a Dorset town.

Colonel Reymes's esteemed partner was born Constance Wise: a name
of Bunyanesque appropriateness. In June 1635 Constance Wise married
George Pley at Melcombe Church in Melcombe Regis, Dorset.[14] George
Pley fought in the Civil War, reaching the rank of captain on the Parliamentary side; later he was to become Puritan Mayor of Weymouth. Under
the Commonwealth he had already begun to supply Cromwell's fine new
Navy with sailcloth, manufactured under his supervision in his cottages in
and around Weymouth. Shortly after the Restoration Captain Pley was
joined in business by Constance, their son George junior and Bullen
Reymes. In the words of Bullen Reymes's biographer, Constance Pley
now became 'the driving force of the enterprise', which was expanded to
include the manufacture of hemp and cordage, and the import of canvas
and other 'stuffs' from France.[15]

These were good times to live in for those involved in the outfitting of
ships – that is, until they came to present the bills for payment. The King
himself, described by Bullen Reymes's friend Evelyn as 'a great lover of
the sea', took an obsessional interest in all the details of shipbuilding and
naval fortification.[16] English foreign policy after the Restoration, guided
by hostility towards the Dutch and nervous rivalry with the French,
demanded ships to implement it in either case, while the expanding empire
– including the new jewel of Tangier – was sea-based. The Pleys, headed
by Constance, were vigorous in their exploitation of this apparently
favourable situation. In March 1664, and later in December, Constance
Pley's name features in a contract with the Navy Commissioners for
different kinds of canvas – the only woman's name to appear. Correspondence was however almost as much a feature of the business as supervision of the work and importation.

Between June 1660 and August 1672 nearly 100 letters were written on
behalf of the joint enterprise to correspondents who included the Navy
Commissioners such as Sir William Coventry and Thomas Middleton at
Portsmouth, Sir John Mennes, the Comptroller of the Navy, and Sir
George Carteret, the Navy Treasurer, as well as Pepys. Constance Pley
herself wrote most of the letters – fourteen to Pepys alone are recorded,
although only one of his has survived.[17] Bullen Reymes wrote of Mrs
Pley's style: 'her oil will be better than my vinegar'. But if Mrs Pley's tone
was never vinegary, it was sometimes highly charged. Most of the letters
are pleas of varying degrees of urgency for payment, in order that the
Pleys and Bullen Reymes should be able to pay their own workmen and

suppliers.

In September 1664 Bullen Reymes himself fired off a furious letter to the Navy Commissioners, having discovered some patterns of canvas known as Noyals (for sails) at the docks supplied by Mr Browne and Le Texer, said to be the same as that used by the French King. It was, he pointed out bitterly, not a jot better than their own – and in any case the partners were owed £20,000! Under the circumstances, Parliament should at least see that they continued to buy the Pleys's sailcloth and cordage; the whole business 'would have been aground long since but for his woman partner'.

The precarious finances of the King's administration were not improved by the prospect of war with the Dutch; this war itself, which broke out in March 1665, plunged the Government's credit downwards while elevating its expenses. The result was catastrophic, at least in financial terms (at the Battle of Lowestoft in June a naval defeat was inflicted on the Dutch by a fleet headed by the Duke of York). Everyone involved in the war, who depended in some way upon payment from a depleted Exchequer, suffered.

The sufferings of the seamen and their dependants, denied their promised pay and given 'tickets' or IOUs, were so acute that in July the following year a maddened mob of women demonstrators – over 300 of them – surged into the yard of the Navy Office, and stayed there, in Pepys's words 'clamouring and swearing, and cursing us'. Then the women broke into the garden which gave them access to Pepys's closet window 'and tormented me'. Many were demonstrating on behalf of their husbands, who had been taken prisoner and were lying penniless and starving in foreign prisons.[18] The extent to which these complaints were justified can be seen by the fact that this was one female mob from which officialdom did not shrink in disgust. Pepys himself felt sorry for the women and called one back to give her extra money as they were departing; she blessed him. When the Navy Board ordered the relief of the prisoners, it was to be done 'without any trouble to be given to any of their relations in attendance here [demonstrating] for the same'.[19]

In 1665 the plight of the sail-makers, desperate for payment for work done for which the Pleys had no money to give them, was not much better; then there was the question of paying for goods imported from France (George Pley junior was now at St Malo supervising that end of the business). Mrs Pley bombarded Sir George Carteret with requests for payment, couched in language which would surely have brought forth recompense, had any recompense been available. At one point she worked out that the Navy Board owed her well over £8,000 and she invoked God himself to move Sir George Carteret's hard heart.[20]

Young George Pley's position at St Malo also concerned her as the 'breach' with France was seen to be approaching: Constance Pley wrote to Pepys demanding a convoy home for £10,000's worth of hemp and other goods, lest they become the object of 'nefarious plundering'. But when the precious cargo did arrive, still Constance Pley was not paid for it – as she told Sir John Mennes on 3 August, this was a poor requital for all her tedious waitings, the great risk she had taken, and the care. In the absence of payment, she had to draw £500 upon her son's credit, something she was loath to do, but 'necessity hath no law'.[21]

The twentieth of August brought an anguished letter from Constance Pley to Pepys: £15,000's worth of goods delivered, and still no payment! From this she 'can apprehend nothing but an approaching ruin, unless speedy relief be granted; £6,000 owing is wanted this month and next'. She 'must end her days in sorrow for meddling in this affair, and bringing in Colonel Reymes and other friends to suffer with her'.[22]

The summer of 1665 was one of gathering crisis, and not only for the Government's many creditors. The first ominous signs of plague were seen in London in June; by August the capital was paralysed. Pepys, making his will, wrote on the tenth that the town was so 'unhealthy' that a man could not reckon on surviving more than two days. The King and the court had already gone to Oxford; even more to the point the Exchequer had moved to the old palace of Nonsuch in Surrey. The King's minister, Arlington, engaged in finding funds for a spring campaign, complained of the difficulty of raising money at that distance.[23] For Mrs Pley it was the difficulty of getting paid.

Trade was of course as adversely affected as everything else dependent on the busy working hum of a capital city. The rich merchants and their families, like the courtiers, fled. Many of them took refuge on ships moored on the river Thames from Greenwich to Limehouse.[24] Mrs Pley heard from one of her correspondents, Richard Fuller, that every day was like Sunday in the City of London; not one merchant in 100 was left. She enclosed Fuller's letter with her own, since Fuller was one of those who protested that health and rest were being 'snatched from him' because Mrs Pley could not meet her obligations, and that she was 'going about to murder him'. At all points Mrs Pley took the responsibility for the business upon herself; payment *must* be forthcoming, so that 'the reputation of her husband and Colonel Reymes, who were drawn into the business by her advice, were not shipwrecked'.

In the meantime George Pley at St Malo, animated by something of his mother's determined spirit, seized every opportunity to trade despite the French 'vapour' or threat of impending war. A small English ship which had sailed on to the French rocks in error, and thus had the right to ask for help to get on its way, was used to send canvas, yarn and hemp back to England. But as Constance Pley told Pepys in December, things brought in by 'stealth' inevitably cost more; she must be paid something out of the Prize Office, for that at least was enriched by the proceeds of wartime capture at sea.[25]

At last some payment came. Mrs Pley's immediate ambition, after she had recovered from her abundance of joy, was 'once more to fill the King's storehouse which is very empty'. But the new year brought with it no halcyon period either for England or the Pleys. In January 1666 Mrs Pley was once more begging on her knees for £500 out of £2,000 owed for goods manufactured in the West Country, to 'stop the mouths of the poor people in her employ'. By late February she described herself as so short both in purse and credit, that she 'scarce dares show her face'. She suffered from a conviction that her appeals were being neglected just because they were so perpetual, but necessity left her no choice. As she told Pepys, if only a special clerk could deal with her on business matters, she could avoid these endless personal applications. Her ultimate threat was that she would come up to London herself and sort matters out.[26]

All the time the people at the centre were not without sympathy for Mrs Pley's case: in the middle of April Thomas Middleton wrote to Pepys, 'Madam Pley complains much for want of money; it would be a pity to let so good a manufacture of English canvas fail for want of encouragement.' The trouble was that the King's financial situation, and that of the country as a whole, was parlous; the Fire of London, coming in high summer to cleanse away the dreaded plague, was in a financial sense a further disaster. In the summer of 1667 the Dutch successfully raided the Medway. Mrs Pley was given 'assignments', i.e. first call, on the Navy tallies at the Guildhall; but in March 1668 Sir William Coventry was telling Pepys that Mrs Pley had written in despair that she could not even secure these payments. Surely 'the burning of London cannot go so deep in the Royal aid ... as to hazard her money', Coventry commented. In 1669 there appear to have been some orders to pay.

The business intimacy between Colonel Reymes and Constance Pley, the respect which he felt for his 'woman partner', led to another venture being arranged between them. In the spring of 1666, a marriage was brought about between Tabitha Reymes and George Pley junior, the girl receiving a portion of £1,000. Public prosperity came to the Pley family following Colonel Reymes's elevation as Vice-Admiral of Dorset. Captain Pley was made his deputy; George Pley junior Collector of Customs at Lyme.

The name of the son born to George and Tabitha, Reymes Pley, commemorated the unusual – for its time – business association between the boy's paternal grandmother and his maternal grandfather. Was there another more romantic aspect – more usual for the time – to this association? Colonel Reymes, left a widower while still a vigorous man, was both attractive to women and susceptible to their charms; for example there was a neighbouring Widow Rodney whose 'fair hands' he wished to kiss, having had much delight from her 'sweet and pleasant conversation' in the course of a journey by stagecoach from London to Salisbury.

The Colonel never remarried, and at his death he instructed his son via his faithful maid Hester Clinch to 'burn all Woman's letters' that he found among his papers. The directive to his son to 'keep fair with Mrs Pley' was however the first and therefore most important instruction in this document; the letter-burning directive comes two paragraphs lower and is not connected to it.[27] The Colonel's attitude and language to Constance Pley was not that of a lover: she was formally and gratefully addressed as his 'sister'. In his will he wrote: 'I give to my sister Constance Pley (my very intimate dear friend and one whom I greatly value and do acknowledge to have been highly obliged by and as having received many obligations from her ever since I knew her) my great Diamond Ring already in her possession, desiring her to accept of it in Testimony of my thankfulness and constant owning her as such to my very last.'[28]

Constance Pley was a 'sister' who was in a position to help Colonel Reymes with a series of loans when times were hard, such as at the beginning of the Dutch War; he borrowed as much as £400 at a time from her, although the amounts were always repaid. When Reymes wrote to Captain Cocke, Receiver for the Sick and Wounded, urging payment for Mrs Pley, he pleaded: 'Pray be punctual with her, she being as famous a she merchant as you have met with in England, one who turns and winds thirty thousand pounds a year, and that even with ... Sir George Carteret.' He added: 'She is also my friend.' There is surely no need to doubt the truth or deny the strength of that description.

And what of the she-merchant herself, what was her motivation? Beyond the particular family circumstances in which she found herself at the Restoration, part of the unusually small family unit, so that every member was needed to act, if the family business was to expand. Fortunately the inimitable and inquisitive Pepys was on hand to ask her. On 16 January 1666 Mrs Pley replied to one of his letters, which does not survive, but clearly contained an inquiry. She explained that several of her family had died years before – 'being formerly deprived of her children' – and more recently her surviving daughter 'within the space of four months was married and buried'. Since then, Mrs Pley wrote, business had been her 'sole delight in this world.... It is a charity to keep her in full employment.'[29]

*   *   *

William Hazlitt reported a conversation among his friends in which all agreed that Oliver Cromwell 'with his fine, frank, rough, pimply face, and wily policy' was the only statesman in history they would wish to have seen.[30] In any similar discussion concerning women born in the seventeenth century, Cromwell's granddaughter Bridget Bendish must certainly have a strong claim to be selected on curiosity value alone. By general consent she bore an alarming – or exciting, depending on your point of view – physical resemblance to her grandfather.

It was one pleasing aspect of the Restoration that no vengeance was exacted from the Protector's large tribe of relatives (although they had all, like putative princes and princesses, benefited from his supremacy). The Lady Protectress ended her days in peace in Northamptonshire with her son-in-law John Claypole; in general this particular Cromwell family sank back into the ranks of the gentry from which it had suddenly and so blazingly emerged. By 1670 King Charles II, in his genial way, was accepting the hospitality of Oliver's second son Henry at his house near Newmarket. Mary Cromwell, who married the Yorkshire magnate Viscount Fauconberg towards the end of the Commonwealth period, went on superbly to enjoy the life of a great lady at court.

Nevertheless the baleful image of Old Noll, warts – or pimples – and all, continued to fascinate the post-Restoration society which had survived him; the 1660s saw a number of plays in which Cromwell featured as tyrant, usurper and so forth, but always as the central character. After 1670 there were still plenty of people alive who could not only testify to Bridget Bendish's physical likeness to her infamous progenitor – 'if their imaginations can add a female dress, a few years in age, and a very little softening of the features' – but also found in this resemblance a subject of cosy fascination.[31] It was an added titillation that in her nature too, as well as her appearance, Bridget Bendish seemed to derive much from her grandfather, and some of the wilder, stranger elements in it; all this in the person of a married woman, later widow, living in Yarmouth and running a salt-works.

Bridget Bendish, born Bridget Ireton in 1649 or 1650, was the fourth child of Cromwell's eldest daughter Bridget, his anxious scrupulous 'dear Biddy', always worrying over the state of her own soul. Her father was Henry Ireton, Cromwell's brilliant dedicated right-hand man. Ireton was left behind by Cromwell to rule over conquered Ireland, a career cut short by his death in 1651 at the age of forty. Young Bridget, who would have been eight or nine when her grandfather died in 1658, was thus quite old enough to remember him. In addition, Bridget was largely brought up by her grandmother the Protectress during the absence of her mother in Ireland; for Bridget Cromwell's second husband Charles Fleetwood, another of her father's associates, was also given command there.

Bridget's childhood memories then consisted of life in the protectoral palace of Whitehall (where incidentally something approaching royal state was kept, at least where the position and prestige of the Protector himself was concerned). At the age of six, she sat between her grandfather's knees during a session of the Council of State. When one of those present objected, the Protector loftily replied: 'There is nothing I would discuss with any one of you which I would not equally confide to that child.'[32]

After the Restoration, Bridget lived for a while with her mother and step-father Fleetwood at Stoke Newington. In 1670 she married Thomas Bendish, a leading member of the Independent Church at Yarmouth on the Norfolk coast (a connection of that Sir Thomas Bendish, the Ambassador at Constantinople who had wearily ejected the Quaker Mary Fisher). Her grandfather, such a prominent supporter of the Independents during the Civil War period, would surely have been gratified by Bridget's choice of bridegroom. In any case, Bridget Bendish, helped on by her early memories and fortified no doubt by a physical resemblance which grew stronger with the passing years, now constituted herself the unofficial guardian of her grandfather's memory. 'Ah, that was what I learned from my grandfather' was a favourite observation[33] – a good or at least impressive remark to be able to make, if your grandfather happened to be Oliver Cromwell.

There was a famous incident when one of her fellow passengers in a stagecoach made some slighting remark about Cromwell, unwitting of the identity of his neighbour. On arrival in London Mrs Bendish challenged him – unsuccessfully – to a duel with a sword. Her aunt Mary Viscountess Fauconberg was, as has been mentioned, a great lady at the court of Charles II, her husband leading a distinguished diplomatic career under his auspices; although aunt would subsequently leave niece a sub-stantial legacy, there was a moment when Bridget Bendish flew into a fury with Mary Fauconberg, on hearing her grandfather (and Mary's father) disparaged under the Fauconberg roof. Bridget, with her usual passion, declared that if her grandmother had not been the most virtuous woman in the world, she would have believed Mary to have been a bastard. As to Oliver Cromwell 'next to the twelve apostles, he was the first saint in heaven'.[34]

It must be said that few, even among his most perfervid admirers, would have agreed with such a remark at any period in Cromwell's lifetime. As to Oliver himself, his quizzical reception of the ecstatically reverential Lady Eleanor Davies ('But we are not all Saints,' - see p. 250) shows that he would certainly have dismissed his granddaughter's overweening cham-pionship with a smile and a shake of his head.

The Bendishes settled down in South Town (once known as Little Yarmouth) on the outskirts of Great Yarmouth. There, on a marshy tract known as Cobham Island, for several centuries the property of the cor-poration and sold by it in 1657, lay the old-established salt-pans and refineries. The importance of the North Sea herring trade in the seven-teenth century led to an equivalent emphasis being placed on salt. The 'good red herring' which abounded off the east coast of England (for which English and Dutch fishing-fleets competed) was either smoked or salted at the ports; salted fish was both a necessity in winter in the absence of fresh meat, and a profitable export to Catholic (Friday-fish-eating) Europe.[35]

Salt-works being good business - indeed, the fishermen complained of the stranglehold which the shorebound salt-providers exerted upon their trade - the Bendishes lived in a handsome mansion nearby. Thomas Bendish owned farms as well as salt-works; until his death in 1707, Mrs Bendish worked alongside him in the conduct of his two businesses (in-cluding actual physical labour) as well as running her own household and raising three children. Her incessant love of drudgery, as it was seen by observers, reminded some of her grandmother the Protectress who had not allowed protectoral state to rob her of the pleasures of her own kitchen and household work. On Thomas Bendish's death, his widow inherited an income of £2,000 or £3,000 a year and the handsome mansion, as well as the farms and salt-works with whose management she was already closely concerned.[36]

For all the drudgery, there was something scintillating, even charismatic about the personality of Mrs Bendish, when she chose to exhibit that facet of herself. One who had known her described how she would be among her workmen 'from the earliest morning to the decline of day; insensible to all the necessities and calls of nature, and in a habit and appearance beneath the meanest of them and neither suiting her character or sex'. After that, 'having eaten and drunk almost to excess' of whatever was put before her 'without choice or distinction', Mrs Bendish would throw herself down on to the nearest couch or bed, and fall into a deep sleep. Then she would rise 'with new life and vigour', and proceed to dress herself 'in all the riches and grandeur of appearance' with a view to attending the assembly at Yarmouth. Here she would regularly appear, 'one of the most brilliant there', sparkling in the company 'as a lady who once expected ... to have been one of the first persons in Europe'.[37]

In later life Mrs Bendish was remembered in company as a striking presence attired in black, what was by now being termed 'the Quaker's colour'; her dress would be of silk, with a scarf or hood (not then fashionable) of the same material. But among her workmen she was seen 'stumping about with an old straw hat on her head, her hair about her ears, without stays, and when it was cold an old blanket about her shoulders and a staff in her hands – in a word, exactly accoutred to mount the stage as a witch in Macbeth'.[38]

Politics continued to interest Mrs Bendish under the Stuarts, provided it was possible to strike out for the ideals she imagined her grandfather would have approved. She was involved to a small degree in that murky tangle, the Rye House Plot of 1683 (which led to the execution of William Lord Russell) and is said to have lobbied for the accession of William III. Queen Mary allowed Mrs Bendish to be presented to her by Archbishop Tillotson and there was some talk of a pension, although the Queen's death put an end to the project.[39]

In religion, she was an extreme Calvinist, some of her religious habits certainly bearing a strong resemblance to those of her grandfather in his early days: 'she would retire to her closet, where, by fasting, meditation and prayer, she would work up her spirit to a degree of rapture, and then inflexibly determine her conduct by some text of Scripture that occurred to her, which she regarded as a divine revelation'. It was said that once 'the vapours' were raised by this method and 'the animal spirits brought up to an unusual ferment', no one could sway Mrs Bendish from her course, not even the 'plainest evidence of the same Scripture against it'.[40]

Was there a streak of the same depression in her nature which had caused Oliver as a young man to be categorized as *valde melancholicus* by Sir Theodore Mayerne? Dr Isaac Watts, a friend to Mrs Bendish, dedicated an ode to her entitled 'Against tears'. If so, Mrs Bendish certainly possessed in full measure the other side of Cromwell's complex character, the upswing which led Richard Baxter in *Reliquiae Baxterianae* to describe him as 'naturally of such a vivacity, hilarity and alacrity as another man is when he hath drunken a cup too much'.[41] As Mrs Bendish grew older, she developed a tendency to call on her friends at nine or ten at night (if the house was not shut up) and would often stay on till one in the morning; 'she would on her visits drink wine in great plenty', wrote a young man who remembered them. Hewling Luson was connected to the Cromwell family because his aunt Hannah Hewling (the brave Baptist maid of the West Country) had married one of Henry Cromwell's sons. 'The wine used to put her tongue into brisk motion, though', he added quickly, 'I do not remember that she was ever disgracefully exposed by it.'

Hewling Luson thought Bridget Bendish was like the Protector in her 'restless unabated spirit'; the difference was that in him this spirit 'by the coincidence of a thousand favourable circumstances' brought him to the summit of power and fame; in Mrs Bendish, the same spirit generally entangled her in disasters.

It was true that Mrs Bendish was no Constance Pley when it came to business. Her profuse, even wild, generosity whatever her financial circumstances got her into trouble with her business creditors, who took the line that their claims should precede those of the poor. We owe our original knowledge of Mrs Bendish to the character sketch by the Rev. Samuel Say, a Dissenting minister in Ipswich who was inspired to take up his pen by the publication of Clarendon's *History*, including his epitaph on Cromwell: 'a brave bad man'. The sketch is however hostile in tone; it has been suggested that Mr Say quarrelled with Mrs Bendish over her disposition of her aunt Fauconberg's legacy, which she wanted to distribute among the poor and he thought should be used to reimburse her equally deserving creditors.[42] He certainly reproached her for her behaviour on this occasion (without, it seems, swaying her) and admits that he felt by turns 'her friendship and resentment'. Subsequent chroniclers of the Cromwell family history dug out other witnesses who were kinder and more sympathetic towards her manifest eccentricities.

Dr Jeremy Brooke, paying tribute to her courage in helping Dissenters in a period of persecution, believed that this extraordinary woman, born into another sphere, would have been 'among the most admirable heroines'; another Zenobia, she would have supported an empire or defended a capital. He praised her charitable endeavours (with less thought to her creditors than Mr Say).[43] Hewling Luson suggested by implication that it was difficult for a mere woman to accommodate the Cromwellian character. He wrote that she had as much of Cromwell's courage 'as a female constitution could receive, which was often expressed with more ardour than the rules of female decorum could excuse'.[44]

It cannot be denied that Bridget Bendish's behaviour was often bizarre. Hewling Luson describes her leaving these late-night sessions of drink and talk on the back of her old mare, known locally as 'the old lady'. On these occasions Mrs Bendish often raised her voice in one of Watts's versions of the Psalms: thus 'the two old souls, the mare and her mistress, one gently trotting and the other loudly singing' jogged home to Yarmouth in the small hours of the morning.

As the years passed, the mare was employed to pull Mrs Bendish's chaise. Still avid in the cause of business, Mrs Bendish took a particular interest in the subject of cattle-grazing. She would travel overnight in her chaise to attend the fairs, expeditions which 'afforded exercise at once for her courage and enthusiasm'. Night to her, she said, was like day; surrounded by the most frightful storm, she would feel a particular happiness, sing this or that Psalm 'and doubted not that angels surrounded her chaise'.[45]

So the odd combination of a sacred monster as a grandfather and a prosperous businessman as a husband, produced a way of life which, however strange it appeared to outsiders, was satisfying to the lady herself in its independence.

20 *Wanton and Free*

'Some Men are of that Humour, as they hate Honest, Chaste
Women ... they love the Company and Conversation of
Wanton and free Women.'

MARGARET DUCHESS OF NEWCASTLE, *CCXI Sociable Letters*,
1664

In the late seventeenth century what is sometimes described (on no particular evidence) as the oldest profession was not necessarily the most
disagreeable one for a woman to adopt – provided she was able to adopt
it at an economically high level. The King – Charles II followed by his
brother James II, equally lecherous but more neurotic about it – constituted
the apex of the social pyramid; it was a pyramid which any audacious
pretty woman might aspire to scale if she caught the monarch's eye.

A handsome upstanding young man in the reign of Elizabeth with a
taste for poetry and adventure might dream of catching the old Queen's
eye; the same young man's son might dream of catching the eye of old
King James twenty years later. Let us imagine this cavalier's granddaughter, the fortune culled from the immoral earnings of her ancestors lost in
the Civil Wars. In her turn she might dream of catching the eye not only
of the King himself but of any of the rich and famous protectors who aped
his behaviour; she might become what a character in one of Aphra Behn's
plays described as 'that glorious insolent Thing, That makes Mankind such
Slaves, almighty Curtezan'. When Richard Allestree in *The Ladies Calling*
of 1673 expatiated on the unhappy lot of harlots ('Their most exquisite
deckings are but like the garlands on a beast designed for sacrifice; their
richest gowns are but the chains, not of their ornament but of slavery') he
was protesting against the luxury in which such women so evidently
lived.[1]

There was a universal truth expressed by Margaret Duchess of New-
castle: 'Some Men are of that Humour, as they hate Honest, Chaste
Women ... they love the Company and Conversation of Wanton and free
Women.'[2] This truth was a positive advantage at this period to the women

concerned if the men were powerful enough, and the women sufficiently bold, cynical or just plain desperate.

After all, it was not as if the economic alternatives for women of all classes who had to provide for themselves were really so very enticing. Not everyone was as high-minded as the poet Jane Barker, who described herself in 1688 as indifferent to the charge of being an 'Old Maid'. (The phrase was probably first used in the pejorative sense in *The Ladies Calling*: 'An Old Maid is now thought such a curse.') She was content to lead the existence of a good (single) woman:

> Suffer me not to fall into the Pow'rs
> Of Mens almost Omnipotent Amours;
> But in this happy Life let me remain
> Fearless of Twenty five and all its train.

More than one gentlewoman without a portion found herself able to sacrifice the much-vaunted respectability of being a waiting-woman or housekeeper for the pleasanter if less moral life of being a kept woman – a 'Miss' or mistress. The exquisite Jane Roberts, mistress to Rochester amongst others, was a clergyman's daughter. She died young (in 1679) with 'a great sense of her former ill life', but there is no suggestion that this was anything more than a deathbed repentance;[3] if Jane Roberts, to whom Aphra Behn dedicated *The Feign'd Curtezans*, had lived, she would undoubtedly have continued to pursue her career among the other 'insolent Things'.

If there was a shortage of husbands, it appears there was no shortage of protectors. Mary Evelyn in *Mundus Muliebris*, laying down the rules by which a gallant should conduct his courtship, took it for granted that he had a choice 'whether his Expedition be for Marriage or Mistress'. *The Womens Complaint against their Bad Husbands*, a satiric piece of 1676, complained that in 'this frivolous Age' many preferred the novelty of the mistress however painted her face, to the established wife, although the writer (unlike the more worldly Margaret Duchess of Newcastle) could not see what 'temptations or allurements' were couched in 'the Monosyllable Miss' which were not also to be found in the word 'wife'. Palamede, in Dryden's play of 1672, *Marriage-à-la-Mode*, complained that 'all Mankind' was setting up with mistresses, so that the demand was beginning to exceed the supply; as a result 'poor little creatures, without beauty, birth or breeding, but only impudence, go off at unreasonable rates: and a man, in these hard times, snaps at 'em'.[4]

It was not a purely literary conceit. Francis North, Lord Guilford, was seriously advised to 'keep a Whore' because he was being frowned upon 'for want of doing so'. The playwright Mrs Mary Manley used the form of a novel, *Rivella*, to give a true account of her own early romantic life. At the age of fourteen she was 'Married [bigamously], possessed and ruined' by her perfidious guardian. He finally abandoned her. Mrs Manley then went into the service of Charles II's erstwhile paramour Barbara Duchess of Cleveland; here a former admirer surfaced with the proposition that she should live in the country as his mistress, an offer which 'could no longer do her an Injury in the Opinion of the World' because of her disgrace.[5] In rejecting the offer on the grounds that she needed to feel herself in love with the protector (she subsequently lived for love as the mistress of another much less well-off man, a lawyer named John Tilly), Mrs Manley showed herself for the first, but not the last time, to be a highly eccentric woman by the standards of her time.

The characters in Aphra Behn's play of 1676 *The Town-Fop* included Betty Flauntit, a kept woman or 'a Person of Pleasure' as she was termed. While Betty Flauntit complained that 'a Miss has as painful a life as a Wife; our Men drink, stay out late, and whore, like any Husbands', for those who could not find husbands the conditions of life, like those of marriage, were not disagreeable unless the protector chose to make them so.[6] The children of such unions were often mentioned quite openly and publicly in the father's will, and in general provision was made for them.

Henry Sidney, always said to be the handsomest man at the Restoration court, was exceptional in that when he died unmarried in 1704 he left numerous illegitimate children for whom he refused to provide. The brother of Dorothy Countess of Sunderland (but born almost a generation later), he showed none of her charm of character, especially when dealing with Grace Worthley, his mistress of twenty years' standing. Mrs Worthley was a widow, but a poor one, her husband having been killed at sea in 1665 during the second Dutch War. She was gently born, living originally at Stoke Hall in Cheshire. The role of kept mistress to Henry Sidney was therefore an opportunity for support for one who might not otherwise have found it easy to survive; she bore Sidney a son. But it is clear that Mrs Worthley also adored her debonair protector for his own sake. Writing to him in 1689 she referred to herself as 'a poor, deluded woman, that hath loved you above myself, nay, above heaven or honour'.[7]

The trouble was that Sidney had acquired a new mistress at the beginning of the 1680s: Diana Countess of Oxford, wickedly attractive, one of the almighty courtesans of the court. By 1682 Grace Worthley was lamenting her dismissal after so many years, at the orders of one whom she described as 'the common Countess of Oxford' with 'her adulterous bastards'. Her son by Sidney was no longer acknowledged: 'all this to please his great Mistress'. Desperate for lack of money, Grace Worthley threatened to shoot Sidney.

Sidney's reaction was to depute his servant to pay Mrs Worthley £12 10s a quarter. If there was any more fuss, he threatened her with a warrant for arrest, which as a Privy Councillor he assured her he would be able to secure.

A few years later the discarded mistress heard that Sidney might be visiting her old neighbourhood in company with the new King William III. The news provoked a pathetic letter of nostalgia for country innocence: 'That I might once before I die make a visit to the good old wooden house at Stoke ... where I was born and bred.... I wish your Lordship would do what is reasonable by me, that I might go into Cheshire and there end my days. I should enjoy more happiness in one month in Cheshire than I have done in all the twenty-five years I have mis-spent in London.' Two years later Grace Worthley was still pleading for money to return to Stoke Hall, having in the meantime been escorted away from her lover's door by a constable and a beadle. Part of this petition of 1694 consisted of a pathetic list of Grace Worthley's relatives to prove that she had originally come of a respectable family.

While a measure of such tragedies were inherent in the insecurity of the situation (although wives as well as mistresses were deserted) Henry Sidney was rated at the time to be specially hard-hearted as well as handsome. Betty Becke, the mistress of Lord Sandwich, had an altogether jollier time, either because her own nature was more resilient or because his was more susceptible. In the spring of 1663 Lord Sandwich, Pepys's patron, while recovering from a serious illness, lodged at the house of a merchant's wife named Mrs Becke in Chelsea. Mr Becke was a merchant who had come down in the world; Mrs Becke, acting as a landlady, had the reputation of being a good and gracious manager, with her food well dressed and presented. Other comforts were provided by her daughters.

By the August of 1663, Pepys heard that his patron doted on one of the Becke girls; his days were spent at court but he passed all his evenings with her, as well as dispensing a great deal of money. Lord Sandwich was at this point a man approaching forty, in a powerful official position; although Pepys was in a sense not surprised that Lord Sandwich should show himself 'amorous' when everyone else at court was busy doing so, in another way he was deeply shocked to see his patron 'grossly play the beast and fool'. Lord Sandwich's 'folly', he was horrified to discover, included taking Betty Becke out in public, playing on his lute under her window 'and forty other poor sordid things'.[8]

At this point Pepys was convinced that Lord Sandwich was dabbling with one who was 'a Common Strumpet'. Another report spoke of Betty Becke as 'a woman of very bad fame and very impudent'. In November therefore Pepys was moved to write his patron a magisterial letter of reproof on the subject: how the world took a grave view of Lord Sandwich's continued sojourn in a house of 'bad report' when his health was clearly mended; Betty Becke was charged with being 'a common Courtesan' there being places and persons to whom she was all too well known; the notorious wantonness of 'that slut at Chelsea', as Pepys assured his patron Betty Becke was commonly known, was causing scandal to adhere to the name of Lord Sandwich.[9]

The following June Lord Sandwich did try the well-known adulterous expedient of using his daughters as a cover for visiting Mrs Becke; unfortunately the girls in question were well able to 'perceive all'. In consequence they hated the place, and complained that their father's one aim was to 'pack them out of doors to the park'; while he stayed behind with Betty Becke.[10]

The next move – on the part of Lord Sandwich's wife – was an equally time-honoured one in the great game of adultery. Lady Sandwich was suddenly inspired to go down to Chelsea herself in order to pay a call upon Mrs Becke the landlady. As Lady Sandwich told Pepys: 'And by and by the daughter came in ...'. By some extraordinary chance – 'for she never knew they had a daughter', let alone more than one – Lady Sandwich found herself feeling very troubled, and 'her heart did rise as soon as she appeared ...'. As for Betty Becke, by another surprising coincidence, she seemed 'the most ugly woman' that Lady Sandwich had ever seen. As Pepys commented tersely, all this, if it was true, was very strange; 'but I believe it is not'.[11]

However when the Becke family – invited by Lady Sandwich – came to call upon the Sandwiches in London, Pepys found that his own view of Betty was radically altered. She was neither 'a Common Strumpet' nor remarkably ugly. Although she did not have one good feature, Betty was nevertheless 'a fine lady', with a good figure, altogether 'very well carriaged and mighty discreet'. Pepys made a point of trying to draw her out in the company of Lord Sandwich's hostile young daughters. When she did contribute to the conversation, as she did from time to time, she spoke 'mighty finely'. Pepys reversed his verdict. Betty Becke was now 'a woman of such an air, as I wonder the less at my Lord's favour to her'; he saw that Betty's true charm lay in her intelligence – 'she hath brains enough to entangle him'. Two or three hours were spent in her company, Pepys and the rest of the ladies adjourning to Kensington where, in the famous garden with its fountain where Anne Conway had played as a little girl, now belonging to her elder step-brother, they all enjoyed some 'brave music' and singing. All in all, Pepys was delighted with the day's work: 'Above all I have seen my Lord's Mistress.'[12]

Five years later, as the intimate record provided by the diary draws to a close, Pepys reported that one of Lord Sandwich's daughters was recovering from sickness in her turn in the Becke house in Chelsea. Lord Sandwich intended to visit her; but Pepys still suspected that it was 'more for young Mrs Becke's sake than for hers'.[13]

*   *   *

Economics apart, there was the subtler question of independence for the mistress. When the Duchess of Newcastle referred to the allurements of women who were wanton and free, she had in mind their conduct rather than their status. Nevertheless it was true of the seventeenth century as people imagined it had been in ancient Rome: it was possible in theory at least for a courtesan to enjoy a measure of independence denied to her married sister, for whom security and adherence to the social norm were accompanied by the need for absolute subordination to her husband, legally and in every other way. Courtesans were sympathetically and even admirably treated in Restoration plays: Otway's Aquilina in *Venice Preserv'd* – 'Nicky Nacky' scornfully trouncing her elderly admirer at his own request – or Aphra Behn's much courted Angelica Bianca in *The Rover* who vowed that 'nothing but Gold shall charm my Heart'. (Although even the spirited courtesan Aquilina received a sharp put-down from her lover Pierre when she attempted to discuss politics: 'How! A woman ask Questions out of Bed!')[14]

In 1695 Rachel Lady Russell wrote a long letter of maternal advice to her nineteen-year-old daughter Katherine Lady Roos, interesting because it reveals such a very low expectation of female happiness even for a nice young lady married to a highly eligible young man. 'Believe me, child,' wrote Lady Russell, 'life is a continual labour, checkered with care and pleasure, therefore rejoice in your portion, take the world as you find it, and you will I trust find heaviness may endure for a night, but joy comes in the morning.'[15] (Admittedly Lady Russell had endured an exceptional sorrow, but then she had also been granted an exceptionally happy marriage.) For most women of this time life was indeed a continual labour – literally as well as metaphorically so. Even so, there were deep springs of strength and independence within the nature of certain females in this as in every other age, which would continue to bubble inextinguishably forth whenever the circumstances were propitious. For some of these, taking the world as they found it meant something a good deal more high-spirited, if less moral than the noble but essentially passive course advocated by Lady Russell. For such a woman, the life of 'that glorious insolent Thing . . . almighty Curtezan' brought rewards beyond the merely financial.

For this reason Catherine Sedley is the most personally fascinating among the numerous royal mistresses because as an heiress, the alternative of a good marriage was open to her in youth. Instead of the 'dull manage of a servile house' in Anne Countess of Winchilsea's phrase, she chose the more testing career of mistress to James II, when Duke of York. Moreover the weapons at her disposal included neither beauty nor any other form of attraction evident to the outward eye; even in youth Catherine Sedley was not reckoned to be pretty. She had a long nose and an unfashionably big mouth at a time when the ideal was a delicate rosebud; her complexion was too pale, lacking the carmine tint which made the approved beauties a contrast of 'white and red'; a cast in her eye enabled her enemies to describe her gleefully as squinting. Above all, she was considered much too thin at a time when the contemporary taste ran to the luscious: 'Fubbs' – for chubby – was Charles II's tender nickname for Louise de la Kéroualle, Duchess of Portsmouth. *'D'une extrême maigreur'*, wrote the French envoy Barillon of Catherine, although he admired her vivacity.[16] Skinny as a girl, Catherine Sedley became positively gaunt as the years passed.

Catherine Sedley conducted her campaign for a place – and a high place too – in society through her wits. In an age when both sexes combined to praise the dulcet female voice expressing softly modest feminine sentiments, Catherine Sedley triumphantly made herself feared by an exceptionally sharp tongue.

This strong vessel was born on 21 December 1657, the only child of the poet, playwright and Restoration Wit Sir Charles Sedley and Lady Catherine Savage, the heiress daughter of Earl Rivers. The mother was wealthy but she was also unstable; a few years after Catherine's birth she was mad enough to be placed under the care of a doctor – a Catholic because she herself, unlike her husband and daughter, was a Catholic. Catherine's mother began to suffer from delusions that she was the Queen, having to be addressed by those who attended her as 'Your Majesty'. She was finally confined in a Catholic convent abroad.[17]

What was to become of Catherine, her father's sole legitimate heiress and, in the conditions which made divorce and remarriage virtually impossible, likely to remain so? It was decided to place the girl at court as a Maid of Honour; after an unsuccessful attempt to enter the Queen's household, Catherine was placed in that of Mary of Modena, then Duchess of York. Catherine seems to have made her mark early on along the path on which she intended to travel; in June 1673, when she was still only fifteen, Evelyn described her when she visited him at home as 'none of the most virtuous but a wit'.[18]

Still, the witty Catherine did have a portion of £6,000, according to popular repute, and a further £4,000 at her father's death; there would have been more but for her father's liaison with Ann Ayscough. Catherine Sedley's arms when she reached the age of twenty-one described her as 'sole daughter and heir' of her father.[19] Yet after a series of affairs Sir Charles had formed a permanent liaison with Ann, the penniless daughter of a Yorkshire gentleman, which resulted in the birth of an illegitimate son. Catherine's mother outlived her husband but Sir Charles firmly termed his relationship with Ann Ayscough a 'marriage' and called the boy his heir. In his own words:

> What a priest says moves not the mind
> Souls are by love, not words, combined.

All the same £10,000 was no small sum as a portion. In 1677, for example, Sir Winston and Lady Churchill were interested in the prospect of Catherine as a bride for their son John (later first Duke of Marlborough), to the disgust of his sweetheart and eventual wife Sarah Jennings. Barillon described Catherine then as very rich and very ugly; but Sarah, after Marlborough's death, called her a 'shocking creature'.[20] This however being eminently an age when cash counted more than scandal, such a wealthy young woman, however provocative, could easily have secured a husband had she so wished.

Instead, Catherine Sedley remained unmarried. When she did eventually take a husband nearly twenty years later, it was as a mature woman approaching forty with a remarkable past behind her; she also had a further sizeable fortune to accompany her, as a souvenir of that past. As an unmarried girl she was entitled to keep her post as Maid of Honour to the Duchess of York and that was certainly a position of which Catherine Sedley, unlike those other more sensitive plants in the same household, Anne Killigrew and Anne Countess of Winchilsea, made full worldly use. By the time she was twenty 'Dorinda', as she was nicknamed in satiric verse, was a celebrated if not popular character at court.

> Dorinda's sparkling Wit, and Eyes
> United, cast too fierce a Light,
> Which blazes high but quickly dies
> Pains not the Heart but hurts the Sight . . .

wrote the poet and Wit Lord Dorset, playing on her alleged squint. Dorinda's personal Cupid was said to be no 'wingéd God' but 'a Black-Guard Boy' – one of the troop of insolent urchins loosely attached to the lower ranks of the royal household.[21]

Most important of all, at the beginning of 1678, Catherine Sedley became the mistress of the Duke of York, supplanting Arabella, the sister of her proposed suitor, John Churchill. The mistresses of the Duke became a legend for their ugliness, once King Charles II had ventured the sly opinion that they must have been prescribed for his brother by his confessors. In fact several of those favoured by the Duke gave the lie to the joke: Susan Lady Belasyse was an acknowledged beauty, while the doe-eyed Elizabeth Countess of Chesterfield (she whom her jealous husband carried off to The Peak) was one of the loveliest women ever to be painted by Lely. It was a combination of the King's wit with Catherine Sedley's own which gave rise to the legend. For Catherine was one of those clever women who created a style out of her own lack of conventional attractions. Dorset hammered the point of her plainness in verse (Dorset's especial venom towards Catherine Sedley was probably due to the fact that she rejected his advances, hell having no fury like a satirist scorned):

> For tho' we all allow you Wit
> We can't a handsome face.
> Then where's the pleasure, where's the Good,
> Of spending Time and Cost?
> For if your Wit be'ent Understood
> Your Keeper's Bliss is lost.

But Catherine made the same joke herself with more economy: 'We are none of us handsome,' she declared of the Duke's harem, 'and if we had wit, he has not enough to discover it.'[22]

The crudity of some of the Wits' printed attacks on women of the court who had incurred their displeasure make them literally unprintable: Sir Carr Scroope, merely describing Catherine as being 'as mad as her mother and as vicious as her father', was using language which under the circumstances was comparatively mild.[23] A vein of morose dislike for woman-kind – 'the silliest part of God's Creation' in Rochester's words – except during the act of sexual congress, runs through their works, including poetry as well as lampoons. And if it can be argued that the maddening feminine silliness referred to earlier (see p. 328) provoked some of it, it is noticeable that Catherine Sedley, an undeniably intelligent woman, provoked even more.

None of this prevented James Duke of York from falling passionately in love with his wife's Maid of Honour. Sir Charles Sedley once inquired of a new arrival at court whether she would turn out to be 'a Beauty, a Miss, a Wit, or a Politician'. Catherine Sedley triumphantly combined the activities of a Miss and a Wit without the helpful attribute of being a Beauty. Sometime before March 1679 she was known to have borne a daughter, known as Lady Catherine Darnley, whose paternity was officially ascribed to the Duke. Mary of Modena, Duchess of York, was said to be 'very melancholy' at this news, especially as the Duke was presently being obliged by the course of Exclusionist politics to leave England. The satirists too marked the event: 'little Sid, She who lately slipped her Kid'.[24]

Catherine was to bear several other children to the Duke, including a son, James Darnley; none of them survived infancy. There seems however some doubt as to whether the Duchess's melancholy over the arrival of little Catherine Darnley was fully justified. To Colonel James Grahame, another member of the Duke of York's household – he was Keeper of the Privy Purse – was also ascribed the honour of her paternity; in later years Lady Catherine Darnley bore a strong physical resemblance to his legitimate daughter. As the wife of John Sheffield, Earl of Mulgrave and in 1703 created Duke of Buckingham, Lady Catherine Darnley was so haughty as to be nicknamed 'Princess Buckingham' but according to Walpole there were still those who muttered that she was nothing but old Grahame's daughter.[25] Grahame, who was Catherine Sedley's confidant in her intrigues and remained so, was almost certainly also her lover. However, Mary of Modena never displayed any of that kindly tolerance towards her husband's mistresses which so signally marked the wise character of Charles II's wife Catherine of Braganza. Perhaps it was because she was so much younger than her husband – nearly twenty-five years – or perhaps it was because Mary of Modena was herself a very pretty young woman. By the summer of 1680 she was declared to be once more 'very melancholy' on the subject of Mrs Sedley by her women: 'She prays all day almost.'[26]

Alas, piety was not necessarily the best way for an 'Honest, Chaste' woman to combat the attractions of a 'Wanton and free' one. It was said of Catherine Sedley that 'there was no restraint in what she said of or to anybody'.[27] Like Nell Gwynn, she was a licensed jester, wit in their mistresses being one taste the two Stuart brothers had in common. As a Protestant herself, she regularly made jokes about the Duke's Catholic priests which one suspects secretly delighted the middle-aged royal roué, torn between guilt and concupiscence.

The death of Charles II in early February 1685 transformed the lives of James and Mary of Modena, now King and Queen of England. A few days later a message to Catherine from the new monarch broke the news that her life too was to be transformed: warned by his brother's example, King James had decided to lead another kind of life. It was to be a life without Catherine Sedley. She should therefore either go abroad or depart for the country; he would provide for her 'but he would see her no more'.[28]

Catherine however refused to go. Her emaciation at this point struck all observers; there was nothing else frail about her. In the end a compromise was reached by which Catherine was installed in a house which had belonged to the King's former mistress Arabella Churchill, and for which he now paid £10,000: No. 21 St James's Square. (The locality was considered sufficiently removed from the royal palace at Whitehall.) She also received a pension of £4,000 from the Privy Purse. Armed with this, Catherine, who had a taste both for music and the arts, proceeded to employ the finest sculptors and painters to adorn her new residence.[29]

It is not known precisely how long the King's good resolution lasted. Little James Darnley, born the previous September, died on the eve of the King's coronation. One story connected the King's resumption of the affair with his remorse at the child's death. James Darnley was certainly given a royal burial. He was placed in the vault at Westminster Abbey created for Mary Queen of Scots, where the King's many legitimate dead infants were already buried, along with such august personages as Elizabeth of Bohemia and Rupert of the Rhine; the plate on his coffin described him as 'natural son to King James the second.... Aged about eight months.'[30] At any rate before very long Catherine Sedley was being conducted up that notorious Privy Staircase leading to the King's apartments in Whitehall which had more than justified its existence during the previous reign.

Was Catherine Sedley also 'a Politician' as well as 'a Wit' and 'a Miss'? At one point the Protestant faction were accused by Lord Sunderland of using her to forward their interests with the King just because Catherine was a 'Protestant whore', as Nell Gwynn had once insouciantly termed herself. But the allegation was unfounded, according to James II's biographer, John Miller.[31] The next real drama in Catherine's life concerned rank rather than politics. In mid-January the King took the decision to make his mistress Countess of Dorchester and Baroness Darlington in her own right. (Henry Pierrepont, the irascible Marquess of Dorchester who was the father of Lady Anne Roos, had died in 1680 without male heirs – his second wife, Katherine Stanley, daughter of the heroic Countess of Derby, had no children – and the title was extinct.)

There was uproar at the court. The rumour that Catherine would also be granted the convenient apartments which had once belonged to Louise Duchess of Portsmouth, *maîtresse en titre* of Charles II in his last years, did nothing to allay the Queen's fury. On 19 January, shortly after 'Mrs Sedley (concubine to—)', as Evelyn discreetly called her in his diary, was officially created a Countess, the diarist noticed that Mary of Modena neither spoke nor ate during the course of two dinners.[32] King James was weakly astonished when his wife threatened to enter a convent if Catherine was not compelled to quit the court.

Catherine for her part had very different plans for herself. She was determined to be received by the Queen in her new rank as a countess. She was in fact already dressed to attend the formal royal reception known as the Drawing-room, when a message came saying that she was refused admittance. 'The hearts of all virtuous ladies and honest wives were filled with inexpressible joy,' wrote a contemporary. The King's act generously attested 'their matrimonial privileges'.[33] The King had once more bowed his head to the pressures of his wife and his priests; he indicated that Catherine should go, and did not even grant her that final interview which she had once made him promise would precede any final parting.

Passivity under stress was as alien to Catherine's nature as discretion in triumph. Once more she declined point-blank to move, posing as a martyr to the machinations of the Jesuits because she was a Protestant. A joke went the rounds that Catherine was taking her stand on her rights under Magna Carta and was refusing to be deported without her consent. Meanwhile 'L'Affaire de Mademoiselle Sidley' as the French envoy called it, continued to preoccupy not only the court Wits, but also the King's various advisers who, even if Catherine had played no political role, saw in her departure 'a trial of their interest with their great Master'.[34]

At one point Catherine either suffered or pretended to suffer a miscarriage to delay matters. She also clamoured loudly against the prospect of being exiled to any Catholic country, saying that Hortense Duchesse de Mazarin had warned her against all convents, and she feared to spend the rest of her life among nuns. (Her mother's fate must have played some part in heating up her imagination on this subject.) Lastly she discovered a neat way of circumventing another proposal to send her to Holland: if she went there, Catherine said, she would insist on being received there at court by James's married daughter, Mary Princess of Orange.[35]

In the end the lot fell upon Ireland. Here Catherine did have some friends and she also had some lands granted to her by the King. This made Ireland in her opinion 'the less invidious as well as the more obscure part of the world'. Catherine left on 17 February in a retinue of four coaches-and-six; by March she was installed in Dublin, posing a problem for English officials. They feared to receive her too courteously lest they incur the Queen's displeasure (as it was, even their sketchy greetings offended Mary of Modena).[36]

It was not long, however, before rumours of the volatile Countess's imminent return, fuelled by the refurbishment of her St James's Square house, were causing the Queen's 'pious mind' to be thoroughly 'discomposed'. Catherine wondered aloud in letters to her English friends why the Queen worried so much over her supposed powers of fascination: 'She thinks much better of me than I deserve.' All the same Catherine pined for England and good English gossip: 'Send the news true or false, I care not. I love an English lie ...'. As for Ireland: 'The English have generally a humour I do not approve of, which is affecting to like nothing but their own country; so were it possible, I would commend this place.' Unfortunately she found it intolerable. 'I find them not only senseless, but a melancholy sort of people,' she wrote tartly, 'and speak all in the tone of the cripples of London.'[37] (Many of whom were of Irish origin and thus begged in an Irish accent.)

November 1686 saw the Countess back at court once more, taking her place unchallenged and with her usual aplomb. She also bought Ham House near Weybridge from the widow of the sixth Duke of Norfolk. Although her influence with James was considered to have declined, Mary of Modena at Windsor could still be relied upon to weep if the King was late returning, convinced that he had been with the Countess of Dorchester.

The revolutionary events of 1688 and 1689 which resulted in the displacement of King James by his son-in-law William and daughter Mary placed Catherine, at least in theory, in an extremely awkward position. Catherine herself was certainly frank enough about it: 'Nothing curbs me in wishing well to the present King [William] but the fear his success may turn to my rueing.' It was true. On the one hand her royal protector had vanished; on the other hand the new Queen Mary was liable to look but coldly on her father's erstwhile mistress. Meanwhile the fact that Sir Charles Sedley was a prominent supporter of William of Orange gave a joyous opportunity to the Wits:

> But Sidley has some colour for his Treason
> A daughter Ravished without any Reason . . .
> And she to keep her Father's honour up
> Drinks to the Dutch with Orange in her Cup.[38]

'Never anybody, sure, was so unfortunately misunderstood as me,' wrote Catherine. The trouble was that Catherine's letters to King James abroad, asking for money for herself and her daughter, *were* liable to be misunderstood as Jacobite plotting; especially as she was obliged to use the Jacobite conduits to dispatch them, including the network headed by Lord Preston, brother of her confidant Colonel Grahame. No evidence has been found that she took a more active part in the Jacobite conspiracies than seeking money; and the counter-suggestion that she was placed among the conspirators as a Williamite spy is equally unproven.[39] What is clear is that Catherine's prime instinct was for survival, that instinct which had already carried her along successfully on her somewhat perilous course for fifteen years. 'My lord,' she wrote to the Williamite Earl of Nottingham in September 1689, whose aid she implored, 'I can't travel with a bundle under my arm tho' the King [William] is pleased to use me like a woman of that rank.' By December 1689 she was desperately refuting any suggestion that she had meddled in politics: 'knowing myself very unfit for it'.[40]

Admission to court in view of Queen Mary's hostility was once more the problem, as it had been during the previous reign, with the previous Queen Mary (of Modena). 'I believe the Queen thinks legion [i.e. the devil] is my name,' wrote Catherine. She was indignant to hear that every day ladies were being admitted whom Catherine 'would be very sorry to be compared to'. She instanced Hortense Duchesse de Mazarin, Barbara Duchess of Cleveland, Diana Countess of Oxford (Mrs Worthley's successful rival) and Susan Lady Belasyse. Full of injured innocence, Catherine told Lord Nottingham that 'the jury might possibly acquit me that would whip [for being whores] every one of the ladies afore mentioned'.[41] In the end Catherine Countess of Dorchester did secure admission.

Where the Queen's icy looks were concerned, Catherine proved herself equal to the occasion. Queen Mary's Regan-like indifference to her ageing father's sufferings was the talk of London at the time; even those who had supported King James's ousting were taken aback by her lightheartedness, her lack of filial honour for her father as prescribed in the Ten Commandments. Catherine told Queen Mary blandly that she was much surprised at her disapproving demeanour towards her adulterous self. 'For,' she said, 'if I have broke one commandment, you have another; and what I did was more natural.' It was left to King William to give her a more sympathetic audience, not out of passion but because he 'feared the lash of her tongue'. He also granted her a pension of £1,500 a year. That left Catherine unable to decide where her political sympathies lay: 'for both the queens us'd her badly, and both kings, she said, were civil to her'.[42]

As well as the wit, the spirit was also undiminished in Catherine. Some of Catherine's lands in the reclaimed Fens, granted to her in 1683 by the Duke of York, were granted after the Revolution by King William to the Earl of Torrington, more out of confusion than malice. Catherine took the case to the High Court of Chancery and won, but Torrington brought in a Bill by leave of the House of Commons to confirm his grant. At which Catherine 'prayed' the House of Commons in her turn, appearing on her own behalf at the Bar of the House. She was successful. The House added a clause to Torrington's Bill granting the Countess of Dorchester £4,000 arrears in rents, and an annuity of £600.[43]

Finally in August 1696, when she was thirty-eight years old, Catherine married Sir David Colyear, a veteran Scots soldier who had served under William III in Flanders. The Wits had a field-day: 'Proud with the Spoils of Royal Cully', they called her, adding: 'The Devil and Sir David take her.' The thick paint now applied to the appearance of the 'Wither'd Countess' was also the subject of much comment, nor did Catherine's sharp tongue escape censure:

> Too old for lust and proof against all Shame
> Her only business now is to defame.

Sixteen years before, Dorset had already gloated over her decline:

> Tell me, Dorinda, why so gay...
> Wilt thou still sparkle in the box,
> Still ogle in the ring?
> Canst thou forget thy age and pox?
> Can all that shines on shells and rocks
> Make thee a fine young thing?

But Dorset was premature in his rejoicing. Sir David was later created Earl of Portmore; Catherine bore him two sons, one of whom inherited the title. It seems that her style as a mother was no more hypocritical than her style as a mistress had been, for she told the boys: 'If any body call either of you the son of a whore you must bear it for you are so: but if they call you bastards, fight till you die; for you are an honest man's sons.' At the court of Queen Anne, Dorinda was still to be seen sparkling away in 'great splendour', covered in diamonds. At the coronation of George I, when the Archbishop of Canterbury, according to custom, went round the throne formally demanding the consent of the people, it was Catherine who was heard to say: 'Does the old Fool think that Anybody here will say no to his Question when there are so many drawn Swords?'[44]

Catherine was still tottering round Bath in her finery in 1717, and finally died in the October of that year. If a mis-spent life by most standards, hers could hardly be termed a wasted one.

*   *   *

The life of Mrs Jane Myddelton, like that of Catherine Sedley, was founded on masculine support in return for sexual favours, although of Sir Charles Sedley's categories Jane Myddelton was regarded as 'a Beauty' rather than 'a Miss'. She performed the functions of a mistress, it was true, to a variety of eligible men – men eligible to keep a 'great Mistress', that is. But the role of a beauty, which Jane Myddelton was so admirably fitted by nature to play, somehow elevated her beyond anything contemptible in the popular esteem; her affairs were seen more as a tribute paid to her great beauty, as the affairs of certain very beautiful and essentially passive women have been seen all through history.

The daughter of Sir Robert Needham, Jane married Charles Myddelton of Ruabon in June 1660 when she was fifteen. He was ten years her senior and a widower, a man of good family but small fortune, being the sixth son of Sir Thomas Myddelton Kt. Jane bore her husband two daughters: another Jane, born the following year, and Althamia. At first the newly-married pair lived with Sir Robert Needham in Lambeth. There seems to have been some plan for settling in Plas Newydd or New Hall in the parish of Ruabon with the help of Sir Thomas Myddelton; in 1664 Charles Myddelton wrote to his father: 'I long for nothing more than to be with you.' But at Easter 1668 the Myddeltons settled in Charles Street, in the parish of St Martin-in-the-Fields, where they were still living nearly twenty years later.[45]

It was the court which was the centre of the Myddeltons' life. Jane soon won a reputation as 'the most beautiful woman in England – and the most amiable', one which she preserved for the rest of her life: in 1683 when she was approaching forty, Evelyn was still able to write of her, the 'famous and indeed incomparable beauty, Mrs Myddelton'.[46] Jane never amassed a great fortune as did some of the avaricious royal mistresses, but the indisputable asset of the wife's dazzling appearance enabled both Myddeltons to enjoy an agreeable life at the court, without any official position, quite beyond their normal financial expectations.

In Jane Myddelton's features, in total contrast to those of Catherine Sedley, were to be found the ideal of seventeenth-century beauty as laid down in the rules of the time. Here was the perfect oval face with the lofty smooth forehead – 'the high temples' of *The Ladies Dictionary* – completed by a neat little chin. Here was the nose neither too big nor too small, the little mouth with its cupid's bow upper lip, the well-marked arched brows. Here too was the well-rounded figure, the milky white *décolletage* above the plump round high breasts – 'two little worlds of beauty' – which caused Pepys, admiring her from afar at the theatre, to rate her as having 'a very excellent face and body, I think'.[47] Above all Jane Myddelton was blonde.

Although men of course continued to fall passionately in love with dark women as they had always done, there was no doubt that the spectacle of a blonde beauty aroused a particular poetical reverence in observers, as though some extraterrestrial being, the Venus of the *Aeneid* perhaps, was passing that way: 'a tint of rose glowed on her neck and a scent of Heaven breathed from the divine hair of her head'. This was the language used about the lovely blonde Maid of Honour Frances Jennings (sister of Sarah Duchess of Marlborough) by Anthony Hamilton: 'To sum up in a few words – her face reminded one of the dawn, or of some Goddess of the Spring....'[48] Dark ladies had to contend with the conviction that saturnine looks concealed a saturnine temperament: Sir Henry Cholmley of Scarborough was proud that his blonde mother had brought about 'the whitening of black shadows' in his family's physical inheritance, while of Henry Oxinden of Deane's intended bride Elizabeth Meredith it was written that her outward fairness was 'a fair ambassador of a most fair mind.'[49]

Equally Hamilton wrote of Jane Myddelton that she was all 'white and golden', and that she was magnificently made. Her thick blonde ringlets surrounded a face which Lely loved to paint. 'Fair and foolish', wrote Margaret Duchess of Newcastle angrily of blondes in general (she was not one); Henrietta Maria Blagge, Margaret Godolphin's sister, another blonde Maid of Honour, was accused of being 'whey-faced' and 'yellower than a quince' by the Comte de Gramont, who reserved praise for those ladies who accepted his advances. For all these jealous carpings, contemporary handbooks were full of recipes for dyeing the hair blonde as well as whitening the complexion. And from the point of view of Jane Myddelton's lovers, the warning of *The Ladies Dictionary* that yellow hair had been since the time of the Danes a sign of lustfulness – 'golden Flames' sparkling without might indicate similar flames burning within - was no doubt enticing rather than the reverse.[50]

All the same it must be said that a look of cow-like complacency stamps Jane Myddelton's fair face, even at the deft hands of Lely. Despite her famous amiability, her air of indolent languor was not to everyone's taste. Her refinement and her pretensions to intelligence irritated everyone not madly in love with her, and even a few who were - 'she was the most tiresome when she wished to be most brilliant' - being one of those who larded her talk with French expressions. A rival beauty also told Pepys (who was always fascinated to hear such details about the belles of the court) that Jane Myddelton gave off 'a continued sour base smell', especially if she was a little hot. Nevertheless her protectors included Ralph Montagu, that notable ladies' man, who finally married another blonde beauty, but a wealthy one, Elizabeth Countess of Northumberland; Richard Jones, later Viscount Ranelagh, reprobate son of the esteemed Katherine Viscountess Ranelagh; and Francis Russell, brother of William, fifth Earl of Bedford, who took her to visit Evelyn at Sayes Court. She was after all, as Saint-Evremond's epitaph declared of her, 'illustre entre les belles'. She died in 1692 at the age of forty-seven. It was said of her decease that she died gracefully, as though she had studied how to do it; and so in a sense the 'incomparable' beauty had.[51]

*   *   *

For the women of the poor, the career of the common prostitute certainly promised the possibility of what the great Irish historian Lecky in his sonorous passage on her suffering figure - 'the most mournful, and in some respects the most awful, upon which the eye of the moralist can dwell' - described as 'disease and abject wretchedness and an early death'. Compared to this, the style of Mrs Myddelton - all white and gold - was shimmering and luxurious indeed. Yet to be realistic the lives of 'your common jilts who will oblige everybody' should be contrasted not with that of Mrs Myddelton but with the daily round of their social equals. Women who supported themselves as manure-gatherers, salt-spreaders and the like[52] (not the pleasantest of jobs) might well envy the financial rewards of prostitution, even if their superior morals prevented them from turning to it.

The figures for these financial rewards are of course so infinitely variable, and also obtained in such a random fashion from the records and literature of the time, that it is difficult to be precise. At the beginning of the seventeenth century, 6d a 'bout' - Pepys's word - was quoted in the country, and up to 20d in the city. In 1649 Ann Morgan of Wells was overheard being offered 1s by a client to 'lie with thee'; she proceeded to demand 18d because he had torn her coat and 'hindered me the knitting of half a hose'. But Ann Morgan was known to charge 2s 6d, double the usual fee, to soldiers. Robert Hooke, picking up a 'call girl' as he termed her, at a coffee-house in Change Alley, Cornhill, in the 1670s, paid her 5s. If an average rate for a female weeder or spinner of between 2d and 4d a day is borne in mind, or for a domestic servant between £2 and £4 a year, it will be seen that under certain circumstances prostitution was at least financially tempting. Most tempting of all economically was the prospect of trade in the New World: when conditions were bad (the Fire of London, for example, had a most depressing effect on the market and the whores had to lower their prices) enterprising ladies set off for Barbados or Virginia where the general shortage of women aided business.[53]

Returning to Lecky's picture, it must be said that disease and abject wretchedness and an early death at this level were not solely the fate of the prostitute, nor indeed of the female sex as a whole. Venereal disease was so widespread – having been spreading since the late fifteenth century – that the dreaded 'pox' received a certain amount of social tolerance. After the Restoration the poet and courtier Dorset wrote a good-humoured letter on the subject to one of his 'Misses' – probably a well-known prostitute called Moll Hinton – enclosing a small sum of money: 'a Little Advice', he wrote, 'and a great deal of Physick may in time restore you to that health I wish you had enjoyed a Sunday night instead of – your humble suffering servant'. Remedies and recipes against the pox would be given where in the same publication measures against conception were not mentioned.[54]

Furthermore, for the harlot there was always the possibility of upward social mobility, another prerogative following her traditional one of power without responsibility. Nell Gwynn, for example, was the daughter of old Madam Gwynn, who kept something very close to a bawdy-house. Her original profession, that of an orange-girl at the theatre, was one distinguished from prostitution more by its additional duties of fruit-selling than anything else; but her son by Charles II was created a duke. (And from pretty witty Nelly, who towards the end of her life could barely manage the two letters E.G. as a signature,[55] an English ducal house descends today.) This was an encouraging story, if not to the chaste.

In 1660 a list of common whores in London mentioned Orange Nan and Mrs Watson an orange-seller, as well as Betty Orange, prepared to do business at home at Dung Wharf. Where Nell was concerned, it was relevant that the orange-girls at the theatre needed a good deal of natural wit and spirit to ply their trade. There was considerable competition: from the women known as 'vizard masks' for example, from the accoutrement which became the badge of their calling, who also used the pit to pick up their clients; to say nothing of the actors on the stage, whose spectacle generally took place in competition with, rather than as an alternative to the activities of the orange-girls. Disease apart, the profession was not without its dangers: in 1679 the playwright Thomas Otway challenged the young John Churchill to a duel for 'beating an orange wench' in the Dorset Garden Theatre; 'and both were wounded, but Churchill most' (we do not learn the fate of the orange wench). At the Theatre Royal, however, few would have ventured to tackle the regular orange-girl, 'Orange Betty' Mackarel, alluded to as 'the Giantess Betty Mackarela' and a byword not only for her strength and her promiscuity but also for her impudence: the Wits jostling with her in the pit would be 'hot at repartee with Orange Betty'.[56]

In the 1660s Frances Jennings, she whose face reminded one of the dawn, and another Maid of Honour, Goditha Price, decided to disguise themselves as orange-girls in order to consult a fortune-teller anonymously.[57] It was easy to disguise the rather swarthy and distinctly stumpy Mrs Price; but Frances, just because of 'her brilliant fairness' and her particular grace of manner, was rather more difficult. All the same the two girls purchased some oranges, and thus equipped hired a hackney-coach. It was a night on which their mistress the Duchess of York had gone to the theatre (Frances pleading illness) and somehow it was irresistible for the two girls to stop there and begin to sell their oranges under the very noses of the court. Mrs Price accosted Henry Sidney, looking more of an Adonis than ever and even more splendidly dressed than usual; Frances tackled the famous libertine Harry Killigrew (Anne Killigrew's cousin).

Seeing two women together, one older and rather plain and the other very pretty, Killigrew made the assumption, natural to the time and place, that one was the other's bawd or manager. Asked if he would like to buy some oranges, Killigrew replied: 'Not just now but if you like to bring me this little girl tomorrow, it shall be worth all the oranges in the shops to you.' His hand, which he had kept under Frances's chin, began to stray downwards towards her bosom. Frances furiously rebuked him.

'Ha! Ha!,' exclaimed Killigrew, 'but this is strange upon my honour! A little whore who tries to raise her fee by being ladylike and unwilling!'

Only one man present recognized them and that was Henry Brounck-ner, known as the best chess-player in England, who combined this hobby with that of keeping a house of pleasure near London, stocked with 'several working-girls'. Brounckner's attention was caught by the good quality of the girls' shoes, as well as Frances's 'prettiest imaginable leg' (which originally he fancied would merit her inclusion in his harem). Brounckner however kept his peace, hoping to have material with which to twit Frances Jennings's fiancé later.

Prostitutes in an infinite variety of forms were omnipresent in seventeenth-century England, something taken for granted even by a Puritan counsellor like William Gouge, who suggested that a husband might be driven to visit them if a wife did not perform her marital duties. Cases of prostitution and scandalous lewdness, having been in the control of the church, gradually developed into indictable offences under the common law as the century progressed. It was felt that the church's administration was inefficient and corrupt, while the punishments meted out by the ecclesiastical courts to those presented to them were inadequate. Local ordinances for the suppression of brothels were founded in the doctrine that such places constituted a breach of the peace, a view promulgated by Coke, who described bawdy-houses as 'the cause of many mischiefs'.[58]

Whores – and whorehouses – being a fact of life, from the customer's point of view it was a case of striking some kind of balance between what his purse could afford and what his sensibilities could stand. The opportunities were infinite, ranging from Oxford Kate's in Bow Street, a public eating-place as well as a covert bawdy-house (Sir Ralph Verney visited it under the Commonwealth because they dressed meat so well) down to the drabs on the mean streets 'like Copper Farthings in the Way of Trade, only used for the convenience of readier Change'.[59]

An Act of Charles I for their suppression described how wayfarers in Cowcross, Turmil Street, Charterhouse Lane, Saffronhill, Bloomsbury, Petticoat Lane, Wapping, Ratcliff and divers other places were 'pestered with many immodest, lascivious, and shameless women generally reputed for notorious common and professed whores'. Sitting at the doors of their houses, sometimes at the doors of sack-houses, these women were 'exposing and offering themselves to passengers'.[60] Others acted with butchers and poulterers, selling themselves in markets on Sabbath days. Others still were involved in robberies, and thus entered the criminal records as a thief as well as a whore.

The Wandering Whore was a publication, probably written as well as published by John Garfield, of which five numbers appeared between 1660 and 1661, taking advantage of the newly permissive atmosphere following the Restoration. It used as its form a favourite device in this particular literary market, a conversation between a young whore and old bawd, and included what has been taken to be a comprehensive list of streets noted for prostitution and for brothels, such as Fleet Lane, Long Acre and Lincoln's Inn Fields. Other favourable districts for this kind of enterprise in London were Lewkenor's Lane, Whetstone's Park, Cheapside or Moorfields.[61]

Outside London, organized prostitution was mainly concentrated in the bigger towns, to which visits could be paid. Cambridge for example in 1676 had no fewer than thirteen bawdy-houses. It should not for this reason be seen as an unchecked centre for disrepute. Elizabeth Aynsworth had kept a loose house at Cambridge in the 1660s, but was banished thence at the instigation of the university proctors. She settled down again at the Reindeer Inn at Bishop's Stortford, to which 'all the goodfellows' of the county speedily repaired. She once served the very proctor responsible for her dismissal 'a most elegant supper' on silver plate. His party dared not touch the meal for fear they would have 'a lord's reckoning' to pay, but Mrs Aynsworth then appeared and observed with some style that it was a gift, since she was so grateful to the proctor for contributing to her advancement. Ale-houses and inns generally provided a natural network for such needs, knowing what local talent could be called upon.[62]

Then there were the looser arrangements. Thomas Heath of Thame, a maltster, was presented before the ecclesiastical court for having 'bought' the wife of George Fuller of Chinner for three weeks; he paid 2d per pound of her weight, which, after Mrs Fuller had been weighed in, resulted in 29s and one farthing changing hands. (In court the maltster admitted the sale, but denied that intercourse had taken place as a result.)[63]

Pepys's relationship with Betty Lane, later Martin, was certainly not a straightforward one of client and prostitute: Betty Lane and her sister Doll, with whom Pepys also dallied, were linendrapers in Westminster Hall, from whom Pepys purchased his linen 'bands'; they were distinguished sharply in Pepys's canon from the 'sluts' at the Black Spread Eagle in Bride Lane, who turned his stomach. On the other hand Betty granted Pepys the most intimate sexual favours over a long period of time, more or less whenever he demanded them; neither her marriage to the Exchequer clerk Samuel Martin nor pregnancy proving any impediment. In return she received entertainment of wine and chicken and cake when that was her prime need, and Pepys's patronage when Samuel Martin wanted a post. Pepys in his diary consistently criticized Betty for her lack of 'modesty' in what she permitted him to do to her and equally consistently resolved not to see her again. 'I perceive she is come to be very bad and offers anything', he wrote piously in February 1666. By June however Pepys was recording that he had had Betty 'both devante and backwards which is also muy bon plazer'. His utilitarian attitude to Betty Martin was not to be equated with his romantic feeling for the banished 'companion', poor little Deb Willet. When Pepys encountered Deb by chance years after her dismissal, he took her into an alley-way and forced her to touch him intimately. Deb's reluctance to do this happily convinced Pepys that she was still 'honest and modest'.[64] For Betty Martin's part, sex was simply one of a number of ways in which she tried to keep afloat. She too used or attempted to use Pepys; although he seems to have had rather the best of the bargain, at least according to the diary.

Famous madams included Mistress Damaris Page, given by Pepys the honorific title of 'the great bawd of the seamen'. Then there was Madam Cresswell, who had her house pulled down by the London apprentices in the riots of 1668. (Why did the apprentices frequent the bawdy-houses, if they were to pull them down? inquired Charles II, sensibly enough.) There were frequent references to Madam Cresswell in the literature of the time, from the high of Otway's *Venice Preserv'd* ('To lewdness every night the lecher ran.... Match him at Mother Creswold's if you can') to the low of the satires. The apprentices' attitude to the bawdy-houses was indeed ambivalent. *The Whore's Rhetorick* was another fictional dialogue of 1683 in which the old bawd 'Madam Cresswell' instructed the young whore 'Dorothea' in her duties; these included keeping herself free for the apprentices on Sundays, when their masters gave them the day off.[65]

The real Madam Cresswell lived to be convicted in 1681 of 'above thirty years' practice of bawdry'. By the time she died towards the end of the century, she had turned optimistically to a public parade of piety. Madam Cresswell bequeathed £10 for an Anglican clergyman to preach her funeral sermon, but with that caution inculcated by the thirty years of business in her particular profession, she made it a condition that he spoke 'nothing but well of her'. The clergyman solved the problem by mentioning her name only briefly in the course of his oration, and in these terms: 'She was born well, she lived well, and she died well; for she was born with the name Cresswell, she lived in Clerkenwell and Camberwell, and she died in Bridewell.'[66]

The fictional Madam Cresswell of *The Whore's Rhetorick* was described as 'livid' in appearance, with hoary eyebrows, yellow gummy eyes, sagging breasts and a beard: in short the prototype of the menacing witch-like female, frightening because she was ugly and ugly because she was old. Dorothea, on the other hand, as a virginal gentlewoman, represented someone for whom a more hopeful future was proposed. She was described as one whose father 'had much more Nobility in his Veins than Money in his Purse', her dowry having been sacrificed in the Civil Wars. Unable to go out to work like her brothers, Dorothea was advised by Madam Cresswell to put her beauty up for sale and become 'a Woman of the Town'.[67]

The ancient bawd pointed out to Dorothea that 'Liberty was the first and the greatest benefit of nature', and that in consequence she should look on it as 'the great business' of her life to please others and enrich herself. That way Dorothea could look forward to retirement in the country, or even contemplate marriage, so long as she secured a third of her husband's estate as a dower: 'the most precious Jewel, next to life and liberty'. A rich merchant or some other honest citizen was probably the best hope for setting her up: 'these are the golden lovers', better than 'a score of ranting Blades'.[68]

Where her work with old men was concerned, Dorothea was adjured to bear in mind England's historic past: 'It is odds if sometimes in a rapture a-Bed, he do not get astride of thy Back, to demonstrate how he managed his horse at Naseby fight' (some forty years earlier). With all her lovers, it was essential for Dorothea to add to her lover's pleasure by simulating her own: 'You must not forget to use the natural accents of dying persons.... You must add to these ejaculations, aspirations, sighs, intermissions of words, and such like gallantries, whereby you may give your Mate to believe, that you are melted, dissolved and wholly consumed in pleasure, though Ladies of large business are generally no more moved by an embrace, than if they were made of Wood or stone.' Blushing was also a useful accomplishment: 'it is a token of modesty, and yet an amorous sign'.[69]

It is not suggested that all whores enjoyed the rich standard of life suggested by Madam Cresswell for Dorothea, or that they were equally salubrious. 'A trading lady', said the old bawd, needed 'a small convenient house of her own', with one or two maids, otherwise she would not be content; everything within had to be exceptionally neat and clean (including Dorothea's own person). Jenny Cromwell, Jenny Middleton, Moll Hinton, Sue Willis and Doll Chamberlain, the celebrated women of the town to be found at the New Exchange, were likely to lead a more rackety life. *The Wandering Whore*, listing the well-known prostitutes of 1660, gave exotic names such as the Queen of Morocco as well as some more homely: Welsh Nan Peg the Seaman's Wife, Long-Haired Mrs Spencer in Spitalfields, Mrs Osbridge's Scolding Daughter (catering clearly for some special masochistic taste) and Mrs Osbridge herself, who practised within Bedlam.[70]

In 1671 the Earl of Dorset announced that he was bored by the constant sentimental addresses to ladies of the court under pastoral names. Instead he proposed to serenade 'Black Bess' – the notorious prostitute Bess Morris:

> Methinks the poor town has been troubled too long
> With Phillis and Chloris in every song
> By fools, who at once can both love and despair,
> And will never leave calling 'em cruel and fair;
> Which justly provokes me in rhyme to express
> The truth that I know of bonny Black Bess.
>
> . . .
>
> The ploughman and squire, the arranter clown,
> At home she subdued in her paragon gown;
> But now she adorns both the boxes and pit,
> And the proudest town gallants are forc'd to submit;
> All hearts fall a-leaping, wherever she comes
> And beat day and night, like my Lord Craven's drums.

In Restoration society Bess Morris had her place as well as Phillis and Chloris, and was well aware of it. When 'a great woman' named Bess to her face as Dorset's whore, Bess Morris answered that she was proud of the fact that she pleased at least 'one man of wit'; let 'all the coxcombs dance to bed with you!' she retorted.[71]

21   *Actress as Honey-Pot*

> ' 'Tis as hard a matter for a pretty Woman to keep herself honest
> in a Theatre, as 'tis for an Apothecary to keep his Treacle from
> the Flies in Hot Weather; for every Libertine in the Audience will
> be buzzing about her Honey-Pot. . . .'
>
> TOM BROWN, 'From worthy Mrs Behn the Poetress to the famous
> Virgin Actress'

According to John Evelyn, Margaret Godolphin was so mortified to find
herself 'an Actress' in 1674, in the court masque *Calisto*, that she spent all
her time off stage reading a book of devotion; she could hardly wait for
the performance to end before rushing to her oratory to pray. This distaste
was recorded with ecstatic approval by Evelyn: in her dress worth nearly
£300, and £20,000's worth of borrowed jewels his favourite looked like
'a Saint in Glory'; even when on the stage, she had the air of abstracting
herself from it.[1]

The behaviour of the rest of the cast did not live up to this high standard.
The 'tiring-room' was crowded with gallants, with whom the lady performers passed the time agreeably between entrances. The celebrated
singer Mrs Knight, whose services had been called upon to supplement the
somewhat weak voices of the amateurs, was an ex-mistress of the King.
Renowned for the range of her voice, she had recently been 'roaming' in
Italy, as a result of which her range was still further extended. Mrs Knight
sang 'incomparably' on this occasion; nevertheless she was not a particularly welcome sight at court to the royal ladies. Another professional
invited, Moll Davis – 'Dear Miss, delight of all the nobler sort' – had cast
such enchantment over the King with the sweetness of her singing on stage
that he had made her his mistress on the strength of it; she had recently
borne him a child.

Although Evelyn was carrying prudery a little far in suggesting that
Margaret Godolphin condemned a masque – the real cause of her pique
lay elsewhere[2] – nevertheless it was true that in the 1670s a respectable

woman could not give her profession as that of 'Actoress' and expect to keep either her reputation or her person intact.

It was a royal warrant of 21 August 1660 which brought Englishwomen on to the English stage for the first time, so that plays should become 'useful and instructive representations of human life', from being merely 'harmless delights'. Before that, women had been seen on stage – but they had been foreigners, and as such highly suspect. Some of these were more travelling performers, mountebanks in the original sense of the word (*monta in banco* – mount on the bench), than actresses: in the time of Queen Elizabeth for example the honest town of Lyme had felt both thrilled and threatened by the 'unchaste, shameless, and unnatural tumbling of Italian women'. In 1629 a troupe of genuine actresses had arrived from France and had performed at Blackfriars, in the Red Bull and Fortune Theatres; they had been hissed off the stage by the English as being immoral. Later William Prynne in *Histriomastix* denounced them as 'notorious whores'.[3]

Under the Protectorate, when Sir William Davenant performed the brilliant conjuring trick of persuading the music-loving Cromwell that the new dramatic form of opera bore absolutely no relation to the scandalous theatre, a woman, Mrs Edward Coleman, had sung the part of Ianthe in the 'opera' *The Siege of Rhodes*. (Later, conveniently, *The Siege of Rhodes* turned out to be a play, and a very popular one too. Mrs Betterton made the part of Ianthe so much hers that she was generally referred to under that name rather than her own.) The conception of the court masque, so beloved of Queen Henrietta Maria and King Charles I, was also preserved during the Protectorate, because in that too music played its soothing part. At the wedding of Mary Cromwell a masque, with pastorals by Marvell, graced the protectoral court in which the young bride appeared; Cromwell himself may have played a non-speaking part.[4] However, a masque – for all Margaret Godolphin's megrims – was not a professional theatrical performance and nor was an opera – by protectoral decision.

It was a few months after the warrant – sometime in November or December 1660 – that one young Englishwoman actually stepped on to the London stage as the first swallow to signify the long hot summer of the English actress. We do not and shall presumably never know her name, although we know the play – *The Moor of Venice* – and the part – Desdemona. (Before that, as it was wittily said, with men of forty or fifty playing wenches of fifteen, when you called Desdemona: 'enter Giant'.)[5] Two companies had been given the monopoly of the London stage by the King's warrant, following the Restoration: The King's Company under Thomas Killigrew and The Duke's Company under Davenant. Although on balance of probability the claim of The King's Company to provide the first actress has been allowed, both companies actually claimed it; which means that the honour lies between Anne Marshall, Mary Saunderson (Mrs Betterton) and Katherine Corey, who became a specialist in old women's roles, famously creating that of the Widow Blackacre in Congreve's *The Double Dealer*. If Katherine Corey is ruled out as an unlikely Desdemona for this reason, the choice lies between Anne Marshall and Mary Saunderson.[6]

Mary Saunderson, who married the great actor-manager Thomas Betterton in 1662 when she was about twenty-five, would be a worthy founder of her profession; since she was the famous exception to the rule that all actresses of this period were to be considered potential prostitutes. 'Having, by nature, all the accomplishments required to make a perfect actress,' wrote Betterton's biographer Charles Gildon, 'she added to them the distinguishing characteristic of a virtuous life.' So wondrous was her virtue that she was actually engaged to coach the young Princesses Mary and Anne in *Calisto*, a task for which those participants Mrs Knight and Moll Davis would certainly not have been held suitable. Shortly before Mrs Betterton's marriage Pepys was ravished by her performance in the title role of *The Duchess of Malfi* (Betterton played Bosola), the play itself being one of the most popular tragedies in the repertory of The Duke's Company. A long career in the theatre at her husband's side ended with the admirable Mrs Betterton training up other younger actresses, including Anne Bracegirdle.[7]

Most of her colleagues presented a very different image to the public. By 1666 Evelyn was finding the professional theatre increasingly distasteful, because audiences were abused by an 'atheistical liberty', to wit, 'foul and indecent women, now (and never till now) permitted to appear and act'; he much preferred the special court performances. In the 1680s the word actress was virtually synonymous with that of 'Miss' or kept woman, at least in the expectations of the public.[8] The burden of proof otherwise fell upon the individual actress, but there were very few who essayed to make the point. The trouble was that those 'useful and instructive representations of human life', the kind of new plays inspired by the opportunity of putting women on the stage, might be brilliant comedies of manners or turgid tragedies of emotion or some combination of the two, but in general they were extremely frank in their depiction of promiscuity. Inevitably and excitedly, the public merged the personality of the actress with that of her character on stage.

As a result, the convenient identification of actress and 'Miss' led to young ladies becoming actresses precisely in order to secure a rich admirer. Now contemporaries pitied the 'little playhouse creatures', as Mrs Squeamish termed them in *The Country Wife*, only if they did not manage to pick up a protector. The casting-couch made its first appearance in our social history when a young woman was sometimes obliged to sacrifice her virtue in order to obtain a coveted place in the theatre from one of its patrons. It was an investment she expected to recoup in the shape of the desired wealthy keeper, once she could display her pretty face to advantage on the stage itself. The beaux of the court expected in their turn to keep a pretty actress; it figured along with all their other expenses in the cause of public display, such as gaudy clothes and fine horses. In this way George Porter kept Mrs Jane Long, Sir Robert Howard (the nephew of his namesake, the lover of Lady Purbeck) Mrs Uphill, Sir Philip Howard Mrs Betty Hall, and the Earl of Peterborough Mrs Johnson.[9]

The *louche* atmosphere of the times is well caught by a joyful letter of 1677 from Harry Savile to Lord Rochester, then ill in the country. Savile tried to tempt Rochester to London with the prospect of a sweet new French *comédienne* called Françoise Pitel: 'a young wench of fifteen'. Savile declared 'it were a shame she should carry away a maidenhead she pretends to have brought', but unfortunately the price was so steep that no one currently in London could afford it.[10]

This two-way traffic called forth many references in the plays of the time. Some of these took the rueful side of management: 'our Women who adorn each Play, Bred at our cost, become at length your prey'. Others pointed to the actress herself as predator, since she intended:

> With open blandishments and secret art
> To glide into some keeping cullies heart
> Who neither sense nor manhood understands
> And jilt him of his patrimonial lands.[11]

Be that as it may, by the 1670s the word actress had secured in England that raffish connotation which would linger round it, for better or for worse, in fiction as well as fact, for the next 250 years.

It had not always been so. The first actresses often concealed their origins, while the honorific appellation 'Mrs' pronounced mistress, which they were granted – as opposed to the opprobrious 'Miss' – sometimes makes their marital status hard to unravel. Yet it is clear that they were neither 'Misses' nor the daughters of 'Misses'. Some, like Peg Hughes, came from actors' families. Others were drawn from that same penurious segment of society which supplied waiting-women and the like, where the daughters were likely to go husbandless if they had no dowry. Singing and dancing being the prerequisites of a ladylike education, such as that provided by the Chelsea girls' schools, there were plenty of pupils in the early days from which to choose; some of whom later came to form part of what Anthony Hamilton called 'the whole joyous troop of singers and dancers who ministered to His Majesty's slighter pleasures'.[12]

Hannah Woolley, advocating the role of gentlewoman in *The Queen-like Closet* as being the best option available to the unendowed girl, drew attention to the alternatives: 'Some who have apt Wits and that Dame Nature hath been favourable to, they are courted to be Players.' The fact was those who had been favoured by Dame Nature did not necessarily share Hannah Woolley's particular sense of priorities. Mrs Pepys's gentlewoman, Gosnell, was one of these. Finding the post of gentlewoman too restrictive, she left to find her freedom (see p. 315). A few months later, in May 1663 'Who should we see come upon the stage', wrote Pepys, 'but Gosnell, my wife's maid'. Unfortunately Gosnell 'neither spoke, danced nor sung; which I was sorry for. But she becomes the stage very well.' The following year Pepys saw Gosnell again, singing and dancing finely at first, but finally falling out of tune. Poor Gosnell! Her career never amounted to much more than being an understudy and an occasional singer. Four years later she was singing the performance 'meanly' throughout, and had lost her looks: Sir Carr Scroope characterized her as 'that old hag'. Finally Gosnell was discharged and vanished from view.[13]

Gosnell had been the daughter of a widow with very little money but genteel connections. Among the first actresses there were plenty of Gosnells, who preferred the liberty and adventure of the stage to a life of doing shell-work with Mrs Pepys, only they turned out to be more talented. Anne and Rebecca Marshall were the daughters of a country parson, who as chaplain to Lord Gerard had been married off to the illegitimate daughter of a Cheshire squire. Mrs Shadwell's father was either a Norwich public notary or 'a decayed knight'; Charlotte Butler was the daughter of a widowed shopkeeper. Accounts of Mrs Barry's origins varied: she was either an orphan brought up by Lady Davenant to be her 'woman' in Norfolk, or the daughter of a barrister called Robert Barry who ruined himself fighting for the King.[14]

Wherever they began, the first actresses – and their managers – were not slow to take advantage of their unique opportunities for display, and profit from that display. Inheriting the famous pre-Restoration female 'breeches' parts from the men who had previously played them, they made of them something yet more titillating. Actresses with pretty legs, like Peg

Hughes and Nell Gwynn, welcomed this legitimate opportunity for show-ing them off in public, not otherwise granted to them by the costume of the time; then there were the infinite enjoyable possibilities of the *double entendre*. New plays were rapidly written employing the old device for a new reason: it has been estimated that nearly a third of all the plays first produced after 1660 and before 1700 contained one or more breeches roles.[15] Audiences, unused to such bonanzas, were enchanted when Betty Boutel, playing Fidelia disguised as a boy in Wycherly's *The Plain Dealer*, had her peruke pulled off and her breasts felt by the actor playing Vernish.

The costumes for the more straightforward women's parts offered opportunities for self-advertisement too.[16] The actress would first don a loose smock of Holland linen falling below the knees, with short sleeves and a very low-cut draw-string neck (it was in these smocks that they spent their hours resting off stage; a convenient costume it might be thought for receiving the gallants who pestered the tiring-rooms with their attentions, including during the performances, to judge from the frequent prohibitions issued against such behaviour). After the smock came wood or whalebone stays. Holland drawers followed for those who in-tended to dance: Nell Gwynn had a habit of wearing 'Rhinegraves' for the King's delectation, special short wide divided skirts which flew up as she danced.[17] Thread or silk stockings, gartered above and below the knee, were worn with high-heeled shoes and buckles. Two or three petticoats, a tight bodice and an over-skirt completed the outfit; this left the bosom more or less bare (so that actresses generally wore a scarf – 'a whisk' – out of doors).

What with the Holland smocks and the low-cut dresses, the opportun-ities for actors on stage – in the course of plays which made frequent use of such gestures – and the gallants off stage, to 'towse and mowse' with a willing actress were virtually unlimited. Pepys was shocked by the back-stage incidents he witnessed, including the bad language of the actresses.[18] Only the leading actress had a room to herself.

Nor were the financial rewards of being an actress such as to make additional income unnecessary. For one thing actresses had to supply their own petticoats, shoes, stockings, gloves and scarves as well as other living expenses; the introduction of liveries paid for by the King was thus a welcome economy, not a humiliation. (When the King, the Duke of York and the Earl of Oxford lent their coronation robes for Orrery's *Henry V*, in which Betterton played Owen Tudor and Mrs Betterton the Princess of France, it was as much to do with economy as with the close informal relationship which existed between the court and the theatre; the court supplying the Lord Chamberlain, whose duty it was to license the players.) Runs of plays were often as short as two or three days and it has been estimated that no one worked for much more than thirty or thirty-five weeks in the year.[19] The shutting of the London theatres for eighteen months at the time of the Great Plague brought about further hardship.

A young actress would receive 10s to 15s a week and would be expected to work for nothing at the beginning of her career. Even the great Mrs Barry only received 30s at the height of her fame, although she also received much larger sums from benefit performances. Mrs Betterton, paid the enormous sum of 50s a week in 1691, was the wife of the principal actor, who was also incidentally the man who ran the company. There were rules which prevented actresses (and actors) from moving between the two companies without permission; the amalgamation of The King's Company and The Duke's Company between 1682 and 1695 as The United Company increased the problems of actors by setting up a monopoly.

Unmarried actresses lived as close as possible to the theatre, the Fleet Street and Covent Garden area for The Duke's Company and Drury Lane for The King's Company; Davenant originally boarded some of his leading actresses, including Moll Davis, in his own apartments. As against these conditions, the life of the kept woman with her own house, best of all her own settlement from her protector, offered innumerable advantages unknown to the virtuous. It is hardly surprising that a large number of actresses succumbed to the temptation.

It was not the talentless who adopted this code of behaviour, rather the reverse. Of the eighty women, who appeared on the Restoration stage, listed by name by J. H. Wilson in his comprehensive study of the subject,[20] twelve who enjoyed an enduring reputation as courtesans or 'Misses' included the most celebrated performers such as Elizabeth Barry and Betty Boutel, an innocent-looking Fidelia, but off stage known as 'Chestnut-maned Boutel, whom all the Town F—ks'. The ladies, it should be said, thrived on this combination of public and private acclaim: Betty Boutel spent twenty-six years on the stage and Elizabeth Barry thirty-five. As for Mrs Bracegirdle, who made a special parade of her virtue, she was described as one that had got 'more Money out of dissembling her Lewdness than others by professing it'; and it seems that she was kept at different times by both Congreve and Lord Scarsdale.[21]

At least another twelve, either lazier, unluckier or less successful, are known to have left the theatre to become straightforward kept women or prostitutes. Another thirty are mentioned so briefly as being on the stage, that it is likely that many of them also vanished into prostitution. 'Mistaken Drab, back to thy Mother's stall'; with these cruel words the pretensions of Sarah Cooke, Rochester's protégée, to be an actress were dismissed by a satirist in the 1680s. In fact 'Miss Sarah's' origins were not so low as indicated; nor was she quite devoid of talent, since she was wanted by Dryden to play Octavia in *All For Love*.[22] Nevertheless the supposition that an unsuccessful actress, having come from the stews, would return to them, was a characteristic one of the period.

Roughly a quarter of these actresses lived respectable lives, so far as we know, and most of these, like Mrs Betterton, were married to fellow-actors; it seems that in the seventeenth century show-business marriages reversed the modern trend and were more stable than otherwise. In general, as the jovial satirist Tom Brown wrote in *Letters from the Dead to the Living* (this letter was headed: 'From worthy Mrs Behn the Poetress, to the famous Virgin Actress'): ' 'Tis as hard a matter for a pretty Woman to keep herself honest in a Theatre, as 'tis for an Apothecary to keep his Treacle from the Flies in Hot Weather; for every Libertine in the Audience will be buzzing about her Honey-Pot....'[23]

*   *   *

Hester Davenport, widely known as 'Roxalana' after her performance in that part in *The Siege of Rhodes* in 1661, was 'a charming, graceful creature and one that acted to perfection'. She was about twenty at the time of her first fame. With her exceptional looks – a beauty that made men 'take ill courses' wrote Anthony à Wood – she captured the heart of the Earl of Oxford, then a childless widower of forty-four. He was a Knight of the Garter, handsome, famously rich, notoriously proud; he was also a lover of the theatre (as his loan of his coronation robes would evince). However, these were the early years before the identification of actress and 'Miss' had thoroughly set in, and there is reason to believe that Roxalana herself attached as much importance to her talent as to her looks; she was after all in proper employment and as the darling of the stage able to support herself.[24] She therefore began by refusing Lord Oxford's tender of protection.

Offers of services and presents were of no avail, so were insults, so, in the last resort, were 'spells' and incantations. Lord Oxford could neither smoke nor gamble as a result of his obsession. Various contemporary accounts agree that Hester Davenport only finally succumbed because Lord Oxford made it seem lawful for her to do so (an elaborate process which neither of them would probably have thought necessary ten years later). In Anthony Hamilton's words, where Love had failed, he 'invoked the aid of Hymen'.[25] First Lord Oxford displayed to his Roxalana a signed contract of marriage. He then enacted that scene which was to become a commonplace of Restoration drama, the fake wedding ceremony, with the minister played by his own trumpeter and the witness by his kettle-drummer. A fellow-actress, who was not in the plot, stood witness for Roxalana.

The next morning, according to the most colourful description of the episode (by the Baroness d'Aulnoy), Lord Oxford aroused his 'bride' with the surprising words: 'Wake up, Roxalana, it is time for you to go.' At which the betrayed woman burst out screaming and wounded her husband-lover with his own sword. The trumpeter and the kettle-drummer vanished; the actress-witness was told Roxalana had merely been playing a part in a play. Whatever her initial revulsion, Roxalana did continue the relationship; she left the stage and bore Lord Oxford a son, Aubrey de Vere, a couple of years – not nine months – later.

Nevertheless Anthony à Wood wrote of Roxalana as having married 'the Earl of Oxon', and another account criticized Lord Oxford for 'marrying his whore' as well as 'spending his estate'. Roxalana complained to the King that she had been deceived and secured a large pension of 1,000 crowns per annum. She also continued to term herself the Countess of Oxford for the rest of her life: at the time of her second – or first – marriage, which occurred after Lord Oxford's death in 1703, she was termed Dame Hester, Dowager Countess of Oxford; she signed her will Hester Oxford.[26] None of this prevented Lord Oxford himself from marrying, in 1673, that fascinating if promiscuous beauty Diana Kirke, successful rival to Mrs Grace Worthley for the affections of Henry Sidney (see pp. 395-6).

The solution may lie in the loose nature of marriage at the time. Given that Roxalana was joined together with Lord Oxford in some kind of union in some kind of ceremony, perhaps she herself did not inquire too closely into its validity. 'You may think she was but an actress . . .' observed Mrs Hobart to her fellow Maid of Honour Mrs Temple, telling this cautionary story about the evil intentions of the opposite sex;[27] yet in the early sixties, this mere actress might put up considerable resistance before sinking into the role of 'Miss'.

Peg Hughes, on the other hand, arrived on the stage five years later 'a mighty pretty woman' but not a modest one, for she had a reputation already for being Sir Charles Sedley's mistress.[28] She proceeded to capture the heart of that old warhorse, the King's cousin, Prince Rupert. Peg

Hughes's brother was a minor comedian (later killed in a brawl at Windsor over the relative claims of his sister and Nell Gwynn to be 'handsomer'). Her first appearance may have been as Desdemona in an *Othello* seen by Pepys in February 1669; she probably replaced another actress called Davenport, Frances, no relation to Hester, who had vanished 'to be kept by somebody' a few weeks earlier. Peg Hughes was certainly acting by the summer – in May Pepys was granted a back-stage kiss – although her first recorded performance was as Panura in Fletcher's *The Island Princess*.

Like Roxalana, Peg Hughes resisted her elderly royal admirer in the first place, although unlike Roxalana, she was hardly concerned to preserve her virtue. The fatal encounter took place at the fashionable spa of Tunbridge Wells; Queen Catherine had sent for the players from London to divert the court. To the ribald glee of the younger gallants and the open pleasure of the King, Prince Rupert became quickly obsessed by the 'mighty pretty' actress, deserting all his habitual scientific pastime. It was 'farewell to alembics, crucibles, furnaces and the black tools of alchemy; farewell to mathematical instruments and speculations! Powder and perfume now filled his whole mind ....'[29] At first Peg seems to have been reluctant to leave the fun of the stage and to have regarded the Prince's passion as rather ridiculous (perhaps he was one of those who, as in Madam Cresswell's advice to Dorothea, recalled 'Naseby fight' in moments of amorous excitement).

The following year more worldly counsels prevailed. Peg Hughes became the Prince's mistress, being installed by him in a substantial house at Hammersmith (George IV's spurned Queen, Caroline, later lived there). She bore him a daughter named Ruperta in 1673, at which point she quitted the stage for three years. It should be said that Peg Hughes, whose acting had been widely praised by her contemporaries, also proved an admirable concubine. At first there were local difficulties: in 1674 Peg Hughes was suspected of acquiring some of the jewels which had once belonged to Prince Rupert's mother, Elizabeth of Bohemia. But as the years wore on, Prince Rupert's sister, the Electress Sophia, grew to appreciate the good care which Peg took of her elderly protector. The Electress described Mrs Hughes as '*très modeste*', or at least the most modest of that not conspicuously modest English court; she wished 'Mistress Hus' (or sometimes Hews) had produced a son for her brother, but in any case wished to embrace 'pretty Ruperta'.[30]

In 1682 Prince Rupert's health began to give way. He praised Peg Hughes's solicitude in a letter to the Electress which also conveyed a picture of the happy family life enjoyed in Hammersmith: 'She [Peg] took great care of me during my illness', he told his sister, 'and I am obliged to her for many things.... As for the little one [Ruperta] she cannot resemble me, she is turning into the prettiest creature. She already rules the whole house and sometimes argues with her mother, which makes us all laugh.' Prince Rupert died at the end of November. In his will, for which the Earl of Craven was trustee, he divided his property between 'Margaret Hewes' and 'Ruperta my natural daughter begotten on the body of the said Margaret Hewes'. In addition Ruperta was charged to be a good obedient daughter and not to marry without her mother's consent.[31]

Ruperta carried out her father's dying commands. She made a suitable match to Lieutenant-General Emmanuel Scroope of Norfolk, and had children.† Peg Hughes was the giddy one, and in the end Ruperta had to look after her mother (Peg lived till 1719). Despite receiving the huge sum of £6,000 from the will of Prince Rupert, Peg Hughes gambled it all away. Another of Tom Brown's fictional dialogues in *Letters from the Dead to the Living* took place between Peg and Nell Gwynn, her rival for 'handsomeness'. Nell Gwynn's sentiments were probably based on truth. Nell was made to reproach Peg for losing by gambling what she had acquired by whoredom: 'for a woman who has enriched herself by one, to impoverish herself by the other, is so great a fault, that a harlot deserves correction for it'.[32]

*   *   *

Anne Marshall, who shares with Mary Betterton the claim to be the first professional English actress, was one of a pair of striking dark-haired sisters; later in her career she acted under her married name of Mrs Anne Quin, leaving the title of 'Mrs Marshall' to her younger sister Rebecca or 'Beck'.[33] The equation of dark tints with tragic grandeur marked both women out for the proud and passionate female roles created pre-eminently by Dryden, in the new type of 'heroic drama', the opposite pole to the brightness and lightness (and lewdness) of Restoration comedy. Rebecca Marshall had the additional advantage for queenly roles – of which there was a plentiful supply – of being very tall. 'Behold how night sits lovely on her Eye-brows While day breaks from her eyes!', or 'Her quick black eye does wander with desire', or 'Her long black locks, on her fair shoulders flow'; these contemporary allusions commemorate the saturnine beauty of the Marshall sisters.

† Today Sir Rupert Bromley Bt represents the direct line of descent from Ruperta, Prince Rupert and of course Peg Hughes.

Anne Marshall, as a founder member of The King's Company and a leading lady there from 1661 onwards, played Zempoalla in *The Indian Queen* which Dryden co-wrote with Sir Robert Howard, and then Almeria in Dryden's *The Indian Emperor*. Pepys praised her Zempoalla and thought it done 'excellently well, as ever I heard woman in my life', even if Anne Marshall's voice was not quite so sweet as Mrs Betterton's.[34] But in depicting the character of Zempoalla, 'the usurping Indian Queen' of Mexico who fell in love with her enemy Montezuma, a little stridency would not have come amiss, for she habitually expressed herself in lines like these:

> Great God of vengeance, here I firmly vow,
> Make but my Mexicans successful now,
> And with a thousand feasts thy flames I'll feed;
> And that I take, shall on the altars bleed. . . .[35]

At the end of the play, defeated and her love scorned, Zempoalla killed herself. Almeria in the sequel was Zempoalla's daughter, equally beautiful, equally tempestuous, equally proud. Catching the eye of the new Emperor of Mexico, Montezuma, who proposed to take her as his wife, Almeria vowed to use his passion to avenge her mother:

> If news be carried to the shades below
> The Indian queen will be more pleased, to know
> That I his scorns on him, who scorned her, pay.[36]

At the end of *The Indian Emperor* however it was Almeria's destiny, like that of her mother, to die. She killed herself at the feet of the Spanish conqueror Cortez, the object of her unrequited love, as Montezuma had been that of Zempoalla.

Rebecca Marshall joined her sister at The King's Company sometime in the summer of 1663 but seems to have been a mere apprentice up until the closure of the theatres in June 1665. Besides being always plagued with debt she had a stormy character: in real life her adventures, if not on such a lofty level, were at least as tempestuous as those of Dryden's 'barbarian Princesses'. In 1665 she complained about the attentions of a certain Mark Trevor of the Temple to the Lord Chamberlain (considered the protector as well as the licenser of the theatrical profession); Mark Trevor responded by assaulting her. This brought a second complaint from Rebecca Marshall: that Mark Trevor had 'affronted her both on and off the stage, attacked her in a coach with his sword etc., and threatens vengeance for her complaining of him to the Lord Chamberlain'.[37]

Two years later there was further trouble with Sir Hugh Middleton. Having insulted the women of The King's Company as a whole, he had the temerity to come round to their tiring-room at the Theatre Royal. Beck Marshall forthwith and roundly denounced him. Sir Hugh Middleton denounced *her*, calling her 'a jade'. Beck then went to the King and secured his promise of protection. Unfortunately she proceeded to boast of this moral victory. Whereupon Sir Hugh Middleton hired some ruffians who waylaid the actress on her way home and rubbed the most disgusting filth all over her. In general Beck Marshall could look after herself: in a further row with Orange Moll, plying her wares at the theatre, both sides gave as good as they got in language and blows.

Naturally her morals were not elevated. She had for example a liaison with the famous fop Sir George Hewell, to whom she bore a daughter. A satire of 1683 suggested that the daughter was no more virtuous than the mother:

> Proud Curtizan Marshall, 'Tis the time to give o'er
> Since now your Daughter, she is turned whore.

Beck Marshall also acted as go-between or procuress to Barbara Duchess of Cleveland, who conceived a passion for the well-known actor Charles Hart.

At the reopening of the theatres in November 1666, the position between the sisters was reversed. The interregnum had given an opportunity to the younger actresses to come to the fore, prominent among them the ex-orange-girl Nell Gwynn with her pretty legs and her talent for comedy, and the 'mighty pretty and fine and noble' Beck Marshall: 'very handsome near-hand' wrote Pepys, sitting close to her at the theatre. In December 1666 Beck Marshall played the part of Evadne, the corrupted heroine of Beaumont and Fletcher's *The Maid's Tragedy*, a part hitherto considered the prerogative of her sister. Pepys noted that 'the younger Marshall' had become 'a pretty good actor'. Early the next year it was Rebecca Marshall who played the lead part of the Queen of Sicily in Dryden's *Secret Love or The Maiden Queen* – 'very good and passionate' – while Anne, having been transformed into Mrs Quin by marriage at some unknown date in between, was condemned to play the secondary part of Candiope, Princess of the Blood; Nell Gwynn incidentally scored a great success in the 'comical' part of Florimel, the Maid of Honour.[38]

The situation was not to be borne, at least from the elder sister's point of view. Nor did Anne Marshall Quin attempt to bear it. She left the theatre once more shortly afterwards and petitioned the Lord Chamberlain to restore her to her old roles – and her old stature as a leading lady. This included the privilege of a dressing-room for her own private use. As a result on 4 May 1667 the Lord Chamberlain instructed The King's Company to admit Mrs Anne Quin 'to Act again at Theatre Royall and that you assign her all her own parts which she formerly had and that none other be permitted to act any of her parts without her consent. And that you assign her a dressing room with a chimney in it to be only for her use and whom she shall admit.'[39]

The petition worked. In a performance of Boyle's *The Black Prince* in October 1667, elder sisters will be relieved to learn that Anne Quin played the romantic part of Alizia Pierce, while younger sisters will burn to hear that Rebecca Marshall played the dull part of Plantagenet. The important part of Donna Aurelia in Dryden's *An Evening's Love* followed for Anne Quin in 1668, with Rebecca Marshall uncast. Anne Quin also re-created her famous part of Zempoalla in June 1668; if Pepys no longer doted upon her quite so much, the rest of the world was full of praise.[40]

However, by October 1669 Mrs Quin had left The King's Company once more, to reappear some years later in The Duke's Company, where she played the part of the courtesan Angelica Bianca in Aphra Behn's *The Rover* and a whole list of other important parts in the late seventies and early eighties (she is last heard of in 1682). These included Lady Knowall, Aphra Behn's caricature of Mary Astell, in *Sir Patient Fancy*; Lady Squeamish in Otway's *Friendship in Fashion*, and Queen Elizabeth in Banks's *The Unhappy Favourite* (a role to which her regal appearance and manner were especially well suited).

The departure of her sister left Rebecca Marshall in full command at The King's Company. She took over the part of Donna Aurelia, and continued as a leading actress there until 1677 when she briefly caught up with her sister again at The Duke's Company for a few months before leaving the stage for good.

It has to be borne in mind that for all the worldly advancement of a Roxalana, a Peg Hughes, and the busy Marshall sisters there were many actresses who fell through the net, were not fought over at court, or ended their lives as 'Dame Hester, Countess of Oxford', but like Gosnell, faltered and disappeared. Elizabeth Farley, generally known as Mrs Weaver, was one of these. She was born about 1640, and as a member of The King's Company from 1660 to 1665, played secondary roles at the Theatre Royal.

According to Pepys's actress friend Mrs Knepp, Elizabeth Farley was 'first spoiled' i.e. seduced, by the King himself. If true, the relationship did not last very long, for by the winter of 1660 Elizabeth Farley was living

with James Weaver, a gentleman of Gray's Inn.[41] Although she was never
married to Weaver, Elizabeth Farley ran up bills of credit as his wife, and
was also generally listed as Mrs Weaver in the cast lists of the theatre.
Weaver not only cast off his mistress but also sought permission of the
Lord Chamberlain to sue her for the return of £30; and she had other
debts. Furthermore Elizabeth Farley was by now pregnant, although she
continued desperately to act, since so long as she was a member of The
King's Company, she was immune from arrest.

The visible signs of her pregnancy could not be concealed for ever. 'Mrs
Weaver' was finally discharged. Carefully misrepresenting the cause of her
dismissal, Elizabeth Farley appealed to the King for reinstatement. Sir
Henry Bennet, on behalf of the King, was ordered to see to it. At this
point Sir Robert Howard, the principal shareholder in The King's Company, issued an indignant protest. Mrs Weaver, he said, had been dismissed
because she was 'big with child' and 'shamefully so' since she was not
married. Women of quality were declaring that they could not possibly
come to the theatre to watch an actress in such a condition. 'Truly, Sir, we
are willing to bring the Stage to be a place of some Credit, and not an
infamous place for all persons of Honour to avoid', protested Howard.[42]
(This was at a moment, incidentally, when the King's *maîtresse en titre*,
Barbara, future Duchess of Cleveland, was just recovering from the birth
of the second of the five bastards she bore to the King; admittedly she was
legally married to Roger Palmer at the time; nevertheless the genteel
protest was striking evidence of the double standard which operated.)

Elizabeth Farley did return to the stage, and played the part of 'fair
Alibech', Almeria's sympathetic younger sister, in *The Indian Emperor* of
1665, a secondary but not unimportant role. Debts continued to pursue
her. When the theatres closed in the summer of 1665 owing to the plague
she effectively vanished from view. It is possible she returned to the stage
from time to time in the 1670s, under her own name; but if she is the 'Mrs
Farley' named in a poem of Rochester's she became a prostitute.

*   *   *

Elizabeth Barry – 'famous Madam Barry' – was by acclaim the greatest
actress of the Restoration period and beyond, her reign extending from
the 1670s until 1710, when she made her last appearance on the stage. Yet
the beginnings of her story are such as to encourage any first-time failure
on the stage to persevere. What was more, she might never have pursued
her career further had not the most notorious libertine of the age, the Earl
of Rochester, come 'buzzing about her Honey-Pot'.

Mrs Elizabeth Pepys, wife of the diarist.

Lady Isabella Thynne, who according to
Aubrey was 'most beautiful ... but she
could not subdue one thing'. The wife of Sir
James Thynne of Longleat, she was formally
separated from him in 1653; her talent for
music was commemorated by Waller's
poem 'Of my Lady Isabella playing on the
Lute'. From the School of Van Dyck.

Basua Makin, governess to Princess Elizabeth, daughter of Charles I, before the Civil War. She later founded a school in which she hoped to inculcate the classics.

Below: Mary Duchess of Beaufort and her sister Elizabeth Countess of Carnarvon, holding a flower painting, with her initials 'E.C.' and a coronet in the left-hand corner. Flower-painting, unlike the study of the classics, was considered a proper feminine accomplishment. Painted by Sir Peter Lely.

Rachel Lady Russell, wife of the Whig Martyr William Lord Russell who was executed in 1683.

Above: The poet Anne Kingsmill, Countess of Winchilsea, by Lawrence Crosse.

Anne Killigrew. A self-portrait used in the book of her poems published in 1686, after her death.

Elizabeth Barry. A portrait after Kneller.

A painting by Samuel van Hoogstraeten thoug[ht]
to portray Anne Viscountess Conway.

The actress Peg Hughes, mistress of Prince Rupert of the Rhine. By Lely.

Right: A London courtesan, by Laroon. She holds a mask, the badge of her profession, in her hand.

Diana Kirke, later Countess of Oxford, one of the celebrated courtesans of the English court. By Lely.

Diana Kirke
Css. of Oxford.

Catherine Sedley, Countess of
Dorchester, mistress of James II. A
portrait from the studio of Lely.

The 'incomparable' Mrs Jane Myddelton.
An engraving after Lely.

The Figure Explained:

Being a Dissection of the Womb, with the usual manner how the Child lies therein near the time of its Birth.

B B. The inner parts of the *Chorion* extended and branched out.

C. The *Amnion* extended.

D D. The Membrane of the Womb extended and detached.

E. The Fleshy substance call'd the *Cake* or *Placenta*, which nourishes the Infant, it is full of Vessels.

F. The Vessels appointed for the Navel string.

G. The Navel string carrying nourishment from the *Placenta* to the Navel.

H H H. The manner how the Infant lieth in the Womb near the time of its Birth.

I. The Navel string how it enters into the Navel.

Above. An illustration from *The Midwives Book* by Jane Sharp (1671): this was the first book on the subject written by a woman in English and went through many editions.

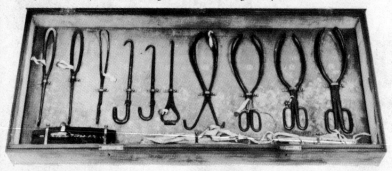

The set of gynaecological instruments, including forceps, owned by Dr Peter Chamberlen which were discovered in the nineteenth century concealed in a box.

A medal struck to commemorate the birth of Prince James Edward Stuart to James II and Mary of Modena in 1689.

A satirical version of the birth of Prince James which draws on the legend of Erichthonius, half man, half monster, who appears out of a basket. The implication is that, hideous and deformed, he could not be of royal blood and must be a pretender. It was suggested by the Whigs that this baby (known to history as the Old Pretender) had been smuggled into the palace in a warming-pan.

No one ever pretended Mrs Barry numbered beauty among her gifts: 'middle-sized' with 'darkish Hair, light eyes, dark Eye-brows ... indifferently plump', was one unenthusiastic description.[43] She also had a mouth which was slightly drawn up on one side, which she used to try to conceal by composing her face as though about to be painted. Her portrait by Kneller shows a face which is distinctly plain, with a Roman nose and thick lips; even if there is an air of intelligence about it, and more than a hint of determination.

It is easy to believe from such a picture that Mrs Barry at the height of her fame was held to be 'the Finest Woman in the World upon the Stage, and the ugliest Woman off on't'.[44] Nevertheless it was not likely that the homely creature she represented as a girl would have caught Rochester's eye had Mrs Barry not belonged to the traditionally promiscuous profession of actress. It can be argued therefore that this aura of promiscuity, while it ruined some young women, helped to advance Mrs Barry.

The story of Mrs Barry, like her origins, has to be pieced together from various (often conflicting) accounts.[45] It seems that she first appeared on the stage in 1674 when she was sixteen. Mrs Barry was thus some twenty years younger than Mrs Betterton and Hester Davenport, the founders of her profession. She played Isabella Queen of Hungary in *Mustapha*, by Roger Boyle, Earl of Orrery (brother of Mary Countess of Warwick and Katherine Viscountess Ranelagh). This début was a disaster. According to Colley Cibber, Mrs Barry was considered so feeble that she was discharged from the company at the end of her first year. Anthony Aston wrote: 'for some time they could make nothing of her; she could neither sing nor dance', not even in a country dance. Mrs Barry was not the only actress-goose whom Rochester determined to turn into a swan. Had he not attempted the same transformation on Sarah Cooke – 'Miss Sarah' – that 'Mistaken Drab' so utterly unable even after Rochester's tuition to impress the critical Wits, that she was ordered back to her 'Mother's stall'? It would therefore not be right to credit Rochester with an unerring eye in this respect: he struck unlucky with 'Miss Sarah' for all her ravishing looks; with Mrs Barry, much less easy on the eye, he struck very lucky indeed.

What should be credited to him without reservation is the manner of his tutorage. This, which might be described as an early form of method-acting, in the hands of the amazing Mrs Barry enabled her to give a proper reality, something rare indeed at the time, to the whole range of female parts in Restoration drama: 'solemn and august' in tragedy, 'alert, easy and genteel' in comedy.[46] As we have seen, the first generation of actresses (with the exception of Mrs Betterton) tended to be admired in one or the other.

The original failing of Mrs Barry was that while she had 'an excellent understanding' she lacked a musical ear: thus she could not catch 'the sounds or emphases taught her; but fell into a disagreeable tone, the fault of most young stage-adventurers'. Lord Rochester's solution was 'to enter into the meaning of every sentiment; he taught her not only the proper cadence or sounding of the voice, but to seize also the passions, and adapt her whole behaviour to the situations of the characters'. He would rehearse her in a part more than thirty times. As a result Betterton said that she could transform a play that would disgust the most patient reader, calling her 'incomparable': 'her action was always just, and produced naturally by the sentiments of the part'. At a time when artificial heroics were considered an inevitable concomitant of such heroines as those created by Dryden, Mrs Barry could wipe away real tears when acting out a tragic death scene.[47]

Rochester had taken over Mrs Barry's career in the first place for a bet: after the disastrous début, he vowed he would make her the most accomplished performer at the Dorset Garden Theatre (the new home of The Duke's Company) within six months. He certainly won his bet. *Alcibiades*, the first tragedy by Thomas Otway, performed in September 1675, featured Thomas Betterton in the title role, with Mrs Betterton as his betrothed Timandra; it was in the small part of Alcibiades' sister Draxilla that Mrs Barry reappeared on the London stage. It was probably after this and before her appearance as Leonora in *Abdelazar* by Aphra Behn the following July that Rochester coached her, although the precise sequence is uncertain.[48] At all events, the new improved Mrs Barry captured more than critical attention: she also won the heart of Thomas Otway. As a result, he laid at her feet the type of bouquet which only a playwright can bestow upon an actress – a series of plays. Mrs Barry dazzled in such varied parts as Monimia, the pathetic eponymous heroine of *The Orphan*, and Lavinia (Juliet) in Otway's adaptation of *Romeo and Juliet*. This was an unpopular play, at least in Shakespeare's version, after the Restoration. Otway's adaptation, which also drew on Plutarch, was entitled *The History and Fall of Caius Marius*; which led to Mrs Barry as Lavinia pronouncing (to her lover, known as Marius junior) the interesting line: 'O Marius, Marius, wherefore art thou Marius.'[49] Most striking of all Mrs Barry's creations in the first flush of her success was that of 'beauteous Belvidera', the plangent heroine of *Venice Preserv'd*.

In all however Mrs Barry created over 100 roles, at The Duke's Company, as the leading lady of The United Company after 1682, and at the breakaway Lincoln's Inn Fields Company after 1695; although by now she was surrendering the juvenile leading parts to a rising young actress called Anne Bracegirdle. Her parts included that of Hellena in Aphra Behn's *The Rover* (a 'breeches' part), Arabella in Ravenscroft's *The London Cuckolds*, Lady Brute in Vanbrugh's *The Provok'd Wife* and Cordelia in another of those bastard versions of Shakespeare which audiences so much preferred to the glorious originals, Nahum Tate's *Lear* (Cordelia finally married Edgar and lived happily ever after). In 1694 Thomas Southerne, author of *The Fatal Marriage*, paid a graceful tribute to her handling of Isabella, his ill-fated heroine: 'I made the play for her part, and her part has made the play for me.'[50]

In *Venice Preserv'd*, Thomas Betterton as Jaffeir gave Mrs Barry as Belvidera, on her first entrance, this lyrical salutation which sums up the romantic view of the female in the late seventeenth century:

> Sure all ill-stories of thy sex are false:
> O woman! lovely woman! Nature made thee
> To temper man: we had been brutes without you:
> Angels are painted fair, to look like you;
> There's in you all that we believe of heaven,
> Amazing brightness, purity and truth![51]

It was ironic under the circumstances that Mrs Barry herself, angel painted fair on stage as she might be, was the focus of so many 'ill-stories' off it, which if only half of them were true, more than justified the opposing cynical view of the female sex. Mrs Barry was dissolute ('She has been a Rioter in her time', wrote Gildon): that in itself was not unusual. She was bad-tempered and at times even violent. Although her good breeding – more or less – was said to make her on stage 'Mistress of that Behaviour which sets off the well-bred Gentlewoman', Mrs Barry was capable of exhibiting quite another side to her character, stage or no stage. In a famous incident, Mrs Barry and 'Chestnut-maned [Betty] Boutel', acting in Lee's *The Rival Queens*, quarrelled over a scarf as the play was about to begin. On the all-too appropriate line:

> Die, sorceress, die and all my wrongs die with thee!

Mrs Barry as Roxana struck Mrs Boutel playing the rival queen Statira with such force that her blunted stage dagger managed to penetrate Mrs Boutel's stays, and pierce the flesh beneath.[52]

Furthermore Mrs Barry was mercenary. Where her professional life was concerned, that was understandable, in view of the low salaries paid to actresses at the time: for example, she insisted on receiving the proceeds of a benefit at the theatre, hitherto generally reserved for writers. But she was also mercenary where her affections were concerned, to an extent that amazed even this worldly age. It was not so much the settlement she was supposed to have secured from the playwright Sir George Etherege (Mrs Barry could see for herself what happened to the unendowed actress), but Tom Brown wrote: 'Should you lie with her all night, she would not know you next morning, unless you had another five pounds at your service.' The lampoons which blasted the private lives of all the famous actresses and courtesans of the time (with the ever glowing exception of Mrs Betterton) showed in later years a particular bitterness towards the 'slattern Betty Barry'.

> At thirty eight a very hopeful whore,
> The only one o 'th' trade that's not profuse,
> (A policy was taught her by the Jews),
> Tho' still the highest bidder she will choose.

At the same time it had to be admitted that Mrs Barry was one whom 'every fop upon the stage admires'.[53] It was as though her defiant combination of talent and calculation was especially exacerbating.

Thomas Otway despaired of Mrs Barry's treatment of him: while accepting the parts, it is said that she would not even requite his besotted love with a kiss. Otway referred to himself as being fobbed off 'with gross, thick, homespun friendship, the common Coin that passes betwixt Worldly Interests'. He addressed a series of agonized letters to his beloved, confessing that since the first day he saw her, 'I have hardly enjoy'd one Hour of perfect Quiet'; and yet he could not break loose: 'though I have languished for seven long tedious Years of Desire, jealously and despairingly; yet, every Minute I see you, I still discover something new and bewitching'.[54]

Otway was bitter in the knowledge that Rochester had succeeded where he had failed: 'I have consulted my Pride, whether after a Rival's Possession I ought to ruin all my Peace for a Woman that another has been more blest in, though no Man ever loved as I did: But Love, victorious Love, o'er throws all that, and tells me, it is his Nature never to remember; he still looks forward from the present hour, expecting new Dawns, new rising Happiness, never looks back, never regards what is past, left behind him, but buries and forgets it quite in the hot fierce pursuit of Joy before him.' On the other hand Rochester, on the evidence of his own letters (thirty-four survive, although they are undated and the originals have vanished), suffered equally from jealousy where Mrs Barry was concerned, for all the consummation of his desire. It was thought by contemporaries that Mrs Barry was the great love of Rochester's life: she was 'his passion', wrote one, and another claimed that he never loved anyone else 'so sincerely' as Mrs Barry.[55]

In poetry Rochester could serenade 'The Mistress' with elegance:

> An age in her embraces past
>   Would seem a winter's day,
> Where life and light with envious haste
>   Are torn and snatch'd away.
>
> But, oh! how slowly minutes roll,
>   When absent from her eyes,
> That fed my love, which is my soul,
>   It languishes and dies.

The letters were less controlled: 'Madam, There is now no minute of my life that does not afford me some new argument how much I love you; the little joy I take in every thing wherein you are not concern'd, the pleasing perplexity of endless thought, which I fall into, wherever you are brought to my remembrance; and lastly, the continual disquiet I am in, during your absence, convince me sufficiently that I do you justice in loving you, so as woman was never loved before.' And again: 'Seeing you is as necessary to my life as breathing; so that I must see you, or be yours no more; for that's the image I have of dying. . . .' Writing to Mrs Barry at three in the morning, a letter of furious expostulation, Rochester ended: 'I thank God I can distinguish, I can see very woman in you. . . . 'Tis impossible for me to curse you; but give me leave to pity myself, which is more than ever you will do for me.'[56]

Rochester's relationship with Mrs Barry lasted for about four years; towards the end of it, in 1677, she bore him a daughter. Rochester was by this time immured in the country, crippled and virtually blind from disease, moving towards that classic reprobate's deathbed in which he would abandon his wicked ways for the consolations of religion. Savile broke the news to him: 'Your Lordship has a daughter born by the body of Mrs Barry of which I give your honour joy.' Savile added that the mother's lying-in was not being held in 'much state' since Mrs Barry was living in great poverty in the Mall. The woman who had taken her in was 'not without some gentle reflections on your Lordship's want either of generosity or bowels [compassion] towards a lady who had not refused you the full enjoyment of her charms'.[57]

Rochester was however at this point pursued by his creditors as well as cut off from London by his physical condition, so that it is difficult to see how he could in fact have helped his mistress financially. He contented himself with writing to her: 'Madam, Your safe delivery has deliver'd me too from fears for your sake, which were, I'll promise you, as burthensome to me, as your great belly could be to you. Every thing has fallen out to my wish, for you are out of danger, and the child is of the soft sex I love. ....' The child, mentioned in Rochester's will under the name of Elizabeth Clarke, where she was left £40, died in 1689 at the age of twelve. At some point before Rochester's death in 1682 little Elizabeth Clarke was taken away briefly from her mother's care because of her want of 'discretion' in bringing her up. Rochester wrote firmly but kindly on the subject: 'Madam, I am far from delighting in the grief I have given you, by taking away the child: and you, who made it so absolutely necessary for me to do so, must take that excuse from me, for all the ill nature of it ...! I hope very shortly to restore to you a finer girl than ever.'[58]

Doubtless Mrs Barry did show lack of discretion in her way of life: 'You have a character, and you maintain it', wrote Rochester in one of the anguished letters.[59] Yet her legendary rapacity and even her coldness and severity towards her admirers are at least explicable when one bears in mind the alternative: the wretched downfall experienced by an actress like Elizabeth Farley. Famous as Mrs Barry was, she had no alternative but to give birth to her child in poverty, without support from husband or lover, and only the help of a 'protectress'; that was the predictable fate of an actress who became pregnant. A little rapacity may be pardoned under the circumstances.

Mrs Barry retired to Acton – then pleasant countryside – when she finally left the stage in her fifties after her long reign. She died there in 1713. She is said to have been the victim of a bite from a pet lap-dog, which she did not know had been 'seized with madness'.[60] If the story is true, it was an appropriately bizarre and tragic end for the first of the great English dramatic actresses, a line of descent leading down to Mrs Siddons in the next century.

Although her plain memorial stone is still to be seen in the church at Acton where she lies buried, the words of Colley Cibber himself constitute her best epitaph: 'Mrs Barry, in Characters of Greatness, had a Presence of elevated Dignity, her Mien and Motion superb and gracefully majestick;

her Voice full, clear, and strong, so that no Violence of Passion could be too much for her: And when Distress or Tenderness possess'd her, she subsided into the most affecting Melody and Softness. In the Art of exciting Pity She had a Power beyond all the Actresses I have yet seen, or what your Imagination can conceive.'[61]

22   *The Modest Midwife*

> 'It is observable that in all the ages of the world and throughout all countries in the world, the help of grave and modest women (with us termed Midwives) hath ever been useful for release and succour of all the daughters of Evah, whom God hath appointed to bear children into this world.'
>
> JACOB RUEFF, *The Expert Midwife*, 1637

In the seventeenth century every woman who had the opportunity to conceive was likely to give birth at least once during her lifetime: the heiress, the Quaker, the prostitute and the actress were all equal in this respect. And if a woman did not actually give birth, she had some other form of obstetrical experience. In the absence of any form of birth control (even coitus interruptus being notoriously uncertain) it was celibacy not marriage which was the relevant fact. Under the circumstances there were few women of the time from the idealistic Margaret Fell to the exotic Elizabeth Barry who did not fall at some point into the hands of those 'grave and modest women (with us termed Midwives)' in the words of Jacob Rueff's textbook of obstetrics.[1] The midwives could also be the agents of drama beyond the mere expedition of birth. It was the midwives' brutal 'search' of Frances Lady Purbeck, to prove her adultery with Sir Robert Howard, which caused her to flee her mother-in-law's roof. Witches were also subject to a routine search by the local midwives to discover the devil's marks; as were those women who sought to escape punishment on the grounds that they were pregnant.

The all-pervasive presence of the midwife in women's lives may be illustrated by the indignant sentiments of *The Midwives Just Petition* of January 1643: let war cease, men return again to their wives so as to 'bring them yearly under the delivering power of the midwife'. *The Midwives Just Complaint* of 22 September 1646 echoed the thought: to the midwives, 'whereas many miseries do attend upon civil wars', nothing was worse than the gross interruption to their trade: 'For many men, hopeful to have begot a race of soldiers, were there killed on a sudden, before they had performed anything to the benefit of midwives.' Such a development was to be lamented: 'We were formerly well paid and highly respected in our parishes for our great skill and midnight industry; but now our art doth fail us, and little getting have we in this age, barren of all natural joys, and only fruitful of bloody calamities.'[2]

At first sight there is something wonderfully solipsistic about this interpretation of recent military events in England as being aimed at the overthrow of the midwives' 'midnight industry' rather than more political changes. Yet to most women of the time, caught up in their cycle of perpetual parturition, the complaint would have been perfectly comprehensible. For they too were caught up in the 'midnight industry' which touched most females far more closely than politics.

It could be said that nothing was more crucial to the life of the average woman than the character and skills of her midwife. Doctors were rarely in attendance at births, and when they were, concentrated on the rich, for obvious reasons. The rise of the so-called 'Man-Midwife' in the course of the seventeenth century, once again affected only the tiny percentage of people who could afford his services.[3] For most women, lying-in meant the attendance of a female, whom it was devoutly hoped would be skilled enough to bring about an easy birth and leave behind a live mother and live child when she left.

There were thus a vast range of professional helps available, from the grand midwives who attended the royal *accouchements* down to the humble helpmates of the poor. Where the latter were concerned a shilling or two was a normal fee at the beginning of the seventeenth century; whereas towards the end of it the anonymous business diary of a midwife shows a prosperous trade with some form of sliding scale.[4] In 1696 this midwife recorded about two deliveries a month, for payments varying from 5s to 10s. On 24 August 1698 Mrs Rowell paid her 12s 6d for the delivery of a daughter at the awkward time of seven o'clock on a Sunday morning – but since the midwife was also able to record that she 'laid Mrs Clarke next door' in the course of the same visit, she only charged the latter 2s 6d. By 1719, this midwife was attending approximately three confinements a month and charging an average of £1 a visit; all of which amounted to a handsome income. The midwife had a large practice in the Old Bailey area of the City of London, but a connection with the Barnardiston family – she attended to a number of their confinements – took her as far as Cornwall where she 'laid Madam Barnardiston'. All the same, the midwife was also aware of her social duty: when she 'laid a woman in the market' no payment was recorded, presumably because the mother was of the poor.

Then there were the payments traditionally made by the godparents to the midwife as well as the nurse (for this, if for no other reason, the midwife had a vested interest in delivering a live infant, for no baby meant no baptism, no 'gossip', and thus no present). In 1661 Pepys as godfather made a payment of 10s to the midwife. At the end of the century Sir Walter Calverley Bt was in the habit of giving a guinea or 20s regularly to the midwives of his godchildren.[5]

Attendance at a royal birth brought heavy responsibilities, a fact acknowledged by the handsome rewards which followed. James 1's Queen, Anne of Denmark, gave birth to a number of children both before and after her arrival in England from Scotland: Alice Dennis, an English midwife, was paid £100 on two occasions. Another English midwife, Margaret Mercer, set off for Heidelberg in 1616 with a train of attendants in order to deliver the baby of Elizabeth of Bohemia, the Queen's daughter; for this she received a total of £84 4s.[6]

On the other hand Charles 1's Queen, Henrietta Maria, as a French Princess, preferred a French midwife. In May 1629, Henrietta Maria was confined with her first child ten weeks prematurely; this was unfortunately far too early for the attendance of the famous French midwife Madame Péronne, who was much in demand – the baby died. The royal doctor Sir Theodore Mayerne hastened to send a message to France that Madame Péronne's services were now no longer needed in England; she should be directed instead to the bedside of the Princess of Piedmont. The next year the Queen was pregnant again. This time Madame Péronne arrived well in advance, dispatched by Henrietta Maria's mother, Marie de Medici. The successful delivery of a healthy boy – the future King Charles 11 – after a labour of eight hours, was rewarded by the elated royal father with a payment to Madame Péronne of £1,000.[7]

Henrietta Maria had the advantage of her English in-laws because midwifery was in a more advanced state in France, with a noted school for midwives being established at the Hôtel-Dieu in Paris, including six weekly lectures on anatomy. The first midwife to enjoy an international reputation had indeed been a Frenchwoman named Louise Bourgeois, who published several books on obstetrics in the early seventeenth century.[8] One of England's most celebrated midwives in the first part of the seventeenth century was herself of foreign origin: Aurelia Florio, one of the midwives who examined the supposed witches of Lancashire, was the daughter of the scholar John Florio, Groom of the Privy Chamber and Reader in Italian to Anne of Denmark. She married the surgeon James Molins, member of a celebrated English medical family, and herself bore seven children, all of whom, no doubt as a result of their parents' combined abilities, grew to adulthood. Aurelia Florio died in 1641, but recent research in the registers of St Andrew, Holborn, has shown that her accomplished handling of her patients was commemorated by the unusual name Aurelia being bestowed on at least seven girls she had delivered, who were not apparently related to her.[9]

Alas, the very tribute indicated how few English midwives approached the standards and skill of an Aurelia Florio. The problem was partly one of language – as it so often was where women were concerned in this period. Only a handful of women could read Latin, the language of medical textbooks, and very few of the midwife class were to be counted among their number. But there was a remarkable scarcity of manuals written in English. The first one printed in England, entitled *The Byrth of Mankind*, had actually been translated from the Latin, which in turn had been translated from the German; after publication in 1540, it ran through thirteen editions, the last in 1654.[10] Such a long reign without medical updating demonstrated not only the desperate need for such sources, but also the primitive, virtually stationary nature of obstetrical knowledge at this time.

Jacob Rueff's textbook *The Expert Midwife*, printed in an English translation in 1637, first appeared in Latin under the title *De Conceptu et Generatione Hominis* in 1554. Rueff, himself an expert surgeon, paid tribute in his Introduction to the ancient origins of the midwives' profession: 'It is observable that in all the ages of the world and throughout all countries in the world . . .' such women had ever been useful 'for release and succour of all the daughters of Evah, whom God hath appointed to bear children into this world.' At the same time he pointed to the undeniable weakness of women as active obstetricians: the two methods of learning being the use of books or 'conference with the skilful', women were unhappily liable to fall behind in the former, since they were traditionally unable to understand anything except their native tongue.

Rueff's book, in its English translation, was intended to remedy this state of affairs. Nor did it approve in principle of the rise of the 'Man-Midwife'. On the contrary, it stated that some men had already gone far too far – 'perhaps for private profit' – in encroaching 'upon women's weaknesses and want of knowledge in these their peculiar businesses'.[11]

Rueff's argument that midwifery was the peculiar business of women (only sacrificed to men by default of learning) was certainly one with which the midwives themselves agreed. 'We knowing the cases of women better than any other', wrote a famous London midwife, Mrs Hester Shaw. Jane Sharp was another experienced midwife; in 1680 she either died or retired after forty years of active work. *The Midwives Book* of 1671, based on her experiences, was the first book of its sort written by an Englishwoman in English and as such is an interesting guide to women's own preoccupations on the subject. Like Rueff's book, that of Jane Sharp went through many editions, the last appearing in 1725 under the title of *The Compleat Midwife's Companion*, by popular demand, according to the printer. Jane Sharp was at pains to point out the range of her own studies: that she had had French, Dutch and Italian books on the subject translated in order to consult them. Like many others in her period, Jane Sharp took her stand on the Bible, and the fact that midwifery as a craft had been designed by God exclusively for the practice of women: 'Men-Midwives are forced to borrow the very name they practise by.... The holy Scriptures hath recorded Midwives to the perpetual honour of the female Sex, there being not so much one word concerning Men-midwives mentioned there.'[12]

Jane Sharp then quoted the story of Shiphrah and Puah, the heroic midwives of the Israelites, in the first chapter of Exodus, who were instructed by the Egyptian King to get ready to kill any boy babies when they saw a Hebrew woman 'upon the [birthing] stools'. (It was this order which led to the concealment of the baby Moses in the bulrushes by his sister Miriam.) Shiphrah and Puah however 'feared God, and did not as the king of Egypt commanded them, but saved the men children alive'. They pretended to the Egyptian King that Hebrew women, unlike the women of the Egyptians, had a habit of giving birth before they could be reached by a midwife. The story ended: 'Therefore God dealt well with the midwives ... he made them houses.'[13] (This text, in the hands of women, was to the concept of exclusive female midwifery what the famous text of St Paul in the hands of men was to the concept of exclusive male preaching.)

According to Jane Sharp, the very fact that men enjoyed a superior education and could unlike women gain a knowledge of anatomy at university, demonstrated God's support for women as midwives. Without divine approval in the role, how should women have managed to preserve their reputation down the ages? 'It is not hard words that perform the work,' wrote Jane Sharp, 'as if none understood the Art of midwifery that cannot understand Greek.'[14] Like the heroism of Shiphrah and Puah, the innate and essentially natural skills of the midwives, handed down from generation to generation of women, were another cardinal point in the fierce discussions which broke out as to whether 'Men-Midwives' had any right to function at all.

This belief in the natural, inherited skill of a woman (as opposed to a man) to deliver a baby safely and healthily was implicitly supported by society; just as nursing in general was regarded as the prerogative of the weaker but tenderer vessel – 'woman's work' wrote Sir Ralph Verney (see p. 201). At the beginning of the seventeenth century, the mistress of the household would count among her accomplishments not only cooking and the use of medicinal herbs, but also the ability to attend to her servants and neighbours in childbirth (Elizabeth Walker, for example, counted this among her good works). Lady Margaret Hoby was the pattern of the great lady ordering her servants and her estates, although unusual in that she kept a diary, half personal half spiritual, between 1599 and 1605 (the first known British woman's diary).[15] Of one particular Wednesday she wrote: 'In the morning at six o'clock I prayed privately: that done, I went to a wife in travail of child, about whom I was busy till one o'clock, about which time, she being delivered and I having praised God, returned home and betook myself to private prayer.' There are numerous other references to her attendances at the labours of local women; delivery being a basic female skill it was not considered relevant that Lady Margaret Hoby was herself childless. Mrs Pepys for example, who also had no children, was summoned to the bedside of Betty Mitchell in July 1668 'when she began to cry out'; she helped to deliver the child, and when it proved to be a girl, acted as her godmother.[16]

None of this emphasis on the archetypal role of women in the great drama of childbirth could however obliterate the unpleasant fact that all too many professional midwives were but ill-equipped to play it; since 'the business whereunto God hath ordained them [was] of so great and danger-ous consequence as concerns the very lives of all such as come into the world', Rueff wrote, and numbers of mothers and infants died unneces-sarily or were mutilated or otherwise injured as a result.[17] Jane Sharp was after all herself writing to remedy ignorance, while stoutly defending the exclusive right of her own sex to the work. As we shall see, a noted and independent-minded midwife of the time, Mrs Elizabeth Cellier, writing in the 1680s, ascribed an extraordinarily high figure of infant mortality to the mishandling of the midwives.

*   *   *

Horror stories of women and their babies being literally pulled apart, with fearful damage to both parties, abounded. Dr Percival Willughby, the son of Sir Percival Willughby of Wollaton in Cheshire, was a celebrated and skilful obstetrician. He published an account of his cases, the *Country Midwife's Opusculum*:[18] in which he cited one incident which took place in Threadneedle Street, in the City of London, where the midwife tugged the mother one way and the other women present tugged the emergent child the other. There were plenty of other tales of the protruding limbs of infants being cut off because they were holding up the process of birth.

Such stories fell into two main groups. In one the midwife accelerated the course of the labour unduly, instead of letting what Dr Willughby called 'Dame Nature, Eve's friend' do her own work, with far more satisfactory results: for example Dr Willughby related how 'poor silly Mary Baker' produced a perfectly good child on the bare freezing ground, having avoided being 'miserably tortured' by the midwives. In the other group, the midwife or midwives proved incapable of helping forward a highly difficult birth. Alice Thornton described in her autobiography how her son died in 1657 because the midwife lacked the skill to 'turn' him. Mrs Elizabeth Freke was another diarist, who wrote from 1671 to 1714, her literacy being due to the solicitude of her father, a Fellow of All Souls, who educated all his four daughters.[19] She gave a chilling description of the birth of her son Ralph Freke in Wiltshire in June 1675: the labour lasted an agonizing five days, with four midwives in perpetual attendance, including a 'Man-Midwife' who half-way through the proceedings pronounced the baby dead. Mrs Freke's benevolent neighbour Lady Thynne was also in attendance as a charitable duty, and it was Lady Thynne who eventually secured the services of yet another midwife, Mrs Mills; she it was who successfully delivered a living child. (Little Ralph Freke even survived another seventeenth-century peril a few months later when a careless nurse broke his leg, and hid him in bed to conceal the fact, pretending he was teething.)

Expert practitioners were highly prized: Dr Willughby educated his two daughters so well – once again in the great seventeenth-century tradition of benevolent educative fathers – that they both enjoyed thriving careers as expert midwives. One 'Mrs' Willughby began by accompanying her father on his rounds, with the advantage of being able to call in her father in a particularly difficult case. One such dilemma occurred with the confinement of the 'wife to one of Oliver's creatures', under Cromwell's Protectorate; Mrs Willughby hastened to call in the senior doctor for fear of the political implications. By 1658 she was practising in London with great success. Her sister specialized in the delivery of twins, never forcing the pace of the second birth. (Both Willughbys, incidentally, married, like most midwives of the time. The antiquary George Ballard and his clever sister were the children of a midwife.)[20]

The fame of a Quaker midwife in Reading, Frances Kent, was sufficient for the Verney family after the Restoration to consider employing her despite her awkward beliefs (they were assured that Mrs Kent never discussed religious matters with her patients) and her price: she could command as much as £25. In 1684, however, when Sarah Fell was about to be delivered of her first child at the age of forty-two, Frances Kent's Quakerism was of course an added bonus. 'She is a fine woman', wrote Sarah, following her successful *accouchement*. 'It was the Lord sent her to me. It was the Lord's mercy that I had her, who is a very skilful and tender woman for that employment.'[21]

The overseeing of Quaker midwives was one of the responsibilities of the Women's Meetings: in February 1675 at Swarthmoor, a Meeting was informed that Mabel Brittaine had been so lacking in skill that the child was born dead. On examination, Mabel Brittaine was found sufficiently deficient in medical knowledge to be told to hire an assistant (if she did not, people who employed her did so at their own risk).[22]

The care of the Quakers was not matched in other sections of society. The midwife was by the nature of her profession a powerful social figure, but she was not necessarily a particularly edifying one. A traditional connection with drink – 'red-nosed midwives' – existed in the popular imagination, which was not unfounded. Dr Sermon in *The Ladies Companion, or The English Midwife* of 1671 suggested that midwives should be sober and discreet, 'not quarrelsome nor choleric', above all not 'rash and drunken women'. His picture of the ideal midwife – 'very cheerful, pleasant, and of a good discourse, strong, not idle, but accustomed to exercise, that they may be the more able (if need requires) to watch' – makes it clear that the contrary was all too often to be found: that 'pitiful, old, ugly, ill-bred woman in a hat' for example, who married Pepys's Uncle Fenner in 1662 and was a midwife.[23]

A midwife's business, of its very nature, offered her the opportunity for certain murky sidelines, of which abortions were the most obvious; it was for fear of this that the authorities were zealous in their requirements that midwives were to report stillborn births. A practical woman who was not too particular might also most conveniently pursue the combined careers of midwife and procuress: several of the 'Crafty Bawds' mentioned in numbers of *The Wandering Whore*, such as Mrs Davies and Mrs Barber of Holborn, were also listed as midwives.[24]

Under the circumstances, the most important gynaecological advance of the seventeenth century was the invention of the forceps, by the beneficial use of which in a difficult and prolonged labour the infant could be skilfully delivered without damage to either mother or child. In the absence of the forceps, types of instruments available were as crude as the techniques by which they were employed. Richard Gough, in *The History of Myddle*, described how the village blacksmith made some 'iron hooks' at the direction of the local midwife; she was then able to draw forth a dead child from its mother successfully. The sensible Dr Willughby condemned the use of 'pothooks, pack-needles, silver spoons, thatcher's hooks and knives' to speed on 'Dame Nature' unnecessarily.[25] But of course where a birth was not straightforward, some form of instrument might have to be employed if mother and child were not to perish, immutably joined together (as so many did).

The man responsible for the invention of the forceps was a member of the Chamberlen family, probably Peter the Elder (so called to distinguish him from his brother and nephew, both also called Peter).[26] Unfortunately the character of Peter Chamberlen the Elder was that particular mixture of enlightenment and professional jealousy which has marked many inventors. On the one hand he called on King James I in 1616 to found a Society of Midwives: 'That some order may be settled by the State for [their] instruction and civil government.' On the other hand he deliberately and successfully guarded the secret of the forceps within the Chamberlen family: his motives being clearly financial, as were those of the Chamberlens who followed him and jealously kept up the tradition of secrecy. (Another member of the Chamberlen family, author of *Dr Chamberlain's Midwives practice* of 1665, which attacked other 'quacking' obstetrical textbooks, defended his refusal to give details of the forceps on the disingenuous grounds that they were by now 'a family secret' and not his to reveal.) As a result the forceps had to be reinvented quite separately in the eighteenth century.† In the seventeenth century much ammunition was given by this professional selfishness to those indignant midwives who protested that doctors and others tried to control and license them purely in order to restrict their activities and preserve their personal monopoly.

Many doctors were considered greedy and selfish, but many midwives were held to be ignorant, and there was something to be said for both points of view. Hitherto the licensing of the midwives had been performed

---

† In the nineteenth century Dr Peter Chamberlen's famous forceps were discovered, still tucked away in their box.[27]

by the bishops – Bishop Bonner is said to have been the first to do so[28] – a practice which had arisen in the previous century more for religious than for medical reasons. In an age of high infant mortality, it was very often left to the midwife, with mother and child *in extremis*, to perform the rite of baptism; it was her responsibility that the correct (Protestant) form should be used. At the same time, the ecclesiastical authorities were anxious that midwives should not invoke the darker powers of witchcraft to their aid; although the poor state of medical knowledge at the time, and the desperate sufferings of so many patients, must have made the invocation of supernatural aid where natural aid had failed irresistible to many caring midwives not otherwise connected with evil. (As early as 1486 *Malleus Maleficarum* had urged an oath upon midwives to eliminate the possibility of witchcraft being used.)[29]

The oath administered to Eleanor Pead, seeking a licence as a midwife from the Archbishop of Canterbury in 1567, is the earliest which has survived.[30] She promised among other things to help the poor as well as the rich, and not to allow a woman to name a man falsely as the father of her child; some significance being attached to these allegations of paternity, extracted as it were by the pangs of labour, which put a responsibility upon the midwife either to remember them or forget them. In addition she had to swear to use no sorcery or incantation, to employ a simple form of baptism if necessary and to register the child's birth with the curate, and not to use any cutting or dismembering in the course of the delivery.

The trouble with the bishops' licensing was that their interests were all in the supernatural: in the course of ecclesiastical visitations, it was customary to ask after the use of prohibited sorcery rather than the progress of deliveries. Dr Peter Chamberlen, son of Peter the Younger, cried out vigorously against a system whereby any woman 'with the testimony of two or three gossips' could pay a fee for her licence, and then hasten into practice. It was a system, he averred, which produced innumerable and 'uncontrolled female-arbiters of life and death'. In 1634 he attempted in his turn to form a Corporation of Midwives, with himself as governor; towards this end he seems to have held monthly meetings of midwives for the purpose of instruction at his home.[31]

This innovation aroused angry protests from the midwives at the interruption of their age-old business. Dr Chamberlen, it was asserted, had no greater skill than anyone else save for his 'iron instruments'. Chamberlen was also accused of bargaining with the rich for larger fees, and neglecting the care of the poor altogether. Among those midwives who petitioned was that Mrs Hester Shaw who may have been the violent midwife of Threadneedle Street criticized by Dr Percival Willughby.[32]

Hester Shaw, towards the end of her career, got into a dispute with Mr Thomas Clendon, the minister of Allhallows, Barking, over some stolen goods: her houses, and the other houses in her row, having been accidentally destroyed by gunpowder, a great deal of Hester Shaw's property had, according to her version, ended up in the minister's possession and stayed there.[33] The details of the case revealed incidentally how substantial could be the rewards of a lifetime of midwifery: two bags of silver, worth over £100 each, and quilted rolls of gold were mentioned as missing, as well as a quantity of silver plate. Hester Shaw was also described by the minister himself as of 'a good education, and volubility of tongue, and natural boldness, and confidence'. In herself therefore she also stood for the midwife as an independent female professional, secure (as she had hitherto always believed) in work which a man was quite unable to perform.

The midwives argued in front of Archbishop Laud and the Bishop of London at Lambeth Palace on 22 October 1634. Their case rested in essence on the importance of experience: 'it must be continual practise in this kind that will bring experience, and those women that desire to learn must be present at the delivery of many women and see the work and behaviour of such as be skilful midwives who will shew and direct them and resolve their doubts'. On the other hand there was a certain lack of logic in the way the midwives added that they also possessed books in English on anatomy, and 'most of them being able to read' (or so they claimed), these books would benefit them more than Dr Chamberlen's lectures on anatomy.[34]

After 1662, in the reversion to old ways brought about by the Restoration, the midwives proceeded as they had done formerly, taking an oath, paying their money, and returning home, in the words of a critical contemporary, 'as skilful as they went thither'. Parts of the oath still conveyed a chilling impression of contemporary abuses through ignorance: 'I will not destroy the child born of any woman, nor cut, nor pull off the head thereof, or otherwise dismember or hurt the same, or suffer it to be so hurt or dismembered.'[35]

*   *   *

The power struggle between the midwives and the doctors was finally resolved by the victory of the latter. Education, as ever in the seventeenth century, was the real key to woman's weakness. Members of the male sex were always likely by definition to have a far greater knowledge of medicine and anatomy than the average woman, if only for their ability to read Latin (as the midwife Jane Sharp herself admitted).[36] As for women doctors, some women did continue to practise medicine on a casual basis – in 1683 one Prudence Ludford of Little Barkhampton was presented at court for unlawful surgery – but the examinations required by the Faculties of Medicine and Surgery in the City of London excluded women.[37]

By the end of the century it had become customary to call in a 'Man-Midwife' for difficult cases. It has been suggested that the vogue for the 'Man-Midwife' among the upper classes may have spread from France (like other customs of an intimate nature such as the use of the prophylactic sheath), after one of the mistresses of Louis XIV, Louise de la Vallière, had been attended by one. In 1780 the honouring of Sir David Hamilton by King George III, the first knighted obstetrician, indicated the course of the future in the medical profession. Those murmurs of feminine modesty at male examination which had persisted in the seventeenth century – Dr Willughby mentions cases where he was not permitted to gaze on the patient's face – and had been evinced by the vocal midwives as support for their traditional claims, died away in view of the superior need for truly skilled attention.[38] And that, it came to be agreed, could not be supplied by women.

Ironically enough there was far more substance to the midwives' claims to represent the correct – because it was divinely-ordained and thus natural-approach to labour than many people, including the doctors, realized at the time. Recent research has come to criticize the 'meddling' male doctors who with their forceps intervened with the natural process of childbirth.[39] It is of course impossible (as was pointed out on p. 76), to estimate with any certainty the figures for mortality in childbirth at this period; even the hazy figures available give no clue as to the relative responsibility of midwife, doctor, let alone that other important figure present at every childbed, 'Dame Nature' herself.

Obstetrics in any modern sense was in its infancy where doctors as well as midwives were concerned. This was an age when the Caesarean delivery was popularly – if not quite correctly – believed to result in the inevitable death of the mother. The key work *De Generatione Animalium* by Dr William Harvey, described as 'the father of English midwifery',[40] was published in Latin in 1651 and, with a thirty-nine-page section 'Of the Birth', translated into English in 1653 (it had a strong influence, for example, on Dr Percival Willughby). But even Harvey was capable of harbouring such misconceptions as attributing to the foetus an active role in breaking out of the womb, in addition to the mother's contractions, on the analogy of the chicken breaking out of the egg.

While some of the notions cherished by the midwife Jane Sharp have a ludicrous sound to modern ears, others are sensible enough. On the one hand she believed the liver rather than the heart to be the fountain of the blood, that boys were begotten from the right 'stone' (testicle) and girls from the left, and that after conception boys lived in the right of the womb and girls on the left. On the other hand Jane Sharp believed in sustaining the strength of women during labour and in keeping them warm after-wards, both sound principles. She was much against hurrying on labour, warned against the difficulty of a breech presentation, and she was aware of the threat of haemorrhage with the need to remove the 'after-burden' (placenta). Her chosen covering for a recently delivered woman – the newly flayed skin of a sheep and a hare-skin on her belly – may sound bizarre, but William Sermon, a doctor, enunciated the same principle in 1671 in *The Ladies Companion* (though Dr Sermon preferred the skin of an ox).[41]

As for Dr Sermon, he too had his capricious notions: for example, he believed one flat breast to be a sign that one twin would be miscarried. Like many doctors and scientifically-minded people in the seventeenth century, he attached much importance to obtaining that popular talisman of the time, an eagle-stone, to aid an easy delivery. Lord Conway, husband of Anne Viscountess Conway and a Fellow of the Royal Society, took enormous trouble to find exactly the right size and shape of one before her delivery in December 1658; fabled to be found in the birds' nests, an eagle-stone was in fact merely an accidental configuration of an ordinary hollow pebble.[42]

In such a primitive state of medicine, the midwives were not so far out in their emphasis on the importance of womanly experience. An accom-plished sensible midwife like Jane Sharp would not really do much less well than a doctor like William Sermon, because in so many cases both of them were effectively helpless. Dr Sermon himself recognized this when he suggested that the 'discreet Midwife' should encourage her patient to call on the Almighty for help: 'and let them call to mind what God hath said with his own mouth; for it would be almost a miracle to see a woman delivered without pain'.

In another passage however, Dr Sermon did draw attention to a re-markable instance of childbirth without pain which he himself had wit-nessed by chance in 1644. The doctor was lurking in the hedgerows, hoping to shoot a hare, when he saw a woman on her way back from market 'delivered of a lusty Child in a Wood by herself'. Presently she encased the infant in some oak leaves and wrapped it in her apron. She then marched 'stoutly' for half a mile to what happened to be the doctor's uncle's house. Within two hours the woman felt well enough, having secured some proper linen for the child, to proceed on her way 'not in the least discouraged'. Dr Sermon knew of other examples in history of women delivered without pain. He also fondly believed that the contemporary women in America sprang out of a bed and ministered to their own husbands immediately after giving birth out of gratitude 'because they [the American husbands] take some pains to beget them with Child'. If only Englishwomen were equally unselfish, reflected Dr Sermon, their husbands would give up kissing their 'handsome Nurses' and generally misbehaving themselves with the neighbours in a similar situation.[43]

But such 'natural' childbeds were rare indeed in the conditions of seventeenth-century England. The real point about obstetrics and midwifery during this period (and for nearly 200 years to follow, until the invention of disinfectant by Joseph Lister in 1867 caused maternal mortality to decline sharply) was that the nature of bacterial infection itself was not understood. Here both doctors and midwives were alike in their ignorance.

Dr William Harvey called for cleanliness to prevent the onset of fever. Handbooks advocated common-sensical measures of hygiene for midwives. Jane Sharp called for pared nails, and Dr William Sermon for comely and neat midwives, hands small, fingers long not thick, 'nails pared, very close'. As for Jane Sharp's recipe for a herbal bath at the onset of labour, to include hollyhocks, bettony, mugwort, marjoram, mint, camomile, linseed and parsley boiled up together, that must at least have involved cleansing the patient; if her recommendation that the woman's 'privities' should be anointed with a compound of oil of sweet almonds, lilies, violets, duck's grease, hen's grease and wax, with butter, ground quince kernels and gum optional is less instantly appealing to modern sensibilities.[44] But none of the endless herbal remedies recommended in handbooks and household books alike for the inexorable female ordeal of childbirth had any real relevance to the problem of sepsis.

It was from septicaemia that the suffering patients died in their hundreds and thousands. This septicaemia was sometimes brought about by the unhygienic conditions of the home (although some immunity must have been established to those); more often it was brought about by that concomitant of most labours, 'the examining hand'.[45] Here both doctor and midwife were equally guilty. The doctor blithely and unknowingly brought with him infection from other cases which might include scarlet fever; the midwife from a daily round which might include the cow-byre and the farmyard generally as well as the lying-in of a neighbour.

It was a hideous truth that progress in this field could lead to greater not lesser mortality, as the examining hand of the doctor grew more skilful, and the importance of internal examination was increasingly stressed. The establishment of the first lying-in hospitals led to the first epidemics of puerperal fever, the first one accurately recorded being in the middle of the seventeenth century.[46]

It was in this sense that the least skilful of the midwives, lacking the knowledge to do much more than concentrate on their herbal remedies in the patient's own home, might actually do less harm, by not spreading infection, than the most practised of the doctors.

*　　*　　*

The ideal midwife (from the point of view of a masculine-dominated society, and no doubt from the point of view of most patients as well) might be 'modest and grave', but there was something about the intimate power of the position, the fact that most midwives acted throughout their careers as 'uncontrolled female arbiters' in the indignant phrase of Dr Peter Chamberlen, which could lead to the development of an altogether bolder type of woman. Mrs Elizabeth Cellier was that outspoken midwife who in 1687 announced that over 6,000 women had died in childbed within the last twenty years, more than 13,000 children had been abortive, and another 5,000 had died in the first month of their life; about two thirds of these had, 'in all probability perished, for want of the due skill and care, in those women who practise the art of midwifery'.[47]

Her career previous to the initiation of her campaign for better training in midwifery had been equally bold, if not quite so judicious. For the details of her early life, we have to choose between the tales of her enemies – that she was born Elizabeth Marshall, the daughter of a brazier or tinker living near Canterbury – and her own account in one of her self-justificatory pamphlets.[48] According to the latter, she was brought up by parents who were fervent Royalists – Protestants, but accused of papistry and idolatry on account of their Royalist sympathies. These perverse accusations led the young Elizabeth to inquire into the truths of the Catholic religion, as a result of which she herself became converted to it.

Elizabeth's first husband seems to have been an English merchant who went to Leghorn and died (the broadsheets had her indulging in a tripartite love affair the while with an Italian and his negro servant, as a result of which an illegitimate son was born). Her second husband vanished to Barbados leaving her with five children; whereupon Elizabeth moved to the City of London and set up as a midwife. Finally she married a French merchant named Pierre Cellier. At which point the dramatic part of her story began.

Clearly there were exciting opportunities for an expert Catholic midwife in London in the 1670s when so many great ladies, including the wife of the heir to the throne, were Catholics: Mrs Cellier ministered to Mary of Modena as well as other Catholic aristocrats. The autumn of 1678 however brought public tragedy into these domestic circles: the false accusations of Titus Oates and others concerning a 'Popish Plot' resulted in the arrest of five ancient Catholic noblemen, including the Earl of Powis and Lord Arundell of Wardour, on the highly unlikely charge that they had been conspiring to kill Charles II. Other Catholics, Jesuit priests, were also arrested on the same charge, possibly with slightly more substance. When witnesses for the defence of the Jesuits were brought from St Omer for their trial in the summer of 1679, it was natural that Mrs Cellier, with her intimate knowledge of the York household, and her continental connections through her husband's business, should lodge them. She also visited the prison and attempted to alleviate the lot of some of her humbler co-religionists there.

The details of the aftermath of the 'Popish Plot' are virtually impossible to disentangle.[49] First, plots had become good business, and any rascal was likely to invent them if he discerned profit in it. Second, both factions, that of Whig courtiers, headed by Shaftesbury, determined to exclude the Duke of York from the eventual succession, and that of the Catholics anxious to preserve him in it, were at the mercy of *agents provocateurs*. Unfortunately it was one of these, Thomas Dangerfield (although he masqueraded under a false name), that Mrs Cellier encountered in the course of one of her merciful visits to Newgate, where he lay in the debtors' prison.

When Dangerfield confided to Mrs Cellier the details of a plot that involved the Earl of Shaftesbury, he found a ready listener; not only was the Catholic York household under threat, but the husband of one of her patrons, the Earl of Powis, was actually in prison, for all of which Shaftesbury was to be blamed.

Mrs Cellier was kind to Dangerfield. She paid off his debts; she spent 16s redeeming his coat out of pawn. She took him into her employ. From this vantage point a plot was said to have been hatched, by which material, incriminating the Earl of Shaftesbury in a plot to kill the King, was planted in the rooms of Mansell, a leading Whig; other conspirators included the Countess of Powis. That at least was Dangerfield's story, for, being re-arrested for debt once more, and carried back to Newgate, Dangerfield quickly turned his plot on its head, and made it a conspiracy of the Catholics against Shaftesbury.

Mrs Cellier, on the other hand, stuck stoutly to her original story. When incriminating documents were found concealed in 'a Meal-Tub' in her house (hence the appropriately ludicrous nickname given to this plot-that-never-was) she maintained that it was indeed information written by Dangerfield which had been found 'between the Pewter in my Kitchen', but this information contained details of a real conspiracy by the Whigs against the King: 'and as the Father of Lies did once tell the truth, so he hath inserted this one truth in his lying Narrative'. She added: 'From my part it was no motive but my Loyalty and Duty to his Majesty, and Love to Truth and Justice, that engaged me in this affair.'[50]

The Jesuit Father John Warner, who later gave a full account of these events from the Catholic point of view, described Mrs Cellier as a woman of strong and 'almost' masculine temperament. It was a fatal caveat:'Nature had endowed her with a lively, sharp and clear mind, but her powers of judgement were not of the same order; as was to be expected in the weaker sex.'[51] Certainly it is possible to see in Mrs Cellier's unwise championship of Dangerfield the rashness of one who was accustomed to trust her own decisions in one important if domestic sphere with success, and could not believe she would not be equally successful in the much wider world of politics and intrigue.

At all events she paid the penalty. The Meal-Tub Plot as a whole, with its alternative versions, was considered too fantastic even for this plot-hungry age. But Mrs Cellier was arrested and flung into Newgate, where of course she encountered her old protégé and new-found betrayer, Dangerfield. A prolonged pamphlet war subsequently broke out between Dangerfield and Mrs Cellier, when both were once more at liberty. Dangerfield, in *The Grand Impostor Defeated*, referred to Mrs Cellier as 'Mother Damnable' (the nickname of a notoriously foul-mouthed character who dispensed ale in Kentish Town).[52] Mrs Cellier for her part gave a superb version of the dialogue which ensued when she met Dangerfield in prison (even if it owed something to *esprit de l'escalier*, one hopes that she delivered at least a few of the following lines at the time):

DANGERFIELD: 'Madam, Madam, Pray Madam speak to me, and tell me how you do.'

MRS CELLIER: 'I am sick, very sick of the Bloody Barbarous Villain.'

DANGERFIELD: 'Pray Madam speak low, and do not discompose yourself.'

MRS CELLIER: 'Nothing you do can discompose me: I Despise you so much, I am not Angry. . . .'

DANGERFIELD: 'I am very sorry for your Confinement, but I could not possibly help what I have done.'

MRS CELLIER: 'Bloody Villain, I am not confined, for *Stone Walls and Iron Bars, do not make a Prison, but a Guilty Conscience*: I am Innocent. . . .'[53]

Dangerfield was pardoned by the King, in response to political pressure. But despite constant petitions, it was not until June 1680 that Mrs Cellier was brought to trial at the King's Bench Court on a charge of high treason, having been a prisoner in Newgate for thirty-two weeks, for much of this in close confinement, unable to see her husband and children. Her conduct at her trial showed however that her spirit at least was unbowed. For example she demanded that Dissenters be excluded from the jury, on the grounds that the plot of which she was accused had been aimed against their interests. It was however in her vigorous attack upon the whole basis of Dangerfield's testimony that Mrs Cellier showed most courage – and enjoyed most success. She argued that Dangerfield might have been pardoned for his part, whatever it was, in the so-called Meal-Tub Plot, but he was still a convicted felon for other previous offences including burglary and perjury, which had brought upon him an unpardoned sentence of outlawry. 'The King cannot give an Act of Grace to one subject', argued Mrs Cellier, 'to the prejudice of another.'[54]

So Mrs Cellier was acquitted of high treason.

Before that, she had given good account of herself in the course of the trial, before the Lord Chief Justice and King Charles II, among others. A piece of broadsheet verse commemorated her courage:

> You taught the judges to interpret laws;
> Shewed Sergeant Maynard how to plead a cause;
> You turned and wound, and rough'd them at your will.[55]

Humour as well as courage was one of the weapons at her disposal, a weapon incidentally always likely to disarm King Charles II. At one point Mrs Cellier was accused of jesting about the alleged 'Presbyterian' plot in a tavern, in the course of which she told a bawdy story thought too immodest to repeat in court.

'What!' exclaimed the King, scenting some sudden possibility of distraction in this interminable and boring tangle: 'Can she speak Bawdy too?'

The King refused to lose sight of the subject. 'What did she say?' he repeated. 'Come, tell us the story'.

Mrs Cellier's official interlocutor began to stammer.

'She said – she said – she said – that so long as she did not lose her hands, she would get money as long as – '

It was Mrs Cellier who completed her own sentence: 'So long as Men kissed their Wives.'

At this the cross-examiner thought he perceived an opening. He swiftly added: 'By the oath I have taken, she said their Mistresses too.'

Mrs Cellier was more than equal to that. 'Did I so?' she inquired. 'Pray what else do they keep them for?'

'That was but witty', said the Lord Chancellor drily, in the presence of his philandering sovereign.

''Twas natural to her Practice', commented the kindly King.[56]

All would perhaps have been well for the triumphant Mrs Cellier following her acquittal, had not the temptation to be a petticoat-author, as well as an uncontrolled female arbiter, overcome her. She had already pushed her luck by refusing to pay the traditional guinea apiece to the jury upon her acquittal. (Had she been convicted the King would have been obliged to pay up.) Instead she wrote to the foreman with a gracious offer of payment in kind: 'Pray Sir accept of, and give my most humble Service to Your self, and all the Worthy Gentlemen of your Panel, and Yours and Their Several Ladies. And if You and They please, I will with no less Fidelity serve them in their Deliveries, than You have done me with Justice in mine. . . .'[57]

Soon after the trial she had her own narrative in pamphlet form 'Printed for Elizabeth Cellier, and to be sold at her House in Arundel Street near St Clements Church.' Entitled *Malice Defeated*, it was said to be 'for the satisfaction of all Lovers of undisguised Truth'. *Malice Defeated* not only related all the circumstances of Mrs Cellier's acquaintance with Danger-field, and the course of her trial, but it also included some trenchant criticisms of conditions within Newgate prison itself. She described hearing the groans of prisoners under torture, which so much resembled those of a woman in labour that Mrs Cellier innocently offered her services in relief. She wrote of a special chamber for prisoners whose crime consisted in adhering to the wrong religion, known sarcastically to the gaolers as 'The Chapel'; a grating permitted paying members of the public to witness their agonies. She wrote of instruments known as the shears, weighing forty to fifty pounds, affixed to the limbs of prisoners, which wore the flesh through to the bone. All of this made (and makes) *Malice Defeated* nothing if not a good read. As Sir Charles Lyttelton wrote to a friend in September: 'if you have not seen Mrs Cellier's narrative, 'tis well worth it'.[58]

Mrs Cellier concluded with an ingratiating acknowledgement of her own weakness: 'And as to my own Sex, I hope they will pardon the Errors of my story, as well as those bold Attempts of mine that occasioned it ... though it may be thought too Masculine, yet was it the effects of my Loyal (more than Religious) Zeal to gain Proselites to his Service. And in all my defence, none can truly say but that I preserved the Modesty, though not the Timorousness common to my Sex.'[59]

This did not save her from a further trial, once more before the King's Bench – this time for libel. And this time Mrs Cellier was found guilty. She was fined £1,000, and sentenced to three sojourns in the pillory – from twelve to one at the Maypole in the Strand on market day, at Covent Garden and similarly at Charing Cross – while on each occasion a parcel of her publications was to be burnt by the common hangman. Even now Mrs Cellier was not quite vanquished. When the time came for her to take up her perilous position – the lot of a 'Popish' conspirator held at the mercy of the mob in the pillory in September 1680 was hardly enviable – Mrs Cellier began by feigning sickness. Unfortunately she was tricked into taking the emetic which she had procured for the purpose a day early. Then – at the age of fifty-odd – she declared that she was pregnant. Her groans and shrieks, as the women came to dress her for her fate, resulted in the calling of a physician; a pig's bladder full of blood, with which Mrs Cellier had intended to implement her imposture, was then discovered. (This pig's bladder proved an absolute boon to the writers of the broadsheets.)

Finally captive in the pillory, Mrs Cellier was greeted by a hail of stones. She carried a board, a piece of wood something like a battledore, with which to defend herself, otherwise she would surely have been brained. She also managed to keep her head one side of the board instead of poking it through as intended, so that she had some measure of protection. And as Rachel Lady Russell (no friend to this enemy of the Whigs) noted in a letter to her husband: 'All the stones that were thrown within reach, she took up and put in her pocket.'[60]

Mrs Cellier returned to publishing with renewed zest. As the anonymous author of *The Midwife Unmask'd* complained: 'This She-Champion, and Midwife ... now being cleared by the law', she 'rants and scratches like another Pucel d'Orleans or Joan of Arque; handling her Pen for the Papistical Cause, as the other did her Lance; and it is pity she has not likewise the Glory of her Martyrdom'.[61]

Nor was that the end of Mrs Cellier's public career. For all the hopeful 'searches' of other midwives, Queen Catherine of Braganza had never produced an heir for Charles II. Her own more successful midwifery had brought Mrs Cellier into that dangerous prominence where she had meddled, to her cost, with politics. Now with the succession of James II to his – officially – childless brother, Mrs Cellier was back in the centre of things again.

In June 1687 she took the opportunity of this newly favourable climate of opinion to float a scheme for a midwives' college.[62] By this she hoped to reduce those fearful casualties of unskilled carelessness on the part of midwives which had disquieted the Chamberlens and others since early in the century. Mrs Cellier's scheme was for a royal 'corporation' to be endowed to the tune of £5,000 or £6,000 a year 'by and for midwives', which in addition would serve as a hospital for foundling children.

Mrs Cellier's plan was on the surface well worked out. Women – to the limit of 1,000 – who were already skilled midwives were to be admitted on the payment of £5; they would then serve as matrons to twelve lesser houses or assistants to the governess. The next 1,000 would pay 50s on admission, and 50s per year in fees; as their training proceeded, they would join the ranks of the matrons and assistants to the governess. The entire income of the first year (which according to these terms would be considerable) would be devoted to the building of the foundling hospital.

There were other provisions: no married person was to be admitted to the government of the hospital, in order to protect the interest of the foundlings. A woman sufficiently expert in writing would act as secretary to the governess of the hospital. The principal physician or male midwife would give a monthly lecture in public at which attendance would be compulsory; afterwards all the lectures would be entered in a book to which the midwives would have free recourse.

In a subsequent pamphlet the following year, Mrs Cellier showed herself capable of a humanitarian imagination where her foundlings were concerned.[63] Their surnames, she wrote, were to be chosen from the 'several Arts or Mysteries', or from 'Complexions and Shapes' or even on a more mundane level from the days of the week; but such children were not to be stigmatized by such opprobrious surnames as 'Bastard', so that in after life they would be capable of any employment, or even honour, without reference to the misfortune of their birth.

Combating the murmurs of the doctors in a pamphlet entitled *To Dr— An Answer to his Queries, concerning the Colledg* [sic] *of Midwives*, Mrs Cellier turned once more to the story of those enterprising Israelite midwives Shiphrah and Puah and expanded it. She argued that they could not have been merely midwives, for two women could not have coped with the whole tribe; therefore they were also teachers, and the scene of such consultations 'might well be called a College'. With that verve which the King's Bench Court would have recognized, Mrs Cellier said that since the Bible stated God had built these midwives 'houses', then the midwives' 'college' antedated the College of Physicians. For good measure, she threw in the fact that there had been colleges of women practising physic, coeval with the bards, before the arrival of the Romans; and that a college of women had centred round the Temple of Diana in London.[64]

The flaw in Mrs Cellier's scheme was the same flaw that had vitiated the corporation, suggested half a century earlier by Dr Peter Chamberlen. Without being granted a monopoly, it would be impossible for this new foundation to impose higher standards, since too many midwives would simply continue in their same bad old ways. On the other hand Mrs Cellier's foundation was envisaged on far too small a scale to deal with the enormous number of midwives required by the female population of England, even if they had been willing and able to afford the fees.

For all this, and for all the queries raised by the doctors, King James II lent a sympathetic ear to Mrs Cellier's propositions. He evidently promised to enrol the midwives into a corporation by his Royal Charter.[65]

When Mrs Cellier published her second pamphlet on the subject of the foundation in January 1688, the Queen, Mary of Modena, was herself in the early stages of pregnancy. Her fruitful condition was a matter of some personal satisfaction to Mrs Cellier: had she not predicted that 'her Majesty was full of Children', and that therapeutic baths at a spa would assist her 'breeding'? Mrs Cellier's satisfaction was certainly shared by the royal parents-to-be, since Mary of Modena, who had lost a number of children at birth and in infancy, had not conceived for some years.

But this was a pregnancy of more than personal importance. Catholic subjects like Mrs Cellier viewed the prospect of the birth of a male heir – who would be a Catholic – with enthusiasm, while Whigs and fanatical Protestants envisaged with equal dismay the blighting of the succession hopes of Mary and Anne, James's Protestant daughters by his first marriage.

Mrs Cellier ventured further prophecy concerning the many ways in which her corporation of midwives would bring benefits to the King their founder: 'And I doubt not but one way will be by giving him a Prince to his Royal consort, who like another Moses may become a mighty Captain to the Nation; and lead to Battle the Soldiers which the Hospital will preserve for him.'[66]

Alas, this time Mrs Cellier's prophecy was singularly wide of the mark.

A prince *was* duly born to Mary of Modena – James Edward Stuart, born on 10 June 1688 – but he went into exile shortly after his birth; having by that birth precipitated the crisis which led to his father's downfall and flight. Known to history as the Old Pretender, in no conceivable sense was this prince another Moses, and the soldiers whom he ordered to battle in his various unsuccessful attempts to recapture the throne of his father were generally drawn from other sources and other nations than the foundlings of England. With the departure of her royal patron, Mrs Cellier's plans for a foundation collapsed.

So determined were King James's political enemies not to accept a Catholic succession – as represented by the baby prince born to Mary of Modena in June – that it was found convenient to believe that the baby himself was an impostor, smuggled into the palace in a warming-pan. Even Princess Anne (who should have known better) affected to credit this absurd story, because it conveniently supported her in her opposition to her father. At the time there were two midwives in attendance, Mrs De Labadie and Mrs Wilkins, both of whom received 500 guineas for what seemed to those within the royal chamber the joyful achievement of delivering the long-sought male heir (a daughter would have followed her Protestant step-sisters Mary and Anne in the succession and therefore would not have posed a threat). There were also doctors and a host of non-medical attendants, ladies of the court, many of them Protestants, amounting to a total of over sixty.[67]

But as luck would have it, one royal obstetrician, the latest member of the Chamberlen dynasty, Dr Hugh Chamberlen, was not actually present at the birth, being away attending to a patient at Chatham. This simple chance, added to the fact that the doctor was himself a strong Whig, played into the hands of another strong Whig, Gilbert (later Bishop) Burnet: he spread the story that the Queen had deliberately sent away her doctor in order to facilitate the smuggling in of the changeling.

Years later Dr Chamberlen wrote to the Electress Sophia of Hanover about the events of that dramatic day, angry that he had been dragged into the scandal.[68] He explained that there was nothing sinister about the fact that the footman sent to St James's to fetch him when the Queen's birth pangs started had not found him there. The plain truth was that the Queen gave birth earlier than was expected; not the first woman to do so. Had the footman reached him, as he must certainly have expected to do, Dr Chamberlen would in fact have arrived just in time to interrupt the act of smuggling – supposing such a stratagem had actually been planned.

Dr Chamberlen's clinching argument was the presence of another vociferous Whig at the scene of the birth – the midwife, Mrs Wilkins. She, who was wont to cry out against the Jesuits who infested the place (finding a sympathetic ear in Dr Chamberlen), had been in no doubt about the circumstances of the baby prince's birth. To Dr Chamberlen now she expatiated indignantly on these rumours of substitution: 'Alas, will they not let the poor infant alone! I am certain no such thing as the bringing of a strange child in a warming-pan could be practised without my seeing it: attending constantly in and about all the avenues to the chamber.'

Lecky regarded the prostitute as 'the eternal priestess of humanity'. But in the seventeenth century it was the midwife who could best claim that title: grave if not always modest, pursuing her profession in and about all the avenues to every chamber, where history was made and where poverty was rampant, from the palace of St James (for 500 guineas) to the market-place where a busy midwife noted in her diary that she 'laid a woman' for nothing.

Epilogue: How Strong?

A prophetess observing the 'brave Viragos' of the Leveller movement who petitioned outside the House of Commons in April 1649, despite the pained astonishment of its male inmates, might have predicted that women would be still 'stronger grown' half a century later.

The prophetess would have been wrong. By 1700 women were not in fact 'stronger grown'. In 1649 one Member of Parliament had exclaimed indignantly: 'it was not for women to Petition, they might stay at home and wash the dishes', an answer treated at the time with energetic disdain.[1] Fifty years later however women were staying at home and washing the dishes as they had always done, as though this eruption of an all-female body – thrilling or menacing depending on your point of view – had never taken place.

In fact where the status of the so-called weaker vessel was concerned, the seventeenth century saw very little improvement in real terms. On the contrary, since the general disturbance of society in the middle decades brought about a temporary unplanned elevation of certain women's authority, the graph of female progress, far from ascending in a straight line from the death of Queen Elizabeth to the accession of Queen Anne, rose during the middle decades to dip again with the restoration of the old order in 1660. (This cyclical pattern, whatever the special factors which brought it about in the seventeenth century, is perhaps worth bearing in mind; as with all forms of liberation, of which the liberation of women is only one example, it is easy to suppose in a time of freedom that the darker days of repression can never come again.)

It so happened that Anne, while still a princess, identified herself with the great Elizabeth; ill-educated and unhistorically-minded as she might be, the youthful Anne equated her own aggravation by her brother-in-law William III with that of Elizabeth by Mary Tudor: 'the Pr. discoursing her sufferings often made a parallel between herself and Qu. El.' wrote Abel Boyer, who tutored her son. Shortly after she ascended the throne, Queen Anne adopted the Latin motto *Semper Eadem* – Always the same, on the explicit grounds that it had been used by 'her predecessor of glorious memory'.[2] But in many ways *Semper Eadem* was a more appropriate motto for the fate of women in general in 1702, than for this one woman monarch in particular – not least because Queen Anne, unlike Queen Elizabeth, had been taught no Latin.

Of course there had been certain advances. But most of them, being shared equally with men, did not affect the relative standing of the sexes in respect to each other.

Literacy came into this category: there was an advance among women as a whole from the virtual illiteracy which prevailed (outside members of a tiny class) in 1600. But with progress came peril. The new differentiation between the types of education thought suitable for the respective sexes meant that male and female education, two ships sailing from the same harbour, now set very different courses, and it was only in rare instances in the future that they would catch sight of each other's sails.

The lack of Latin instruction in particular was a miserable handicap – remember the desperate plea of Basua Makin that 'tongues are learnt in order to [learn] things'. One historian has written of this period: 'Not to be able to read Latin was to go in blinkers.'[3] Such a lack could even affect those areas of traditional womanly skill such as midwifery and nursing: inevitably the woman (unskilled beause she could not study in Latin, the language of medicine) lost out to the man (skilled because he could). As for those few females who did gamely surmount these obstacles, they also had to put up with 'those wise Jests and Scoffs that are put upon a Woman of Sense and Learning, a Philosophical Lady as she is call'd by way of Ridicule', in the words of Mary Astell in 1706;[4] these constituted a hazard undreamt of by the philosophical ladies of the late sixteenth century.

Women were no longer put to death for being witches in eighteenth-century England; although Jane Wenham, who was condemned to die in 1712 but subsequently reprieved, must have had some anxious moments, unless she was magically aware that to Alice Molland of Exeter in 1685 had already fallen the dubious honour of being the last witch to be killed in this country. Nevertheless the fact that the old women of the poor were able to relapse into their traditional practice of 'white' witchery, as 'cunning women' and healers, without fear of ugly reprisals based on primitive forces beyond their own control, certainly constituted an advance, albeit a somewhat negative one.

In general the war of words concerning the precise nature of woman's 'weakness' was being won by those who saw in this weakness something which entitled her to the special tenderness and protection of the male; there was no longer held to be something spiritually inferior about it. Indeed the notion of the 'softer sex', 'the gentle sex', which might actually be finer than its masculine opposite was growing in literature as the century drew to a close. A work of Cornelius Agrippa, *Female Pre-eminence or the Dignity and Excellency of that Sex, above the Male*, originally written in Latin in the early sixteenth century for the benefit of Margaret of Austria, daughter of the Emperor Maximilian I, appeared in an English version in 1670, adapted by Henry Care. Here it was boldly stated that where the soul was concerned there was 'the same innate worth and dignity' in both male and female, 'the Image of their Creator being stamped as fairly, and shining as brightly in one, as 'tother'; but in all other respects 'the noble and delicate Feminine Race, doth almost to infinity excel that roughhewn boisterous kind, the Male'.[5] Here was a line of reasoning which would lead eventually to the Victorian notion of woman as a creature too pure to be sullied by man's gross appetites.

When on 11 May 1699 the Rev. John Sprint preached a wedding sermon at Sherborne, *The Bride-Woman Counseller*, which trotted out all the old reproaches towards womankind, he was much attacked for it. He admitted himself that his views were by now largely old-fashioned, although he could wish to see them restored to currency. Sprint blamed women for all the faults of their husbands since Man's previously sweet nature had been soured by the Fall: 'You may thank your Mother Eve for it', he declared, 'who, when she had gotten a good Natur'd and Loving Husband, that was easy to be pleas'd, could not then be contented, but must try Practices with him.' Under these disgraceful circumstances, Sprint advocated the example of certain 'Persian Ladies who have the resemblance of a Foot worn on top of their Coronets' in order to indicate that 'the height of their Glory, Top-Knot and all, does stoop to their Husband's feet'.[6]

If few English ladies at the turn of the seventeenth century would have contemplated sporting 'the resemblance of a Foot' upon their Top-Knots, the lack of such an outward symbol of submission should not obscure the fact that their position at law with regard to their husbands was exactly the same in 1700 as it had been 100 years earlier: the authority of the husband remained, as it was then, absolute.

The Lawes Resolutions (probably written by lawyers in the late sixteenth century, but printed in 1632) had pointed out that a man might beat 'an outlaw, a traitor, a Pagan, his villein, or his wife because by the Law Common these persons can have no action'. In 1696 the author of *An Essay in Defense of the Female Sex* (anonymous except for her sex) evoked an even more piteous comparison: 'Women, like our Negroes in our western plantations, are born slaves, and live prisoners all their lives.'[7] As against the lack of legal rights within marriage which applied to the vast majority of Englishwomen, the small amelioration brought about to heiresses by the development of Chancery, or the increased choice of marriage partner (within socially prescribed limits) allowed to the young, were but limited advances.

Women remained weak at law, tied by what Samuel Hieron had called 'this blessed knot of matrimony', something which did not always live up to this enthusiastic description, but was nevertheless the binding which every girl was expected to accept if she was to fulfil her role in society.[8] In this connection legal bewilderment prevailed when any woman who did not admit such a state or something related to it encountered the authorities: 'Are you a maid, or a widow or a wife?' inquired the magistrate of the Catholic nun, Mary Ward's colleague,[9] unable to accept the concept of chosen celibacy in a female. It is significant that two new types of woman which imposed themselves upon public attention in the second half of the seventeenth century, the Quaker and the actress, were both in their different ways outside the law as it had stood up till 1660.

In another area, even more crucial to their daily lives, women were as weak (if not weaker) at the end of the century as at the beginning. It was no one's fault that one of the consequences of the development of gynaecology (before the nature of infection was appreciated) meant that maternal mortality rose slightly by the end of the century, with outbreaks of puerperal fever. The fact remained that women's lot was 'a continual labour' in more senses than one, as Rachel Lady Russell told her daughter Katherine,[10] and with high maternal mortality, no proper means of controlling conception, high infant mortality and high expectations of childbearing from their spouses, it was difficult to see how it could be otherwise – with all the attendant family joys that such persistent child-bearing also brought.

Men of course shared all the other physical miseries of women induced by poverty and disease (having the additional privilege of dying on the battlefield): life expectancy overall fell in certain places in England after 1625 for a period,[11] another example of the cyclical nature of progress. Then there were the emotional sufferings equal for both sexes, including the deaths of infants; as is made clear by the lamentations of such multifathers as William Brownlow, with his twenty-two years of recorded grief.[12] Nevertheless being Adam's sons rather than Eve's daughters, they could not and did not suffer what the poet Waller had once jocularly called down upon Dorothy Sidney when she chose another suitor: 'the first curse imposed on womankind – the pains of becoming a mother'.[13]

For all this, women in the seventeenth century were as they had always been, strong vessels where they had the opportunity: that is to say, where a particular combination of character and circumstance enabled them to be so. In this of course they were exactly like their male counterparts, no more no less. Who can tell what imponderable freak of character inspired the girl soldier Anne Dymoke to pursue such a courageous course after the death of her lover at sea, ending up in a Scottish garrison, when most other girls of her time and class would have remained quietly melancholic in the country in the first place? It was just that women, given the structure of society at the time, had vastly fewer public opportunities to demonstrate their worth and resourcefulness.

It was the unexpected arrival of these opportunities which gave to the Civil War period its peculiar character for women; although even here one should note that the boldest she-soldier could not count on being free from 'the first curse'. Such heroines were often only detected by the unconcealable fact of pregnancy, as unavoidable a lot, it seemed, in uniform as out of it. The ballad of 'The Female Warrior', she who was 'at push of Pike ... As good as ever struck', commemorated this hazard:

> This valiant Amazon with courage fill'd
> For to Display her Colours was well skill'd
> Till pregnant nature did her Sex discover
> She fell a pieces, and was made a Mother.[14]

As for those women 'solicitors', they too lay under the first curse: from Mary Lady Verney, alone and gravid as she pleaded in vain with 'Old Men's Wife' to aid her husband's cause, to Elizabeth Lilburne, baptizing her baby Tower because he had been born in the Tower of London (John Lilburne's current prison).

It is however an almost universal fact of history that women have done well in wartime when they have been able or compelled to act as substitutes for men, showing themselves resourceful, courageous and strong in every sense of the words; in short displaying without much difficulty all those qualities generally described as masculine. It is another fact that the post-war period has generally seen a masculine retreat from this view of the female sex when the vacuum no longer needs to be filled. Post-Restoration

England was no exception to this rule; indeed as early as 1657 Dr Jeremy Taylor, discoursing on friendship *In a Letter to the most Ingenious and Excellent Mrs Katherine Phillips* (the Matchless Orinda), attacked those morose cynics who would not admit women to this state: 'a man is the best friend in trouble,' he wrote, 'but a woman may be equal to him in the days of joy ... in peaceful Cities and times vertuous women are the beauties of society and the prettiness of friendship'.[15] His views were flattering enough considering the low opinion of women then prevalent, most men arguing against the mere possibility of friendship with the opposite sex, but the terms in which he couched them paid but scant attention to the realities of recent history.

On the other hand most women were undoubtedly pleased to see the return of peaceful conditions, the old order as it seemed, without analysing its social consequences for themselves. The fact that John Lilburne may (or may not) have included women in the natural order which endowed natural rights, and that John Locke thirty years later certainly did not, was of little importance to their 'continual labour'. While the fact that John Lilburne, revolutionary thinker concerning natural rights in public, was in private one of the most trying husbands a woman ever had to bear, goes perhaps some way to explaining the slow pace of the development of women's position in the ensuing centuries.

The public ideal of womanhood towards the end of the seventeenth century is given in a panegyric, preached as a sermon after the death of Queen Mary on 28 December 1694, and later printed.[16] Nothing is rarer than to find the heroic character in a woman, declared the panegyrist, the Rev. James Abbadie, minister at the French church in the Savoy, while going on happily to discover such heroism in the character of the deceased sovereign. Only the heroism which distinguished her and which conjured forth his admiration was entirely based on modesty: it was modesty which had marked out Queen Mary from first to last, including modesty in abasing herself before her husband, William III; all kinds of modesty, ending with the notion that her own palace was 'a true temple of modesty'.

Yet this was an age which produced the quick-witted 'She-Champion and Midwife' Mrs Cellier as well as the modest Mary, born to rule, content to serve. Carving out a nursing career despite her dubious origins, holding her own against the officers of the law while on trial at the Old Bailey, indulging in *badinage* with Charles II on the same occasion, coolly storing the stones thrown at her in the pillory in her pocket and later ambitiously attempting to found a college of therapeutic midwifery, Mrs Cellier was also characteristic of a century when woman was widely held to be the weaker vessel.

To those that have come after, Mrs Cellier is a more engaging, and even perhaps a more admirable character than the submissive Queen – if not to her own society, which threw the stones.

References

Prologue: How Weak?

1 e.g. Hieron, *Helpe unto Devotion*, p. 270.
2 Wilkinson, 'Merchant-Royal', p. 130.
3 Rowse, *Shakespeare's Dark Lady*, p. 103.
4 Perkins, *Discourse of the Damned Art*, p. 168.
5 Josceline, 'Mothers Legacy', BL Add MSS, 27, 467.
6 Swetnam, *Arraignment of Women*, p. 15.
7 See Camden, *Elizabethan Woman*, pp. 23-4.
8 *Fox Journal*, p. 8.
9 Austin, *Haec Homo*, p. 5.
10 Allestree, *Ladies Calling*, Preface.
11 *As You Like It*, Act II, scene IV; Sharp, *Midwives Book*, p. 250.
12 cit. Illick, *Child-Rearing*, p. 320; *Ladies Dictionary*, p. 136.
13 cit. Stone. *Family, Sex and Marriage*, p. 495.
14 *Letters In Honour of the Dutchess of Newcastle*, p. 166; Newcastle, *Worlds Olio*, Preface.
15 *Lawes Resolutions*, p. 6.
16 *Lawes Resolutions*, p. 6.
17 Salmon, *Aristotle's Masterpiece*, p. 3.
18 *Hoby Diary*, p. 47.
19 Dante's *Inferno*, Book I, Canto III.

Chapter 1: A Wife Sought for Wealth

1 Wilkinson, 'Merchant-Royal', p. 20.
2 Nichols, *Progresses of King James I*, pp. 105-21.
3 Wilkinson, 'Merchant-Royal', p. 18; Dedication.
4 Gataker, 'Good Wife Gods Gift', p. 8.
5 *Lawes Resolutions*, p. 144.
6 HMC, Hastings MSS, IV, p. 332; *Cromwell Writings*, I, pp. 585-92; II, p. 8.
7 *Hatton Correspondence*, I, pp. 15-16.
8 Kenny, *History of the Law of England*, Part III, Chapter III.
9 Powell, *Domestic Relations*, p. 5 and note 2.
10 *Lawes Resolutions*, p. 146.
11 Willson, *King James VI and I*, p. 388.
12 Willson, *King James VI and I*, p. 286.
13 The 'courtship' is dealt with at length in Norsworthy, *Lady Hatton*; Lockyer, *Buckingham*, adds the findings of modern scholarship.
14 Ben Jonson, *The Gypsies Metamorphosed*, p. 139.

15 *Hic Mulier: Or, The Man-Woman.*
16 cit. Norsworthy, *Lady Hatton*, p. 55; Gardiner, *History of England*, III, p. 87.
17 Norsworthy, *Lady Hatton*, p. 39.
18 See Stone, *Family, Sex and Marriage*, pp. 31, 33-4.
19 Norsworthy, *Lady Hatton*, p. 43.
20 Norsworthy, *Lady Hatton*, pp. 49-50.
21 cit. Norsworthy, *Lady Hatton*, p. 29; HMC, Salisbury MSS, XXII, p. 52.
22 MacDonald, *Mystical Bedlam*, p. 21; CSP Domestic, 1619-23, p. 405.
23 Lockyer, *Buckingham*, p. 408.
24 May, *Social Control of Sex Expression*, p. 132.
25 Norsworthy, *Lady Hatton*, p. 125.
26 On 20 October 1624 according to Burke's *Extinct Peerages*, p. 559; Lockyer,
     Buckingham, p. 285, gives the birth as 'early in 1625'.
27 Norsworthy, *Lady Hatton*, p. 151.
28 *Conway Letters*, p. 25.
29 Burke's *Extinct Peerages*, p. 559.
30 For the marriage of Mary Blacknall see *Verney Papers*, pp. 138-46.
31 See Stone, *Family, Sex and Marriage*, pp. 30-37.
32 *Verney Memoirs*, II, p. 421.
33 *Verney Memoirs*, III, p. 30.
34 CSP Domestic, 1637, p. 422.
35 CSP Domestic, 1637, p. 423.
36 CSP Domestic, 1637, p. 423.
37 CSP Domestic, 1637, pp. 404, 547.
38 CSP Domestic, 1637, p. 565.
39 CSP Domestic, 1637-8, p. 499.

Chapter 2: Affection Is False

1   cit. Schücking, *Puritan Family*, pp. 25-6; Rogers, *Matrimoniall Honour*, p. 32.
2   See Sensabaugh, *Love Ethics in Platonic Court Drama*; Ben Jonson, *The New Inn*, Act I,
     scene V.
3   *Houblon Family*, I, Appendix A, p. 346.
4   cit. *Collins' Peerage*, II, p. 491.
5   HMC, Salisbury MSS, XXII, p. 239.
6   Swetnam, *Arraignment of Women*, pp. 12-13; Gataker, 'Good Wife Gods Gift', p. 18.
7   cit. Scott Thomson, *Noble Household*, p. 28.
8   McElwee, *Murder of Overbury*, pp. 238-41.
9   cit. Scott Thomson, *Noble Household*, pp. 28, 30.
10 Scott Thomson, *Noble Household*, pp. 28, 30.
11 Duncon, *Vi-Countess Falkland*, p. 149; Duncon, *Returns of Spiritual Comfort*, p. 1.
12 Duncon, *Vi-Countess Falkland*, p. 152.
13 *Clarendon Life*, I, p. 44.
14 *Clarendon Life*, I, p. 45.
15 Clarendon, *History of Rebellion*, III, p. 180.
16 Duncon, *Vi-Countess Falkland*, p. 153; Aubrey, *Brief Lives*, ed. Powell, p. 335. I
     discount Aubrey's secondhand gossip concerning Falkland's death (p. 356), preferring
     the account given by Clarendon, who knew him intimately.
17 Clarendon, *History of Rebellion*, III, pp. 189-90.

18 Duncon, *Vi-Countess Falkland*, pp. 155, 157.

19 Duncon, *Vi-Countess Falkland*, pp. 176, 195.

20 Duncon, *Vi-Countess Falkland*, p. 205.

21 Newcastle, *True Relation*, p. 12.

22 cit. Grant, *Margaret the First*, p. 81.

23 See E. A. Parry's edition for the letters and Lord David Cecil's biography of Dorothy Osborne in *Two Quiet Lives*.

24 *Osborne Letters*, pp. 181-2, 182.

25 *Osborne Letters*, p. 197.

26 *Osborne Letters*, p. 163.

27 Newdegate, *Muniment Room*, p. 36.

28 *Lismore Papers*, v, p. 101; *Warwick Autobiography*, p. 3.

29 *Warwick Autobiography*, p. 8.

30 See Gardiner, *Oxinden and Peyton*, pp. xxvi-xxvii and 'Oxinden Correspondence', v, BL Add MSS, 28, 003.

31 Fell Smith, *Warwick*, p. 336; *Osborne Letters*, p. 115.

32 'Oxinden Correspondence', v, BL Add MSS, 28, 003, fo. 147, 143.

33 'Oxinden Correspondence', v, BL Add MSS, 28, 003, fo. 143.

34 'Oxinden Correspondence', v, BL Add MSS, 28, 003, fo. 173.

35 'Oxinden Correspondence', v, BL Add MSS, 28, 003, fo. 173.

36 See Gardiner, *Oxinden and Peyton*, pp. 113-14, 155, 171.

37 Woolley, *Gentlewomans Companion*, p. 104.

38 MacDonald, *Mystical Bedlam*, p. 90.

39 *Martindale Life*, p. 16.

40 See Laslett, *World we have lost* (1983), pp. 81-3.

41 cit. Duffy, *Inherit the Earth*, p. 88; *Overbury Works*, pp. 169-70.

42 *Herrick Poems*, pp. 229-30.

43 *Osborne Letters*, p. 85.

Chapter 3: Crown to her Husband

1   Walker, *Holy Life*, p. 39 quoting Proverbs, 12, vs. 4; Hieron, *Helpe unto Devotion*, p. 386; Walker, *Holy Life*, p. 40; Hookes, *Amanda*, p. 116.

2   Knevet, *Funerall Elegies to the memory of Lady Paston*; Ballard, *Memoirs of Several Ladies*, p. 285.

3   Markham, *English Huswife*, II, p. 3.

4   Brathwaite, *English Gentlewoman*, p. 397.

5   Walker, *Holy Life*, p. 39.

6   *Houblon Family*, Appendix A, p. 346; *Evelyn Diary*, II, pp. 237, 128, 173.

7   i.e. *Pepys Diary*, VI, p. 316; IX, p. 204; *Hic Mulier: Or, The Man-Woman*.

8   cit. Notestein, *English Woman*, p. 94; Bridenbaugh, *Vexed Englishmen*, p. 119 and note; Fuller, *Worthies*, II, p. 294.

9   Gardiner, *Oxinden Letters*, pp. 40-41.

10 cit. Notestein, *English Woman*, p. 94.

11 Howell, *Familiar Letters*, p. 76; *Memoriae Matris* in Herbert, *Works*, p. 422 (translation by Edmund Blunden in *Essays and Literature by Members of the English Association*, XIX, pp. 32-3).

12 cit. Clark, *Working Life*, pp. 44-5.

13 *Stout Autobiography*, p. 3.

14 cit. Fussell, *English Countrywoman*, p. 62; Clark, *Working Life*, p. 51.
15 *Queen's Closet Opened*, Preface; see especially pp. 7, 44.
16 Kent, *Choice Manuall*, see especially pp. 107–8, 174, 4.
17 Kent, *Choice Manuall*, p. 198.
18 Brathwaite, *English Gentlewoman*, p. 397.
19 Walker, *Holy Life*, pp. 14, 67.
20 Walker, *Holy Life*, p. 67.
21 Walker, *Holy Life*, p. 72.
22 Walker, *Holy Life*, pp. 67, 88.
23 Ambrose, *Works*, pp. 117–18.
24 Fell Smith, *Warwick*, pp. 322–41; *Warwick Memoir*, pp. 292–4.
25 Walker, *Holy Life*, p. 27.
26 Evelyn, *Mundus Muliebris*, Preface; Gardiner, *Oxinden Letters*, p. 299.
27 Nash, *Worcestershire*, I, p. 500.
28 See Stone, *Family, Sex and Marriage*, pp. 489–90; Sharp, *Midwives Book*, p. 33.
29 Gouge, *Domesticall Duties*, p. 223; Milton, *Paradise Lost*, Book IV, lines 338–9.
30 cit. Bowle, *Evelyn*, p. 177.
31 Capp, *Astrology*, pp. 120–21.
32 *Oglander Notebook*, p. 5.
33 Whitelocke, *Memorials*, III, p. 32.
34 See Christie, *Shaftesbury*, p. lii.
35 Fell Smith, *Warwick*, p. 302.
36 *Heywood Autobiography*, I, pp. 61, 177.
37 *Harley Letters*, pp. 1, 3.
38 Denbigh, *Royalist Father*, pp. 197, 202, 199.
39 *Lovelace Poems*, p. 17.
40 See Lady Fanshawe's account in *Halkett and Fanshawe*, pp. 110, 102.
41 *Halkett and Fanshawe*, p. 114.
42 *Halkett and Fanshawe*, p. 115.
43 *Halkett and Fanshawe*, pp. 115–16.
44 *Halkett and Fanshawe*, pp. 123, 128.
45 *Halkett and Fanshawe*, pp. 130–31.
46 *Halkett and Fanshawe*, p. 103.
47 *Halkett and Fanshawe*, p. 103.
48 Fanshawe, *Shorter Poems*, p. 6.

Chapter 4: The Pain and the Peril

 1 See Schücking, *Puritan Family*, p. 67.
 2 Hookes, *Amanda*, p. 1.
 3 Walker, *Holy Life*, pp. 44, 33.
 4 See Appendix, 'A Chronology of Sir Richard Fanshawe', *Halkett and Fanshawe*, pp. 95–9.
 5 Hieron, *Helpe unto Devotion*, p. 148; I Timothy, 2, vs. 14–15.
 6 Hieron, *Helpe unto Devotion*, p. 148.
 7 *Halkett and Fanshawe*, p. 22.
 8 Sermon, *Ladies Companion*, p. 7.
 9 *Cust Family Records*, series II, p. 97; *Pepys Diary*, V, p. 222.
10 Grant, *Margaret the First*, p. 96; Newcastle, *CCXI Letters*, p. 94.
11 Sackville-West, *Clifford*, p. 107; Newcastle, *CCXI Letters*, p. 95.

12 *Heywood Autobiography*, I, p. 70.

13 *Mordaunt Private Diarie*, p. 21.

14 *Mordaunt Private Diarie*, p. 3; Clarendon, *History of the Rebellion*, VI, p. 59.

15 HMC, Salisbury MSS, 1612-88, p. 433; see Fraser, *Cromwell*, pp. 478-82.

16 Mordaunt, *Private Diarie*, pp. 28, 38, 152, 183.

17 Himes, *Contraception*, pp. 168-70, 183, 191-2; *Pepys Diary*, VIII, p. 318.

18 See Schnucker, 'Elizabethan Birth Control'; 'New Bill in Reply to the Ladies and Batchelors', p. 449.

19 Defoe, *Conjugal Lewdness*, p. 155; Capp, *Astrology*, p. 122.

20 Capp, *Astrology*, p. 122; Schnucker, 'Elizabethan Birth Control', p. 657.

21 Schnucker, 'Elizabethan Birth Control', pp. 657-9; Eccles, *Obstetrics in Stuart England*, pp. 26-32.

22 Macfarlane, *Josselin*, p. 201.

23 cit. Wrigley, 'Family Limitation', p. 105, note 3.

24 See Wrigley, 'Family Limitation'; Henry, *Anciennes Familles Genevoises*.

25 *Warwick Autobiography*, p. 32.

26 Josceline, 'Mothers Legacy', BL Add MSS, 27, 467; Reynolds, *Learned Lady*, p. 29.

27 Josceline, 'Mothers Legacy', BL Add MSS, 27, 467; Reynolds, *Learned Lady*, p. 29.

28 Sharp, *Midwives Book*, p. 170; Newcastle, *CCXI Letters*, p. 189.

29 *Harcourt Papers*, I, p. 106; Pilkington, *Celebrated Female Characters*, p. 199.

30 See Evelyn, *Mrs Godolphin*, for her story; esp. pp. 79, 144-51.

31 Black, *Folk-Medicine*, pp. 162-3; *Pepys Diary*, IV, p. 339 and note 2; Eccles, *Obstetrics in Stuart England*, p. 20.

32 Evelyn, *Mrs Godolphin*, p. 156.

33 Hartmann, *King's Friend*, p. 205.

34 Hieron, *Helpe unto Devotion*, p. 270; Cartwright, *Sacharissa*, p. 74.

35 Gardiner, *History of England*, IX, p. 80; Higgins, 'Women in the Civil War', p. 50.

36 See Stone, *Family, Sex and Marriage*, esp. pp. 105-14; MacDonald, *Mystical Bedlam*, pp. 77-82.

37 *Verney Memoirs*, II, p. 296; *Heywood Autobiography*, I, p. 45; Souars, *Orinda*, p. 89.

38 *Cholmley Memoirs*, p. 31.

39 Clarke, *Lives of Eminent Persons*, p. 158.

40 Duncon, *Vi-Countess Falkland*, p. 175; Sidney, *Diary*, I, p. lxxxv.

41 *Cust Family Records*, series II, p. 120; see Stone, *Family, Sex and Marriage*, p. 60 for 'an average family' of four, five, or six children of whom two or three would die young.

42 *Thornton Autobiography*, p. 126.

43 *Thornton Autobiography*, p. 94.

44 *Thornton Autobiography*, p. 145.

45 Peter Laslett, in *World we have lost* (1983), p. 129; cit. Illick, *Child-Rearing*, p. 305 and note 10, p. 333; Stone, *Crisis of the Aristocracy*, p. 619.

46 See McLaren, 'Nature's Contraceptive'.

47 *Stout Autobiography*, p. 14; McLaren, 'Nature's Contraceptive', p. 432.

48 Ross, *Margaret Fell*, p. 335; *Collins' Peerage*, II, p. 81; *Conway Letters*, p. 124.

49 Fildes, 'Infant Feeding Practices', seminar.

50 Sharp, *Midwives Book*, pp. 349, 365; *Verney Memoirs*, II, p. 94.

51 *Heywood Autobiography*, I, p. 58; Clark, *Working Life*, p. 27; CSP Domestic, 1661-2, p. 221; 'Farthing affidavit', *Notes and Queries*, V, 11th series, 1912, p. 508; Fildes, 'Infant Feeding Practices', seminar.

52 McLaren, *Nature's Contraceptive*, p. 433.
53 Schnucker, *Puritans and Pregnancy*, p. 648; Sharp, *Midwives Book*, p. 353.
54 Newdegate, *Muniment Room*, pp. 20, 88.
55 See 'Lincoln's Nursery', esp. pp. 25, 27, 205, 31.

Chapter 5: Are You Widows?

1 'Warwicke Specialities' BL Add MSS, 27, 357.
2 Duncon, *Returns of Spiritual Comfort*; Clarke, *Lives of Eminent Persons*, II, p. 148.
3 Newdegate, *Muniment Room*, pp. 86, 156, 126.
4 Macfarlane, *Marital and Sexual Relationships*, pp. 120, 213.
5 *Herbert Autobiography*, pp. xix, 10 and note 3.
6 See Cartwright, *Sacharissa*, for the story of Dorothy Sidney; *Waller Poems*, I, p. 128; Cartwright, *Sacharissa*, p. 74.
7 Cartwright, *Sacharissa*, pp. 104–6.
8 *Osborne Letters*, p. 44.
9 *Pepys Diary*, I, p. 60.
10 Laslett, *World we have lost* (1983) Table 10, p. 108, gives 38.1 in 1601, declining to 35.7 in 1661 and 32.5 in 1721.
11 Stone, *Family, Sex and Marriage*, p. 56.
12 *Verney Memoirs*, I, p. 242.
13 *Verney Memoirs*, I, p. 257.
14 *Verney Memoirs*, I, pp. 265, 268.
15 *Verney Memoirs*, I, p. 274; *Warwick Autobiography*, p. 27.
16 Fell Smith, *Warwick*, p. 11.
17 Fell Smith, *Warwick*, pp. 109–10.
18 *Herbert Autobiography*, pp. 46–7.
19 Blundell, *Cavalier's Notebook*, p. 242; Brailsford, *Quaker Women*, p. 137; *Harley Letters*, p. 117.
20 Notestein, *English Woman*, p. 107, note 16.
21 *Osborne Letters*, p. 123.
22 Kirkman, *Unlucky Citizen*, p. 163.
23 Price, *London Bankers*, pp. 151, 31; Price, *Marygold*, p. 23.
24 See Lang, 'Greater Merchants of London', Chapter V; *Chamberlain Letters*, II, pp. 572, 576; *Pepys Diary*, VI, p. 215.
25 See the Rev. L.B. Larking in *Proceedings, Principally in the County of Kent, In Connection with the Parliaments called in 1640*, for the story of the Widow Bennett.
26 Philip Massinger, *City Madam*, Act IV, scene IV.
27 John Webster, *Duchess of Malfi*, Act I, scene I; Swetnam, *Arraignment of Women*, p. 31.
28 Larking, *Proceedings*, p. xxxiii.
29 See *Verney Papers*, pp. 199–223 for the second marriage of Margaret Poulteney.
30 *Verney Papers*, p. 221.
31 Allestree, *Ladies Calling*, p. 42.
32 'Twysden Notebooks', BL Add MSS, 34, 163, fo. 211.
33 'Twysden Notebooks', BL Add MSS, 34, 163, fo. 211.
34 'Twysden Notebooks', BL Add MSS, 34, 163, fo. 210, 28.
35 G.E.C., *Complete Peerage*, XII/2, p. 775, note D.
36 Sackville-West, *Clifford*, p. xxxviii; Rowse, *Shakespeare's Dark Lady*, p. 139.
37 Notestein, *Four Worthies*, p. 128; Sackville-West, *Clifford*, p. 28.

38 Sackville-West, *Clifford*, p. xxxix; Whitaker, *History of Craven*, p. 277; Cocke, 'Clifford'.

39 Notestein, *Four Worthies*, p. 149; cit. Ballard, *Memoirs of Several Ladies*, p. 317.

40 Notestein, *Four Worthies*, p. 154; see Ballard, *Memoirs of Several Ladies*, p. 314, writing within living memory of Lady Anne.

41 Even if these rights, up till the end of the seventeenth century, were only effective in practice in the City of London, the province of York and Wales (see Stone, *Family, Sex and Marriage*, pp. 195–6).

42 *Thornton Autobiography*, p. 247.

43 See Stenton, *English Woman*, pp. 100–105.

44 See Clark, *Working Life*, pp. 10, 150, 104.

45 Clark, *Working Life*, pp. 20–31, 233, 215; cit. Thompson, *Women in Stuart England*, p. 217, note 86.

46 Stenton, *English Woman*, p. 219; Clark, *Working Life*, p. 161.

47 Brathwaite, *English Gentlewoman*, p. 332.

Chapter 6: Poor and Atrabilious

1 HMC, Hastings MSS, IV, p. 325; the third Earl of Warwick was the proposed bridegroom, cit. Fell Smith, *Warwick*, p. 145.

2 See Laslett, *World we have lost* (1983), pp. 90–98; Thomas, *Religion*, pp. 560–67.

3 Pearl, 'Social Policy', p. 129.

4 cit. Smith, 'Growing Old in Early Stuart England', p. 127.

5 Ballard, *Memoirs of Several Ladies*, p. 361; *Collins' Peerage*, IV, p. 106; Smith, 'Growing Old in Early Stuart England', p. 127.

6 John Milton, *Comus*, l. 453; John Ford, '*Tis Pity She's a Whore*, Act II, scene v; *Hic Mulier: Or, The Man-Woman*.

7 cit. Thomas, *Religion*, p. 464.

8 Perkins, *Discourse of the Damned Art*, p. 168; Burton, *Anatomy of Melancholy*, I, p. 210; Quaife, *Wanton Wenches*, p. 152.

9 See Ewen, *Witchcraft*, Index (Marks); also Macfarlane, *Witchcraft*, p. 19 for increasing stress placed on marks at trial; Thomas, *Religion*, pp. 445–6.

10 cit. George, ' "Goodwife" to "Mistress" ', p. 161; Eyre, *Dyurnall*, p. 46; Proverbs, 25, vs. 24, cit. for example in Allestree, *Ladies Calling*, p. 48.

11 Roberts, *Social History*, p. 156; see Capp, *Astrology*, pp. 124–5.

12 Bridenbaugh, *Vexed Englishmen*, pp. 357–8.

13 Thomas, *Religion*, pp. 503–5; Dekker, Ford and Rowley, *Witch of Edmonton*, Act II, scene I.

14 Woolley, *Gentlewomans Companion*, p. 42; see Burstein, 'Psychopathology of Old Age'.

15 Thomas, *Religion*, p. 557; Macfarlane, *Witchcraft*, p. 161; Stearne, *Discovery of Witchcraft*, p. 12.

16 Thomas, *Religion*, p. 565; Burstein, 'Psychopathology of Old Age', p. 65.

17 Scot, *Discoverie of Witchcraft*, Epistle to Readers, p. xxiii.

18 See *Complete History of Magick, Sorcery and Witchcraft* (1715), I, pp. 177–95 for a version of the Belvoir witches' story written when witchcraft was still part of contemporary belief.

19 Ewen, *Witchcraft*, p. 231; Scot, *Discoverie of Witchcraft*, p. 5.

20 *Macbeth*, Act I, scene I; Dekker, Ford and Rowley, *Witch of Edmonton*, Act V, scene I; Nichols, *Leicestershire*, p. 49, note 12; see Ewen, *North Moreton*, p. 4.

21 *Complete History of Magick*, I, p. 179.

22 Ewen, *Witchcraft*, p. 233.

23 Notestein, *Witchcraft*, p. 134, note 19.

24 See *Complete History of Magick*, I, pp. 177–95; Ewen, *Witchcraft*, pp. 232–3.

25 Nichols, *Leicestershire*, p. 49, note 12.

26 Nichols, *Leicestershire*, p. 49.

27 *Complete History of Magick*, I, p. 193.

28 Ewen, *Witchcraft*, p. 233; *Complete History of Magick*, p. 195.

29 HMC, Rutland MSS, 12th Report, IV, pp. 514, 516.

30 CSP Domestic, 1619–23, p. 71; Lockyer, *Buckingham*, p. 58.

31 Lockyer, *Buckingham*, p. 59; Stone, *Family and Fortune*, p. 197.

32 *Wilson Life*, p. 476.

33 See Larner, *Enemies of God*, p. 20, for a summary of recent work on the subject.

34 Macfarlane, *Witchcraft*, p. 163; Stearne, *Confirmation of Witchcraft*, p. 10; Scot,
    Discoverie of Witchcraft, p. 42; Larner, *Enemies of God*, p. 20; Burton, *Anatomy of
    Melancholy*, I, p. 210.

35 e.g. *Middlesex County Records*, III, p. 287; Ewen, *Witch Hunting*, p. 33; cit. Burstein,
    'Psychopathology of Old Age', p. 64.

36 cit. Notestein, *Witchcraft*, p. 272, note 6.

37 See Ewen, *Witchcraft*, pp. 365–7, for the trial.

38 cit. Ewen, *Witchcraft*, p. 372.

39 Notestein, *Witchcraft*, p. 272, note 6.

40 cit. Macfarlane, *Witchcraft*, p. 114, and see pp. 114–30 for 'cunning folk' in general;
    Verney Memoirs, IV, p. 172.

41 cit. Burstein, 'Psychopathology of Old Age', p. 64; Gardiner, *Oxinden Letters*,
    pp. 220–21.

42 Hill, *Intellectual Consequences of the Revolution*, p. 64.

43 *Athenian Oracle*, III, p. 336.

44 Dekker, Ford and Rowley, *Witch of Edmonton*, Act II, scene I.

Chapter 7: Unlearned Virgins

1 Josceline, 'Mothers Legacy', BL Add MSS, 27, 467; *Mordaunt Private Diarie*, Appendix,
   p. 228; *Harcourt Papers*, I, pp. 153, 173.

2 Quaife, *Wanton Wenches*, p. 95.

3 *Verney Memoirs*, II, p. 76; IV, p. 255.

4 Newcastle, *Worlds Olio*, Preface; p. 72.

5 Newdegate, *Muniment Room*, p. 150; Josceline, 'Mothers Legacy', BL Add MSS, 27,
   467; Reynolds, *Learned Lady*, p. 29.

6 *Osborne Letters*, p. 100.

7 *Letters in Honour of the Dutchess of Newcastle*, pp. 4–5, 11.

8 *Bradstreet Works*, p. 361; Oman, *Elizabeth of Bohemia*, p. 22.

9 Fraser, *Mary Queen of Scots*, p. 180.

10 Reynolds, *Learned Lady*, pp. 9, 23; cit. Notestein, *English Woman*, p. 82.

11 Clarke, *Lives of Eminent Persons*, pp. 201–2.

12 Eyre, *Dyurnall*, p. 34; Duncon, *Vi-Countess Falkland*, p. 152; Fell Smith, *Warwick*,
    pp. 170–71; *Cholmley Memoirs*, p. 52.

13 Leigh, *Mothers Blessing*, pp. 4, 56.

14 cit. Gardiner, *Girlhood at School*, p. 194.

15 Matthew, *Lady Lucy Knatchbull*, p. xiv.

16 Memo of Mary Ward, cit. Chambers, *Mary Ward*, I, p. 376, note iii.

17 For the life of Mary Ward, see M.C.E. Chambers' biography (1885), and post 1945 shorter studies, pamphlets and articles by James Brodrick SJ, Joseph Grisar SJ, Margaret Mary Littlehales IBVM, Pauline Parker IBVM, and Immolata Wetter IBVM.

18 cit. Littlehales, *Mary Ward*, p. 13.

19 Chambers, *Mary Ward*, I, pp. 410–13.

20 cit. Littlehales, *Mary Ward*, p. 14.

21 Wetter, *Apostolic Vocation*, p. 89.

22 Littlehales, *Mary Ward*, p. 27.

23 cit. Wetter, *Apostolic Vocation*, p. 91.

24 *Italian Life* (probably written by Mary Poyntz), cit. Littlehales, *Mary Ward*, p. 28.

25 *Heywood Autobiography*, p. 49; Walker, *Holy Life*, p. 96; Ballard, *Memoirs of Several Ladies*, p. 310.

26 *Thornton Autobiography*, pp. 233, 342; *Verney Memoirs*, II, p. 228.

27 Cressy, *Literacy*, pp. 119, 128, 145.

28 Scott Thomson, *Noble Household*, p. 120.

29 Scott Thomson, *Noble Household*, pp. 75–6.

30 Scott Thomson, *Noble Household*, p. 305.

31 Reynolds, *Learned Lady*, p. 266; *Hearne Remains*, p. 307.

32 *Oglander Notebook*, p. 74.

33 *Conway Letters*, pp. 15, 5.

34 Masson, *Milton*, V, p. 232; *Collins' Peerage*, VII, p. 167.

35 Fell Smith, *Warwick*, p. 38.

36 *Warwick Autobiography*, pp. 14, 22.

37 Masson, *Milton*, V, pp. 233–4.

38 Fell Smith, *Warwick*, p. 37; Budgell, *Lives of the Boyles*, I, Appendix, p. 5; I, p. 147.

39 Masson, *Milton*, V, p. 457.

40 Fell Smith, *Warwick*, p. 315.

41 Fell Smith, *Warwick*, p. 357.

42 *Locke Correspondence*, II, p. 219; Fell Smith, *Warwick*, p. 347.

43 Walker, *Holy Life*, p. 39; Clarke, *Lives of Eminent Persons*, p. 201.

44 *Halkett and Fanshawe*, pp. 10, 110; *Thornton Autobiography*, p. 8.

45 *All's Well That Ends Well*, Act I, scene III.

46 See Lucy Hutchinson, *Memoirs of Col. Hutchinson*, ed. James Sutherland, pp. 28–35 and 288–9 for her account of her education.

47 cit. Hutchinson, *Memoirs*, pp. 278–89.

48 Hutchinson, *Memoirs*, p. 33.

49 Hutchinson, *Memoirs*, p. 48.

50 Roberts, *Social History*, p. 378; Thompson, *Women in Stuart England*, p. 204; Gardiner, *Girlhood at School*, pp. 276–94.

51 Thompson, *Women in Stuart England*, pp. 192–3.

52 Mulcaster, *Positions*, cit. Cressy, *Education*, pp. 109–11.

53 Thompson, *Women in Stuart England*, pp. 189–90.

54 Gardiner, *Girlhood at School*, p. 181.

55 Gardiner, *Oxinden and Peyton*, p. 128; *Thornton Autobiography*, p. 8; Gardiner, *Girlhood at School*, p. 159.

56 F. P. Verney, 1892, *Verney Memoirs*, I, p. xiii; Dorothy Gardiner 1933, *Oxinden Letters*, p. xxviii.

57 cit. Goreau, *Aphra*, p. 31.
58 Lambley, *French Language*, pp. 263–4, 299; *Harley Letters*, p. 13.
59 *Artamenes*, Dedication.
60 *Verney Memoirs*, III, p. 66.
61 *Verney Memoirs*, III, pp. 72–4.
62 *Verney Memoirs*, III, p. 74.
63 Dr Denton had sat on the Council of the Girls' Public Day Schools Company, *Verney Memoirs*, I, p. 72.

Chapter 8: Living under Obedience

1   See Batchiler, *Virgin's Pattern*; Gardiner, *Girlhood at School*, pp. 211–13.
2   Batchiler, *Virgin's Pattern*, Epitaph.
3   Theodore Spencer in 'History of an Unfortunate Lady'.
4   Batchiler, *Virgin's Pattern*.
5   Batchiler, *Virgin's Pattern*.
6   Batchiler, *Virgin's Pattern*.
7   Milton cit. Goreau, *Aphra*, p. 76; Clarke, *Lives of Eminent Persons*, p. 135; Chambers, *Mary Ward*, I, p. 210.
8   Newcastle, *CCXI Letters*, p. 124; Evelyn, *Mrs Godolphin*, pp. 75, 121.
9   See Halkett and Fanshawe, pp. 12–20.
10 Gibbon, *Decline and Fall of the Roman Empire*, I, Chapter 3; Chambers, *Mary Ward*, I, pp. 203–5; Clarke, *Lives of Eminent Persons*, p. 135.
11 Warner, *Alone of All Her Sex*, pp. 246–7.
12 Stafford, *Femall Glory*, pp. 25, 32.
13 Stafford, *Femall Glory*, p. 168.
14 Laslett, *World we have lost* (1983), p. 27, describes the gentry class and above as one twenty-fifth or at most one twentieth of the population; OED; Bridenbaugh, *Vexed Englishmen*, p. 147.
15 *Pepys Diary*, VIII, p. 193 and note 2; Ashley, *Life in Stuart England*, p. 27; HMC, Salisbury MSS, 1612–88, p. 394.
16 Laslett, *World we have lost* (1983), p. 12.
17 Chambers, *Mary Ward*, II, p. 33.
18 I Corinthians, 14, vs. 35; *Verney Memoirs*, III, p. 74.
19 Macfarlane, *Josselin*, p. 147; Laslett, *World we have lost* (1983), p. 13.
20 Laslett, *World we have lost* (1983), p. 82, suggests a 'mean age' of about twenty-three and a half.
21 Wage of £2 cited for 1685 by Goreau, *Aphra*, p. 73; *Cust Family Records*, series II, p. 63; Scott Thomson, *Noble Household*, p. 301.
22 Fell Smith, *Warwick*, p. 348; Stuart, *English Abigail*, p. 40.
23 For *Mary Woodforde's Book*, see *Woodforde Papers*, pp. 3–34.
24 Blundell, *Cavalier's Notebook*, p. 158; Halifax, *Complete Works*, p. 292.
25 *Twysden Diary*, pp. 119, 122, 134; Scott Thomson, *Noble Household*, p. 120.
26 *Wilson Life*, p. 462.
27 Scott Thomson, *Noble Household*, p. 309.
28 Kirkman, *Unlucky Citizen*, p. 127; HMC, Salisbury MSS, XXII, p. 425.
29 Kirkman, *Unlucky Citizen*, p. 99.
30 *Thornton Autobiography*, p. 277; *Diary of Robert Hooke 1672–1680*, cit. Stone, *Family, Sex and Marriage*, pp. 561–3.

31 See *Martindale Life*, pp. 6-8, 17-18.
32 See Spufford, 'Portraits of Society'.
33 Hogrefe, *Tudor Women*, pp. 89-90; *Mistress Mary Firth*.
34 See CSP Domestic, 1628-9, pp. 530-1.
35 Thomas, *Religion*, p. 137.
36 Carte MS, Vol. LXXVIII, fo. 410, no. 175.
37 For the career of Lady Eleanor Davies see especially Spencer, 'Unfortunate Lady', and 'Dougle Fooleries'.
38 Spencer, 'Unfortunate Lady', p. 43.
39 CSP Domestic, 1619-23, p. 400.
40 'Dougle Fooleries', p. 95.
41 HMC, Hastings MSS, IV, p. 343.
42 Spencer, 'Unfortunate Lady', p. 48.
43 CSP Domestic, 1633-4, pp. 266, 345; 'Petition of Lady Eleanor (Davies)', Thomason Tract, 669, fo. 10/2.
44 CSP Domestic, 1633-4, p. 261.
45 Spencer, 'Unfortunate Lady', p. 51.
46 CSP Domestic, 1633-4, p. 346.
47 'Dougle Fooleries', p. 97.
48 'Dougle Fooleries', p. 94.
49 Tract no. 18, HMC, Hastings MSS, IV, p. 344.

Chapter 9: Courage above her Sex

1 Newcastle, *Worlds Olio*, p. 215.
2 cit. Bankes, *Dorset Heritage*, p. 55; Washbourn, *Gloucestrensis*, part I, p. lxxxvii.
3 HMC, Bath MSS, I, p. 27; still to be seen on the wall of the chancel in St Martin's Church, Ruislip, Middlesex.
4 *Cholmley Memoirs*, p. 42; *Cholmley's Narrative*, p. 583.
5 cit. Coate, *Social Life*, p. 30; *Cromwell Writings*, II, pp. 378-9.
6 'Lathom Siege Journall', p. 163.
7 'Dyve Letters', p. 67.
8 See Fraser, *Cromwell*, p. 335; 'Dyve Letters', p. 73; Foster, 'Digby', p. 23.
9 Denbigh, *Royalist Father*, p. 224.
10 *Harcourt Papers*, I, p. 168; see the anonymous 'A Briefe Journal of the Siege against Lathom', Ormerod's *Civil War Tracts in Lancashire*, pp. 159-86, for a first-hand account of its course.
11 'Lathom Siege Journall', p. 167.
12 'Lathom Siege Journall', p. 177.
13 See Powicke, 'Hastings Manuscripts', pp. 262-7.
14 Lloyd, *Memoires of Noble Personages*, p. 572; Blundell, *Cavalier's Notebook*, p. 151; *Fox Journal*, p. 464.
15 See Godwin, *Civil War in Hampshire*, pp. 84-370.
16 Clarendon, *History of Rebellion*, III, p. 410.
17 Godwin, *Civil War in Hampshire*, p. 347; *Cromwell Writings*, I, p. 341.
18 Lloyd, *Memoires of Noble Personages*, p. 586; Clarendon, *History of Rebellion*, II, p. 536.
19 Hutchins, *Dorset*, I, pp. 504, 488-9.
20 Hutchins, *Dorset*, I, p. 495.

21 Hutchins, *Dorset*, I, p. 489; for a contemporary account of the siege, see *Mercurius Rusticus*, No. XI, cit. Hutchins, *Dorset*, I, pp. 504–7.

22 Hutchins, *Dorset*, I, p. 507.

23 Hutchins, *Dorset*, I, p. 506.

24 Hutchins, *Dorset*, I, p. 508; Vicars, *Burning-Bush*, p. 372.

25 Hutchins, *Dorset*, I, p. 509.

26 cit. Bankes, *Dorset Heritage*, p. 94.

27 HMC, Bath MSS, I, p. 4.

28 *Harley Letters*, p. xiii.

29 *Harley Letters*, pp. 7–9, 13, 16, 20.

30 *Harley Letters*, p. 24.

31 *Harley Letters*, pp. 104, 158, 167, 178, 181.

32 *Harley Letters*, p. 183.

33 *Harley Letters*, p. 186.

34 *Harley Letters*, p. 188–90.

35 *Harley Letters*, p. 204; HMC, Bath MSS, I, p. 8.

36 HMC, Bath MSS, pp. 8–9.

37 HMC, Bath MSS, pp. 12–13.

38 HMC, Bath MSS, pp. 4, 6.

39 HMC, Bath MSS, pp. 14, 17.

40 HMC, Bath MSS, p. 17.

41 HMC, Bath MSS, p. 27.

42 *Harley Letters*, pp. 206–7, 209.

43 The exact date of her death is not known; see her entry in DNB.

44 HMC, Bath MSS, pp. 29–32.

45 *Harley Letters*, pp. 230, xxxv.

46 Washbourn, *Gloucestrensis*, Part II, p. 227; Butler, *Hudibras*, p. 148.

47 Higgins, 'Women in the Civil War', p. 38; Burghall, 'Providence Improved', p. 166.

48 Bayley, *Civil War in Dorset*, p. 174; Strong, *Joanereidos*, 1645; 'Tobie Trundle', in *Joanereidos*, 1674.

49 Bayley, *Civil War in Dorset*, p. 127; Kaufman, *Conscientious Cavalier*, p. 154.

50 Kaufman, *Conscientious Cavalier*, p. 154.

51 Bayley, *Civil War in Dorset*, p. 150 note 1, p. 172.

52 'Tobie Trundle', in *Joanereidos*, 1674.

53 Bayley, *Civil War in Dorset*, p. 191.

54 Vicars, *Gods Arke*, pp. 246, 259.

Chapter 10: His Comrade

1 *Verney Memoirs*, II, p. 96; 'Scourge of Civil War', Thomason Tract, 669, fo. 10/27.

2 Higgins, 'Women in the Civil War', p. 29; *Cromwell Writings*, I, p. 248.

3 CSP Domestic, 1645–7, p. 260; Gregg, *Charles I*, p. 361; *Athenae Oxonienses*, I, p. xxviii.

4 *Athenae Oxonienses*, I, p. xxviii; IV, pp. 15–41.

5 Gregg, *Charles I*, p. 411.

6 *Lilly's History*, p. 139.

7 Hillier, *Narrative*, pp. 142, 130, 140.

8 Note by P. Bliss, *Athenae Oxonienses*, I, p. xxix; Gregg, *Charles I*, p. 443.

9 See J. Loftis, Introduction, *Halkett and Fanshawe*, p. xii.

10 See *Halkett and Fanshawe*, pp. 23-30.
11 *James II Memoirs*, p. 41.
12 *Verney Memoirs*, I, p. 293.
13 *Warwick Autobiography*, p. 20.
14 See Denbigh, *Royalist Father*, pp. 165-95.
15 *Crashaw Poems*, p. 236.
16 *Staffordshire and Great Rebellion*, p. 132.
17 Everitt, *Kent and Great Rebellion*, p. 26.
18 Quaife, *Wanton Wenches*, pp. 125, 133.
19 cit. Clark, *Working Life*, p. 80.
20 *Verney Memoirs*, II, p. 176.
21 *Verney Memoirs*, II, pp. 199-200.
22 *Verney Memoirs*, II, p. 203.
23 *Mercurius Aulicus*, 9 September 1643.
24 cit. Godwin, *Civil War in Hampshire*, pp. 121-2.
25 Godwin, *Civil War in Hampshire*, p. 122.
26 On the exaggeration of horrors including this incident, Brig. Peter Young to the author; *Luke Letter Books*, p. 204.
27 Bayley, *Civil War in Dorset*, p. 188 and note 1.
28 Young, *Edgehill*, p. 11; Whitelocke, *Memorials*, I, p. 188.
29 BL Harleian MSS, 6804, fo. 75/6.
30 Higgins, 'Women in the Civil War', pp. 46-7; Firth, *Cromwell's Army*, pp. 298-9.
31 Young, *Marston Moor*, p. 166, and letter to the author.
32 Lacy, *Old Troop*, pp. 150, 141, 155.
33 Lacy, *Old Troop*, p. 141; 'Gallant She-Souldier', *Roxburghe Ballads*, VII, pp. 728-9.
34 Higgins, 'Women in the Civil War', p. 42.
35 Firth, *Cromwell's Army*, pp. 80, 73-4, 116-17; 'Female Warrior', *Douce Ballads*, I (79); 'Famous Woman Drummer, *Roxburghe Ballads*, VII, pp. 730-32.
36 Higgins, 'Women in the Civil War', p. 45.
37 Higgins, 'Women in the Civil War', p. 42; CSP Domestic, 1639, pp. 146, 282.
38 *Mrs Christian Davies' Life*, pp. 2, 20.
39 HMC, Leyborne-Popham MSS, p. 112 for Col. Sawrey's letter; extensive researches in local records have unfortunately failed to produce an Anne Dymoke of the right age.
40 *Verney Memoirs*, IV, p. 256.
41 *Venables Narrative*, p. 102.
42 Firth, *Cromwell's Army*, pp. 259-60.
43 Hutchinson, *Memoirs*, p. 99.
44 Macdonald, *Alkin*, p. 21; CSP Domestic, 1652-3, p. xxxi; Frank, *English Newspaper*, p. 204.
45 Firth, *Cromwell's Army*, p. 264; Clark, *Working Life*, p. 243.
46 Firth, *Cromwell's Army*, p. 265.
47 *Halkett and Fanshawe*, p. 75.
48 *Halkett and Fanshawe*, p. 82.

Chapter 11: A Soliciting Temper

1 Makin, *Essay on Education*, p. 25; Newcastle, *True Relation*, p. 20.
2 Gardiner, *Civil War*, I, pp. 100-101, 244.
3 Higgins, 'Women in the Civil War', p. 110 and note 1.

4 Gardiner, *Civil War*, III, p. 197; Higgins, 'Women in the Civil War', p. 15.
5 Fraser, *Cromwell*, p. 504.
6 Beard, *American Civilization*, I, p. 25; Nash, *Worcestershire*, I, p. 492; Foster, 'Digby', p. 4.
7 CSP Domestic, 1640-41, pp. 249-50; Clark, *Working Life*, pp. 23-4.
8 Gardiner, *Civil War*, III, pp. 197-9.
9 *Knyvett Letters*, p. 147.
10 See *Twysden Family*, pp. 172-3 and *Cholmley Memoirs*, pp. 44-8. .
11 *Twysden Family*, p. 148.
12 For the story of Dame Isabella Twysden, see her *Diary*, ed. by the Rev. F. W. Bennet, and 'Twysden Notebooks', BL Add MSS, 34, 163.
13 See *Twysden Diary*.
14 'Twysden Notebooks', BL Add MSS, 34, 163, 1, fo. 332.
15 'Twysden Notebooks', BL Add MSS, 34, 163, 1, fo. 332.
16 *Verney Memoirs*, II, p. 238.
17 *Verney Memoirs*, II, p. 225.
18 *Verney Memoirs*, II, pp. 231-2, 234-5.
19 *Verney Memoirs*, II, pp. 239-40.
20 *Verney Memoirs*, II, p. 239.
21 *Verney Memoirs*, II, pp. 244, 253.
22 Newcastle, *True Relation*, p. 20.
23 Newcastle, *True Relation*, p. 20; *Verney Memoirs*, II, p. 248.
24 *Verney Memoirs*, II, pp. 249-58.
25 See *Verney Memoirs*, II, pp. 255-82, 292-3, 316-17 for Mary Verney's dealings with the Committee, visit to Claydon and return to France.
26 *Verney Memoirs*, II, p. 411.
27 *Verney Memoirs*, II, pp. 414-16.
28 *Verney Memoirs*, II, pp. 422-3.
29 *Verney Memoirs*, III, p. 30.

Chapter 12: Sharing in the Commonwealth

1 Higgins, 'Women in the Civil War', p. 146.
2 Neville, *Ladies Parliament*; *Ladies, A Second Time, Assembled*; *Commonwealth of Ladies*.
3 CSP Venetian, 1643-7, p. 135; *Venables Narrative*, p. xl.
4 Gibb, *Fairfax*, p. 181; *Mercurius Pragmaticus*, 26 December 1648.
5 Clarendon, cit. Stone, *Family, Sex and Marriage*, p. 340; *Verney Memoirs*, III, pp. 318, 341.
6 Newcastle, *Worlds Olio*, pp. 74-5.
7 Taylor, *Sex in History*, p. 277; Knox, *Enthusiasm*, p. 140.
8 Brailsford, *Quaker Women*, p. 246; Ross, *Margaret Fell*, p. 108.
9 cit. Stone, *Family, Sex and Marriage*, pp. 627, 626.
10 cit. Owen, 'Lincolnshire Women', p. 34; Fraser, *Cromwell*, p. 54; Higgins, 'Women in the Civil War', p. 142.
11 Kerridge, 'Revolts in Wiltshire', pp. 68-9; Higgins, 'Women in the Civil War', p. 144.
12 George, ' "Goodwife" to "Mistress" ', p. 152; *Womens Sharpe Revenge*, pp. 37-42.
13 See Mitchell and Leys, *London*, pp. 397-8; Herbert, *History of Livery Companies*, p. 21.

14 Lupton, *London Characters*, pp. 91–4.
15 See OED (see also Mary Ward's use of Billingsgate, p. 128 *ante*); Timbs, *Curiosities of London*, pp. 54–5; Butler, *Hudibras*, p. 44.
16 Higgins, 'Women in the Civil War', pp. 154–67; 'Certaine Informations', E. 65 (8); Gardiner, *Civil War*, I, p. 187.
17 *Kingdomes Weekly Intelligencer*, E. 65/II; Higgins, 'Women in the Civil War', p. 168.
18 Carlyle, *Critical Essays*, IV, pp. 327, 333.
19 See Hirst, *Representative of the People?*, pp. 18–19.
20 Chapman and Chapman, *Status of Women under Law*, p. 23; Hirst, *Representative of the People?*, p. 18.
21 Coke, *Institutes*, Part 4, p. 4.
22 Fieldhouse, 'Parliamentary Representation in the Borough of Richmond', pp. 207–8.
23 *Clarke Papers*, I, pp. 299, 302; Gregg, *Free-Born John*, p. 215.
24 Thomas, 'Women and Sects', p. 56.
25 Astell, *Reflections*, pp. 43–5.
26 cit. Appendix C, Berens, *Digger Movement*, p. 252.
27 *Middlesex County Records*, III, pp. xxii, 287.
28 Gibb, *Lilburne*, pp. 171, 174; Gregg, *Free-Born John*, on the other hand, makes no such suggestion: see p. 215.
29 Higgins, 'Women in the Civil War', pp. 178–87.
30 'Overton Appeal and Petition', E. 381/10, pp. 3–4, 6–9, 174.
31 Gregg, *Free-Born John*, p. 398.
32 Gregg, *Free-Born John*, p. 90.
33 Gregg, *Free-Born John*, p. 103.
34 Lilburne, *Freemans Freedome Vindicated*, p. 6.
35 Gibb, *Lilburne*, p. 192.
36 Gibb, *Lilburne*, p. 192.
37 Rushworth, *Collections*, VIII, p. 1257.
38 *Mercurius Militaris*, 22 April 1649.
39 *Petition of Women*, 1649, E. 551 (14).
40 Gibb, *Lilburne*, p. 174; Higgins, 'Women in the Civil War', p. 178; *To the House of Commons for Lockier*, 5 May 1649, BL 669, fo. 14/27.
41 Higgins, 'Women in the Civil War', pp. 180–81; *To the Parliament for Mr J. Lilburn*, 24 June 1653, BL 669, fo. 17/24; *Unto every individual Member of Parliament*, 26 July 1653, BL 669, fo. 17/37; Clarendon MSS, Vol. 46, fo. 110.
42 Clarendon MSS, Vol. 46, fo. 131.
43 Gibb, *Lilburne*, pp. 272–3.
44 Gregg, *Free-Born John*, p. 314.
45 Gregg, *Free-Born John*, p. 321.
46 CSP Domestic, 1655, pp. 263–4; Gregg, *Free-Born John*, p. 340.
47 Gregg, *Free-Born John*, p. 340.
48 Gibb, *Lilburne*, p. 342.
49 *Petition of Elizabeth Lilburne*, CSP Domestic, 1657–8, p. 148.
50 CSP Domestic, 1658–9, pp. 260–61.
51 Pauline Gregg, *Free-Born John*, p. 348, thinks he would not have approved.
52 Lilburne, *Jonah's Cry*, p. 4.

Chapter 13: When Women Preach

1 Duncon, *Vi-Countess Falkland*, p. 205; Brathwaite, *English Gentlewoman*, p. 82.
2 *Verney Memoirs*, III, p. 72.
3 Thomas, 'Women and Sects', p. 47; Higgins, 'Women in the Civil War', p. 88; Williams, 'Women Preachers', p. 563.
4 Higgins, 'Women in the Civil War', p. 93; Edwards, *Gangraena*, cit. Higgins, 'Women in the Civil War', p. 89.
5 Williams, 'Women Preachers', p. 563.
6 Vicars, *Schismatick Sifted*, p. 34; Edwards, *Gangraena*, p. 84.
7 BL Add MSS, 31, 116, fo. 254-4v (I owe this reference to Dr Maurice Ashley); cit. Williams, 'Women Preachers', p. 564.
8 cit. Higgins, 'Women in the Civil War', p. 83; Thomas, 'Women and Sects', pp. 50, 60, note 66.
9 Warren, *Old and Good Way vindicated*, Preface; Warren, *Spiritual Thrift*, p. 81.
10 Williams, 'Women Preachers', p. 563; Ballard, *Memoirs of Several Ladies*, p. 281; Edwards, *Gangraena*, p. 170.
11 Williams, 'Women Preachers', p. 566; Chidley, *Justification*, p. 26.
12 Chidley, *New Yeares Gift*, E. 23(13); Chidley, *Good Counsell*, 669, fo. 10/39.
13 Williams, 'Women Preachers', pp. 567-8.
14 Edwards, *Gangraena*, cit. Weigall, 'Women Militants', p. 437.
15 'Puritan Congregation Minute Book', 1654, Rawlinson MSS, D. 828, fo. 30/32.
16 Spencer, 'Unfortunate Lady', pp. 56-8.
17 Ballard, *Memoirs of Several Ladies*, p. 280; Spencer, 'Unfortunate Lady', pp. 56-9.
18 See Powicke, 'Hastings Manuscripts', pp. 267-74.
19 See Carte MSS, Vol. LXXVII, fo. 201, 417.
20 Clarendon MSS, Vol. 29, fo. 102.
21 Thomas, *Religion*, p. 139 and note 1.
22 See *Clarke Papers*, II, pp. 150, 154, 163-5; Fraser, *Cromwell*, pp. 227-8.
23 Capp, *Fifth Monarchy*, p. 174.
24 See Capp, *Fifth Monarchy*, Appendix 1, p. 266 for summary of Anna Trapnel's career.
25 See Trapnel, *Legacy for Saints*, pp. 1-43.
26 1 Samuel, vs. 12-18; *Trapnel's Report and Plea*, Preface.
27 Trapnel, *Legacy for Saints*, Preface; Trapnel, *Cry of a Stone*, p. 42; Burrage, 'Trapnel's Prophecies', p. 531; 'Anonymous Folio Volume', Bodleian Library, S.1.42. Th; Dobell, 'Unique Book: Trapnel', p. 221.
28 *Strange News from Whitehall*, pp. 4-6.
29 *Cromwelliana*, p. 133.
30 *Strange News from Whitehall*, p. 8.
31 Capp, *Fifth Monarchy*, pp. 262, 101; CSP Domestic, 1653-4, p. 393.
32 'B.T. 21.10.54' cit. Burrage, 'Trapnel's Prophecies', pp. 531-2; Thurloe Papers, XXI, Rawlinson MSS, A 21, fo. 323.
33 *Osborne Letters*, p. 222.
34 See *Trapnel's Report and Plea*, pp. 1-20.
35 Trapnel, *Legacy for Saints*, p. 49.
36 CSP Domestic, 1654, pp. 86, 89, 134.
37 *Trapnel's Report and Plea*, pp. 21-37.
38 CSP Domestic, 1654, p. 436; *Trapnel's Report and Plea*, p. 38.
39 CSP Domestic, 1654, p. 438; Trapnel, *Legacy for Saints*, p. 59.

40 See 'Anonymous Folio Volume', Bodleian Library, S. 1.42. Th; note by Bertram Dobell, 'Unique Book: Trapnel', p. 221.

41 'Anonymous Folio Volume', Bodleian Library, S.1.42.Th, p. 1.

42 Dobell, 'Unique Book: Trapnel', p. 223; 'Anonymous Folio Volume', Bodleian Library, S.1.42.Th, pp. 256, 649, 697.

43 cit. Capp, *Fifth Monarchy*, p. 142.

44 Capp, *Fifth Monarchy*, p. 266.

45 *Charles II Letters*, p. 92.

46 *Clarendon State Papers*, II, p. 383; Ross, *Margaret Fell*, p. 39.

47 See Brailsford, *Quaker Women*, pp. 103–6.

48 *Fox Journal*, p. 96.

49 cit. Thomas, 'Women and Sects', p. 47.

Chapter 14: Worldly Goods

1 *Verney Memoirs*, II, p. 480; *As You Like It*, Act III, scene v.

2 *Verney Memoirs*, II, pp. 361, 365.

3 *Verney Memoirs*, II, pp. 372, 215, 390; III, pp. 213–15; II, p. 383.

4 *Verney Memoirs*, IV, pp. 33–7.

5 See Habakkuk, 'Marriage Settlements'; Stone, 'Social Mobility in England', p. 52; Stone, *Crisis of the Aristocracy*, pp. 637–45.

6 G.E.C., *Complete Peerage*, II, p. 53.

7 cit. Coate, *Social Life*, p. 25; cit. Habakkuk, 'Marriage Settlements', p. 23; *Pepys Diary*, I, p. 269; Hollingsworth, 'Demographic Study of the British ducal families', p. 9, cites 6 per cent of ducal female offspring umarried eventually, 1480–1679, compared to 17 per cent, 1680–1729 (at the age of twenty-five the relative figures were 19 per cent to 37 per cent).

8 King, *Natural and political observations*, p. 39; Graunt, 'Natural Observations upon bills of Mortality', II, p. 375.

9 *Marriage Promoted in a Discourse*, p. 27.

10 cit. Appendix C, Berens, *Digger Movement*, p. 252.

11 cit. Cartwright, *Madame*, p. 153; Hamilton, *Gramont Memoirs*, p. 108.

12 *Oglander Notebook*, p. 95; *Killigrew Poems*, p. 31.

13 Aphra Behn, *Feign'd Curtezans*, Act IV, scene II; Aphra Behn, *The Rover*, Part I, Act I, scene I; Charles Sedley, *Bellamira*, Act V, scene I.

14 Hamilton, *Gramont Memoirs*, p. 232; Index, p. 367.

15 *Verney Memoirs*, IV, pp. 273–80.

16 *Verney Memoirs*, IV, pp. 207, 452–4.

17 Newcastle, *Worlds Olio*, p. 211.

18 HMC, Salisbury MSS, 1621–88, p. 420.

19 Allestree, *Ladies Calling*, Part II, p. 177; *Warwick Autobiography*, pp. 35–6.

20 *Cust Family Records*, series II, p. 74.

21 Woolley, *Gentlewomans Companion*, p. 89.

22 See Finch MSS, I, pp. xxv, 461–4; III, p. 139.

23 *Athenian Oracle*, II, p. 155.

24 cit. Hiscock, *Evelyn and Mrs Godolphin*, p. 166.

25 Although *Collins' Peerage*, V, p. 516 gives 14 October 1679, I have followed Sidney, *Diary*, II, p. 11, and Cartwright, *Sacharissa*, page 247, which make it clear the ceremony took place in March.

26 Cartwright, *Sacharissa*, p. 247; Fraser, *King Charles II*, pp. 348–9.
27 Cartwright, *Sacharissa*, p. 247.
28 Cartwright, *Sacharissa*, p. 215; Sidney, *Diary*, I, p. 286.
29 Sidney, *Diary*, I, pp. 238–9.
30 Sidney, *Diary*, I, pp. 250–51.
31 Cartwright, *Sacharissa*, p. 244.
32 Sidney, *Diary*, II, p. 39; Cartwright, *Sacharissa*, p. 247.
33 Cartwright, *Sacharissa*, pp. 248–9.
34 Sidney, *Diary*, II, p. 25; George Farquhar, *The Beaux' Stratagem*, Act II, scene I.
35 *Verney Memoirs*, IV, p. 231; Newdegate, *Muniment Room*, p. 178.
36 *Evelyn Diary*, II, p. 160; *Pepys Diary*, VIII, p. 139.
37 *Hatton Correspondence*, I, p. 53.
38 Shannon, *Discourses and Essays*, Preface; cit. Jameson, *Beauties of Charles II's Court*, p. 168.
39 See Jameson, *Beauties of Charles II's Court*, pp. 169–70.
40 Sidney, *Diary*, I, p. 302.
41 *Life of Lady Russell*, p. 75.
42 *Hatton Correspondence*, I, p. 236.
43 *Evelyn Diary*, II, p. 160; *Life of Lady Russell*, p. 75.
44 *House of Commons*, I, p. 716.
45 Fea, *Some Beauties*, pp. 40–50; *Hatton Correspondence*, II, p. 8; Newdegate, *Cavalier and Puritan*, p. 154.
46 DNB (Thomas Thynne); *Evelyn Diary*, II, p. 386.
47 Newdegate, *Cavalier and Puritan*, p. 160.
48 cit. Fea, *Some Beauties*, p. 69.
49 *Life of Lady Russell*, pp. xvi, xcviii.
50 Scott Thomson, *Russells in Bloomsbury*, pp. 14, 17.
51 Scott Thomson, *Russells in Bloomsbury*, p. 62.
52 *Lady Russell Letters*, I, p. 36; *Life of Lady Russell*, p. 36.
53 Fraser, *King Charles II*, p. 429.
54 *Life of Lady Russell*, p. xxv; Pilkington, *Celebrated Female Characters*, p. 311.
55 Burnet, *History*, II, p. 380; *Life of Lady Russell*, p. xxvi.
56 See Strong, *When did you last see your father?*, p. 21; Appendix, p. 167.
57 *Life of Lady Russell*, pp. xxiv–xxxv.
58 *Life of Lady Russell*, p. xliii.
59 *Life of Lady Russell*, p. xcvi.
60 Mary Berry, anonymous editor, *Life of Lady Russell*, p. viii.
61 *Evelyn Diary*, II, p. 173; *Life of Lady Russell*, p. lxxviii; G.E.C., *Complete Peerage*, II, p. 81.
62 *Life of Lady Russell*, p. lxxix.
63 *Life of Lady Russell*, p. 93.
64 *Lady Russell Letters*, p. 223.

Chapter 15: Divorce from Bed and Board

 1 Cripps, *Elizabeth of the Sealed Knot*, pp. 89–90.
 2 Gardiner, *Oxinden and Peyton*, pp. 219, 265, 344.
 3 MacDonald, *Mystical Bedlam*, p. 101.
 4 Norsworthy, *Lady Hatton*, p. 30.

5 *Osborne Letters*, p. 169; *Waller Poems*, I, p. 90; Aubrey, *Brief Lives*, ed. Powell, p. 295.

6 Carte, *Ormonde*, IV, p. 701; Burghclere, *Ormonde*, I, p. 41.

7 Longleat NMR MS, 1847.

8 *Verney Memoirs*, III, p. 435; Carte MSS, Vol. LXXVIII, fo. 412; *Giffard Correspondence*, p. 4.

9 Fell Smith, *Warwick*, pp. 284-90.

10 *Verney Memoirs*, III, pp. 430-32; IV, p. 199.

11 *Pepys Diary*, II, p. 6 and note 6.

12 Hogrefe, *Tudor Women*, p. 89.

13 Whateley's tracts, cit. Stenton, *English Woman*, pp. 107-8; see Milton, *Doctrine and Discipline of Divorce*; Thompson, *Women in Stuart England*, pp. 169-77.

14 *Ladies Dictionary*, p. 165; HMC, Denbigh MSS, Part V, p. 14.

15 Aphra Behn, *The Town-Fop*, Act V, scene IV; *Sir Patient Fancy*, Act V, scene I.

16 Houldsworth, *English Law*, I, p. 623.

17 Robinson, *Dukes of Norfolk*, pp. 145-7.

18 Thomas, 'Double Standard', p. 201; *Athenian Oracle*, I, p. 428.

19 Devereux, *Earls of Essex*, II, pp. 304-6.

20 *Pepys Diary*, IV, p. 254 and note 2.

21 G.E.C., *Complete Peerage*, XI, pp. 262, 109-12.

22 *Clarendon Life*, III, p. 17; G.E.C., *Complete Peerage*, XI, p. 263; HMC, Rutland MSS, IV, · p. 519.

23 HMC, Rutland MSS, IV, p. 540.

24 *Clarendon Life*, III, p. 172.

25 *Clarendon Life*, III, p. 172.

26 *Clarendon Life*, III, p. 172.

27 *Clarendon Life*, III, p. 173.

28 *Clarendon Life*, III, p. 174.

29 *Dorchester's Letter to Lord Roos, with his Answer*.

30 *Dorchester's Letter to Lord Roos, with his Answer*.

31 *Clarendon Life*, III, p. 175.

32 HMC, Salisbury MSS, XXII, p. 441.

33 HMC, Salisbury MSS, XXII, p. 442.

34 HMC, Rutland MSS, IV, p. 547.

35 HMC, Salisbury MSS, XXII, p. 442.

36 HMC, Salisbury MSS, XXII, p. 444.

37 G.E.C., *Complete Peerage*, IV, p. 406 and note A.

38 *Journal of the House of Lords*, XII, pp. 17, 28.

39 *Journal of the House of Lords*, XII, pp. 41-52.

40 *Journal of the House of Lords*, XII, p. 95.

41 HMC, Rutland MSS, II, p. 8.

42 G.E.C., *Complete Peerage*, XI, p. iii and note C.

43 *Journal of the House of Lords*, XII, p. 324; Burnet, *History*, I, p. 471, note 2.

44 HMC, 8th Report, Appendix, p. 117.

45 Burnet, *History*, I, p. 472; Matthew, 5, vs. 32; 19, vs. 9; Mark, 10, vs. 11-12; Luke, 16, vs. 18; *Case of my Lord Roos*.

46 *Journal of the House of Lords*, XII, p. 323.

47 HMC, Rutland MSS, IV, p. 547; *Journal of the House of Lords*, XII, p. 350.

48 *Case of Divorce and Remarriage Discussed*.

49 i.e. Dorothy Lady Stanhope on behalf of her niece Lady Betty Livingstone, cit. Stone, *Family, Sex and Marriage*, p.184; HMC, Rutland MSS, IV, p. 551.

50 G.E.C., *Complete Peerage*, IV, p. 406; X, p. 422; *Hatton Correspondence*, I, p. 159.

51 HMC, 12th Report, Appendix, Part V, p. 140.

52 *Life of Lady Russell*, p. lxxiv.

53 Nichols, *Leicestershire*, II, Part I, p. 62.

54 HMC, 12th Report, Appendix, Part V, p. iv.

Chapter 16: Benefiting by Accomplishments

 1 Woolley, *Queen-like Closet*, Part II, p. 340.

 2 Sidney, *Diary*, I, p. 191 and note ii, p. 22.

 3 *Waller Poems*, I, p. 56; Grant, *Margaret the First*, pp. 195, 229; *Osborne Letters*, p. 50; Stuart, *English Abigail*, p. 51.

 4 Evelyn, *Mrs Godolphin*, p. 154.

 5 Cripps, *Elizabeth of the Sealed Knot*, pp. 10, 36, 59, 190.

 6 Reid, *John and Sarah*, p. 141.

 7 Green, *Queen Anne*, p. 99.

 8 DNB (Abigail Masham).

 9 *Pepys Diary*, I, p. 288; II, p. 232 and note 2, p. 4.

10 *Pepys Diary*, II, p. 139.

11 *Pepys Diary*, III, p. 223.

12 *Pepys Diary*, II, pp. 11, 204.

13 Her Christian name was probably Winifred; see *Pepys Diary*, III, p. 256 and note 2; III, p. 277; *Verney Memoirs*, IV, pp. 20–21.

14 *Pepys Diary*, IV, pp. 79, 280.

15 *Pepys Diary*, V, p. 152; Lambley, *French Language*, pp. 366–70; John Vanbrugh, *Provok'd Wife*, Act II, scene II; *Pepys Diary*, V, pp. 265, 274.

16 *Pepys Diary*, VI, pp. 252, 163–4; VII, p. 138.

17 *Pepys Diary*, VIII, pp. 471, 475; IX, p. 210.

18 *Pepys Diary*, VII, p. 311; VI, p. 235; VIII, p. 212.

19 *Pepys Diary*, IX, pp. 337–8, 344, 367.

20 DNB (Woolley); see Woolley, *Gentlewomans Companion*, pp. 15–17.

21 See Wallas, *Before the Bluestockings*, pp. 17–54.

22 Woolley, *Gentlewomans Companion*, p. 10.

23 Woolley, *Gentlewomans Companion*, p. 288.

24 Woolley, *Gentlewomans Companion*, p. 65.

25 Webster, *Great Instauration*, pp. 219–20; Turnbull, *Hartlib*, pp. 120–21.

26 Reynolds, *Learned Lady*, pp. 270–80; Lambley, *French Language*, p. 381; Makin, *Essay on Education*, p. 23.

27 cit. Green, *Queen Anne*, p. 99; Lambley, *French Language*, p. 392.

28 Hamilton, *William's Mary*, p. 19.

29 *Winchilsea Poems*, p. 5.

30 *Pepys Diary*, V, p. 45; Ede, *Arts and Society*, pp. 84–6; see Greer, *Obstacle Race*, pp. 255–7; *Ladies Dictionary*, p. 434.

31 Makin, *Essay on Education*, p. 22.

32 Birch, *Anna van Schurman*, p. 73; van Schurman, *Learned Maid*, p. 5.

33 Stuart, *Girl through the Ages*, pp. 196–7.

34 Fraser, *King Charles II*, p. 194.

35 Makin, *Essay on Education*, Postscript.

36 Makin, *Essay on Education*, pp. 3-7.

37 Bowle, *Evelyn*, p. 213; Hiscock, *Evelyn and Mrs Godolphin*, p. 167.

38 *Locke Correspondence*, III, p. 105; II, p. 485; DNB (John Locke); cit. Illick, 'Child-Rearing', p. 320; Masham, *Occasional Thoughts*, p. 197.

39 HMC, Hastings MSS, IV, p. 348.

40 *Fox Journal*, pp. 520, 748; see Cressy, *Literacy*, p. 145.

41 BL Add MSS, 5858, fo. 213-21.

42 *Verney Memoirs*, IV, p. 221.

43 'The New Letanie', Thomason Tract, 669, fo. 10/120; cit. Grant, *Margaret the First*, p. 37.

44 Cressy, *Literacy*, p. 37; Cressy, *Education*, p. 114.

45 Makin, *Essay on Education*, p. 33.

46 *Poems by Eminent Ladies*, I, p. 215; Rochester, *Works*, p. 18.

47 Halifax, *Complete Works*, p. 289; Evelyn, *Mundus Muliebris*, p. 8, Preface.

48 *Life of Lady Russell*, p. xcviii.

49 *Sedley Works*, II, p. 112; cit. Utter and Needham, *Pamela's Daughters*, p. 23.

50 *Verney Memoirs*, IV, pp. 225-6.

51 Barksdale, *Letter touching a College of Maids or a Virgin Society*; see Florence Smith, *Mary Astell*, for this and other biographical details.

52 See Hartmann, *Vagabond Duchess*, for the life of Hortense Mancini.

53 Astell, *Reflections*, pp. 4-5.

54 Burnet, *History*, 2 June 1708, cit Smith, *Mary Astell*, p. 22.

55 Astell, *Reflections*, Preface.

56 'The Saxon Nymph'.

57 Elstob, *English-Saxon Family*, Preface, p. ii.

58 'The Saxon Nymph'.

59 'The Saxon Nymph'; DNB (Elizabeth Elstob).

Chapter 17: Petticoat-Authors

1 Masham, *Occasional Thoughts*, p. 199; *Winchilsea Poems*, p. 5.

2 Aphra Behn, *Sir Patient Fancy*, Act I, scene I.

3 Thomas Wright, *The Female Vertuosos*, Act III, scene I; William Congreve, *The Double Dealer*, Act III, scene x.

4 Gildon, *Comparison Between Two Stages*, pp. 26-7.

5 Needham, 'Mrs Manley', p. 265.

6 Mary Manley, *The Lost Lover*, Prologue, cit. Needham, 'Mrs Manley', p. 263; Duffy, *Passionate Shepherdess*, p. 138.

7 There are two recent biographies of Aphra Behn: Maureen Duffy, *The Passionate Shepherdess* (1977) which casts fresh light on the mystery of her birth, and Angeline Goreau, *Reconstructing Aphra, A Social Biography* (1980).

8 *Life of Mr Joseph Alleine*, Printer's Note.

9 Barham, 'Discovery of the Authorship of the *Whole Duty of Man*'; *Winchilsea Poems*, p. xxxviii; Ballard, *Memoirs of Several Ladies*, p. 363.

10 See her biography by P.M. Souars, *The Matchless Orinda* (1931).

11 cit. Souars, *Orinda*, p. 189.

12 cit. Souars, *Orinda*, p. 91; *Aubrey's Brief Lives*, ed. Lawson Dick, p. 242.

13 cit. Souars, *Orinda*, pp. 91, 98.

14   Souars, *Orinda*, p. 253.

15   cit. Souars, *Orinda*, pp. 110, 43.

16   Taylor, 'Treasures of Friendship', pp. 63-5.

17   Souars, *Orinda*, p. 277.

18   *Killigrew Poems*, Publisher's Note; Dryden's 'Prefatory Ode'.

19   *Killigrew Poems*, p. 85.

20   *Killigrew Poems*, p. 79.

21   *Killigrew Poems*, p. 32.

22   *Killigrew Poems*, p. 51.

23   *Killigrew Poems*, ed. Morton, p. xi.

24   *Killigrew Poems*; Dryden's 'Prefatory Ode'.

25   *Killigrew Poems*, p. 13.

26   See Greer, *Obstacle Race*, p. 255, where it is pointed out that her Christian name was Joan, not Anne, as stated previously.

27   Greer, *Obstacle Race*, pp. 255-7.

28   *Woodforde Papers*, p. 5.

29   Sir Oliver Millar in a letter to the author; Millar, *Lely*; Blunt, *Botanical Illustrations*, pp. 129-30.

30   See *Winchilsea Poems*, Introduction by Myra Reynolds, for biographical details.

31   *Winchilsea Poems*, p. 21.

32   *Winchilsea Poems*, p. 4.

33   *Winchilsea Poems*, pp. 268-70, lxxvi.

34   i.e. by Dale Spender in *Man Made Language*, pp. 194-5, 230.

35   cit. *Winchilsea Poems*, p. lxii.

36   M.H. Nicolson in *Conway Letters*, p. xxv.

37   *Conway Letters*, p. 47.

38   *Conway Letters*, p. 57, note 7.

39   *Conway Letters*, p. 152.

40   *Conway Letters*, p. 53.

41   Sacks, *Migraine*, p. 241.

42   See *Conway Letters*, esp. pp. 113, 91 note 1, 114, 79.

43   *Conway Letters*, pp. 106, 116.

44   *Conway Letters*, pp. 248-9.

45   *Conway Letters*, p. 282.

46   *Conway Letters*, p. 168.

47   *Conway Letters*, p. 337.

48   cit. *Conway Letters*, pp. 299-300.

49   *Conway Letters*, p. 278.

50   *Conway Letters*, p. 412.

51   *Conway Letters*, p. 413.

52   By M.H. Nicolson, *Conway Letters*, p. 378.

53   *Conway Letters*, p. 433.

54   *Conway Letters*, p. 436.

55   *Conway Letters*, pp. 456, 481.

56   *Conway Letters*, pp. 451, 457.

57   *Conway Letters*, p. 159; *Principles of the most Ancient and Modern Philosophy*, Preface.

58   *Principles of the most Ancient and Modern Philosophy*, pp. 3, 11, 14.

59   *Principles of the most Ancient and Modern Philosophy*, p. 77.

60 *Conway Letters*, p. 451; *Principles of the most Ancient and Modern Philosophy*, Preface; *Conway Letters*, p. 456.
61 *Conway Letters*, p. 457.
62 *Conway Letters*, pp. 465–8.

Chapter 18: Helping in God's Vineyard

1 *Conway Letters*, pp. 412, 433.
2 Brailsford, *Quaker Women*, p. 70.
3 Brailsford, *Quaker Women*, p. 324.
4 Ross, *Margaret Fell*, p. 35; *Trapnel's Report and Plea*, p. 24; see Brailsford, *Quaker Women*, pp. 159–76, 213–16.
5 Nalson, *Countermine*, p. 93.
6 cit. Brailsford, *Quaker Women*, p. 15.
7 See Brailsford, *Quaker Women*, pp. 16–41 for the story of Elizabeth Hooton.
8 *Fox Journal*, p. 9.
9 Brailsford, *Quaker Women*, p. 19.
10 Brailsford, *Quaker Women*, p. 333.
11 cit. Manners, 'Elizabeth Hooton', pp. 14–15.
12 See Brailsford, *Quaker Women*, pp. 94–113.
13 See Scales, 'Quaker Women in Dover, New Hampshire'.
14 *Pepys Diary*, v, pp. 12–13; Bryant, *Pepys, Years of Peril*, p. 204 and note.
15 Roberts, *Monmouth*, II, p. 205.
16 Scales, 'Quaker Women in Dover, New Hampshire'.
17 *Fox Journal*, II, pp. 213, 436 and note.
18 See Braithwaite, *Beginnings of Quakerism*, pp. 422–4; Brailsford, *Quaker Women*, pp. 114–32 for Mary Fisher's expedition.
19 Braithwaite, *Beginnings of Quakerism*, p. 423.
20 Marsh, *New Survey of Turkish Empire*, Part 2, p. 33; Paul Ruycaut (later English Consul in Smyrna), *Ottoman empire*, p. 120.
21 Taken from the account of Willem Sewel, in his *History of the Quakers*, first published (in Dutch) in 1717. According to M.R. Brailsford, *Quaker Women*, p. 128, Sewel may have heard the details directly from Mary Fisher.
22 Thurloe Papers, VII, p. 287; Brailsford, *Quaker Women*, p. 116.
23 G.E.C., *Complete Peerage*, XII/2, p. 778, note 1; *Collins' Peerage*, pp. 384–5.
24 Ross, *Margaret Fell*, p. 226; see this biography in general for details of her life.
25 Ross, *Margaret Fell*, p. 24.
26 cit. Knox, *Enthusiasm*, p. 161.
27 Ross, *Margaret Fell*, p. 37.
28 Ross, *Margaret Fell*, p. 170.
29 Ross, *Margaret Fell*, p. 138.
30 Spufford, 'Portraits of Society', p. 12; *Fox Journal*, p. 421.
31 *Athenian Oracle*, I, p. 33.
32 *Fox Journal*, p. 554.
33 Ross, *Margaret Fell*, p. 220.
34 Ross, *Margaret Fell*, pp. 228 note 2, 226.
35 *Sarah Fell Account Book*, pp. xx, xix.
36 Thomas, *Women and Sects*, p. 48.
37 Margaret Fell, *Womens Speaking*, pp. 3 (sic: Joel 2, vs. 28 differs slightly), 4, 10.

38 Margaret Fell, *Womens Speaking*, p. 5.
39 Margaret Fell, *Womens Speaking*, p. 14.
40 Braithwaite, *Second Period of Quakerism*, pp. 270–72, 286–8.
41 Letter of Isabel Yeamans, 8 August 1676, MSS, Religious Society of Friends, Nottingham Meeting.
42 *Fox Journal*, pp. 629, 647, 666–8.
43 Ross, *Margaret Fell*, pp. 313–14; Katz, *Readmission of the Jews*, p. 238.
44 Ross, *Margaret Fell*, p. 318.
45 Ross, *Margaret Fell*, p. 370.

Chapter 19: The Delight of Business

1 Ede, *Arts and Society*, p. 14; see Clark, *Working Life*, pp. 32–3 for Joan Dant's story.
2 Brailsford, *Quaker Women*, p. 15.
3 Ballard, *Memoirs of Several Ladies*, p. 287; Anderson, *Friends and Relations*, p. 68.
4 See *Sarah Fell Account Book*.
5 Scott Thomson, *Noble Household*, pp. 189, 199.
6 Miranda Chaytor and Jane Lewis in Clark, *Working Life*, p. xxxi.
7 *Pepys Diary*, I, p. 30; X, p. 241.
8 i.e. see *The Diary of Roger Lowe*; its editor, William L. Sachse (p. 7), describes the alehouse of this period, on the diary's evidence, as 'the unofficial club' of both poor man *and* poor woman.
9 cit. Bridenbaugh, *Vexed Englishmen*, p. 195; cit. Pinto, *Sedley*, p. 58; Gough, *Myddle*, pp. 197–8.
10 Finch MSS, III, p. 438.
11 *Pepys Diary*, V, p. 62.
12 *Pepys Diary*, V, p. 266.
13 The story of Mrs Pley and Colonel Reymes is told in Helen Andrews Kaufman's biography of the latter, *Conscientious Cavalier*.
14 Hutchins, *Dorset*, II, p. 459.
15 Kaufman, *Conscientious Cavalier*, p. 182.
16 Fraser, *King Charles II*, p. 223.
17 Kaufman, *Conscientious Cavalier*, pp. 182, 247 note 7.
18 *Pepys Diary*, VII, pp. 199–200.
19 *Pepys Diary*, VII, p. 200 note 2.
20 Balleine, *All for the King*, p. 127.
21 CSP Domestic, 1664–5, pp. 500–501.
22 CSP Domestic, 1664–5, p. 525.
23 *Pepys Diary*, VI, p. 187; *Carlingford Papers*, II of III, Osborn Collection, Yale.
24 Defoe, *Journal of the Plague Year*, p. 120.
25 CSP Domestic, 1665–6, p. 108.
26 CSP Domestic, 1665–6, pp. 219, 244; 1666–7, 66; 1665–6, pp. 357, 272.
27 Kaufman, *Conscientious Cavalier*, p. 237.
28 Kaufman, *Conscientious Cavalier*, p. 184.
29 CSP Domestic, 1665–6, p. 207.
30 'Of Persons one would wish to have seen', in *Hazlitt Selected Essays*, p. 532.
31 See Howell, 'Image of Cromwell in Restoration Drama'.
32 Waylen, *House of Cromwell*, p. 81.
33 Waylen, *House of Cromwell*, p. 77.

34 Noble, *Cromwell Memoirs*, II, p. 337.

35 Nall, *Yarmouth*, p. 154; Ogg, *England of Charles II*, pp. 72–3.

36 Collins, *Salt and Fishery*, p. 61; Waylen, *House of Cromwell*, p. 77.

37 Costello, *Eminent Englishwomen*, III, p. 55.

38 Waylen, *House of Cromwell*, pp. 82–3.

39 Waylen, *House of Cromwell*, pp. 82–3.

40 Noble, *Cromwell Memoirs*, II, p. 332.

41 Sloane MSS, 2069, fo. 96 B; Baxter, *Reliquiae Baxterianae*, p. 57.

42 The Rev. Samuel Say's account is printed in full in Noble, *Cromwell Memoirs*, II, pp. 329–33, first published in 1727; the Rev. James Waylen in *The House of Cromwell*, 1880, suggests the explanation for Say's hostility.

43 Dr Jeremy Brooke's account in full in Noble, *Cromwell Memoirs*, II, pp. 333–8.

44 Hewling Luson's account in full in Noble, *Cromwell Memoirs*, II, pp. 338–46.

45 Noble, *Cromwell Memoirs*, II, p. 346.

Chapter 20: Wanton and Free

1 Aphra Behn, *The Feign'd Curtezans*, Act IV, scene I; Allestree, *Ladies Calling*, p. 26.

2 Newcastle, *CCXI Letters*, p. 76.

3 Allestree, *Ladies Calling*, p. 157; OED; Barker, *Poetical Recreations*, Part I, pp. 12–13; Fraser, *King Charles II*, p. 285.

4 Evelyn, *Mundus Muliebris*, Preface; *Womens Complaint*; John Dryden, *Marriage-à-la-Mode*, Act I, scene I.

5 North, *Lives*, II, p. 164; Needham, 'Mrs Manley', p. 276.

6 Aphra Behn, *The Town-Fop*, Act IV, scene II.

7 See Sidney, *Diary*, I, pp. xxviii–xxxiv, for the sufferings of Mrs Worthley.

8 *Pepys Diary*, IV, pp. 114, 270, 303.

9 *Pepys Diary*, IV, pp. 281, 387–8.

10 *Pepys Diary*, V, pp. 173–4.

11 *Pepys Diary*, V, p. 184.

12 *Pepys Diary*, V, p. 179.

13 *Pepys Diary*, IX, p. 455.

14 Thomas Otway, *Venice Preserv'd*, Act III, scene I; Act II, scene I; Aphra Behn, *The Rover*, Part I, Act I, scene I.

15 HMC, 12th Report, Appendix, Part V, p. 158.

16 cit. Pinto, *Sedley*, Appendix III, p. 355.

17 Pinto, *Sedley*, pp. 120–25.

18 *Evelyn Diary*, II, p. 84.

19 BL Add MSS, 30, 382.

20 cit. Pinto, *Sedley*, p. 129; Wolseley, *Marlborough*, I, pp. 188–9.

21 Dorset, *Works*, XI, p. 16.

22 Dorset, *Works*, XI, p. 209.

23 Wilson, *Court Wits*, p. 113; Pinto, *Sedley*, p. 137.

24 cit. Pinto, *Sedley*, p. 140 note 2.

25 Burke's *Extinct Peerages*, p. 492; Pinto, *Sedley*, p. 140.

26 Turner, *James II*, p. 142.

27 Pinto, *Sedley*, p. 238.

28 Pinto, *Sedley*, p. 158.

29 Pinto, *Sedley*, Appendix III, p. 355.

30 Stanley, *Memorials of Westminster Abbey*, Appendix, p. 507.

31 Miller, *James II* (1978), p. 151; F.C. Turner in his biography *James II* (1948), p. 294, also thought the evidence came from Sunderland and was therefore suspect.

32 *Evelyn Diary*, II, p. 248.

33 cit. Turner, *James II*, p. 300.

34 Pinto, *Sedley*, Appendix III, pp. 355–60.

35 Pinto, *Sedley*, Appendix III, p. 360.

36 Turner, *James II*, p. 300.

37 Pinto, *Sedley*, Appendix III, pp. 346–7.

38 Finch MSS, III, p. 347; cit. Pinto, *Sedley*, p. 174.

39 See Pinto, *Sedley*, pp. 204–5 and note 2.

40 Finch MSS, III, p. 34.

41 Finch MSS, III, pp. 348, 351.

42 *Hatton Correspondence*, II, p. 128 and note A; p. 129.

43 *Case of the Countess of Dorchester relating to the Torrington Bill.*

44 Dorset, *Works*, XI, p. 198; Pinto, *Sedley*, pp. 218–19; DNB (Catherine Sedley).

45 See Myddelton, *Chirk Castle Accounts*.

46 *Pepys Diary*, VI, p. 64 and note 2; *Evelyn Diary*, II, p. 183.

47 *Ladies Dictionary*, pp. 219, 63; *Pepys Diary*, VIII, p. 46.

48 *Aeneid*, Book 1, l.402 (trans. J. Middleton Murry); Hamilton, *Gramont Memoirs*, p. 204.

49 *Cholmley Memoirs*, p. 12; Gardiner, *Oxinden Letters*, p. 164.

50 Hamilton, *Gramont Memoirs*, pp. 109, 131; Newcastle, CCXI *Letters*, p. 215; *Ladies Dictionary*, p. 212.

51 *Pepys Diary*, VIII, pp. 286, 251; Myddelton, *Chirk Castle Accounts*; cit. Jameson, *Beauties of Charles II's Court*, p. 163.

52 Lecky, *History of European Morals*, II, pp. 220–30; Mary Pix, *The Innocent Mistress*, cit. Morgan, *Female Wits*, p. 266; Clark, *Working Life*, Introduction, p. xxxi.

53 Macfarlane, *Marital and Sexual Relationships*, p. 104; Quaife, *Wanton Wenches*, p. 150; cit. Stone, *Family, Sex and Marriage*, pp. 561–3; *Wandering Whore*, No. 1, p. 12.

54 Macfarlane, *Marital and Sexual Relationships*, p. 105; May, *Social Control of Sex Expression*, p. 110; Wilson, *Court Wits*, p. 79.

55 Pierpont Morgan Library MSS, R. of E., box IX, Part 2, fo. 55, 57, 62, 64.

56 *Wandering Whore*, No. 1, p. 10; No. 2, pp. 4–6; *Otway Works*, I, p. lxx; Wilson, *King's Ladies*, p. 167.

57 See Hamilton, *Gramont Memoirs*, pp. 131–220.

58 Gouge, *Domesticall Duties*, cit. Laslett, *World we have lost* (1968), p. 131 and note p. 267; see May, *Social Control of Sex Expression*, p. 132.

59 *Verney Memoirs*, III, p. 51; *Humble Remonstrance of the Batchelors*, p. 481.

60 *Middlesex County Records*, III, p. 13.

61 *Wandering Whore*, Prefatory Note, and No. 2, p. 9; Wilson, *King's Ladies*, p. 18.

62 Stone, *Family, Sex and Marriage*, pp. 616, 619; *Pepys Diary*, VIII, p. 466, note 1; Quaife, *Wanton Wenches*, p. 150.

63 Hair, *Before the Bawdy Court*, p. 136.

64 *Pepys Diary*, VII, pp. 62, 142; IX, p. 521.

65 *Pepys Diary*, IX, p. 132; Thomas Otway, *Venice Preserv'd*, Prologue; *Whore's Rhetorick*, p. 117.

66 *Wandering Whore*, Prefatory Note; DNB (Cresswell).

67 *Whore's Rhetorick*, pp. 29, 24.

68 *Whore's Rhetorick*, pp. 58, 117.

69 *Whore's Rhetorick*, pp. 108, 148, 96, 62.

70 *Wandering Whore*, No. 3, p. 11.

71 Dorset, *Works*, XI, p. 205; cit. Greene, *Rochester*, p. 121.

Chapter 21: Actress as Honey-Pot

1 Evelyn, *Mrs Godolphin*, p. 97 (still Blagge in fact); *Evelyn Diary*, I, p. 332.

2 Having to appear in public still unmarried, see Hiscock, *Evelyn and Mrs Godolphin*, p. 113.

3 Nicoll, *English Drama*, I, pp. 70–71; Roberts, *Social History*; Gregg, *Charles I*, p. 275; *Pepys Diary*, II, p. 5, note 2.

4 Marvell, *Poems*, I, pp. 125, 331.

5 cit. Findlater, *Player Queens*, p. 12; Nicoll, *English Drama*, I, p. 70.

6 See Wilson, *King's Ladies*, pp. 5–8 (although he does not totally dismiss the claim of Katherine Corey).

7 Gildon, *Betterton*, p. 7; Hamilton, *William's Mary*, p. 25; *Pepys Diary*, x, p. 86.

8 See Wilson, *King's Ladies*, pp. 17–19.

9 William Wycherley, *Country Wife*, Act II, scene 1; Wilson, *King's Ladies*, p. 14.

10 cit. Wilson, *Court Wits*, p. 80.

11 cit. Wilson, *King's Ladies*, p. 16.

12 Wilson, *King's Ladies*, pp. 9–10; Hamilton, *Gramont Memoirs*, p. 314.

13 Woolley, *Queen-like Closet*, p. 134; *Pepys Diary*, IV, p. 162; V, p. 267; IX, p. 268 and note 5; Wilson, *King's Ladies*, p. 146.

14 *Pepys Diary*, VIII, p. 503, note 1; Wilson, *King's Ladies*, pp. 110–11, summarizes the various stories.

15 By J.H. Wilson in *King's Ladies*, p. 73.

16 See Wilson, *King's Ladies*, pp. 68–70 for details of the actresses' costumes.

17 Wilson, *Nell Gwynn*, p. 288.

18 *Pepys Diary*, VII, p. 463.

19 *Pepys Diary*, V, p. 240 and note 3; Wilson, *King's Ladies*, p. 34.

20 See Wilson, *King's Ladies*, Appendix I, pp. 109–92, for a list of actresses, 1660–89, including biographical details.

21 Wilson, *King's Ladies*, p. 127.

22 Wilson, *King's Ladies*, p. 130; 'Commentary', C.H. Hartmann in Hamilton, *Gramont Memoirs*, p. 338.

23 *Brown Works*, II, p. 303.

24 Hamilton, *Gramont Memoirs*, pp. 233–4.

25 'Commentary', C.H. Hartmann in Hamilton, *Gramont Memoirs*, pp. 361, 233; Wilson, *King's Ladies*, pp. 12–13.

26 Wilson, *King's Ladies*, p. 14.

27 Hamilton, *Gramont Memoirs*, p. 234.

28 For the correct dating of her career, see J.H. Wilson's article, 'Pepys and Peg Hughes'.

29 cit. Morrah, *Prince Rupert*, pp. 400, 415.

30 cit. Morrah, *Prince Rupert*, p. 415.

31 cit. Morrah, *Prince Rupert*, pp. 416–17, 426.

32 *Brown Works*, II, p. 241.

33 See J.H. Wilson's article, 'Marshall Sisters and Anne Quin', where their careers are disentangled.

34 *Pepys Diary*, v, p. 34 and note 1.

35 John Dryden, *The Indian Emperor*, Act I, scene II.

36 John Dryden, *The Indian Emperor*, Act v, scene I.

37 CSP Domestic, 1665-6, p. 157.

38 *Pepys Diary*, VIII, pp. 91, 235.

39 cit. Wilson, 'Marshall Sisters and Anne Quin', p. 106.

40 *Pepys Diary*, IX, p. 250.

41 *Pepys Diary*, IX, p. 19 and note; see Wilson, *King's Ladies*, Appendix A, pp. 142-4.

42 CSP Domestic, 1664-5, pp. 139-40.

43 Aston, 'Brief Supplement', in Cibber, *Apology*, II, p. 302.

44 Gildon, *Comparison between Two Stages*, p. 18.

45 van Lennep, *London Stage*, I, p. 210; DNB (Elizabeth Barry); Cibber, *Apology*, I, p. 159; Aston, 'Brief Supplement', in Cibber, *Apology*, II, p. 303.

46 Aston, 'Brief Supplement', in Cibber, *Apology*, II, p. 303.

47 Curll, *Betterton's History*, pp. 14-16.

48 See van Lennep, *London Stage*, I, p. 245; Treglown, *Rochester's Letters*, p. 29 for the point that it is unlikely Rochester saw *Alcibiades* as he was in the country.

49 Thomas Otway, *Caius Marius*, Act I, scene II.

50 Thomas Southerne, *The Fatal Marriage*, Dedication, 1694.

51 Thomas Otway, *Venice Preserv'd*, Act I, scene I.

52 Gildon, *Comparison Between Two Stages*, p. 18; Wilson, *King's Ladies*, pp. 115-16, 61-2.

53 *Brown Works*, III, p. 39; cit. *Otway Works*, I, p. lxiv.

54 *Rochester Familiar Letters*, pp. 90, 88.

55 *Rochester Familiar Letters*, p. 82.

56 Rochester, *Works*, pp. 11, 269, 277, 280. There is no direct evidence linking Rochester's poem 'The Mistress' with Mrs Barry, despite its title; none of Rochester's poems are dated by him and their dating from other evidence presents difficulties (Treglown, *Rochester's Letters*, p. 25). Graham Greene in *Rochester*, p. 132, suggests the connection with Mrs Barry.

57 cit. Pinto, *Rochester*, p. 189.

58 Rochester, *Works*, p. 274.

59 Rochester, *Works*, p. 280.

60 DNB (Mrs Barry).

61 Cibber, *Apology*, I, p. 160.

Chapter 22: The Modest Midwife

1 Rueff, *Expert Midwife*, Introduction.

2 *Midwives Just Petition; Midwives Just Complaint*, 1646, cit. Aveling, *English Midwives*, p. 30.

3 Eccles, *Obstetrics in Stuart England*, p. 121.

4 See 'Anonymous Business Diary of a Midwife', Rawlinson MSS, D. 1141.

5 *Pepys Diary*, II, p. 110; *Calverley Memorandum Book*, pp. 62, 67.

6 Aveling, *English Midwives*, pp. 31-4.

7 Hamilton, *Henrietta Maria*, p. 95; Fraser, *King Charles II*, p. 13.

8 Clark, *Working Life*, p. 274.

9 See G.C.R. Morris, 'Which Molins treated Cromwell for stone?', p. 431, and letter to

the author concerning girls baptized Aurelia, 1618-39, in the registers of St Andrew, Holborn.

10 Eccles, *Obstetrics In Stuart England*, p. 12.

11 Rueff, *Expert Midwife*, Introduction.

12 cit. Cutter and Viets, *Midwifery*, p. 48; Sharp, *Midwives Book*, pp. 2-3; Sharp, *Compleat Midwife*, Preface.

13 Exodus, I, vs. 15-21.

14 Sharp, *Midwives Book*, p. 3.

15 Walker, *Holy Life*, p. 86; *Hoby Diary*, p. 63.

16 *Pepys Diary*, IX, p. 260.

17 Rueff, *Expert Midwife*, Introduction.

18 See Willughby, *Country Midwife's Opusculum*, Sloane MSS, 529.

19 Willughby, *Country Midwife's Opusculum*, Sloane MSS, 529; *Thornton Autobiography*, p. 96; see *Freke Diary*, pp. 24-5.

20 Aveling, *English Midwives*, pp. 55-6; Stenton, *English Woman*, p. 228.

21 *Verney Memoirs*, IV, p. 169; Ross, *Margaret Fell*, p. 351.

22 Ross, *Margaret Fell*, p. 292.

23 *Humble Remonstrance of the Batchelors*, p. 479; Sermon, *Ladies Companion*, p. 5; *Pepys Diary*, III, p. 16.

24 i.e. *Wandering Whore*, No. 2, p. 5; No. 5, p. 13.

25 Gough, *Myddle*, p. 173; Willughby, *Country Midwife's Opusculum*, Sloane MSS, 529.

26 See Cutter and Viets, *Midwifery*, pp. 44-7 for the early history of the Chamberlen family.

27 Cutter and Viets, *Midwifery*, p. 50.

28 Aveling, *English Midwives*, p. 8.

29 cit. Thomas, *Religion*, p. 259.

30 cit. Aveling, *English Midwives*, pp. 8-9.

31 Cutter and Viets, *Midwifery*, p. 47.

32 Cutter and Viets, *Midwifery*, p. 49.

33 See *Mrs Shaw's Innocency Restored*.

34 cit. Cutter and Viets, *Midwifery*, p. 49.

35 cit. Illick, *Child-Rearing*, pp. 306, 333, 13.

36 Sharp, *Midwives Book*, p. 3.

37 Clark, *Working Life*, p. 263.

38 Shorter, *Women's Bodies*, pp. 141-3, 123-38; Eccles, *Obstetrics in Stuart England*, pp. 123-4.

39 Donnison, *Midwives and Medical Men*, p. 190.

40 By J.H. Aveling (founder of *The Obstetrical Journal of Great Britain and Ireland*) in *English Midwives*, 1872, p. 39.

41 Sharp, *Midwives Book*, pp. 6, 13, 38; Sermon, *Ladies Companion*, p. 94.

42 Sermon, *Ladies Companion*, p. 94; *Conway Letters*, p. 153.

43 Sermon, *Ladies Companion*, p. 94.

44 Aveling, *English Midwives*, p. 39; Sharp, *Midwives Book*, p. 184; Sermon, *Ladies Companion*, p. 5.

45 Shorter, *Women's Bodies*, pp. 125-6.

46 Aveling, *English Midwives*, p. 112.

47 Cellier, 'Scheme for the Foundation of a Royal Hospital', p. 136.

48 Kenyon, *Popish Plot*, pp. 189-90; Cellier, *Malice Defeated*, Preface.

49 But see J.H. Kenyon, *Popish Plot*, for the clearest summary of the various facts and suppositions.
50 Cellier, *Malice Defeated*, p. 10.
51 Warner, *English Persecution of Catholics*, I, p. 314.
52 Caulfield, *Portraits*, I, pp. 25–6.
53 Dangerfield, *Grand Impostor*, p. 4; Cellier, *Malice Defeated*, p. 19.
54 Cellier, *Malice Defeated*, p. 38.
55 cit. Aveling, *English Midwives*, p. 64.
56 Cellier, *Malice Defeated*, p. 28.
57 Cellier, *Malice Defeated*, p. 42.
58 *Hatton Correspondence*, I, p. 236.
59 Cellier, *Malice Defeated*, p. 32.
60 *Life of Lady Russell*, p. 44.
61 *Midwife Unmask'd*, p. 134.
62 See Aveling, *English Midwives*, pp. 76–7.
63 Cellier, 'Scheme for the Foundation of a Royal Hospital', p. 137.
64 See Cellier, *To Dr—, An Answer*, pp. 1–2.
65 Cellier, *To Dr—, An Answer*, p. 7.
66 Cellier, *To Dr—, An Answer*, p. 8.
67 Strickland, *English Queens*, V, pp. 214–26.
68 Dr Chamberlen's Letter, Sloane MSS, 4107, p. 150.

Epilogue: How Strong?

1 *Mercurius Militaris*, 22 April 1649.
2 cit. Green, *Queen Anne*, p. 111.
3 Makin, *Essay on Education*, p. 11; Notestein, 'English Woman', p. 83.
4 Astell, *Reflections*, p. 85.
5 Agrippa, *Female Pre-eminence*, pp. 1–2.
6 Sprint, *Bride-Woman Counseller*.
7 *Lawes Resolutions*, p. 144; *Essay in Defense of the Female Sex*, p. 38. (Probably written by Mrs Judith Drake, see Reynolds, *Learned Lady*, p. 297.)
8 Hieron, *Helpe unto Devotion*, p. 386.
9 Chambers, *Mary Ward*, II, p. 33.
10 HMC, 12th Report, Appendix, Part V, p. 158.
11 Seaver, *Seventeenth-Century England*, p. 9.
12 *Cust Family Records*, series II, p. 120.
13 Cartwright, *Sacharissa*, p. 74.
14 'The Female Warrior', *Douce Ballads*, I (79).
15 Taylor, 'Treasures of Friendship', p. 53.
16 Abbadie, *Panégyrique de Marie, Reine d'Angleterre*, see esp. pp. 2, 7, 8, 13, 31; it was also printed in English.

Reference Books

This is not a complete list of all works consulted (which would be impossible for reasons of space) but a list of those books to which allusion is made under short titles in the References. The place of publication is London unless otherwise stated.

Abbadie, J., Docteur-en-Théologie, Ministre de la Savoye, *Panégyrique de Marie, Reine d'Angleterre, d'Ecosse, de France et d'Irlande, de glorieuse et immortelle mémoire, Décédée à Kensington le 28 décembre 1694.*

Adair, John, *Roundhead General, A Military Biography of Sir William Waller*, 1969.

Agrippa, Henry Cornelius, *Female Pre-eminence or the Dignity and Excellency of that Sex, above the Male*, Done into English with Additional Advantages, H.C. (Henry Care), 1670.

The Life and Death of that Excellent Minister of Christ, Mr Joseph Alleine, 1672.

Allestree, Richard, *The Ladies Calling. In Two Parts. By the author of the Whole Duty of Man etc.*, 5th impression, Oxford, 1677.

Ambrose, Isaac, *Works, including Prima, Media & Ultima*, 1674.

Anderson, Verily, *Friends and Relations. Three Centuries of Quaker Families*, 1980.

'Anonymous Business Diary of a Midwife', Rawlinson MS. D. 1141, Bodleian Library, Oxford.

'Anonymous Folio Volume' (of Anna Trapnel's verse), S.1.42. Th., Bodleian Library, Oxford.

Artamenes or The Grand Cyrus. An Excellent new Romance, Written by that famous Wit of France, Monsieur de Scudéry ... and now Englished by F.C., Gent, 2 Vols, 1653.

Ashley, Maurice, *James II*, 1977.

Ashley, Maurice, *Life in Stuart England*, 1964.

Ashley, Maurice, *The Stuarts in Love*, 1963.

Astell, Mary, *Reflections upon Marriage*, 3rd edition, To which is Added a Preface, in Answer to some Objections, 1706.

Athenae Oxonienses, ed. P. Bliss, 1813.

The Athenian Oracle, Being an Entire collection of all the Valuable Questions and Answers in the Old Athenian Mercuries, 1703.

Aubrey, John, *Aubrey's Brief Lives*, ed. and with a life of John Aubrey, Oliver Lawson Dick, 1968.

Aubrey, John, *Brief Lives and Other Selected Writings*, ed. and with an Introduction, Anthony Powell, 1949.

Austin, William, *Haec Homo. Wherein the Excellency of the Creation of Woman is described. By way of an essay*, 1637.

Aveling, J.H., MD, *English Midwives. Their History and Prospects*, 1872.

Ballard, George, *Memoirs of Several Ladies of Great Britain Who have been celebrated for their Writings or skill in the learned languages arts and sciences*, Oxford, 1752.

Balleine, G.R., *All for the King. The Life Story of Sir George Carteret (1609-1680)*, Channel Islands, La Société Jersiaise, 1976.

Bankes, Viola, *A Dorset Heritage, The Story of Kingston Lacey*, 1953.

Barham, Francis, 'Discovery of the Authorship of the *Whole Duty of Man*', *The Journal of Sacred Literature*, Vol. 5, 4th series, July 1864.

Barker, Jane, *Poetical Recreations Consisting of Original Poems, Odes, etc*, 2 parts, 1688.

Barksdale, Clement, *Letter touching a College of Maids or a Virgin Society*, 1675.

Batchiler, John, *The Virgin's Pattern: in the Exemplary Life and lamented Death of Mrs Susanna Perwick*, 1661.

Reliquiae Baxterianae, or Mr Richard Baxter's Narrative of the Most Memorable Passages of his Life and Times, 1696.

Bayley, A.R., BA, *The Great Civil War in Dorset, 1642-1660*, Taunton, 1910.

Beard, Charles A. and Mary R., *The Rise of American Civilization*, Vol. 1, New York, 1929.

Behn, Aphra, *The Works*, 6 Vols, 1904.

Berens, Lewis H., *The Digger Movement in the Days of the Commonwealth*, 1906.

Birch, Una, *Anna van Schurman. Artist, Scholar, Saint*, 1909.

Black, W. George, *Folk-Medicine*, 1883.

Blundell, William, of Crosby, Lancashire, Esquire, *A Cavalier's Notebook, Being Notes, Anecdotes and Observations*, ed. with introductory chapters, Rev. T. Ellison Gibson, 1880.

Blunt, Wilfrid, *The Art of Botanical Illustrations*, 1950.

Bowden, James, *The History of the Society of Friends in America*, 2 Vols, 1850.

Bowle, John, *John Evelyn and his World*, 1981.

The Works of Anne Bradstreet in Prose and Verse, ed. John H. Ellis, Charlestown, 1867.

Brailsford, M.R., *Quaker Women, 1650-1690*, 1915.

Braithwaite, W.C., *The Beginnings of Quakerism*, 1912.

Braithwaite, W.C., *The Second Period of Quakerism*, 1919.

Brathwaite, Richard, *The English Gentlewoman, Drawne out to the full Body: Expressing what Habilliments doe best attire her, what Ornaments doe best adorne her, what Complements doe best accomplish her*, 3rd edition, 1641.

Bridenbaugh, Carl, *Vexed and Troubled Englishmen 1590-1642* (pbk), Oxford, 1976.

Brodrick, James, SJ, *Mary Ward 1585-1645*, Society of St Paul, Langley, Bucks, 1945.

Works of Mr Thomas Brown, 5 Vols, 1719.

Bryant, Arthur, *Samuel Pepys, The Years of Peril* (pbk), 1961.

Budgell, E., Esq., *Memoirs of the Lives and Characters of the Illustrious Family of the Boyles*, 3rd edition, 1737.

Burghall, Edward, 'Providence Improved', A Manuscript by the Puritanical Vicar of Acton, 1628-1663', in T.W. Barlow, *Cheshire: Its Historical and Literary Associations*, 1855.

Burghclere, Lady, *The Life of James, First Duke of Ormonde 1610-1688*, 2 Vols, 1912.

Burke, Sir Bernard, *A Genealogical History of the Dormant, Abeyant, Forfeited and Extinct Peerages of the British Empire*, 1883.

Burnet, Gilbert, *History of my own Time*, ed. Osmund Airy, 2 Vols, with supplement, Oxford, 1897.

Burrage, Champlin, 'Anna Trapnel's Prophecies', *English Historical Review*, Vol. 26, 1911.

Burstein, Sona Rosa, MA, 'Aspects of the Psychopathology of Old Age. Revealed in

Witchcraft Cases of the Sixteenth and Seventeenth Centuries', *British Medical Bulletin*,
Vol. 6, Nos. 1-2, 1949.
Burton, Robert, *The Anatomy of Melancholy*, ed. Holbrook Jackson, 1936.
Butler, Samuel, *Hudibras*, ed. John Wilders, Oxford, 1967.

(CSP Domestic) Calendars of State Papers, Domestic.
(CSP Venetian) Calendars of State Papers, Venetian.
Memorandum Book of Sir Walter Calverley Bart, Surtees Society, LXXVII, 1883.
Camden, Caroll, *The Elizabethan Woman*, 1952.
Capp, Bernard, *Astrology and the Popular Press, English Almanacs 1500-1800*, 1979.
Capp, B.S., *The Fifth Monarchy Men - A Study in Seventeenth-Century English
Millenarianism*, 1972.
Carlingford Papers, Osborn Collection, Yale University.
Carlyle, Thomas, *Critical and Miscellaneous Essays*, 4 Vols, 1847.
Carte MSS, Bodleian Library, Oxford.
Carte, Thomas, *A Collection of Original Letters and Papers . . . Found among the Duke of
Ormonde's Papers*, 2 Vols, 1739.
Cartwright, Julia, *Madame. A life of Henrietta, daughter of Charles I and Duchess of Orleans*,
1891.
Cartwright, Julia, *Sacharissa - Some Account of Dorothy Sidney, Countess of Sunderland, her
Family and Friends 1617-1684*, 1937.
Cary, Mary, *The Resurrection of the Witnesses*, 1648.
*The Case of Divorce and Remarriage thereupon Discussed by a Reverend Prelate of the Church of
England and a private Gentleman Occasioned by the late Act of Parliament for the Divorce of
the Lord Rosse*, 1673.
*The Case of the Right Honourable Katherine Countess of Dorchester relating to the Bill lately
brought in for the confirming the Grant made to the Right Honourable Arthur Earl of
Torrington, by his present Majesty King William, and the late Queen Mary.*
*The Case of my Lord Roos. Printed with an Act touching the Lord Marquess of Northampton and
the Lady Elizabeth his wife*, Anno V, Ed. VI, Thomason Tract, 669 fo. 24/34.
Caulfield, James, *Portraits, Memoirs and Characters of Remarkable Persons, from the Reign of
Edward the Third, to the Revolution*, 2 Vols, 1794.
Cellier, Mrs Elizabeth, *To Dr—An Answer to his Queries, Concerning the Colledg of
Midwives*, 16 January 1688.
Cellier, Mrs Elizabeth, *Malice Defeated, Or a Brief Relation of the Accusation and Deliverance
of Elizabeth Cellier etc.*, 1680.
Cellier, Mrs Elizabeth, 'A Scheme for the Foundation of a Royal Hospital, and Raising a
Revenue of Five or Six-thousand Pounds a year, by, and for the Maintenance of a
Corporation of skilful Midwives, and such Foundlings or exposed Children, as shall be
admitted therein, etc.', 1687, Harleian Miscellany, IV, 1745.
'Certaine Informations', E. 65 (8), British Library.
Dr Hugh Chamberlen to the Princess Sophia, 4 October 1713, Sloane MSS, 4107, British
Library.
The Letters of John Chamberlain, ed. N.E. McClure, 2 Vols, Philadelphia, 1939.
Chambers, M.C.E., *The Life of Mary Ward, 1585-1645*, 2 Vols, 1885.
Chapman, A. Beatrice Wallis, and Chapman, Mary Wallis, *The Status of Women under the
English Law*, 1909.
The Letters of King Charles II, ed. Sir Arthur Bryant, 1968.

Chidley, Katherine, *Good Counsell to the Petitioners for Presbyterian Government that they may declare their faith before they build their Church*, 1645, Thomason Tract, 699, fo. 10/39.

Chidley, Katherine, *The Justification of the Independent Churches of Christ, Being an Answer to Mr Edwards his Booke etc.*, 1641.

Chidley, Katherine, *A New Yeares Gift, or a Briefe Exhortation to Mr Thomas Edwards*, 1645, E. 23 (13), British Library.

The Memoirs of Sir Hugh Cholmley, Knt and Bart, 1870.

'Sir Hugh Cholmley's Narrative of the Siege of Scarborough, 1644-5', ed. C.H. Firth, *English Historical Review*, Vol. 32, 1917.

Christie, W.D., *A Life of Anthony Ashley Cooper First Earl of Shaftesbury, 1621-1683*, 2 Vols, 1871.

Cibber, Colley, *Apology*, ed. R.W. Lowe, 2 Vols, 1887.

Clarendon, Edward Earl of, *The History of the Rebellion and Civil Wars in England*, 6 Vols, Oxford, reissued 1969.

The Life of Edward Earl of Clarendon in which is included A Continuation of His History of the Grand Rebellion, 3 Vols, Oxford, 1827.

Clarendon MSS, Bodleian Library, Oxford.

State Papers collected by Edward Earl of Clarendon, commencing 1621, ed. R. Scrope and T. Monkhouse, 3 Vols, Oxford, 1767-86.

Clark, Alice, *Working Life of Women in the Seventeenth Century*, ed. Miranda Chaytor and Jane Lewis, reissued 1982.

Clark(e), Samuel, *The Lives of Sundry Eminent Persons in this Later Age, in Two Parts*, 1683.

The Clarke Papers, ed. C.H. Firth, 4 Vols, 1891-1901.

Clyde, William M., *The Struggle for the Freedom of the Press. From Caxton to Cromwell*, Oxford, 1934.

Coate, Mary, *Social Life in Stuart England*, 2nd edition, 1925.

Cocke, Thomas, 'Classical or Gothic? Lady Anne Clifford Reconsidered', *Country Life*, 31 January 1980.

Coke, Sir Edward, *Institutes of the lawes of England*, 4 Vols, 1628-44.

Cole, Susan, 'A Flower of Purpose – A Memoir of Princess Elizabeth Stuart (1635-1650)', *Royal Stuart Papers* VIII, The Royal Stuart Society, 1975.

Collins, John, *Salt and Fishery. A Discourse thereof*, 1682.

Collins' Peerage of England, ed. Sir Egerton Brydges, 9 Vols, 1812.

A Complete History of Magick, Sorcery and Witchcraft, 2 Vols, 1715.

Conway Letters. The Correspondence of Anne Viscountess Conway, Henry More and their Friends 1642-1684, ed. M.H. Nicolson, 1930.

Costello, Louisa Stuart, *Memoirs of Eminent Englishwomen*, 4 Vols, 1844.

The Poems, English, Latin and Greek, of Richard Crashaw, ed. L.E. Martin, Oxford, 1957.

Cressy, David, *Education in Tudor and Stuart England*, Documents of Modern History series, 1975.

Cressy, David, *Literacy and the Social Order – Reading and Writing in Tudor and Stuart England*, Cambridge, 1980.

Cripps, Doreen, *Elizabeth of the Sealed Knot*, Kineton, 1975.

Cromwelliana, A Chronological detail of events in which Oliver Cromwell was engaged from the year 1642 to his death, 1810.

'Oliver Cromwell's Cousin's Diary', transcribed by Rev. William Cole, Additional MS, 5858, fo. 213-21, British Library.

Writings and Speeches of Oliver Cromwell, with an Introduction, notes and a sketch of his life, W.C. Abbott, 4 Vols, Cambridge, Massachusetts, 1937-47.

Curll, Edmund, *Betterton's History of the English Stage*, 1741.

Records of the Cust Family, series II, *The Brownlows of Belton, 1550-1779*, compiled by Lady Elizabeth Cust, 1909.

Cutter, S., and Viets, Henry R., *A Short History of Midwifery*, 1964.

Dangerfield, Thomas, *The Grand Impostor Defeated*, 1682.

The Life and Adventures of Mrs Christian Davies, commonly call'd Mother Ross ... Taken from her own mouth when a Pensioner of Chelsea Hospital, 1740.

'The humble petition of the Lady Eleanor (Davies)', 21 March 1644, Thomason Tract, 669, fo. 10/2.

Defoe, Daniel, *Conjugal Lewdness; or, Matrimonial Whoredom*, 1727.

Defoe, Daniel, *A Journal of the Plague Year*, London, 1950.

Denbigh, Cecilia Countess of, *Royalist Father and Roundhead Son - Being the memoirs of the First and Second Earls of Denbigh 1600-1675*, 1915.

Derby, James Earl of, 'The History and Antiquities of the Isle of Man', in *Desiderata Curiosa*, Francis Peck, Vol. II, 1770.

Devereux, Walter B., *Lives and Letters of the Devereux, Earls of Essex*, 2 Vols, 1853.

(DNB) *Dictionary of National Biography*.

Dobell, Bertram, 'A Unique Book: Anna Trapnel', *Notes and Queries*, 21 March 1914.

Donnison, Jean, *Midwives and Medical Men: A History of Inter-professional Rivalries and Women's Rights*, New York, 1977.

The Lord Marquesse of Dorchester's Letter to the Lord Roos With the Lord Roos's Answer thereunto. Whereunto is Added the Reasons why the Lord Marquess of Dorchester published his letter of the 25 of Feb, 1659. Dated the 13 of the same moneth. With his Answer to the Lord Roos his Letter, 1660.

Dorset, Charles Sackville, Earl of, 'Poems', in *Works of the English Poets*, ed. Samuel Johnson, Vol. XI, 1779.

Douce Ballads, Bodleian Library, Oxford.

'Dougle Fooleries' (S.G.W.), *Bodleian Quarterly Record*, VIII, 1932.

Duffy, Maureen, *The Passionate Shepherdess; Aphra Behn 1640-1689*, 1977.

Duffy, Maureen, *Inherit the Earth*, 1980.

Duncon, John, *A Letter containing Many Remarkable passages in the most Holy Life and Death of the Late Lady, Letice, Vi-Countess Falkland. Written to the Lady Morison at Gt Tew in Oxfordshire*, 2nd edition, 1649.

Duncon, John, *The Returns of Spiritual Comfort and Grief in a Devout Soul. Represented (by entercourse of Letters) to the Right Honourable the Ladie Letice, Vi-Countess Falkland in her life time etc.*, 2nd edition, enlarged, 1649.

'The Life and Letters of Sir Lewis Dyve', ed. H.G. Tibbutt, *Bedfordshire Historical Record Society*, Vol. XXVII, Luton, 1946.

Eccles, Audrey, *Obstetrics and Gynaecology in Tudor and Stuart England*, 1982.

Ede, Mary, *Arts and Society in England under William and Mary*, 1979.

Edwards, Thomas, *Gangraena*, 1646.

Elstob, Elizabeth, *An English-Saxon Homily on the Birth-Day of St Gregory*, trans. with Notes, 1709.

An Essay in Defense of the Female Sex, 1696.

Essays and Literature by Members of the English Association, XIX, Oxford, 1934.

Diary and Correspondence of John Evelyn FRS, ed. William Bray, 4 Vols, 1850.

Evelyn, John, *The Life of Mrs Godolphin. Now first published and ed. Samuel Lord Bishop of Oxford*, 1848.

Evelyn, Mary, *Mundus Muliebris: Or, The Ladies Dressing-Room Unlock'd and her Toilette spread In Burlesque etc.*, 1690.

Everitt, Alan, *The Community of Kent and the Great Rebellion, 1640–1660*, Leicester, 1966.

Ewen, C. L'Estrange, 'A Noted Case of Witchcraft at North Moreton, Berks, in the early 17th century', *Berkshire Archaeological Journal*, Vol. 40, No. 2, 1936.

Ewen, C. L'Estrange, *Witchcraft and Demonianism, A Concise account derived from sworn depositions and confessions obtained in the courts of England and Wales*, 1933.

Ewen, C. L'Estrange (ed. with an Introduction), *Witch Hunting and Witch Trials. The Indictments for Witchcraft from the Records of 1373 Assizes held for the Home Circuit, A.D. 1559–1736*, 1929.

Eyre, Adam, *A Dyurnall, or Catalogue of all my Accions and Expences, from the 1st of January 1646–7, Surtees Society*, LXV, 1877.

Fanshawe, Sir Richard, Bt, *Shorter Poems and Translations*, ed. N.W. Bawcutt, Liverpool, 1964.

Martha Farthing's affidavit', *Notes and Queries*, V, 11th series, 1912.

Fea, Allan, *Some Beauties of the Seventeenth Century*, 1906.

Fell, Margaret, *Womens Speaking, Justified, Proved and Allowed of by the Scriptures, All such as speak by the Spirit and Power of the Lord Jesus*, 1666.

The Household Account Book of Sarah Fell of Swarthmoor Hall, ed. Norman Penney, FSA, Cambridge, 1920.

Fell Smith, Charlotte, *Mary Rich, Countess of Warwick 1625–1678, Her Family and Friends*, 1901.

Fieldhouse, R.T., 'Parliamentary Representation in the Borough of Richmond', *Yorkshire Archaeological Journal*, XLIV, 1972.

The Journeys of Celia Fiennes, ed. and with an Introduction, Christopher Morris, 1649.

Fildes, Valerie, 'Infant Feeding Practices in the Sixteenth and Seventeenth Centuries', seminar, University College, London, 14 January 1981.

Report on the Manuscripts of Allan George Finch Esq., HMC, 3 Vols, 1913–61.

Findlater, Richard, *The Player Queens*, 1976.

Firth, C.H., *Cromwell's Army, A History of The English Soldier during the Civil Wars, the Commonwealth and the Protectorate*, 1912.

Life and Death of Mistress Mary Firth, 1662.

Foster, Michael, 'Major-General Sir John Digby "Peerlesse Champion and Mirrour of Perfect Chivalrie",' *Royal Stuart Papers* XX, The Royal Stuart Society, 1982.

The Journal of George Fox, Revised by John L. Nickalls, with an epilogue by Henry J. Cadbury, and an introduction by Geoffrey F. Nuttall, Cambridge, 1952.

Frank, Joseph, *The Beginnings of the English Newspaper, 1620–1660*, Cambridge, Massachusetts, 1961.

Fraser, Antonia, *Cromwell: Our Chief of Men*, 1973.

Fraser, Antonia, *King Charles II*, 1979.

Mrs Elizabeth Freke. Her Diary. 1671 to 1714, ed. Mary Carbery, Cork, 1913.

Fuller, Thomas, *History of the Worthies of England*, ed. J. Nichols, 2 Vols, 1811.

Fussell, G.E. and K.R., *The English Countrywoman, A Farmhouse Social History*, 1953.

Gardiner, Dorothy, *English Girlhood at School. A Study of Women's Education through Twelve Centuries*, 1929.

Gardiner, Dorothy, ed., *The Oxinden Letters, 1607-1642*, 1933.

Gardiner, Dorothy, ed., *The Oxinden and Peyton Letters, 1642-1678*, 1937.

Gardiner, S.R., *History of England From the Accession of James I to the Outbreak of the Civil War 1603-1642*, 10 Vols, 1883-4.

Gardiner, S.R., *History of the Great Civil War, 1642-9*, 3 Vols, 1886-91.

Gataker, Thomas, 'A Good Wife Gods Gift', in *Two Marriage Sermons*, 1624.

G.E.C. (Cokayne), *The Complete Peerage*, 6 Vols, Gloucester, reprinted 1982.

George, Margaret, 'From "Goodwife" to "Mistress": the Transformation of the Female in Bourgeois Culture', *Science and Society*, 37, 1973.

Gibb, M.A., *John Lilburne the Leveller, A Christian Democrat*, 1947.

Gibb, M.A., *The Lord General. A Life of Thomas Fairfax*, 1938.

Martha Lady Giffard. Her Life and Correspondence. 1664-1722, ed. Julia G. Longe, 1911.

Gildon, Charles, *A Comparison Between the Two Stages, with an Examen of the Generous Conqueror; in Dialogue*, 1702.

Gildon, Charles, *The Life of Mr Thomas Betterton*, 1710.

Godwin, Rev. G.N., *The Civil War in Hampshire (1642-45) and the Story of Basing House*, Southampton, 1904.

Goreau, Angeline, *Reconstructing Aphra - A Social Biography of Aphra Behn*, Oxford, 1980.

Gouge, William, *Of Domesticall Duties. Eight Treatises*, 3rd edition, 1634.

Gough, Richard, *The History of Myddle* (pbk), 1981.

Grant, Douglas, *Margaret the First. A Biography of Margaret Cavendish, Duchess of Newcastle 1623-1673*, 1957.

Graunt, John, 'Natural and Political Observations mentioned in a following index and made upon the bills of mortality', 1662, in *Economic Writings of Sir William Petty*, ed. C.H. Hull, New York, 1964.

Green, David, *Queen Anne*, 1970.

Greene, Graham, *Lord Rochester's Monkey, Being the Life of John Wilmot, Second Earl of Rochester*, 1974.

Greer, Germaine, *The Obstacle Race - The fortunes of women painters and their work*, 1979.

Gregg, Edward, *Queen Anne*, 1980.

Gregg, Pauline, *Free-Born John, A Biography of John Lilburne*, 1961.

Gregg, Pauline, *King Charles I*, 1981.

Grisar, Joseph, SJ, 'Mary Ward 1585-1645', *The Month*, 1945.

Habakkuk, H.J., 'Marriage Settlements in the Eighteenth Century', *Transactions of the Royal Historical Society*, XX, 1949.

Hair, Paul, (ed.) *Before the Bawdy Court, Selections from church court and other records relating to the correction of moral offences in England, Scotland and New England, 1300-1800*, 1972.

Halifax, George Savile, Marquis of, *Complete Works*, ed. and with an introduction by J.P. Kenyon (pbk), 1969.

The Memoirs of Anne, Lady Halkett and Ann, Lady Fanshawe, ed. John Loftis, Oxford, 1979.

Hamilton, Anthony, *Memoirs of the Comte de Gramont*, translated by Peter Quennell, 1930.

Hamilton, Elizabeth, *Henrietta Maria*, 1976.

Hamilton, Elizabeth, *William's Mary: A Biography of Mary II*, 1972.

The Harcourt Papers, ed. E.W. Harcourt, Vol. I, Oxford, 1880.

Harleian MSS, British Library.

Letters of Lady Brilliana Harley, with an Introduction and Notes, Thomas Taylor Lewis, MA, Camden Society, 1854.

Hartmann, C.H., *The King's Friend, A Life of Charles Berkeley, Viscount Fitzhardinge Earl of Falmouth, 1630-1665*, 1951.

Hartmann, C.H., *The Vagabond Duchess*, 1926.

Correspondence of the Family of Hatton, 1601-1704, ed. E.M. Thompson, Camden Society, 2 Vols, 1878.

Selected Essays of William Hazlitt 1778-1830, ed. Geoffrey Keynes, FRCS, 1970.

The Remains of Thomas Hearne. Reliquiae Hearnianae, Being extracts from his MS Diaries, compiled by Dr Bliss, now newly revised by John Buchanan-Brown, 1966.

Henry, Louis, 'Anciennes Familles Genevoises', Étude démographique: *XVIe-XXe siècle, Travaux et Documents*, cahier no. 26, Presses Universitaires de France, 1956.

The Autobiography of Edward, Lord Herbert of Cherbury, ed. Sidney Lee, 1886.

Works of George Herbert, ed. F.E. Hutchinson, 2nd edition, 1945.

Herbert, William, *History of the Twelve Great Livery Companies of London*, 1836.

The Poems of Robert Herrick, ed. L.C. Martin, 1965.

The Rev. Oliver Heywood B.A., 1630-1702; His Autobiography, Diaries, Anecdote and Event Books, 3 Vols, ed. J. Horsfall Turner, Brighouse, 1882.

Hic Mulier: Or, The Man-Woman and Haec-Vir; Or, The Womanish-Man, 1620, reprinted Exeter, The Rota, 1973.

Hieron, Samuel, *A Helpe unto Devotion; Containing Certain Moulds or Forms of Prayer, fitted to several occasions; and penned for the furtherance of those, who have more desire than skill, to poure out their soules by petition unto God*, 4th edition, 1613.

Higgins, P.M., 'Women in the English Civil War', MA thesis (unpublished), Manchester, 1965.

Hill, Christopher, *Antichrist in Seventeenth-Century England*, 1971.

Hill, Christopher, 'Clarissa Harlowe and her Times', *Essays in Criticism*, IV, 1955.

Hill, Christopher, *Some Intellectual Consequences of the English Revolution*, 1980.

Hillier, George, *A Narrative of the Attempted Escapes of Charles the First from Carisbrook Castle ... Including the letters of the King to Colonel Titus now first deciphered and printed from the originals*, 1852.

Himes, Norman E., *Medical History of Contraception*, 1936.

Hirst, Derek, *The Representative of the People? Voters and Voting in England under the Early Stuarts*, 1975.

Hiscock, W.G., *John Evelyn and Mrs Godolphin*, 1951.

HMC (Historical Manuscripts Commission), Bath MSS, Vol. I, 1904.

HMC (Historical Manuscripts Commission), Denbigh MSS, 7th Report, Part V, 1911.

HMC (Historical Manuscripts Commission), 8th Report, Appendix, 1881.

HMC (Historical Manuscripts Commission), R.R. Hastings MSS, 4 Vols, 1928-47.

HMC (Historical Manuscripts Commission), Leyborne-Popham MSS, Norwich, 1899.

HMC (Historical Manuscripts Commission), Rutland MSS, 12th Report, IV-V, 1888-91.

HMC (Historical Manuscripts Commission), Salisbury MSS, Vol. XXII, 1612-68, 1971.

Diary of Lady Margaret Hoby, 1599-1605, ed. Dorothy M. Meads, 1930.

Hogrefe, Pearl, *Tudor Women - Commoners and Queens*, Iowa, 1975.

Hollingsworth, T.H., 'A Demographic Study of the British Ducal Families' in *Population in History*, ed. D.V. Glass and D.E.C. Eversley, 1965.

Hookes, Nicholas, *Amanda, A Sacrifice to an Unknown Goddesse, Or, a Free-will offering of a loving Heart to a Sweet-Heart*, 1653.

Houblon, Lady Alice Archer, *The Houblon Family, Its Story and Times*, 2 Vols, 1907.

Houldsworth, W., *A History of English Law*, 3rd edition, 5 Vols, 1942.

The House of Commons 1660-1690, ed. Basil Duke Henning, *The History of Parliament* series, 3 Vols, 1983.

Howell, James, *Ho-Elianae or Familiar Letters*, ed. J. Jacobs, 2 Vols, 1892.

Howell, Roger, ' "The Devil cannot match him": the Image of Cromwell in Restoration Drama', *Cromwelliana*, Cromwell Association, 1982-3.

'A humble Remonstrance of the Batchelors, in and about London, to the honourable House, in Answer to a late Paper, intitled, A Petition of Ladies for Husbands', Harleian Miscellany, IV, 1747.

Hunter, Joseph, *The History and Topography of Ketteringham*, Norwich, 1851.

Hunter, Rev. Joseph, FSA, *The Life of Oliver Heywood 1630-1702*, 1842.

Hutchins, John, MA, *The History and Antiquities of the County of Dorset*, 3rd edition, 4 Vols, 1861.

Hutchinson, Lucy, *Memoirs of the Life of Colonel Hutchinson*, ed. James Sutherland, reprinted 1973.

Illick, Joseph E., 'Child-Rearing in Seventeenth Century England and America', in *The History of Childhood*, ed. Lloyd deMause, 1976.

Memoirs of James II, 2 Vols, Colchester, 1821.

Jameson, A., *The Beauties of the Court of King Charles the Second*, 1833.

Johnson, G.W., *The Evolution of Woman. From subjection to comradeship*, 1926.

Jonson, Ben, *The Gypsies Metamorphosed*, ed. from original and unexpurgated sources by George Watson Cole, New York, 1931.

Josceline, E., 'The Mothers Legacy to her Unborn Child', Additional MSS, 27, 467, British Library.

Journals of the House of Lords.

Katz, David S., *Philo-Semitism and the Readmission of the Jews to England, 1603-1655*, Oxford, 1982.

Kaufman, Helen Andrews, *Conscientious Cavalier, Colonel Bullen Reymes, MP, FRS, 1613-1672*, 1962.

Kenny, C.S., *The History of the Law of England as to the Effects of Marriage on Property and on The Wife's Legal Capacity*, 1879.

Kent, Countess of, *A Choice Manuall of Rare and Select Secrets in Physics and Chyrurgery*, 2nd edition, 1653.

Kenyon, John, *The Popish Plot*, 1972.

Kerridge, Eric, 'The Revolts in Wiltshire against Charles I', *The Wiltshire Archaeological and Natural History Magazine*, Vol. 57, 1958-60.

Poems by Mrs Anne Killigrew, 1686.

Poems (1686) by Mrs Anne Killigrew, facsimile reproduction with an Introduction, Richard Morton, Gainesville, Florida, Scholars' Facsimiles and Reprints, 1967.

King, Gregory, *Natural and political observations and conclusions upon the state and condition of England. To which is prefixed a life of the Author by George Chalmers*, 1810.

Kingdomes Weekly Intelligencer, British Library.

K(irkman), F., *The Unlucky Citizen*, 1673.

Knevet, Ralph, *Funerall Elegies; Consecrated to the Immortall memory of the Right Honourable the Lady Katherine Paston, late wife to the truly noble and heroicke, William Paston of Oxned Esquire*, 1637.

Knox, R.A., *Enthusiasm. A Chapter in the History of Religion*, Oxford, 1950.

Knyvett Letters, 1620-1644, ed. Bertram Schofield, Norfolk Record Society, 1949.

Lacy, John, *The Old Troop, or Monsieur Raggou*, 1672, in *Dramatists of the Restoration: John Lacy*, Edinburgh, 1875.

The Ladies Dictionary being a General Entertainment for the Fair-Sex. A Work never attempted before in English. Printed for John Dunton, 1694.

Lambley, Kathleen, MA, *The Teaching and Cultivation of the French Language in England during Tudor and Stuart times*, Manchester, 1920.

Lang, R.G., 'The Greater Merchants of London in the Early Seventeenth Century', D. Phil. thesis (unpublished), Oxford, 1963.

Larking, Rev. Lambert B. (ed.), *Proceedings, Principally in the County of Kent, In Connection with the Parliaments called in 1640*, Camden Society, 1862.

Larner, Christina, *Enemies of God - The Witch-hunt in Scotland*, 1981.

Laslett, Peter (ed.), with Oosterveen, Karla, and Smith, Richard M., *Bastardy and its Comparative History*, 1980.

Laslett, Peter, *Family Life and Illicit Love in Earlier Generations*, 1977.

Laslett, Peter, *The World we have lost* (pbk), 1968.

Laslett, Peter, *The World we have lost - further explored*, 3rd edition, 1983.

'A Briefe Journall of the Siege against Lathom', see under Ormerod. *Tracts Relating to Military Proceedings in Lancashire during the Great Civil War*.

The Lawes Resolutions of Woman's Rights, or the Lawes Provision for Women, 1632.

Lecky, William, *History of European Morals*, 2 Vols, 1869.

Leigh, Mrs Dorothy, *The Mothers Blessing*, 7th edition, 1621.

Lennep, W. van, *The London Stage*, Vol. I, Illinois, 1960.

Lewenhak, Sheila, *Women and Work* (pbk), Glasgow, 1980.

Lilburne, John, *The Freemans Freedome Vindicated*, 1646.

Lilburne, John, *Jonah's Cry out of the Whale's Belly*, 1647.

William Lilly's History of his Life and Times. Reprinted for Charles Baldwin, 1822.

'The Countess of Lincoln's Nursery', Oxford, 1622, Harleian Miscellany, IV, 1747.

The Lismore Papers, First Series, Viz. Autobiographical Notes etc., of Richard Boyle, First and 'Great' Earl of Cork, ed. A.B. Grosart, Vol. V, 1886.

Littlehales, Margery Mary, IBVM, *Mary Ward (1585-1645)*, Catholic Truth Society, 1974.

Lloyd, David, *Memoires of the Lives, Actions, Sufferings and Deaths of those Noble, Reverend and Excellent Personages that Suffered ... for the Protestant Religion etc.*, 1668.

The Correspondence of John Locke, ed. E.S. de Beer, 4 Vols, Oxford, 1976-9.

Lockyer, Roger, *The Life and Political Career of George Villiers, First Duke of Buckingham 1592-1628*, 1981.

Longleat MSS, Longleat, Wilts.

The Poems of Richard Lovelace, ed. C.H., Wilkinson, Oxford, 1930.

The Diary of Roger Lowe, of Ashton-in-Makerfield, Lancashire, 1663-1674, ed. William L.

Sachse, Foreword by Professor Wallace Notestein, Yale University Press, New Haven, 1938.

The Letter Books 1644-45 of Sir Samuel Luke, ed. H.G. Tibbutt, FSA, HMC, HMSO, 1963.

Lupton, Donald, *London and the Countrey Carbonaded and quartred into severall Characters*, 1632.

McArthur, Ellen A., 'Women Petitioners and the Long Parliament', *English Historical Review*, XXIV, 1909.

Macdonald, Isabel, *Elizabeth Alkin*, 1934.

MacDonald, Michael, *Mystical Bedlam. Madness, anxiety and healing in seventeenth century England*, Cambridge, 1981.

McElwee, William, *The Murder of Sir Thomas Overbury*, 1952.

Macfarlane, Alan, *The Family Life of Ralph Josselin. A Seventeenth Century Clergyman. An Essay in Historical Anthropology*, Cambridge, 1970.

Macfarlane, A.D.J., 'The Regulation of Marital and Sexual Relationships in Seventeenth Century England, with special reference to the county of Essex', M. Phil. thesis (unpublished), London, 1968.

Macfarlane, Alan, *Witchcraft in Tudor and Stuart England - A Regional and Comparative Study*, 1970.

McLaren, Dorothy, 'Nature's Contraceptive. Wet-Nursing and Prolonged Lactation: The Case of Chesham, Buckinghamshire, 1578-1601', *Medical History*, 23, 1979.

Makin, Basua, *An Essay to Revive the Antient Education of Gentlewomen, In Religion, Manners, Arts and Tongues. With an Answer to the Objections against this Way of Education*, 1673.

Manners, Emily, 'Elizabeth Hooton, first Quaker Woman preacher, 1600-1672', *Journal of the Friends Historical Society*, Supplement No. 12, 1914.

Markham, Gervase, *The English Huswife: containing the inward and outward vertues which ought to be in a compleate Woman* (Book 2 of *Countrey Contentments*), 1615.

Marriage Promoted in a Discourse of its Ancient and Modern Practice etc., By a Person of Quality, 1690.

Marsh, Henry, *New Survey of the Turkish Empire*, 1663.

The Life of Adam Martindale. Written by himself, ed. Rev. Richard Parkinson, Chetham Society, 1845.

The Poems and Letters of Andrew Marvell, ed. H.M. Margoliouth, 2 Vols, Oxford, 1971.

Masham, Damaris, *Occasional Thoughts in reference to a Vertuous or Christian Life*, 1705.

Masson, David, *The life of John Milton*, 7 Vols, 1859-94.

Matthew, Sir Tobie, *The Life of Lady Lucy Knatchbull*, Introduction by Dom David Knowles, 1931.

May, Geoffrey, *Social Control of Sex Expression*, 1930.

Mercurius Militaris.

Mercurius Pragmaticus.

Middlesex County Records, ed. J.C. Jeaffreson, Vol. III, 1888.

The Midwife Unmask'd: or The Popish Design of Mrs Cellier's Meal-Tub plainly made known: being a Second Answer to her Scandalous Libel, in short Remarques upon the same etc., 1680.

The Midwives Just Petition: or, A complaint of divers good Gentlewomen of that faculty; Shewing to the whole Christian world their just cause of their sufferings in these distracted Times, for their want of Trading, 25 January 1643.

Millar, Oliver, *The Age of Charles I: Painting in England 1620–1649*, Tate Gallery, 1972.

Millar, Oliver, *Sir Peter Lely, 1618–1680*, National Portrait Gallery Exhibition Catalogue, 1978.

Miller, John, *James II – A Study in Kingship*, 1978.

M(ilton), J., *The Doctrine and Discipline of Divorce, Restor'd to the good of both Sexes, etc.*, 1645.

'Minute Book of a Puritan Congregation, 1654', Rawlinson MSS, D. 828, Bodleian Library, Oxford.

Mitchell, R.J., and Leys, M.D.R., *A History of London Life*, 1958.

The Private Diarie of Elizabeth Viscountess Mordaunt, Duncairn, 1856.

Morgan, Fidelis, *The Female Wits – Women Playwrights of the Restoration*, 1981.

Morrah, Patrick, *Prince Rupert of the Rhine*, 1976.

Morris, G.C.R., 'Which Molins treated Cromwell for Stone – and did not prescribe for Pepys?', *Medical History*, 26, 1982.

Myddelton, W.M., *Chirk Castle Accounts 1666–1753*, privately printed, Horncastle, 1931.

Nall, J.G., *Great Yarmouth and Lowestoft*, 1867.

Nalson, John, *The Countermine*, 3rd edition, 1678.

Nash, Thomas, *History and Antiquities of Worcestershire*, 3 Vols, 1781.

Needham, Gwendolyn B., 'Mrs Manley: An Eighteenth Century Wife of Bath', *Huntingdon Library Quarterly*, No. 3, April, 1938.

Neville, Henry, *The Ladies Parliament*, 1647.

(Neville, Henry), *The Ladies, a Second Time, Assembled in Parliament. A Continuation of the Parliament of Ladies*, 2 August 1647.

Nevil(l)e, Henry, *Newes from the New Exchange, or the Commonwealth of Ladies, Drawn to the Life, in their severall Characters and Concernment*, 1650.

'A New Bill, drawn up by the Committee of Grievances, in Reply, to the Ladies and Batchelors Petition and Remonstrance, etc.', 1693, Harleian Miscellany, IV, 1745.

Letters and Poems In Honour of the Incomparable Princess Margaret, Dutchess of Newcastle, 1676.

Philosophical and Physical Opinions Written by the Thrice Noble, Illustrious and Excellent Princess, the Lady Marchioness of Newcastle, 1663.

CCXI Sociable Letters written by the Thrice Noble, Illustrious and Excellent Princess The Marchioness of Newcastle, 1664.

A true relation of the Birth, Breeding, and Life, of Margaret Cavendish, Duchess of Newcastle, written by herself, with a Critical Preface, etc. by Sir Egerton Brydges, MP, Kent, privately printed, 1814.

The Worlds Olio. Written by the Right Honourable the Lady Margaret Newcastle, 1655.

'The New Letanie', 15 March 1647, Thomason Tract, 669, fo. 10/120.

Newdigate-Newdegate, Lady, *Cavalier and Puritan in the Days of the Stuarts, Compiled from the Private Papers and Diary of Sir Richard Newdigate, second Baronet, etc.*, 1901.

Newdigate-Newdegate, Lady, *Gossip From a Muniment Room – Being Passages in the Lives of Anne and Mary Fytton 1574–1618*, 1897.

Nicoll, Allardyce, *A History of English Drama, 1660–1900*, Vol. I, *Restoration Drama*, Cambridge, 1952.

Nichols, John, FSA, *The History and Antiquities of the County of Leicester*, 2 Vols, 1795.

Nichols, John, *The Progresses, Processions and Magnificent Festivities, of King James the First*, 4 Vols, 1828.

Noble, Mark, *Memoirs of the Protectoral-House of Cromwell*, 3rd edition, 2 Vols, with improvements, 1787.

Norsworthy, Laura, *The Lady of Bleeding Heart Yard. Lady Elizabeth Hatton 1578-1646*, 1935.

North, Roger, *The Lives of Francis North, Baron Guilford. .... Sir Dudley North; and Rev. Dr John North etc;* ed. A. Jessopp, 3 Vols, 1890.

Notestein, Wallace, 'The English Woman, 1580-1650', in *Studies in Social History*, ed. J.H. Plumb, 1955.

Notestein, Wallace, *Four Worthies*, 1956.

Notestein, Wallace, *A History of Witchcraft in England from 1558 to 1718*, 1911.

Ogg, David, *England in the Reign of Charles II* (pbk), 3rd edition, Oxford, 1963.

A Royalist's Notebook. The Commonplace Book of Sir John Oglander Kt. of Nunwell, ed. Francis Bamford, 1936.

Oman, Carola, *Elizabeth of Bohemia*, 1964.

Ormerod, George (ed.), *Tracts Relating to Military Proceedings in Lancashire during the Great Civil War*, Chetham Society, Manchester, 1844.

Letters from Dorothy Osborne to Sir William Temple (1652-54), ed. E.A. Parry, 1914.

The Complete Works of Thomas Otway, ed. Montague Summers, 3 Vols, 1926.

Miscellaneous Works in prose and verse of Sir Thomas Overbury, with a memoir of his life, 1756.

'The Appeal and Petition of Mary Overton', 24 March 1647, E. 381/10, British Library.

Owen, Dorothy M., 'Lincolnshire Women in History', *The Lincolnshire Historian*, Vol. 2, No. 6, 1959.

'Family of Oxinden Correspondence', Vol. v, 1652-7, Additional MSS, 28, 003, British Library.

Parker, M. Pauline, IBVM, *The Spirit of Mary Ward*, Bristol, 1963.

Pearl, Valerie, 'Social Policy in Early Modern London', in *History and Imagination. Essays in honour of H.R. Trevor-Roper*, ed. Hugh Lloyd Jones, Valerie Pearl and Blair Worden, 1981.

The Diary of Samuel Pepys, ed. with Companion and Index, Robert Latham and William Matthews, 11 Vols, 1970-83.

Perkins, William, *Discourse of the Damned Art of Witchcraft; so far forth as it is revealed in the Scriptures and Manifest by True Experience*, 1608.

The Humble Petition of divers well-affected Women inhabiting the City of London, Westminster, the Borough of Southwark, Hamblets and places adjacent, 1649, E. 551 (14), British Library.

Pierpont Morgan Library MSS, New York.

Pilkington, Mrs, *Memoirs of Celebrated Female Characters etc.*, 1804.

Pinto, V. de Sola, *Rochester. Portrait of a Restoration Poet*, 1935.

Pinto, V. de Sola, *Sir Charles Sedley, 1639-1701*, 1927.

Poems by Eminent Ladies, 2 Vols, 1755.

Pope, Mary, *A Treatise of Magistracy, shewing The Magistrate hath been, and for ever is to be the cheife Officer in the Church etc.*, 1647.

Powell, C.L., *English Domestic Relations, 1487-1653*, New York, 1917.

Powicke, F.M., 'Notes on Hastings Manuscripts', *Huntingdon Library Quarterly*, No. 3, April 1938.

Price, F. Hilton, FSA, *A Handbook of London Bankers*, 1890-91.

Price, F. Hilton, *The Marygold at Temple Bar*, 1902.

The Principles of the most Ancient and Modern Philosophy. A little Treatise published since the Author's death, translated out of the English into Latin ... and now again made English by J.C. Medicinae Professor, printed in Latin, Amsterdam, 1690, reprinted, London, 1692.

'Puritan Congregation Minute Book', 1654, Rawlinson MSS, D. 828, fo. 30/32.

Quaife, G.R., *Wanton Wenches and Wayward Wives*, 1979

The Queens Closet Opened. Incomparable secrets in Physick, Chirurgery, Preserving, Candying and Cookery, As they were presented to the Queen. Never before published. Transcribed from the true Copies of her Majesties own recipe books, by W.M., one of her late Servants, 1655.

Rawlinson MSS, Bodleian Library, Oxford.

Reid, Stuart, *John and Sarah*, 1913.

Reynolds, Myra, *The Learned Lady in England 1650-1760*, New York, 1920.

Roberts, George, *The Life, Progresses, and Rebellion of James Duke of Monmouth*, 2 Vols, 1844.

Roberts, George, *The Social History of the People of the Southern Counties of England*, 1856.

Robinson, John Martin, *The Dukes of Norfolk – A Quincentennial History*, Oxford, 1982.

Familiar Letters Written by the Right Honourable John late Earl of Rochester, And several other Persons of Honour and Quality. With Letters written by the most Ingenious Mr Thomas Otway and Mrs K. Philips, etc, 1697.

Rochester, John Wilmot, Earl of, *Collected Works*, ed. John Hayward, 1926.

Rogers, Daniel, *Matrimoniall Honour*, 1642.

Ross, Isabel, *Margaret Fell. Mother of Quakerism*, 1949.

Rowse, A.L. (ed. and with an Introduction by), *The Poems of Shakespeare's Dark Lady*, 1978.

Roxburghe Ballads, 9 Vols, Ballad Society, Hertford, 1871-99.

Rueff, Jacob, *The Expert Midwife, or An Excellent and most necessary Treatise of the generation and birth of Man, etc*, 1637.

Rushworth, John, *Historical collections of private passages of state etc.*, 7 Vols, 1659-1701.

The Letters of Lady Russell, ed. Lord John Russell, 1853.

The Life of Rachael Wriothesley, Lady Russell; followed by a series of letters to her husband 1672-1682. With eleven letters from the Countess of Sunderland to the Marquis of Hallifax, ed. anonymously by Mary Berry, 1819.

Ruycaut, Paul, *Present state of the Ottoman empire*, 1668.

Sacks, Oliver, *Migraine. Evolution of a common disorder. A practical guide to treatment and relief*, revised edition, 1981.

Sackville-West, V., ed., *The Diary of Lady Anne Clifford*, with an Introductory Note, 1923.

Salmon, W., *Aristotle's Masterpiece*, in Two Parts, 1697.

'The Saxon Nymph' (Elizabeth Elstob), *Times Literary Supplement*, 28 September 1933.

Scales, John, 'The Quaker Women who were whipped in Dover (Noted women of Old Dover, New Hampshire)', Dover Public Library MSS, New Hampshire, USA.

Schnucker, R.V., 'Elizabethan Birth Control and Puritan Attitudes', *Journal of Interdisciplinary History*, v, 4, 1975.

Schnucker, R.V., 'The English Puritans and Pregnancy, Delivery and Breast Feeding', *History of Childhood Quarterly*, i, 1973-4.

Schücking, Levin L., *The Puritan Family. A Social Study from the Literary Sources*, 1969.

Schurman, Anna van, *The Learned Maid; or whether a Maid may be a Scholar?*, 1659.

Scot, Reginald, *Discoverie of Witchcraft, 1584*, ed. Brinsley Nicolson, 1886.

Scott Thomson, Gladys, *Life in a Noble Household 1641-1700* (pbk), 1965.

Scott Thomson, Gladys, *The Russells in Bloomsbury, 1669-1771*, 1940.

'The Scourge of Civil War and the Blessing of Peace, 1645', Thomason Tract, 669, fo. 10/27.

Seaver, Paul S. (ed.), *Seventeenth-Century England, Society in an Age of Revolution*, New York, 1976.

The Poetical and Dramatic Works of Sir Charles Sedley, collected and ed. by V. de Sola Pinto, 2 Vols, 1928.

'The Arms of Katherine Sedley', Additional MSS, 30, 382, British Library.

Sensabaugh, G.F., 'Love Ethics in Platonic Court Drama, 1625-1642', *Huntingdon Library Quarterly*, No. 3, April 1938.

Sermon, William, *The Ladies Companion, or The English Midwife*, 1671.

Shannon, Francis Boyle, Viscount, *Discourses and Essays, Useful for the Vain Modish Ladies and their Gallants*, 2nd edition, with new additions, 1696.

Sharp, Mrs Jane, *The Compleat Midwife's Companion etc.*, 4th edition, 1725.

Sharp, Mrs Jane, *The Midwives Book. Or the whole art of Midwifery Discovered etc.*, 1671.

Mrs Shaws Innocency restored, and Mr Clendons Calumny retorted, Notwithstanding his late Triumphing, 1653.

Shirley, John, *The Illustrious History of Women*, 1686.

Shorter, Edward, *A History of Women's Bodies*, 1983.

Sidney, Henry, *Diary of the Times of Charles the Second*, 2 Vols, ed. and with notes by R.W. Blencowe, 1843.

Sloane MSS, British Library.

Smith, Florence, *Mary Astell*, New York, 1916.

Smith, Steven R., 'Growing Old in Early Stuart England', *Albion*, Vol. 8, 1976.

Souars, P.M., *The Matchless Orinda*, Cambridge, Massachusetts, 1931.

Spencer, Theodore, 'The History of an Unfortunate Lady', *Harvard Studies and Notes in Philology and Literature*, XX, 1938.

Spender, Dale, *Man Made Language* (pbk), 1980.

Sprint, John, *The Bride-Woman Counseller, Being a Sermon Preach'd at a Wedding, May the 11th, 1699 at Sherbourn in Dorsetshire*.

Spufford, Margaret, 'Portraits of Society, Popular fiction in 17th-century England', *History Today*, February 1982.

Stafford, Anthony, Gent., *The Femall Glory or The Life and Death of our Blessed Lady, the holy Virgin Mary, Gods owne immaculate Mother*, 1635.

Staffordshire and the Great Rebellion, Staffordshire County Council, 1964.

Stanley, Dean, *Memorials of Westminster Abbey*, 1867.

Stearne, John, *A Confirmation and Discovery of Witchcraft*, 1648, reprinted Exeter, The Rota, 1973.

Stenton, D.M., *The English Woman in History*, 1957.

Stone, Lawrence, *Crisis of the Aristocracy 1558-1641*, Oxford, 1965.

Stone, Lawrence, *Family and Fortune. Studies in aristocratic finance in the sixteenth and seventeenth centuries*, 1973.

Stone, Lawrence, *The Family, Sex and Marriage in England 1500–1800*, 1977.

Stone, Lawrence, 'Social Mobility in England 1500–1700', *Past and Present*, No. 33, April 1966.

Autobiography of William Stout of Lancaster, 1665–1752, ed. J. Harland, 1851.

Strange and Wonderful News from Whitehall, proceeding from Mistris Anna Trapnel . . . With her Declarations concerning the State Affairs of Great Britain etc., 1654.

Strickland, Agnes, *Lives of the Queens of England*, facsimile edition, 8 Vols, 1972.

Strong, James, Batchelour, *Joanereidos: or, Feminine Valour Eminently discovered in Westerne Women, etc.*, 1645.

Strong, James, *Joanereidos: or, Feminine Valour Eminently discovered in Westerne Women, at the Siege of Lyme etc.*, reprinted 1674 ('with additions for the Satisfaction of his Friends').

Strong, Roy, *And when did you last see your father? The Victorian Painter and British History*, 1978.

Stuart, D.M., *The English Abigail*, 1946.

Stuart, D.M., *The Girl through the ages*, 1933.

Swetnam, Joseph, *The Arraignment of Lewd, Idle, Froward, and Unconstant Women: Or, the vanitie of them; chuse you whether*, 1634.

Tannahill, Reay, *Sex in History*, New York, 1980.

Tanner, John, 'Lucius Cary, Viscount Falkland – Cavalier and Catalyst', *Royal Stuart Papers* v, The Royal Stuart Society, 1974.

Taylor, G. Rattray, *Sex in History*, new edition, 1959.

Taylor, Jeremy, 'The Treasures of Friendship', in Bp Taylor's *Opuscula*, 1678.

Thomas, Keith, 'The Double Standard', *Journal of the History of Ideas*, xx, 1959.

Thomas, Keith, *Religion and the Decline of Magic, Studies in Popular Beliefs in Sixteenth and Seventeenth Century England*, 1971.

Thomas, Keith, 'Women and the Civil War Sects', *Past and Present*, 13, 1958.

Thomason Tracts, British Library.

Thompson, Roger, *Women in Stuart England and America*, 1974.

The Autobiography of Mrs Alice Thornton of East Newton, Co. York, Surtees Society, Vol. LXII, Durham, 1873.

'Thurloe Papers', xxi, 1654, Rawlinson mss, A. 21, Bodleian Library, Oxford.

Timbs, John, *Curiosities of London*, 1869.

To the House of Commons for Lockier and other Leveller prisoners from women of London and parts adjacent, 5 May 1649, 669, fo. 14/27, British Library.

To the Parliament of the Commonwealth . . . petition of afflicted women in behalf of Mr J. Lilburn, 24 June 1653, 669, fo. 17/24, British Library.

Trapnel, Anna, *Cry of a Stone, or a Relation of Something spoken in Whitehall by Anna Trapnel*, 1654.

Trapnel, Anna, *A Legacy for Saints; being several Experiences of the dealings of God with Anna Trapnel, In, and after her Conversion . . . together with some letters of a later date*, 1654.

Anna Trapnel's Report and Plea, Or, a Narrative of her Journey from London into Cornwall . . . Whereto is annexed a Defiance against all the reproachful, vile, horrid, abusive and scandalous reports raised out of the bottomless pit against her etc., 1654.

'Anna Trapnel's verse', anonymous folio volume, S.I. 42, Th., Bodleian Library, Oxford.

Treglown, Jeremy (ed. with an Introduction), *The Letters of John Wilmot, Earl of Rochester*, 1980.

Turnbull, G.H., *Hartlib, Dury and Comenius. Gleanings from Hartlib's Papers*, 1947.

Turner, F.C., *James II*, 1948.

'The Diary of Isabella, wife of Sir Roger Twysden, Baronet, of Royden Hall, East Peckham 1645-1651', Rev. F.W. Bennet, MA, *Archaeologia Cantiana, Transactions of the Kent Archaeological Society*, Vol. LI, 1939.

The Family of Twysden and Twisden. Their History of Archives from an original by Sir John Ramskill Twysden, 12th Bt, completed by C.H. Dudley Ward, DSO, MC, 1939.

'Sir Roger Twysden's Notebooks', 2 Vols, Additional MSS, 34, 163, British Library.

Unto every individual Member of Parliament, the Humble Representation of afflicted Women Petitioners on behalf of Mr John Lilburne, 26 July 1653, 669, fo. 17/37, British Library.

Upham, A.H., 'English *Femmes Savantes* at the end of the seventeenth century', *Journal of English and Germanic Philology*, Vol. XII, 1913.

Utter, R.P., and Needham, G.B., *Pamela's Daughters*, 1937.

The Narrative of General Venables, ed. and with an introduction by C.H. Firth, 1900.

Verney, Frances Parthenope, *Memoirs of the Verney Family During the Civil War*, 4 Vols, 1892.

Letters and Papers of the Verney Family, down to the end of the year 1639, ed. John Bruce Esq., Camden Society, 1853.

Vicars, John, *The Burning-Bush not Consumed Or the Fourth and Last Part of the Parliamentary Chronicle*, 1646.

Vicars, John, *Gods Arke Overtopping the Worlds Waves, or The Third Part of the Parliamentary Chronicle etc.*, 1646.

Vicars, John, *The Schismatick Sifted: Or, a picture of Independents freshly and fairly washt over again*, 1646.

Walker, Anthony, DD, *The Holy Life of Mrs Elizabeth Walker*, new edition, abridged and revised by the Rev. J.W. Brooks, 1823.

Wallas, Ada, *Before the Bluestockings*, 1929.

The Poems of Edmund Waller, ed. G. Thorn Dury, 1905.

The Wandering Whore, numbers 1-5, 1660-1661, reprinted Exeter, The Rota, 1977.

Warner, John, *History of English Persecution of Catholics and the Presbyterian Plot*, 2 Vols, Catholic Record Society, Vol. 48, 1953.

Warner, Marina, *Alone of All Her Sex, The Myth and the Cult of the Virgin Mary*, 1976.

Warren, Elizabeth, *The Old and Good Way vindicated in a Treatise etc.*, 1645.

Warren, Elizabeth, *Spiritual Thrift, Meditations, wherein humble Christians (as in a mirror) may view the Verity of their saving Graces etc.*, 1647.

Autobiography of Mary Countess of Warwick, ed. and with an Introduction, T.C. Croker, Percy Society, 1848.

Memoir of Lady Warwick: also Her Diary from AD 1666 to 1672, now first published, to which are added Extracts from her other Writings, The Religious Tract Society, 1847.

'Some Specialities in the life of M. Warwicke' (autobiography of Mary Lady Warwick), Additional MSS, 27, 357, British Library.

Washbourn, John (ed.), *Biblioteca Gloucestrensis*, Gloucester, 1825.

Waylen, Rev. James, *The House of Cromwell and the Story of Dunkirk*, 1880.

Webster, C., *The Great Instauration*, 1975.

Wedgwood, C.V., *The Trial of Charles I*, 1964.

Weigall, David, 'Women Militants in the English Civil War', *History Today*, June 1972.

Wetter, Immolata, IBVM, 'Mary Ward's Apostolic Vocation', *The Way*, Supplement 17, Autumn 1972.

Whitaker, T.D., *The history and antiquities of the deanery of Craven*, 3rd edition, by A.W. Morant, 1878.

Whitelocke, Bulstrode, *Memorials from the Beginning of the Reign of Charles I to the Restoration*, 4 Vols, Oxford, 1853.

The Whore's Rhetorick, 1683, reprinted 1960.

Wilkinson, Rev. Robert, 'The Merchant-Royal or Woman a Ship', 1607, in *Conjugal Duty: Set forth in a Collection of Ingenious and Delightful Wedding-Sermons*, 1732.

Williams, E.M., 'Women Preachers in the Civil War', *Journal of Modern History*, Vol. I, Chicago, 1929.

Willson, David Harris, *King James VI and I*, 1956.

Willughby, Dr (Percival), *De Puerperio Tractatus, Country Midwife's Opusculum*, Sloane MSS, 529, British Library.

The Life of Mr Arthur Wilson the Historian, Written by Himself, in *Desiderata Curiosa*, a collection by Francis Peck, Vol. II, 1779.

Wilson, J.H., *All the King's Ladies, Actresses of the Restoration*, Chicago, 1958.

Wilson, J.H., *The Court Wits of the Restoration*, Princeton, 1948.

Wilson, J.H., 'The Marshall Sisters and Anne Quin', *Notes and Queries*, March 1957.

Wilson, J.H., *Nell Gwynn: Royal Mistress*, 1952.

Wilson, J.H., 'Pepys and Peg Hughes', *Notes and Queries*, October 1956.

The Poems of Anne Countess of Winchilsea, ed. Myra Reynolds, Decennial Publications, Vol. V, second series, Chicago, 1903.

Wolseley, Sir Garnet, *Life of John Churchill, Duke of Marlborough*, 2 Vols, 1894.

The Womens Complaint Against their Bad Husbands, Or the good Fellows Anatomized by their Wives, 1676.

The Womens Sharpe Revenge, 1640.

Woodforde Papers and Diaries, ed. and with an Introduction, Dorothy Heighes Woodforde, 1932.

Woolley, Hannah, *The Gentlewomans Companion, or a Guide to the Female Sex ... With Letters and Discourses upon all occasions, Whereunto is added, a Guide for Cook-maids, Dairy-maids, Chamber-maids, and all others that go to service*, 1675.

Woolley, Hannah, *The Queen-like Closet or, Rich Cabinet ... To which is added a supplement presented to all Ingenious Ladies and Gentlewomen*, 5th edition, 1684.

Wrigley, E.A., 'Family Limitation in Pre-Industrial England', *Economic History Review*, 2nd series, Vol. XIX, 1966.

Letter of Isabel Yeamans, 8 August 1676, MS, Religious Society of Friends, Nottingham Meeting, 35 Clarendon Street, Nottingham.

Young, Peter, *Edgehill 1642 - The Campaign and the Battle*, Kineton, 1967.

Young, Peter, *Marston Moor 1644 - The Campaign and the Battle*, Kineton, 1970.

Index

THE WARRIOR QUEENS

A panoramic work of history that looks at women who led armies and empires, from the first century A.D. to the modern day. Here are Boadicea, Cleopatra, Isabella of Spain, Jinga Mbandi, Margaret Thatcher, Indira Gandhi, and Golda Meir, among others, "rescued from their own myths, and given their due as individuals" (Margaret Atwood, *Los Angeles Times Book Review*).

"An intelligent and artful study of women rulers who commanded in battle.... Ms. Fraser at once clarifies history and suggests the many ways that myths betray history.... She holds our attention and she misses nothing."

—*The New Yorker*

History/Women's Studies/0-679-72816-3/$14.00

THE WIVES OF HENRY VIII

Interweaving passion and politics, and deftly capturing the spoiled yet charismatic personality of Henry himself, this multiple biography unravels the web that raised Henry's consorts to the throne—and sometimes brought them to the chopping block.

"Admirably succeed[s] in bringing to life the six women who married England's ruler...[a] deeply engaging portrait of a marriage—in serial."

—*The New York Times Book Review*

History/Biography/0-679-73001-X/$14.00